TOBRUK

ALSO BY PETER FITZSIMONS

Basking in Beirut

Little Theories of Life

Hitchhiking for Ugly People

Rugby Stories

Everyone But Phar Lap

Everyone And Phar Lap

Nick Farr-Jones: The Authorised Biography

FitzSimons on Rugby

Beazley: A Biography

Nene

Nancy Wake: A Biography of Our Greatest War Heroine

The Rugby War

John Eales: The Biography

The Story of Skilled Engineering and Frank Hargrave

Kokoda

Steve Waugh

TOBRUK
PETER FITZSIMONS

HarperCollins*Publishers*

Cover images reproduced by courtesy of the Australian War Memorial, Canberra.
Front cover: (*top*) Veterans of Tobruk NX36694 Corporal Alexander Robert McHutchison of
Northcote, Vic. (*left*), and NX35323 Private Patrick Joseph McKenna of Griffith, NSW, both
of the 2/13th Battalion (AWM 010982); (*bottom*) a patrol from the 2/13th Infantry Battalion
making its way through a gap in the barbed wire entanglements protecting its unit position,
8 September 1941, Tobruk (AWM 020780). Back cover: a wounded Australian, evacuated from
Tobruk, on a stretcher after he had been taken from a Royal Navy cruiser, Alexandria, Egypt,
27 September 1941 (AWM 020469). Endpapers: General Field Marshal Erwin Rommel,
1 July 1942 (Getty Images 3275648); Corporal John Edmondson of the 2/17th Battalion,
AIF, who was posthumously awarded the Victoria Cross for action on 13 April 1941 at
Tobruk (AWM P00426.003).

HarperCollins*Publishers*

First published in Australia in 2006
by HarperCollins*Publishers* Australia Pty Limited
ABN 36 009 913 517
www.harpercollins.com.au

HarperCollins*Publishers*
25 Ryde Road, Pymble, Sydney NSW 2073, Australia
31 View Road, Glenfield, Auckland 10, New Zealand
77–85 Fulham Palace Road, London W6 8JB, United Kingdom
2 Bloor Street East, 20th floor, Toronto, Ontario, M4W 1A8, Canada
10 East 53rd Street, New York NY 10022, United States of America

National Library of Australia Cataloguing-in-Publication data:

FitzSimons, Peter.
 Tobruk.
 Bibliography.
 Index.
 ISBN 978 0 73227 645 4.
 ISBN 0 7322 7645 4.
 1. Tobruk, Battles of, 1941–1942. 2. World War, 1939–1945 –
 Campaigns – Africa, North. 3. World War, 1939–1945 –
 Participation, Australian. I. Title.
940.54231

Cover and internal design by Matt Stanton
Relief drawings by Matt Stanton
Maps by Laurie Whiddon, Map Illustrations
Typeset in 11 on 15pt Bembo by Kirby Jones
Printed and bound in Australia by Griffin Press on 79gsm Bulky Paperback White

7 6 5 4   06 07 08 09

To my late parents, Lieutenant Peter McCloy FitzSimons (pictured below, in Cairo, 1941) and Lieutenant Beatrice Helen Booth, OAM, both of whom proudly served with the AIF in World War II — my mother with the 2/7th Australian General Hospital in New Guinea and Bougainville, and my father with the 4th Light Ack-Ack Regiment in North Africa, most notably at the Battle of El Alamein, and then in New Guinea at Finchhaven and Dumpu.

And to you, mighty Rats of Tobruk . . .

Us Blokes

Only a crowd of civilians
From every walk of life,
We left our homes and our loved ones
For we felt it our duty to fight.

We think of our wives and sweethearts
Back on our sunny shores;
We think of the boys who could help us
Bring victory to our cause.

But we carry on, midst the heat and the dust,
Not that we want to, but we know that we must.
It's square your shoulder and pick up your pack,
For the sooner it's over, the sooner we're back.

POEM PUBLISHED IN THE 2/48TH BATTALION NEWS SHEET
ON 27 AUGUST 1941, WHILE THE BATTALION WAS IN TOBRUK

Contents

MAPS viii

FOREWORD BY MANFRED ROMMEL xiii

INTRODUCTION xv

1 IN THE BEGINNING 1

2 HIS STRUGGLE 21

3 A WORLD AT WAR 43

4 ROMMEL RISES 69

5 ENTER THE AUSTRALIANS 96

6 TAKE TOBRUK 123

7 ENTER, *THE* GERMAN GENERAL 154

8 ATTACK!!! 184

9 FIRST STRIKE 213

10 ALL SET 243

11 THE EASTER BATTLE 265

12 TO FIGHT ANOTHER DAY 295

13 THE BATTLE BUILDS 322

14 THE BATTLE OF THE SALIENT 350

15 THE DIGGERS DIG IN 383

16 MANOEUVRES POLITICAL 419

17 END GAME 456

EPILOGUE 493

AUSTRALIAN UNITS AT TOBRUK
    APRIL–DECEMBER 1941 525

ENDNOTES 527

BIBLIOGRAPHY 549

INDEX 557

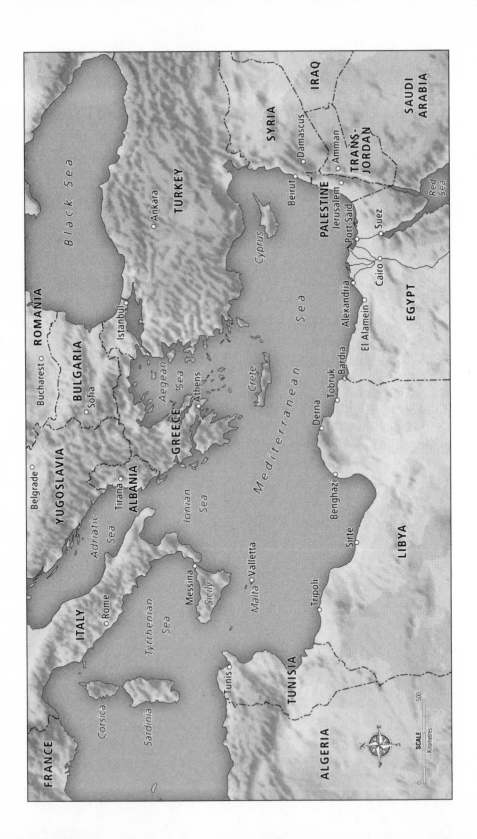

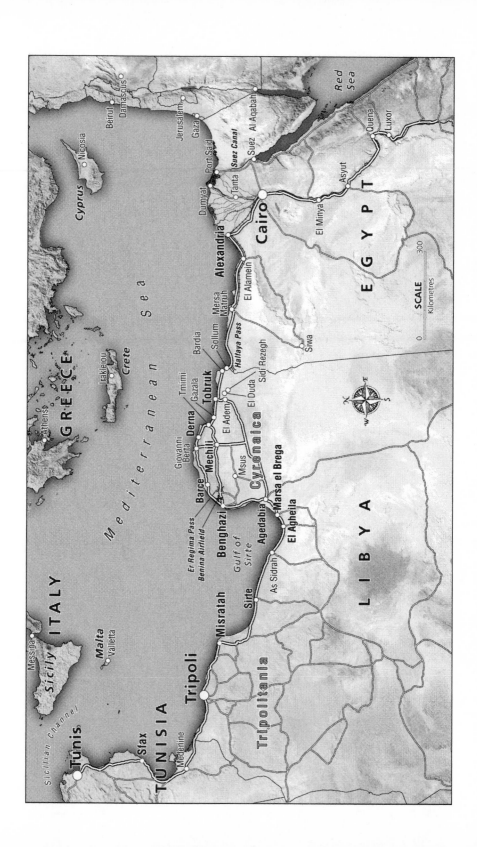

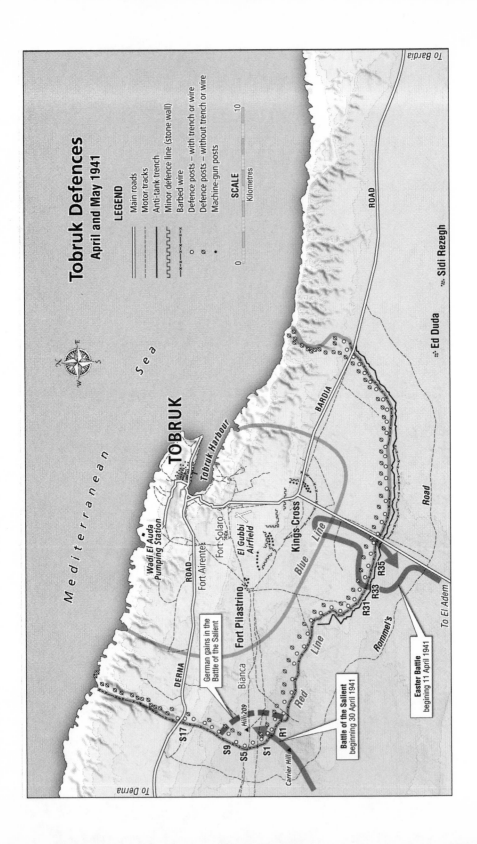

Tobruk Defences
April and May 1941

LEGEND

Main roads
Motor tracks
Anti-tank trench
Minor defence line (stone wall)
Barbed wire
Defence posts – with trench or wire
Defence posts – without trench or wire
Machine-gun posts

SCALE
0   10
Kilometres

Mediterranean   Sea

TOBRUK

Tobruk Harbour

Wadi El Auda
Pumping Station

Fort Airente

Fort Solaro

El Gubbi
Airfield

Fort Pilastrino

Kings-Cross

Blue Line

Bianca

Red Line

Hill 209

Carrier Hill

DERNA ROAD

ROAD

BARDIA

Rommel's

R31
R33
R35

S17
S9
S5
S1
R1

German gains in the
Battle of the Salient

Battle of the Salient
beginning 30 April 1941

Easter Battle
beginning 11 April 1941

To Derna

To Bardia

ROAD

Sidi Rezegh

Ed Duda

To El Adem

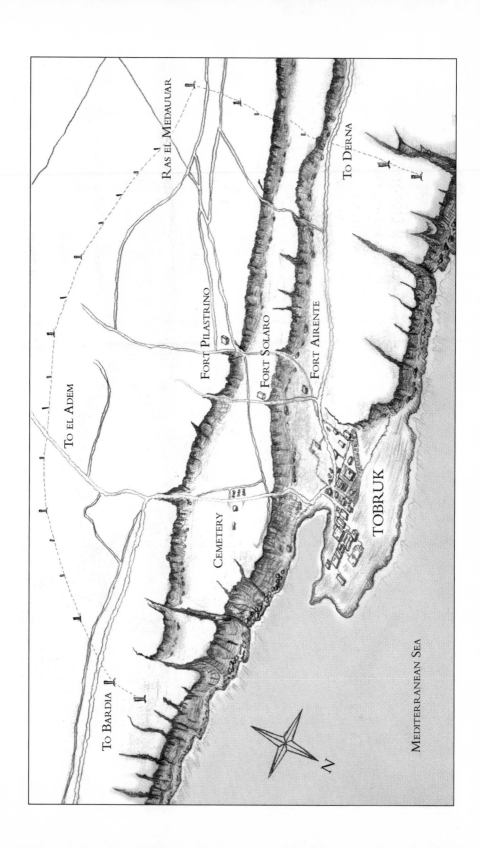

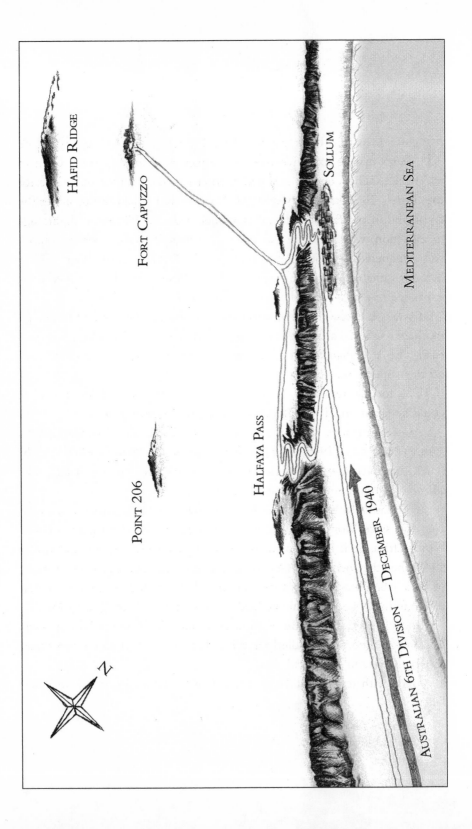

Foreword

The title of the book by Mr Peter FitzSimons, *Tobruk*, refers to the events that lie sixty-five years in the past, the battles between German and Italian soldiers on one side and Australian soldiers on the other side, for the fortress Tobruk in the year 1941. German and Italian troops under the command of my father, General Rommel, had in a *Blitzaktion* (lightning-speed action) won back the part of Libya that Field Marshal Wavell's troops had conquered — with the exception of Tobruk, a small town with a harbour suitable for deep-water vessels, whose surroundings had been expanded to a half-circle-shaped fortress system by the Italians.

Grown careless, due to his previous successes in France and in Africa, my father suffered a defeat during the attempt to take Tobruk in a *coup de main*. The Australian defenders withstood, and the Axis forces had to break off their operation.

The fortress remained in the hands of the British 8th Army until it could be taken on 21 June 1942 by the German–Italian troops ...

Australian troops were at this time not in the fortress. But five months later, in November 1942, Tobruk fell back to the 8th Army without a fight when the German–Italian Panzer army withdrew towards Tunis after Montgomery's victory in the Battle of El Alamein.

The Australian troops, whose fighting value had been well known to the Germans since World War I, played a great part in the British successes in North Africa, be it in Tobruk, also during the battles in autumn and winter 1941 when they, behind the German–Italian front, represented a massive threat; or be it when they contributed in summer 1942 so that the German–Italian march to the Nile delta could be held up; or in the Battle of El Alamein.

Today we are friends. But the graves of our soldiers in the Libyan desert not only remind us of soldierly heroism, but also urge us to do everything to retain peace in the world.

Filled with respect, I take off my hat to the Australian Army and their fallen.

Manfred Rommel
Stuttgart,
March 2006

Introduction

It was one of those things, I suppose ...

Often when I have just finished a book I go into an odd kind of state, bouncing somewhere between exhaustion and exhilaration, swearing on the holy skulls of my ancestors that I'll never put myself through such an arduous process again, and yet knowing on the other hand that I will because it feels so good and satisfying when it's done. I was in precisely such a condition in late 2003 when, after having just finished my book *Kokoda*, I was briefly visiting my aunt and uncle, Ted and Mary Carter, in Napier Street, Tamworth. After sleeping in their spare room, in the first light of dawn the following morning I spied something interesting on the wall, slowly taking shape as more light seeped in.

It was a framed certificate of some kind, featuring the title 𝕽𝖆𝖙𝖘 𝖔𝖋 𝕿𝖔𝖇𝖗𝖚𝖐 𝕬𝖘𝖘𝖔𝖈𝖎𝖆𝖙𝖎𝖔𝖓.

Was my Uncle Ted a 'Rat of Tobruk'? I don't even remember him ever talking about it! But then my dad never talked much either about fighting with the 9th Division at the Battle of El Alamein, and my uncle Jim was long dead before I knew he'd fought in the last part of the Battle of the Kokoda Track. Mum would mention her service with the AIF in Bougainville and Lae — helping rehabilitate injured soldiers — if it came up, I suppose, but no more than that. For that generation of Australians just weren't big talkers — most especially after the war was over; but in any case, a seed had been planted for my next book.

True, I knew next to nothing about what happened at Tobruk, but in many ways that was the whole point. *Why* didn't I? Why didn't we all know more of it? How was it that, like Kokoda — which I had also known very little about beforehand — most details of what had happened at Tobruk had so faded from the wider public consciousness that all that was left was the name? Perhaps it was with the twentieth rerun of *Patton* on Australian television, or perhaps it had been simply the corrosive influence of Coca-Colonisation generally, but somehow a significant chunk of a proud part of our past really had been lost to view. While we'd been remembering the Alamo with the Americans, we'd forgotten so much of our own stuff, leaving only the legend of Gallipoli intact. And yet Gallipoli consumed all, occupying such space that there was room for little else.

I had been stunned at how inspiring a story Kokoda proved to be, so might Tobruk be the same, I wondered.

A quick chat with Uncle Ted over the bacon and eggs — with a liberal sprinkling of the 9th Division's 2/1st Pioneers, Panzers, minefields, General Erwin Rommel, anti-tank ditches, patrols and something called the Easter Battle — before heading to the airport, and I was at least resolved to read a bit more about it. No, I didn't want to start another book so soon after finishing Kokoda, but on the other hand, when you're working on something that feels like a great yarn, it doesn't always feel like work.

And so it began. Nudging up to two and a half years later, here we are.

This book is the result of what seemed like an enormous journey for me, but it is of course as nothing compared to the journey embarked upon by the people whom this book is about. I have been privileged to meet many of the soldiers from Australia, Britain and Germany and have been met with universal warmth and hospitality.

In Germany, the survivors of the Afrika Korps could not have been more open or hospitable to me, and for me the scene was set when, on the evening after I arrived in Stuttgart in October 2005, I attended one of their small dinner reunions. Invited politely by an ex-Colonel to state my business, I stood up and said that I was writing a book, and that though my uncle had fought against them at Tobruk and my father at El Alamein, both had told me how much they respected the men of the Afrika Korps as soldiers ... at which point my hosts all applauded, and made it clear they wished to send their own best wishes to the Australian soldiers who were still alive.

Three members of the Afrika Korps, particularly, simply could not have been more helpful, from driving me to meet their former comrades, to taking me into their own homes, to spending many hours explaining various facets of the campaign and helping to dig out some of the information that I needed about their comrades. My special thanks go to Rolf Völker, Rolf Munninger and Wilhelm Langsam. And of course a particular thanks to Field Marshal Erwin Rommel's son, Dr Manfred Rommel, who so very kindly wrote the foreword to this book.

Similarly, in Australia both Jack Harris of the 2/17th Battalion and John Searle of the 2/13th Battalion were very kind, inviting me to their reunions, introducing me to their fellow veterans, helping me to follow leads, and I am indebted to both good men. Bill Noyce of the 2/13th Battalion was also very good to me, as was his comrade Bert Ferres who, though he was initially too modest to say much about it, had an extraordinary tale to tell, as did Doug 'Snowy' Foster of the 2/17th Battalion, and Keith Secombe of the 2/3rd Australian Anti-tank Regiment. A thought that occurred to me time and again while working with them all was what a magnificent thing it was that, a good six decades after the war was over, the veterans were still so tight with each other and with the widows of those who hadn't survived — and none bore any ill will towards their former enemies. None of them complained that Tobruk had come to be forgotten over the years, but they were certainly pleased I was doing the book.

As a working journalist with the *Sydney Morning Herald* and the *Sun-Herald*, while also broadcasting every morning on Sydney radio station 2UE, I mentioned from time to time the project I was involved in, and every time the result was the same: seemingly from everywhere, I was contacted by veterans' families, either wanting me to look at diaries or letters they had in their possession, or saying I must talk to the veteran himself. This was wonderful and turned up absolute treasures of previously uncovered information.

One lot particularly stands out. Early in my research I was contacted by a Gary Parsisson, wanting to know if I would like to look at his natural father's account of what life at the time of Tobruk was really like. Yes, please.

Bingo! Gary father's name was Ivor Hancock, Ivor was with the 2/24th Battalion, and from the first I was riveted by his extensive account, not just because he was in a lot of the front-line action, but because his eye for detail was so extraordinary, and he was brutally honest about the things he experienced, both on and off the battlefield, giving a completely unsanitised flavour of the time.

Too, early in my research I came across the letters, held by the Australian War Memorial, that flowed between John Johnson of the 2/23rd Battalion and his wife, Josie, and their eight children at home in Walwa, northern Victoria. The book, *War Letters 1940–41*, was gripping from first to last. I subsequently made contact with the fifth son, Len, who had done so much not only to ensure that the letters went to the War Memorial, but also an extraordinary amount of research to ensure that they were put in their right perspective. I cannot thank him enough for his help in telling his parents' story, as well as for providing the photos of them you will see herein.

At a sports dinner I was speaking at in Noosa Heads, Queensland, I met a fellow by the name of Robert Mrozowski who had heard I was writing a book about Tobruk and told me I had to meet his father, Adam, who was a

Polish Rat of Tobruk. Done. I interviewed Adam Mrozowski extensively, was richer for the experience, and knew immediately I had the man I was looking for to tell that part of the story. Out of the blue, after I wrote a small piece in the *Herald* about Elizabeth Edmondson and her son, Jack, who was a Digger, I was contacted by two women: Mrs Dariel Larkins of Sydney's northern suburbs and Mrs Sue McGowen from Sydney's east, who knew the Edmondson family well sixty years ago, and both were wonderful in helping me to reconstruct certain crucial details of what the Edmondsons were like, as well as their house, their farm, their very lives. I record my warm appreciation to them both.

Never in the course of writing a book have I had to call on the expertise of so many different people from so many different countries. In England, my researcher Matthew Hope delved into some of the deepest recesses of Britain's Imperial War Museum to get me some precise details of individual actions at Tobruk, as did historian Dr Oliver Hemmerle in Mannheim, Germany.

From Australia, I particularly thank Sonja Görnitz, who was magnificent in organising my trip to her homeland of Germany, and putting her language skills at my disposal. Time and again I was not only calling upon her to translate particular documents — such as large chunks of reminiscences by Afrika Korps soldiers of the 8th Machine-gun Battalion in the book *Nur ein Bataillon*, and Hitler's Nuremberg Rally speech of 1938 — but also to use her extraordinary research and journalistic skills to isolate the things I was looking for, the illustrative nuggets that hopefully held the whole. While I did the preliminary interviews with Rolf Völker in Stuttgart, Sonja did the follow-up ones, and she — as a German of a younger generation — was constantly expressing amazement to me about the kinds of things she was hearing about for the first time. Questions that were normal for me to put to Rolf had always been *tabu* for her, just as I gather some of the answers he gave her were things rarely discussed in post-war Germany, and never by one who had fought in the war with one who had been raised to revile everything about it. Sometimes I felt both privileged and yet even a little intrusive, as two generations of Germans discussed frankly issues of the most extraordinarily sensitive nature. That discussion, nevertheless, has immensely enriched this book, and I warmly thank them both for their trust, of each other and of me. Another who was extremely helpful on the German side of the story was Neal Pritchard, a Sydneysider with an extraordinary passion for German history, a library to back it, and the generosity of spirit to place both at the service of this manuscript. I owe him, and will do for some time.

A journalist mate of mine, Mick Toal, who is a fiend in the field of World War II weaponry, was very generous with his expertise to the point of painstakingly building small models of various bits of weaponry so I could better understand what I was writing about, and I am in his debt.

The *éminence grise* of the *Sydney Morning Herald,* Max Prisk, is also a World War II buff, and one day I arrived at work to find he had put on my desk all the Tobruk jewels that were to be found in the Fairfax archives. I owe him, and I thank him.

My friend Dr Michael Cooper, with whom I walked the Kokoda Track, did for me with this book the same as he did for Kokoda: researched the medical side of the battles, and sent me a lot of material which proved to be invaluable.

The noted historian Neil McDonald, who edited the book *Chester Wilmot Reports* — which I drew on heavily — and is currently writing Wilmot's biography, was a great source of advice throughout my writing of this book and I was privileged to be able to constantly tap into his great scholarship.

In Canberra, while constantly calling on the copious resources of the Australian War Memorial and National Library, my researcher Glenda Lynch continued to send me package after package of fresh transcripts, photocopies and books — to the point that the whole thing was a foot deep on my dining room table — while also promptly answering my endless emailed queries. To her, my gratitude, as ever, for going way above and beyond the call of duty.

My gratitude too, to the official Royal Australian Navy historian, Duncan Perryman, for reviewing some of the material I had come up with, and also to his counterpart in the Royal Australian Air Force, Dr Christopher Clark, who did the same on matters pertaining to the RAAF and RAF.

In April of 2006, I was privileged to be able to go to Tobruk itself — after two previous attempts had gone awry — in the company of the greatest North African battlefield expert of them all, Stephen Hamilton. In a four-wheel-drive, in a very low gear, I was able to visit all the places I had been writing about and make changes to this book accordingly. You will see, for example, reference to Hill 209 in the chapters to come, and yet it was only while standing upon it that I was truly able to appreciate its significance. Equally, it was only while standing at Post R33 that I could really get a sense of the sheer windswept *desolation* of that part of the desert, or standing at the base of Ed Duda Hill that I could hear the barest eerie echo of what it must have been truly like, and this book is all the better for it. I record my deep appreciation to Stephen Hamilton, both for going to such efforts to get me to all those places and more around Tobruk, and for subsequently reading my battlefield accounts and making suggestions accordingly.

In essence, I have tried to do in this book much what I tried with *Kokoda,* which was to take as many established points of historical fact and tiny detail as I could find and then join them together to the point that I would be able to build it into a book that has hopefully a novel-like feel. Certainly, in an effort to achieve this to my own satisfaction, I have had to very occasionally take out my poetic licence — surmising the feelings of a soldier who has just received a mortal wound, for example — but not often, as I hope the pages of endnotes at the end of this book will attest to. Each endnote gives the main source of the material used, and I have chosen endnotes in preference to footnotes to prevent the manuscript looking like a textbook while still giving full acknowledgment. What you will see in the following pages is in rough, though not precise, chronological order, the better for the story to be told in a hopefully easily comprehensible structure.

The happiest circumstance of all for me, though, was just how much extraordinary material there was to build the account from, in that in this battle some of the key protagonists had been great letter writers, diarists and note-takers.

General Erwin Rommel not only wrote to his wife, Lucie, daily, but as an already extremely successful author before World War II for his account of his actions in World War I, he took even more copious notes this time around, with a view to publishing another book when the war was over. As B. H. Liddell Hart wrote in the introduction to the book that gathers all those notes in one precious volume, *The Rommel Papers* (which Liddell Hart so assiduously edited), 'No commander in history has written an account of his campaigns to match the vividness and value of Rommel's.'

And just as Johnson had his Boswell, Rommel had his Schmidt — his adjutant, Lieutenant Heinz Schmidt, who wrote *With Rommel in the Desert* after the war was over, recording a great many fascinating incidents and words from Rommel at crucial times in the course of the campaign. I might say in passing on the subject of the two aforementioned books that the serious scholar — and me besides — will find it completely impossible to make Rommel's and Schmidt's accounts of the campaign mesh together perfectly as, in my view, Schmidt's timing is sometimes confused, and I have almost always deferred to Rommel's timing — as he was writing a lot of it contemporaneously — while still greatly valuing Schmidt's reminiscences.

If serious scholars do follow this, I note that the best German overview is provided by Wolf Heckmann, who wrote *Rommel's War in Africa* in 1978, and he struggled with the same problems with Schmidt's timing as I did — coming to much the same conclusions as I have as to how it best fits together. I particularly valued his account of the initial storming of Tobruk, the Italian experience in North Africa, and the May Day battle. Herr Heckmann, though in hospital, was very kind in offering guidance to Sonja over the phone from Germany, and he is another I must thank.

(I might say on the general subject of *precisely* defining when a given event occurred, it is not even possible to make the official Battalion histories synchronise perfectly with Barton Maughan's official account of the whole campaign, *Tobruk and El Alamein*, and to resolve timing conflicts I have gone with the memory of the surviving Diggers and *Panzergrenadiere* whom I have talked to.)

On the Tobruk side of the perimeter, Australia's own Lieutenant General Leslie Morshead had no interest in writing a book after the war, and so did not take a lot of detailed notes during the battle, but he did, by God, leave something almost as good, and I will for ever mark down as one of the great thrills of my authorial life an episode that occurred when I met his octogenerian daughter, Mrs Elizabeth Kidd, in May 2005. Having been provided with an introduction by a woman who was a great friend of my mother's, I went to Mrs Kidd's elegant Sydney apartment and explained my project, wondering if perhaps her father — who had been my own father's Commanding Officer — might have left some written account of what happened at Tobruk that had not yet seen the light of day? With barely a word, she disappeared into her bedroom and returned with a shoebox full of his letters that she kept in her top cupboard, all perfectly preserved and kept in chronological order.

'Is this what you're looking for?' she asked brightly.

With somewhat fevered brow, I turned to the letter with the date of the first Battle of Tobruk, and there, written in his own hand, were Lieutenant General Morshead's exact feelings, confided in the silent watch of the night, to the person closest to him in the world — his wife, Myrtle — and most of these letters unseen or examined since Myrtle Morshead read them all those decades ago. Eureka!

There was more, much more, and I am endlessly grateful to Mrs Kidd for allowing me access to those precious letters, as well as the previously mentioned eminent Australian historian Neil McDonald, who painstakingly went through those letters at my request, with a magnifying glass in one hand and sharpened pencil in the other, taking extensive notes. He will, I hope, be able to use some of those notes for his own forthcoming biography about Chester Wilmot, but it was nevertheless an act of great generosity and of enormous value to this manuscript, and I am in his debt. On the subject of Chester Wilmot, allow me to say that I am more convinced than ever that he was a journalistic giant of his time, as well as a great author, and all who write about Tobruk must do as I did and make as a starting point his raw reports and his wondrous book, *Tobruk 1941*, which came out in 1944. Of the authors who followed Wilmot, I would particularly cite Barrie Pitt, who wrote *The Crucible of War: Western Desert 1941*, as another of the greats, and his writings about the first taking of Tobruk were particularly valuable for this book.

On that subject, while I have a full bibliography at the end of the book, allow me to say that — just as it was with my book about Kokoda — Professor David Horner's book about Australia's most senior officer in World War II, *Blamey, the Commander in Chief,* was a great resource, as was David Day's book *The Politics of War.* I thank both men for their advice on certain aspects of the story that I was finding difficult to understand, and checking that I had details correct. For the raw quality of life of the Diggers, I found Jack Barber's book, *The War, The Whores and The Afrika Korps,* to be an absolute gem, and also a treasure trove of great details.

All of that said, whatever mistakes that remain in this book are mine and mine alone.

As a rule I refer to the metric system of measurement when referring to the Germans and Italians, and the Imperial system when my account is about the British and Australians.

This is my seventeenth book, and by this time I have been blessed to have a very good team of people helping me to put it together. My thanks, as always, to my principal researcher, Kevin Brumpton; my transcriber of interviews, Margaret Coleman; and my help in all things to do with the form and texture of the book, my indefatigable and treasured colleague at the *Sydney Morning Herald*, Harriet Veitch, who put many weekend and evening hours into the project and was a constant fount of both ideas and information.

I record my appreciation and professional respect to everyone I worked with at HarperCollins, most particularly Shona Martyn, Alison Urquhart and Sophie Hamley, who was commendably malleable with her deadlines. With a firm deadline before us that would kill a brown dog, Mary Rennie joined the project at the end and was wonderful, as was Tracey Gibson, the picture editor, and Matt Stanton with his creative flair. And I might offer a particular thanks to Graeme Jones, a typesetting genius of extraordinary patience who was there when I needed him most.

Before I hand any of my books to the publisher, they are always vetted by my wife, Lisa Wilkinson, whose professional background is editing women's magazines, but who is also blessed with a bent for determining what works and what doesn't in storytelling, and she has more than my usual appreciation as she has worked harder on this book than any other book.

As have I, I must say. Enough, though.

I hope you enjoy the read, and as I write this with dawn not too far away, my primary feeling is that I should stay well away from Napier Street, Tamworth ... but I am certainly glad I visited there last time.

Peter FitzSimons
Sydney
April 2006

PS. On the afternoon of 24 April 2006, I conducted my last interview for this book, with Jack Harris of the 2/17th Battalion. A fortnight earlier I had given him a large slab of the manuscript, and he had wanted me to correct certain details. Now, we sat together in the Liverpool Library in Sydney's southwest having coffee and cucumber sandwiches, after a plaque to one of his fellow soldiers of the 2/17th had just been unveiled — and I read to him my new and corrected account. I am happy to say Jack approved in every detail, and when we were done I shook his hand and told him that I looked forward to seeing him and his wife, Jean, on the morrow at the Anzac Day reunion of his battalion in downtown Sydney. Sadly, just twenty minutes later, while I was on my way home, Jack collapsed then died a short time afterwards. He was a very good man; like so many of the Diggers of his generation that I met in the course of this book, he was an officer and a gentleman and I was privileged to know him. Vale.

CHAPTER ONE

In the Beginning . . .

And Crispin Crispian shall ne'er go by,
From this day to the ending of the world,
But we in it shall be remember'd —
We few, we happy few, we band of brothers.

— WILLIAM SHAKESPEARE, HENRY V

They called it Tobruk.

On the north coast of Africa, nestled neatly by the Mediterranean Sea, it simmered in the sun for centuries, substantially unchanged, with the only drama occurring every few centuries or so, when the local potentates of a distant and fading empirical power would fight an always-losing battle against either the incoming potentates of a rising empire or the Tobruk natives themselves. Arab tribes had been obliged to give way to the Greeks, who had colonised the area six centuries before the time of Christ, who had given way to the Arab tribes once more, who then had to give way to the Romans, who had at least been there long enough to have given Africa its name: *Africa terra*, 'land of the Afri'. Somewhere in the decline and fall of the Roman Empire, though, the Arab tribes had again taken it back, and so it had continued.

In those parts, during those times, those tribes had swirled around Africa in much the same manner as the dust storms, moving fast across the landscape, briefly settling and then moving again, leaving little trace of where they'd been. And yet, Tobruk had always been a place to come back to, and fight for, by virtue of the fact that it had springs of fresh water. Later on, the fact that it had a deep harbour would also become significant.

The rise of the Ottoman Empire from the early sixteenth century saw Tobruk become a kind of outer satellite of the capital, Benghazi, which lay about two weeks away to the west (on a fast camel). At the end of the eighteenth century, no less a personage than Napoleon Bonaparte had strutted ashore, after his ships called in there on their way to conquer Egypt.

•

By the dawn of the twentieth century, when everything was so old it was new again, it was the Romans who once again came to visit — or, more precisely, the Italians, as they began to settle many of the North African towns in those parts from 1911 onwards, and kicked out the Turks for their trouble. The Arabs tried to kick out the Italians in turn, forming a resistance movement against their colonisation, but the Italians were too strong and the local rebels — and, frequently, their families — were brutally suppressed.

To Great Britain in that first flush of the new century, Tobruk — and, indeed, all of Libya, in which it was found — meant next to nothing. Not only did the tiny outpost and port not feature on the part of the map that was red — signifying it as just one more part of the British Empire on which the sun never set — but it was actually in one of those extremely rare parts of the world that the Brits didn't have the slightest design on.

When Italy successfully fought Turkey for control of all Libya in 1912, it barely registered in Whitehall. As far as they were concerned, the Dagos could bring in their troops, build up their villages and towns, and call it their own if they wanted, but it wasn't as if such a godforsaken country actually counted for much — not like Egypt to the east, which was firmly in the British camp and was extremely important, because whoever controlled the Suez Canal effectively controlled the crossroads of the world's shipping.

The Germans had a similar attitude. Those with Teutonic blood looked perhaps with acid amusement upon the vainglorious attempts of silly Italians to revive their Roman empire, but no more than that.

Australia? As the nineteenth century clicked over into the twentieth, and the continent became one country for the first time — as opposed to six separate colonies — it would not be straining credibility too much to think that from Sydney to Perth, from the mighty Kimberley in the north to the southern tip of Tasmania, there might not have been a single person who had even *heard* of Tobruk, let alone been glad they'd never been there.

Ah, but the forces would grow in this new century that would begin to bring the interests of all those countries into a common focus ... and for a brief moment events in Tobruk would be crucial as to which way one significant part of the river of history would run.

A proper starting point for the story, some of its key characters and the forces that helped to shape and steer them all, then, is probably around 1914 ...

•

It was everywhere.

That day, an enormous dust storm like no one had ever seen swirled and whirled its way across the bone-dry Australian desert and engulfed them all down Wagga Wagga way. It bathed everything first in an ethereal glow and then in an extraordinarily fine terrestrial talcum. And on the afternoon of 8 October 1914, right in the middle of it all, plumb in the eye of the dusty dynamo, a child was born to Elizabeth Edmondson and her husband, Will. Though John Hurst Edmondson arrived during a difficult time, with a deadly drought squeezing the life out of everything it touched — the grass had long ago died, the wheat had wilted and their cattle were showing more ribs than meat — John's own life was, from the beginning, nothing but a joy for his parents.

They had waited a long, long time for the good Lord to bless them with a baby, and this quiet, gentle boy was their reward. Their pride soon turned into a good-looking toddler, with the classic combination of very red hair, milky complexion, and finely chiselled features which yet belied a robust spirit. He was given a horse, Black Bess, for his third birthday; broke his right elbow while riding shortly afterwards; and despite the fact that before he had turned four the drought had driven the family from Wagga Wagga to another 670-acre farm just off the Hume Highway near Liverpool — complete with a small weatherboard farmhouse, surrounded by poinsettias and carefully nurtured roses trained on wires between the veranda posts, which they called 'Forest Home' — still nothing could dim the boy's own bubbling happiness. Jack, as he soon became known, was an only child — with 'Robinson Crusoe' a frequent and favourite game — and he was all the more precious for it. Nothing could dim Elizabeth's joy — not even the Great War, which had first smouldered and then blazed into life at much the same time as her Jack had been born . . .

•

For Australia, the real action had started in 1915, on that legend of a landing called Gallipoli, where at dawn on 25 April no fewer than 17 000 ANZACs hit the beaches all at once and, in the face of withering fire, had still somehow held on, and continued to cover themselves in glory, despite the terrible conditions.

One soldier landing on that first morning was a young Australian bloke by the name of Captain Leslie Morshead of the Australian Imperial Force's 2nd Battalion. Though Morshead had started his adult life as a Ballarat-born schoolmaster with just a sideline interest in the cadets, he was already beginning to make a name for himself as a military man of the highest order. Fearless, without yet being reckless, Morshead was so highly regarded by his superiors that from enlisting just a few days after the war had begun and taking his first commission as a lieutenant, he was swiftly promoted. Though never a one-of-the-boys type of military leader, he remained very popular with his troops, in part because, on top of the many successes under his leadership, they had a sense that he valued their lives highly and would do all he could to make them an effective fighting unit and get them home safely. And he wasn't a bloke to muck around lightly, with a later description of him seeming to have relevance for all of his military career: 'He has dark eyes, piercing, incisive, unrevealing; a clear crisply toned voice; an ability to speak at length on military matters, disdaining either a crescendo or diminuendo, so that his words can become a drum-fire of fact and phrases calculated to impress friends and annihilate enemies.'[1]

In many ways Morshead's schoolmaster background showed up in his military approach, as he seemed always to be endeavouring to garner as much information as possible about every battlefield before framing his attack; to learn whatever lessons he could from every action; and to spread the information to his superiors and among those under his command while also doing what he could do to improve the latter's skills. Physically, he was by no means a robust man, but his mental acuity, courage and presence made of him such that the great Australian war historian C.E.W. Bean would later say that Morshead was a man 'in whom the traditions of the British Army had been bottled from his childhood like light-corked champagne'.[2] And yet, a fairly small champagne bottle it was. As a matter of fact, he was only 10-and-a-half stone for a 5-foot 7-inch frame, and his chest circumference was just 33 inches with a deep breath and a further puffing up at the thought of serving his country. This was one inch smaller than the army deemed allowable, and he'd had to do some fast-talking to make it into the army in the first place.

But Morshead proved to be so successful as a leader of men in the dreadful battle conditions of Gallipoli that he was then ordered to move on to France for the campaign there, where he commanded the 33rd Battalion — a unit he had founded and raised from the ground up — and was always right in the thick of it.

The Australian Army culture that Morshead was growing and prospering in was one where nothing was more highly valued than resolution, initiative and refusal to budge, even when against seemingly superior forces. Personally, Morshead so embodied this attitude that, despite being severely wounded in the course of his actions, occasioning a long period of rehabilitation in a hospital, he had still become a Lieutenant Colonel by war's end, had won a Distinguished Service Order from Australia and the *Légion d'Honneur* from the French, and had been 'mentioned in dispatches' on an extraordinary six occasions. Before he was thirty years old, Morshead had been wounded three times and spent as many years in command of an infantry battalion of the line.

Of the Australian military men of note to emerge from that Great War — including the likes of Iven Mackay, Gordon Bennett and Arthur 'Tubby' Allen — Leslie Morshead was close to the best and brightest of the rising generation, with only one Thomas Blamey outshining him. Blamey, four years older than Morshead, had begun World War I as a major, had also hit the beaches of Gallipoli on the morning of 25 April 1915, shone throughout the war, and finished it as a Brigadier General. The two would end up working closely together, but in the meantime the reputation of the younger man as a leader was further confirmed by something else Bean had written about him: 'Morshead had the nearest approach to a martinet among all the young Australian colonels, but able to distinguish the valuable from the worthless in the old army practice ... he had turned out a battalion which anyone acquainted with the whole force recognised ... as one of the very best'.[3]

Somehow it was just in his bones. Morshead had a passion for, and a remarkable ability in, all things military — with the only other competing passion being the one he was developing for the woman who would become his wife, Myrtle Woodside (the sister of one of his pupils, and eight years his junior).

•

Within the German Army in the meantime, a German officer in his late twenties, by the rank and name of Lieutenant Erwin Rommel, was also making a reputation for himself — through the successive theatres of France, Romania and Italy — as a great and courageous leader of men, however tender his years. Though not of the classic Prussian stock from which most of the high German officer class was drawn — he was one of five children of a mathematics teacher based in the small village of Heidenheim, 100 kilometres east of Stuttgart — Rommel was able to boast of something even better. That is, he had a growing record of bringing off stunning military manoeuvres that he alone seemed to be able to conceive, let alone execute with such extraordinary results.

His first biographer, Desmond Young, would later say of him, 'From the moment that Rommel first came under fire he stood out as the perfect fighting animal, cold, cunning, ruthless, untiring, quick of decision, incredibly brave',[4] and there is much to back this up — most particularly, his affinity with the very fox he kept as a pet.[5]

Rommel's *modus operandi*, which he refined throughout the course of the war, was to slip through enemy lines then attack the enemy from the rear. In the subsequent panic, confusion and freewheeling havoc, he would turn himself and his men into a tornado of terrible devastation, moving quickly and hitting again and again before moving to a new target, always before the defence had a chance to draw a bead on them, and frequently from positions so difficult to attain that the defenders had not thought to prepare defensive positions against such angles. As he later defined it, 'The deeper we penetrated into the enemy's defences, the less ready they were to confront us, and consequently the fighting became less intense.'[6]

If a full-on frontal assault was the only way to proceed, Rommel would always pick what he felt to be the weakest point of the enemy defences and concentrate overwhelming firepower on it, before leading equally overwhelming forces to attack it. Once the breach was made, the aim was to widen it by peeling back the edges, and then it was as before: his forces poured through, sowing havoc behind the rest of the enemy lines and then reaping their many rewards from there.

Of all his many exploits, the most outstanding came in the capture of Monte Matajur, just southwest of the northern Italian town of Caporetto, in late October 1917. In command of just 300 of his own men, as part of the famed German Alpine Korps, Rommel first captured an Italian gun battery high up on a heavily defended Italian stronghold, before swinging around and capturing a further 2000 crack Italian troops. Yes, his nominal orders had required of him nothing more than to maintain a holding position on the left flank of the Bavarian Regiment, but Rommel had precisely *no* interest in purely defensive orders. Having seen an opportunity he had taken it, and as it happened, he now saw another opportunity, and, again, did not hesitate.

For, still not done, and not resting for sleep, with just a couple of senior officers and a handful of his own best men, he took another 1500 Italian troops prisoner by convincing them that his force was in the vanguard of thousands more, and then — still without sleep — he and his men stormed the high Italian citadel and overpowered the last defenders at bayonet point. His net 'bag' was 132 Italians killed, 4000 captured and one key line of Italian defence entirely knocked out. On his own side of the ledger, Rommel had lost just one man, killed. But still he was not done. Now, gathering more of his own men to him, and despite not having slept for the previous 45 hours, Rommel pushed on for the Italian garrison town of Longarone, and, with extraordinary audacity — which involved at one point charging across a booby-trapped bridge and removing explosives as they went, just before they could explode — the Rommel-led troops took another 8000 Italian prisoners. Though Rommel had just lived through the defining episode of his early military career, it would much later be said of him by one of his military comrades, 'Basically Rommel always remained that lieutenant, making snap decisions and acting on the spur of the moment.'[7]

Though it took some time and much lobbying from Rommel himself, he was eventually awarded the German Army's curiously French-named highest award for bravery, the Pour le Mérite — its youngest recipient at that point — and it was a wonderful addendum to the Iron Cross, 1st Class and 2nd Class that he had already won. (All of which went a treat with his new uniform of captain, after his promotion on the strength of this exploit.)

Somehow it was just in his bones. Rommel had a passion for, and a remarkable ability in, all things military — with the only other competing passion being the one he felt for his wife, Lucie, the beautiful daughter of a landowner in West Prussia, whom he married while on a brief leave home, in 1916.

Though proud of what he had achieved in the Battle of Monte Matajur, one thing Rommel could never fathom then, or ever afterwards for that matter, was just why the Italians gave up so easily. How could it be that on that particular exercise, he could assign just two men — *two* men! — to take back a thousand Italian prisoners without the Italians either trying to make a break for it, or overpowering his soldiers? Did they have absolutely no stomach for the fight?

•

On the Italian side of things, Corporal Benito Mussolini, for one, had no further stomach for the fight.

A highly influential political activist and journalist/publisher before the Great War — one of his most famous writings was a thunderous editorial in the first issue of his newspaper, *Il Popolo d'Italia*, calling for Italy to declare war on Germany and Austria, which it shortly did thereafter — Mussolini had only just survived his part in the front lines of that conflict. He returned to Milan embittered, determined that the world would change. Of the Germans who had given Italy such a pounding in the war to that point, he felt something akin to complete contempt. In one of his writings before the war, Mussolini had acquired the view that Germany was nothing less than a nation of 'robbers and murderers', and that it was their very 'bestial pride' that had caused the war in the first place[8] — and nothing of his experience in this war had changed this view.

Mussolini's antipathy for the Germans though, did not come close to the rage he felt towards an Italian government that had so badly mismanaged the war from the start. He was determined that everything would change, and used his splendid powers of communication to promote the idea of *la trincerocrazia*, the aristocracy of the trenches. As detailed by biographer Nicholas Farrell, 'Mussolini first used the word "*trincerocrazia*" in an article published in *Il Popolo d'Italia* on 15 December 1917. Italy would be divided, he wrote, after the war "between those who were there and those who were not there; those who fought and those who did not fight; those who produced and the parasites." These men — *trinceresti* — had the moral right and the necessary strength he said to create the new post-war Italy.'[9]

•

Perhaps, oddly enough, Mussolini's nearest equivalent on the German side of the fight was a young corporal by the name of Adolf Hitler ...

Born and raised in provincial Austria, the son of a customs officer — whom he would later describe as an 'irascible tyrant' — before the war Hitler had been a frustrated bohemian, a poorly educated, would-be artist who had twice failed to get into Vienna's Academy of Fine Arts despite his fervent applications. Nevertheless, he had *just* managed to survive, by painting postcards and advertisements, sleeping in dosshouses and frequently eating in soup kitchens, before moving in 1913, at the age of twenty-four, to Munich, where his luck changed. For when the Great War broke out, Hitler was standing in Berlin's main square, the Odeonsplatz, to hear the announcement, and was thrilled as never before in his life. *Purpose!* He quickly joined the 16th Bavarian Reserve Infantry Regiment, and though he was not one to rise through the ranks as Rommel and Morshead had done, making it only to the level of corporal, Hitler was not without courage.

In fact, for the conspicuous bravery he displayed in two separate actions as a *Meldegänger*, a battalion runner — ferrying messages back and forth between Company and Regimental Headquarters, frequently under fire — he was awarded the Iron Cross, 2nd Class, and Iron Cross, 1st Class. Beyond such awards, he was noted as a very good soldier who never questioned orders and remained calm even when under enormous pressure. Perhaps most importantly, with various of the remarkable escapes he had in battle, Hitler came to believe that he was ordained to survive the war, and that there was a higher purpose he was destined to fulfil.

Indeed, one of the more amazing stories to emerge from that war — albeit disputed — is that on one occasion, early in the battles in France, a British private by the name of Henry Tandey — who'd previously been decorated for a combination of his superb marksmanship and his extraordinary bravery — came face to face with a defenceless Hitler emerging from the smoke of battle, presenting the Englishman with an easy kill if he just pulled the trigger. But somehow it was *too* easy, with Hitler close enough that his features would be permanently etched in Tandey's memory — just as Hitler would never forget Tandey's face. For a reason that Tandey never quite understood, but would often have cause to wonder about in years to come, he simply felt that he couldn't shoot an injured, unarmed man at such close range. Slowly — so the story goes — almost as if he was the one who was defeated, the Englishman lowered his rifle. Hitler, himself stunned, nodded in thanks and moved on.

On another occasion, as Hitler would rather mystically recall many times ever afterwards, he was in a dugout when, for no obvious reason, he decided that he wanted to be elsewhere and reacted to the impulse immediately. Just seconds after he left, a shell scored a direct hit on the dugout and killed everyone inside.[10]

Among those of his comrades who survived the war — and at one point 2900 soldiers of the 3500 soldiers of his regiment had been wiped out — Hitler was respected without being particularly popular. Part of the problem was that he was never quite at home carousing with the others, as he detested smoking, drinking and whoring and said so, and he was also obsessed with things political, perpetually blaming Jews and Marxists for everything — not only for the war, but up to and including the terrible food and bitter cold. *Everything!* But survive he did.

Wounded in action in 1916, Hitler was gassed two years later when his List Regiment found itself in action just to the south of Ypres in Belgium and the British exploded gas canisters all around them on the night of 13 October 1918. Taken by stretcher-bearers in gas masks to safety and clean air, he was put in a hospital in Pasewalk, Germany. Despite the damage done to his lungs, Hitler was not, at this point, consumed with bitterness. Whatever else, the massive conflict of the Great War had given to him what civilian life had not: a purpose, a passion, camaraderie, a sense of belonging, and an intensity of experience that he would ever after use as a point of reference by which he could steer. This sense of general equilibrium was about to be shattered, however . . .

For on the morning of 10 November 1918 — a cold, dank and dark day in Pasewalk — an elderly priest turned up in the military hospital where Hitler was recovering, to tell the patients some extraordinary news that he had just heard. As the soldiers gathered around — some missing limbs, others having trouble breathing, still others being obliged to listen only, as they could no longer see — the old man told them that by tomorrow the war would be over. Even though German soldiers were still out in the field and quite capable of fighting on, their political masters had agreed to lay down arms and surrender![11]

The armistice came into effect at eleven o'clock the following morning, and the Kaiser would abdicate, making way for a government based on democratic elections. Germany was to be changed for ever, by the demands of *foreigners*. The priest's own feelings about this matter were clear from the fact that he was crying as he told the soldiers of Germany's complete humiliation, and his misery was surely matched by Corporal Hitler's own.

Stunned, reeling, Hitler staggered and stumbled his way back to his ward and, as he later described it, 'buried my aching head between the blankets and pillow'.

He started to cry.

Everything he believed in — the supremacy of German arms, of the German race, of the fact that the rightness of their cause would *have* to triumph against the evil of those who opposed them — was coming apart.

How could it be so? The more he wrestled with the question, the more his misery deepened. For as bad as he felt when he first found out, he would later admit, 'the following days were terrible to bear and the nights still worse . . . During these nights my hatred increased, hatred for the originators of this dastardly crime.'[12]

Those originators were a mixed bunch, 'a gang of despicable and depraved criminals!', but they included left-wing politicians, Social Democrats, Communists and Jews.

And still neither Hitler nor the rest of Germany knew the worst of it. That would come when the terms of peace were known, under conditions imposed by the Treaty of Versailles. Those conditions were worked out at a gathering of the victorious powers in the summer of 1919 at the Palace of Versailles in France, around a table in the magnificent Hall of Mirrors, and just along from the former apartments of Marie Antoinette — a table at which the losing Germany had *no seat*. (Let them eat cake.)

The terms were specifically designed to both humiliate Germany and to weaken it, to ensure it would never be able to launch itself into such a destructive war again.

Entirely ignoring every other cause of the catastrophic conflagration, Germany was forced to acknowledge total guilt for starting the war in the first place, and also had to agree to pay punitive reparations to Allied countries totalling a rough sum of 132 billion Goldmark, approximately 47 000 tonnes of gold at a value today of approximately 780 million Euros. Even worse, Germany was to lose various parts of its territory, with whole chunks — totalling 13.5 per cent of her land and 12.5 per cent of her population — being carved off and given to Czechoslovakia, Poland, France, Denmark and Belgium, while the Rhineland right next to France was to be a demilitarised zone, meaning Germany would not be able to place any forces at all there. Not that it would have many forces in the first place: Germany was ordered to have a limit of just 100 000 soldiers in its army, the *Reichswehr*, no submarines in a navy restricted to just six battleships, and no air force whatsoever. Too, all of its overseas territories were confiscated and given to one of the victorious powers as part of the spoils of victory.

It is difficult to overstate the outrage that much of the German populace felt for such terms, and yet what could Germany do? It had surrendered in good faith, believing that by complying with United States President Woodrow Wilson's famous Fourteen Points — which he had put before his Congress in January of 1918 — the world could once again be at peace and Germany could rebuild its prosperity. But the only alternative to signing the Versailles Treaty was to once again take up arms, and that was simply out of the question.

So, the representatives of the newly installed *democratic* government of the Weimar Republic were obliged to sign. The result was that both the Weimar Republic and the whole concept of democracy in general would be forced to wear the opprobrium of the German people, as their unhappiness over the consequences of the Versailles Treaty continued to grow. Irrespective of the fact that the wretched French were loudly moaning that the terms of the treaty were nowhere near harsh enough on Germany, the Germans themselves felt that it was not a 'treaty' at all but a *Diktat*, and they would not forget. Or forgive.

•

The wash-up of the Great War created different effects, as it hit different shores around the world . . .

In France, on the evening of the day the news came through from Versailles that the treaty had been signed, there were great celebrations. The Champs Elysées and all major thoroughfares in Paris were festooned with flags and cheering crowds for nine torchlit processions of military men, and there were lights everywhere, from those turned on all over the metropolis in celebration to the enormous searchlight from the Eiffel Tower sweeping over the city. Hallelujah, the famed City of Lights was shining again, even as, just 200 miles to the east, all the principal peaks of the mighty Vosges Mountains had bonfires lit upon them.

As to Britain, a similar sense of celebration seized the people with the news of the signing. As a nation they were thrilled with the terms of the Versailles Treaty, and when the news flashed up on cinema screens, for example, many people spontaneously jumped to their feet and sang *God Save the King*.

In Australia, the signing was formally celebrated with a synchronised 101-gun salute fired by various military establishments around the country, as well as on many ships. Generally, with the Allies' victory and Australia's part in it, a new kind of energy had been released across the continent, a binding force on a nation that had only achieved Federation almost two decades earlier, but had now been tested in battle in a worthy cause and had not been found wanting. Certainly no one was deluded into thinking that Australia now carried weight enough for it to be compared to the great powers, but certainly it had enough weight to forthwith insist on being heard.

This new-found confidence had appeared, for example, at Versailles, in an exchange between the seemingly all-powerful President Wilson and Australia's irascible Prime Minister, Billy Hughes. At issue was who would now have control of the former German colony in New Guinea. Wilson favoured Japan, which had fought on the side of the Allies in the war, while Hughes was equally insistent that it should be Australia — in part, as a buffer against what he suspected might be Japan's future territorial ambitions across Southeast Asia and into the South Pacific. When a frustrated Wilson noted that in Hughes' role as Australian Prime Minister, 'after all, you speak for only five million people', Hughes cut him short with, 'I speak for 60 000 dead. For how many do you speak?'[13]

It was an acute reminder of what kind of sacrifices Australia had made in the war, and of the fact that his nation had earned in blood the right to be heard at this high table. Still, President Wilson wouldn't back down in his insistence that New Guinea should go to the Japanese, and he was fully supported by the other victorious nations present. But nor would Hughes, the 'Little Digger', back down, and he continued to put his view with some force.

Shocked, President Wilson broke in: 'Mr Prime Minister of Australia, do I understand your attitude aright? If I do, it is this: that the opinion of the whole of the civilised world is set to nought.'

In response, Hughes adjusted his hearing aid for a moment, ruminated on what the President had just said, and then came back: 'Very well put, Mr President. You guessed it. That is just so.'[14]

Australia ended up with New Guinea as its protectorate.

By this time nearly all of the Australian soldiers who had survived the Great War had returned home, and were for the most part trying to settle back into civilian lives. As a nation, there was a sense of great debt to such men, and many an individual career was subsequently powered by the public desire to repay some of what was felt was owed to those who had served the country so well. And while, of course, to those who had paid the ultimate price — of their lives — there could never be repayment, at the least they could and would be remembered with reverence. In those first few years after the Great War, just about every town in Australia worthy of being called a town constructed an Anzac War Memorial where, every Anzac Day, those who had served marched proudly down the main street of their towns, and were warmly applauded by all who attended.

It was natural enough under such circumstances, then, that the young lads of Australia growing up in those mid 1920s viewed serving your country in a war as a high calling.

•

If the result of the Great War was a new dawn of hope and prosperity rising in Great Britain, and new pride and unity in such countries as Australia, it was quite the reverse in the defeated and humiliated land of Germany. There, the initial desolation at their outcome had deepened, while outrage at the conditions imposed upon them had heightened. The strains placed upon the nation as a whole created precisely the kind of instability which meant that the body politic was always going to be susceptible to tumours of a particularly virulent nature.

In Munich, for example, an otherwise nondescript locksmith by the name of Anton Drexler had had enough. In January 1919, appalled at the suffering of the country during and since the war and the way it was heading, Drexler founded *Deutsche Arbeiterpartei,* the German Workers' Party, which was devoted to righting the wrongs visited upon Germany by the victors of the Great War. And that, make no mistake, was a war that Germany had *never* surrendered in! Germany had simply ceased hostilities, under the orders of a corrupt political leadership! As to the Versailles Treaty, which was imposed shortly after the party was formed, that also had never been agreed to by the people, but rather imposed upon them, and was only now being executed and observed by the traitorous government of the Weimar Republic.

All of this had to be changed, and done away with — by force of arms if necessary — and in a town like Munich, which had somehow become a magnet for the restless elements left over from the war, there were many who were willing to listen. In those turbulent times, Drexler's party put forward just one of many alternative visions for the future, and in that maelstrom it was something close to pure chance that caused Corporal Adolf Hitler to attend one of the first Workers Party meetings, where just twenty-five people were gathered.

By this time Hitler had become an Education Officer with the German Army, and had been sent by his masters to this seemingly left-wing meeting to monitor precisely what was going on. Were they possibly the most dangerous, threatening group of all — the Communists? (In another part of Germany a few months later, another German Army officer, in the form of Erwin Rommel — one of the few career officers from the Great War to have survived the post-Versailles culling of the ranks — would instruct his troops to turn on high-pressure fire hoses and aim, using them 'like machine-guns, to stop revolutionaries storming the town hall of Gmund'.[15])

In this case, though, not at all. As a matter of fact, Hitler — already a man of extremely strong political views — found that many of the ideas expressed in this meeting concurred with his own, and at one point he simply couldn't help himself. In response to something that had been said by another attendee, Hitler stood up and made a passionate point of rebuttal. The meeting paused and considered the twitchy stranger with the toothbrush moustache. Whoever this newcomer was, there was no doubt that he could speak, and equally no doubt that he was speaking their kind of language in a very certain, and curiously alluring, fashion. There was no hesitancy about him; he seemed so sure of what had to be done. Hitler ended up making further discourses throughout the evening, and by meeting's end both the German Workers Party and Hitler were mightily impressed with each other.

Somehow, Hitler had a way of speaking that was just mesmerising, demonstrating a capacity to tap into the wellspring of German greatness, to imply that simply to embrace his ideas was to ensure that Germany would be great again! His oratory was strong, and always to the point.

'We want to call to account the November Criminals of 1918', was a phrase typical of his thrusts. 'It cannot be that two million Germans should have fallen in vain and that afterwards one should sit down as friends at the same table with traitors. No, we do not pardon, we demand — vengeance! The dishonouring of the nation must cease. For betrayers of the Fatherland and informers, the gallows is the proper place.'[16]

Never before to this point had Hitler realised quite how much he loved oratory, nor what a powerful elixir it was to see the mood of a whole body of people sway to his will. Shortly after the initial meeting, he formally joined the party, just the fifty-fifth person to do so, and so he took the membership number 555, as Drexler had started membership numbers at 500 in an effort to make the party look bigger than it was. Hitler went so well from the first that — at about the time the nascent party embraced the swastika, a curiously modified symbol of Hindu origins, for their flag — he was asked by Drexler to join his Executive Committee, to have a direct say in the guiding of the party's fortunes, even as Hitler continued to address meetings.

So it was that with his communication skills, and his background as a decorated common soldier of the war who had been wounded in battle and had earned the right to be heard, Hitler's influence on Drexler and the leadership of the German Workers Party soon grew to the point that the former corporal was able to persuade Drexler to change the name of the party to the National Socialist German Workers Party, or *Nationalsozialistische Deutsche Arbeiterpartei* — which became known as 'Nazis' for short.

One who was stunned the first time he heard Hitler speak was Rudolf Hess, a similarly restless veteran of the Great War who felt passionately that Germany had been betrayed. After listening to Hitler speak, Rudolf rushed to find his girlfriend.

'You must come with me the day after tomorrow,' he burst out, 'to a meeting of the National Socialist party. I have just been there with the General. An unknown man spoke. I don't remember his name. But if anyone will free us from Versailles, this is the man — this unknown will restore our honour.'[17]

Hess clearly believed in Hitler from the first, and many others were similarly struck, as the meetings where Hitler was going to speak continued to get larger as the word spread. Such was his power that, by the autumn of 1921, Hitler took over from Drexler, who would be gone from the party within two years.

Now the Nazis fell fully in behind a 25 Point plan that Hitler had formulated, with some input from Drexler, the year before. Intensely nationalistic, these 25 Points broadly called for Germany to formally abrogate the terms of the Versailles Treaty. It was now time to re-arm, and bring together all of the chosen race, the Germanic people of Europe. This *Herrenvolk*, this master race, needed one super-state encompassing a *Grosswirtschaftsraum* (large, unified economic space) and it especially needed *Lebensraum* (living space) while also eliminating from German society all *Untermenschen* — subhumans — most particularly Jews, and such human detritus as gypsies, homosexuals and Slavic immigrants.

While Karl Marx had seen the history of the world as an ongoing clash between economic classes, and proposed a final seizing of power by the working class, Hitler's vision was that history was a clash between races, and he proposed that the superior Aryan race must seize control of its own destiny and force its will on the weaker races by pure right. And, after all, didn't they have the recent example before them of how it could be done?

When the great colonial age had been at its height, European powers like Britain, France, Holland, Portugal and Spain had claimed — while ruthlessly crushing all resistance — vast tracts of the world's surface and peoples for themselves. This was while the Germanic peoples, just like the Italians, had not yet united into one powerful state and therefore had not been able to effectively participate. But, Hitler made clear, that age should now be upon them and, just as all those countries had done in the past, the Germans would now take those lands.

This *Lebensraum* lay most obviously to the east of Germany — Poland, Czechoslovakia and Russia — where the bulk of the Slavic subhumans lived. This would ensure a barrier to the filthy and voracious Communists just beyond them, and with that land the German people could become entirely economically self-sufficient and capable of withstanding attacks from all the lesser races. All was possible once the German master race had made its conquests and positioned itself atop a hierarchy of subordinate peoples.

•

At this point, Hitler was far from the only one beating the drum that things must change. Around the world, a movement known as Fascism was taking hold, the broad brush strokes of which were all similar to Hitler's plans: the primacy of the state being valued above all other things, under the command of a strong, unquestioned leader atop a highly militaristic culture, with severe punishment for all dissenters. Whereas Communism, of course, attacked the business and land-owning classes, Fascism was quite the opposite, and enjoyed strong support from the business classes because of it — and in many ways was at its strongest when the fear of Communism could be harnessed to the cause.

The word 'Fascism' had an Italian derivation, and no one evinced it more than the same Benito Mussolini who had, just a few years before, been merely a disaffected corporal in the army, like Hitler.

No matter that Mussolini did not enjoy the support of 51 per cent of the nation, or even remotely close to that. The point in this instance was that, in a nation where all the cards had been thrown into the air because of the upheaval caused by the Great War, there was a growing belief that ordinary democracy could not work any more — because no one could achieve a majority of popular support — and, therefore, it was not the most popular who would, should or could rule, but the strongest. With the forces of Mussolini, this strength showed up not just in his preparedness to use violence to quell opposition, but in his ability to attract the kind of men who would provide that violence and put it onto the streets, at his service. That was never better demonstrated than in his march on Rome in late October 1922.

Loudly, violently, Mussolini's followers — distinctive because of the black shirts they used as a uniform — showed up on all roads leading to Rome, even though Mussolini himself took the train (*prima classe*). On that train, at one point, he was asked what he was thinking about, and he immediately replied, 'I am thinking about my dad.' Which was appropriate: some twenty years earlier his father, Alessandro, had been arrested and sent to prison for six months for smashing the ballot box in their native village on election day. Now, Benito was about to demonstrate that he had little more respect than his father for the classic workings of democracy.[18]

Within days the Italian government had collapsed, and Mussolini was the new leader.

Inspired, one year later the 33-year-old Hitler tried the same in his infamous Beer Hall Putsch, hoping to arrest the legitimately elected leaders of Bavaria, take control of communications and suspend the constitution, in the belief that the Nazis' followers around the nation would equally rise up and the Weimar Republic would be extinguished.

'I propose,' he told his roaring supporters in the lead-up to the putsch, 'that until accounts have finally been settled with the November criminals [the signatories of the Versailles Treaty], the direction of policy in the National Government be taken over by me.'[19]

True, once the putsch had collapsed — after a battle lasting just a minute, with fourteen Nazis and three policemen killed — Hitler was not, in fact handed the keys to the Chancellor's office. Instead he was to find himself in a prison cell in the Bavarian fortress of Landsberg am Lech for the next nine months — without any key whatsoever — but even the court case that had put him there had provided him another opportunity to make his case that Germany and his fellow Germans deserved better. And, just as sixty years earlier Chancellor Otto von Bismarck had first led Germany to greatness with the cry, 'The great questions of the day will not be solved by speeches and majority resolutions, but by blood and iron', so too did Hitler, an aspiring German Chancellor, express a similar sentiment now.

Germany had been betrayed, he said, and he and his band had been set upon saving it. 'In such a critical movement *ein Volk* (a people) cannot be saved by quiet reflection ... only fanaticism, hot, reckless, and utterly brutal fanaticism offers the means to rescue *ein Volk* from enslavement.'

It was strong stuff, and there was plenty more to come in a trial that lasted six weeks and received a lot of publicity and coverage across Germany. Every day, more Hitler, Hitler, Hitler! And even though the Bavarian court didn't *also* acquit them, Hitler's short spell in prison made him something of a martyr, and also gave him time to develop his ideas with the help of his fellow prisoner and now great friend, Rudolf Hess.

While Hitler talked and walked back and forth in the cell spouting on — 'The army is to be the ultimate school for patriotic education. In this school the youth shall become a man!' — Hess took notes. Slowly, the turgid and ungrammatical form of Hitler's virulent autobiography — which he wanted to call *Four and a Half Years of Struggle against Lies, Stupidity, and Cowardice* — took shape. Instead, the publisher to whom it was eventually handed decided to call it *Mein Kampf* — 'My Struggle'.

And so it went. The penniless prisoner Adolf Hitler continued to rant while the equally pathetic Rudolf Hess continued to faithfully write it all down, the latter genuinely convinced he was in the presence of a very great man who really would one day be able to lead Germany. ('I am more devoted to him than ever!' Hess gushed to his girlfriend. 'I love him!'[20])

Hitler raved on. And on. And on ... developing the kind of words and cadences that would before long have an even greater resonance ...

Ein Volk, ein Reich, ein Führer! One people, one state, one leader!

Outside the prison as he ranted, the conditions were turning ever more favourably towards Nazism flourishing. Such a radical belief system could only bloom in desperate times, when moderate forms of government were clearly not working, and this proved to be the case for the ill-fated Weimar Republic.

One of the Republic's worst weeping wounds was a continuing inability to meet the crippling payment schedule for the reparations imposed upon it by the Versailles Treaty. The problem was not just that the level of payments was so high, it was that much of Germany's heaviest industry and many of its crucial resources — like coal — had been in precisely those chunks of territory now donated to other countries. Desperate to try to bridge the gap, the government of the Weimar Republic notoriously attempted the solution of simply printing more money, which resulted in hyper-inflation and the currency ultimately becoming almost worthless, with a simple piece of bread costing four million marks on a *good* day. What had been a recession became a forerunner of the worldwide Depression, with unemployment rising, starvation taking hold and Hitler's popularity rising with every notch of suffering of the German people.

At the least, he was offering an alternative: revenge on those who had betrayed the country; the chance for Germany to be powerful again; and ruthless punishment to those who had so humiliated it.

•

Jack Edmondson was turning into a very special child, notable for a curious combination of great gentleness and extraordinary resolve, possessed of a fiercely independent spirit while still enjoying an enormous bond to both his parents, especially his mother.

Elizabeth had stood out among her woman friends for being the only one to never, ever smack her boy, but they all acknowledged that she did not spoil him despite the enormous attention she paid him. This attention included Elizabeth personally teaching her Jack for the first two years of his schooling, from when he was six years old, as the Austral Public School was a full 5 miles away and she was flat-out not prepared to have him ride that far on his own, even if he had been riding Black Bess since the age of three. And a good teacher she was, too, with Jack quickly picking up a great love of both reading and writing, and conceiving a great passion for learning about ancient Greek and Roman history. He particularly liked the Greeks, he told his mother, because they seemed 'kind and brave'. With his father, Jack shared a passion for horses, though the younger Edmondson male was looking after Bess on his own by the age of five — including changing her shoes — just as he could milk the cows by that age. When Jack turned eight, Black Bess was replaced by

Bonnie Doon, and Elizabeth finally deemed that he was ready to ride to school proper for the first time.

On the other side of the country in the southwest of Western Australia, in a woebegone place by the name of Mullalyup, the experience of young Ivor Hancock could not have been a greater contrast. Mullalyup was the kind of town where, although a train line went through it, no one seemed quite sure where the line came from, where it went, or if there had ever been a train along it. Way back when, people supposed, Mullalyup must have counted for something, to have had such an important thing as a train come to visit, but progress had long passed it — and them — by.

Ivor was the older of two boys of an extremely poor family of pioneers living on a farm 5 miles outside the town, and only a few shillings more above the subsistence level. Father was an embittered Great War veteran who had been gassed in France and never quite recovered, and mother was the daughter of a man of similar description. Home was a dirt floor, surrounded by some rough-hewn slabs of timber, with internal hessian walls to make 'rooms', covered by corrugated iron — and none of it warmed by familial love.

As a matter of fact, when, at the age of three, Ivor had broken his ankle and the first bout of treatment had gone wrong, his parents had taken him to a Perth hospital and just left him there, like a sack of rotten potatoes they had no use for. For months Ivor mostly lay on his back, staring at the cracks in the ceiling and trying to take his mind off the *maddening* itching beneath his plaster cast, waiting for his parents to return. At last his mother turned up, and he thought he was saved, but then she disappeared and didn't come back. *She didn't come back.* The lack of contact was so terrible that the hospital simply had to mark him down as an Abandoned Child, although that didn't seem to worry anyone noticeably. No one came to take him to a foster home or an orphanage or the like, as it was probably easier to let him just continue to lie there. Finally, late the following year — a full eighteen months after he had been admitted — Ivor's father dropped by, as he happened to be passing the hospital, only to be told that young Ivor had been able to go for months.

So, after some discussion, his father took the lame five-year-old home, but things were never the same again, and from then on Ivor always felt a great distance between himself and his family, and perhaps even a certain deadness or ache where he felt his heart should have been.

CHAPTER TWO

His Struggle

*In an era when the earth is gradually being divided up among states, some
of which embrace almost entire continents, we cannot speak of a world
power in connection with a formation whose political mother country is
limited to the absurd area of five hundred thousand square kilometres.*

— ADOLF HITLER MAKING GERMANY'S CASE FOR LEBENSRAUM[1]

*While [Italy] was conquering or seeming to conquer, the dictatorship
remained a nervous regime ... talking big because it was always
most likely that it was little ...*

— RICHARD BOSWORTH, MUSSOLINI'S BIOGRAPHER[2]

Upon Hitler's release in December 1924, the Nazi Party prospered, progressively attracting more of the disaffected segments of German society; and, from its beginnings in Munich, the swastika started fluttering first in other parts of Bavaria and thence around the German nation.

In fact, so well did things go that, by the end of 1925, the Nazis were able to boast 25 000 signed-up members. Moreover, a certain organisational genius on Hitler's part had seen the party establish the *Gauleiter*, or district leader, throughout Germany, whose job it was to harness and grow local support as well as begin to contest municipal, state and federal elections.

•

A girl!

On 4 March 1923, Myrtle Morshead gave birth to a healthy baby girl, Elizabeth. She would be Leslie and Myrtle's only child, and was perhaps all the more cherished because of it. Certainly, Daddy was always very busy, either because of his involvement with the 'weekend warriors' of Australia's Citizens Military Force, or pursuing his career in the burgeoning industry of shipping, with the prestigious company known as the Orient Line — a place where he could further hone his abilities to move men and machinery around with maximum efficiency — but he was nothing if not a devoted father.

•

A boy!

After many years of waiting, and hoping, Lucie Rommel gave birth to a healthy baby boy on Christmas Eve, 1928. Manfred would be Erwin and Lucie's only child, and was perhaps all the more cherished because of it, being very close to both his parents. Certainly, all through his early years there was a great sense of his father's importance — as a recognised expert on military tactics, Erwin Rommel was teaching first at Dresden Infantry School and then at the prestigious Potsdam War Academy — but Erwin was nothing if not a devoted father.

•

By 1929, the Nazi Party had 180 000 members and was a powerful, and growing, force in national affairs. If there was to be any stopping of Hitler, it was unlikely to come from within the Nazi Party, and certainly not from Rudolf Hess. For it was in that last gasp of the 1920s that Hitler had a long conversation with the ever-faithful Hess, and unleashed an idea so strong that Hess reported to his wife, 'He gave me a lecture on the solution to the Jewish problem which inwardly astounded me . . .'[3]

Meanwhile, in Britain the seeds of a similar kind of politics had been planted and were growing. On 1 October 1932, Sir Oswald Mosley (whose title was hereditary), had combined a number of smaller parties into the British Union of Fascists (BUF), devoted to the proposition that simple, traditional democracy was not going to be strong enough to resist the challenge posed by those who sought to mount in Britain a revolution like the one wrought in Russia. The BUF proposed instead to have a government strong enough to provide complete control over the markets, and to ensure full employment and better wages — including equal pay for women, though they also promised that under the British Fascist system men would make high enough wages that if their wives wanted to stay at home, that was equally to be encouraged. They foresaw a utopia so strong that no one would want to turn to drab Communism.

One of Mosley's first members was a certain William Joyce, an odd kind of man who had enough passion for English literature to gain a first-class honours degree in the subject from London University, but also loved physical violence enough to be constantly involved in brawling. (His curiously nasal drawl, as a matter of fact, had come from having his nose badly broken when he was engaged in a fierce fight while at school.) Initially, Joyce was a good man for Mosley to have on board for such a venture; he showed boundless energy, moving around the country from meeting to meeting, always encouraging the people to rise as one against the current weak democracy and embrace the full-blooded, strong spirit of Fascism. He was soon promoted to become the BUF's Director of Propaganda, as well as Deputy Leader of the Party.

•

Though Australia never had a figure remotely like either Hitler or Joyce rising to public attention, there is no doubt that there was an echo of their kind of dynamic let loose in the land — at least in the sense that the rise of Communism was greatly feared and there was a nagging doubt whether the normal democratic processes could be strong enough to withstand the rise of the Bolsheviks. So it was that an informal paramilitary group called the Old Guard arose in New South Wales (later effectively becoming the New Guard when the Young Turks established their own organisation), just as the White Guard flourished in Victoria. Both groups were essentially a rough coalition of former soldiers from the Great War, together with ideologues of the right and those who just loved the idea of a paramilitary group devoted to regular meetings and drill sessions, mixed with firebrand speeches where the common theme was the Armageddon to come if something wasn't done. Broadly, the groups were manifestations of what Australian historian Geoffrey Serle would later call 'a right-wing variation of Australian nationalism ... based on the new patriotism and pride of race of the protestant middle class'.[4]

In 1932, in New South Wales alone, there were as many as 75 000 members of the New Guard. Among other things, they were committed to thwarting the will of the NSW Labor government, notwithstanding the fact that it was precisely the government that the majority of people of New South Wales had chosen in the previous election.

Apart from many meetings and massed rallies, including in the Sydney Town Hall, the New Guard's most visible manifestation came with the opening of the Sydney Harbour Bridge. The NSW Premier, Jack Lang, was about to cut the ribbon when ...

When suddenly a member of the New Guard, Captain Francis de Groot, charged out from the ranks on horseback and cut it first! When de Groot was interviewed by NSW Police after he had cut the ribbon, one of the names he mentioned in passing was that of the then Victorian Police

Commissioner, and one of the key Australian heroes of the Great War, Thomas Blamey — heightening suspicions that Blamey was either a secret member of the White Guard, or even its principal commander.[5] This was not altogether surprising, as men of that ilk were certainly involved in the movement. In New South Wales it was even said — though there was never proof — that Leslie Morshead had been a part of the Old Guard.

What there could be no doubt about, however, was that both Blamey and Morshead at least shared the view of the paramilitary groups that the lack of expenditure by the Australian government since the Great War on the nation's defence was nothing short of disgraceful — and Morshead, in particular, frequently spoke out against it. In fact, so lax was the Australian military and political establishment's response to the way the world was turning that, half a century later, the eminent Australian historian Professor David Horner would write, 'It is now generally agreed that the Australian defence policy between the wars ... was at the best, naively optimistic, and at the worst, some might say, close to treason.'[6]

Australia was not the only country where this rather benign approach to military expenditure held sway. For while Germany had been moving progressively closer to outright militarism at this time — pushed along by the Nazis, who in 1932 had registered a staggering fourteen million votes in the national elections, which provided them with 230 elected representatives out of a total of 608 in the Reichstag — in places like Great Britain and the United States, the Great War really had had the opposite effect. That is, exhausted morally, spiritually and financially — and with the feeling that the war to beat all wars had already been fought and won — defence budgets were slashed as, figuratively, people went and did the Charleston instead.

•

In 1934, even the small counterweight to Hitler's control of German politics was removed with the elderly President Hindenburg's death, and Hitler formally became *der Führer*, as in, 'the Leader', which he most certainly was by virtue of holding the Chancellorship, as well as the position of Commander in Chief of the armed forces — with all members now swearing personal fealty to him:

'I swear by God this holy oath: I will render unconditional obedience to the Führer of the German Reich and People, Adolf Hitler, the Supreme Commander of the Armed Forces, and will be ready, as a brave soldier, to stake my life at any time for this oath.'

With Hitler's hands now on all crucial levers of government, Nazism soon permeated every last part of the German state. For, within months, it became compulsory for all those in the highest echelons of the civil service to also be members of the Nazi Party. Hitler's control was complete ... and the resources now poured into expanding the Army, particularly, were massive. Within a year of Hitler becoming Chancellor, the size of the German Army had trebled to 300 000 men. Within two years all youth organisations other than Hitler Youth became illegal — with the plan that by 1936 every child in Germany between the ages of ten and eighteen would be a member. A large part of the focus of Hitler Youth for both boys and girls was playing little military war games, with the youth dividing up into platoons and skirmishing with each other, trying to live up to the Hitler Youth's credo of *Blut und Ehre* (Blood and Honour).

As well, they engaged in marches, sang heavily nationalistic songs and revelled in animated discussions that examined exactly why it was that Aryans were the master race and precisely who it was who had most wronged them. One very popular measure by the Nazis had been to reduce the age when you could get a driver's licence from twenty-one to eighteen, and they had made it a lot cheaper to boot!

On some glorious occasions, the best of the Hitler Youth were able to see Hitler *personally*, as had happened at a gathering of the organisation in 1934, when, in the manner of a kindly but stern father, he made a mesmerising speech, his voice ringing around the stadium:

'Regardless of whatever we create and do, we shall pass away, but in you, Germany will live on ... And I know it cannot be otherwise because you are flesh of our flesh, blood of our blood, and your young minds are filled with the same will that dominates us ... And when the great columns of our movement march victoriously through Germany today, I know that you will join these columns. And we know that Germany is before us, within us, and behind us ...'[7]

It was, all of it, vintage Hitler, and there would be much more to come in similar vein:

'It is the army which has made men of us all, and when we looked upon the army our faith in the future of our people was always reinforced. This old glorious army is not dead; it only slept, and now it has arisen again in you!'

•

In *Mein Kampf,* Hitler had maintained that when it came to the forming of German youth 'his entire education and training must be designed to convince

him of his absolute superiority over others', and radical steps were now taken
to ensure that that was precisely what happened, including at school itself.

Biology became, at least in part, a study of why the Aryan race was
superior to all other races, starting with the Jews at the bottom — of whom
half a million were German — with emphasis placed on why racial purity
was so important. (And girls bleaching their hair blonde on the quiet
became very prevalent indeed.) In the subject of history, a great deal of time
was now spent looking at how Jews and Marxists had betrayed Germany to
deliver up the Treaty of Versailles, while when it came time to study
geography, the first thing on the agenda was a look at the lands that
Germany had had removed from her because of Versailles, land that was
still part of her *Lebensraum*. Science focused a great deal on the dynamics of
military aviation, the trajectory of missiles and so on. A good exam question
could even cover the lot:

> *A bomber aircraft on take-off carries 12 dozen bombs, each weighing*
> *10 kilos. The aircraft takes off for Warsaw, the international centre for Jewry.*
> *It bombs the town. On take-off with all bombs on board and a fuel tank*
> *containing 100 kilos of fuel, the aircraft weighed 8 tonnes. When it returns*
> *from the crusade, there are still 23 kilos left. What is the weight of the*
> *aircraft when empty?*[8]

When it came to Physical Education, Hitler's instructions were specific.
They had to be *Flink wie Windhunde, zäh wie Leder, und hart wie Kruppstahl*
(as fast as greyhounds, as tough as leather and as hard as Krupp steel).
Boxing was compulsory for boys, and at least one hour a day at school was
given over to PE. Such measures were rarely resisted by the people, least of
all by the youths themselves.

Down in Stuttgart, for example, the young teenager Rolf Völker found
the Hitler Youth terrific. He was a softly spoken, gentle lad, and his
enjoyment of the Hitler Youth had nothing to do with him having a
particularly militaristic bent. After all, his father had only survived his bitter
experience of fighting for the German Army against the British in Palestine
in the Great War by just long enough to conceive him, and his stepfather
had lost part of his arm and a good deal of his sanity fighting against the
Russians in the same war — so Rolf hardly aspired to emulate their
experience. Rather, it was the sudden opportunities that opened up for him
and his friends that he enjoyed. For Rolf, who was raised as a puritanical
Protestant, going on camps and picnics with the *Christliche Deutsche Jugend*

(Christian German Youth) had been fine as far as it had gone — he had particularly enjoyed going to green meadows on many picnics, to play his guitar and sing with his friends — but it hadn't really been exciting (though he had felt sorry for a Jewish schoolfriend who had cried because he had not been allowed to join the Hitler Youth like everyone else, nor to wear the brown shirts). When Rolf was thirteen and Hitler had come to power, everything changed.

Of course, the wholehearted embrace of the Nazi values of *Arbeit und Ordnung* (work and order) wasn't necessarily easy for schoolboys, but there was also fun to be had, and a lot of that came after the Christian German Youth had been folded into the Hitler Youth. Suddenly, *everything* was possible for these young lads, all dressed the same in brown shirts and black shoes, all feeling an extraordinary oneness.

The boys only had to express an interest in flying, and they would be taken to the local military airfield, where they could climb all over a plane, and some lucky lads could even be taken up in one. So too with the army, where they were shown machine guns and invited to fire them, and they were taken to look at barracks and meet real live *generals*, while those who thought the navy might be for them soon found themselves on ships. With opportunities like that, it wasn't long before the prayer groups and picnics were completely passé and entirely unlamented. Now they were learning martial skills, singing songs and reciting poems with the common theme being that there was no greater honour than to die for the Fatherland. They were told, and gloried in, the fact, that they weren't just kids — they were the next generation of Germany, and it was going to be up to them to make Germany great again.

Rolf soaked it all up. As a young boy he had spent a few years in the occupied part of the Rhineland, in the Frankenthal area, and humiliation at the hands of French soldiers had been their everyday lot. When a French soldier was on the footpath, you had to get off and walk on the road to let him walk through, and their every bit of swagger never let you forget that Germany had lost the war so badly that it had had to sign the Versailles Treaty. And now Hitler was offering a way to tear up that treaty? Well, he had Rolf's support.

•

In Australia, Jack Edmondson's own education could not have been in greater contrast. He was now at Austral Public School, situated about 40 miles southwest of downtown Sydney, and his teacher, Mr Rae — who had been impressed with the job Elizabeth had done with Jack's home tutoring — regarded him as a 'sturdy, earnest little schoolboy'.[9] Still, when a new government school moved in nearby with a specifically agricultural bent, a place called Hurlstone Agricultural High School, Jack was the first student enrolled, on the first day it was open for business on its new premises. This was because that school offered strong tuition in all things farming — Jack's great dream was to one day take over the family spread from his father — as well as allowing the softly spoken young man to indulge his passions for such things as the writings of Charles Dickens and the music of Mozart and Beethoven, which he delighted in playing on the piano. (At a later point, when he turned twenty-one, the present he requested of his parents was the complete collected works of Dickens.)

Muscular without being enormous, Jack became a valued member of the school's First Rugby XV, and outside of school he was a very keen member of the Liverpool–Cabra Vale Rifle Club. His prowess with a rifle became such that at the age of seventeen he won a highly coveted marksmanship prize from the National Rifle Club.[10] Though he had flat-out refused to go hunting for such things as rabbits — because he just liked them, that's all, and as a kid had always caught them and made them pets rather than eating them — he would sometimes knock crows and hawks out of the sky, as they were particularly damaging pests on the property.

On weekends, if Jack was not playing rugby or off shooting, he could usually be found going for long walks with his mother, or helping his father on the farm.[11] Things military were far, far away.

•

On the other side of the country, and at a far lower socioeconomic level, the experience of Ivor Hancock could not have been more different again to that of Jack Edmondson. Whereas Jack was attending the finest school in his district and prospering there, just as he did at home in the bosom of his family, the still slightly limping Ivor had dropped out of school at the age of only fourteen on the grounds that he hated it, and in all likelihood it hated him. What did he do after that? The best he could, mostly hiring himself out for cheap labour and working on the dairy farm ...

By this time, after Ivor's father had finally given up the unequal struggle to make a living off the land, the family returned to Victoria after ten years in Western Australia, with only the clothes they stood up in, and began by settling in the tiny town of Pura Pura, just west of Melbourne.

•

In his Sydney office, meantime, Australia's most high-powered Nazi in residence, a diplomat by the name of Dr Rudolf Asmis, finished the report he had been asked to write on how Australia organised its own race relations, before sending it off to Berlin. Based on an extensive trip he had just completed to the Northern Territory and Western Australia, he titled it 'Australian Aboriginal Policy', and made many points:

'Segregation is the catch-cry,' he wrote. 'The government has gradually decided to allocate certain areas to the Aborigines as reserves where they are kept in as though in a national park. Unfortunately the borders of these reserves do not appear to have been established in any final sense and if a valuable mineral deposit is discovered in the reserves, as recently occurred at Tennant Creek, the borders are simply moved and the Aborigine has to give way ...

'I was able to observe the accommodation, food provisions and employment of Aborigines on cattle stations at first hand ... If they refuse to work, they receive no food rations; should they become rebellious, paternal floggings might well be meted out. Running away from the station is hardly possible, as the neighbouring stations have an agreement among themselves not to employ a black man from another station ...

'For the station owner, the Aborigine is no more than an animal, with no wish other than to have a full belly, and which he cares for as long as it is necessary in his own interest. But there is no doubt that what has been achieved on these stations is that the Aborigines have become accustomed to work, and heavy work at that, and that they know that they will not obtain food and clothing unless they work.'

Which in his view was to the good, and perhaps there was something the Nazis could learn from this.

When it came to disciplining them, though, the Nazi doctor wasn't quite so sure that the white Australians were doing things in the right way.

'In the opinion of most experts, imprisonment is pointless for Aborigines, as it has no deterrent or educative effect, so that even the Royal Commissioner charged with investigating the living conditions of Aborigines in Western Australia recommends whipping as a more appropriate punishment in so far as it is carried out without undue harshness and in the presence of as many members of the tribe as possible ...'

The diplomat even found some Australian treatment too harsh, saying, 'When they are employed outside the gaols, and while being transported, coloured prisoners are chained together, or they are handcuffed. This latter seems to me to be an unnecessary hardship in view of the fly-plague prevailing in the entire interior of the continent ...'

Then there was the troubling matter of whether killing them off entirely really was a good idea.

'The possibility of employing [the Aborigines] in the work force would permit an economic development of the country which would not exist with the use of white labour alone,' the doctor wrote. 'While it is true that the extermination of a whole people has enabled a relatively small number of persons to take possession of enormous areas of land and provided them with large fortunes with a minimum of effort, it is also true that the most important branch of industry in Australia, the wool industry, presupposed pushing most of the Aborigines out of the sheep country. Nonetheless, to me, it is very doubtful whether it would not have been much wiser and much more farsighted — completely regardless of an ethical obligation towards an indigenous population — had they adopted all possible measures from the time of the division of the land between white and black to try to maintain this population, measures which the Government now sees itself forced to take at the last moment as a result of attacks by humanitarians, had they educated and developed the Aborigines for work gradually from the very beginning. Plantations, mining and farming would have had cheap coloured labour ...'[12]

Dr Asmis sent the whole report off to Berlin, in the hope that it would provide food for thought for the Foreign Office, of which Joachim von Ribbentrop had just arisen as the Nazi minister in charge.

•

Slowly, slowly, and then with ever greater force, things that Hitler had first proposed in *Mein Kampf* began to take shape. The military was revitalised with progressively more resources being put towards it, the laws against the Jews in Germany became ever more vicious, and the power of both Hitler and Germany was growing by the month.

While in some respects Italy was developing on a parallel course to Germany — both under Fascist regimes — there was no doubt that the kind of Fascism developing in the two countries was entirely different. In Germany its foundation stone was a hard-baked militarism, avaricious for power and territory at any cost, whereas in Italy Fascism had a far softer, more languid way about it. Perhaps it was the Mediterranean sun, or the wonderful pasta or the wine, or the mostly voluptuous approach Italians took to life, but to observers it often appeared as if the Italians were much more into the spectacle of full-blown Fascism rather than totally committed to building a machine with genuine, whirring steel blades that could cut down anything, as the Germans were so clearly doing.

When, for example, Mussolini visited Hitler in Munich, what impressed him most was neither the state-of-the-art Panzers, nor the high-powered artillery weaponry that he inspected. Rather, he loved the impressive high goose step of the marching German soldiers, and it wasn't long before the Italian dictator made his desires known that his troops should begin practising their own version of it, which became known as the *passo Romano*.[13] (As to Hitler himself, however, Mussolini was never, particularly in the early years of their association, an admirer. And if Hitler must sometimes have wondered whether Mussolini had a problem with his genitalia, it is worth noting that the Italian was a deeply, *deeply* superstitious man, and whenever he encountered someone whom he thought possessed 'the evil eye', he would furiously engage in the traditional defence, which was to scratch his testicles.[14])

True, in real military terms it was extremely difficult for Italy to keep in step with Germany, but they did the best they could ...

In March 1936, Hitler sent in forces to militarily reoccupy the Rhineland, to regain what Germany had lost from the Great War, in strict contravention of the Versailles Treaty which had removed it; his actions caused loud and strident protests from Britain and France, but no more than that. Shortly afterwards Mussolini made his own highly militaristic move by sending Italian forces to invade Eritrea and Abyssinia, the better to foist his own Fascist vision upon the world, of a modern *Imperium Romanum*, complete with its own colonies. Again, leaders in Britain and France made more angry speeches, and imposed some half-hearted sanctions, which did not include the thing that Italy needed most: oil. And yet far from dissuading Italy in its territorial ambitions, these responses rather pushed Italy closer to Germany, resulting in Mussolini declaring a 'Rome–Berlin Axis'.

One concrete thing did change for a spectator country. Because Egypt now started to look askance at Italy's intention in Egypt's part of the world, it allowed Britain to base a large number of forces in its territory, including a base for Britain's naval fleet at Alexandria — something that would prove significant in coming years.

•

If Australia watched Italy's — and especially Germany's — slide into totalitarian militarism with a small sense of foreboding as to what it would mean for the British Empire, still it was all so far away that it was quite possible to ignore it entirely — and a large chunk of the population did exactly that. Some, though, were placed in a situation where Hitler was just impossible to ignore, and in that case their mood did indeed turn ugly.

One such was an Australian cyclist by the name of Edgar 'Dunc' Gray, who, at one frozen moment in time in 1936, looked at the pointy end of his spear, looked at Adolf Hitler swanning past just 15 yards away, and in a moment of madness thought that he would probably be doing a very good thing if he just bloody well drove the spear into Hitler's heart and so be done with it. But then sanity returned.

Gray was Australia's flag bearer at the Berlin Olympic Games of 1936, and the Opening Ceremony was about to get under way. For all that, Gray was not alone in the Australian Olympic team in feeling a great deal of antipathy towards both Hitler and his Germany, as they had come to see a Fascist state close up. From the moment they'd arrived for the Games, there just seemed to be a bad feeling in the air, with more Nazi flags displayed everywhere than there were Olympic flags, armed soldiers omnipresent, and the knowledge that the newly constructed Olympic Village they were staying in was going to be — what else but? — officers' barracks after they left.

What's more, the Australian team couldn't help but notice that the German people generally gave the serious impression of being right into this cove Hitler, who all of Europe and the world were talking about. You'd never believe it if you hadn't seen it with your own eyes, but when the Germans met each other in the street, instead of shaking hands or giving a Teutonic version of 'How ya going?', they would throw their arm out and yell 'Heil Hitler!' and all that sort of malarkey.

Sure, the Australian Olympic team got into it, too, after a while, and started shouting out 'Hail Mary!' at each other as they passed in the corridor … or even 'Haile Selassie!' in reference to the Emperor of Ethiopia, then in the news for leading the resistance to an invasion of his country by the absurd little Italian dictator, Benito Mussolini. But the whole thing was a worry, all right.

In the stadium, while Dunc Gray was fuming outside, Rudolf Hess was settling in to watch the Opening Ceremony himself. Despite his exalted position as Deputy Führer to Hitler, he was far from universally admired. He was sometimes known as 'Fräulein Anna'[15] by party homosexuals for his curious manner and slavish devotion to the Führer, and Hitler regarded his loyalty as so rock-solid that he was an ideal defender of the Führer's throne. On this day, though, whatever might have been his own inadequacies when he was not shining from the reflected light of Hitler's power and proximity, Hess was surrounded by many dignitaries from around the world. One of them was a young, good-looking British Member of Parliament and famous aviator, whose title was the Marquis of Clydesdale, later to become the Duke of Hamilton. Whether Hess, himself a very enthusiastic pilot, met the Marquis on this occasion was later to become the subject of great conjecture, but there is no doubt that this was a significant crossing of life trajectories ...[16]

•

Not so very far away and only a short time later, the accomplished Sydney businessman Leslie Morshead happened to be in Britain, in his capacity as Sydney Passenger Manager for the Orient Line. As he was also one of the leading lights of the Citizens Military Force — whose job it was to give Australia some reserve of military skills, against the day they might be needed for another war — while over there he made sure to make time to update his military knowledge. Most importantly, he went to watch the British 5th Brigade and 2nd British Division engage in war exercises in some of the more picturesque fields of East Anglia, north of London, and was immensely impressed. The firepower and versatility of their guns! The way one of these new Brens could go from a single shot to automatic with the simple flick of a switch! In personal expression Morshead was rarely a man given to exclamation marks, but on this occasion nothing else would do.

Most of all, though, the Australian businessman was taken by the extraordinary speed of the British brigade's movement across the terrain. Whereas in the Great War he and his comrades had marched endlessly, what the modern soldier needed to move from one position to another, he realised, was wheels and plenty of them. And not just any wheels — they needed wheels like the British had, with armoured vehicles all around, capable of taking direct hits in battle and still keeping going. In one exercise that really impressed Morshead, two infantry brigades had started a mock clash some 60 miles apart, but within two hours were at each other. And together with this speed of movement, the British had also wondrously improved their communications so that decisions could be taken, literally, on the run, and sent to all parts of the battle theatre to create a hopefully cohesive action.

The British were a long, long way ahead of what Australia possessed militarily at this time, and Morshead didn't mind saying so upon his return. In various reports and addresses to audiences with varying degrees of clout he insisted that it was time for the Australian Government to put resources towards modernising its forces since, effectively, the whole game had changed.

'Modern warfare, as I see it,' he said in a speech to the United Services Institute in Sydney in early 1937, 'places a premium on dash and audacity. If you are overcautious you will be overtaken ... everything will be much more scattered and much more open than in the past. In the early stages of a major European war, mechanisation and "motorisation" will play a vital part, and, at the outset, there will be a great deal of jockeying for position.'[17] Alas, few were taking serious note.

•

In Germany, meanwhile, one man who was working hard to ensure that Germany's own military tactics and strategies were state of the art, across the board, was Erwin Rommel. For, even as Morshead continued to sound the alarm in Australia, Rommel was nearing completion of a book that had been gestating for a couple of decades, and that he'd been actively working on for several years. A lot of it was made up of lectures that he'd been giving at the War College in Potsdam, just southwest of Berlin, that he'd now edited to fit the book format.

Entitled *Infanterie Greift An* — 'Infantry Attacks' — it was a compendium of everything he knew about military tactics in specific battle situations, liberally laced with anecdotes and accounts of actions he had figured in during World War I. Whatever else, no one could say that he had pulled any punches.

When discussing the Italians, for example — against whom he had fought so ferociously in the Great War — Rommel was scathing: 'In the battles from October 24 to 26, 1917, various Italian regiments regarded their situation as hopeless and gave up fighting prematurely when they saw themselves attacked on the flank or rear. The Italian commanders lacked resolution. They were not accustomed to our supple offensive tactics, and besides, they did not have their men well enough in hand.'[18]

Luckily — given that Italy was now a very close ally of Germany, and effectively their only brother in arms — Rommel's view was that things had now changed. 'Today,' Rommel wrote, with perhaps more confidence than he surely felt, 'the Italian Army is one of the best in the world ...'

For the rest, there were many stories in the book of his own battles, the orders he had given, what had subsequently happened, together with what he had learned from the whole exercise. In general, he believed in leadership operating from as near to the front lines as possible, the virtues of constantly pushing the attack and, always, the importance of flanking movements, perpetually probing around the enemy's main defences, finding the weak point and launching everything at that.

The book was an immediate success when it was first released early in 1937, with one reader being more important than all the rest put together: Chancellor Adolf Hitler loved the book from the first. (While it certainly wasn't the equal of the masterpiece *Mein Kampf*, it wasn't bad.) It was on the strength of this, together with a brief but impressive dealing the Chancellor had already had with the rising military commander, that Hitler arranged to meet Rommel to discuss a possible new role for him ...

•

It was a moonless night, exactly the way Billy Wright liked them. Just as lizards are drawn to sunshine, so are thieves to the darkness. Carefully, oh so carefully, Billy made his way across the roof of the Pyrmont warehouse in Sydney's inner west, right to the spot where he knew the skylight to be. A quick jemmy with the tyre lever he carried with him and it opened. Securing the heavy rope he also carried to a nearby chimney, in no time at all he was lowering himself to the floor below, and then making his way to where he knew the safe was. This was always his favourite part. Removing the satchel from his shoulder, he took out his torch, fuses, explosives and detonators, and got to work. After packing the safe door with the explosives, he went and found the bags of coarse salt that he knew were located elsewhere in the warehouse, and packed them close around the dynamite, knowing that this would make the explosives have a much greater effect. Now setting the timer for fifteen minutes, he was quickly up and away, back on the roof and down on the street safely.

The folks who lived around said it felt like an earthquake. In any case, it was an extraordinary explosion, and from the moment it happened Billy knew that he might have overdone it just a tad. The telltale sign was that the entire front wall of the warehouse had come down, and the safe bounced out into the street right in front of him! That last was the good part; the bad part was that everyone who lived within a bloody bull's roar was soon there in their pyjamas, dressing gowns and slippers, trying to work out what had happened, bringing the cops with them, and there was simply nothing that could be done. After mingling with all the stickybeaks, Billy slunk away into the night, his hands jammed hard into his still-empty pockets, back to the mean streets of Glebe.

•

If Hitler was particularly manic in September 1938, even by his own lofty standards, it was perhaps because he had had such a remarkable year thus far. In February he had consolidated, to the point of total domination, his hold over the German military forces by establishing the *Oberkommando der Wehrmacht*, known as the 'OKW', to replace the former War Ministry. It was a domain that was answerable to him and him alone — his decree setting it up had plainly stated: 'Command authority over the entire Armed Forces is from now on exercised directly by me personally.' Most particularly — and this was in many ways the point of it — the OKW was designed to control the last bastion of the old-style Prussian military German Army High Command, known as the OKH (*Oberkommando des Heeres*).

Only a month after establishing himself as a completely unchallengeable political and military dictator, Hitler then realised part of his long-held dream of at least partial reunification of the German people, by giving Austria a stark choice between annexation or annihilation. Austria reluctantly chose annexation, and after being absorbed into greater Germany — in a process which became known as *der Anschluss* — ceased to exist as a separate country.

Another Hitler triumph!

And still there was more to come, as the German Chancellor would make clear in a speech to the Nuremberg Rally, which was held in the famous German city from 6 to 12 September 1938, swelling the population from 500 000 to about 1.5 million for the duration. These rallies, as a hard-rising Australian Broadcasting Commission (ABC) radio journalist by the name of Chester Wilmot described them, were 'more than a mere party meeting ... it is almost the Nazi Holy Week ... the time when pilgrims from all parts of Germany come to worship their Lord and Führer, and to work themselves into such an unreasoning frenzy that by comparison a meeting of the hot-gospellers in Harlem looks like a pleasant Sunday afternoon.'[19]

Wilmot, twenty-eight years old and the son of a famous journalist, was on his way to becoming the cream of the ABC crop. Educated at Melbourne's Church of England Grammar School and Melbourne University, he was every bit as worldly, articulate and forthright as might be expected of one who had captained the university debating team to great success on a tour encompassing universities in Britain, continental Europe,

East Asia and North America, before returning to Australia, and —
convinced there was going to be a world war — deciding to become a
journalist. And after just one week in Nuremberg, he viewed the coming
war as a certainty, as it appeared that the bulk of the citizenry believed that
their militarism was fully justified, and Germany really did have a right to its
Lebensraum, and if other races had to be forcibly moved aside to achieve it,
then so be it.

•

Yet, while the rest of Europe was not nearly so compelled by the same
argument, the bottom line was that they were not prepared to fight to stop
Hitler achieving his aims. That, at least, was the purport of what became
known as the Munich Agreement, a treaty signed in Munich on 29 September
1938 by Hitler of Germany, Benito Mussolini of Italy, Prime Minister Neville
Chamberlain of Britain and Premier Edouard Daladier of France, whereby the
latter two nations agreed that Hitler could march his troops into the
Sudetenland and in return Hitler would make no further claims on any other
territory in Europe.

The following day Chamberlain flew back to London, walked down the
steps of his aircraft, waving the agreement to massive cheers, and then made
his way in his motorcade through rain-sodden but applauding crowds all
the way to Buckingham Palace, where he appeared on the balcony with
King George VI and Queen Elizabeth, to acknowledge yet more acclaim
from a grateful populace for a man of peace, who had delivered exactly that.
Returning to 10 Downing Street, he was persuaded to appear at the first-
floor window to greet still more crowds who had gathered and utter the
words which would become his most famous: 'We regard the agreement
signed last night . . . as symbolic of the desire of our two peoples never to go
to war with one another again. We are resolved that the method of
consultation shall be the method adopted to deal with any other questions
that may concern our two countries, and we are determined to continue
our efforts to remove possible sources of difference, and thus to contribute
to assure the peace of Europe. My good friends, for the second time in our
history, a British Prime Minister has returned from Germany bringing
peace with honour. I believe it is *peace for our time*. Go home and get a nice
quiet sleep.'[20]

However, the agreement did not meet with universal acclaim. To begin
with, the Czechoslovakians were outraged that their country had effectively
been sacrificed on the altar of peace at any cost — *their* cost — and all at a

conference of powers that they were not even invited to attend! As Czechoslovakia's Ambassador to Great Britain, Jan Masaryk, put it in a note, 'Your people have finished us — let me down. You advised us to mobilise; then you told us to give up our defences — and now we cannot defend ourselves against any brigand.'[21]

Equally, beyond just the outrage visited upon Czechoslovakia, many influential people in Britain were convinced that the Hitler beast would never be sated, and that giving in to him only made him and Germany stronger, meaning that the bill that would have to be paid later would be all the higher. One who felt that very strongly was the imperious British parliamentarian Winston Churchill, who rather theatrically walked out of the House of Commons while Chamberlain was attempting to justify the treaty by saying, 'Ever since I assumed my present office my main purpose has been to work for the pacification of Europe, for the removal of those suspicions and those animosities which have so long poisoned the air. The path which leads to appeasement is long and bristles with obstacles. The question of Czechoslovakia is the latest and perhaps the most dangerous. Now that we have got past it, I feel that it may be possible to make further progress along the road to sanity.'[22]

Churchill himself, however, thought the whole thing was insanity and would not be appeased with fine sentiments or high hopes, making his own reply in the House two days later. He was scathing about Chamberlain's 'agreement', noting: 'The utmost he has been able to gain for Czechoslovakia and in the matters which were in dispute has been that the German dictator, instead of snatching his victuals from the table, has been content to have them served to him course by course.'[23]

And he held out no hopes for a peaceful future: 'We have sustained a total and unmitigated defeat,' he thundered, 'and ... France has suffered even more than we have ...

'We are in the presence of a disaster of the first magnitude which has befallen Great Britain and France ...

'And do not suppose this is the end,' he warned. 'This is only the beginning of the reckoning. This is only the first sip, the first foretaste of a bitter cup which will be proffered to us year by year unless by a supreme recovery of moral health and martial vigour, we arise again and take our stand for freedom as in olden times.'[24]

Around the Commonwealth, others took up the cry that the Munich Agreement was a total disaster, and that far from meaning peace for our time, it had in fact created a terrible slide into inevitable war, as Hitler must now be convinced that Britain, on the tragic example of Neville Chamberlain, was simply not prepared to fight to stop him.

•

One who read of Churchill's reaction with particular interest was Robert Menzies, the Australian Attorney General in the conservative government of Joseph Lyons. A keen observer of British politics, Menzies had met Churchill on one of his trips to Britain, three years earlier, when the celebrated British Cabinet Secretary Maurice Hankey had taken his Australian friend to see the eccentric Churchill at his estate 25 miles southeast of London, Chartwell. When they had got there, they found Churchill wallowing in a swimming pool he had built himself, looking rather like a hippopotamus in a mud pond, fat and contented. Over tea, Menzies had been obliged to listen for a long time as Churchill divested himself of his views of how shocking Britain's defences were and how it was near criminal that they had been let go to that extent, all while Hitler's Germany was building its military might up! For all that, Menzies was not overwhelmed with awe.

'My impression,' Menzies wrote in his diary that night, 'is of a man who lives too well and lacks that philosophical mental self-discipline which prevents a man from going to excesses of either mind or body. But an arresting person — and I had no delusions of grandeur in his presence!'[25]

•

Back in Australia, the rise of the Nazis and the sheer violence and power of their rule at last focused attention on the likelihood that the world was on the precipice of a war that Australia would almost certainly follow the motherland, Great Britain, into, and that preparations had to be made to ensure that the Australian military would have the requisite manpower and firepower. Of course, after two decades of solid neglect, this was no small matter to organise. Yet on 27 October 1938, in the wake of the Munich Agreement — and in part because of the thunderings of former Prime Minister Billy Hughes, who remained in parliament and was constantly sounding the alarm — the government of Australian Prime Minister Joseph Lyons announced that it would double the size of the Citizens Military Force to 60 000 men, and a month later this number was increased to 70 000. Recruitment campaigns were launched and the plan was to have a body of men trained and substantially ready to go, against the day that a war was declared — without, yet, having to go to the budget-breaking expense of having an enormous army on stand-by. Germany had introduced the universal draft in 1935, with every young man of suitable age compelled to join one of the three services, but that was not the Australian way. The government wanted first and foremost the men who wished to fight for their country, and the call went out ...

Quite a few Australian males answered that call, and they included young Jack Edmondson, now a strapping 25-year-old. Though he was prone to bad asthma attacks, that didn't stop him. And nor did it matter that Jack had no real desire to learn how to kill other people. Simply put, he felt it was his duty, and from early 1939 he was attending weekly drill sessions and training weekends away, totalling twelve days a year, with the 4th Battalion of the Citizens Military Force, which was based at Merrylands, not too far from his home in the southern suburbs of Sydney. In short order he rose to the rank of Corporal.

Close by, one who had already been a part of the CMF for two years at this time — even though he was only sixteen years old — was a mere slip of a lad by the name of Bert Ferres, who had joined the 45th Battalion of Arncliffe, which used to meet right opposite the dusty factory where he worked making radio cabinets. Civilian life had been very tough for young Bert, obliged as he was to work from seven-thirty in the morning to five o'clock in the afternoon, being bullied by foremen for much of the time, and then going home to the thin fibro shack with a tin roof that the government provided for destitute families in Culver Street, Ramsgate, in Sydney's southern suburbs. Bert's embittered father had been a successful businessman simply wiped out by the Depression, who now got by the best he could with a bit of labouring work. Most nights, the best meal the family of six could afford was bread and dripping. It was, for the most part, a drab, dull existence for young Bert — all for the slave wages of 17 shillings and sixpence a week — and he hated it.

But in the Citizens Military Force it was different! Maybe they had guessed Bert was only fourteen when he'd joined two years earlier, in 1937 — he'd lied about his age to get in — but they didn't seem to care. For Bert — who'd dreamed of being a soldier from the age of eight onwards, when he'd first picked up a pistol in the travelling carnival penny-a-pop sideshows at Brighton le Sands — there was a real sense of belonging with the 45th Battalion, filled as it was with good, decent men whom he admired. Too, for the first time in his life he had a chance to do exciting things, like bayonet drills, firing real .303 rifles on the Randwick rifle range, and even occasionally, on weekends, firing a Lewis machine gun. Suddenly Bert was really good at something. At school he had never been any good at the three Rs, nor sport, and as a worker he had been no more than average. But with a .303 in his hands, he felt like he'd grown an extra limb, was comfortable with it, and could just about wing a passing sparrow if he had to. It was the same with the Lewis. He just knew what to do.

Sure, when his father found out what he had done, Bert caught hell, as Ferres senior was a committed pacifist and didn't want to lose his boy as 'cannon fodder' in some useless war, as had happened to so many in the Great War; but that was by the by. Bert loved his time with the 45th Battalion too much to even think of giving it up, and he only hoped there would be a war. Please, let there be a war . . .

•

And then, the last part of the jigsaw puzzle of Neville Chamberlain's worst nightmare fell into place. On 23 August 1939, the Soviet Union of Josef Stalin and Adolf Hitler's Germany signed a non-aggression pact, the effect of which was that neither country would attack the other, and would help the other if attacked. The transparent design was for both countries to attack Poland and divide it, for starters, between them, before likely moving on to the rest of Europe. And even though just the following day Neville Chamberlain's Britain announced the formation of the Anglo–Polish pact — whereby Britain reaffirmed its commitment of five months earlier to unilaterally guarantee Poland's security if it was attacked — for most it appeared to be too little, too late. Those who knew the parlous state of British defences at that time, with only 620 combat-ready aircraft, 259 tanks and not even that many anti-tank guns, were even more fearful about what might happen.

It seemed clear to many international observers, under such circumstances, that just about nothing could prevent another world war, with the Soviet Union now joining Germany's Fascists — and possibly those of Italy if Mussolini came on board. They would be lined up against Britain and France and the rest of Europe not yet under the Nazi yoke.

With such inevitability, there was a lot of last-minute scurrying as many of those who still could — including some Jewish families — fled Germany. But, too, there was at least some movement the other way. One such traveller was the noted British Fascist William Joyce, who, with his family in tow, began a journey to Berlin on 26 August 1939. He'd been tipped off that if he stayed in England and war broke out, he would have been interned as an enemy of the state until hostilities were over. In previous months Joyce had been more vocal than ever to the effect that the Chamberlain government was entirely at fault, and that the only way forward was for Britain to become an *ally* of Germany, and embrace the Nazi model. Joyce arrived in Germany in the last days of August, was warmly welcomed, and immediately set about finding a way he could make himself useful to the Nazis.

And, as it turned out, he had escaped from Britain just in time . . .

CHAPTER THREE

A World at War . . .

An infantry battalion at battle strength was made up of about six hundred men. But six hundred men do not make a battalion. The six hundred men have to learn the soldiers' trades and disciplines. Even then they are not a battalion. An effective battalion in being ready to fight, implies a state of mind — I am not sure if it is not a state of grace. It implies a giving and a taking, a sharing of almost everything — possessions, comfort, affection, trust, confidence, interest. It implies a certain restriction, and at the same time a certain enriching and widening of the human spirit. It implies doing a hundred things together — marching to the band, marching all night long, being hungry, thirsty, exhausted, filthy; being near but never quite mutinous. It involves not the weakening but the deferment of other bonds and interests; the acceptance that life and home are now with the battalion. In the end it is possible to say 'the battalion thinks' or 'the battalion feels' and this is not an exaggeration.

HISTORIAN HENRY GULLETT[1]

If it moves, salute it; if it doesn't move, pick it up; and if you can't pick it up, paint it.

A COMMON SAYING AMONG ALLIED SOLDIERS IN WORLD WAR II

At 8 o'clock on the night of 31 August 1939, a company of German soldiers that answered to *dem Reichssicherheitshauptamt* (the Reich Security Central Office) staged an attack on their own radio station at a place called Gleiwitz, right beside the Polish border. While one of the German soldiers who spoke Polish made a brief inflammatory address into the microphone, claiming Gleiwitz for Poland, others brought forward some prisoners from a nearby concentration camp who had been drugged and dressed in Polish military uniforms for the occasion. Then the Germans shot them dead, and scattered their bodies around the station, before the press arrived. Radio Cologne had already reported that German police were

then and there fighting off a force of Polish invaders at Gleiwitz. The stage
was set . . .

•

For in the early hours of 1 September 1939, following exactly to the
schedule set out by Hitler himself — a schedule that had never included
anything so prosaic or old-fashioned as a 'Declaration of War' — the first of
2000 Panzers crossed the border with Poland and, together with 2000
planes and well over a million German soldiers, unleashed devastation the
likes of which the world had never seen.

It famously became known as *Blitzkrieg* and it was that — with
everything done *Blitzartig schnell* (at lightning speed) — as a massive
armoured force was brought to bear on a specific point of the enemy's
defences, followed up by highly mobile infantry and artillery units working
together in a co-ordinated fashion to totally overwhelm all resistance by
attacking from many directions at once with a wide range of weaponry, not
least of which was usually a massive array of bombers and fighters hitting
precise targets at equally precise times. The Panzers, however, remained at
the prow and it was the role of the infantry and artillery to ensure that the
tanks could keep advancing, regardless of what resistance there might be.

Like many young Germans at that time, Rolf Völker heard on the radio
many of the stirring words that Hitler said to the soldiers of the German
Army on the day of the invasion: 'The Polish State has refused the peaceful
settlement of relations which I desired, and has appealed to arms. Germans
in Poland are persecuted with bloody terror and driven from their houses.
A series of violations of the frontier, intolerable to a great power, prove that
Poland is no longer willing to respect the frontier of the Reich. In order to
put an end to this lunacy, I have no other choice than to meet force with
force from now on. The German Army will fight the battle for the honour
and the vital rights of the reborn Germany with hard determination.' It
seemed right. Rolf, like so many of his peers, believed in *Führer, Volk und
Vaterland*, and if Hitler said that the aggressive Poles had to be brought to
heel for the greater good of the German people and the Fatherland, then
Rolf for one believed him. Before Hitler appeared, as a people they had
been hungry, miserable and trodden upon. Now they had food in their
bellies, were proud, and were able to tread on others if they wanted.

Even though Rolf's schooling was over and he was studying to be an
engineer — meaning he was now old enough to serve in the military — it
didn't seem likely that his life would radically change because of Poland.

Germany had simply taken back what had been stolen from it, and like the situations before in Austria and Czechoslovakia, that was likely to be the end of the matter. Despite its *fait accompli* feel, Rolf volunteered to serve in the Army for, in his certain view, Germany had right on its side, and it was his job to add to that might, just as he had been taught through most of his adolescence.

Yes, Rolf's mother worried for him — given what had happened in wartime to both his father and his stepfather — but, as he explained to her with the kind of philosophical detachment that marked his generation, it was destiny, and all they could do was hope that he would come through.

•

Poland had almost nothing to counter the German invasion with bar the courage of its people, which it had in plenty, but that proved not to be remotely enough.

For, time and again, brave Polish soldiers found themselves face to face with German tanks, mighty Panzers, with machine-gunners coming in behind on foot and in lorries, and from that point on it was no longer a matter of bravery. For what could one do, however brave, against a 20-tonne machine, protected by as much as 114 millimetres of armour, with a 320-horsepower Maybach engine to power it, dozens of machine-gun belts, and 100 shells ready to fire out of a 75-mm cannon?

Sanity dictated surrender. And surrender many of the soldiers of Poland did, albeit with pockets here and there of brave fighters who refused to give up, no matter what, and so either found their way into the resistance or fled across the borders with the hope that they could re-form into an army of Polish soldiers fighting the Axis powers outside Poland, in whatever field the Allied High Command cared to place them (though it would hopefully be somewhere that they could shoot Germans). Across the country, the Polish Army was obliged to fall back in the face of this overwhelming force, as the nation's soul cried out at witnessing new levels of horror and barbarity. Jews were rounded up, synagogues burnt down, women frequently raped, and many Poles showing the smallest signs of resistance summarily shot.

The stories of such atrocities soon spread among the Polish population at large, heightening the fury with which they regarded the German Army. The strapping blond seventeen-year-old student Adam Mrozowski, living just outside the city of Starachowice, was among them. With his family, he had immediately done what he could to help thwart the German invasion.

When a general mobilisation order had gone out, he and his uncle had gathered some horses from their property and tried to take some wagons full of provisions to the front line to assist the soldiers — only to be met on the road by a solid stream of retreating soldiers and refugees spreading the news that the Germans were already in the next town and coming their way. It scarcely seemed credible that the Germans could have moved so far, so quickly, but there was no doubting it, and the Mrozowskis reluctantly turned back. In the first instance it was apparent that the Polish Army was not going to be able to stop the Germans, and it was everyone's hope that other countries would come to their aid ...

•

In response to the German invasion of Poland, both France and Britain — at last galvanised to action — demanded that the Germans withdraw. And yet Hitler refused, assured by his Foreign Minister, Joachim von Ribbentrop, that when it came right down to it, Britain and France would back down once more.

So it was that at precisely nine o'clock on the morning of 3 September, the British Ambassador to Germany, Sir Neville Henderson, arrived at the German Foreign Ministry on Berlin's regal thoroughfare, the Wilhelmstrasse. Because von Ribbentrop had declined to receive him, he actually met a mere German–English translator by the name of Paul Schmidt, and the reason the latter seemed a little out of breath was not just the gravity of the occasion. (In fact, with all the tumult and meetings going through much of the night, Schmidt had overslept and arrived at the Foreign Ministry in a taxi just in time to see the purposeful Ambassador heading up the stairs. Racing around to the back entrance, he had made it to von Ribbentrop's office to formally receive the Englishman with barely a moment to spare.)

The Ambassador shook Schmidt's hand, but solemnly declined an invitation to be seated, rather in the manner of a man who knew that what he had to say was of the gravest import and the only appropriate way to deal with it was to stand and deliver.

'I regret,' he began with deep emotion, 'that on the instructions of my government I have to hand you an ultimatum for the German Government. More than twenty-four hours have elapsed since an immediate reply was requested to the warning of September 1st, and since then the attacks on Poland have been intensified. If His Majesty's Government has not received satisfactory assurances of the cessation of all aggressive action against Poland,

and the withdrawal of German troops from that country, by eleven o'clock British Summer Time, from that time a state of war will exist between Great Britain and Germany.'

The formal part out of the way, the Ambassador then shook Schmidt's hand once more and said he bore no personal ill will towards him, as he had always seemed a rather decent chap, and he wished him well for what was to come. Good day to you.

And to you, Mr Ambassador.

Schmidt then made his way across the street to Hitler's Chancellery, where most of the members of the German Cabinet were gathered in the room next to the Führer's office, anxiously awaiting news, and now crowded around Schmidt to get it. They would have to wait — such was the import of the ultimatum Schmidt had to impart, it was only proper for it to first be delivered to Hitler himself. Schmidt was soon ushered into the presence of Germany's leader, who proved to be sitting quietly at his desk, while von Ribbentrop was a small distance away, standing by the window.

This time Schmidt stood ramrod straight in front of Hitler, and after delivering a very crisp 'Heil Hitler!' salute with his arm raised at the regulation 45-degree angle, he carefully translated the British Government's ultimatum, finishing with '... by 11 o'clock British Summer Time, from that time a state of war will exist between *Grossbritanien und Deutschland*.'

When he had finished ... absolutely nothing happened. Hitler simply sat there, apparently turning over in his mind all the implications of what he had just been told. For all his sometime frenzy when speaking before a large audience, in person and one-on-one he was equally capable of being very quiet and reflective, and this was just such an occasion. Clearly, however, after Hitler had thought over what he had just heard, the implications were not to his liking, for after a period which, to Schmidt, 'seemed like an age', Hitler turned to von Ribbentrop, still standing by the window, and said, 'What now?' accompanied by a savage look.

To Schmidt, it was as if Hitler 'was implying that his Foreign Minister had misled him about England's probable reaction'.

Which was as may be.

Nevertheless, von Ribbentrop could only answer quietly: 'I assume that the French will hand in a similar ultimatum within the hour ...'

Schmidt left them to it, pausing only long enough to tell those who gathered outside Hitler's office, and now crushed in on him once more, 'The English have just handed us an ultimatum. In two hours a state of war will exist between England and Germany.'[2]

Again, the response to this stunning bit of information was complete and utter silence.

•

Finally, it had come to this.

At exactly 11.15 on the morning of Sunday, 3 September, the British Prime Minister, Neville Chamberlain, took to the radio to address the British nation and, indeed, those many countries that formed part of the wider British Empire.

'I am speaking to you from the Cabinet Room at 10 Downing Street,' he began in his clipped, but now rather unsteady voice.

'This morning the British Ambassador in Berlin handed the German Government a final note stating that unless we heard from them by 11 a.m., that they were prepared at once to withdraw their troops from Poland, a state of war would exist between us. I have to tell you that no such undertaking has been received, and that consequently this country is at war with Germany ...

'At such a moment as this the assurances of support that we have received from the Empire are a source of profound encouragement to us ...

'Now may God bless you all. May He defend the right. It is the evil things that we shall be fighting against — brute force, bad faith, injustice, oppression and persecution. And against them, I am certain that the right will prevail.'

The speech was followed by the playing of *God Save the King*, and almost immediately after that air-raid sirens sounded, wailing across London. The bloody Germans hadn't taken long about it. (Though, mercifully, this time it proved to be a false alarm.)

•

That night all across Australia, people gathered around their radio sets, knowing that an announcement of some kind was coming from the new Australian Prime Minister, Robert Menzies, who had taken over shortly after Joseph Lyons had died just five months before.

Down Liverpool way, by the Hume Highway, Elizabeth and Will Edmondson went three miles over to the home of their neighbours, the Scotts, to listen to such a momentous address together. Just a few seconds before Prime Minister Menzies came on, Jack arrived and just stood there, not wanting to disturb anyone, as everyone leaned forward to hear the Prime Minister's words. The clock on the mantelpiece showed it to be just after 9.15 p.m. — just after 12.15 p.m. in London of the same day.

'Fellow Australians,' the Victorian said in his highly educated but grave tones, 'it is my melancholy duty to inform you officially that in consequence of a persistence by Germany, and her invasion of Poland, Great Britain has declared war upon her and that as a result Australia is also at war . . .'

After the speech was over everyone just sat there, not saying a single word, just going over and over the implications of it all in their minds. Finally, it was Jack who broke the spell. Walking over to his mother, he sat beside her, put his arm around her, and said, 'The Prime Minister should bring in compulsory service at once, and not wait a year before acting. Put every man where they are best suited to further the war effort — and *no* exemption for only sons . . .'[3]

Elizabeth could barely breathe. They were the kind of words she most expected Jack to say, but also the ones she most feared.

And Jack wasn't mucking around, either. That night, when they got home, the whole family stayed up till two o'clock, packing Jack's things, as by happenstance he had duties with his Citizens Military Force battalion the next day, and under the circumstances it seemed appropriate to turn up more ready than ever. As a family they began to apply spit, polish and elbow grease to his already sparkling uniform. The brass became more shining. The white webbing blazed whiter still. His boots began to look like black mirrors. No matter that Jack was wheezing a little as he was doing it, with a bad case of asthma.

'I'll be all right soon,' he said.

But would the world? Only a short time after Mr Menzies' announcement, New Zealand had taken a similar stance, with Prime Minister Michael Savage declaring to his own nation, 'Behind the sure shield of Britain we have enjoyed and cherished freedom and self-government. Where she goes, we go. Where she stands, we stand.'[4]

The New Zealanders, too, were at war against Nazism, and they were followed six hours later by the French declaration, with the Edmondson family listening to some of the developments on the radio, even as they continued to polish away.

•

The next morning, 4 September 1939, at seven o'clock — not even twelve hours after Mr Menzies had declared war — Jack was at Liverpool station and then on his way to Merrylands, where the HQ of his 4th Citizens Military Force Battalion was situated. From there Jack and his battalion would head to a base at Narrabeen on the northern beaches of Sydney, from where they could undertake their assigned task of guarding Barrenjoey Lighthouse, at the northern end of Palm Beach.

All over the country at this time, the Prime Minister's words of the night before were immediately affecting lives — with some men gathering at barrack gates at dawn in their eagerness to join up[5] — as the drums of war that had been beating in the distance for so many months, now came so thrillingly close. Some men would join up out of a simple sense of duty, others because whatever the army was offering would have to be better than their current jobs and lives. And yet there were still others, too — most particularly those whose fathers had fought in the Great War — for whom joining up was done more in the spirit of adventure. They'd heard the stories, all right, of how their dads had hit the beaches at Gallipoli, faced down the Germans on the Western Front, marched with the Froggies and all the rest, and do you reckon they were going to miss out on fighting such a war now that they had a chance? Not bloody likely they weren't!

In droves, they began to join up across the nation. And that would be one in the eye for old dad. No matter that their fathers had fought in the 'war to end all wars' — who knew whether this one just might be bigger than that?

Nor, for all that, was there any real surprise that Australia was also now involved. From the moment that Britain had declared war, it followed that Australia — her loyal dominion — would also go to war.

Australia was, in fact, so loyal to Britain that in short order, as had been agreed to by treaty, Australia's navy was soon effectively placed under the control of the British Royal Navy and sent to northern climes, while much of the resources of the Royal Australian Air Force was also placed at the service of King and Empire. This seeming servitude to Britain went right to the point of replacing the longtime chiefs of staff of both the Australian Army and RAAF with British officers, while the Royal Australian Navy also had a senior British officer commanding it. Menzies even went so far as to say, 'We shall be guided by the [British] Chiefs of Staff in what theatre of war our troops are used.'[6] (Not that any of this approach was particularly new. Back in 1922, when a disarmament conference was held in Washington between Japan, Britain, France, Italy and the United States, a resolution was passed to reduce the size of each power's navy. As part of the observation of that treaty, Australia was asked by Britain to take its finest warship, *Australia*, out through Sydney Heads and sink it to the bottom of the Pacific Ocean — and it was done!)[7]

Still firmly within this frame, it would not be long before an entire division of the Australian Army, which was then and there being quickly raised, was also put essentially at the service of British interests.

To get that division up and running, one of Menzies' first moves had been to appoint Major General Thomas Blamey to be the General Officer Commanding, and it would be Blamey's most urgent task to get the '6th Australian Division' gathered, trained, equipped and sent on its way. (The 1st Australian Imperial Force which had been formed for the Great War had consisted of five infantry divisions — with each division numbering 14 000 men — and this, the 2nd Australian Imperial Force, had continued the numerical tradition, with the first division formed for this war becoming the 6th Division, the next one forming the 7th Division, and so on. Perhaps the government's naming it that way heralded the leadership's view that this was to be a similar conflict to the Great War, with many countries involved and likely many casualties. And perhaps, also, it was a challenge to the men of this generation to be as good and as worthy of deep respect as their famous fathers.)

One of Blamey's first concerns was getting the right senior officers in charge of the various battalions and brigades that would make up this division, as well as determining the right leader for the division itself. Late in the afternoon of 6 October, for example, one Leslie Morshead received a telegram at his Vaucluse residence, the sun sparkling off the harbour as he read it:

Confidential stop selected for appointment as Comdr 18 Inf Bde special force stop telegraph desire re acceptance of appointment stop letter confirming follows stop if you accept required report for conference Melbourne for one day next week date to be advised.

Adjutant General.[8]

If it wasn't quite the fulfilment of a dream, it was close. General Blamey had formally offered Leslie Morshead command of the 18th Brigade, one of the three brigades that was to make up the 6th Division. As he did with most important decisions, Morshead talked the offer over with his wife, Myrtle.

On the one hand he could honourably decline on the grounds of his age, fifty, and the fact that he had already more than done his duty in the last war — and could therefore stay safe in his comfortable life in Vaucluse right beside his beloved wife and sixteen-year-old daughter, while continuing his extremely lucrative career as a shipping executive. Or he could leave that all behind to devote himself to training up 5000 mostly raw recruits and turning them into Australian soldiers, before heading overseas to risk his life and be responsible for all of their lives, while fighting against an extremely powerful enemy that had already proved its ruthlessness and willingness to massacre all who stood in the way.

Of course he chose the latter, and had his wife's blessing to do so. The army was simply in his blood, and to be asked to become a brigadier by General Blamey was an enormous honour. More than anything, though, Morshead felt that it was no less than his duty to answer that call. He had already seen too much of war to have stars in his eyes about the 'adventure' of it all, and knew he would miss his wife and child terribly, but it was certainly a job that had to be done.

Within four days of receiving that telegram, Morshead had resigned his shipping job — where at that very time he had been engaged in turning the Orient Lines cruise ships into troop transport — and formally signed up.

●

In Poland over much of the previous month, Erwin Rommel had also been greatly missing his own wife and eleven-year-old child, but could get home to them soon, as on the same day that Morshead received his telegram, the last of the Polish resistance finally crumpled. At the Führer's request, Rommel — newly promoted to Major General — had from the beginning of the invasion been seconded from his posting as commandant of the officer cadet school at Wiener Neustadt, near Vienna, and sent to organise the *Führerbegleitbataillon*, the Führer Escort Battalion. It was as the commanding officer of that unit, then, that Rommel had made his way into Poland close by Hitler's side, as the head of his bodyguard, and had remained so throughout, even eating at Hitler's table twice a day.

For three weeks Rommel escorted Hitler right to where much of the battle action was taking place, with both men observing closely how modern warfare was executed. While Rommel was in many ways overqualified to be commanding just 385 men in the bodyguard when others of his military generation were in command of many thousands of soldiers — and right at the front line at that — the advantage for him was that he was further able to gain Hitler's trust, which could be useful. Rommel did not have the pure Prussian bloodlines that traditionally filled

Germany's highest military echelons — was not a 'von' or 'Graf' or 'Baron' — but nor was Hitler, and to a certain extent this might have been something that helped to bond the two. For, just as Hitler was sometimes referred to in a sneering whisper by the Prussian Old Guard as 'the Austrian corporal', so too was Rommel viewed as an upstart by certain of his contemporaries, and the moreso when his book, *Infantry Attacks*, began to be so successful. And, though, while many in that Old Guard of the German military never embraced the Nazi ethos, Rommel deeply admired the leadership that Hitler displayed and, like so many veterans of the Great War, had felt that Germany really had been betrayed when the armistice had been signed while they were still in the field. In Rommel's view, Hitler had dared to reunite a troubled nation, and return it to its position of former glory. (Rommel also respected Hitler for the Iron Cross that the Führer proudly displayed on his uniform — the only military decoration he ever wore — which had been awarded for his bravery in the Great War. As distinct from other high German officers, Hitler had really done his time on the front line, and had done well, and the two sometimes talked of their battle experience.)

At one point in their close association in Poland, Hitler asked Rommel the question that would entirely alter the direction of his military career. '*Rommel, sagen Sie, was wollen Sie in der Armee erreichen?*' — Tell me, Rommel, what do you want to achieve in the army?

In reply, Rommel had no hesitation in stating his wishes: 'Command a Panzer division,'[9] he said simply to his Führer.

The brilliant military officer and instructor had seen enough of what had happened in Poland to realise that in modern land warfare, there was nothing more powerful than the use of massed Panzers working in tandem with motorised infantry and heavy support, and despite the fact that he had never commanded an armoured division — or even been in a tank before that point — Rommel had equally no doubt that the same general principles of warfare that he had elucidated in the last quarter century could equally be applied to tank warfare.

Hitler, although not quite promising on the spot that Rommel could have what he requested, promised that upon their return to Berlin he would see what could be done.

•

Behind them on that return, however, they left a nation that had been entirely devastated. In the five weeks between the German invasion and the

Polish capitulation, whole sections of cities had been razed to the ground, factories and railways destroyed and, at German hands alone, over 50 000 Poles had been killed and over 100 000 wounded. How many had been killed by the Russians — who had made a shocking invasion from the east just three weeks after the Germans, in accordance with an otherwise secret appendix of Stalin's treaty with Hitler — could never be properly calculated, but it was in the many tens of thousands. Some Polish soldiers escaped, to live to fight another day, but as a country Poland would wear the bitter scars of the German and Soviet invasions for many decades to come.

(And, in fact, there were those in Germany who were unhappy with what had been done to Poland — even some of those close to the highest ranks of the German military. Much of the plan for the Polish invasion had been formulated by the Chief of the General Staff, General Franz Halder, with the help of a man he considered to be something of an administrative genius, General Friedrich Paulus. When the wife of Paulus — a beautiful woman of high Romanian aristocratic birth by the name of Helena — found out what he was involved in, she expressed in very strong terms that she thought it was completely immoral to do such a thing. Paulus's reply was almost a model of the time — it was not his decision, he said. He was a soldier, and he was following orders. The only query for him was how to follow those orders to the best of his ability.)

•

In England, Neville Chamberlain was making his own key appointments, including putting men in charge of what would likely be the most important theatres of war. In the Middle East, for example, looking after the major British possession in the area — the Suez Canal — General Sir Archibald Percival Wavell became Britain's Commander in Chief for the Middle East.

Wavell was a curious cove, and the Australian journalist Alan Moorehead, who came to know him well over this period, would later describe him in clear terms: 'He never failed to impress and puzzle everyone who met him. His voice was high, rather nasal, and unless he was actually engaged upon some definite business he seldom said anything at all. His dark deeply tanned face was lined and heavy to the point of roughness. His thinning hair was grey, and the one good eye left him from the last war gleamed brightly from a face that was usually as expressionless as a statue.'[10]

Yet beyond Wavell being merely a member of the Old School, he figuratively had the credentials to be the headmaster of that school, so perfect was his pedigree as a scion of the military establishment. He had attended the venerable Winchester College before going off to the famous Sandhurst, and then won the first of his many military spurs in the second of the Boer Wars, before shining as a high-ranking officer during the Great War. A Colonel Blimp type, however, Wavell most certainly was not, and many of his military escapades had had a very un-English daring about them.

One who admired him was the author of *Infantry Attacks*, Erwin Rommel, who, before long, would be reading and studying a German translation of Wavell's writings from the Great War called *Generals and Generalship*. Indeed Rommel would later declare that, of all the British generals, 'the only one who showed a touch of genius was Wavell'.[11]

In this instance, now that Wavell was in charge of all Allied army operations in the Middle East, his chief strategic concern was the Italian forces of Benito Mussolini in Libya, which were well established in both Tripolitania (Western Libya) and also Cyrenaica (Eastern Libya), nudging right up to the Egyptian border.

Nevertheless, for the moment Mussolini decided to keep his powder dry, declaring that, just like Switzerland, Italy would remain in a state of *neutralità* in the current conflict, a 'non-belligerent', and that therefore the 1.2 million men he had under arms would stay above the fray.

•

It had taken a while, but the newly promoted Lieutenant General Blamey had finally got it all sorted out. Based on his experience in the Great War where, too often, Australian soldiers had been used as little more than cannon fodder by their British commanders, he wanted a veritable insurance policy that it would not happen again in this war. With that in mind, Blamey had begun a process whereby the Australian and British governments agreed to the conditions under which Australian soldiers could be sent into, and remain in, a battle under British command. The key to the protocol, substantially written at Blamey's behest by High Court Judge Sir Owen Dixon, was that in any struggle between the Commander of British and Australian forces over the disposition of Australian troops, the Commander of the Australian forces — General Blamey himself, of course — would be the one holding four aces. To wit: in the opening paragraphs of what was effectively a charter, signed off on by both governments, it was established in the first point that:

a) The Force to be recognised as an Australian Force under its own Commander who will have a direct responsibility to the Commonwealth Government with the right to communicate with that Government. No part of the Force to be detached or employed apart from the Force without his consent.[12]

Four aces? With a clause like that, it was writ in stone that in the event of any future dispute, Blamey would also be holding the joker, able to trump anything the Brits threw at him. And he knew it.

•

In the meantime, William Joyce had landed on his feet. After arriving in Berlin just before the war had begun, a friend within the Fascist movement had introduced him to Dr Erich Hetzler, the Private Secretary to Germany's Foreign Minister, Joachim von Ribbentrop, and Joyce was able to offer his services, in whatever capacity the Germans cared to use him, at the highest level. So it was that just two weeks after setting foot in Germany, with the world at war, Joyce was effectively put in charge of broadcasting German propaganda back to Britain, from the powerful transmitters situated in the western Berlin suburb of Charlottenburg.

His job was to highlight Germany's successes, and weaken British resolve and morale. From late September 1939, then, his nasal drawl began to envelop Britain, sneering and jeering at the Empire's chances of stopping the Nazi war machine, while cheering his own new masters on.

Sadly for Britain and her allies, it would not be long before Joyce — soon to be known as Lord Haw-Haw — would have a great deal to cheer about when it came to both German and Soviet successes, including the latter's successful invasion of Finland.

•

Ah, but still, there remained the hope that the Brits would soon surely sort them out, likely with the help of the French. That was almost for certain, or at least that remained the hope in Britain itself and in far-flung parts of the Empire. All over Australia people crowded into the picture theatres and thrilled to the newsreels before the main movie showing the soldiers of the British Expeditionary Force getting off the ships that had just deposited them in France, and in the process assuring the audiences of all the Commonwealth in their wonderful sing-alongs that they would soon be hanging out their washing on the Siegfried Line, the defensive

wall built by the Germans along the most vulnerable part of their border
with France.

Mother dear I'm writing you from somewhere in France,
Hoping to find you well,
Sergeant says I'm doing fine, a soldier and a pal,
Here's a song that we don't sing, this'll make you laugh.

We're going to hang out the washing on the Siegfried Line.
Have you any dirty washing, mother dear?
We're gonna hang out the washing on the Siegfried Line
'cause the washing day is here.

•

Every day, every hour, sometimes every few *minutes* — another problem.
Up at the Rutherford training camp just outside Maitland, on this
December day of 1939, Brigadier Leslie Morshead was doing all he could
to whip his charges into shape, but sometimes the problems hit where they
were least expected. While his 18th Brigade was dominated by
Queenslanders, South Australians and Western Australians, there was also a
smattering of Tasmanians put together with Queenslanders in the 2/12th
Battalion, and it was fair to say that they didn't always mix together quite as
well as he'd hoped ...

For example, on one hot, summery day a group of Queensland soldiers
had returned to their barracks after the day's training to find 'two strangers
in our hut'. But still, that was nowhere near the worst of it. The worst of it
was, they were *Tasmanians*. The Queenslanders refused to parade until the
two Tasmanians were shifted.[13]

That sort of thing could be dealt with in the form of a simple
command — like it or lump it, follow orders and fit in — but in the
meantime what Morshead most wanted to see out of his troops was work
and discipline. Many of his new recruits, upon first spying their new
commander, had taken him to be a rather dapper little chappie unlikely to
give the likes of them a hard time, and yet they were quickly in for a rude
awakening. For ever and always, Morshead took the view that there was no
problem in the formation of an army that enough work couldn't put right,
and he was a stickler for the troops rising early, getting stuck into their drills
and then doing more and more and more drills, together with weapons
instruction and physical fitness exercises, saluting all the while, and certainly

not doing any swearing within earshot of him. He was the type to say what he meant, and mean what he said, or look out. When, on the Christmas break, some of his new recruits misbehaved and were late to return to camp, Morshead curtailed future leave, shut the canteen, worked them harder and ensured that all men attended lectures on exactly what a court martial consisted of, focusing on how very unpleasant it could be. This was a war they were preparing for, and there were to be no half measures. Mistakes meant men died and battles were lost; discipline and hard work put together meant a fine fighting army that ensured that it was the enemy who died, while they were the ones who triumphed.

The reality that they were likely to get to grips with the enemy at some point was emphasised by the fact that, in early April 1940, Germany made its next move by invading Denmark and Norway — signalling the end of what some people had called the 'Great Bore War', and the beginning of Germany's wider campaign to dominate all of Europe. And even beyond ...

•

Adam Mrozowski and his cousin, Czeslaw Kreowski, could barely believe it. The previous few months in their Polish town had been a complete nightmare under German occupation, with many workers rounded up and sent to labour camps, and man after man arrested by the Gestapo and then shot. All the while, through their town came a continuing stream of refugees from the provinces of Silesia, Posnan and Pomerania — the western parts of Poland that Germany had long claimed were naturally its — as all those of non-German ethnicity had simply been expelled. They had been given just fifteen minutes to pack one suitcase and then been loaded into cattle trucks and shipped east. Adam had personally seen an old Jewish man try to give some of those refugees a bottle of milk through the train window, only to get a German rifle butt to his face for his trouble, with the subsequent blood so copious it flowed over the edge of the platform.

And now this. Walking along towards them on the footpath was Maria Jakubowska, a beautiful girl from their class at school, whom Czeslaw had always been particularly keen on, and there she was walking, promenading with a young German soldier! (Always, the German soldiers walked in a manner that told you to get out of the way. They *never* let you forget you had lost the war.)

But Maria! After everything the Germans had done, it was simply unimaginable that she would get involved with one of them, and yet the proof was right before their eyes. This called for action, and though there was little they could change, at least they did something. Both eighteen-year-olds summoned a glob of phlegm and — on behalf of all decent Poland, unaccustomed as they were — expertly *spat* at the feet of the couple as they passed, and accompanied it with looks of contempt that they hoped would sear the girl's soul for ever. The response was a howl of outrage from both the girl and the German soldier, who reached for his gun — and may very well have shot them dead in the street were it not for the girl's intervention. Even then the hot-headed Czeslaw wanted to go on with it, so boiling was his fury, but Adam dragged him away.

It was apparent that neither of the cousins was going to survive long in this country with their attitude, so they began to examine other possibilities. Really, there was only one: to run away, slip across the Polish border into Hungary, and find a way to get from there to Palestine, where the word was that a Polish Army Brigade was forming up to fight with the Allies, to kill the Germans first in other countries and then come back to Poland to kill them here, to liberate their homeland. Once the idea took hold, it simply wouldn't release them. None of their parents would ever agree to it, they knew, but they would have to live with that. Their parents still thought of them as boys, whereas they knew they were now men, and as men they were going to fight. Bit by bit, their plans became more detailed . . .

•

It was a dream — a nightmare, to be more precise — and it had an enormous impact on Elizabeth Edmondson when she first experienced it, shortly after Denmark had fallen to the Germans. She was in a kind of dark, circular enclosure formed by strong, high posts that surrounded her. She didn't like it there, and kept trying to climb out, attempting vainly to dig the points of her shoes and then her toes into the posts to try to get enough purchase to claw her way upwards. Always, she made it just a few steps higher before she slipped and fell back. Repeatedly she tried, fighting the rising panic, but it was to no avail. There was no gate out, and no way up. She looked around — and there in the centre stood her Jack. He was deathly pale and dressed in a grey suit, watching her, not attempting to help, but surely because he couldn't, which would explain the expression of sheer agony on his face. Elizabeth did not try to speak to her son, nor he to her. The dream seemed to go on all night and was so vivid that every detail of it came back to her when she recorded it in her diary.[14]

A few days after that, on 22 April 1940, Elizabeth had one of her worst fears confirmed. The Army doctors had given their official verdict on the state of Jack's health.

They said he was okay ...

Jack had passed his medical for the AIF, and was now free to join the 7th Division, the formation of which the government had just announced. (The first brigade of the 6th Division had already left for the Middle East in January 1940 — so following the rough pattern of the Great War, in which Australians divisions trained in Palestine, before being deployed either elsewhere in the Middle East and North Africa, or sent to Europe.) The way Jack had told her his medical had proceeded, the doctor had only tapped his chest once and asked if he had any illnesses.

Jack had replied 'No', and of course that was that. *No* mention of his crook elbow, or his serious bronchial asthma. And Elizabeth knew how bad it was, all right, despite Jack's strenuous denials that his asthma was a problem. One of her son's fellow soldiers — Jack Tully, a local chap —who camped with him in the wet lowlands of Narrabeen had even told Elizabeth that some nights Jack's coughing was so bad that he feared that Jack would *die*. Her Jack had also told Tully, 'Don't let mother know', but Tully had felt it was so important that she did know that he told her.[15] And of course Elizabeth had remonstrated with her son, but Jack had steadfastly maintained that he would do his duty come what may, and no amount of coughing or strangled wheezing was going to stop him.

In any case, the fact that Jack had passed the medical meant that he was now officially out of the Citizens Military Force, into the Australian Imperial Force and able to be sent overseas as soon as he completed his training. While this was devastating for Elizabeth, the one saving grace was that he could leave the wretched camp of Narrabeen, two hours' drive away, and move to the Ingleburn camp just 12 miles by road from their Liverpool property (or a couple of miles across the back paddocks), where she felt she would be much more capable of taking care of him. From there he could return home much more often, just as she and her husband, Will, would be able to visit him.

Could Elizabeth simply ask Jack not to go, as she knew her heart would break to be separated from him for so long? She could not. As she later put it in a letter to a friend, 'I did not ask him to stay at home — nor could I wish him to stay here and shirk his duty.'[16] It was a precise summation of the way Jack himself felt. Though, as he confided to his mother at the time, he hated the idea of going overseas, and leaving the farm and his parents behind, what he hated more was not doing everything he could do to defend the country, and that meant more than just staying relatively safe at the camp in Australia.[17]

So it was that in no time, Jack was formally signing his enlistment papers . . .

> I, John Hurst Edmondson, swear that I will well and truly serve our Sovereign Lord, the King, in the Military Forces of the Commonwealth of Australia until the cessation of the present time of war and twelve months thereafter or until sooner lawfully discharged, dismissed or removed, and that I will resist His Majesty's enemies and cause His Majesty's peace to be kept and maintained, and that I will in all matters appertaining to my service faithfully discharge my duty according to law.
>
> So Help Me God
>
> Signature of Person Enlisted . . .
>
> *John Hurst Edmondson*

. . . and shortly thereafter descended from a bus at the vast Ingleburn training camp. Carrying a small kit which contained, as required by his call-up notice, a comb, hairbrush, shaving brush, razor, fork, knife and spoon, he was reporting for duty with the just-formed 2/17th Battalion. The camp itself was a fairly unprepossessing kind of place. It was really not much more than an enormous, glorified cow paddock, albeit without fences, with the main road to Sydney going right through the middle of it. The major structures were various barracks, huts — Jack found himself assigned to a bare-earthed shack called Hut 33 — 'mess halls' and 'latrines' that were dotted here and there, while for the newcomers it was populated mostly by bellowing Sergeant Majors who seemed to be just about everywhere. And yet they weren't the only ones calling out.

'You'll be *sorrrrrrry!*' chortled the 'veterans' — some of whom had been there as long as a month! — and in the short term quite a few of the 2/17th Battalion's new recruits really were sorry to be there, just as were the recruits of their sister battalion, the 2/13th, a little way down the road. Side by side, frequently in direct manoeuvres against each other, the two battalions began to go hard at it.

For the training at Ingleburn was nothing if not intense, designed to turn boys into men and men into soldiers as quickly as possible. Every day started well before dawn with reveille and a sergeant's shout in the barracks: '*Righto! Righto! Feet on the floor! Feet on the floor!*' Then they had a short amount of time for their ablutions, making their bed with proper hospital tucks — and Gawd help anyone who got it wrong — followed by breakfast, followed by an inspection, rifle cleaning and then ... FALL IN! ... the training day proper could begin.

This included bayonet training, which, apart from having the men stab at straw dummies with the 'toothpicks' they attached to the end of their rifles, also involved them in a more confrontational exercise. It required an experienced soldier, usually the Sergeant, to hold a short pole with a wooden bayonet on one end and a small ring on the other. First the Sergeant would try to stab the recruits with the wooden bayonet, so they could learn how to parry and thrust, and then he would hold out the ring to one side as a target that they could vigorously stab at to improve their accuracy.

One who shone in such drills — because he'd been doing much the same for three years with the CMF — was seventeen-year-old Bert Ferres, who had newly joined the 2/13th Battalion, after having tried and failed previously to enlist as soon as the war started. In September 1939 they had simply refused to believe that Bert was much older than the sixteen years of age he really was, but by May 1940 he had succeeded in convincing them he was born on 12 December in 1919, and not 1922, which was his true birthdate.

That, of course, still didn't make him twenty-one, which he would have needed to be to sign up without parental permission, but he had then wheedled his blessed mother — who would have done anything for him — into signing the relevant permission forms, and had got around the absence of his father's signature by steadfastly maintaining that the old man had abandoned the family and couldn't be found. True, as soon as his outraged dad found out, he threatened to expose to the authorities Bert's true date of birth, but Bert still had some hope that he could work things out with the old man. In the meantime, the young man was simply revelling in the thrill of it all. There he was, just over seventeen years old, and because of his background in the CMF he was able to show the way, bayonet training and all, to much older blokes who respected him for his knowledge. In addition, what he had hoped for had happened: a war, a real *war*, and he was already off to a flying start, all on the wonderful wage of five shillings a day!

•

Many other young soldiers though, who were fresh to the military, were now struggling to learn not just the new skills, but also to make sense of the building blocks of the army structure for the first time, and how it worked roughly in multiples of three. You see, men, the base unit is a 'section', made up of a Corporal, a Lance Corporal and eight Privates — which includes two scouts whose job it is to get themselves in forward positions and act as the eyes and ears for the others, as well as two machine-gunners and four riflemen. Three sections then make up a platoon, commanded by a Lieutenant; three platoons form a company, commanded by a Major; four companies form the essence of a battalion, under the command of a Lieutenant Colonel; three or four battalions make a brigade, and three or four brigades a division — which by now usually consists of about 14 000 men, when you add ancillary units like the anti-tank regiment, field artillery regiment, engineers, signals and so forth. In command of a division was not God Himself, but not far off — usually a Major General. All put together, it could get very complicated, and for many of the new recruits the only safe way forward was to snap off myriad salutes at anyone with insignia indicating they weren't a Private, and try to work out just what their rank and significance were later on ...

•

After they'd all got through their tuberculosis shots — with Jack having a particularly bad reaction to his, as his inner forearm where the needle had entered swelled up terribly[18] — training was constant and intense, and covered such things as weaponry, sentry duty, night manoeuvres, infantry drill, bayonet practice and many, many long marches to lift their mobility, toughen them and make them physically fitter.

Together with all these there were frequent — sometimes daily — battalion parades, where the young soldiers would have to turn up exactly on time, positively gleaming in their neatness, and then march and manoeuvre around the parade ground — by the *riiiiiight*, quick *march* — like clockwork. True, it did seem to some of them that there was little chance they would beat the Germans, or whoever they fought, by out-parading them and doing more 'square-bashing', as it was called, than the enemy, but the military reckoning was that it was only by learning the kind of discipline necessary to parade perfectly that battalions could later turn into truly effective fighting forces. As it was explained to them, it was all about imposing a discipline so that in a battle the soldier's reflexes to obey a command from a superior officer would be instant and automatic. In battle, they were told, there were 'the quick and the dead', and this training was about ensuring that they would be quick in both the response to the order and the execution of it. If an officer told you to turn left, you turned left, *Suh!*; if he told you to turn right, you turned right, *Suh!*; and if in battle he told you to advance 50 yards and attack on the right flank, then that is what you did, *Suh!*

Some blokes hated it regardless, but no one in the 2/13th, particularly, complained too loud, for fear of having to face the 2/13th's commanding officer, The Bull.

Lieutenant Colonel 'Bull' Burrows probably had a formal Christian name, but no one quite knew what it was, and they wouldn't have been at all surprised if he had been 'Colonel' from birth. The whole aura of the bloke was that of a soldier who had been out there, and fought with everything from guns and grenades to bayonets and bare knuckles, in places like Gallipoli and Pozières. He was, therefore, one who knew what a good battalion was made of, and by God he was clearly going to make one himself — and woe betide anyone who didn't look like they wanted to get with the program. He was a bloke with a jaw so square and strong that it could have been used to split a log, and he had a voice to go with it that could probably have felled the tree in the first place ...

From their first assembly as a battalion, Bull meant business, as would be fondly recorded in the battalion history: 'By personal example, by his keen personal interest in, and his uncanny knowledge of everything going on in the Unit, together with his terrific energy and drive, the Commanding Officer kept all members of the Unit constantly on the alert. Resplendent in immaculate uniform, with shining leggings, swagger cane under arm, he was a striking figure in those days. He would be up before "Digger" Burgess sounded reveille, prowling through Company lines and kitchens, seeing that early morning administrative parades were properly attended and carried out. Woe betide any officer or Non Commissioned Officer whose men were a fraction late on parade, or if there was any slackness in dress or discipline ...'[19]

·

And now there was mortar training, loved by many for the very simplicity of the firing action and the fiery results thereafter. For many, the favourite trainer of all was a gnarled old soldier by the name of 'Ned' Kelly, who certainly got to the heart of the matter without any fanfare: 'You drops the bomb in here, and *whoooosh!* out she comes ...'

Yet, for all the excitement that many of the men felt when dealing with live ammunition, both with such things as mortars and firing live bullets, a very few just froze up and found they couldn't fire, regardless of whatever encouragement or threat of punishment they received. They just . . . *couldn't* . . . do it, and were quietly transferred to non-combat duties.

As to the rest — naturally enough, as they trained, learning the mechanics of military killing, each and every man thought about death. What would it be like to launch a mortar bomb down there, knowing that it was aimed at real flesh and blood on the other side of the trenches? What about firing a rifle at another man, or taking a bayonet to him, slicing him open and ending his life? It was one thing to do that on stuffed dummies at bayonet practice, but would you really be able to do it to another living, breathing human being? These were not the kinds of thoughts any man expressed out loud, but they were there all right.

Bit by bit, though, things started to gel. When the men had started this caper they had been a motley mix of teachers, timber workers, taxi drivers, carpenters, con men, lawyers, labourers, illiterates, butchers, bakers, candlestick makers . . . together with one Rhodes Scholar who fitted in with all the rest.

Now what were they? Why, they were all now *Diggers*, soldiers of the 2/17th Battalion, the 2/13th Battalion, the 2/15th Battalion and so on . . . and proud to be so! Over the weeks a certain *esprit de corps* — or whatever that French saying was — had grown up between them, and it was at a particularly high pitch one afternoon early in the piece, when hundreds of members of the original 13th Battalion from the Great War came to visit.

It had been The Bull's idea, and what a very fine one it was too.

For the 2/13th's first outing in public, they paraded in full battledress before these men whose deeds they hoped to emulate.

Presssssent . . . arms.

With a single, fluid movement, the sun flashing off bayonets moving in perfect unison, the 2/13th Battalion presented arms to their founding father forebears and were presented with two things in return.

The first was warm applause. It really had been an impressive display for young soldiers only two months into their training, and the old ones were experienced enough to know it boded well. To parade like that took enormous reservoirs of pride, discipline and cohesiveness, all essential ingredients of a powerful fighting force.

But the older men had also come to solemnly present the young'uns with the mighty flag of their battalion, and express their firm hope that the new lads would carry it forward to the same glory that they had. And they meant it, too. In the first war the 13th Battalion had been a byword for 'guts and gumption', and their sobriquet of the 'Fighting 13th' had been well earned in such places as Gallipoli, Messines, Ypres and the legendary Pozières. Now it was for the 2/13th to live up to the legend of their predecessors.

The 2/17th trained on, and would soon have their own moving ceremony with the original 17th Battalion from the Great War.

●

Elsewhere, others were still contemplating whether or not to join the AIF. In the tiny town of Walwa, for example — three hours' drive to the east of Albury on a very rough track, in the western lee of Mount Kosciuszko, and up where the mighty Murray River rises — a chippie by the name of John Johnson was at this time talking late into most nights with his darling missus of the last sixteen years, Josie, all while their six sons and one daughter slept in various nooks and crannies of their windy, three-roomed cottage. Should he go, or shouldn't he? John was all of thirty-eight years old, and Josie was petrified that if he went he wouldn't come home, but on the other hand John felt he had a duty.

Plus, there was this — and this is important, Josie: after the Great War, returned soldiers had got first dibs on newly released land from the government, to make their own soldier settlement farms. If he got back from this war okay, it just might be that the government would release some acreage to him, and the family could escape their poverty for ever and have their own big block. They could maybe even build their own house, to replace the one the bank had foreclosed on during the Depression. And in the meantime, for the first time in years, the family would have a regular income, with his basic army wage topped up by a marriage-and-children allowance. She and the kids could at last afford to be eating something better than a constant diet of rabbits and golden syrup dumplings. If everything really worked well, maybe the kids could even be educated in Melbourne, Josie?

Josie …?

Josie would not easily give way, but they had overcome tough times before, not least when they had first fallen in love. Because she was a Catholic and John was a Protestant, their parents had refused their consent, but so great had been their love that they decided to conceive a baby. That had forced the issue all right, with their first child being born just seven months after the wedding, and neither of them ever regretting the decision for a moment, despite their abject poverty. They all had each other, and that was the main thing.

But if John went away, they wouldn't all have each other, don't you see, John?

With no easy resolution available, they did the only thing they could do, which was to keep talking about it, though careful to keep most of it from their children.

·

On every trip to the city, Elizabeth Edmondson passed through Liverpool station, and every time it seemed like there were more and more troops heading every which way, as the war had shifted from something happening in the distance to something happening now, requiring massive movement. Sometimes Elizabeth would sit there on one of the benches, examining the faces, wondering if perhaps one of them would be the best-loved face of all. But it wasn't easy, not by a long shot. One day in early May she was there, knitting Jack some thick socks, and this wretched old fellow next to her kept watching the troops, while lugubriously repeating, over and over, 'They won't come home, none of them.'

Elizabeth kept knitting, concentrating furiously on her needles, hoping he would either take the hint from the *click-click-click* that she didn't care for that kind of talk or, failing that, that it would take her mind off the wretched thing that he was saying.

But even as the soldiers kept going back and forth, the fellow kept saying it — 'They won't come home, none of them' — and finally Elizabeth could stand it no more.

'My *son* is a soldier,' she said, with some feeling, 'and he is going overseas too.'

Still the man would not be put off.

'Well, I don't care,' he said. 'He won't come back either.'[20]

In response, there was really nothing Elizabeth could say, so she simply kept knitting, though managed to turn her back on him — lady that she was, it was as much as she could do to indicate her extreme displeasure while maintaining her dignity.

Knit one, purl two. Knit one, purl two. *Drat* that man.

·

As the men of this nascent next division of the Australian Army trained at such scattered bases as Puckapunyal, Ingleburn, Rutherford, Greta, Albury,

Enoggera, Holsworthy, Swanbourne and Singleton they all kept at least one eye trained on world events, trying to follow the course of the war, and determine just which side was winning. One thing was certain: it wasn't the British Prime Minister, Neville Chamberlain. He had never recovered from the moment Germany had declared war, with his many critics hurling his 'Peace for our time!' return from Germany the year before at him as a sarcastic insult.

Having lost the confidence of both his party and the British people, and perhaps even confidence in himself, Chamberlain resigned on the evening of 10 May 1940 — a day which had begun with Germany invading Belgium, Luxembourg and Holland. The new British leader was the same man who had been so bitterly critical of Chamberlain's Munich Agreement with Hitler, which betrayed Czechoslovakia: one Winston Churchill, and at the least everyone knew he could make a speech. As a matter of fact, the first speech he made in the House of Commons as British PM was a *corker*, and widely reported in the Australian papers.

'I say to the House as I said to ministers who have joined this government,' Churchill said, 'I have nothing to offer but blood, toil, tears, and sweat. We have before us an ordeal of the most grievous kind. We have before us many, many months of struggle and suffering . . .'

And there was no time to get started like the present, for even as he spoke, the Nazi assaults were continuing apace, with now France itself reeling under the heavy tread of the German jackboot . . .

CHAPTER FOUR

Rommel Rises

*The art of concentrating strength at one point, forcing a
breakthrough, rolling up and securing the flanks on either side,
and then penetrating like lightning deep into his rear, before the
enemy has time to react — [is Blitzkrieg].*

ERWIN ROMMEL

*Pitch thy behaviour low, thy projects high;
So shall thou humble and magnanimous be.
Sink not in spirit: who aimeth at the sky,
Shoots higher much than he that means a tree.
A grain of glorie mixt with humblenesse
Cures both a fever and lethargicknesse.*

GEORGE HERBERT, 'THE CHURCH-PORCH' (1633), LIEUTENANT GENERAL MORSHEAD'S
FAVOURITE POEM, WHICH HE FREQUENTLY RECITED TO HIS SENIOR STAFF

In all of the many German actions in Europe, one general had stood out. He
was the once-again newly promoted *Generalleutnant* Erwin Johannes Eugen
Rommel, now commander of the 7th Panzer Division. His appointment early
in 1940 to such a prestigious post at Hitler's personal behest, leapfrogging far
senior men who actually had experience with armoured warfare, had caused
consternation among the German High Command — Rommel later
reminisced dryly that 'my appointment did not suit the gentlemen of the
OKH'.[1] And yet it had since been fully vindicated, as he had captured the
German people's imagination with his daring thrusts across northern France,
continually pushing forwards and personally being the first man across both
the Meuse and Seine rivers. Though he'd had no background in commanding
the massive Panzers before the war had begun, Rommel had found that much
the same principles that he had established in infantry warfare applied.
Reconnaissance, probe, *attack*. Peel back the flanks at the point of penetration,
and pour through. If you're running out of supplies, don't worry too much, as

the chances are that in the newly captured territories to come you will find some more and effectively be able to live off the land.

Yet Rommel was a lot more than a mere theoretician far removed from the real action, and he quickly won the deep respect of his men for his courage under fire, and his preparedness to take the same risks they did. On one occasion, when it was necessary for his troops to build a pontoon across the River Meuse while under fire, it was Rommel himself who had no hesitation in wading into the waters with the engineers and the sappers — the privates whose job it was to help the engineers — hauling the pieces of timber necessary and getting them secured.[2] When enemy artillery started to draw a bead, Rommel gave word to set nearby houses on fire, and the work continued under the subsequent smoke screen. And, later, when it proved that the 7th Division's own 75-mm anti-tank guns and the guns of its Panzers were incapable of penetrating the particularly thick armour on the 24-ton British 'Matilda' tanks — so-called, affectionately by the British, because they had a protective metal 'skirt' around their tracks — it was Rommel who embraced a completely devastating solution: just outside of the northern French town of Arras, he sited his very powerful anti-aircraft 88-mm guns to shoot on a flat trajectory, and then had his tanks manoeuvre in such a way that the British tanks came right to them and were completely wiped out.[3] It mattered nothing to Rommel that he was using the 88s for a purpose they were not designed for. All that mattered was what they could do: penetrate enemy armour from an enormous distance, with an extremely high rate of fire to boot.

•

How could the soldiers not be inspired by such a man?

Always, he guided them towards speed in attack, to keep moving, to hit the enemy with so many blows at once, from so many directions — especially from behind, once their first defences had been breached — that the enemy would almost automatically crumble.

It was inherent to the concept of modern German arms that their Panzer Divisions consisted of a lot more than just 218 Panzers, as it came complete with a motorised infantry brigade; four rifle battalions, totalling some 2400 specially trained soldiers known as *Panzergrenadiere*; anti-tank and artillery regiments together with reconnaissance; and military-engineering battalions and service units, all in radio contact with each other. To organise such a disparate array of forces and co-ordinate it in such a fashion that, whatever the obstacle, the right parts of the division could attack a target so cohesively that it could be quickly overcome, was not easy, but after nigh on thirty years of being both a student and deadly practitioner of the military art, Rommel accomplished it brilliantly, and with an élan that no other German commander had ever boasted. Not for nothing would he be awarded the highly coveted Knight's Cross of the Iron Cross for his accomplishments in just this early part of the whole French campaign.

•

Against Blitzkrieg, the British and French simply had no answer, and through the astonishing capacity of Rommel's division to cover enormous distances and show up where it was least expected before disappearing again to hit somewhere else, some 470 Allied tanks had been destroyed and 97 000 prisoners had been taken in the space of just a rough month, for the loss of only forty-two German tanks. (As was always the case with every unit Rommel commanded, one of the greatest logistical problems for the 7th Panzer Division was what to do with all the prisoners they had captured. Other German Generals — especially of the SS — had solved such problems by simply having the prisoners shot, but Rommel was always chivalrous in such matters and insisted that his prisoners be treated with respect, the more so if they had fought well.)

And the possibility of entirely wiping out most of the British Army now beckoned. For, by late May 1940, some 340 000 British and French troops were pinned on the beaches around the northwestern French town of Dunkirk, as seemingly the entire German Army and Luftwaffe bore down upon them. On the edge of complete catastrophe, a flotilla of tiny English boats, ferries, large ships and just about anything that could stay above the water made its way across the English Channel to assist the Royal Navy and, due to the extraordinary courage of all the captains and crews, successfully plucked the troops to safety back in England. Certainly, in some ways the exercise was a massive defeat for the British, in that their forces had been so comprehensively routed in the face of the German Blitzkrieg through Holland, Belgium and France.

On the other hand, the fact that the evacuation had been successful, and that such a large number of troops had escaped to fight another day, was inspirational to the Allied cause. What was clear was that Britain was going to need help, and it was for the sons and daughters of the English-speaking world to answer the call.

An editorial in the *New York Times* immediately after Dunkirk reflected the overwhelming joy with which the success of the amazing operation was greeted, and the hope it generated.

So long as the English tongue survives, the word Dunkirk will be spoken with reverence. For in that harbour, in such a hell as never blazed on earth before, the rags and blemishes that have hidden the soul of democracy fell away. There, beaten but unconquered in shining splendour, she faced the enemy. They sent away the wounded first; men died that others might escape. It was not so simple a thing as courage, which the Nazis had in plenty. It was not so simple a thing as discipline, which can be hammered into men by a drill sergeant. It was not the result of careful planning, for there could have been little. It was the common man of the free countries rising in all his glory from mill, office, mine, factory and shop and applying to war, the lessons learned when he went down the mine to release trapped comrades; when he hurled the lifeboat through the surf; when he endured hard work and poverty for his children's sake. This shining thing in the souls of men Hitler cannot attain nor command nor conquer. He has crushed it where he could from German hearts. This is the great tradition of democracy. This is the future. This is victory.[4]

•

In the short term, however, for Brigadier Morshead's 18th Brigade — then on the high seas on board the *Mauritania*, heading to the Middle East — what the whole German thrust into France had meant was a sudden change of course. Even before the evacuation at Dunkirk, a cable to the ship in the middle of the night informed Morshead that he and his men were now urgently required in Britain, to bolster the home defences against a possible, even likely, German invasion. The strong view at the time was that not only was the Hun at the gate, but he would very shortly be crashing through the door, and the more soldiers Britain had on the other side of that door, the better.

With the Germans now rampant throughout northern Europe, however, all eyes turned to Mussolini. Would he now declare that Italy too was at war, or would he stay clear? France was still vowing to fight on, but was clearly wobbling, and the question was whether the temptation would be too great for Mussolini or not ...

It was General Sir Archibald Wavell, the commander of all the Allied armies in the Middle East, who proved to be the most prescient and eloquent in his appraisal, as documented in a letter to a military colleague in London: 'Italy still seems to be hesitating on the brink, but I think must take the plunge soon. Musso looks to me rather like a man who has climbed up to the top diving board at a swimming pool, taken off his gown and thrown his chest to the people looking on. I think he must do something. If he cannot make a graceful dive he will at least have to jump in somehow; he can hardly put on his dressing-gown and walk down the stairs again.'[5]

And so it proved. For it was no coincidence that, just as General Erwin Rommel's 7th Panzer Division forces broke through to the shores of the English Channel — and it seemed obvious to many that the war had now reached 'end game' stage — Mussolini made his move, and on 10 June 1940 promptly declared war on both Britain *and* France. He did so with high confidence, assured by Hitler that Germany would be invading Britain itself by mid July. Part of the Italian dictator's reasoning was explained in his remark at the time to the Italian Army's Chief of Staff, Marshal Pietro Badoglio: 'I only need a few thousand dead so that I can sit at the peace conference as a man who has fought.'

For her part, Britain was not unduly panicked by the Italian move. As a matter of fact, when her Ambassador to Italy, Sir Percy Loraine, was summoned to the Foreign Ministry and informed by Mussolini's Foreign Minister and son-in-law, Count Galeazzo Ciano, that as from midnight Italy would be at war with Britain, it was documented by the Count in his diary that Loraine 'received my communication without batting an eyelid or changing colour . . .' It is equally the stuff of legend that, just before Loraine left the ministry, he drew himself up and said with equal measures of gravity and dignity, 'I have the honour to remind Your Excellency that England is not in the habit of losing her wars.'[6]

That level of sangfroid was nearly matched by the coolness with which the Italian population as a whole received the news. When Mussolini himself appeared on the balcony of Rome's Palazzo Venezia to give them the news —

. . . Men and women of Italia, of the empire and of the Kingdom of Albania! Listen! An hour marked by il destino *beats in the sky of our country. The time of the irreversible decisions . . . The declaration of war has been already delivered to the ambassadors of Great Britain and France . . .*

— he could practically hear his own echo, for he was *not* drowned out by cheering. And yet was Mussolini really that surprised? It was, after all, the honest estimation of the German Ambassador to Rome that Mussolini 'must know that Italy cannot fight a world war either militarily, materially, or morally'.[7]

•

It was a beautiful day for doing what Elizabeth Edmondson most loved doing in the entire world. That was, going for a long walk together with her son, Jack, on his day-leave return from the army camp at Ingleburn in New South Wales. Whenever he returned home for a full day — sometimes he could only get away for an hour or two, though he always said that even if he could only stay for five minutes it would be worth it just to be momentarily home and see them — the two would walk around and about the paddocks, often arm in arm, heads bowed, happily chatting, catching up with each other's news of the previous week. On this sunny day, it was so lovely that they decided to really make an afternoon of it. Jack prepared the cordials and put them in bottles; Elizabeth made the cream puffs and ginger sponge with cream filling, the sandwiches and scones. And then they put the lot in a basket and took it with them to have a picnic in the shade of a particularly lovely tree.

Only two things spoiled an otherwise perfect happiness for the mother and son: the first was that Jack would have to soon leave his mother and return to camp; the second was that, just as he had been leaving camp that morning, a rumour had begun to swirl that France had either capitulated, or was just about to, under the sheer weight of German guns and jackboots. Nothing was yet confirmed, but even without that confirmation it was already clear that the German war machine was powerful beyond belief — way beyond anything that the world had ever seen before. Looking at Jack in the sunlight, happily munching on his scone and smiling at her, Elizabeth tried vainly to fight the chill thought that it might be her boy, with so many other mothers' sons, who would have to try to stop the Germans.

Jack was at this time having a burst of rare good health in what had otherwise been a long spate of terrible attacks of asthma, and if he had really taken himself off to a Medical Officer when the attacks were at their worst, then his honourable discharge from the army would have been little more than a formality — but he just wouldn't do it. Quite the reverse: Jack did everything he could to hide his condition, and lived in fear that he would be discharged on medical grounds, even though he was still dreading going overseas.

•

At precisely the same time as Jack and Elizabeth were walking through the sunny paddock of their Liverpool property, a long, long way to their northwest, on the opposite side of the planet, Adam Mrozowski and his cousin Czeslaw were equally walking, but freezing to the very marrow of their bones in the thick Polish night. In the company of a smuggler they had paid to show them the way, they were trekking at night across the small section of the Carpathian Mountains that separated Poland from Hungary, trying to dodge German patrols and keep moving, moving, moving into Hungary and away, hopefully to join the free Polish army in the Middle East. Neither lad had told his parents he was going, but running away for this purpose was just something that had to be done, as the German grip on the Polish throat had tightened even further, just as it had across Europe. The cousins' chief hope — apart from that of their own survival — was that on the other side they would hear the news that the much-vaunted French army had not only stopped the Germans, but also hurt them really, really badly. They prayed that this would be so, even through their chattering teeth, and also that the lights way down there in the distant valley would indeed prove to be those of the Hungarian village they had picked as their first port of call.

•

'READ ALL ABOUT IT!'

Just as he did every morning, the young newspaper boy moved between the barracks at Ingleburn training camp, doing a brisk business with most soldiers he came across, but this morning there was an extra edge to his voice — because he had real news, *big* news, news that was guaranteed to sell him a lot of papers very quickly. FRANCE SURRENDERS! read the big, black headlines.

Of the 2/13th Battalion, it was 'Turk' Heard who was seen to get to the kid first, but strangely enough he entirely ignored the front page and went straight to the back, to the comic section. Turk was known to be a bloke who loved the 'Joe Palooka' comic strip like few other things, and today there was a certain feverishness to the speed with which he tore through the pages to find it ... before reading it and emitting a long sigh of relief.

'Joe got out of it okay,' he informed the others as he handed the rest of the paper over. 'Struth, was that boy in bother.'[8]

Unfortunately, it was soon clear to his fellow soldiers that Joe wasn't the only one in bother. For the terms that France was obliged to agree to, following her surrender, put in train a dreadful turn of events that completely gutted the Allied war effort. Just a few days later, on the afternoon of Saturday, 22 June, the famous American war correspondent William Shirer — in the company of many of his professional ilk — focused his binoculars upon an extraordinary and most upsetting scene taking place just a short distance away from where he was standing. There was a railway carriage standing in a clearing in the forest of Compiègne — the same carriage, in the same spot, where just over two decades earlier France's Marshal Ferdinand Foch had forced the defeated Germans to agree to bitterly punitive terms after their own defeat in 1918. But now the wheel had turned. Now, it was none other than Adolf Hitler whom Shirer could see through the opening, surrounded by his generals and about to lay down terms to the French delegation, led by Marshal Henri Philippe Pétain. Shirer recorded in his diary:

> *The time is now three-eighteen pm. Hitler's personal flag is run up on a small standard in the center of the opening. Also in the center is a great granite block which stands some three feet above the ground. Hitler, followed by the others, walks slowly over to it, steps up, and reads the inscription engraved in great high letters on that block. It says*

**HERE ON THE ELEVENTH OF NOVEMBER 1918
SUCCUMBED THE CRIMINAL PRIDE
OF THE GERMAN EMPIRE ...
VANQUISHED BY THE FREE PEOPLES
WHICH IT TRIED TO ENSLAVE.**

> *Hitler reads it and Göring reads it. They all read it, standing there in the June sun and the silence. I look for the expression on Hitler's face. I am but fifty yards from him and see him through my glasses as though he were directly in front of me. I have seen that face many times at the great moments of his life. But today! It is afire with scorn, anger, hate, revenge, triumph.*[9]

All of which, in fact, were manifested in the terms of the treaty that Hitler now imposed on France, which he signed himself and forced Pétain to sign, before he left abruptly.

Under the terms of the armistice, two-thirds of France would be formally occupied and governed by the German Army while the two million French soldiers still under arms would be interned in mass prison camps. All of that would, of course, be very expensive, but no problem — Pétain agreed that France would make payment to Germany of 400 million francs *per day* for their own supreme humiliation.

With France's disappearance as their one fighting friend on the continent, and Italy's ascension as Germany's Fascist ally, Britain had many more problems than just having been comprehensively beaten and isolated in Europe. For the situation in and around the Mediterranean, particularly with reference to the Middle East and North Africa, had also changed overnight. Vast swathes of territory that had been either nominally neutral or firmly French (meaning they were pro-British) were suddenly gone on the other side of the ledger.

•

For all that, France's defeat was greeted by the British forces with dismay, but by no means despair. Their stoical attitude was best exemplified by a young Royal Air Force pilot who, upon hearing the news, is reputed to have said, 'At least that puts us in the bloody *final!*'[10]

Meanwhile, General Sir Archibald Wavell himself was not quite so flippant, but he did do a nice bit of modern mimicry of Sir Francis Drake, who, when he learned on the afternoon of 19 July 1588 that the Spanish Armada was on its way, had first finished his game of bowls before doing anything. In this case, the news of the French defeat came to Wavell when he was handed a telegram while playing golf at Cairo's Gezirah Club. Almost as a point of honour, Wavell played the final two holes on the course that remained to him.

Bogey.

Bogey. [11]

But still . . .

•

In the meantime, those 'common men of the free countries' continued to join up in great numbers, not least in Australia, where the German advance across Europe, right to the ramparts of England itself, was now viewed with growing alarm. In June 1940 alone, just a little fewer than 49 000 Australian men signed up for the armed forces. One of them was Ivor Hancock, now an itinerant labourer who, with his great mate Norm Graham, turned up with hundreds of others at Caulfield Racecourse in Melbourne, which had recently been transformed into an Army Induction Centre. Just what had propelled Ivor to sign up was never quite certain, even to him, though he was ever after sure there was a lot more to it than just wanting to preserve King and Country — and in his own case it had nothing to do with the fact that his father had served in the Great War. One thing neither Ivor nor a lot of blokes could help noticing, for starters, though, were the blokes in uniform with snazzy slouch hats pulled low to one side, strutting down Collins Street — sometimes with a girl on each arm! There was an aura about these blokes, like there was men's work to be done, and these were the men to do it; and there really were plenty of blokes who wanted to earn the right to have an aura like that — and if that involved enlisting, then so be it.

Now that they were here, the first step was to form up into a long line and be put through a medical to see if they were fit enough to join the Army. (And an extremely nominal medical it was, too, given that one bloke who passed with Ivor and Norm had a glass eye, while another confessed to them privately that he had fought in the Boer War, in the last gasp of the nineteenth century!)

In response to the regulation question as to whether they had any preference for a particular branch of the army — as in, Artillery, Signals, Armoured Vehicles (not that Australia had any yet), Machine Guns, etc — both Ivor and Norm replied that they didn't particularly mind, and so quickly found themselves assigned to the Infantry. Sworn in on the spot — 'You're in the army now, son!' — they were then sent off to the Quartermaster's store, where their arms were piled high with boots, socks, underwear, shirts, belt, pants, shirts, gaiters and various paraphernalia, all of it topped off with a slouch hat on their head. They were then ushered to a rough kind of changing room where they were told to change out of their 'civvies' and into their new gear, and with that their Army adventure had begun!

•

Another man who would shortly be going through a similar experience was John Johnson, who at last, with his wife Josie's blessing, had decided that he would indeed go. Though they really had agonised for months, she had ended up being overwhelmingly proud of his decision, his patriotism and his courage. The children who were old enough to understand mostly took their cue from their parents and felt the same, though young Barry remained deeply upset by it, no matter what the others told him: Dad didn't want to go away, but it was just something that had to be done.

So it was decided. A hitched ride to Albury with a couple of the other blokes from Walwa who had also decided to join up, and it was done. John Johnson was now a member of the 2nd Australian Imperial Force, in what in short order would become the 2/23rd Battalion, and the first night he spent in the camp set up at the old Albury Showgrounds — with the few wooden huts reserved for administration, dining and Quartermaster's stores, while he and the rest of the men slept in tents — was the first night he had spent away from Josie in the sixteen years of their marriage.

•

After arriving in Hungary from their trek across the mountains from Poland, it became quickly apparent to Adam and his cousin that they were not yet safe, and to be identified as a Pole was to risk being immediately turned in as an illegal refugee, and possibly handed back to the Germans. In the face of that terrible danger, Adam turned to the Hungarian Jews — easily identifiable by their long beards and black hats — reckoning that, given the way the Nazis had treated their own people across Europe, they would be unlikely to turn two Poles in. And he was right. They gave the cousins food and drink to survive, and the Poles tried to blend in with the local Hungarian population as best they could while they contemplated their next move — and yet, something of his Polishness must have been showing.

For now, feigning sleep while sitting on a park bench, there was a light touch on Adam's knee and he opened his eyes to see an old Jewish man right beside him, though studiously avoiding any eye contact. Out of the corner of his mouth, the Jew said — in a rough version of Adam's own language — 'Are you Polish?'

Deep breath. Big risk. Long pause.

'*Tak*,' Adam finally replied. *Yes.*

Now the Jew said, 'Look, I will show you where the Polish Consulate is. Walk just a little way behind me, and when I stop, I will point to you the building. Go in there, and they should be able to help you get away to fight the Germans.'

It was done.

Within a week, Adam and his cousin were standing before a Polish Army officer in the Polish embassy in the Hungarian capital of Budapest, which was all to the good. What was to the bad was Adam's reaction when the rather supercilious officer asked Adam why he had crossed the border from Poland into Hungary, *as if there could be any other possible answer.*

Young, headstrong and proud of what he had already achieved by escaping, Adam looked the officer right in the eye and said, with more arrogance than he knew he had in him, 'Not to be like you, sitting behind a *desk* ...'

Wrong answer. The upshot was that the officer marked something down on Adam's newly issued papers, and while his cousin was given a train ticket to take him south towards where the Polish Carpathian Brigade was forming up, Adam was taken to a refugee camp.

•

Well, they didn't call it a 'mess' for nothing.

As Sergeant Bill Merrikin looked out on the mess hall that was his primary province of operations at the Ingleburn army camp, he saw the usual devastation wrought by a thousand hungry men eating in too confined a space, well away from wives, girlfriends or mothers who might have induced in them a more genteel manner of taking their food. A smear of tomato sauce here, a broken cup there; what looked to be crushed peas up one end and what was obviously squashed carrot up another. There were knives and forks that had fallen to the floor, and even a few overturned chairs, caused by men in such a hurry to report back to their posts that they had simply stood and let the chairs collapse back behind them. (And aware that it would be somebody else's job to pick them up, so why bloody bother?)

Sighing, the good sergeant — a 45-year-old from the Sydney suburb of Concord — realised it was going to be a long afternoon of cleaning up, when he looked up at the entrance of some late arrivals. Were these some more hungry mouths to feed, who would no doubt be making more mess? No, it was that fellow Jack Edmondson, the one the other soldiers sometimes called 'Meggsy' — because of his red-haired resemblance to the comic-strip character of the same name — who had arrived with five lads from his platoon.

'Fatigue reporting for duty, Sergeant,' Jack said with a smile.

'But I had not asked for a fatigue duty,' the sergeant replied, mystified.

'Well, we're here anyways,' Jack replied with a laugh, and without further ado he and his men pitched in to clean the whole place thoroughly, from top to bottom. After dinner, they did it again. In his whole time in the army, this had never happened to Sergeant Merrikin, and he never forgot it. In his opinion, Jack Edmondson was one soldier in a thousand.[12]

•

For Ivor Hancock and Norm Graham, the training had been singularly intense. First put in the training camp out at Colac, they had been through an exhausting variety of marching exercises, together with running, jumping and clambering through and over all sorts of obstacles. Even in their sleep, they could hear the endless cadence: 'Fall in ... quick march ... right turn ... left turn ... about face ... right wheel ... left wheel ... on the double ... form fours ... form threes ... by the right ... quick *march*!' As they proceeded, they were frequently encouraged by Sergeant 'Jock' Wilkie to bellow marching songs, which would both lift their morale and help them to keep in step. A particular favourite dated from the time of the Great War ...

> *Pack up your troubles in your old kit bag and smile, smile, smile!*
> *While you've a Lucifer to light your fag,*
> *Smile, boys, that's the style!*
> *What's the use of worrying!?!?*
> *It never was worthwhile ...!*
> *So, pack up your troubles in your old kit bag*
> *and smile, smile, smile!*

From Colac, they'd been taken in July to another army training camp, at a place called Rokeby in country Victoria, where the wind seemed to blow even colder, the mattresses were harder, and every Sergeant Major had a voice that was part foghorn and part air-raid siren. It was there, too, that they were issued with rifles and bayonets for the first time — all of the weapons taken out of storage, where they had lain since the Great War, which meant they went well with large parts of the men's uniforms, which also dated from that time. (As in, they might not yet be Anzacs, worthy of hitting the beach at Gallipoli, but there really wasn't two bob of difference in the way they *looked*.)

By this time Ivor was getting a lot more used to the army life, and while strengthening the bonds even further with his old mate Norm, he had formed some strong friendships with a new bunch of knockabout blokes, perhaps best distinguished by the fact that for the most part they'd rather have a fight than a feed. There was the bloke from northwestern New South Wales they called 'Pudden Head' Poidevin, because he had the most enormous melon for a head anyone had ever seen, though they could equally have called him 'Ape' for the amount of thick, jet-black body hair he had. Blokes swore that Pudden Head had a five-o'clock shadow even at seven o'clock in the morning, right after he'd shaved, and though he was such a tough bastard no one wanted to say anything, everyone quietly thought he was a dead ringer for Benito Mussolini, squat, rough mongrel that he was.

Another rough diamond of a bloke went by the name of Frankie Barlow, and though Ivor had initially warmed to the Melburnian because they shared a common interest in motorbike racing, Frankie was deeply admired by everyone for the fact that he was always getting into, and then out of, scrapes, where you knew — you just bloody knew — he was gone a million, and then he'd be all right, and not even get busted!

Yet one more who Ivor liked a lot, who stood out as one of the most colourful characters in their company — soon to become D Company of the 2/24th Battalion of the 7th Division — was 'Cocky' Walpole. He was from up Mildura way, and despite having the short, slight build of the bush jockey he had been, Cocky, as Ivor would later describe him, 'had been in so many drunken fights that his face looked like a rugged map of Australia'.

The son of Polish immigrants, Cocky had a wicked sense of humour and a laugh that would make the hair on the back of your neck stand up — even Frankie Barlow's, if it hadn't been so damn thick. Cocky loved nothing better than getting out on the piss and getting as full as a butcher's pup, was an incurable gambler, had a bit of a criminal record and, rumour had it, had once been up on a murder charge over gambling, but nothing could be proved. He was also the company 'scrounger'; as one who could provide almost anything from anywhere, Cocky was a very useful bloke to have around.

Just a few months prior, Ivor had never laid eyes on any of them bar Norm, but now they were more than merely his best mates, and they all stuck to each other 'like shit to an army blanket', as the expression went. Among a hundred other babbling voices on the parade ground, Ivor could have picked Cocky's rather nasal drawl in an instant; at dusk on a cloudy night he was able to distinguish Pudden's head at a distance of 200 yards, just as he could pick in an instant, by the curious way Frankie stood — with one knee angled out like a pelican in the mud — which one was him in a bunch of blokes doing sentry duty right on the edge of camp. These weren't like the 'friends' he had back in Melbourne, who he might see once or twice a week, at the pub or a game of Aussie Rules. These were like brothers he saw all day, every day, who depended on him and he depended on in turn; and Ivor enjoyed the intimacy of it all, after the barrenness of his past family life.

Some things in military life though, Ivor just couldn't cop. One of these was what was known in the army as the 'short arm inspection', which meant the whole Company lining up in three rows with their flies undone and their penises exposed. Then a Medical Officer would come along, place a cane under the penis and closely examine it for signs of infection. If the member was uncircumcised, the MO would bark 'foreskin back', and again, if there were any signs of dirtiness, the humiliating order would come: 'Take it away and wash it!'

The sheer indignity of it! And yet it wasn't just insufficient washing that the MO was looking out for: there was also the growing problem of venereal disease.

The thing was, the soldiers would get a weekend's leave every fortnight, whereupon most of them would head off into Melbourne, and it was amazing how well a bloke in uniform could go with the ladies there. They were soldiers, see; soldiers in the Australian Army, about to go off to fight a war, to maybe die for their country, and as such were due an immediate deference from their fellow Australians. And as such, if you played that deference right with comely females, you could be already well on your way to doing a little horizontal foxtrot with them.

Ivor would frequently go on his weekend leave with Norm, and the two soon became very serious with a couple of ladies who greatly pleased them, whom they'd met at a Saturday night dance at the Essendon Rowing Club: Dorothy Poynton and Jean Coles. Ivor really liked Jean — a very fetching shop girl from Edmont's Variety Store — a great deal. There was just something about her, her *spark*, her look — her *bloody curves!* — and he couldn't even think straight when he was around her. She certainly liked Ivor well enough to let him into her bed. Norm felt much the same about Dorothy, and for both couples things progressed from there.

•

Whose move?

In Libya, the highest-ranking Italian military man on site, Marshal Rodolfo Graziani, Marchese di Nogheli, had at his command some 250 000 troops of the Italian 10th Army, and was staring across the savage Western Desert at General Sir Archibald Percival Wavell, who, with his 100 000 British troops defending Egypt and its Suez Canal, as well as the prized naval base at Alexandria, was staring right back. While the desert itself was of no particular value — there was little there bar lots of sand, a few roaming Arabs and some Italian outposts — it was enormously important as the flank of Egypt. Across it all, just one metalled road stretched along the relatively narrow coastal strip, with a few other desert tracks meandering in the manner of the camels that forged them, through the rest of the vast swathes of desert that lay inland.

The expectation of Wavell was that the Italians would launch their own full-blown attack, as opposed to the few small argy-bargy clashes there had been so far, but as July turned into August, still there was nothing ... and Wavell was not the only one wondering what was going on. For Mussolini, too, was keen that Italian arms be seen to be doing something — now that they were officially at war — and so encouraged Graziani to move on the British. After all, on the maps in Mussolini's spacious sparkling War Room in Rome's magnificent Palazzo Venezia, it looked like a fairly straightforward exercise, and *Il Duce* waited impatiently for action to be taken.

Still nothing.

Finally, on 10 August 1940 — by which time Mussolini was convinced that the German invasion of Britain was imminent and that it was urgent that Italy earn its place to share in the spoils of victory — he cabled Marshal Graziani a direct order:

```
The day on which the first platoon of German soldiers
touches British territory, you will simultaneously attack.
Once again, I repeat that there are no territorial
objectives, it is not a question of aiming for Alexandria,
nor even for Sollum. I am only asking you to attack the
British forces facing you. I assume full responsibility for
this decision of mine.[13]
```

•

Marching, marching, marching. Marching till they wanted to drop ... but still they didn't, on this twelfth day of August. For they were the 2/13th Battalion, marching all the way from their Ingleburn camp up to Bathurst, 132 miles away — with 34-pound packs on their backs — as part of their last preparations before they would be ready to head overseas. The mighty 2/17th Battalion, their brothers in arms, had cheered them out of the camp, knowing that they would very shortly be following in their weary footsteps. The 2/13th appreciated it, as noted in their official history: 'Men of the 2/13th had already realised the sterling worth of its sister battalion, the 2/17th, and as their band picked up the step and played the 2/13th through the gates, new-found soldierly grimness was somewhat relaxed and the 2/13th allowed itself a grin and a cheer in answer to the hearty farewell ... Any man wearing the other's colour patch was to be made wholeheartedly welcome among men of the other unit, everywhere and at all times.'[14]

For now, though, the march, the march, the march . . .

The men of the 2/13th were proud of how well they had prepared themselves over the previous two months, and when it came to feeling pride, they weren't the only ones. For along the way to Bathurst, as they proceeded, droves of schoolchildren came out in every town they passed through, waving their Australian flags and cheering the soldiers to the echo. And nor was it just the kids — journalists seemed to jump out from behind every second bush, as did photographers, and cinematographers getting footage for the newsreels. By one report the whole thing had been staged as a wonderful publicity opportunity for the newsreel cameras in the first place.[15] The feeling seemed to run that with the way things were going in Europe, maybe these were the boys who could help fix things up. Fair dinkum, it'd make a bloke feel like a hero, and they hadn't even done anything yet!

Still, that feeling of heroism was enhanced on that first night, when the battalion pulled into the tiny town of Wallacia, 17 miles from Ingleburn, to find that a dance had been organised in their honour and that, right after the dance was over, they were to be bedded down as billets among the locals, before forming up and heading off again the following morning, feeling refreshed and ready to go.

Just wait till they had a crack at those Germans, then those bastards would see a thing or two!

Few felt this more strongly than Bert Ferres, who was practically skipping his way to Bathurst, so relieved did he feel. His troublesome father had now said that if he could make it all the way to the inland town, he would give his final blessing to Bert joining the AIF and wouldn't dob him in for having lied about his age, and the young man knew that, with that kind of incentive, he would waltz it in . . .

•

Following just two days behind the 2/13th, the attention given to the 2/17th was understandably slightly less, though up Springwood way all were interested to observe that one young girl was noticeably keen to get as many of their autographs as possible, and was very carefully writing down their names beneath the sometimes unclear signatures. When asked why she was being so careful, she replied cheerfully enough that she wanted to check their names off later on, when the casualty lists came out, so she could see how many of the dead and wounded she knew.[16]

Oh.

Well, it was fame of a sort.

•

For John Johnson, still camped with the rest of the 2/23rd Battalion at the Albury Showground, it was the best time of all — mail call. Usually it would bring him a letter either from his dear Josie, or from one of his six sons or his daughter — either written by them, or with the help of an older brother or Josie herself. This one, dated 6 September, was from his nine-year-old, Barry, and it may well have been written in crayon.

Dear Dad,
I hope you are well we are good. Jim came home tonight. I made a traler for Des little car and it s a goodey. It was good up at Hunts. I think Id had bedder go now.
Goodbye,
Your loving Son Barry.

Such simple words, but they made him want to weep with a mixture of joy for hearing from Barry, and sadness at being away from them all. The whole thing had been even tougher for John Johnson than he had imagined — and he knew that it was equally tough for them — but the letters helped a lot. This one, as with every one he received, John carefully secreted in a special waterproof spot in his kitbag with all the others, whence at odd moments he could fish them out to read them again and again. It helped.

•

Despite all the *realpolitik* of obeying Mussolini's order to attack the British forces in North Africa, Marshal Graziani still remained reluctant, feeling that his troops were not yet ready. But finally — a full month after first being ordered to do so by *Il Duce* — Graziani felt he really had no choice, and knew that he must either order the attack or face being removed from his position and replaced by someone who would give such an order.

One important thing had to be done first, though ...

So it was that on the morning of 8 September 1940, the British forces assembled near the HQ of the 7th Armoured Brigade — situated at Sidi Barrani, right near the so-called 'front line' of this strangely inactive war to date — had a message bag dropped upon them. Inside, neatly typed, was a list of all the British prisoners the Italians had so far managed to snare in their various skirmishes, the state of their health, and even a letter from the most senior British officer in captivity, affirming that they were being treated well.[17]

Of course, it was jolly decent of the Italians and all, but if you didn't know better you'd think it was a message from the Italians to the effect, 'We are treating *your* prisoners very well, so should *we* fall into your clutches in coming days and weeks, would you mind doing the same for us, *per favore . . .?*'

Proprieties now observed, Graziani gave the order to . . . *ATTA—*, well . . . at least *advance*.

And so they did.

On 13 September, six divisions of the 10th Army, 200 light and medium tanks — most of which were too light to make much of an impact — and many hundreds of enormous lorries, all of which were too heavy to proceed if ever they left the safety of the road, carefully rumbled east across the Egyptian border, and began firing salvos upon the assembled British forces. As recorded by the astute Italian Foreign Minister, Count Galeazzo Ciano, 'Never has a military operation been carried out so much against the wishes of its commander . . .'[18]

Bemused rather than bedazzled by all this Italian military might, the British did indeed fall back under the sheer weight of numbers, while nevertheless firing enough Parthian shots from their many artillery units that they created havoc among the advancing Italians. In one gratifying episode, which occurred near Sollum, the retreating British looked back to see an interesting thing on the distant hillside. At one point on a bend, the windshield of the Italian trucks caught the sun and flashed across the valley. Then, some ten seconds later, the same vehicle would appear a little lower down at the next bend. Therefore, by timing their high explosive shells to land at the second bend exactly ten seconds after they saw the flash, the result was carnage!

•

For all that, within days the Italians were right to Sidi Barrani, 90 kilometres inside the Egyptian border, some 480 kilometres to the west of Alexandria, at which point they ran out of gas, figuratively and almost literally . . .

Not only had they chewed up much of their precious oil supplies but, just ahead, the main British forces were now dug in and well defended at Mersa Matruh, with a very clear attitude of *This far and no further*. Which was fine with the Italians.

For a while the front line now settled down and became static, even though Wavell had only committed 36 000 British troops to defending the position — shrewdly judging that the Italians were unlikely to press the issue, and would likely have no idea just how weak the forces opposing them were.

A cautious man by nature — and feeling that he had done enough to get Mussolini off his back for a while — Graziani decided to stockpile his supplies of gasoline, keenly aware that his problems of supply would get exponentially worse the further his forces pushed from their Tripoli base. Fortunately, though, there was also a lot of materiel coming through the Italian-held small port of Tobruk, just 220 kilometres back . . .

•

While the forces of Fascism were on the march in North Africa, so too were the forces of democracy at work in Australia, particularly in the lead-up to the federal election, held on 21 September 1940. It was Robert Menzies' first chance to be confirmed by the Australian people as their chosen Prime Minister, and his approach was clear. As later described by the eminent Australian historian David Day, the way Menzies presented himself during the campaign was 'A vote for Menzies was a vote for Churchill'.[19] Clearly, however, that approach by Menzies — against a Labor Party led by John Curtin that was running on an entirely different platform which stated that, when it came to Australian Government policy, it actually should be Australian interests that counted first of all (which was the reason Curtin and his party had opposed the deployment of Australian troops to the Middle East in the first place) — was now teetering on the razor's edge to oblivion.

For when the counting was over, the Menzies men had won thirty-six seats in the House of Representatives, while John Curtin's Labor Party had won . . . thirty-six seats, too. With the two sides deadlocked, the fate of the government was in the hands of the two independents: Alex Wilson from the electorate of Wimmera in northwestern Victoria and Arthur Coles, who held Henty in east Melbourne. After some prevarication, both backed Menzies, but it was clear to all that Menzies — who had seen the sixteen-seat majority he had inherited from Joseph Lyons evaporate — was flagging, and that Curtin was closing fast.

Still, with the Italians now on the march in North Africa and the Germans continuing to shackle Europe to their tyrannical yoke, one of the first Menzies moves after the election was to approve a request by Winston

Churchill to form up yet one more Australian division to fight for the British Empire in foreign climes — this one to be the 9th Division. The plan was that it would initially see action in the Middle East and, after some kerfuffle, it was decided that the new division would be composed of spare parts put together from elsewhere. Morshead's 18th Brigade and the nascent 25th Brigade — both from the 6th Division and still in training in Britain — would form the core of the new division.

•

It was 30 September 1940. Father had gone to bed early, and in the kitchen of their rambling weatherboard farmhouse, mother and son were eating the toasted sandwiches Jack had made for their late supper and drinking Elizabeth's tea as they chatted over the serious matter of just what might happen in the war, and how Jack might deal with it.

'Whatever will you do, Jack,' Elizabeth said at one point, 'if you get in a tight spot, say a bayonet charge, say someone coming at you with a bayonet?'

Momentarily, Jack was slightly nonplussed.

'Why do you say such things? Why do you ask me questions like that?'

'Because I am afraid for you and I hate the bayonet.'

'So do we all, Mother. We all loathe it.'

'Why, then, don't you seem to be more afraid of it, fear it more?'

'Because I know how to use it . . .'

He was odd like that, her Jack. So sweet, so sensitive, so gentle, such a loving son, and yet when it came to talk of battle and the like, he always evinced a sense of quiet confidence that he would acquit himself well. Which was good, she supposed; but, as ever, the same fear came back. Possibly he was too confident, to the point of needlessly putting himself in danger. They sat there for a while longer, quietly, as their cat, Stuffy, purred around 'doing his laps' — perpetually going from hers to his and back again, as if he couldn't decide which one he loved more — and then Elizabeth heard herself say it.

'Jack . . . never any decorations.'

Jack replied quietly and seriously, and it was clear he really meant it: 'No, Mother, I *want* to come back.'[20]

Just five days later, and it was the eve of his departure. Again father had gone to bed, and mother and son had supper together and quietly sat in front of the fire, warming themselves at home and hearth. Then Jack got up and, without a word, walked into the lounge room, opened the piano and began to play the haunting strains of the *Maori Farewell*.

Barely able to contain herself, Elizabeth mouthed the well-loved words, knowing that they had never had as much force as right now.

On a moonlit night
I see in a dream
You going
To a distant land

Farewell,
But return again
To your loved one,
Weeping here

•

The following morning, it was time.[21] Jack's home leave was over, and he had to return to his camp in preparation for departure overseas. On this occasion, Elizabeth decided she wouldn't go with him to Liverpool station, as she just couldn't bring herself to put them both through the agony of another goodbye, enduring the terrible moments when the train first lurched into life and began pulling away, each turn of the wheel taking her son further and further away from her. At least if they said goodbye here at home, her agony was more private.

Terribly conscious of how hard his mother was going to find it while he was overseas and away from her, Jack embraced her tightly and begged her to promise that she would 'put up a good fight', that she wouldn't simply give in to her misery — which she faithfully did. Jack was not to worry, she said. She would be fine, she assured him.

'Mother, it may be harder for you than you think …'

Elizabeth started to cry, Jack to tear up. Finally there was nothing for it. This had to end, and there was only one way. He *had* to *go*.

'Mother, keep your chin up,' he said, kissing her, and then without another word got into the car, which was to be driven by his father to the station, leaned out the open window and snapped off a formal military salute.

'Good luck …' he called, and then the car left. Elizabeth watched it till the last moment it disappeared around the distant corner. Her boy was gone.

As she went back inside a house that suddenly felt cavernous in its cold emptiness, she caught sight of the birthday cake she'd baked him a fortnight early for his twenty-sixth, on the grounds that he would be on the high seas by the time it actually fell. Jack had had too much luggage to take his birthday cake as well, and neither had any appetite to eat it.

•

It was the *Queen Mary*, but it was not the '*Queen Mary*'.

That is, while everyone knew what the big ship anchored off Bradley's Head in Sydney Harbour was called, its normal painted name had been removed — to be replaced by *HMT QX*, whatever that was — and it was against the law to refer to it by any other designation, for reasons of security. In these troubled times, the byword was that 'loose lips sink ships', and there was a strong reckoning that by not even naming those ships in the first place, there was less chance they would be sunk. (It made sense at the War Cabinet level of government.)

In any case, it was a mighty big ship (the second largest cruise liner afloat) and on this afternoon of 19 October 1940, the men of the 2/13th and 2/17th — which, together with the 2/15th Battalion, still training up in Darwin, made up the 20th Brigade of the 7th Division — were awed by the size of the thing as they approached the harbour. Fresh from a long journey by train, and then a short trip by ferry, they began filing up the gangplank into the belly of the beast and finding their positions from there. The luckiest of the troops settled into cabins fit for dinki-di royalty, with, among other things, real mother-of-pearl on the dunny seats! It almost seemed criminal to sit on them, but the Diggers — geez, they loved being called that now — knew they'd manage.

The following morning, just after 10 a.m., the mighty and magisterial ship raised both anchor and steam, and started gently pulling away from its previous anchorage, making for Sydney Heads. Around and about her as she left on this sparkling Sunday in Sydney Town were hundreds of small yachts, tooting ferries, jostling tugboats and pleasure craft, running and fussing for all the world like baby dolphins encircling a massive whale, wanting to be close but not *too* close for fear of being swamped. In the boats was a fair sprinkling of Sydneysiders come out to wish the troops well — smiling and waving and giving them three cheers *hip-hip-hurrah!*

The bulk of those on the water, though, were the wives, girlfriends, parents and families of the troops, wanting to give the men a proper send-off, as well as get one last, precious look before they left. Some of the onlookers were crying, others trying to put on a brave face, while others still were holding up signs that said things like 'GOOD LUCK BOBBY! WE LOVE YOU!', 'BYE DADDY', signed 'JENNIFER B', 'GO WELL, JOHN FROM COOTAMUNDRA' and so forth. From one yacht the strains of *Auld Lang Syne* could be heard, led by an elderly couple — perhaps grandparents of one of the young soldiers, wondering if they would still be there when their grandson got back. *If* he got back.

The troops in turn smiled down, waving, blowing kisses, and despite their own emotions at leaving their families running high, generally their mood was euphoric. They were off! No, they didn't yet know where they were going, as that too was a secret, but what they did know was that it already felt like an adventure. From the Finger Wharf at Woolloomooloo on the opposite side of the harbour, now came the good ship *Aquitania* (albeit under its code name), another enormous cruise liner equally laden down with troops, and both ships had as escort the cruiser HMAS *Perth*. As Watsons Bay appeared to their — what was that word again? — *starboard*, the three ships now fell into line, even as the troops they carried shifted to the stern, straining for last looks at both the small dolphins that were falling back, and at the shining city itself. The Sydney Harbour Bridge was now looking no bigger than a kid's Meccano set in the far, far distance, and even the people on the nearby southern shores who were waving at them looked like no more than tiny dots with matchstick legs.

And yet, even as some 5000 of the soldiers crowded the now low-in-the-water stern, one soldier stood right up high on the bow with a British sailor who happened to be there. For Bert Ferres of the 2/13th Battalion, it was perhaps the most exciting moment in his young life, as he strained to see what lay ahead, already feeling entirely disconnected from what he felt was the dreary existence that lay behind him. *Bliss was it in that dawn to be alive, but to be young was very heaven.*[22]

Sydney fell away, and the convoy slid quietly down the east coast, where other troopships were beginning to congregate off Port Phillip Bay, ready to carry away in their own turn the cream of Victoria's military manhood.

•

John Johnson had arrived home to Walwa just the day before — on his final leave before embarkation — in the company of his fellow 2/23rd Battalion men and good mates from the rural town, Alan Kelly and Pat Joy.

And now John was walking with his oldest son, fourteen-year-old Jack, up by the bridge near Ernie Murray's place, and the two were having a quiet father-and-son talk in the afterglow of that hot spring day. John knew he had to leave on the morrow and there were some things that needed to be said, the things that maybe had to be said now, 'cos there may not be a 'later' to say them.

'Like girls, son. Don't fret too much about them, particularly not over the next few years, because when the right one comes along, you'll just know, just like I did with your mother.'

'Yes, Dad.'

They kept walking, the freshly fallen gum-tree blossom lightly eddying in their wake, and then another thing came to John.

'The main thing is, son, *look after your mother and your brothers and sister.* Whatever happens, you make sure you look after them.'

Now, just what got into his father that day, young Jack couldn't be sure, but the next words were particularly clear:

'I don't think I will be coming back, son,' his father said. 'If I get killed, just tell your mother everything will be all right.'

With words like that, there wasn't a whole lot more to be said, and the two kept walking in silence, until they got to within cooee of the family cottage — at which point all the other kids rushed out to meet them, eager not to waste their last precious hours with their now all-laughing, all-singing, all-rouseabout, tumble-in-the-grass father. *Playing in Walwa for one night only, so get him while he's here!*

The following morning at the crack of dawn, the tiny town awakened to the sound of a haunting trumpet playing reveille. It was Alan Kelly, and he played at it as never before, the timeless tones ringing across the valley and beckoning to arms all those who were willing to carry them, a clarion call to tell his fellow soldiers and the rest of Walwa that this was the day that the town's patriotic sons were off to war.[23]

At the Johnson household, they were all soon up and about and around their father, looking so strong and proud in his slouch hat and khakis, his kitbag over his shoulder, readying to catch the mail bus with the others. Before he went, he gave each of them, and Josie — including the growing mound in her tummy, because she had fallen pregnant again just before John had joined the Army — a special hug, kiss and a few intimate words goodbye. It was a bit tough when little Barry slowed things by clinging to his father's legs and with great big sobs *begged* him not to go, but his father was equal to the task. He gently extricated himself, explained to Barry that although he didn't want to go, he had to, and Barry had to try to understand that.

A quick photo with all the family out the front of the house, and then he was gone.

The Johnson kids went off to school half sad and half cock-a-hoop. Yes, their dad was gone, and yes, they were going to miss him terribly, but not to forget: their father was a *Digger*. And he had gone away to fight for Australia. No, it wasn't quite the same as 'playing for Australia' in your baggy green cap like Don Bradman and Tiger O'Reilly did, but it was still something, something to be really proud of and they walked tall because of it.

•

Well away from such strong familial scenes, Ivor Hancock was AWL, holed up in Jean's place. Bored beyond all redemption with having to wait in the camp for the embarkation orders for the 2/24th, he'd decided to jump the fence, hitch a ride and spend precious time with his girlfriend, figuring he'd take his chances with whatever punishment the Army gave him, if indeed it found out. As it was, he reckoned he was still a fair chance of getting away with it, as the boys were all covering for him, including good ol' Corporal Roy McKenzie, a canny Scot known as Macca who was responsible for doing the daily head count.

But then came the knock on the door, and the cable boy. It was a telegram from Corporal Macca saying the orders to move out the following day had come, and Ivor had to get his arse back immediately or he'd end up being charged with being a deserter.

An intimate embrace for Jean, and then with all the others Ivor was soon on his way on the high seas on one of P&O's finest, the *Strathmore* — in the company of the *Orion*, also bearing Australian troops, and the *Batory*, carrying some Kiwis — heading west in the wake of the 20th Brigade, just three weeks behind it . . .

Also on the *Strathmore* was John Johnson, and though he generally mixed easily with the rest of the Battalion, he remained very tight with Pat Joy and Alan Kelly, his mates from Walwa. Pat was a slim 25-year-old farm labourer of intelligent disposition, while Alan was the forever-laughing only son of a large Irish family who doted on him. A good decade older than both men, John took an almost paternal interest in them, though the relationship was not one way. For John, too, drew no small measure of solace from the younger men, at least in part because they were the only ones on the ship who knew Josie, knew his kids and properly understood just how badly he was missing them all. Somehow, homesickness hurt just a little less when you were talking to your own blokes from home, and the three of them stuck closely together, a trio of best friends.

•

Who knows quite how to define the common thread of many men's thoughts at such a time, leaving their homeland as seagulls cawed and swooped all around? For, of course, their thoughts were so many and varied that the thread is not easily visible, and yet . . .

And yet most of the men, with the certain exception of John Johnson, seemed to have one certainty, which was that they would be coming back. Yes, of course, they were engaged on a dangerous venture, going up against powerful enemies, and of course it was only logical that a good percentage of them — 10 per cent, 30 per cent, who knew? — would likely be killed in action. After all, it was for a very good reason that the army had ensured that each of them, before departing, had filled out a dull cream form which was their last will and testament. Most often a bloke would just sign everything over to his parents or his wife, in just a couple of lines, get a handy mate to witness it, and Bob was your bloody uncle.

Two of the blokes in Ivor's platoon, for example, were a laid-back fellow by the name of Dougie Smythe from Wentworth in southwestern NSW, and his equally quiet mate, Lou Gazzard, a school teacher from Condah in the green rolling hills of southwestern Victoria. Typically, Dougie got Lou to witness his will — where he 'bequeathed all personal property & estate' to his mother, 'Mrs Elizabeth Smythe of Adam Street, Wentworth, NSW' — and then Lou did the same for Dougie. That made everything *neat*. If they got killed, their mums could inherit all their worldly possessions, up to and including their old kitbag.

And yet, of course, each man felt sorry that some of his mates wouldn't make it. But against all that was the mostly silent conviction that, somehow, some way, there was an ordination that their own cards were not so marked. They would be okay. It wasn't something you talked about out loud, 'cos the other blokes'd go you, but they felt it, all right.

All together now, they were on their way.

CHAPTER FIVE

Enter the Australians

*These men from the dockside of Sydney and the sheep stations of the
Riverina presented such a picture of downright toughness with their gaunt
dirty faces, huge boots, revolvers stuffed in their pockets, gripping their rifles
with huge shapeless hands, shouting and grinning — always grinning —
that the mere sight of them must have disheartened the enemy troops.'*

AUSTRALIAN JOURNALIST ALAN MOOREHEAD, OBSERVING THE FIRST AUSTRALIAN
TROOPS LANDING IN THE MIDDLE EAST[1]

All, *all* is context. There have doubtless been many occasions in the history
of the world when a man who was convinced he was an 'emperor'
waited impatiently for another man, who was convinced he was the
undisputed leader of the world's 'master race', to arrive on an official visit,
even as the 'emperor' waited to hear news of whether his empire has been
satisfactorily expanded. The difference in this case, however, was that it was all
real. Or real enough ...

On this morning of 28 October 1940 it was Benito Mussolini waiting
on the platform of Florence's stunning and newly constructed Santa Maria
Novella railway station — all high stone walls and cathedral ceilings
punctuated by vast skylights — ready to greet Adolf Hitler when he arrived
after his long trip from Berlin. And the Italian leader had news. Over the last
four months he had become more mightily annoyed than ever that the full
march of history was taking place without him being seen right beside
Hitler at the front of the throng — and he was nothing less than
embarrassed at how slowly the Italian advances in North Africa were
proceeding. So he had decided on a bold new course of action ... which he
had initiated just hours earlier, by ordering the Italian troops based in
Albania to cross the border into Greece that very morning at dawn.

Now, as he waited for Hitler, he was constantly agitating his staff for
news of whether or not the Italian troops had yet won 'a great victory'.[2]

Sadly, there was no such news, and when Hitler's train pulled up and the

German dictator emerged from his specially constructed carriage, Mussolini could only expostulate: 'Führer, we are on the *march!*'

Hitler's reply has gone unrecorded by history, but his thoughts have not. Having already heard on the train that morning what Mussolini had done, the German dictator was furious. Though it would not do to give full vent to his feelings for such a close ally, the German leader just could not believe that Mussolini would launch such an action, first without giving Germany any advance notice, and second at such a time when surely any fool knew that the autumn rains were at their heaviest in Greece and in rough country any advancing army would find themselves caught in one giant quagmire.

And nor — though he did not know it at this time — would Hitler have been surprised to know of Winston Churchill's immediate response to the Italian invasion, which had taken the form of a cable to the Greek leader General Ioannis Metaxas:

We will give you all the help in our power!

Metaxas was more than a little underwhelmed. This was one Greek who wasn't sure if he even wanted this particular gift. His view was that, unless the British could give them major help — say, six divisions — it would be better for his country to deal with the Italians on their own, and not risk attracting the Germans, in which case Greece would be in real trouble.

Still, within just a few days Mussolini had his news from the front. And it was not good. Despite his proud boasts of what would happen, the reality was that the broad mass of the Greek citizenry and soldiery were in fact conspicuous for not greeting his troops as 'liberators' from the cruel rule of their own government. The truth was that they were against the Italian presence from the first. Actually, the Greeks were suddenly united as never before and had practically risen as one, and taken up arms, and they were now coming at the soaked, sodden and stuck Italian troops from all angles ...

In short, far from taking over all of Greece, as Mussolini had hoped, in the space of only a week the invading Italians had been cleared out of the country and beaten so far back into Albania that the Greeks threatened to clear them out of there, too, already controlling one-third of the former Italian territory. Equally disastrous for the Axis cause, Metaxas had welcomed the Royal Air Force onto Greek territory in the short term, and with British bombers now operating from Athens' airfields, it suddenly meant that the crucial oil fields of Romania — veritably Germany's petrol station for the entire Nazi war machine — were now within range of British bombers.

•

Elizabeth Edmondson had just stopped in at Fitzpatrick's store at Liverpool when a lady, whom she knew did some sewing at the Ingleburn camp, walked in with what she thought was a bit of very interesting gossip. This lady had been talking to a young priest who had been talking to some senior army officers, who had told him — who had told her — that the *Queen Mary* had been sunk! The blood drained from Elizabeth's face and she could barely speak. In fact, as she couldn't trust herself as to what she might say, she just kept mum, and left the store trying not to scream.

By the time Will picked her up a short time later she had decided on her course of action: she wanted to go *straight* to the Ingleburn camp and ask whether there was any possible foundation to the rumour. Will favoured going home to await developments, but Elizabeth would have none of it. She insisted they go, and so go they did.

The couple was received by the Commanding Officer of the camp, Colonel Moore, who, mercifully, assured them that as far as he knew there was nothing to the rumour at all; that he was not holding anything back from them; and that he would personally come to see them and tell them the very instant he heard any news to the contrary. They left, at least partly satisfied that their beloved boy was still alive and on the high seas.[3] (And in fact he really was okay, notwithstanding the fact that at one point he and his mates had been convinced they had just seen a whole heap of submarines about to surface right beside their ship in the middle of the Great Australian Bight — only to find out that they were enormous whales![4])

•

In the meantime, the men of the Australian 6th Division continued their training in Palestine, though it had not been easy for them. The Australian journalist Alan Moorehead later gave one particularly illustrative account of what was ailing them. 'The first Australian division, sent to the Palestine deserts, was cursing and complaining. They wanted action instead of route marches in the sand. They were said to be so poorly equipped at this early stage that they were using sticks tied with red flags as anti-tank guns and sticks tied with blue rags as Brens. A sergeant, so the story ran, was court-martialled for cynically demanding a new anti-tank gun of the Quartermaster, on the grounds that his old one was eaten by white ants . . .'[5]

At least they were there, on site in the Middle East, which was a whole lot better than the likes of Jack Edmondson, Ivor Hancock, John Johnson and their fellow freshly trained troops, who at this point were still continuing their journey across the Indian Ocean to the west, and their destiny. Each ship in the convoy was spaced out far enough from the others that it would only be a lucky bomb that would hit more than one of them, but they were still close enough to protect each other. The ships, however, were the only things that did have any space. With each ship as full as a googy egg, crowding of the troops was so bad that fights would sometimes break out over just who had first dibs on a coveted bit of deck space. And just as the seas shimmered with the heat, so did the days, blurring around the edges and kind of melting into one another, until in all the stinking humidity one day looked little different from the next. Dinkum, it nearly killed the soldiers when every two or three days they would be instructed to wind their watches back by half an hour, so giving up time that had been bloody hard won.

The only thing a fella could be certain of in such circumstances was that they must be closer to their destination, because the heat was marginally more intolerable today than it was yesterday ...

•

Among all the soldiers was Chester Wilmot, equipped with his pen, his notebook, his typewriter, talent, drive and fine journalistic eye, all of which he put to the service of making broadcasts for the ABC on just what the mood and manner were among these Australian warriors on their way to a great battle.

Cooped up himself aboard the *Indra Puera*, Wilmot started to record for posterity their experience. For the men rising every morning to the sound of reveille played by bugles and a half-strangled bagpipe, each day aboard ship was a kind of bored blur of routine, meals, callisthenics, inspections and instructions on such things as health and hygiene, and how to survive gas attacks — as the Indian Ocean sailed backwards behind them. There were few interruptions to this way of life, though a welcome one was in the afternoons, when the aspiring 'Ack-Ack' — the Anti-Aircraft gunners — would trail enormous kites off the back of the ship and then set about bringing them down with the accuracy of their fire.

Early on, this could be quite entertaining, as the men watched and ironically cheered as either the kites were missed entirely or barely winged — followed by a real cheer when they were knocked from the sky, exactly as they hoped any enemy plane that made it through the defences of their escort might be. After just a couple of weeks, though, this daily entertainment didn't last long, as the Ack-Ack boys would no sooner put the kites up than they were knocked down again in nothing flat.

Despite the difficulties of life and training in such a confined space, there was a growing sense among the Australian soldiers that if they ever got a chance at the Jerries or the Ities, they really might be able to give them a bit of what-for. Chester Wilmot's reports home of his ship-board experience were upbeat and optimistic, sounding a tone that the boys were on their way and that there seemed every chance they would be able to put on a 'good show' if given the chance.

On 30 October, just off the Cocos Islands, there was something new under the sun, as recorded in the 2/17th Battalion history: 'At midday, HMAS *Perth* handed over her escort duties to HMAS *Canberra*, and went racing down the convoy line in farewell. The blue water danced about her in the sunlight; her ensigns were spread; all in white the sailors lined her decks; white bow waves folded away in a perfect symmetry of lazy foam; a boiling white wake spread behind her like a fan. In her was all the gallantry of the sea — and not a single watching soldier but felt this. The soldiers cheered the sailors as they went racing past; the sailors cheered in reply. And then the Perth wheeled on her course and set off back for Australia, signalling "Goodbye", and the *Queen Mary* replied, "Thank you; goodbye. Success against the enemy".'[6]

Among the soldiers of the 2/13th, Bert Ferres was standing with his best mate, Bill Walmsley, a big gangly country lad from up Inverell way in northern New South Wales, and both were waving their hats and cheering with the best of them. For his part, Bert could still barely believe his luck. On his way to a real, live war, he was sleeping in what had been a luxury cabin with seven other blokes, complete with a bathroom that had hot and cold running water; and getting three decent meals a day! Life had never been so good, and on the rare occasions that he did think about his previous life in the fibro shack at night, and the dusty factory during the day, it was only with a shudder.

•

In London, Churchill's War Cabinet viewed the situation in the part of the world the Australians were heading to with growing alarm. With the Allies having been comprehensively routed in mainland Europe, it now looked like they were under an extreme threat of suffering similar humiliation in

North Africa and the Middle East, something that would surely have a catastrophic effect on the public's morale. But morale, a mere problem of the spirit, wasn't really the worst of it ...

If the Axis powers were to get to the Suez Canal, they would control much more than just the world's crossroads — they would also control a good chunk of the oil supply that the Allies were using to keep their own war machine going. For, without the Suez Canal, Allied ships heading to such places as India and Singapore would have to go all the way around the Cape of Good Hope, adding six weeks to the journey and effectively stretching the supply line to their front line by a distance of some 6000 miles ...

The result would be that Britain's relationship with the rest of its empire, in the lands lying around the Indian Ocean and western Pacific, would be strained and at the immediate mercy of the Axis powers. With all of that in consideration, it seemed likely that if the Suez Canal did fall to Rommel and his men, then it was highly unlikely that the United States would join the Allied war effort, as without that crucial aquatic thoroughfare it would almost definitely be a losing proposition.

•

On the good ship *Strathaird*, steaming south from Britain where they had been training for months, Brigadier Leslie Morshead sat in his cabin and composed a letter to his wife, Myrtle. The last few months had been very intense. The famed Battle of Britain had been going on, and it had momentarily looked as though the brave pilots of the Royal Air Force were going to be knocked out of the skies by the Luftwaffe, who came in wave after wave over Britain day after day, and that a German invasion against an all but defenceless island must be imminent. Even when that threat faded, however — with Churchill commenting famously in reference to those pilots that 'never has so much been owed, by so many, to so few' — Morshead had not stopped whipping his 18th Brigade into shape. Now, such was their state of readiness, he felt some satisfaction that they were heading to where some of the action was — to the Middle East.

Their convoy had left Scotland on 17 November, and though there was some risk from U-boats and the like, Myrtle was not to worry, as there were plenty of lifeboats, they were well trained in what to do in case of torpedoes — and in any case, as a high-risk troopship, they were not going through the dangerous waters of the Mediterranean, which the Italians dared to call *Mare Nostrum* (Our Sea), and would instead take over thirty days longer by going the safer way round, down the coast of Africa, around the southern tip and then all the way up to the Suez Canal, before disembarking in Alexandria in Egypt, where they would join the other Australians.

•

In early November the men of the 2/13th and the 2/17th, together with the other troops in their convoy, had spent a brief sojourn in Bombay — the first time in a foreign country for just about every man jack of them — but then had left it behind and pressed on, with still no official word as to their destination.

And yet, one didn't really need to be a genius to work it out. As first land appeared to starboard, and then to port, and started closing in on both sides — even as the sun above didn't merely shine, it *beat* — it was fairly obvious that they were afloat on the Red Sea, heading north, and would shortly be sailing up the Suez Canal.

Sure enough, on 24 November they moved into the Canal proper, and the Diggers were gobsmacked by the amount of work that had so obviously gone into the building of it some seventy years earlier. (And they thought *they* were Diggers!) As their ships moved slowly up the waterway, the Australians stared out on a world they had heard about from their fighting forefathers as a place of legend — the Middle East — and which they were now spying for the first time. Amidst fairly sad mud huts, with chickens running every which way, strange-looking Arabs (or 'Wogs', as the men knew them — some said that was short for 'Western Oriental Gentlemen', others for 'Golliwogs') traipsed along dusty paths beside heavily veiled women, nearly all of whom carried heavy loads, including huge water jars amazingly balanced on their heads. Sometimes you'd even see whole families out and about for what was probably their version of a Sunday afternoon drive: fat dad, squat and complacent on the back of a tiny donkey, while veiled mum walked behind with a load on her shoulders and head, and a huge bunch of snotty-nosed brats all around. Get a load of 'em, would yers?

Visible on the banks were tiny patches of land under cultivation, where you could see a few mangy donkeys tethered, and such workers as the Diggers could see were mostly female — and then mostly guiding old cows drawing *wooden* ploughs![7] The ships kept moving, and the Diggers kept watching, soaking it all up, particularly interested in the ways of the locals. Every now and then there would be a kind of ethereal, haunting wailing coming to them across the waters, which the Diggers worked out was a call to prayer because sometimes they could see the Wogs stop where they were and go to ground, banging their heads towards Mecca or some damn thing.

At night, in full moonlight, the vision of the barren desert and rugged hills stretching away on both sides of their ship, beneath a night sky of impossibly bright but unfamiliar stars, was intoxicating. Somehow, there was a sense that they were entering a timeless land ...

At long last, in the early morning of 26 November 1940, they stopped at a place called El Kantara, with a railway on their left leading to Egypt's capital of Cairo and one on their right to Palestine. Well before they had got there, however, their direction had been decided, for even as the first of the Australian troops had been on their way to the Middle East ten months before, the initial plan had been for them to do their training in Egypt — right up until the time the Egyptian government had put its collective foot down. Essentially, the Egyptians' gripe was that Cairo was still recovering from the after-match victory party of the Australian Light Horse back in 1918 at the conclusion of the last world war, and it would be some years still before they felt ready to lodge more Australians for the long term. They didn't feel the same about the New Zealanders, who were welcome to come to their land, but not the Australians. It was a move endorsed by Wavell, who said that he, too, 'did not want the Australians running riot around Cairo'.[8]

•

So they turned to the right, towards Palestine.

As they disembarked, fully laden with their kit, they were easy targets for the seemingly hundreds of young Arab urchins begging them for 'Baksheeeesh, George, baksheeeesh' or their older brothers offering to sell them carved elephants, cushion covers, scarves or the charms of their sisters — 'very clean, very hygiene' — and if not her, what about at least some 'feeeelthy pictures'? Cheap!

Which was fine, to a point. They had sort of got used to that kind of thing back in Bombay anyway, though there were more than a few Diggers now suffering an excruciating burning sensation every time they relieved themselves, who wished they had contented themselves with just filthy pictures in India, instead of going with the whores on the infamous Falkland Road ...

(This had not included Bert Ferres. As one of the quieter members of the 2/13th, he had been selected to go with a party of soldiers to a girls school for a musical afternoon, and to take tea.)

As to the urchins, though, it was noted that if the Diggers denied *baksheesh* to them, there was every chance that the young Arab lads would smile back at them and say with high hilarity, 'You ... fuck off now', a sure sign that the 6th Divvie had passed this way — and on that subject, many of the Diggers now asked what few white men they could find for news, to have some idea where their friends, brothers and others might now be situated. The answer was a bit vague, but it varied between the 6th being still in training in camps in Palestine, and the thought that they might have already received their marching orders for some hush-hush assignment.

After a hot breakfast in the British canteen — remembered ever afterwards by many Diggers for the hardest hard-boiled eggs they'd ever seen, with an egg white more blue than white and a yolk you just about could have hammered a nail in with — they were directed to the trains awaiting them. (But, Christ, those things sat heavy in your guts, didn't they? And they'd thought the powdered eggs they'd been eating for weeks on the ship — known as 'the yellow peril' — were bad!)

In short order they were divided into lots of twenty-five, and put into carriages designed to carry cattle, and smelling of the same.

Still, there was a certain symmetry in these young Australians being on this particular railway line, as it had been constructed by Australian soldiers of the Great War. A further reminder of those first Diggers — and a sobering one it was at that — came when, just outside of the town of Gaza, the new Diggers passed by the Australian War Cemetery, where many of those original men — once upon a time every bit as young and adventurous as them — still lay.

Dead.

The troops looked as their carriage rolled past, fell quiet, and did their best to shake it off...

That night they moved into a makeshift tented camp called Kilo 89, situated on what was effectively holy ground for the Australian military, atop Gaza Ridge. The 2/13th Battalion were camped on the south side of the ridge, with their sister battalion, the 2/17th, right beside them. Their training in the Middle East had begun, and was altogether more intense than it had been at Ingleburn. Yet much of that intensity now came from the men themselves. (It was marvellous how it could concentrate a bloke's mind, when he thought that sometime in the next few weeks he really might be going into battle and fighting for his life.)

In these weeks all of the Australians learned about digging trenches in the stony desert; how the Bren light machine gun worked; how to load it, fire it, assemble and disassemble it in just half a jiffy; and, perhaps most importantly, how to fix it when it was jammed and clean out the bloody dust which always got into its mechanism. There were lectures on how to steer by the stars if you were alone in the desert, and instruction on how to operate as a company: how to turn your flank without losing your firepower; move into a new position; provide covering fire; tactical thrusts and counter-thrusts, et cetera. They learned such things as that a 'start line' was a designated point where you had to be at a certain time before launching an assault, and that when a battle was on you could keep in touch with Battalion HQ by firing up flares called 'Very lights', with certain colours meaning certain things — red for more artillery fire, green for no artillery fire, white for we've secured the position, and so on — according to what the code was for the day.

Every Saturday they got into full battledress, complete with rifles, and went out on long route marches in the desert, with just ten minutes' break for a smoke every hour or so before going again. Often they marched over the same ground where they knew that the Australian Light Horse had so covered themselves in glory in the Great War. Those small things that looked like so many black pebbles? Look closer — shrapnel. Worn down by the wind and sand, but it was shrapnel all right. Some of the older heads in the Battalion — who had actually served in the Great War — would tell them the story, of 'the last successful cavalry charge in history in the Battle of Beersheba . . .'

It was on the afternoon of 31 October 1917, and under a blazing hot sun, 500 men of the Australian 4th Brigade charged a distance of more than 4 miles, straight at the Turkish guns. Three waves. Thundering hooves. One Aussie soldier who was in a forward position and had to jump out of their way said afterwards 'It was the bravest, most awe-inspiring sight I've ever witnessed, and they were . . . yelling, swearing and shouting. There were more than 500 Aussie horsemen . . . As they thundered past, my hair stood on end. The boys were wild-eyed and yelling their heads off.'

The Turks fired heavily at them, but the Australians kept going hard, see, and as they got closer the fire started to dissipate as some of the panicked Turks turned and ran. Galloping full-on into the Turks, the Australians then 'got to work with the bayonet' while others used their rifles as clubs. The result was a great victory for the Aussies.[9]

Blokes loved hearing that story — only maybe slightly regretting that because horses were now gone from matters military they would never be able to engage in such a glorious charge themselves — and it certainly helped pass the time as they kept marching. All too often, the last two or three miles would be marched in deep sand, just to make sure that they would get back to camp with absolutely nothing left in their tank.

And so they kept training. For Bert Ferres, Bill Walmsley and others in the 2/13th, the best part of the day usually came near dusk, when the Battalion Sergeant Major would tell them it was 'Time to charge Sheepshit Hill'.

Sheepshit Hill, so-called, was a relatively small hill on the edge of the encampment covered in sheep droppings, and the drill was to attach your bayonet to the end of your rifle, and then form up into one long line and charge up the hill, usually screaming at the top of your lungs. It was good for general conditioning, and also good for working out a way of doing it so you didn't stick your bayonet up your mate's arse by mistake, could cover each other's flanks and become a fierce fighting force should you ever have to take a similar hill for real. Best of all, once it was done, generally, so was training for the day ...

•

On a journey to the same part of the world were the Australians of the 26th Brigade, travelling in a convoy on the same route as had been previously taken by the 20th Brigade. It was clear to Ivor Hancock, Norm Graham, Frankie Barlow, Cocky Walpole, Pudden Head Poidevin and their mates that things were getting serious from the moment they were within a stone's throw of the Suez — and the ships' guns were given a test firing, even as a few depth charges were let off into the water to make sure that everything was in order for them to defend themselves. As a matter of fact, on the very day that the convoy had entered the Red Sea, Ivor happened to be on guard duty in the bowels of the ship — ensuring that the munitions store was secure — when he suddenly heard the searing wail of his ship's air-raid siren followed by ... *what the hell was that?* ... the deadly clatter-patter of machine-gun bullets ringing off the decks above! The ship was under attack! What to do? It was quite possibly a life-or-death decision. Ivor had strict instructions that he was not to leave his post whatever happened, which had sounded all right at the time — and yet it could now be his death warrant. The pounding on the decks continued and he knew that where there were bullets, there were likely bombs and torpedoes ... If the ship was hit, then his position confined in a narrow passage well below the water line meant he would be unlikely to escape. *What to do?* Fighting rising panic, Ivor miserably decided to follow orders and stay, ready to make a dash upwards at the first serious explosion, when amid the still-ringing machine-gun fire he — wonder of all wonders — heard the sounds of high hilarity, shrieks of laughter filtering down. What the . . .?

Slowly, carefully, he decided to investigate, and emerged on deck to see two sailors with dessert spoons in their hands, banging away like drummers on the steel bulkheads, while everyone else was positively falling about with laughter.

Dickheads.

•

Back in Australia, a conversation that she had had several months before continued to haunt Elizabeth Edmondson. In the previous July, her Jack had been mercifully home from Ingleburn on sick leave — as his temperature had soared to 104 degrees with the flu — and he was just getting up and about again when a neighbour by the name of Bob Mitchell came over. They had been chatting over this and that and nothing in particular when this fellow Mitchell had asked Jack straight out why he wanted to go to war. And then, before Jack could even answer, Mr Mitchell had followed up by saying, 'I'd rather be a live mouse than a dead lion . . .'

Jack had mildly replied, 'Would you?' and left it at that, but Elizabeth could not forget so easily.

She had missed Jack terribly since the moment he had left, but it was somehow even worse as she faced her first Christmas in twenty-five years without him, and troubling thoughts and memories like the conversation Jack had had with Mr Mitchell kept gnawing away at her very *soul*. Another one was how, back in August, she had attended a ceremony at the Ingleburn camp during which the 17th Battalion from the Great War had presented a set of new drums to the 2/17th, and afterwards she had met the officer who would be most directly in charge of her Jack, one Lieutenant Austin Mackell.

'I was not impressed,' Elizabeth had written in her diary the night after meeting him. 'He is a small lad, and like most small folk, he thought he was the whole 2/17th.' Elizabeth couldn't quite put her finger on it, though recorded that Lieutenant Mackell 'seemed very light and flippant, more suited to an outdoor tennis party I should say, and he talked a lot about making "whoopee", whatever that is, when he gets home.'

Another time, when Jack had been home for a brief spell, the two had sat up talking into the wee hours and the subject of his officers had come up, and Jack had confirmed how much he liked the 2/17th's Captain John Balfe and Colonel John Crawford and Major 'Bluey' Allen — all of them fine officers and fine men — but when the subject had come back to Lieutenant Mackell, Jack's voice had trailed off and he didn't say anything at all for a while, before he said thoughtfully . . .

'Oh, he's a nice little chap . . .'

Again Jack fell into silence, before continuing.

'Mother, he is so young. Not in years. He is twenty-three years old, but actually he is a lot younger than that.'[10]

Night-time provided no relief for Elizabeth, either. Instead of sweet sleep giving her blessed rest from all her fears and nagging anxieties, somehow these multiplied, grew and became worse. For the dream that she had first had earlier in the year — about trying to get out of a tight enclosure, to no avail, while Jack with an infinitely pained expression looked on — was now recurring, and sometimes it was so real she was hard put to determine whether it really was a dream, or whether it was really happening. At other times the dream had a variation in that she entered another enclosure that was so dark she could barely see, and the only source of dim light was the face of her son, lying before her at floor level and looking up at her with a terribly dull-eyed, half-comatose look. She confided to her diary:

> I hurried to him and asked what was the matter? and asked had he been bilious, as his colour had all gone? . . . and just do tell me what is the matter? I seemed to be getting upset. He looked straight at me and his face brightened up, but so white and gave me just the same old big smile then went to speak but I only heard a word or sounded like 'Uh'. I was then awake and just shivering for the rest of the night, and it all seems to me tonight still real.[11]

Maybe if she got out more the dreams would not come on so strong, but in the absence of Jack she simply didn't want to go out, and nor did she feel inclined to receive visitors.[12] And though she couldn't work out why the whole thing had such a powerful effect on her, she consoled herself with a snatch of conversation she had once had with a young clergyman. She distinctly remembered him saying that 'dreams, when very vivid and lasting, usually have a solution which will later reveal themselves . . .'

•

A shot rang out in the night . . .

The 2/13th Battalion, in their camp, Kilo 89, was immediately astir. Who had fired it? Were they under attack? Was someone wounded or killed? Colonel Bull Burrows didn't waste any time and quickly called a muster parade to find out who had fired the shot. As recorded in the 2/13th official history: 'Company Sergeant Major Fyfe fell the Company in and ordered the Platoon Sergeants to make a roll call. This being done, he called for reports.

'"No. 1 Platoon — all correct, Sir!"

'"No. 2 Platoon — all correct, Sir!"

'This was done all down the Company, finally reaching the Transport Platoon, No. 6.

'"No. 6 Platoon — one man missing, Sir!"

'"Who is that man?" asked the CSM.

'"Private Clancy, Sar'nt Major!"

'"Where is Private Clancy?" demanded the CSM.

'All was quiet for a few seconds, but a voice from the dark in the Signal Platoon answered: "Clancy's gone to Queensland droving, and we don't know where he are."

'There was loud laughter, which got the CSM really mad. Striding down the Company's Parade Ground, he bellowed: "Who is that potential Victoria Cross winner?" Finally Private Arty Armstrong established himself as the owner of the offending voice. He was given seven days' pack-drill, a little ceremony which was presided over by the CSM himself.'[13]

•

General Johannes Streich could barely believe it. He had just been reading the book that General Erwin Rommel had recently published about the extraordinary achievements of his Panzer division during the French campaign, and Rommel's own brilliant part in leading them, and had been staggered to see no mention of his own name! As a matter of fact, not only had that upstart Rommel not mentioned the sterling work done by Streich's 15th Panzer Regiment of the 5th Panzer Division but, worse still, he had claimed some of that regiment's efforts as his own! This despite the fact that Streich had been awarded the Knight's Cross in recognition for those very actions![14] Nor was there any mention that one of the reasons

Rommel had been able to go so far so fast was because he had snatched for himself much of the 15th Regiment's common resources of bridging equipment and tanks, while the rest of them had had to scramble for themselves![15] Indeed, he and Rommel had had a heated exchange over just who possessed the rights to the bridging equipment, and the fact that Rommel had ended up with it was something that Streich never forgot or forgave.

Under such circumstances, Streich — sometimes referred to by his troops as 'Papa', mostly because he always seemed so much older than his fifty years — took an extremely dim view of Rommel's book indeed. But what could he do? It was well known throughout the German Army that Rommel was the favourite of the Führer, meaning that the hard-rising young officer was all but entirely invulnerable to being brought down the peg or two that he clearly so desperately needed to be.

For the moment, Streich just let his sense of outrage fester inside ... and yet he was far from the only one who resented the rise of Rommel. Another case in point was General Franz Halder, the Chief of Staff of the German Army and of pedigree perfect enough that he had been almost born and raised to such a high position by a father who had himself been a Major General in the German Army. Not for nothing would Franz Halder be described by the German historian Wolf Heckman as 'the guardian of the Holy Grail of ancient General Staff virtue'. As head of the OKH, which had so recently and effectively been superseded by Hitler's political military bureau, the OKW, it was already natural that Halder and his senior brethren feel some resentment of any move made by the OKW. In Halder's case this went right to the point of occasionally referring — albeit, extremely quietly — to the OKW as 'Corporal Hitler's military bureau'. As to Panzer divisions, Halder remained of the *very* old school, believing that infantry was the be-all and end-all of warfare, and all the rest were mere addendums.[16]

For Halder, that Rommel was a Hitler favourite did not automatically mean that he should be particularly looked after, and as a matter of fact, when the manuscript for Rommel's so-called book on infantry tactics had first come across his desk he had taken some pleasure in refusing Rommel permission to use certain photos on the grounds that in his view they would be a breach of security. Sadly, that hadn't prevented it from turning into a major bestseller, with, 300 000 sales in Germany even before the war began — but it had still been some satisfaction to deny Rommel the photos.

•

Mail van coming!

The Johnson kids at Walwa could hear it gurgling, backfiring as it came down Cooks Hill, slowing as it crossed the first creek, thrashing the gears as it made its way up the next rise. Then, as ever, it backfired again as it slowed into the next creek, and then it was roaring again, coming up past Hughie Hanna's place and reaching a stop outside Walwa's pub, not far from their own place. And there was a letter from Dad! He was on his way west, and sort of north. On the ship. They gathered round their mother as she read the whole thing out to them in a slightly tremulous voice, stumbling only when she came to the words which had been cut out with a razor for censorship reasons, and they tried to work out what he had said . . .

My Dear Family,

I am having a good trip & have not had any sea sickness since leaving the last port from which I last wrote. The ship is rocking a good deal at present but I am in a position which catches the sway. I have just done my washing & have it out on a line on the top deck so here I am keeping an eye on it.

I do hope you are all well as I have not had a word from you since leaving camp, but I hope to be rewarded within 2 or 3 days with a host of letters. I can't tell you how far out we are but we travel at about 20 miles per hour all the time. There's little news aboard ship as we just eat, sleep & attend & give lectures on our work & we see nothing all day but the rest of the ***. One of our **** came round in the night with his *** & I would not *** any raider which ****

I hope no nasty rumours reach you regarding the sinking of any convoy, as they are mostly groundless.[17]

There were several more wonderful pages of news about ship-board life and how all the men were all looking forward to arriving at wherever it was they were going, and then he closed.

Well my dear boys & Sylvia Rose my darling baby, I have no more
news so will close with tons of love to you all & to Mum,
from your loving Dad.

Goodness, they missed him.

At least, though, there was something solid they could do to help to support their dad and his comrades, and like many kids across Australia they were active in penny collections at the end of every month, from all and sundry — a penny, just a penny! — which was then donated to the Red Cross. There were also collections for War Savings Certificates at Walwa Public School, as with many schools, whereby other spare pennies were gathered, and given by the children to their teacher. Then, when a total of five shillings was collected, the teacher would purchase a five shilling-bond from the Walwa Post Office, place the donor children's names in a hat, draw out the winning name, and that child was given the bond, redeemable at the end of the war. Still more fundraising activities were initiated for the Australian Comforts Fund, which was devoted to making the life of the front-line Diggers easier by sending them food, tobacco, toiletries and the like. And for the Johnson kids, a particular favourite was to sometimes stay back after school and help to weave camouflage nets, using the sisal, hemp, hessian and tools provided by the government. Somehow, every one produced made them feel that their father was just that little bit safer, and that he would be able to return home to them.

•

It was while settling into their new digs that the freshly arrived Australian soldiers to the Middle East first started to hear excited reports of what the Brits had been up to. It seemed that at dawn on 9 December 1940, Wavell had given the order to launch a serious counterattack on the Ities, something that was called Operation Compass.

Under the command of that dashing red-headed wisp of a man, British Lieutenant General Richard O'Connor, 36 000 men of the Western Desert Force had crept up to, and in many cases through, the ring of fortified camps that Marshal Graziani had placed around the Italian stronghold of Sidi Barrani, where their army had been parked since those dashing days of September when they had first pushed the British back as much as 90 miles. Now, with the first rays of the sun, the Brits — frequently attacking from the rear of the Italians' prepared defences — opened fire upon these outposts and charged forwards behind the protection of their own Matilda tanks, even as from the skies the mighty Royal Air Force unleashed bomb after bomb. Up against the piss-poor Italian tanks — slow, cumbersome and thinly skinned — the British tanks had as much of a field day as the British infantry. Though the Matildas, which were specifically designed to support advancing infantry, had a top speed of only 12 miles an hour, the main thing was that their armour was 3 inches thick, and the Italian artillery simply bounced off, meaning the British were capable of wreaking terrible destruction on the Italian defenders.

How well did it go? Well enough that — get this! — after just two days Winston Churchill received an official report that, while it was impossible to count the Itie prisoners, there were about '20 acres of officers and 100 acres of other ranks!' (This actually added up to about 38 000 men, while 237 guns were captured together with 73 tanks, as well as the third most prized of all things in desert warfare, after water and petrol: 1000 working vehicles.) It was a wonderful beginning to the British counterattack, even if there remained a lot of hard work to do — most notably to clear the Italians out of their strongholds of Bardia, Tobruk, Derna and the large city of Benghazi — before Cyrenaica (the eastern half of Libya) was once again under Allied control, so giving Egypt and its Suez Canal the western buffer zone it needed. The problem was that, for the next part of the campaign, O'Connor was to lose a large chunk of his troops, in the form of much-valued support units of soldiers from the New Zealand Division and the great warriors of the 4th Indian Division — both of which had been pulled out by Wavell to fight in another theatre. Who could O'Connor get to replace them, for the hard work still to be done?

The Australians. Specifically, the Australians of the 6th Division, who had been in the Middle East now for nigh on a year, done the hard training necessary and were now ready.

Generally, those Australian soldiers in the Middle East not so blessed as to be a part of the 6th wished them well, but were so envious themselves that they could hardly raise spit. Many times they wondered, and discussed between themselves, precisely where the 6th could be ...

•

Sitting high on the escarpment above Sollum on the Egyptian–Libyan border, the Australian war correspondent John Hetherington and a colleague gazed at the splendid vista before them, down onto the plains of Egypt, sitting snug by the enormous blue bay of the Mediterranean, with seagulls diving, gliding, screeching their pleasure too, at the day. But look there ...

Right on the hundredth of the hundred horizons that stretched before them, a small brown stain of something appeared, something that was not part of nature, and was gradually, ever so gradually getting bigger. What could it be . . .? They stood up, and then leaned forward, in the instinctive manner of humans towards curious things seen at a great distance . . .

A nearby Tommy soldier, perhaps better informed, told them in a broad West Country voice, thick with excitement, 'T' Aussies are movin' up! They'll give bloomin' Itie some 'urry-up, them laads will an' all!' Hetherington and his friend weren't sure, but kept watching intently into the desert distance. Was it just a cloud of dust, after all? They decided to investigate, and carefully drove their car down the rutted road that constituted one of only two ways to get from the plateau of Libya to the plains of Egypt along 50 miles of escarpment that stretched into the southern wastelands of desert. Now below, it became clearer. Hetherington wrote: 'The sky darkened, thickened, expanded, like a storm-cloud moving to meet us. We knew then that this rolling sea of dust was not raised by any wind. We knew then that it was raised by men, thousands of men, moving forward, moving on to the battle . . .

'The great cloud of dust rolled on to meet us and presently we saw the vanguard of the trucks. Then behind them, huddling through the dun fog churned and lifted by their own wheels, we saw more trucks stretching away mile on mile. I looked at the men who sat behind the driving-wheels of trucks and the men who perched under the canopies behind, cuddling their rifles. Their faces coated with dust, looked like the faces of film actors made up to go before the camera . . .'[18]

But actors they weren't. This was for real. This was the Australian 6th Division, moving forward, answering the battle siren that had just sounded for them . . .

•

Sundays, wretched Sundays.

Good Lord, how Elizabeth despised them. Sunday had always been the day Jack would come home from camp, and this Sunday — just as it had been every Sunday since he'd left in October — he wasn't there. Elizabeth tried to pass the time as profitably as she could by preparing and then preserving Jack's favourite mushrooms and putting them into twelve large bottles, all ready for when he came home, but really nothing helped. Some of her nervous energy she could expend in her garden (which she was very proud of), but even that was hard, because working the garden was something that she and Jack had done together, and she missed his strong arms to do some of the heavier work. Sometimes it would all get a little too much for her and she would sit down on a garden seat Jack had built for her, beside the screen of jacaranda trees he had planted for her just before he had left, right by the house. She missed him so badly she physically *ached*.

•

Look, it wasn't something you necessarily wanted to talk about with the other blokes, but just on the quiet, many of the newly arrived Australian troops gathered at the training camps in Palestine were so badly missing their families on this Christmas Eve, 1940, that they too just about physically *ached*. For the more religious it was a special privilege to be readying to celebrate the birth of Jesus Christ in the Holy Land, but that still changed naught the fact that they were a long, long way from home and the ones they loved most.[19]

The mood then was bittersweet among a lot of the Australian troops who gathered around a huge campfire on the edge of Kilo 89 and began to sing Christmas carols — their voices soaring high into the cold desert night and then wide, drawing in many others.

Silent night,
Holy night,
All is calm,
All is bright,
Round yon virgin, mother and child . . .

The following day, there were of course no presents under the tree from their parents, wives, children, sweethearts and sundry, but at least there were special hampers sent from the mighty Australian Comforts Fund, and blokes were delighted to get newly knitted scarves, balaclavas and various toiletry items, together with a wonderful Christmas lunch of roast turkey, mince pies, dried fruits and plum pudding — all of it served by their own officers, a once-in-a-year treat. And as well as the lovely cartons of cigarettes, which were always the second-most popular thing among the Diggers (after mail from home), there was even some precious Vegemite that they could take with them!

Another weird thing? For the first time in their lives, a lot of the Australian soldiers were meeting real, live Pommies. They seemed like all right kinds of blokes, oddly enough, but they dressed weirdly. As recorded by the official history of the 2/24th Battalion: 'We realised that we were not very neatly turned out by their standards. The first real surprise was the sight of a Scottish officer in green tartan trews on Gaza station. Then we saw a Tommy with starched shirt and shorts, side-cap with bright brass badge and buttons, and web-belt and gaiters pipe-clayed white!'

Seriously, weird! True, for some strange reason the Pommies and Scotties didn't necessarily take kindly to having their unusual dress pointed out to them, but that at least proved that they could in fact fight, which was promising to the Australians should they ever find themselves in a blue together against Hitler's and Musso's lads.

Out on the open seas, Morshead's 18th Brigade continued to steam towards them all, on its way from England, and was now just a week out from Alexandria, hoping to berth before New Year's Eve ...

•

Maybe this was the week.

Maybe, after all the training, all the waiting, all the training, all the travelling, all the training and waiting again, maybe this was the week that the Australian 6th Division would finally be seeing a bit of action. That certainly seemed to be their hope, anyway, as Chester Wilmot had his breakfast with them on that Boxing Day morning of 1940, while they camped within just a day's march of the Italians holed up in the North African coastal town of Bardia, the first serious settlement in Libya you see coming from the east, about 20 miles from the Egyptian border.

As Wilmot subsequently recounted to his ABC listeners in Australia, in his rather clipped and distinguished tones ...

'Over one of those fires we ate bully-beef cut in slices and grilled on a kerosene tin lid and then served on a toasted biscuit. It was extremely good ... and we washed it down with tea made in a cut-down kero tin. Most of the fellows still had some of their Christmas hampers left, and they finished their breakfast with peaches and cream or the last half of a plum pudding and then turned in for the day. The only thing wrong with their Christmas was their inability to find a fight ...'[20]

That inability, however, would not last long.

The closer the Australian soldiers of the 6th Division got to the Italian perimeters of Bardia, the more evidence the Diggers found of the creeping

collapse of the Italian war effort. For just as in the 'long paddock' at home
— read: on the lost and lonely roadsides that desperate graziers would
sometimes use to feed their sheep and cattle — it was a common sight to
see bleached bones by the side of the bitumen, the scattered remnants of
Italian trucks and burned-out tanks became thicker than fleas on a stray and
mangy dog, and then even thicker still the closer the Diggers got to Bardia.
Other vehicles hadn't been destroyed at all but abandoned outright on the
simple reckoning by the fleeing Italians that one stood a better chance of
survival on foot than inside or on top of a tasty Royal Air Force or Royal
Australian Air Force target like a truck or tank.

   Whatever, for the advancing Diggers, it was clear that the 'Wops' had
already taken a good bashing from the Allied aeroplanes — which, even
then, mostly Hurricanes, were buzzing by overhead in enormous numbers
— and the men were equally sure that once they could get to grips with
the Ities themselves they would give them a real hiding like they'd never
had before. Just cut our blokes loose on the Wops in Bardia, and it would be
all over very quickly, they just knew it!

                                    •

Tonight was the night, and as darkness fell it was time to get ready.
Positions everyone. Make-up on, perfume applied, lights shaded to just the
right intimate atmosphere. The Australians — some of whom had been
placed in Port Said on garrison duty — would soon be here in force, and
if experience counted for anything, they were likely to be wild. It was not
easy running a brothel in Palestine's Port Said — a hot spot for all kinds
of servicemen with a leave pass — but if you got it right, like Madame
Mala of the Golden Slipper, it was lucrative. The main thing was, her girls
were clean, with regular check-ups given by the army doctors ensuring
that they remained so. Venereal disease was so rife in other brothels
throughout the town that the senior officers of the AIF had placed pickets
in front of the entrances, forbidding their soldiers from going inside, and
insisting that they either go to Madame Mala's place or (*sniff*) The
Constantinople down the road.

   In a cloud of perfume, and with her trademark green silk scarf tied
atop her thick black hair, Madame now moved among her beautiful bevy,
ensuring that everything was in order. The girls (but of course) looked
alluring, and none more than her star attraction, Angel, with the long, curly
locks and mesmerising, pneumatic breasts — notable, apart from the
obvious, for boasting 'a ring of brightly coloured butterflies tattooed

around each nipple'.[21] The fact that tonight, as every night, Angel wore a silken dress made out of the Union Jack helped to make her an immediate focal point of attention among the British servicemen, but that certainly wasn't the only thing, and the Australians certainly didn't steer clear of her because of it.

As Madame fluttered among her girls, straightening a stray strand of hair here, pulling a blouse a little lower there, Angel and twenty or so others were lounging around what the Australians and Brits called the 'shufti room' — with *shufti* meaning, in Arabic, 'to look' — listening to music coming from the ancient wind-up gramophone in the corner, frequently playing the Egyptian national anthem, among other things.[22] (It was played so often, as a matter of fact, that many regular brothel patrons learned it off by heart!) If Madame judged that the mood needed it, she would get the girls to do a dance to a different kind of music, sometimes involving a few 'tricks' with each other that were guaranteed to make the soldiers get a head of steam up, while admittedly shocking a few others.

And now the Australians had arrived, all of them still in uniform, most of them with a lot of grog on board, some surveying her girls with practised eyes, while others — the ones Madame most warmed to — were goggle-eyed and scarcely believing what they were seeing. For only seventy-five piastres — just under a pound — they could take a girl into one of the rooms down the hall and have a 'jump' (as the more genteel of them sometimes referred to it!).

It was true, mind, that their superior officers had tried to discourage this behaviour, but so what? In one address to Ivor Hancock's company in the 2/24th Battalion, the Medical Officer had even spelled it out this way: 'When you are at home, your wife or girlfriend is your right hand. Now that you are over here, let your right hand be your wife or girlfriend . . .' All that was forgotten now.

The girls, just as Madame had instructed, were gentle with these younger men, while far bolder with the older, swaying their hips, giggling, bending down and flashing what few parts of their body hadn't already been revealed by their low-cut blouses and fishnet stockings. The key was to get the men to make a choice quickly, get them to the room, get the business done, and get back to the shufti room for the next one.

Yes, it was going to be a big night.

And this was no bad thing either. Some of these boys would surely be dead in the matter of just a few weeks, so why shouldn't they have some earthly pleasures before heading off? Nor was it something that need follow the survivors home. Madame knew from her many talks with the Australians that they all intended to keep to a strict code of 'The Wartime Secrets Act', which specifically stated that whatever happened in such places while they were away from home, it was never to be referred to again once the men returned to those homes, and this was no joke ...

At roughly the same time — on a few days' leave in Jerusalem — Ivor Hancock and some of his mates from the 26th Brigade were incredulous. Sure, they had heard the expression used by some of the veterans of the Great War: 'You couldn't get a job as a Condy's boy in a brothel'. But none of them had known what it had meant to this point. And now they found out — for it was their own experience that you couldn't get *near* any of the Jewish women in the brothels there until young Arab boys who worked at the establishment had made sure you'd seriously washed your penis with a warm Condy's crystals solution, and then they made sure you put a condom on. And even when you'd done the business, the same Condy's boys made sure that you washed your nether regions again before heading out into the night to compare notes with the other blokes. Still, at only seventy-five piastres for a root, it wasn't a bad bargain, if not quite as good a one as that offered by the many hawkers on the street who were reluctantly prepared to part with *genuine* splinters of the very same cross on which Jesus was crucified — or even one of the nails that had gone through his hands and feet — all for just the equivalent of a few pounds! Geez, you could still see the bloodstains!

As it happened, though, on trips to places like that Ivor and his mates preferred to spend their money on grog, women, grog, raising hell and grog, though not always in that order. Around and about them as they caroused, normal life in Jerusalem went on, with its exciting sights and sounds and smells, and 'Gully-Gully' men doing brilliant magic tricks on sidewalks, and urchins, and mysterious veiled women and shoeshine boys and beggars and so many things that to the locals were just everyday, but for the Australians were never-seen-before ...

See, there! On this day, the Australians were obliged to stand back as a Jewish funeral cortege went slowly down the street. Though they might normally have stood back out of respect in any case, on this occasion they stood back for reasons of safety, as they were briefly in danger of being hit by some of the stones that the Arabs, for reasons that the Australians couldn't quite understand, were throwing at the mourners and ...

And were they? Cocky Walpole was always one who could be counted on to help in the raising-hell stakes, and always all the more so when both he and the boys had a fair whack of grog in them. One time four or five of them went rolling drunk into a shop looking for some souvenirs to buy, when ol' Cocky spied a small fishbowl, in which half a dozen little goldfish were happily swimming around. Their happiness soon disappeared, however, when Cocky's big paw suddenly snatched in and grabbed two of them — one of which went straight down Cocky's massive gullet as the other men fell about laughing. He was just about to swallow the second fish when a posse of screaming Arab shop assistants swarmed all over him, yelling threats in that incomprehensible gibberish they spoke, and it was all the Australians could do to fight the Arabs off and free their cobber to get out on the street again . . . where it seemed like a drunken good idea at the time to go for a sightseeing ride on one of the many horse-drawn carriages that abounded in those parts.

'Cept, once they were all on the carriage, the thieving Wog carriage driver wanted too much money, so this time, instead of a couple of fish, Cocky had to take the whole matter into his own hands. Without warning, the old bush jockey had vaulted off the carriage onto the back of one of the horses and was — yee-ha, *giddy*, GIDDYAP! — driving his heels into the animal's side even as he had grabbed the reins of the lead horse. The laughs! The fun! Half the Arabs in Jerusalem were in hot pursuit, but they were no match for the skills of Cocky, who took the carriage twice around the block, lapping his pursuers once, before he steered it to a quiet spot and they were all able to scarper away.

•

Many other Australian soldiers, like John Johnson — newly promoted to Corporal and thrilled at the extra money that would provide for his family at home — steered well clear of the whorehouses, and spent their time visiting the holy places in Jerusalem as well as buying souvenirs for their families. In one package that John sent off to his family there was an assortment of wonderfully mystic presents: miniature carved camels, strange coins, a brooch shaped as a knife, a quill box, illustrated cloths and cards from the Garden of Gethsemane itself! Ah, the wonder of it all for the Johnson kids, as their mother Josie opened it on the dining room table, and they happily bickered over who was to get what.[23]

Not that there was too much time for too much bickering, mind, because without Dad around there was a lot of work to be done, and each child had his or her set chores to do, from chopping the wood to feeding the dogs to fixing the fences to milking the cow, then collecting the eggs, getting the washing in the copper, stoking the fire beneath it, and not to forget making sure that the leak in the roof above the kitchen finally got fixed.

•

All over Australia at this time, the newspapers were full of the triumph of the Australian troops in action — as they had conquered Bardia in the first days of January — and thrilled to the stories that the Australian troops had even sung in unison *The Wizard of Oz* as they had triumphantly entered the township.

In the *Sydney Morning Herald*, succeeding days of headlines told the story:

AUSTRALIANS LAUNCH ATTACK ON BARDIA

BARDIA PRACTICALLY IN BRITISH HANDS

FIRST-CLASS JOB BY AUSTRALIANS

Despite the well-entrenched Italian defences, in just three days these first Australians to fire shots in anger in what was now becoming known as 'World War II' had taken over 40 000 Italian prisoners, and captured over 400 guns and a few serviceable tanks!

The mood of celebration in Australia was so overwhelming, that in Sydney, particularly, many high society people were even holding cocktail parties on the strength of it — toasting the victories as if they'd had something to do with it in even the remotest fashion.

One who did not feel the common euphoria was Elizabeth Edmondson.[24] How could there be celebration of anything to do with this war? Hadn't they followed the ABC reports of Chester Wilmot like she had? Hadn't they seen the casualty lists like she had, studied them every morning, hoping against hope she wouldn't recognise any of the names. Didn't they know that the sons of their own soil were dying? So far, the *Sydney Morning Herald* had it that 120 had been killed and 230 wounded. And yet these idiots were quaffing Champagne!

Whatever the widespread success of the Allied operations in North Africa, however, the situation in Greece was now growing critical as, despite the great resistance provided by the Greeks to the invading Italians, it seemed likely that the Germans would intervene and come to the aid of their allies, invading Greece themselves.

While if this happened it was no certainty that the Allies could do anything to stop them, the fact was that Britain had a treaty with Greece, stipulating that each country must come to the other's aid if they were attacked.

But with those Allied troops already stretched thin across so many theatres, where could Churchill find the manpower to honour that treaty? The answer was it could only come from other fronts, and the obvious one was nearby North Africa, where the job against the Italians had already been substantially accomplished. After some to-ing and fro-ing, it was felt that the best option was to allow the victorious Australian 6th Division to knock over one more key target in Libya and then — rather than have them press on to Tripoli — turn them around and send them north across the Mediterranean. So it was that on 10 January 1941, Churchill sent a cable to Wavell which included the following sentences:

Nothing must hamper the capture of Tobruk; but thereafter all operations in Libya are subordinated to aiding Greece. We expect and require prompt and active compliance with our decisions, for which we bear full responsibility.

CHAPTER SIX

Take Tobruk

[For the Australians] the desert was their sea. Over it they privateered and struck — equipped as lightly as could be for personal comfort, as heavily as could be for the job of discomfiting the enemy.

CHESTER WILMOT[1]

In some indefinable way, the purity of the desert purified the desert war . . .

BRITISH HISTORIAN RONALD LEWIN[2]

Tobruk, Churchill had decided, was a particularly important town to take, as it possessed the sole major harbour on that part of the North African coast for 800 miles, complete with jetties and great depth close to the shore, and it also boasted one of the few reliable supplies of fresh water on the coast for nearly as far. Put together, it meant that in any future action in North Africa, possession of Tobruk — currently an Italian garrison town, 50 miles to the west of Bardia — would be enormously important for both sides because of its potential to facilitate the crucial supply necessary to keep the war effort in those parts going. For when there was really no question of being able to 'live off the land', access to a workable sea port was going to be paramount.

The plan to shift focus from North Africa to Greece after Tobruk had been secured — and with it so many, many resources, including no fewer than 47 000 soldiers, comprising a New Zealand and Australian division, together with an assortment of British troops and a brigade of 100 British tanks — was a singularly momentous one, but at the time Churchill was relatively comfortable with it.

That is, despite the fact that he held little hope that the plan would actually be successful.

At this very time, Harry Hopkins, an extremely influential emissary from President Roosevelt, met Churchill at 10 Downing Street and, whatever else, the British Prime Minister could not be faulted for frankness when discussing the prospects for this new venture, as Hopkins recorded in a diary entry that night:

> [Churchill] thinks Greece is lost — although he is now reinforcing the Greeks — and weakening his African Army — he believes Hitler will permit Mussolini to go only so far downhill — and is now preparing for the [German attack in Greece] — which must bring its inevitable result. He knows this will be a blow to British prestige and is obviously considering ways and means of preparing the British public for it . . .[3]

A blow to British prestige if it did go wrong, certainly, but it was essentially the Australians and New Zealanders who would take the body blows. And if perchance they were successful, the War Cabinet had some hope that both Turkey and Yugoslavia — each nominally neutral, though wavering — might come across to the Allies. This alliance between Greece, Turkey and Yugoslavia, backed by the forces of the British Empire, could possibly help form a 'Balkan front' in the war, thus diluting further the forces of the Axis powers.

True, there was the matter of getting the Australian leadership to agree to the sending of their troops to Greece on what was always going to be a risky venture, but Churchill didn't feel this would be too much of a problem, with the extremely 'loyal' Australian Prime Minister, Robert Menzies, usually amenable to British proposals.

•

And yet — and yet — while Winston Churchill was correct in surmising that the Germans were preparing to attack Greece, he had not reckoned on them moving elsewhere in that part of the globe. For, unbeknownst to him, only the day after Churchill cabled Wavell that resources in North Africa had to be shifted to Greece, Adolf Hitler released his own 'Directive No 22' to his senior military command, whereby he ordered his forces to begin to prepare to support the Italians in both the Greek *and* Libyan fields of operation. Hitler decreed:

> The situation in the Mediterranean makes it necessary to provide German assistance, on strategic, political and psychological grounds. Tripolitania [western Libya] must be held.[4]

For Hitler, too, had been watching events in North Africa (not to mention Greece) with a very close eye. And despite being appalled at the Italians' poor performance in North Africa, and still angry over Mussolini's *dummkopf* invasion of Greece, he had equally taken the view that it was out of the question to let his Fascist ally collapse in both theatres. However disappointing the Italians had been as brothers in arms, they were at least better than nothing — just — and perhaps even more important than sustaining them for their own sake was the possibility of denying the Allies a major victory anywhere.

Besides which, to cede to the British all of North Africa, from Cairo to Tripoli, giving them control of its airfields and ports, would be effectively giving them control over all of the southern Mediterranean, and this result was unimaginable and deeply humiliating for a race that had essentially gone to war on the claim of its natural superiority.

So: however difficult it would be, Italy had to be supported even in as difficult a terrain as Libya — and plans to do so began to be put into place. Hitler had no designs for his troops to establish dominion over North Africa, but what had to be done, and quickly, was to get enough of them there to act as a block, to ensure that Tripoli didn't fall. And though Mussolini had already declined a previous Hitler offer of help in North Africa, this time the Italian dictator not only accepted but acceded to Hitler's insistence that Italy provide three fresh elite divisions of its own: the 132nd Ariete Division with its 80 tanks, and the 27th Brescia Division and the 102nd Trento Motorised Division. Though none of the divisions was at full strength, at least the two infantry divisions had six battalions each, meaning that, all put together, the sum of the Germans and Italians under arms there numbered about 26 000.

In broad terms, that mass of troops that Hitler had been intending to use in the invasion of Britain were now to be redirected, with some to go to Africa, others to the Balkans, while yet more would be sent east, as Hitler also began to look more seriously at invading Russia. That had been detailed as part of Hitler's master plan for the master race in *Mein Kampf*, and though it had been put on hold due to the alliance of convenience to divide Poland up between them, he was now feeling militarily strong enough to do it — and the non-aggression pact he'd signed with Josef Stalin be damned.

•

For all their sterling work laying siege to Bardia three weeks earlier, the next major nut for the 6th Division to crack was Tobruk. While in peacetime the place had had a population of about 7000 — mostly Italian settlers and troops, together with Arab civilians — the joint was now manned by 25 000 Italian soldiers under the command of Generale Petassi Manella, and armed to the teeth, and not only that . . .

The town had long been designated by the Italians as the linchpin of their defensive bulwark in the eastern half of Libya, as well as a key base and safe haven for the Italian Navy to use on the North African coast — hosting three destroyers and two squadrons of submarines.[5] Much of the Italians' energies in the previous three decades, since capturing Tobruk from the Turks, had been given over to constructing strong defences around the town, including an anti-tank ditch, extensive barbed wire and many, many fortifications in which the Italian soldiers could fire from superbly protected positions. It was not going to be easy to take, but by God the Australians were going to give it their best shot . . . and for the previous two weeks had been conducting extensive reconnaissance, working out specifically where those defences were situated, before making their move.

It was to be the job of the Australians to penetrate the perimeter and push on into the town from there, while the Brits would provide bombardment from the Royal Navy, artillery support from their gunners on land and a dozen of their tanks attacking at other parts of the perimeter, to keep the Italian defences diffused.

So it was that in that darkest part of the night, just before the moon rose in the early hours of 21 January 1941, thirty-three men of the 2/1st Field Company donned their balaclavas to top off the blackness of the rest of them and moved forwards on their bellies into the whipping winds of no-man's-land, each of them holding long, willowy sticks. While they had left behind their warm greatcoats as too bulky, they had been given a good drop of rum to put in their water bottles, both to ward off the cold and to steady themselves for the rather delicate task ahead.[6]

Their job was to locate the mines and the booby traps in the 2000-yard stretch that had been designated as the assault point, and then 'de-louse' them. In the case of the mines, this meant first lying on your belly and gently poking ahead with the sticks to locate them, before carefully, oh so carefully, taking the lids off and removing the detonators and percussion caps inside. As to the booby traps, though easier to locate, they were a little more problematic to defuse. Mostly they were canisters filled with shrapnel and explosives, attached to posts a little over a foot off the ground. A small bit of twine joined each booby trap to the other, with the reckoning being that anyone creeping up in the darkness, or hurrying forward in the daylight, would pull the tripwire, causing the canister to explode and either kill or maim its victim. These traps too were capable of being neutralised but it was a time-consuming process, involving slipping a nail back into the 'safety pin' all the grenades came equipped with, and following the twine from there to the next booby trap — its defuser always cognisant that with just one slip-up the canister would go off, likely killing him and, far more tragically, alerting the defenders that an assault upon them was about to be launched. The one thing absolutely sure about all these sappers, as they were known, working to de-louse the mines: not one of them had ever made a mistake. (You could tell as much, just by counting their limbs. Two arms and two legs meant that their record of successfully disarming mines was 100 per cent. On the other hand, the firm rule was that, 'If ever you see one of these blokes running, your best bet is to try to keep up with him!') Painstakingly then, stealthily, the men of the 2/1st Field Company got on with their important work.

As they did so, just a few hundred yards back Chester Wilmot was writing a slightly nervous letter to his parents — beginning 'My dearest Mother and Father' — in which he explained why it was that he intended to accompany the Australian soldiers when they stormed Tobruk at first light . . .

> I can only speak of what they go through if I go through it with them as much as I can . . .
> We all knew that if I did this job properly I would have to take the risks of an ordinary soldier. My conscience wouldn't be clear if I did less than that.[7]

And he meant it, too.

When the dim moon rose, at 1.30 a.m., and the desert was bathed in a curious light that was just strong enough to see by, without quite being able to throw shadows, Wilmot drove slowly among the bulk of the Australian troops, camped some 15 miles from the Tobruk perimeter — at a distance well removed from any possible artillery fire from the Italians — where they had been moved under cover of darkness only a few hours before. Now Chester moved around, soaking up the feel of an army just hours away from the battle's roar.

Softly, softly now, the ABC journalist sometimes stopped and walked among the men, who were mostly grabbing as much sleep as they could in the shallow trenches they had scraped for themselves out of the desert floor . . .

Others, though, were awake, particularly the army cooks, who had dug much deeper trenches to hide the fires they were tending beneath enormous pots, in which they were preparing hot meals. Not far away, tiny lanterns on the lee side of some of the bulky trucks — many of them purloined from the Italians and now rechristened such things as 'Wop 125' and 'Wop 86', 'Dago Dragon', 'Spaghetti Sue', 'Benito's Bus' and so on[8] — revealed officers earnestly studying some of the well-detailed maps discovered in Bardia, where much of the Tobruk layout was clearly marked. Yes, the attack was going to be a risky business, but the more information that could be gleaned from the maps, and the extensive reconnaissance that had been conducted and then entrenched in the heads of the men who would be guiding the attacks, the less risk there was.

All up, Wilmot was amazed at just how extraordinarily calm the men were, and as he later reported to his ABC listeners, based on this visit, the Australians 'might have been more worked up just before a football grand final . . .'[9]

Gradually, though, as the wee hours of the night started to wane, so the wider camp came to life, first with the low growl of trucks carefully nudging along to their positions at assembly areas, then the throatier roaring rumble of tanks also starting to move off, and then the troops themselves, shifting slowly in the moonlight, then rising, then stretching, then murmuring softly to each other . . .

Now was the hour. Boots on. Rifle checked. Bayonet fixed. Get some grub into you, we're moving off in twenty minutes. Good luck, Digger.

Wilmot watched it all, still amazed that on the edge of a battle where it was all but guaranteed that some of these men would soon be lying dead in a ditch, the mood was calm, purposeful, resolute. Like ploughing the top forty on a stinker of a December day, or taking the cattle on a drive through the high country, this was just something that had to be done and they were the men to do it. So let's get on with it. Get to grips. Get this thing over with. Knock off the Ities, clean 'em out, and the sooner that was done, then the sooner we can get home again . . .

And now the RAF bombers were doing their part, roaring overhead and unleashing their loads to soften up the Italian defences on the perimeter, just as, off the coast, twenty warships of the British Royal Navy had poured in their fire in many salvoes before midnight. The dozen British tanks away to their west were also now doing their bit, making something of a diversionary attack, together with some units of the Free French. Then at precisely 5.40 a.m., 'the arty' — as the men called the artillery — opened up, focusing saturation fire on a rectangle measuring 2500 yards wide by 800 yards deep on the southern perimeter of the Tobruk defences. The idea was to ensure that all defenders in this key area would either be blown to bits, or be obliged to keep their heads down, while several companies of Allied engineers and sappers crept closer to a part of the perimeter where it had been determined that the anti-tank ditch was only 2 feet deep. The Allies would continue slowly forwards even as the shells from their own arty hurtled overhead and exploded just several hundred yards beyond them, a 'creeping barrage', as it was known. As Wilmot, a keen and professional observer of the whole action later described it, 'Great clouds of dust like huge waterspouts marked each explosion, and in the still morning air, these took some time to drift away, so that for a few minutes they looked like silver poplars.'[10]

This peaceful image belied the carnage below, as the surviving Italian defenders were indeed obliged to keep their heads down, allowing the Australian engineers and sappers to get right up to the anti-tank barrier without taking too much fire. (One reason for this was that the point of first attack had been selected after extensive examination to determine to the nearest 20 yards where the 137-strong ring of Italian defensive posts was at its most vulnerable.)

While some sappers worked at easing more passages through the minefield, others concentrated on getting the shallowest parts of the anti-tank ditches filled in enough for one of their tanks to get over them. Sometimes the best way to do this was with a shovel and frantic hurling of rocks and sand, while at other times it was better to use explosives to blow the sides of the anti-tank ditch in, to collapse the walls inward and make an effective bridge.[11] In other spots they tried to get in place wooden bridges which they simply dropped over the narrowest part of the ditches, with mixed success.

Suddenly, disaster.

Just as the 'C' Company 2/3rd Battalion was getting near to the first of the anti-tank ditches in preparation for storming forward, a high-explosive shell — likely coming from Italian artillery within the perimeter they were attacking — landed right among the men and exploded. In a split second twenty good men were blown apart, heads severed from torsos, arms flung 30 yards away, whole bodies disintegrating into nothingness where the shell landed. Twenty mothers' sons, killed or wounded.[12]

The medics were quickly on the spot, dragging survivors back for treatment, but what could other nearby companies do? The only thing they could, and that was to keep their own heads down and keep moving towards to their fate, whatever that might be. (Though it is fair to say that after witnessing such carnage, close up, of their mates, the deep certainty that just about all the Diggers had felt back in training camp that they personally would be returning home — now started to waver somewhat.)

•

Getting lighter now. Again, precisely as planned, with everyone having synchronised watches by the BBC time signal, at 6.05 a.m. the barrage of artillery fire ceased, even as the next part of the plan smoothly swung into action. Now, the 'Bangalore Torpedoes' — 12-foot lengths of 3-inch water pipes packed with high explosives — were brought forwards and placed just above the ground amid the rolls of concertinaed barbed wire. At Bardia those little Bangalore beauties had blown gaps 25-foot wide in the wire and the hope was they could do the same here, once they were exploded from a distance, courtesy of a wire that had been carefully attached to their detonators.

And sure enough ... and sure enough ...

Heads down, boys, 'cos we're about to let 'em rip. With great explosions through narrow passages, the wire was suddenly blown to smithereens, and the way was clear.

There was a stunned moment as the assembled Australian troops of the 2/3rd and 2/1st Battalions saw the gap, and then the clear voice of a Lieutenant rang out.

'*Go on, you bastards!*'[13]

And with a mighty roar, so they did. Up there, Cazaly, and into 'em! Charging through the now deloused minefields, across the now even shallower anti-tank ditch, through the blown corridor of barbed wire, the Australian soldiers swarmed.

Some of the stunned Italians had sufficiently recovered from the barrage to quickly return ferocious fire, but the first of these defenders didn't last long. So numerous were the Australians, and so fast were they in charging and firing as they went — with the ground so flat that they could see the flashes of the guns of the defenders ahead, just as they could see the flashes of their own guns behind — that the first of the Italian posts fell almost immediately. With that breach in the Italian perimeter now assured, within minutes six Matilda tanks had traversed the anti-tank ditch, split up into two packs of three, and were aiding the troops to knock over the Italian defences, post by post.

Some posts fell to the rampaging Australians quickly, with the Italian soldiers coming out with their eyeballs rolling, their hands up and frequently holding silky white handkerchiefs that seemed to have been pristine for just such an occasion, while others resisted solidly. These were usually brought under severe artillery fire, causing huge amounts of billowing dust. Into that heavy dust cloud, then, would charge the leading Australians, bayonets drawn and grenades at the ready. Clean 'em out, clean 'em out, clean 'em out, and go again.

It was a busy morning, and the road back from the Australian front lines to the breach in the perimeter was soon thick with Italian prisoners, thousands of them, giving every indication that they were happy to be away from these wild men from the south insanely charging at them with death and destruction pouring from their every barrel, and heading towards the comparative safety of an Australian stockade. Rome Radio had been shrieking for days that the 'Australian barbarians have been turned loose by the British in the desert',[14] and now that these soldiers had seen the Australians close up, few of them wanted any part of it.

Sometimes 500 prisoners at a time would come back under the escort of just two Australian soldiers; at other times they were just disarmed and sent back in the direction of the breach. For there was no time, and no men to spare. (If only they could have done what one Australian officer had in the previous action at Bardia, when the weight of surrendering Italians had been so great that at one point he had told a mass of them, 'Go away. We haven't got time to deal with you; come back in the morning.' And they had!)

Meanwhile, by nine o'clock in the morning, twenty-one posts had fallen at Tobruk, and the stream of prisoners was now at full flood. White flags sprouted like mushrooms before the advancing Australians, followed by the ubiquitous cry of 'Ci rendiamo! Ci rendiamo!' which the Allies soon learned meant 'We surrender! We surrender!'

One thing the Allies couldn't help but notice was that there was never much trouble separating the Italian officers from their soldiers — with each group seeming to have a total contempt for the other — which was perhaps a sign as to why the latter had not seemed so keen to fight for the former.[15]

For all that, the fighting went on through the afternoon, by which time it was clear that Tobruk was going to fall — it was just a matter of when. Generally, the more posts that fell, the more hopeless the Italian position became and the more easily their troops gave up, though there were still some posts that held out remarkably well. Just as the light began to wane on that afternoon of 21 January, Major John Copland of the 2/4th Battalion — a

35-year-old bloke from Sydney's Manly Beach — had just led a successful attack on a post near a road leading down the escarpment towards Tobruk proper, when he was approached by one of the Italian prisoners. This man was an officer, impeccably turned out — and even their greatest critics would argue that no one could quite do 'impeccably turned out' like the Italian officers could — and in broken English he asked to see a senior officer.

Copland made the fellow to understand that he personally was about as senior as it got in these parts at this time, despite the fact that, covered in the dirt, dust and grime of battle, he was near indistinguishable from his soldiers. The Italian officer, once convinced he was indeed talking to a Major, asked Copland to accompany him ...

Curious but careful, Copland did so, going further and further into a complicated tunnel system, until they came to a sad-looking but dignified old man who had all the insignia and air of being a very senior officer himself.

An interesting conversation then took place.

The old man spoke: 'Officer?'

'*Oui*, officer,' Copland replied, reaching for one of the few foreign words he knew, and maybe it even worked because the old man clearly understood, nodding to that effect. Then the old man took out his silver pistol and, with tears streaming down his face, handed it to the young Australian ...

It was the modern equivalent of the ancient ritual of the defeated general handing his sword to his victorious opponent as a symbol of surrender, and it was then that Copland realised the man before him must be the Commanding Officer of the Italian garrison at Tobruk, Generale Petassi Manella.[16]

High officer he might have been, but still so upset, with the tears still coming, that Major Copland even felt moved to say something to comfort him.

'*C'est la guerre* ...' he said softly, now exhausting the only foreign words he had left in his lexicon.

'*Oui*,' the 72-year-old General replied, '*c'est la guerre* ...'

Despite this formal surrender, however, nothing could persuade the Italian commander to issue an all-purpose order for the rest of the Italians at Tobruk who had not yet been captured to lay down their own arms, and spasmodic fighting continued through the night.

Still, a significant clue of what the second day was going to hold came early, when two of the first Italian soldiers spotted were carrying a white flag, ready to give up their section of the defences.

•

Not long afterwards, Lieutenant Hennessy and Sergeant Mills of the 2/4th Battalion were in the advance guard of troops heading into the town proper, warily proceeding in an armoured carrier, when right in front of them another immaculately turned-out Italian officer stepped forwards and, in broken English, indicated that, if the Australians would follow him, he would lead them to the Admiral, who wished to surrender.

Now it was true that this bloke seemed like he was on the up and up, but on the other hand, all across North Africa there were crosses marking the spots of soldiers who hadn't taken every precaution for their own safety. So, just to make *doubly* sure the Itie was dinkum, they put him on the bonnet of their carrier and, following his directions, slowly nosed their way towards the location of the Naval Headquarters, in a large white building beside the harbour. Not too far away, the once proud *San Giorgio* warship was burning fiercely — bombed and beached in the early days of the war, it had been used as an anti-aircraft arsenal since, but on the previous night had been abandoned by her crew and set ablaze — while all around the harbour, the masts and funnels of other ships that had been sunk by the British bombers were poking through the waters like so many aquatic tombstones.

Coming from the headquarters itself there was also a fair amount of smoke, though this emanated from documents that the Italian officers had been burning in anticipation of what was about to happen. (And still more smoke was coming from some of the Diggers themselves, as around and about the township they engaged in a process they called 'rabbiting' — which involved lighting some thick crude oil at the entrance of one of the many underground shelters the Italians had constructed, and then watching carefully to capture the coughing enemy as they emerged from one of the other, inevitable, exits — just like they used to do back in the western plains of Victoria when the numbers of the local rabbit population started to get out of control.)[17]

Yet there, as promised, when Lieutenant Hennessy and his party entered the three-storey Naval Headquarters — awaiting the Australians and standing with several of his most senior officers — was indeed the remaining ranking Italian officer, Ammiraglio Massimiliano Vietina, the commander of the naval garrison. This rather distinguished officer received them standing at attention in his dress whites and weighed down with surely every medal he'd ever won. And now the admiral indicated, with an air of rather theatrical sadness, that he was ready to offer them his sword of surrender.

Lieutenant Hennessy, however, with a highly developed sense of propriety, declined to take it, asserting that only his Commanding Officer, Brigadier Horace Robertson, should have the honour of accepting this formal surrender, and so the two sides waited in a rather uncomfortable silence for Robertson to arrive on the armoured carrier that had been sent back to his Brigade HQ to fetch him — though several of the Diggers with the Lieutenant passed the time by helping themselves to the excellent Champagne the good Admiral had in stock and . . .

And that'll be the Brigadier now.

A big, bluff, rather hail-fellow-well-met kind of gent, Brigadier Robertson entered the room accompanied by his friend and colleague, Brigadier Leslie Morshead of the 18th Brigade. As part of his own education in modern warfare, Morshead had accompanied the 18th's sister brigade, the 19th, on their assault of Tobruk and had observed its method of sending in infantry closely behind a creeping blanket barrage as a way of piercing defences, before the attackers spread out from there.

Now, though, Morshead took very much a back seat as Brigadier Robertson saluted the Italian admiral. That gentleman then stepped forwards and, with a translator making the whole thing even more drawn-out and excruciating, delivered a rather long-winded and florid speech detailing just why the Italians were choosing the better part of valour by giving up, before offering up the sword of surrender. With an absolute bare minimum of his own formality, the Australian Brigadier took it and then got down to tin tacks.

'You have landmines laid in and around the town,' he said firmly. 'I will take reprisals for the life of every one of my men lost on those mines.'[18]

Once translated, there was a quick burst of voluble Italian from Admiral Vietina, and that was clearly quickly sorted out, with some of the other Italian officers present immediately taking some of the Australian officers in tow to show them exactly where those minefields lay. As to various booby traps that had been set up around Tobruk, the Admiral added that these were in the process of being 'sprung', just as were — *massive explosion in the distance* — some of the ammunition dumps.[19]

Well away from such formalities, however, there was another symbol of the predominantly Australian triumph. It came in the form of a Digger who shinnied up the town's flagpole and ran his slouch hat up the mast. And there it stayed. The Australians were in residence, and let those who could try to take the town off them.

•

Not that this particular exercise had come without loss. In the two-day battle the Australians had lost 49 killed and 306 soldiers wounded. Against that, however, they had captured 27 000 Italian prisoners, as well as 208 guns and 23 tanks.

And yet, the general atmosphere among the victorious Australian troops and scattered British forces was one of celebration, and it so happened that they found there was plenty to celebrate with. For as they wandered along Tobruk's wide and pleasant streets — the main thoroughfare of which, Via Mussolini, had already been renamed 'Pitt Street' after Sydney's famous main street — and then began exploring among its many white colonial style buildings, what they found was an absolute treasure trove.

Grog! Warehouses of it! Tinned food, enough to sustain 25 000 men for two months!

Precious delicacies, of Gawd knew what, but she tasted all right! Fancy cheeses! Recoaro water! (Er, whatever that was.) And then there were the silk shirts, the blue cavalry cloaks, elaborate toilet sets in Florentine leather and all manner of a scented kind of hair gunk[20] that'd make you think they were either all pooftas, or at least sat down when they pissed! Fair dinkum, some of those fancy officers had more kit — lots of it plastered in gold braid and weighed down with medals from victories unknown — than you could poke a burned stick at.

With some of their officers, it was almost as if they were going to a fancy-dress party in what an officer should look like — with such extraordinary efforts going into their appearance and comfort — and also, to judge from the battle just gone, with so very little effort having gone into doing what an officer should *do*, which is lead.

Even the common soldiers had their own personal coffee percolators. *Get a load of it, would yers!* Plenty of the Diggers actually did, regarding such finery as the spoils of war — even though most of what they took would have to be discarded within just a few days on the simple grounds that what could be neither eaten nor drunk nor shot from was usually not worth carrying. Still, it was an eye-opener, all right.

A final sign of just what lengths the Italians went to in order to fight their war in complete comfort, was a brothel, which had apparently been doing a roaring business until at least a couple of days previously. The fourteen remarkably cheerful women who had been working there were soon rounded up and sent on their way to sit out the rest of the war in a convent in Cairo — pausing only to kiss the hands of the Diggers they passed, saying in thickly accented English, 'Aussies good!' — and some of the troops took the liberty of adopting the small pet dog of one of the prostitutes as their own. They called him 'Dusty' because when he shook he stirred up enough dust to nearly disappear in the cloud. (A curiosity of Dusty was that he didn't lift his hind leg to relieve himself, but instead squatted. Why? Because, they reckoned, the poor little bastard had never seen a tree in his life on which to learn how to do it![21])

Walking around among the soldiers that morning, getting the feel of the 'morning after' — and already beginning to form up what he would have to say in his next report for the ABC — Chester Wilmot was trying to comprehend just what drove the Italians to live like that. As he later wrote: 'To the Italians such luxurious trappings were natural and necessary. They were an essential part of the illusion Mussolini had fostered in the hope of inspiring them with a warlike spirit and an imperial ambition. In his speeches and propaganda he had glamourised war and sought to sell them the idea that it was a grand adventure, with power, plunder and glory as the prizes. To bolster their faint hearts he had told them that young, virile Fascist legions had only to march and the jaded, effete British would collapse ...'[22]

In the there and then, though, what most amazed Wilmot was just how little damage had been done to the township and its immediate surrounds, despite the massive pounding it had taken from the British and Australian artillery. He had been standing *right* beside some of the more powerful of the artillery batteries when they had first been unleashed, and knew the explosive power of the rounds sent the Italians' way — and yet somehow the solid stone structures in the town had withstood the worst of it. More importantly still, the town's two water purification plants and its sole subartesian well — together capable of providing 40 000 gallons a day — plus the jetty and power stations had been left untouched! (One theory as to why these, and whole warehouses of food, hadn't been blown up by the Italians was that they realised that once they were prisoners they would probably find themselves at the end of a very long queue to get such supplies as there were, so it was as well to keep them plentiful.[23])

Clearly, the biggest damage done must have been to Italian morale — of which there was now just about nothing left. Everywhere, long lines of Italian soldiers were being led away to hastily formed stockades where they would be held until they could be sent back to 'Alex' (Alexandria) or Cairo or wherever more permanent containment could be found for them. The majority of these prisoners wore the hangdog expressions of the truly beaten, in marked contrast to the Diggers leading them, some of whom were now jocularly lighting cigarettes with 50 and 100 lire notes, with smiles as wide as the Sydney Harbour Bridge.

Here now, for example, came a Digger escorting another motley crew of Itie prisoners; he was all bright-eyed and bushy-tailed, surely in part because he was now all newly adorned with the insignia and badges of rank of no less than a *capitano* of the Italian Army!

Upon Wilmot's gentle inquiry of how he got them, the Digger beamed, 'I swapped 'em for a couple of fags. For 'arf a bloody packet, I coulda been a blasted general.'[24]

And so he perhaps could have been — not that Italian Generals were especially highly regarded at this time in history, nor indeed were any of the Italian forces . . .

As to those Italian soldiers, Wilmot's command of their language was just strong enough that he was able to conduct some rough kinds of interviews with them, and he was particularly interested in one theme of their responses: These *australiani*, these are *voluntari*? It is not *obbligatorio*, they are not forced to be here? It was clearly something the Italian soldiery just couldn't quite comprehend, try as they might. As Wilmot faithfully reported: 'They understood their own position. They had been sent to Libya to win glory for Mussolini. They presumed that the Tommies were there merely to defend British Imperial interests. But why were the Australian volunteers there?'[25]

One of the reasons was for a *fight*, and many of the Australians felt short-changed that they hadn't really got one, with another private commenting to Wilmot, 'Fightin'? Call this fightin'? Gawd . . . the police in Tel Aviv give us a better fight than this.'[26]

One thing the Italians had given them that the Tel Aviv police couldn't, however, was brand-bloody-spanking-new Fiat and Lancia trucks — about 200 of the beauties! — which had been captured intact, and these were soon loaded to the gills as the men of the AIF made preparations to move on. The capture of Tobruk and its crucial fresh-water supplies — together with its deep harbour and jetties enabling the port to deliver more food, weaponry and munitions into established storage facilities — had meant that it was now possible to develop a hard power of punch even further to the west of Cairo, and the victorious soldiers had no intention of tarrying.

•

Finally, it was nearly done. The very last of the resistance in Tobruk had been crushed and the Italian soldiers disarmed and rounded up. As it happened, Chester Wilmot was standing, chatting, in the Piazza Vittorio Emmanuelle with the Commanding Officer of the 2/6th Battalion, Lieutenant Colonel Arthur Godfrey, when yet one more lot of Italian soldiers were led by, causing the colonel to remark, 'That's about the last of the 25 000. If we'd had 25 000 Australians inside these defences, not even the Germans would have got us out in six months.'[27]

One person walking around Tobruk with particular interest on that same morning — just as the first of the British ships were starting to nudge into the wonderful harbour, bringing much-needed fresh supplies — was Brigadier Leslie Morshead of the 18th Brigade. Though already well satisfied that he had learned a lot on this trip — with particular reference to the techniques used by the 19th Brigade in their assault — he still wanted to know more.

Over the next three days Morshead continued to reconnoitre around and about this tiny town by the Mediterranean, taking copious notes as he studied the defences that the Italians had built up over the previous twenty-five years of their occupation. Certainly these defences hadn't been sufficient to hold the Australians up for more than a day, but Morshead was of the view that that may well have been because the Italian soldiers didn't really have their hearts in it. As someone who was always keen to improve his knowledge of the art of warfare, of the science of attack and defence, Morshead ranged far and wide looking at the intricacies of the man-made defences, as well as the natural lie of the land.

The focal point of the settlement was a great natural harbour, about one mile wide and two miles long, which had been formed by the penetration of a small finger of the Mediterranean snaking into the African coast at an angle of about 45 degrees northwest from the latitudinal line — in turn making a high thumb out of the peninsula of land that divided it from the Mediterranean proper, and the town was built on the slopes of that thumb. Composed of many solid stone buildings covered in white plaster, including a lot of large and gracious villas for the high officers, and many, many barracks for the common troops, its human footprint resembled a soldier's boot more than anything else.

Now, into the coast on either side of the harbour entrance, other rather more stubby fingers of the Mediterranean had made small dents in the coastline, and on the terrain leading down to those dents were many wadis, essentially dry creek gullies which creased the otherwise fairly flat land near the coast, before the land reared up in two escarpment steps to a plateau. Dotted around that plateau were the ruins of previous civilisations that had essayed to establish a permanent foothold upon the burning sands of this perilous land, but had succeeded only in leaving the fading footprints of ruined castles, shattered synagogues and numerous ancient burial cisterns.[28] There was also the indication that the soil had once been fertile, and yet all that remained of that now were a few scraggy fig trees and one or two tomato plants. For the rest, most of the current human footprint was beaten back to within cooee of the harbour proper. To anyone in a plane looking down, Tobruk appeared as a small settlement 'squatting at the foot of two huge steps of a staircase'.[29]

The contours of the landscape were such that, although Tobruk offered precious little in the way of natural barriers to an invading force, the Italians had cleverly based their defences — especially their elaborately constructed anti-tank ditches — around some of these deeper wadis. Where the wadis — read: huge gullies — had stopped, their bulldozers and dynamiting had continued the enormous ditches regardless, the best they could. Although in some places the rock beneath had been so solid that it hadn't been possible to continue the ditch — at which point the Italians had compensated by laying heavy minefields and enormous rolls of barbed concertina wire 5 feet high in front, as further protection — in other places the ditch was as deep as 12 feet and as wide as 20 feet. Now, on the inside of the whole perimeter, in a broad semicircle going some 30 miles around Tobruk — with a rough distance of 9 miles from the harbour at its outermost point — the Italians had built 150 ground-level defensive positions, enormous concrete constructions buried into the earth with ground-level slots to allow guns to fire. Each post was some 25 yards wide, protected in front by more rolls of barbed wire, while inside were three circular pits in which there was a specially built spot for an anti-tank gun and other spots for machine guns, with many of the pits connected to each other by trenches, and the whole thing designed to hold a platoon. Though they were open to the skies above, at the back of each post was a small bomb-proof room for sleeping, with a very strong roof. Yet so low to the ground were these constructions that in the dusty haze of the desert they would be almost invisible to the enemy until he was right upon them — especially in the shimmering heat of full day. In one final flash of military engineering genius, in some places the anti-tank ditch was narrow enough that it had been covered by thin pieces of timber covered with dirt, meaning that it would be every bit as effective a way to stop a tank as a larger ditch, but would have the advantage of not being seen until the tank had actually tumbled into it.

Cleverly, the posts were placed in a zigzag pattern so that every second one was positioned some 500 yards back, allowing it to cover any flanking move that might be made on the posts 350 yards to the left and right. There was even an identification system, with every post with an odd number on the front line and all the inside posts having an even number. In addition, all the posts situated to the north of the southwest corner of the perimeter had an S in front of them, while all to the east of that had the prefix of R, meaning that if a platoon was sent to, say, R33, they could instantly recognise by that designation alone where it would roughly lie. (Front lines, eastern end of the southern perimeter.)

In short, the Italians had done an extraordinary job of turning Tobruk into a great fortress, even if their soldiers were clearly not the equal of their engineers. Not that the landscape didn't offer some natural advantages. For Morshead also paid attention to the lie of the land on the other side of the ditches. For those attacking, there was precious little cover except for the odd clumps of 'camel-thorn' shrubs — so-called by the troops because the hardy camel was the only thing tough enough to touch it. In most parts of that perimeter a defender could see for miles, precluding all possibility of launching any daytime attacks with any element of surprise.

•

Far, far to the south and east at much the same time — even as the bulk of the men of the 6th Division began to move out of Tobruk and continue to the west to their next targeted Italian stronghold of Derna — the flying boat of the Australian Prime Minister, Robert Menzies, took off from Sydney's Rose Bay at the beginning of a long trip to London, via North Africa . . .

His mission was multifaceted, but high on the agenda for Menzies was simply being in the Mother Country itself, seeing the Australian troops in the Middle East on the way over, having a say while in London as to their disposition, and persuading Churchill of two crucial things. The first was that Singapore needed a stronger British military presence than the scant force it had there at the time — as Singapore, of course, stood at the gateway to Australia, and all Australians were counting on Britain to defend them should the increasingly militaristic and threatening Japanese declare war, as was feared. And the second thing was for Churchill to move some of Britain's industrial capacity to make ships and aircraft to Australia, where it could be free from German bombs, and help the stretched Australian economy.[30]

•

Was it fair that kids had to be around this kind of thing?

At first when, just out of school, he'd joined the Liverpool General Post Office in southern Sydney, it had been exciting to be in such a busy and important environment. Telegrams would arrive with glad tidings of babies born, engagements announced and the blessed news that '*I'll be home soon!*' Now, though, particularly since this whole business in North Africa had started, another kind of telegram was starting to arrive. They were from the government, and always stamped *Personal Acknowledgment of Delivery*, meaning that it was the job of the delivery boy to get the signature of the person to whom it was addressed.

It didn't take anyone long to realise, because pretty soon everyone knew it (and not just those who worked in the GPO), that *Personal Acknowledgment of Delivery* was almost always a death sentence, because the news was invariably that a distant Australian soldier was either Missing In Action, seriously wounded or — and this was the most frequent one — Killed In Action. Sometimes it was all you could do to get the signature out of them, and the scenes you were in the middle of were terrible. Still, it really was worse for some: one day, one of the young fellows had to take a telegram to his own mother telling her that her son — his older brother — had been killed.

•

They were grim and they were determined. These military men with their red caps had already had plenty of experience with the Australians, and felt they were getting closer to having their measure. The thing was, you had to hit them hard and early, and if at all possible get them isolated. The worst of it with these Australians was that if you took one on, you soon had another dozen coming at you, because they stuck together so tenaciously — but if you got the right support from your own comrades it was just possible that it could be done.

It wasn't easy being a British military policeman on the streets of the Palestinian port town of Jaffa, trying to maintain some sense of public order when literally thousands of servicemen were out and about letting off steam, but someone had to do it and they were the ones. Mind you, while drunkenness was one problem with the Australians, it was far from the only one.

Often, at the first sign of the military police, the soldiers from other nations tended to sober up on the spot. But again, not these bloody Australians. With grog in them they could be very aggressive indeed, and they seemed to have very little respect for authority for its own sake. For most soldiers, a bloke with three stripes and a truncheon was a military policeman around whom they should behave carefully. But for a lot of the Australians, when they were three sheets in the wind, he was just a bloke with a truncheon against whom they fancied their chances anyway, so why not 'give it a burl', as they said?

As it turned out, this particular night was a good one, finishing with a new record for the military police. Eighteen Australian soldiers just from the one battalion, the 2/23rd, all securely locked away in the Jaffa Gaol![31]

•

Still, not to worry too much.

True, one of the most senior British Generals, Sir Henry Maitland Wilson, had been a tad pointed when, upon meeting the Australian Prime Minister for the first time in those early days of February 1941, he noted that 'The Australian soldiers have been troublesome', but Robert Menzies had come up with a fair old reply for this soldier, whom he had found from the first to be 'tall, fat, and cunning'.

'Yes,' the Australian Prime Minister said drolly, 'I understand the Italians soldiers have found them very troublesome ...'

Still, the British general would not leave off.

'It's not that,' Wilson replied. 'They're not disciplined, you know.'

'These men,' Menzies returned fire, 'haven't spent their lives marching around parade grounds. They come from all walks of life and they've come over here to do a job and get it over with.'[32]

All of which was a fair defence. Still, it was not necessarily an easy thing for Menzies to be around Australian soldiers fighting in a world war, for the principal reason that when he had been their age and presented with exactly the same opportunity to join up, go overseas and fight for his country in the Great War, he had declined. Some parliamentarians, even from Menzies' own side of the political fence, thought that that fact alone should have disqualified him from becoming Prime Minister. Most famously, just six months before World War II began, the leader of the Country Party, Earle Page, at a time he was Acting Prime Minister following the death of Joseph Lyons, had even said so in parliament — on the occasion of detailing why neither he nor any members of his party would serve in the cabinet of the incoming Menzies government.

It was Page's view that Menzies could not provide the leadership desperately needed by a country facing the prospect of war, and not just because he had been so flagrantly disloyal to Lyons shortly before he had died, though that was a factor. Rather more pointedly, Page — who had himself served in the Great War in the Middle East — asserted that the honourable gentleman had still not 'explained to the satisfaction of the very great body of the people who did participate in the [Great War], his reasons [for not joining up] and because of this I am afraid that he will not be able to get that maximum effort from the people of Australia to which I have referred.'[33]

On that occasion, Menzies had made the dignified reply that the question of whether or not one enlisted in the Great War was one that related 'to a man's intimate, personal and family affairs', and for which no answer can 'be made on the public platform',[34] and yet it still troubled him. He was, after all, on this very trip to the Middle East involved in making decisions by which men would live or die, and it certainly would have been easier to do so had he personally experienced something of the Australian soldiers' lot and had himself faced the like of the trials they were about to.

Nevertheless, on this occasion — inspecting the troops of the 21st Brigade at Julis Camp in Palestine — he was extremely heartened to see that the soldiers themselves seemed to bear him no ill will, and some of the older and bolder of the cooks even called out to him 'How are you, Bob!?'[35] at his very sight. Others came up to him, shook his hand and asked very politely, 'How are things in Australia?' and were transparently delighted at his simple response: 'First rate, and everyone is very proud of you.'

And as a matter of fact, Menzies said just that to the assembled men a short time later: 'I promise and pledge you that Australia will be behind you through good and bad. We all know your sacrifices. I cannot describe the immense pride and affection felt for you at home. Go forward; you are not alone.'[36]

Still, both the magnificence and the possible fate of these men were so strong as he stood on the reviewing stand, surveying some of Australia's toughest fighting men, that he confided to his diary, 'It is a moving thing to speak to thousands of young men, mere boys, in the flower of their youth, many of whom will never see Australia again. War is the abomination of desolation, but its servants are a sight to see. These men are unbeatable.'

That evening, Menzies met with Lieutenant General Leslie Morshead, and the meeting went well, with Menzies very much liking the cut of the general's jib from the first, equally confiding to his diary that Morshead looked 'first rate'.

Which was as well, because Morshead had just been given an enormous job to do: commanding the 9th Division and getting it quickly up to speed. Though Morshead had initially been passed over for the job of running the 9th in favour of Major General Henry Wynter, that officer had fallen sick just a couple of weeks before and returned to Australia, so leaving the way clear for the man from Vaucluse.

Menzies assured Morshead of his full support as the two took leave of each other — Morshead to get back to his men, and Menzies to visit a few more places in North Africa to gauge the Australian war effort, before heading on to Britain and attempting to accomplish his chief aim. With the thinnest of all parliamentary majorities and an Australian public that was ever more worried about the way the war was turning, *and* an opposition led by John Curtin that continued to attack both Menzies and his government for failing to stand up for Australian interests in Britain, *and* a press that believed his performance was sluggish, Menzies needed some demonstrable results. His chief hope was that after long and strong consultations with Winston Churchill and senior British political figures, as well as sitting in on deliberations of the War Cabinet, he would be able to produce them.

•

Two figures, flitting in the dusk of the early evening.

'Halt!' the Australian sentry cried, readying to shoot.

Just in time, two Arabs emerged with their hands held high, but bearing welcome news to the men of the 6th Division. They were emissaries from the Libyan population of Derna ... and they had an important message.

'Italian finish,' they said. 'Libyan peoples want soldiers to come.'

If they were ridgy-didge, it seemed the Ities had given up the important town of Derna without a fight, and the following morning an extremely cautious advance party of the 6th Division entered the town to check it out. Though there was to be some fierce fighting around Derna Aerodrome, the Italian defences collapsed, as Chester Wilmot put it, 'like a pricked balloon', and in short order pretty much the whole division entered the town.

And look at this place! In all of North Africa there surely couldn't be a better spot. As described by Australian journalist John Hetherington, who was there: 'Trees flourished along the streets and in the gardens of the houses. Cabbages, cauliflowers, spring onions, radishes and other vegetables throve in kitchen plots. And there were baths to be had for the turning of a tap.

Desert-grimed men who had been washing, shaving, cooking, drinking and filling their truck radiators from their ration of a gallon of fresh water per man per day for nearly six weeks, wallowed in tubs of steaming water and watched the grime of battle disappear from their bodies.'[37]

Still, all of this was nothing compared to the local Arabs in wonderfully coloured clothing who soon emerged and gave them a welcome for the ages, showering them with handshakes and kisses, making it completely clear that they had hated the Italians all along, that the Australians were their saviours, and by the way would they like to buy some of these trinkets? Some eggs, perhaps, or cakes, or slippers or scarves or necklaces? After what they had been through, for the men of the 6th Division the whole thing was a slice of heaven, and at that moment they wouldn't have bothered to call the King their uncle. It was the Africa of their dreams, and if you didn't have a home to go to, this would be a wonderful spot for a man to stop and put down roots. But no, all too soon, they had to push on ...

•

Meanwhile, at the Julis camp, Lieutenant General Morshead really did get on with the job at hand. With his appointment becoming official the following day, he was immediately a blur of movement, consulting his carefully selected senior staff, trying to organise, equip and bring an entire division — composed of three brigades of infantry with assorted other units of intelligence, artillery, armour, et cetera, totalling 15 000 men — up to cohesive speed. For from the first, it was obvious that things were not everything they might be. While it was true he had some good and capable senior officers — most particularly in the big and bluff form of his senior staff officer, Colonel Charles 'Gaffer' Lloyd, and Brigadiers John Murray, Arthur Godfrey and Ray Tovell — when it came to the men and their equipment, well, that was another matter. In the first part it wasn't even yet clear what the component divisions of the 9th were, as General Blamey continued to form, and then re-form, its composition under his fingertips.[38]

The fact that at this point the 9th Division was a hotchpotch of different brigades and units and raw recruits all thrown together at the last instant was far from its only problem. More importantly, it desperately needed an infusion of such basics for any army as guns, ammunition, trucks and fuel — not to mention training — before it was going to be much chop at anything. Still, there were more than a few of Morshead's senior staff, and perhaps a few in the lower ranks, who seriously asked themselves the question: was there going to be anything left in this part of the world for this division to do, in any case?

For just the day after Morshead had received his appointment, the British and Australian forces clashed with the Italian forces at Benghazi. Though outnumbered by the Italians by about five to one in tanks and men, that only meant that by virtue of the way the war had gone to date, it was a fairly fair fight. And so it proved. For Benghazi had fallen to the Allies by nightfall!

In the previous two months Wavell's forces had advanced 600 miles, wiped out ten divisions of Italians, and taken 130 000 prisoners, all for the loss of 600 of their own men. It was the British Foreign Minister, Anthony Eden, who perhaps summed it up best when talking with Churchill. 'If I may debase a golden phrase,' he said, 'never has so much been surrendered by so many to so few.'[39]

To all intents and purposes, it seemed to be 'Game Over' for the Axis powers in North Africa. None of which slowed Morshead for an instant. A professional, he continued to train his troops hard against the day they might just possibly be needed, if not here in North Africa, then in one of the many other theatres the Allies were involved in.

Which was all right for him. Many of his men, though, were nothing short of devastated. With the bloody 6th Division having done so well in battle in North Africa, just what *was* going to be left for them to achieve? Had they done all this training, and come all this way, only to leave without getting a fair-dinkum fight? Stone the bloody crows!

As it happened, however, something was in fact stirring that might mean Morshead's men were a chance of getting something of a fight after all . . .

•

On the very afternoon that the British and Australian forces had been fighting with the Italians in Benghazi, a singularly important meeting was taking place far, far to the north that would ultimately affect all of them.

After driving through a bustling Berlin, where the new film from the Nazi propaganda unit, entitled *Victory in the West*, was showing everywhere to packed theatres, the man who was the star of the pic, just as he was on the cover of many, many magazines — the dashing General Erwin Rommel of the famed 7th Panzer Division — was shown into the office of the Wehrmacht's Commander in Chief, *Oberbefehlshaber* Walther von Brauchitsch, and shortly thereafter was taken to have an audience with Hitler himself.

They had a new and very important task for him . . .[40]

Instead of returning to western France, where he and his men had been in training for the mooted invasion of England, Rommel was to go to North Africa. He was to take command of a new force that would be forming up there over the next few weeks and months. This force would shortly be named the Afrika Korps — a rare bit of Hitler humour of the ironic variety, as Rommel had first risen to prominence as part of the Alpine Korps in Italy, so the German leader thought it made sense. The Afrika Korps would have at its core two armoured divisions: the 15th Panzer Division, commanded by General Heinrich von Prittwitz und Gaffron, and the 5th Light Division under General Johannes Streich. The 5th Light — boasting 8000 veterans and 150 tanks in its own right, with more than half being the devastating Mark III and Mark IV Panzers with their 50-mm and 75-mm cannon respectively — would leave immediately, while the 15th Panzer would be there by the middle of May. This, the Führer told the ambitious and hard-rising general, would give him some crucial time to get to know the African terrain, as well as his Italian allies, who would be providing two fresh infantry divisions themselves together with the Ariete Armoured Division. After showing him American and British magazines with many photos of Richard O'Connor's successful drive through North Africa to clear out the Italians, the Führer made it clear that Rommel's key job would be use his force only as a *Sperrverband* — a special blocking formation — to stop any further British moves west across North Africa. Further, he was to work with the Italians, whose Generale Italo Gariboldi, the replacement for the unfortunate Graziani, would nominally be Rommel's superior.[41] This was necessary because, after all, Libya was Italian territory and so German intervention had to be structured in such a fashion that they were only there at the *invitation* of Italy, and they would have to remain deferential to Italian wishes. (That, at least, was the theory.)

All up, Rommel would have 25 000 soldiers and 8500 vehicles at his disposal.

When Hitler himself made a request of this nature, there was only one proper response, and Rommel did not miss it. He thanked his leader for the honour done him by allowing him to command such a force for such an important task, clicked his heels, Heil Hitler-ed, and left. So many things to do, so little time.

The most important thing of all, however, was to write a quick note to his wife, Lu — whenever away from her, he wrote to her every day without fail — telling her he had been given a new and very important assignment, and consoling her over the fact that their precious time together would once again be cut short.

'Don't be sad,' he wrote to her at their home, still in Wiener Neustadt, where she had stayed with their twelve-year-old boy, Manfred, 'it had to be . . .'[42]

And though it would be a terrible breach of security if he were to tell her where he was going, he was able to make an oblique reference to it in another note the following day, by saying that at least the new assignment was 'one way of getting my rheumatism treatment . . .'[43]

Frau Rommel recognised the clue by the fact that, the previous year, a doctor who had treated her husband had said to him, 'You need sunshine, Herr General; you ought to be in Africa.'[44]

By the following day Rommel was on his way and was soon conferring in Rome with the Italian *Comando Supremo*. In some ways the timing of the meeting was propitious. For, while in the structure of this new command Rommel was to be answerable to the Italians, the fact that they were meeting at a time when the last of the Italian 10th Army was surrendering to O'Connor and his men at Beda Fomm — about 160 kilometres south of Benghazi on the coast — was a fair indication of just how much Mussolini needed Rommel and his Afrika Korps. In a stunning move, O'Connor had effectively headed the retreating Italians off at the pass, by sending his 7th Armoured Division from its base at Mechili (which boasted an extremely significant spring of fresh water, and an enormous supply depot) sweeping *across the desert* through extraordinarily rough country to cut the coast road east of El Agheila's fort, airfield and watering point, and stop their retreat, while the Australians of the 6th Division kept pushing them from behind, along the coast road from Benghazi, 280 kilometres north of the outpost.

Outgunned, outmanned, outmanoeuvred and blocked in every direction, the Italians had outright collapsed and hauled up and into view every bit of white material available to them. (Seven of the prisoners taken at Beda Fomm were Italian Generals, and O'Connor briefly searched them out to apologise for their temporary shabby accommodation in a dilapidated farmhouse, explaining that 'We haven't had time to make proper arrangements.' One of the prisoners, General Cona, graciously replied, 'Thank you very much. We do realise you came here in a very great hurry.'[45])

The Italians needed Rommel, all right, and listened closely to his plans. A small example of the power dynamic between the German and the Italian leadership was Rommel's reaction when he heard that the Italians had 'ordered' that the 400 aircraft of the *X Fliegerkorps* of the *Luftwaffe* — which had been moved to Sicily so as to be within range of North Africa on their sorties — not engage in bombing Allied forces now installed in Benghazi because that was where the Italian settlers were also concentrated and there was too much valuable property at stake. Rommel rescinded the order on the spot, and the bombing of Benghazi began that night.[46]

The Italians simply had to accept it. Rommel was practically *una forza della natura*, who you got in the way of at your peril.

•

On 9 February 1941, the British Prime Minister, Winston Churchill, made a stirring speech in his famous stentorian tones.

'Give us the tools, and we'll finish the job,' he said. 'The whole British Empire has been proud of the mother country and they long to be with us over here in even larger numbers. We have been deeply conscious of the love for us which has flowed from the Dominions of the Crown across the broad ocean spaces. There is the first of our war aims — to be worthy of that love and to preserve it ...

'The events in Libya are only part of the story. They are only a part of the story of the decline and fall of the Italian Empire. That will not take a future Gibbon so long to write as the original work ...'

•

They muffled the shouts the best they could — as they were breaking regulations — but Christ Almighty, it was *hard*. A bloke approaching those back barracks of the Julis camp in Palestine was left in no doubt that something was going on there from as far as 50 yards away, but the instant they opened the door to slip inside, they were near engulfed by both the roars of their soldiers and the completely intoxicating atmosphere. Well over fifty men were gathered in a tight circle and belting out their encouragement and passion as, time and again, two glittering coins flew skywards — 'COME IN SPINNER!' — to land spinning on the hard wood floors, everyone leaning forward to take in the results.

'He's TAILED 'EM!' came the shout, with half the men cheering raucously because of it, and the other half ruefully handing over money to them even as they set up for the next round.

'I'll have ten a head! Ten a head, who's got me?'

'Tails, twenty for tails!'

'I'll have ya!'

For Ivor Hancock, Cocky Walpole, Pudden Head Poidevin, Norm Graham and many of their mates, playing two-up was no less than one of the great pleasures of their life in the camp, and lately some of them had been playing it furiously — frequently betting many weeks of their military wages on a single toss — and all for a very good reason. The bugger of it was that an edict had come out that unless you had twenty pounds in your pay book, you couldn't go to Cairo — and it was in Cairo that the best brothels of all were meant to be. Forget Jerusalem, this was the *real* promised land! So on and on they played ... and woe betide anybody who tried to welsh on a bet in such games. If you didn't pay up, you had to answer to Max the Axe, a knuckle-man from western Victoria, built like a brick shithouse, who was the key organiser of the two-up games and effectively the battalion enforcer to boot. While it was generally the job of the military police to keep the men in line at an official, external level — dealing with insubordination, public drunkenness and so on — the likes of Max the Axe operated on another level entirely, keeping internal discipline and ensuring that the battalion's code was followed. Debts were to be paid, there was to be no ratting on your mate to a superior officer, no filching another bloke's stuff ... and so on. Max was one tough bastard, and no one wanted to mess with him.

Those who were dead busted broke and couldn't bet money bet everything else, from rum rations to boots to the very shirts off their backs, but under the circumstances what everyone really wanted was money ...

As it happened, the only two who got to the requisite twenty pounds in these first days of February were Cocky Walpole, who did indeed win big on two-up, and another fellow known as 'Nancy', as in 'Nancy boy' — because he neither smoked, nor drank, nor gambled. Nancy, if you can believe it, had managed to save the required amount from his standard pay of eight shillings a day and, even though he had no interest in debauchery, had agreed to accompany Cocky on the grounds that another edict had it that you had to move in pairs in Cairo! Besides, Nancy wanted to see some of the museums in the Egyptian capital, and make a quick trip to the pyramids, which Cocky had agreed to. A more mismatched pair could not have been imagined, and the battalion watched them depart with some amusement. It was their return, however, which caused outright howls of hilarity. From Nancy's fixed impression of a stunned mullet and near inability to speak even after several days, put together with Cocky's stories of all-night drinking and late-night atrocities — with Nancy feeling obliged to stay with Cocky to ensure that the rule about 'staying in pairs' was followed — it was clear that the two hadn't seen many of the museums. (And in fact the Australians weren't even allowed into the major museums, for fear they would steal the gold.)

•

In his whole seven years of life, young Len Johnson had never been this upset. Certainly not on the day his dad, John, had left to go to the war, as Len had been so proud of him in his uniform, with his slouch hat, khakis, Rising Sun badges and shiny black boots, and had never doubted for a moment that he would be coming back. But, still, the agony of it! He hadn't even known how much he'd miss his father until the weeks had started to drag by with no sign of his return, and yet one thing in particular had helped to sustain him. Just before John Johnson had left, he found out that young Len had discovered the magic of books, and so had given him an illustrated copy of Walt Disney's *Dumbo the Flying Elephant*. To young Len's mind it had seemed that the gift belonged to both his father and himself — it was almost a part of the father he was missing so much — and he simply refused to let it out of his sight, reading it over and over again, and always feeling close to his father when he did so.

Then it happened. One night his mother sent him on a quick trip in the horse and gig with Grandma and Grandad, and she put his book carefully on the gig's tray, so it would be there when he arrived. But when they got there, it was gone! Vanished in the night! Most probably it had simply slipped off the back when they had gone over bumps, but no matter how much they looked for it, it was gone.

The sense of loss was overwhelming. Len was instantly inconsolable and wept for days. It was his father's last gift to him before he had left, and Len had not only lost that last gift, but also the last thing that the two of them had shared. If only his father could return soon — even though he dreaded telling him that he had lost their book — that would help make it right.

•

General Richard O'Connor was caught in a curious crossfire between elation and frustration. The elation came, of course, because of the extraordinary success of his troops in the previous two months, advancing west across North Africa and sweeping all the Italians before them, culminating in the Italian surrender at Beda Fomm.

The frustration was because GHQ in Cairo would not let him finish the job. The way to Tripoli was now open, the possibility being that the

Italians could be entirely cleared out of North Africa, and yet the British War Cabinet was insisting that O'Connor's war-hardened troops now be taken from him and sent to a highly dubious venture into Greece instead!

In desperation pure, O'Connor decided to send one of his most trusted senior officers, Brigadier Eric Dorman-Smith, back to Cairo to make a last-minute plea to the Commander in Chief Middle East, General Wavell, to see if there was any possibility that sanity might prevail despite everything. After all, O'Connor felt he already had the tools, and he just wanted to be able to finish the job without having them snatched away!

And so, at ten o'clock on the morning of 12 February, Dorman-Smith arrived at the large, grey, pillared building surrounded by barbed wire in Garden City that housed General Headquarters Middle East — sometimes unkindly known as 'Headquarters Muddle East' — the veritable nerve centre for all the Allied Forces in that part of the globe. He found Wavell in the enormous Map Room, but this was not at all like he had seen it the last time he was there. Then, it had been full of large maps of North Africa, together with minutely detailed maps of various towns and landforms that their troops had fought in along the way. Now, all that was gone. Now, everywhere, were maps of Greece!

Greeting him, Wavell airily waved his hand at all the maps and said, 'You find me busy with my spring campaign.'[47]

And so he was. Despite that, Wavell still heard Dorman-Smith out and was convinced enough to give it one more go, by cabling the British Prime Minister and passing on O'Connor's request.

It was not to be. The cable from Churchill in reply, arriving the following day, was firm: the troops were to go to Greece, and that was that was (*Churchillian growl*) that. It had been Churchill's instruction to his Foreign Minister, Anthony Eden, that it was Britain's 'duty to fight, and, if need be, suffer with Greece',[48] and nothing could change that. And, as there were no British troops available to fulfil that duty, there was nothing for it but for the Australian and New Zealand troops to go and do the suffering.

In the meantime, the gains in North Africa would have to be garrisoned by what Wavell termed 'the minimum possible force'[49] and, after some to-ing and fro-ing, that minimum force turned out to be the Australian 9th Division, together with a small, weak British armoured brigade and some artillery support.

Gutted, O'Connor accepted the ruling extremely reluctantly. He at least, shortly thereafter, became the General Officer Commanding of all the British Troops Egypt, known as BTE. In short order the senior military officer of eastern Libya was one of his close friends, Lieutenant General Sir Philip Neame VC, who based himself in the beautiful small town of Barce — all white stone, broad boulevards, gardens, stone porticos and cool colonnades of classic Italian colonial architecture, surrounded by a wonderfully fertile plain — situated about 90 miles northeast of Benghazi. (The weirdest thing of all for many of the Australian soldiers who passed through the town was that many of Barce's main streets were lined, for reasons unfathomed, with gumtrees and wattles, the latter of which were in bloom. It would fair dinkum make a man *weep* with homesickness, and some of them did.[50])

As a soldier, Neame had been no slouch, having won a Victoria Cross in the Great War in France, in an action in which he had held off the advancing enemy for forty-five minutes single-handedly, then rescued all his wounded. In happier circumstances but with much the same rifle, he had even won an Olympic Gold Medal for shooting in the 1924 Olympics. Yet, as this was his first major command at this kind of level, and he had absolutely no background in desert warfare, it would have to remain to be seen how he would go at it. Neame settled in at his own pace, aware — as he had been told by the Intelligence staff at GHQ in Cairo — that he was in command of a fairly quiet area, or 'passive battle zone, with no possible enemy threats . . .'[51]

CHAPTER SEVEN

Enter, *the* German General

Krieg ohne Hass (War without hate) . . .

ROMMEL IS SAID TO HAVE SO CHARACTERISED THE AFRICAN CAMPAIGN

*This great tract . . . stretched with apparent indefiniteness over the face of
the continent. Level plains of smooth sand — a little rosier than buff,
a little paler than salmon, are interrupted only by occasional peaks of rock:
black, stark and shapeless. Rainless storms dance tirelessly over the hot crisp
surface of the ground. The fine sand, driven by the wind, gathers into deep
drifts among the dark rocks of the hills, exactly as snow hangs about an
alpine summit; only it is fiery snow such as might fall in hell. The earth
burns with the quenchless thirst of ages and in the steel-blue sky scarcely a
cloud obstructs the unrelenting triumph of the sun . . .*

WINSTON CHURCHILL, DESCRIBING NORTH AFRICA DURING THE OMDURMAN
CAMPAIGN IN WHICH HE FOUGHT IN THE LATE NINETEENTH CENTURY[1]

Lights. Huge ones. Down by the harbour. From the rest of Tripoli, enveloped in a strictly enforced total blackout in an attempt to thwart British bombers, it looked as though a volcano was spewing forth light into the night and sending it cascading down upon the wharves. What was going *on*?

It was the Germans. Lots of them — the bulk of them from the 5th Light's 3rd Reconnaissance Battalion — the first in what would be a great series of waves of Hitler's finest hitting North African shores in the next few days and weeks, unloading from the ships themselves, among other things, their twenty-five armoured cars, as they were bathed in floodlights.

Standing a small way off, alone and somehow regal in his bearing, was a man in the military uniform of German High Command, and with something more besides. For around his throat, and catching some of the light, hung the oh-so-coveted glittering blue and gold Maltese Cross of the Pour le Mérite, together with a Knight's Cross.

It was, of course, General Erwin Rommel — who'd flown in two days previously, on 12 February 1941 — and it was a measure of the man, and his command, that for an operation like this he did not need to utter a single word, issue an order, or barely raise an eyebrow. Superbly trained and effortlessly efficient, his troops filed off the ships, immediately formed up into their sections, platoons and companies, and then helped with the unloading of the 6000 tonnes of supplies themselves. By the first light of dawn the following morning the whole job was done, with the locals noting that the Germans had beaten the time it had usually taken for an Italian division to unload, form up and be operational by ten days. It was an impressive effort, and bode well for the immediate future. With the mighty German war machine now landed in Libya, how long could it be before the infernal British were hunted from these parts?

Extraordinarily, despite the arrival of Rommel and the first of his troops — a fact known to damn nigh everyone in Tripoli, especially after the Germans staged a big and showy parade through the main street of the Libyan capital just the morning after their arrival — the high British military leadership in General Headquarters Middle East in Cairo remained entirely unaware of it. In all of Tripoli, they had not a single intelligence agent, informant, spy or set of friendly eyes and ears that they were in touch with. No matter that all of Cairo was awash with Italian agents reporting the Allies' every move — in a full-on attempt to provide not even the *slightest* provocation for Mussolini to declare war on the Allies, the British Intelligence Service chiefs had deliberately not placed any intelligence agents in the Italian colonies, and by the time Italy had declared war it was too late to get up to speed.

The bottom line, however, was that there was now more than one whirlwind on the North African desert, apart from the the infamously dirty wind of the desert, the *khamsin*. For, on the day of his arrival, in his first meeting with his nominal Italian superior, Generale d'Armata Italo Gariboldi — an enormous man with a bristling white moustache who, like so many Italian officers, at least looked the part of a great military leader — Rommel expressed his desire to get stuck straight in and begin to move his troops to the east as soon as they arrived, only to have the Italian attempt to douse his flames.

'*Ma, no!*'

One of the problems, Gariboldi said, with much hand waving and no little force of expression, was that Rommel didn't understand desert warfare and it would take time.

'There is no such thing as "desert" warfare,' Rommel snapped in reply, only just managing to restrain himself. 'War is war, wherever you are. The only difference is that the desert allows more scope for manoeuvre and a war of movement. But only the offensive pays. We must strike where the enemy is least expecting us by outflanking him.'[2]

Still, Gariboldi would not be swayed, insisting that even if all warfare were the same, it would still take Rommel *molto tempo* to get to know the terrain he was fighting on.

This was no problem, Rommel replied.

'It won't take me long to know the country,' he told Gariboldi. 'I'll take a look at it from the air this afternoon and report back to the High Command this evening.'[3]

With which, he left.

It was a significant beginning for the way their relationship would run. For even though Gariboldi was nominally Rommel's superior, the German cared little for such niceties. It wasn't quite that Rommel felt he was entirely his own man, but he was certainly Hitler's man and that, he felt, gave him a great deal of latitude — not to mention longitude — both of which he intended to push as far as he could through North Africa, into Egypt.

Which is exactly the direction Rommel was heading in just a few hours later. In a Heinkel 111 plane, he was sweeping down over the desert east of Tripoli, pushing further east still, and earnestly examining both the terrain and the shabby groups of disconsolate Italian soldiers who seemed to be scattered around in a rough, random manner. Just like all the rest of the Italian infantry Rommel had seen since first arriving, they looked ill disciplined, unkempt, ill led and, most of all, already defeated. He held small hope that the Italians already on the ground in North Africa would prove to be much help in doing what needed to be done, and was more glad than ever that the fresh German and Italian divisions were already on their way.

In parts, however, the terrain itself looked more promising, and he was quite taken with the country around the Gulf of Sirte, where he was able to confirm the view that he had already formed from minutely studying such maps as were available: that it would only take a relatively small, disciplined force to block the road near the coast, and such was the unforgiving nature of the terrain on either side that the Allied forces would not be easily able to go further. The area around the small outpost of El Agheila — 750 kilometres east of Tripoli — was especially significant, as in that whole

Western Desert it was balanced precariously between the Mediterranean to its north and the Great Sand Sea just 10 kilometres to its south. Whoever controlled El Agheila, therefore, controlled a crucial gateway on the east–west axis of North Africa. But why had the British stopped at that gate if they intended to go on with it? Why — particularly when Tripoli itself beckoned before them, just 750 kilometres of good road ahead?

With such a plum there for the plucking, it could only be because they weren't capable of going on, either because their own supply lines were exhausted across such a vast stretch of desert, or because their situation had changed in some other way. Perhaps because of a lack of will to continue by the high British command? Whatever it was, Rommel decided that the sooner he could get the bulk of his men heading east, the better it would be ...

With his senior staff, he began to make plans even as, in short order, the roar of aircraft overhead indicated that the first of the Stuka dive bombers and the twin-engined Messerschmitt 110s, from the Luftwaffe's *Fliegerkorps X*, had begun to arrive in Tripoli to what would be their new base ... for a couple of days, until they too would be sent winging to their east.

•

Whenever Lieutenant General Thomas Blamey was seriously angered, first his moustache would bristle, then his eyebrows would rise and fall, as new aspects of the fresh provocation occurred to him, and soon it seemed as if his whole body was *vibrating* in stiff-backed outrage. This was just such an occasion.

For, ever since this war had begun, he had agitated for Australian troops to remain as far as possible under Australian command. As a veteran of the Great War, Blamey knew better than most that the casualty rate of Australian soldiers when under British command was much higher than that which the British soldiers suffered under their own — with 72 per cent of Australian troops either killed or wounded over the course of the war, as opposed to just 44 per cent of the Brits. So often it had been the Australians who had been given the all-but-impossible line to hold, the extremely well-held hill to storm, the suicidal beach to hit ...

For Blamey it was, too, a matter of national identity and pride. Yes, he was proud that Australia was a part of the British Empire and fighting in its interests, but given that he was confident that both Australian soldiery and its leadership were every bit as good as their British counterparts, why shouldn't they be one corps, under one commander — him?

This view had taken hold to the point that, up until just a few weeks before, the plan had been for the '1st Australian Corps' to be established at Tobruk under his command, but then, when the 6th Division had continued to pursue the Italians to El Agheila under General Richard O'Connor, that had been temporarily put on hold.

And now, *this*. Just when he had thought that the 6th would soon be back in his bailiwick, he had been peremptorily summoned to Cairo to be informed by General Wavell that the 6th was now going to be sent to Greece, *with* the 7th Division *and* his own Corps Headquarters, fighting with Poles and New Zealanders, all of them under the overall command of British General Sir Henry Maitland Wilson. What was more, Wavell claimed that he had discussed it all with Robert Menzies just before he left Cairo, and no significant objection had been raised.

Blamey was stunned. And not just because, as he would later claim in a letter to a colleague, in his view 'The Greek expedition hadn't a dog's chance from the start'.[4]

It was just that four days previously he had himself had a strong conversation with Menzies, during which he had made the point to his Prime Minister that 'Australian forces must be regarded as national, under national command. This does not exclude the use of smaller units in special places, but all must be subject to my own consent, as the General Officer Commanding of the AIF.' And Menzies had seemed to agree. What was incomprehensible, however, and would remain so for generations to come, was why the Australian Prime Minister — who had first heard of the possibility of the Greek venture even before leaving Australia — never discussed the virtues or otherwise of such a campaign while consulting on myriad matters of much lesser importance with his senior military man on site!

At that point, though, all that mattered was that Blamey had been given his orders, and he had to follow them. (And this rather high-handed approach to the Australians was not untypical of Wavell. The Australian journalist Alan Moorehead had been present when the Commander in Chief had addressed the first arrivals on a troopship at Suez, in February 1940. 'I am very glad to have Australian troops under MY command, and I am sure MY orders will be carried out,' said Wavell. As Moorehead noted dryly, 'The capitals are the General's.'[5])

None of this, however, prevented Blamey from subsequently writing a letter to Prime Minister Menzies, raising some points that continued to gnaw at him: 'The whole of the fighting troops are Australian and New Zealand. It is clear that, broadly speaking, the fighting is the function of the

Dominion troops while supply and Lines of Communication is the main function of the British ... Past experience has taught me to look with misgiving on a situation where British leaders have control of considerable bodies of first-class dominion troops while dominion commanders are excluded from all responsibility in control, planning and policy.'[6]

Menzies would not be moved, maintaining then, as he maintained later, that as pertained to the Greek venture, 'Australia was not likely to refuse to take a great risk in a good cause'.[7] And certainly not on his watch.

Besides which, Menzies had only agreed on the express condition that the Australian infantry be given 'a fighting chance', which included the British providing adequate air cover for the Australian troops. It was Menzies' view that it was better that the 6th and 7th be sent to Greece, to honour the British commitment to that country, than stay in North Africa, where there was really very little left to do now that the Italians had been cleaned up.

·

Well, bugger him. In the heated haze of mid afternoon, 17 February, Corporal Harry Short of the King's Dragoon Guards was just doing a routine patrol in his tiny Marmon-Harrington armoured car — oft known as 'a tin can on wheels' — on the coast road just west of El Agheila when he saw what, for the life of him, really looked like a trail of dust even further out to the west. He had the driver stop to get a better squiz, and brought his binoculars to bear.[8]

It was a trail of dust, a tiny wisp of worry on the far, high horizon, that was ... could it really be? ... yes, it certainly seemed to be ... heading towards him. But who the devil could that be? Harry knew he was the westernmost patrol at that moment, and he also knew that the Ities, who'd taken a right royal belting in this area ten days ago, had been last seen heading west as fast as their little legs could carry them. It wouldn't be like the Italians to be coming back this way, so who could it be?

He wouldn't have to wait too long to find out. At some speed the Corporal got his vehicle behind a sand dune and then climbed up the top to see what he could see. Presently the gentle hum of an engine in the distance could be heard, coming in alternate crescendos and diminutions, as its path rose and fell, and then finally in the far distance he saw a vehicle slowly beginning to take shape out of the shimmer. Fading, forming, fading and then forming more solidly, it was soon apparent that it was some kind of enormous behemoth with eight wheels, clearly designed for desert travel, and right in its centre was an enormous gun. Still coming towards him, still coming, still coming, and ... stop.

By pure happenstance, the armed reconnaissance vehicle — for that, it now dawned on him, was clearly what it was — had come to a halt on a dune opposite the one where Harry lay breathing heavily, and men got out. And well-formed, muscular men they were, too, with peaked caps, talking animatedly and looking to the east. If they weren't Germans then Harry was a bloomin' monkey's uncle, that was what he was. They looked like Germans, felt like Germans, and though they were too far away to hear, he was damn sure they would bloody well sound like Germans! And, most importantly, they would go into his report as Germans.

They were Germans, just west of El Agheila, who looked and acted like far-forward scouts who'd come to have a look at just what kind of terrain and defences might be in their way, before turning their vehicle round and heading back again — no doubt to make their own report.

•

It wasn't that Harry was necessarily disbelieved back at camp, but the most that can be said is that his report did not cause alarm bells to ring across North Africa to the effect that *the Germans are coming! The Germans are coming!*

In fact, nothing happened at all — in London, at the very time this encounter had taken place, the War Cabinet had been in the process of formally committing to the dispatch of tens of thousands of soldiers out of the heat of the backblocks of North Africa and Egypt and into the new hot spot of Greece. Still, just a few days later, three British scout cars were amazed to come over the coast road at much the same possie as Harry had, to find three of those strange eight-wheeled vehicles heading straight for them, together with men on motorcycles and a truck with machine guns. Shots were fired from both sides without much bloodshed. Both sides retreated to their corners and quiet reigned, bar one small skirmish that occurred later that night, with a similar result.

Now Harry Short's original report started to carry a little more weight, at least among his own regiment. However, getting people further back from the front lines to start to take these reports seriously proved a little more problematic. For, if nothing else, such reports created great merriment back at GHQ in Cairo, where senior staff positively *fell about* at the news that some of the new arrivals had mistaken Italians for Germans. The very thought!

For, at a meeting of the War Cabinet in London — held, as ever, in the basement of the Office of Works building, opposite St James Park and roughly midway between Parliament and 10 Downing Street — the subject of the El Agheila skirmish came up, and it was Winston Churchill himself who took the lead, as recorded in the minutes.

'It would be a mistake,' he said, from his enormous chair at the head of the table, 'to draw pessimistic conclusions from the fact that British and German armoured vehicles have clashed in Libya. The German forces were driven back; there is no indication that they are preparing for any significant actions, let alone an attack across the Libyan desert. It is not known how many of these German mechanised units have been brought to Libya ...'[9]

In short, it was nowhere near yet time to draw any conclusion that the denuding of eastern Libya of experienced Allied troops and sending them to an ill-fated campaign in Greece was going to see a calamitous advance of the German Army in Africa. And, even if it was a calamity, it wasn't one of Churchill's making.

•

Christ Almighty!

What was going on?

Now bloody Blamey had just made a sudden and rather offhand announcement that the entire make-up of the 9th Division was to be changed. It had been composed of the 18th and 25th Brigades arriving from Britain to join up with the 24th Brigade, which was already in Africa, but Blamey now announced that the 18th and 25th would be transferred to the 7th, while the 20th and 26th Brigades of the 7th Division would now became part of the 9th Division!

It was enough to make a bloke's head hurt, just trying to follow it all — who was who, what was what and who went where. Yes, at the time that Blamey made the announcement he said it was a 'temporary expedient' only, but that didn't make it easier to bear. Look, it all might have been just numbers to some people, but for many of the soldiers those numbers meant a lot, and were a large part of their self-identification. Changing it at the stroke of a pen — and, worse, making that number *higher* — did not sit easily with them.

As a matter of fact, there was an entire culture in the Australian Army at this time, whereby the lower number you had, the more prestige you were due. Everyone got an enlistment number when they joined up, and if your number was lower than another bloke's, it meant you had joined before him. In such stakes, there were only seven men in New South Wales who could have won boasting rights over Lieutenant General Morshead, for example, as his enlistment number of NX8 indicated that he was just the eighth man from New South Wales to join the 2nd AIF. (Had he been from Victoria, the first letters would have been VX, Western Australia WX, Queensland QX and so forth.) Similarly, men cherished the honour of being a part of the lower-numbered battalions and brigades, *and* divisions.

The blokes from the 6th Division, for example, referred to those in the 7th Divvie as 'the deep thinkers', noting how long it had bloody well taken them to make their minds up to join, and the 7th felt themselves up a notch or two on the blokes of the 8th Divvie. What were they going to say about blokes from the 9th Divvie? It bloody well wasn't fair, and there was a good bit of bellyaching about it.

●

Morshead was pleased. He had received a letter from home from his wife and daughter, both clearly thrilled at his elevation to Divisional Commander. He replied to his daughter, in his careful hand:

I am glad that you and mummy got such a thrill and I can well imagine the excitement on discovering the news in the paper. I had heard a few days previously although others knew some time before me because I was right forward at the time where the postman and telegraph boy doesn't call very frequently ... Yes it was a very interesting experience in the desert and I have no doubt that I shall be making its further acquaintance. It's not so bad except for the dust and shortage of water ... The beautiful sky is marred at times by the Boche in his dive bomber — he's a squirt isn't he? Just a nark and spoil sport.[10]

●

Shit. Ivor Hancock wasn't too pleased. His mate Norm had just received a letter from his girlfriend, Dorothy, saying that her best friend, Jean Coles — as in, Ivor's girlfriend — was pregnant with Ivor's child! *Up the duff.* A bun in the oven — and it was his. Due in September. Ivor was shell-shocked and not quite sure what to do. He loved Jean all right, and as a matter of fact his love was so great that, after a recent trip to a brothel in Jerusalem, he had made time to go to a back-alley tattooist and have a beautiful tattoo done — of a heart with a dagger through it, to show the pain of separation from the girl of his dreams way back in Australia — with her name, 𝔍𝔢𝔞𝔫, featuring prominently. The problem was that he had got her *into trouble*, and he wasn't there to make it right. What to do?

Ivor decided to go and see his immediate superior officer, Captain Bird, together with the Regimental Medical Officer, to explain the situation. Fortunately, they — gentlemen both — understood straight away that something had to be done and together they quickly decided on the course of action. Both officers knew about Ivor's weak ankle, which had already played up on a couple of occasions, and it was determined that the best thing would be to see if they could get Ivor sent home because of it, so that he could 'do the right thing' and marry the girl before the child was born. Certainly, it would take a bit of paperwork — and that would include ensuring that some of his army pay was immediately redirected towards her on the same basis as a wife's allowance until he could get home to formalise it all — but it could be done. And, besides, Ivor had always been conscious that his father had met his mother in the early stages of the war, when he'd just joined up as a soldier, so — despite how generally unhappy they had subsequently been — it sort of seemed to fit.

Ivor left the meeting feeling a lot better for it. Maybe he would be going home! It would hurt to be separated from the boys, but he couldn't see any way around it.

And yet, as it turned out for the moment at least, his departure to Oz would have to wait. For Ivor had no sooner reported back to Norm, Frankie, Pudden Head, Cocky and the lads what the lie of the land was, than orders came through. The 2/24th Battalion, and indeed all of the 9th Division, was to move out on the double. Though unconfirmed, there was a rumour doing the rounds that the 6th Division in Libya was going to go to Greece, and it was going to be the 9th's job to take their positions. No matter that the 9th's artillery regiments were still without guns and so couldn't come; that their nominal cavalry had no Cruisers and so would also remain; that as a division they had three-fifths of bugger-all transport to call their own. The infantry brigades, it was decided, would just have to make the best of it and get going on their own — led by the 20th Brigade — and so they did.

For Ivor, Jean and the baby — and everything else for that matter — would just have to wait a while till they got this thing sorted out.

•

Oh, the sheer pleasure of it!

After months and months in the dirty dust bowl of North Africa — all hazy horizons, sandstorms, surly Arabs, shiver-me-timbers nights and boiling hot days — to be once again in Europe was not far short of nirvana. Chester Wilmot had arrived in Greece with the first of the Australian troops of the 6th Division, and as he reported to the ABC listeners at home with as close as he could allow himself to exultation: 'We're in a country where you can walk around the streets for hours without being besieged by touts or by seedy youths selling dirty post-cards. Coming to Greece is like coming to a new world where people wave to you as you go by . . . a country where the people round you are also with you and are fighting for the same cause.'[11]

•

There was movement at the station . . .

Kantara station — the same place the 2/13th and 2/17th had disembarked three months earlier, when their ship had docked there after travelling up the Suez Canal — now saw, in these last days of February and early March 1941, the same soldiers passing through again. This time they were on their way into Egypt, as every third-class carriage groaned with no fewer than seventy-two men, complete with kit. (And you hadn't seen a third-class carriage until you'd seen a third-class Egyptian carriage.) Still, the mood was upbeat. After all that training, at least something was now happening. No, the men didn't know exactly where they were going, but the main thing was that it was somewhere that wasn't just a training camp in Palestine, and was very likely going to be somewhere closer to the fight — in all probability, Greece.

In no time at all they had crossed the mighty Nile — get a load of that, Bluey! — and were heading west into what soon turned out to be, in the words of one of the Diggers, 'miles and miles of fuck-all'.[12]

Seriously, it would make a bloke homesick for the Nullarbor, it would. As they kept moving west, however, the mood lightened a little, as it was now obvious that they weren't heading to Greece or some other place — they were heading to the North African desert that the bloody 6th Divvie had already conquered! After ten months of training, it looked like their job was only going to be to hold on to what had already been won.

That night, arriving at one-thirty in the morning of 2 March, literally at 'the end of the line', the first of the troops bunked down about 200 miles west of Cairo in the bombed-out Egyptian Army barracks — with dust and broken glass inches deep on the floor — at Mersa Matruh. It was a place right on the Mediterranean, and one or two of the more educated of the Australian soldiers recognised it as the same place that Cleopatra used to come to from Alexandria to bathe with the cove called Mark Antony, each seduced by the other, the Mediterranean sun and Mersa Matruh's golden sands. They even reckon Alexander the Great was the one who laid out the town, way back when.

When they woke up, exhausted, the following morning to have a look around, it was clear that if there was a more desolate place on earth they hadn't seen it. The town was perched on the edge of the desert, between the road and the sea, and consisted of a few forlorn little buildings, many of which had taken direct hits from bombs and were now empty shells, encircled by barbed wire and minefields and anti-tank ditches. As for people, all the Diggers could spot were the sad and scattered rump of the Arabs who still lived there, together with some chooks and goats. More than one farmer's son among the Australians looked around, wondering just what it was that those chooks and goats lived on! There was *nothing* there! Not a blade of anything seemed to grow in those parts; the whole place was as dry as a dead dingo's donger, and yet, somehow, just, the local population seemed to hang on.

It was one of the first clues they received as to how important supply was going to be in this North African campaign. In other campaigns it was possible for an army to live off the land, but in this one, in a place where the land gave you just about *nothing*, damn nigh everything needed to keep both men and machinery going — from food to fuel to water, to even something so basic as wood to build their latrines with — was going to have to be brought here from elsewhere. How bad was it? So bad that in this joint you even had to bring your own shade.

Late the next day, the Australians of the 20th Brigade — which is to say, the 2/17th Battalion, 2/13th Battalion and the 2/15th Battalion, which had now joined them — were transferred into the motley collection of clapped-out trucks that awaited them and now motored on, and on and on and on, seventeen men to a truck, going through and past such outposts as Sollum, Fort Capuzzo, Sidi Rezegh, Bardia and Ed Duda.

In that vast ocean of nowhere that seemed to be most of Cyrenaica, the town of Tobruk was at least somewhere, and all the men knew of it as the place that the mighty 6th Division had captured a couple of months earlier. Physically, the place appeared chiefly notable for what looked like a goodish harbour, with a ship by its shore still smoking from some attack or other. Still, it was clear that some ships were now able to get into the harbour and unload, as fully laden trucks were now coming out of it and heading to the front with the Australians. After only a short stop — which included watching some of the extreme optimists scouring a few of the battered and broken buildings to see if maybe the 6th Divvie had overlooked some stocks of Chianti, alas to no effect — they were on their way again and pushing further west, on to Benghazi. Truthfully, the 20th Brigade wasn't too unhappy to leave Tobruk. Even in the short time they had been there, something the Arabs called a 'khamsin' had blown up — which, translated into Australian, meant a 'bloody awful sandstorm where you couldn't see a bloody thing'. This, they were told, was something of a local feature of Tobruk, and they were glad to leave it all in their wake as they continued to the west. Not too far behind, much of the 9th Division was proceeding on the same course.

•

They were a small gathering of the nomadic Bedouin people, in an encampment just a little off the road leading into Derna from the east, on a morning in the early days of March 1941 — not that specific calendar dates meant anything to them. They were of the desert, and measured time only by the passing of the three major seasons of the year: hot and dusty; extremely hot and dusty; not quite so hot, but still very dusty.

The Australians of the 9th Division saw them as they continued in their long truck convoy on their journey west.

And in turn the Bedouin saw the Australians, the colourfully garbed women briefly looking up from their cooking pots . . .

Before looking down again.

Foreigners had come to this land before.

Foreigners had left this land before.

And then more foreigners had come.

But the time would come when they would go too. The Bedouin were a people who lived in a landscape dotted with ruins left by past occupiers, from the Romans to the Greek to the Byzantines and Turks. All had crumbled and gone. So, too, ultimately, would these new occupiers.

So it was. So it had always been.

The Bedouin were still here, though, and pretty happily so, thanks.[13] And would remain, whatever fights these strange newcomers, trailing yet more dust, had between themselves.

•

Lieutenant Heinz Schmidt was caught between being frightfully intimidated and terribly impressed.

Just a couple of hours earlier he had arrived from the Eritrean front in East Africa, and was now due to meet *Generalleutnant* Erwin Rommel for the first time, in his room in Tripoli's luxurious Hotel Uaddan. As the South African-born Schmidt would describe in a book of his reminiscences published a decade later, *With Rommel in the Desert*, Rommel impressed him as a man with 'a powerful handshake. Blue grey eyes. Humour wrinkles. An energetic, vital personality.'

Their first talk had seemed to go fine-ish, to a point. And that point was reached when, in response to Rommel's question about what the situation in Eritrea was like for the German Army, he had reported honestly to his superior officer that it was very bad.

Then, suddenly, the humour lines seemed to flatten and disappear into a tight, taut visage.

'What do you know about it, anyway, *Herr Leutnant?*' Rommel had come straight back at him, standing and leaning forward over him with his hands behind his back in what Schmidt would soon find was his classic manner. 'We shall reach the Nile, make a right turn and win back everything.'

Yes, sir, if you say so.

And Rommel *did* say so, appointing Schmidt as his adjutant — effectively his offsider officer whose job it was to assist him in just about everything.

Now, just a couple of hours later, in a large conference room at the same hotel, Rommel was preparing to say much the same thing to thirty senior German officers of the 5th Light Division, who had just arrived in Tripoli and were getting their bearings. A fine-figured bunch of men, with a long list of extraordinary military successes behind them in Poland and France — the hard-won medals of which now adorned their black Panzer Group uniforms — they all jumped to their feet the moment Rommel entered the room. For many of them, it was the first time they had been able to get a look in the flesh at this man who had recently made more headlines in Germany than just about any other, bar Hitler himself.

But hark . . .

'*Meine Herrn*,' Rommel began, once he had given them permission to sit down and they had carefully done so, 'I am pleased to know that after many strenuous days the gentlemen of the 5th Panzer Regiment are now in Tripoli almost up to full strength. With the arrival of your Panzers the situation in North Africa will be stabilised. The enemy's thrust towards Tripolitania has been brought to a standstill. Our reconnaissance units under Lieutenant Colonel Wegmar have reached the Italians' advanced positions on the Gulf of Sirte at El Agheila, and have morally and materially strengthened the front. It is our task to restore the confidence of the Italian people in their arms, and bolster up the fighting spirit of our allies.'[14]

When Rommel addressed his men in this forceful fashion, he was mesmerising, pausing between sentences for dramatic effect while still remaining short-sharp-and-to-the-point and using energetic facial gestures for emphasis. And while, in the course of his address, Rommel was properly respectful of the Führer, he clearly remained his own man and didn't labour the point, as some senior officers did, that their role was to win victories for the greater glory of Hitler and the Fatherland. They were military professionals, with a job to do, and they must do it. Too, while Rommel was clearly very confident in both his and their abilities, there was no language of hate from him towards the enemy. There was no call to beat the English because they were some bastard race that needed to be wiped out. To the contrary, it was clear the British had Rommel's respect — quite probably much more than the Italians did — and it was for that reason the Germans would have to be all the more assiduous to beat them.

'You will not have very much time to get acclimatised and to get to know the desert,' Rommel said as he began to wind up his address. 'But time is of the essence; we must seize the initiative and keep it. Our campaign begins tomorrow ... the desert is waiting for us. We are about to embark on a great safari!'[15]

At this point, a young officer jumped to his feet once more and shouted, '*Heia Safari!*' Let's go on a safari!

The cry was taken up by most of the others in the room. '*Heia Safari! Heia Safari! Heia Safari!*'

Rommel was clearly held in awe by many of the men he led, with the certain exception of General Johannes Streich, the commander of the 5th Light Division, who still held many reservations about this man who was going to guide them in North Africa. Just two years ago Rommel had been nought but an instructor in the German Army who'd written a book that had gone surprisingly well, and though the same age, back then Streich had been far Rommel's superior in rank. But such were the vagaries of war, Rommel had not only rocketed high in the ranks but had also been turned

ABOVE War photographers swore it was almost impossible to capture the intensity of a sandstorm. The Arabs called it a *khamsin*, the Germans called it a *Sandsturm* and the Australians called it 'bloody awful'. When the wind howled, dirt was blown into eyes, ears, noses and clothing for days, and according to the Aussies, you 'couldn't see a bloody thing!' The British guns coped better with the sand than the German guns.

BELOW Hitler made Rommel *Generalleutnant* and Commander of the 7th Panzer Division in North Africa in 1940. After Rommel's campaign in France, Hitler had great confidence in the man from Heidenheim. Even later, when members of the Führer's General Staff turned against Rommel, Hitler continued to support him.

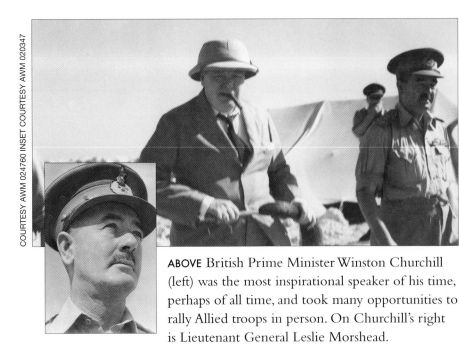

ABOVE British Prime Minister Winston Churchill (left) was the most inspirational speaker of his time, perhaps of all time, and took many opportunities to rally Allied troops in person. On Churchill's right is Lieutenant General Leslie Morshead.

INSET Morshead worked as a schoolmaster before the war, joined the 1st AIF, and was among the initial troops to hit the beaches at Gallipoli on 25 April 1915, where he quickly began to forge a reputation as a first-class military man, and then to rise through the ranks.

BELOW General Sir Thomas Blamey had, like Morshead, landed at Gallipoli on the morning of 25 April 1915. He began the Great War as a Major, finished it as a Brigadier General and was chosen by Prime Minister Menzies to lead the Australian Army in WWII.

ABOVE Jack Edmondson joined the 4th Battalion of the CMF in 1939 when he was twenty-five years old. He came from Liverpool near Sydney, was trained in Ingleburn and left for Palestine from Woolloomooloo on the *Queen Mary* in September 1940. His mother was appalled when people in Sydney celebrated a minor war victory with champagne, even though Australian soldiers had been killed, and there remained so much fighting to do. **RIGHT** Jack Edmondson was an only child. At school he developed a passion for Greek and Roman history. He especially liked the Greeks, whom he considered 'kind and brave'.

ABOVE LEFT John Johnson, father of eight, went to war to do his duty, with the added hope that it might make it easier for him, as a returned soldier, to get a parcel of land for his family. **ABOVE RIGHT** On the day John left, the family posed for a picture in front of their house. **INSET** This photo of baby Jocelyn Johnson was sent to John in North Africa, and he kept it close thereafter. He had not seen his eighth and youngest child before he left Walwa in Victoria.

BELOW John Johnson before his departure from Walwa on Friday, 25 October 1940, standing proudly by the car that would take him away to the war.

ABOVE LEFT AND RIGHT Mates of the 2/23rd Battalion Pat Joy and Alan Kelly were, like John Johnson, from Walwa in Victoria. The three men stuck together in Palestine and Tobruk, sharing the news from home they received in letters from their loved ones, and drawing strength from each other. **BELOW LEFT** Just before the call came for his battalion to go overseas, Private Ivor Hancock of the 2/24th Battalion went AWL to see his girlfriend, rejoining his comrades right before they sailed. **BELOW RIGHT** Rolf Völker of the *Schützenregiment* 104 was sent home to Germany from North Africa to recover after grenade splinters hit him in the back and the buttocks. In the field hospital his comrades joked: 'This happens when you run away from the Tommys!'

COURTESY BERT FERRES

ABOVE As the *Queen Mary* continued on its way bearing the Australian soldiers towards the Middle East, its escort, HMAS *Perth*, went racing down the convoy line in farewell, signalling 'Goodbye'.

BELOW Among Australian soldiers of the 7th Division headed to the Middle East there was generally an impatience to get to grips with the enemy, and a confidence that they would return safely. **INSET** The emblem of the 9th Australian Division.

9th Aust. Division

COURTESY AWM 009532

ABOVE 'I'm proud to be an Aussie,' an Australian soldier wrote to his mother from Tobruk. 'There's something different about them. The Hun fights with grim determination, the Tommies fight by numbers, but the Aussies tear about like kids at a picnic, swearing and laughing the whole time.'

BELOW Locals had seen warriors come and go like desert storms. In WWII, they supported the Allies, then the Axis, then the Allies again, with cheering and much selling of goods, such as clothing and photos.

ABOVE AND BELOW Rommel's camper van, an adapted Opel Blitz bus, from which many orders were issued.

into a bona fide idol of the German people. This was, admittedly, in part because of his exceptional success, but also because Hitler's propaganda genius, Joseph Goebbels, had understood the power of having a hero like Rommel and had ramped up the promotion of his legend to the public.

Now, though Streich could be extremely prickly and was not known for his great diplomacy, he said very little out loud on this occasion. Privately, however, he was far from convinced that Rommel was equal to the position he held, or worthy of such widespread adulation.

For all that, there could be no argument that it was an impressive feat for Rommel to have his men moving eastwards *en masse* within forty-eight hours of their arrival . . .

(And though Tripoli at that time was awash with brothels, they received precious little patronage from the Afrika Korps. Those *Damen*, Rommel made clear, were strictly *verboten*, and that was the end of it.[16])

•

Getting closer to their destination now and the country was starting to look a little easier to the eye. The Australian troops of the 20th Brigade were well west of Derna, in the spot where the Italian settlers had not merely parked themselves and held on — as they had in such places as Tobruk — but in fact had really made something of the land. To the Diggers' amazement, they now saw green farms abounding all around, with neat white houses surrounded by gardens in which bougainvillea flourished beside equally flowery bushes, with fences, hedges, dams, banana plantations, pomegranate groves, goatherds — the lot. And also blooming were many of those Italian settlers and their offspring — sometimes, when the soldiers were lucky, they saw gorgeous young Italian women — who were now all watching the Australians with a wary eye. There were very few, if any, young Italian men there, as they had long ago been called up to the army, but many of the older settlers had been in these parts for forty years, and were proud of what they and the 100 000 other Italian settlers had built up from just about nothing — and their chief hope seemed to be that the war would just go away. Hopefully the Italians and Germans would win, but if the Allies won, so be it, so long as they could be left alone to run their farms, raise their children and live their lives 'neath the African sun.

The Australians kept moving to the west, passing close by the ruins of the Roman town of Cyrene, which for 2000 years had been able to sustain one million people by the food produced in its environs, and the whole area had in fact been known as 'the breadbasket of the Roman Empire'.

•

Getting closer to their destination now — wherever that was. For the latest arrivals of the Afrika Korps, everything had happened so quickly that it was hard to know from one day to the next where they would be by sunup ... and then sundown. Just a few days before they had been training in Germany, before being told to quickly get on trains that had come into the station named Güterbahnhof Angermünde and which were meant to take them to 'exercises in Romania'. (Not that anyone had believed that any more after they had finished loading a whole lot of tropical equipment.) Then, once departed, they were told they were really going to Africa, which had been well received, as many of them had visited the famous Berlin Zoo as kids and were keen to see lions and elephants and hippos in their natural jungle habitat. And then they had landed in grotty Tripoli, with barely any vegetation to be seen, and had been put overnight in Kilometre 5, a camp so disgusting — filthy stone barracks without doors or windows — that most preferred to spend their first night out under the stars. And now here they were, already racing to the east, well out of wretched Tripoli, and seeing different things. Generally, their mood was upbeat, off on *das grosse Abenteuer* (the great adventure), as they referred to it among themselves. As recorded by one of their number: 'Despite all strains — the impressions of the desert remain unforgettable: the unreal, constantly changing colours of the desert, especially in the morning and evening hours, their variety and harsh beauty, even in the glowing midday heat and in the cold nights; the romance of the oases with their palm trees, wells and the quiet, white houses.'[17]

Somewhere up ahead lay the Gulf of Sirte, where they were to supposedly stop for a while, to either train or dig in — they were not yet sure.

•

Lieutenant General Morshead did not really warm to Lieutenant General Sir Philip Neame, the man he was now obliged to answer to. It wasn't anything he could quite put his finger on, but certainly a part of it was a sense the Sydney man had developed that the senior British officer just did not like Australians that much, and was not necessarily confident in the fighting abilities of the 'colonials' when left to their own devices. And that was certainly the impression Morshead got now, after he had come on just ahead of his troops and was meeting Neame at his headquarters in Barce on the morning of 7 March 1941, to discuss where the Australian troops would be situated when they arrived.

In fact, the meeting had got off to a troubled start when Neame informed Morshead rather offhandedly that the newly arrived Australians would be placed up near the border with Tripolitania and shortly thereafter he wanted Morshead and his headquarters to withdraw to supervise the rest of the 9th Division in their training up in the area around Gazala. At that point, he said, Australia's 20th Brigade would be placed under the command of Major General Michael Gambier-Parry of Britain's 2nd Armoured Division — which was then also in the process of replacing a battered and exhausted 7th Armoured Division, which had never quite recovered from its dash cross-country the month before. (In fact, the incoming 2nd Armoured Division was only about half the size of a genuine armoured division, as half of its tanks had already been sent to Greece.)

Appalled that his own brigade would not be under his control, Morshead was upfront with Neame, coming right out and telling him, 'I am not impressed with this arrangement. No mention of such a proposal has been made to me by GHQ or General Blamey.'[18]

Still Neame would not be swayed, insisting that he would personally sort it out with General Blamey when he went to Cairo on the morrow.

But he didn't.

•

If only more dreams could be like that. It was her Jack, all dressed in white for some reason. But he had come to her, and he was *there*, and even in the semi-darkness she could see him. And when Elizabeth Edmondson spoke to him, Jack gave her his usual happy smile in return — beaming, absolutely beaming with his love and his presence. And, yes, it was only a dream, but Elizabeth was somehow nourished by it. Quite where he was — exactly what he was doing — she couldn't be sure, even though she scanned every day's papers assiduously. All she knew was that she missed him terribly, and that dreams like that somehow helped her to get through.[19]

•

They were there. Early in the second week of March, the 20th Brigade — which was the first to arrive from the 9th Division — effectively took over in western Cyrenaica the positions of the remnants of the 6th Division who had not departed for Greece. Inevitably, as they did so there was a lot of, usually, good-natured leg-pulling.

'Well, well, welllllll, here come the "rainbows"!' the blokes of the 6th Divvie often called upon first spying the new arrivals.

'Rainbows?' the new arrivals inquired the first time they heard it.

'Yeah, y'know, *rainbows* — they always come out *after the storm is over!*'

And so it went . . .

'Where the hell have you lot been?' a 6th Division soldier with flaming red hair bellowed out to the convoy in which Bert Ferres and much of the 2/13th were travelling. 'You were a bit long hearing the bugle, weren't you? The war here is bloody *over!*'

Laugh? *Laugh?* The 2/13th and the rest of the 9th Divvie thought they'd never start. Never mind. In short order the men of the 6th — many of them complete with beautiful Italian leather jackets, shining and totally unused Italian bayonets, and lots of other souvenirs of war — were getting in either their own trucks or, as often as not, the very same trucks the 9th had borrowed to come here, and heading east. (Still, the problem of the 9th being without transport to call its own had not been solved. Promises had been made, and that was all.)

So, where the hell were they, exactly?

A⁺ Lieutenant General Sir Philip Neame's specific instruction, the re' ⌐tant Lieutenant General Morshead had had the 20th Brigade dig in up near what was supposedly the 'front line', about 30 miles northeast of El Agheila, the only spot on that whole area of the North African coast where the natural environment lent itself to mounting a defensive position. The 2/17th took the most forward position, taking over from the 6th Division's 2/7th Battalion just south of the village of Marsa el Brega, while the 2/15th was some 10 miles further back and the 2/13th a bit further back again as Brigade reserve. The notion was that if there was any attack, the 2/17th and 2/15th could bear the brunt, with the 2/13th there as backup. With them, the Australians would have the rump of the British 2nd Armoured Division — about twenty-five light tanks, commanded by Major General Gambier-Parry — and a couple of companies of a Free French motorised battalion, as well as some scattered British units including the 1st and 104th Royal Horse Artillery and the 51st Field Regiment.

All up, it was hardly enough to stop any major thrust by the enemy, but it remained Neame's view that the Australians were unlikely to see much action. Certainly at one point on the Diggers' approach to their present positions there'd been a bit of a spray from five enemy aircraft — and they had tragically lost two good men, killed — but that had seemed like a one-off. So, too, with the one or two reports that had been received about some enemy activity to the west — none of it seemed really to have amounted to much, and the thing is, they were only Ities anyway. Yes, there had clearly been some German planes about, but GHQ was of the view that they were there primarily to protect Italian airfields, even though they would regularly swoop down to shoot up the Australians. The main thing was that the new arrivals of the 9th Division would have plenty of time to get all of their equipment issued and working, and all their training completed, before any heavy demands were placed on them.

For the moment there was nothing for it but to make the best of it. The extremely dusty winds of fortune might have blown them to this lost part of the world, on this God-forgotten bit of ground where nothing much was likely to happen, but that was just the way it was.

Theirs not to reason why, theirs but to do or die.

Probably of boredom . . .

•

In the meantime, what was left of real Allied strength in North Africa continued to depart for Greece. Across the desert, the seasoned troops of the 6th Division streamed east, to get on ships leaving from Alexandria to take them north. In the Mediterranean, gunboats and destroyers steamed either directly north, or via Alexandria to pick up the troops that needed a lift. Above them all, most of the planes that had been so crucial in securing the extraordinary victory of O'Connor's forces roared down runways all through the area where the 9th Division was settling in, sometimes waggled their wings in farewell, and also headed to Athens and points north.

Very quickly Neame was left with no more than ten planes to call on, leaving even basic reconnaissance at its most threadbare. On any given day a maximum of just three sorties were sent out to see what the enemy was up to.

•

Back in Palestine at this point with the rest of the 2/23rd, as they got ready to also start moving, John Johnson took the opportunity to pen another letter to his family, shortly after receiving the thrilling news that he had a new baby daughter, little Josie Jacqueline.

My Dear Family,

Had my usual letter today & all the latest from home — Mum
wrote most of it in hospital. Let me see, Alex had an itch, Don was
stabbed with a piece of charcoal & Barry was bitten by a jackal also
Accar had a bad thumb. Well, what a list of casualties. I hope your
various complaints are a thing of the past and that you are all well
again. I imagine Sylvia holding her little hands out and saying
'nothing' when asked what she has. Then asked what Mummy has,
'A baby thister for me . . .'

Typically, upon receiving the letter Josie Johnson would gather her
children round the kitchen table and read it all out slowly, with each child
smiling broadly and feeling a rush of special warmth when singled out by
their dad for special attention. With this letter there were more lovely lines
with stories from North Africa — the older ones had looked up where it
was on the spinning globe at school — and then their mother squeezed out
the last precious drops of love from afar . . .

Well my dears I'll have to close now with love to you all boys and my
two little girls and Mum. Remember me to all at Walwa. I'm glad
John is liking Melbourne. Love to Gran and Grandad.
        Love to all from your loving Dad[20]

Within just four days, John Johnson and the rest of the 2/23rd had got
the word. And the word was good. They were moving out of their camp in
Palestine, and following the rest of the 9th Division, westward ho.

Though Josie continued to worry herself sick that John would be all right,
one thing consoled her at least a little. It was that the three men from Walwa
— her John, Alan Kelly and Pat Joy — would be able to help look after each
other. John made frequent references to the other two, and in one letter from
him Alan had even added a cheerio, addressing Josie very respectfully and
formally as 'Mrs Johnson', and yet signing it 'love and kisses from your friend,
Alan Kelly', perhaps his way of saying that, because he felt a special bond to her
husband, he also felt a bond to her. Josie felt the same bond to both Alan and
Pat and their families in Walwa, and would frequently compare notes with the
latter as to what they had heard and how the trio was going in North Africa.

•

Now that *was* a little worrying.

For as it happened in these middle days of March, some of the blokes of the 2/15th and 2/17th who'd been patrolling just west of El Agheila were beginning to report signs of enemy activity, as more and more vehicles stirred up dust on the hazy horizon. On 13 March, a Lieutenant from the 2/15th Battalion took a sergeant and eight men, together with a couple of armoured cars from the King's Dragoon Guards and went on a long recce out into the desert, going about 45 miles down to the southwestern approaches to El Agheila.[21] Though they didn't see any Germans, they certainly saw a bloody lot of tank tracks, no doubt about that, and big tanks they must be too. Probably *German* tanks.

There was no concerted thrust or anything, just a growing awareness that they were out there, not far away, and growing in numbers. The real problem was that most of the 9th at this point had bugger-all to defend themselves with. The 6th Divvie had taken most of their weaponry with them to Greece, and much of the 9th *still* hadn't been issued with theirs yet. (Indeed, a lot of the weaponry stockpiled for them in Australia had instead been sent to England, to replace what had been lost at Dunkirk. As ever, it seemed to the critics, like Opposition leader John Curtin, that the main priority of Menzies was simply to defend England.) Things were so bad that the only time most of the 9th saw Bren guns was when they were issued for training, at the end of which they had to hand them back.[22]

Fortunately, some of the weaponry started arriving just days after those first reports came in, and the 9th breathed a little easier, but not much. They didn't mind a stoush — in fact wanted a stoush — but they also wanted to have a fair chance to give the Germans a good belting. To make up some of the difference, a lot of the troops busied themselves going through the detritus left behind by the Italians. It was true that their British commander — someone called Neem, Neam or something like that anyway — had issued specific orders that the abandoned Italian weaponry had to remain abandoned, because it was too dangerous to try to find any of it, but stuff that for a joke — that was not the Australian way. The Australian way was to live off the land the best you could, adapt, make do, find a way, and there was no way known that, with insufficient weaponry of their own, they were going to ignore all the Itie guns that were just lying around.

For, amidst all the rubbish and ruin, there were quite a few guns, including machine guns, and the 9th set to with a will to clean them and get them serviceable again. One who was thrilled to find something valuable on the former battlefield was Bert Ferres, who came across an old pistol that had probably first seen service in the Great War — and it was not at all unlike the one he'd fired at the travelling carnival at Brighton le Sands all those years ago, which had first turned his head towards the idea of being a soldier. It was a bloody beauty! Bert carefully cleaned it and then secreted the pistol in his pack, certain that, whatever else, he had a very good souvenir . . .

Signallers, meantime, salvaged a lot of signal wire, while the transport blokes got many of the abandoned Italian trucks working again — and beauties they were, too.

One indication of the necessity of such an approach was provided by the fact that at one point Lieutenant General Morshead sent two trucks back to Tobruk with a long list of spare parts that were needed for trucks, tanks and the like, hoping that the Quartermaster would be able to provide them. When his men returned, they had just one thing from the list — the cable for a truck speedometer.[23]

Nevertheless, the informal Australian policy of scavenging with all the intensity of bull ants working over the carcass of a dead wombat was effective, which was as well under the circumstances . . .

For yet more reports kept coming in, of more enemy activity and rumbling trucks in the night to their west, but still no word as to whether it was Jerries or Ities or Calathumpians. Soon, though, there was no mistaking it. The word came back that they were definitely German armoured cars, while blokes only had to look skywards to see that the planes that were now so very regularly strafing them were Messerschmitts and Heinkels, and there was no mucking around — in the first encounter of the 2/13th Battalion with those Heinkels, they lost two killed and one wounded.

•

Now, what the hell was that?

Following in the wake of the 20th Brigade, the men of the 2/23rd Battalion were making their own way to the west and noticed, near an airfield at Sidi Barrani, a whole lot of what looked from a distance to be Royal Air Force Hurricanes, but close up turned out to be just wooden dummies of the planes! As it turned out, they were only partly wood — and mostly Hollywood, for it was all an elaborate ruse to fool the Germans into thinking that Allied air power was greater than it actually was, and to encourage them to waste precious bombs on worthless replicas of the real thing. The whole thing was taken so seriously that a whole posse of men was retained there to regularly move the planes around to new positions, so the Germans wouldn't cotton on.

Still, maybe the game was up. It was possible they were pulling their legs, but the Poms told some of the soldiers of the 2/23rd Brigade that a few mornings ago they had come out to find that the Germans had dropped some wooden bombs on their wooden planes![24]

•

Up on the edge of Benghazi, where they had been settled in for a week or so, Corporal Stanley Waugh of the 2/3rd Light Anti-Aircraft Regiment and his mates had been looking after 7000 Itie prisoners in a nearby compound, which had been pretty dull duty most of the time — and nowhere near as interesting as firing their guns at Jerry planes, which is what they would have been doing, had they had any guns. But, still, maybe now they could have a bit of fun. For, on the morning of 16 March, they had been told they had the job of doing a bit of 'Wog chasing'. That is, they were told to get rid of the Arabs who were living in and around the Australian camp.

See, the word was that some of the Wogs had been signalling German planes overhead to bring on the bombing the city had been suffering in the last few days, and maybe even doing some Morse coding at night — though to whom, and about what, was never clear. The bottom line was that the senior Australian officers didn't want to take any more chances, and it was for Corporal Waugh and his mates to do the job.

They started out that afternoon down by the waterfront, and with some mirth soon rounded up twenty-six Arabs, whacked them onto the back of the trucks, drove them out of town and told them not to come back. Don't argue, and don't come back — have you got it, you Arabs?

That wasn't so bad, even though a lot of the Arabs weren't too happy about being removed from their town and their homes for what they saw as no good reason. But when the time came to move the Arab women and kids, well, it started to get very grim indeed. The first thing was going into their hovels — literally, mud huts about 15 foot long by 5 foot high — and seeing the conditions in which they lived. The filth! The stench! In Corporal Waugh's view it was no wonder so many of them were blind, with various deformities and lots of skin complaints. And did they carry on! Crying, hugging each other, screaming, trying to hold the Australian soldiers around the legs to stop themselves being moved. Relenting a little, the soldiers allowed them to take their sheep, goats and donkeys with them — putting the lot of them together on the backs of the trucks — but it still made a bloke feel crook in the guts to see women and children going on like that. But it had to be done, and they dropped them out of Benghazi at the same spot where they'd dropped the men, before they returned to grab the Wogs' chooks for a big dinner and a bit of a booze-up they had planned. Still, though, that crook-in-the-guts feeling about what they had had to do wouldn't quite leave them.

As Corporal Waugh confided in his diary that night ...

> We thought we were going to have some fun this afternoon, but it never turned out so funny to me. It sure is a shame to have to shift these wogs as I don't think they do any harm. They have been living here for years I suppose, but it was orders and we have to obey them. I don't think we will have a raid tonight as it is pitch black.[25]

Alas, despite the blackness and the fact that the suspicious Wogs had been removed, he was awoken at five o'clock the following morning by bombing that nearly knocked their barracks over.

The Germans had come anyway. Bombed the bejesus out of them. That morning Corporal Waugh and his men did a little more desultory Wog chasing — grabbing another four — but they didn't really have their hearts in it.

•

Men, with strange hats, running straight at them. Adam Mrozowski had finally made it out of the refugee camp and all the way to the Middle East just three weeks before, to join up with the Polish Carpathian Brigade, and was with some fellow soldiers on a first trip to Jerusalem when, from the other end of the street they were walking down, had come galloping these foreign soldiers on the charge, right for them. The Poles tensed, and half went into a defensive crouch. Was there going to be a massive brawl?

And then the Australians were upon them, all over them, around them.

'Polish boys!' they kept laughing and crying out. 'Polish boys!' Slapping them on the back, shaking their hands, and saying, 'Ozzies! We're Ozzies!'

Then, 'Swop? Swop?' Through sign language and a few garbled words, the Australians made it clear they wanted to swap their own AIF emblem badge of the rising sun for the colourful Polish emblem of a brass eagle. A few of the Polish soldiers did exchange, causing more guttural cries of exclamation from these strange men in their still stranger language, and then it was time for their next query.

'Pub?' the Australians asked.

'Youse COME to the PUB with US and have a DRINK?' they roared, as if yelling out every important word would force a passage across the great dividing range of their different languages ...

And maybe it did, because in next to no time the Polish and Australian soldiers were indeed all drinking together and carrying on. The more beer they drank, the less language mattered at all, and for some reason that Adam could never fathom there just seemed to be a strong bond between the Polish and Australian soldiers from the first. These men from the other side of the world, where they had strange creatures called kangaroos, had so little regard for authority that they thought nothing of setting up a peculiar game of spinning coins and lots of shouting, right on the main intersection of Jerusalem, bringing the entire place to a standstill. And yet nor did they ever seem to stop laughing or offering you another beer. The military police? They could get fuckski, see? Have another beerski! And so they did. Well into the night.

For months afterwards one of Adam's friends, a gunner, had the ability to make their whole Polish battalion fall about with laughter — at any time, be it in the shower or on a route march or in the mess hall — by standing up and doing a rendition of a very odd song some of the Australians had taught him. It involved a lot of high wailing, mixed with a sort of low grunting, and they all knew that to do it the way the Australians did it, you had to sort of wave your arms around a little, with your clenched fist going back and forth before your stomach, and a huge grin on your face as you roared out something that sounded like, '*It's a log, log way to Tipperareeeeeee, it's a log way to go ...*'

Ah, how they laughed. But they liked the Australians, and no mistake.

•

It was now Lieutenant General Morshead who was feeling mightily aggrieved. While other commanders were happy to make decisions from maps and reports alone, it had always been his practice to closely inspect positions held by his men on the front lines, and now that he had done so, he was appalled. It was obvious that if the Germans were coming their way in force, then they would have to come through El Agheila, meaning that Morshead's men of the 20th Brigade — most of whom were situated about 30 miles back from there, near a small Arab village called Marsa el Brega —

would be right in their firing line thereafter. And his men were all on a flat, fairly featureless desert that ran almost all the way back to Benghazi. The more he looked at it, the more he became convinced that in their current position his men were in great danger, as against a determined force they would be too few, too ill armed, with way too few munitions, and too totally exposed to hold a line. Most importantly, the men of the 20th Brigade would be insufficiently mobile without enough trucks to move them to where they needed to go once the shooting started.

Lastly Morshead felt the Germans might be clever enough to do to the Allies what the Allies had done to the retreating Italians — that is, cut across the desert, head off the Australians at the pass and, having isolated them, cut them down. Yes, Neame had some forces placed at the inland fort of Mechili — a very rough structure, made out of stone and mud, that had approximately *no* chance of providing serious shelter from artillery fire or even bullets — in an effort to block any attempt by the Germans to do that, but that would still not be any guarantee of actually stopping them.

Morshead fumed. Though a military man to his very core, and steeped in the sanctity of the chain of command — orders were orders were orders — there was a higher issue at stake. He passionately felt that the safety of his men was at grave risk, and decided that that overruled everything.

Feeling he had no choice but to try to correct the situation, he composed a long memo to Neame pointing out the tactical insanity of leaving his men where they were, and requesting that they be pulled back to the more easily defensible Benghazi–Barce area, while a more mobile force was put in place at the clearly crucial El Agheila.

Just when he was about to send it, however, on 17 March, the word came through.

In the company of General Wavell, no less than the Chief of the British General Staff, General Sir John Dill, had flown in from Cairo to Neame's headquarters in Barce, and now all three of them wanted to meet him at Beda Fomm at 6.15 p.m. that night, to discuss the way their defences were set up against any possible attack by the Axis forces.

Perfect!

•

Wavell began the meeting by turning to Morshead and saying bluntly, 'What is your appreciation?'[26]

The Australian didn't need to be asked twice. In clear, succinct terms, but still with some force, Morshead made his case: unless the 20th Brigade was seriously strengthened with more men, ammo, weaponry, food and, most crucially, transport, the men would have to be pulled back to near Benghazi, where the 26th Brigade were located.

Neame was not convinced, and said so, clearly irritated that the Australian was questioning his placements. He further insisted that, even if he wanted to, he wouldn't be able to organise the transport to take the 20th Brigade back in less than a week.

Still, Morshead would not be put off, and noted, once again, that Australian reconnaissance patrols had picked up the tracks of Panzers just beyond El Agheila! (Which was something Wavell, for one, still refused to believe, insisting that there must have been some kind of mistake.)

To this point Wavell had said very little, and merely sat there listening, but you didn't have to have been in the game as long as Morshead to know when you were losing the argument. Wavell's very calm bespoke a man who was entirely relaxed with the situation as it stood, who was doing Morshead the honour of hearing him out but in no way shared his views.[27] Oh, he accepted that the Australian position was pretty hopeless if there was a sustained German attack, but for the moment he didn't believe the Germans were there, so it followed that there wasn't a problem.

In for a penny, in for a pound, though, and Morshead insisted that the Panzers *were* there, and made no bones about what would happen to his men if the Germans attacked in force.

'In my opinion, sir,' Morshead said, 'the whole area where they are now offers as much scope for a defensive position as a billiard table . . .'[28]

Maybe it was the passion Morshead put into the words, or perhaps the metaphor of the billiard table, but something seemed suddenly to click with General Dill, who was, after all, the highest-ranking man there. And though he had, characteristically, limited his words to this point — his detractors sometimes called him 'Dilly-Dally' behind his back[29] — his words now carried a lot of weight.

He couldn't help but feel that Morshead was right, he said, and perhaps it might be more prudent to pull the 20th Brigade back, to absolutely ensure that at the first enemy move they wouldn't be finished as a fighting force.

Addressing his remarks to his old friend Neame, Dill said frankly, 'You are going to get a bloody nose here, Philip, and it is not the only place we shall get a bloody nose.'[30]

With Dill having asserted his authority and settled the issue, it was at this point that Wavell again asked Neame how soon the Australians could be moved back. Again Neame, now highly miffed, replied that it would be at least one week.

Morshead could stand it no more, and turned to Wavell. 'Sir, I believe it is essential that they start moving before dawn tomorrow.'[31]

With little further ado, Wavell gave the orders for the Australians to be pulled back to the nearest area that was not as flat as a billiard table, a place where it might be possible to make something of a stand — some of the higher country on the approaches to Benghazi — and the meeting closed. While this decision was a relatively severe blow to Neame — whose lack of tactical nous in desert warfare had now been exposed and effectively officially stamped as such by the most senior British officer of all — it was a major victory for Morshead, who left well satisfied. Yes, the lack of sufficient transport meant that the borrowed trucks would have to come and get the 20th Brigade a battalion at a time and piggyback them, step by step, but it was a move in the right direction. He was also pleased to be informed that the two other brigades of his division, the 26th and the 24th, had at last arrived from Palestine, the first to settle at Gazala and the latter at Tobruk.

•

For his part, Wavell returned to Cairo more than a little troubled. While he had noted 'with approval Morshead's quiet and soldierly demeanour, and decided he had the right man to command the 9th Australian Division',[32] he had been obliged to take his estimation of Neame down a peg or two.

The whole issue of where the 20th Brigade was to be placed aside, the problem was the state of preparedness — or lack thereof — of Allied forces in the Western Desert. The communications system between all the separate units was all but nonexistent; such tanks as had been left there, instead of going to Greece, were clapped out and in urgent need of spare parts that simply weren't there — and even if they could find them, there wouldn't be enough mechanics who knew what they were doing to exchange the new parts for the broken parts. True, some of those conditions were inevitable from the moment that Wavell himself had gone ahead with the move of transferring the hard edge of his firepower from North Africa to Greece, but it didn't seem to Wavell as if Neame had done a whole lot to overcome the losses and make the best of a difficult situation. And, yes, with the main supply port of Tobruk being a full 450 miles away, together with there being a major lack of trucks, things were always going to be a little threadbare on the front lines. But even allowing for all that ...

'I came back anxious and depressed from this visit,' Wavell later recounted, 'but there was nothing much I could do about it. The movement to Greece was in full swing and I had nothing left in the bag. But I had forebodings and my confidence in Neame was shaken.'[33]

Upon consideration of the perilous situation, Wavell decided that the best that could be done was to avoid decimation and, if there was a serious attack, his specific instructions to Neame were to simply *harass* the enemy and do what they could. But the most important thing was to keep his forces intact. His subsequent written orders to Neame therefore — formalising what he had told him at his headquarters in Barce — stated that:

> The safe-guarding of your forces from a serious reverse and the infliction of losses and ultimate defeat of the enemy, are of much greater importance than the retention of ground. The re-occupation of Benghazi by the enemy, though it would have considerable propaganda and prestige value, would be of little military importance and it is certainly not worthwhile risking defeat to retain it.

The thrust of that order — which was to retreat from, rather than retain, anything he considered to be useless ground — was something that Neame would observe right down to the very letter.

•

Morshead left Barce to head back to his HQ, satisfied with a job well done. Making his way along the dusty road, with his driver negotiating the small amount of oncoming traffic and a few herds of sheep, he was still touched, as ever, by the friendly waves of the Italian settlers. No doubt recognising his high-ranking insignia, children saluted, the townsfolk waved, and the goatherders and shepherds in the pastures lifted their hands in acknowledgment. They appeared to be a very simple sort of people, whose most earnest desire was just for the whole war to go away, and that they be left to live out their lives in peace.[34]

Still, on this day, there seemed to be an uneasy edge to their waves, almost as if, with the practised sense of generations spent on this strange part of the planet, they could feel a storm building ...

CHAPTER EIGHT

Attack!!!

You must treat your men as men, not as creatures of a lower grade.
You must not be afraid to be unpopular. I would sooner
command a hundred men with their tails up than a
thousand men with their tails down.

GENERAL LESLIE MORSHEAD, IN 1947

The majority of foreign bodies encountered were bone fragments,
which were often literally sprayed deeply into the brain from
a tangential wound. Metallic foreign bodies were nearly all
non-magnetic. The removal of most foreign bodies is a difficult
matter, because the brain gives no resistance against which the
body may be grasped, and clumsy handling will only drive it
further away and may easily cause perforation of the ventricle —
a major tragedy . . .

THE MEDICAL JOURNAL OF AUSTRALIA, 1942, COMMENTING ON
WOUNDS AND TREATMENTS AT TOBRUK

Rommel had rarely been so honoured.

On a lightning trip back to Berlin — arriving on the afternoon of 19 March 1941 — he was ushered once again into the presence of Adolf Hitler in his enormous office at the Chancellery, and the Führer began their meeting by personally presenting the Oak Leaves medal to Rommel in recognition of the extraordinary feats he had achieved with his Panzer Division in France in the previous year. To win the Pour le Mérite in the Great War had been wonderful, but to get this award from Hitler himself was surely the pinnacle of the recognition he had been given thus far. But from the glories of the past he was quickly obliged to move onto the realities of the moment.

Ten days earlier, Rommel had sent a strong signal from his headquarters in North Africa to Berlin, which stated his aims in his typically blunt language: 'The first objective of an attack would be the re-conquest of Cyrenaica, the second ... northern Egypt and the Suez Canal ...'[1]

Of course, Rommel wanted and expected nothing less than to seize the Suez Canal, and apart from receiving his medal, his great focus in coming to Berlin was to convince Hitler, together with the German General and Chief of Staff, Franz Halder, and the Commander in Chief of the Army, Field Marshal von Brauchitsch, that he could achieve great things if he was just given more men and munitions.

As it happened, though, Hitler, Halder and von Brauchitsch were united in their view — and their expression of it — that the only reinforcement Rommel could expect was the already planned 15th Panzer Division, which would be arriving in May, six weeks away, and in the meantime he was *not* to push the attack, for that was not the desired role of the Afrika Korps in Cyrenaica in the first place.

Privately, Rommel did not like highly officious Halder at all, nor von Brauchitsch for that matter, characterising these arrogant German generals of the General Staff — mere desk jockeys and military politicians, as opposed to being real front-line leaders in battle — as 'smooth, cold, black at heart'.[2]

And so it proved on this occasion. In a further meeting with Halder and von Brauchitsch a little later, to go over details of the situation in North Africa, nothing Rommel could say would convince them that he should be allowed to plan to push on to Suez, and for every argument he raised they had a counter-argument.

Still Rommel would not back down, and at one point General Halder could restrain himself no longer and smiled unpleasantly after Rommel had told them of yet one more advantage of securing the Suez Canal.

'And how many more troops do you think you might be needing to accomplish that?' he enquired, his top lip curling.

'Perhaps another two Panzer corps ...' Rommel replied.

Now Halder was acidly amused, and did not bother to hide it.

'Even if we had them,' he said, 'how are you going to supply them and feed them?'

Rommel's reply was one that Halder would never forget (in fact, many of the latter's recollections were bolstered by the fact that he was an inveterate note-taker and detailed diary-keeper), a reply that heightened his hate for this upstart of low birth even more.

'That is quite immaterial to me,' Rommel said, far above such mundane matters that were more in the Quartermaster's province. 'That's your pigeon.'[3]

The upshot was that Rommel returned to Libya with firm instructions that his job was to defend Tripolitania and prepare only for taking over Cyrenaica possibly at the end of May, when all his forces were on the ground. He was not to launch into Cyrenaica. Rommel was made to understand that the Afrika Korps did not have the resources to do this, and he must content himself for the moment with fulfilling a far more defensive role. In the circumstances, Rommel did not like to say that he had already instructed his officers to move the Afrika Korps forward, ready to move on El Agheila when he gave the word upon his return . . .

Never mind. Getting around obstacles to attain the prize — even obstacles as formidable as the German High Command — was what he had always been very good at.

What the German High Command had not told Rommel, although it was significant information, was that one of the reasons they were harbouring their resources at this time was that they were preparing to invade Russia with every spare man and every armoured set of wheels they had.

·

The grand plans of military moves, back and forth, parry and thrust, attack and retreat, flank and outflank, are usually only clear many years afterwards, to historians — and sometimes, on a good day, to the senior officers who initiate them at the time. The common soldiers, following orders from on high, only rarely understand their own part in the overall scheme of things: why a particular march is necessary; why it will be to the greater good of their side of the war effort that they move forward, back or sideways. And 22 March 1941 was not such an occasion for the men of the 2/13th, 2/17th and 2/15th Battalions, all of which made up the 20th Brigade of the 9th Australian Division. All they knew was that trucks would shortly be coming for them, and they were to pile in and go wherever those trucks took them — though they knew that the move would be away from where they thought the Germans to be, and not towards them, which was the direction in which most of the Australians wanted to travel.

When the orders had come through, most of the men of the 20th Brigade were heartily pissed off. They were to pull back. Get on the trucks and hightail it! No reasons were given. No reasons were *ever* given in this man's army. That was why they were called 'orders', because no one had to explain.

Within hours, though, the men were indeed on their way, heading backwards through the night, and most of them still hadn't *seen* any bastard, let alone been shot at by one of them. All that training, all that waiting, all that carry-on and ballyhoo and 'Let us at the Germans!', and now they were turning tails like dingoes and running away from the enemy. After a night spent freezing their balls off waiting for the damn trucks, they were now frying in the back of them as the sun beat down, until at last they halted at some godforsaken place near a village called Ghemines, and could finally get some sleep. The only good thing — when the trucks at last dropped them off and they were told that this was their final destination — was that they could see that they were in a spot where there were some patches of grass and trees, and even a bit of height above the vast, dull plain. With the last came something of a view as, to their southwest, they could spy the distant, shimmering city of Benghazi. This place, the 2/13th was told, was called the Er Regima pass, while the lads of the 2/17th were situated a bit further back, and the 2/15th a bit further back still, near El Abiar.

Behind them all, some of Britain's best forces in Cyrenaica, including the 1st and 104th Regiments and Royal Horse Artillery, had substantially taken over the positions of the 20th Brigade — better equipped than the Australians, as they were, with arms, transport and training to deal with whatever might be coming ... not that they really believed that anything was.

A little further to their north, the men of the 2/24th Battalion had been placed defending a pass called Tocra, which provided a parallel way to the east, to the road that went through Er Regima.

Among them, Ivor Hancock was with his mates Pudden Head, Norm and Cocky, all hungering for a bit of action, a chance to prove that they had what it took to take a crack at the Jerries. Nothing was confirmed yet, but there were more and more stories that the Germans really were out there, and would shortly be coming their way, and Cocky for one could barely think straight in the hope that it was true. Cocky — who was proud of the fact that his people were originally from Poland — felt that it was high time that there was some squaring of accounts, and reckoned that he was just the man for the job.

•

Oh, Christ. Bert Ferres felt sick at heart. One of the men in his unit had borrowed the pistol that Bert had treasured so much, just before he got his hands on some rum or beer or something. The two had made a terrible combination, because he was a bloke who just didn't know how to drink;

who, from the moment he got grog into him, turned violent. How was Bert meant to know that? It was just one of those things. Anyway, it had finished with the bloke taking Bert's pistol into General Neame's cookhouse and then taking two shots at his cook! Mercifully he was so drunk the shots had gone wild, and he'd been subdued before he could do any more damage, but there was going to be hell to pay. Bert had lost his treasured pistol forevermore, and the bloke was going to be court martialled at the very least, even as he now rotted in jail. Bert kept his head down, not sure if he was going to be implicated or not ...

•

Less than twelve hours after Rommel returned to Africa and gave the word, the attack on El Agheila was launched — and it was effectively over in just a few minutes more than nothing flat. In the first daylight hours of 24 March, the 3rd Reconnaissance Battalion of the Afrika Korps' 5th Light Division, backed in part by the hundred 'dummy' tanks made of wood, canvas and cardboard put atop VW cars that formed Rommel's 'Cardboard Division' (two could play at that game), swooped on the thinly defended garrison, and sure enough swiftly overcame what little resistance there was. Yes, there were some minefields that the attacking German force of real Panzers had to overcome, and the time it took to do it allowed most of the British defenders the breathing space they needed to get away, but the key was that one of the two genuine bottlenecks of passable terrain on the entire North African coast — the other was at a place called El Alamein — was now in German hands. What came with it was both a landing strip to give the Luftwaffe a new forward base, and also one of the few sure water supplies in the area. Consequently the move of the Afrika Korps to the east now picked up new momentum ...

•

From London, Churchill was so alarmed at the fall of El Agheila that he cabled Wavell:

> I presume you are only waiting for the tortoise to stick
> his head out far enough before chopping it off. It seems
> extremely important to give them an early taste of our
> quality.

At this point, Wavell might well have been forgiven for sending a blistering reply back to Churchill, but ever the correct military man, he did no such thing. Nevertheless, he did have some cause for complaint. It had been specifically at Churchill's behest that Wavell had sent, from North Africa to Greece over the previous two months, more than 58 000 experienced soldiers and 8000 vehicles. And now Churchill was asking him to stop the advance and chop the tortoise's head off? With *what*? And to what 'quality' did Churchill refer?

In any case, lest the Prime Minister worry too much, Wavell was quick to assure Churchill that he did not believe the reports that it had been a fundamentally German attack, and was quick to cable him to that effect.

```
No evidence yet that there are many Germans at Agheila;
probably mainly Italian, with small stiffening of Germans.⁴
```

•

And yet while the force that took El Agheila was in fact all Germans, it was true that the newly provisioned Italians of the Ariete and the Brescia divisions, who had arrived in North Africa at much the same time as the Afrika Korps, were now advancing with their comrades in the Axis cause. One of the Italian tank commanders in the Ariete was a former mechanic from Milan by the name of Mario, and, all patriotism aside, he was impressed by what his countrymen had accomplished in this part of the world that God had so clearly forsaken. Where there had been just desert and scrub, the Italian settlers had put windmills up to pump the water from beneath the surface, and dug canals thereafter to move it around. They had cleared the ground, planted the trees and made from nothing farms, orange groves and well-tilled fields where crops grew so well they could be harvested three times a year. They had, praise be to the Madonna, carved out of the unforgiving desert, with their energy and ingenuity, a really civilised life. When, for example, the division had stopped at a place just before Derna, the Italian settlers had offered them all bread, cheese and wine of their own making, every morsel of which was as good as you were likely to get in Rome itself. But then one of the settlers, an older man from Napoli, had come up, a very short man with very large hands, and gripped Mario's hand with something close to desperation.

'There was *niente* here but desert when we came,' he said. 'We pray every day that we may stay here. The Germans will stop the British, won't they?'

In spite of himself, and the obvious gentle sincerity of the settler, Mario lost his temper.

'*We* are here, too!' he raged, indicating all his Italian military comrades in their tanks. By God, it wasn't just the Germans who would save them! With which Mario turned on his heel, only to be pursued by the old settler, who embraced him and gave him his good wishes.[5] Mario accepted his apologies, but remained troubled as he and his comrades continued to the east in the wake of the Germans, who always seemed to be far ahead of them.

The Italian settlers were not the only ones who doubted the Italian troops. Mario remembered well when his tank had been unloaded back on the docks in Tripoli, two Germans coming forward to have a closer inspection. They had left, laughing themselves silly at his 'tank'. (And unbeknownst to him, Rommel shared a similar view, later commenting, 'It made one's hair stand on end to think what sort of weapons the Duce had sent his forces into battle with . . .'[6])

•

By now the actions of the Luftwaffe, bombing and strafing the troops pulling back from El Agheila to Benghazi, were so devastating that that particular section of road was referred to as Messerschmitt Alley. Time and again the planes would dive down, like eagles on stray rabbits, and unleash withering fire up and down the length of a convoy. Of course the troops returned fire the best they could, and even had one or two successes by bringing a couple of the planes down, but their true saviours were the men of the RAAF's No 3 squadron, operating out of the Benina airfield just outside Benghazi. Outnumbered five to one, their planes continually hurtled skywards, doing what they could to protect their own and being cheered by the troops below for their trouble.

•

As ever, Lieutenant General Morshead began his letter to his wife with 'My darling Myrtle', and after finishing it read it over, as his own censor, to make sure he hadn't breached any security regulations by giving away information that might be damaging in the hands of the enemy. However careful in the writing, he was not yet above blacking out some of his own scrawl if he thought he might have gone too far, though this particular letter was not an example of that. On the top right-hand corner he had given his own time and place of writing as . . .

26 *March* 1941
In the field.

... and then given a rough outline of what he had been up to, before getting slightly more detailed.

Although there are some extremely comfortable buildings close by, we are living in the open. We need the practice and experience and have the bombing in mind. My tent is similar to those two I had at Rutherford. You remember they were joined one day for use as a bedroom, the other as an office. Here one such tent does both jobs. It is ... comfortable. I have electric light — we have a mobile plant which is very necessary because we have to work at night. Of course one misses a bath.

Then, with a warmth that would possibly have amazed many of the soldiers under him who were rarely allowed to see the more human side of the general, he did what he usually did, which was to express his great love for his wife.

... I miss you very much. At night especially I think of you and long for you. War wouldn't be so bad if one only had to work and fight by day and go home at night except of course it would have to be fought in one's own country. I'd love to be able to put my arms around you sweetheart and have a real love up. One indulges in a great deal of wishing I'm afraid, still my dear girl, there's a good time coming but before it does no doubt we will have to face a serious and difficult time chiefly because we do not heed its obvious warning and adequately prepare. I used to preach that so often. I must have bored you. It is foolish and so terribly risky and it is in the end so unnecessarily costly to give the other fellow the advantage of a flying start. We shall win through but not so quickly and economically.
Goodnight my precious and sweet be your dreams.
Les.[7]

•

In Greece, the situation was becoming more and more tense for the Allies by the day.

On 27 March in Yugoslavia, just north of Greece, a coup against the government by a group in favour of the Allies had been quickly followed by a coup by a group in favour of the Germans. Alas, because the first rule of renegade politics is that it is always the last coup that wins, German forces were even then happily rolling into Yugoslavia and coming perilously close to the Greek border, where, with the Greek Army, the chief defenders were the Australian soldiers of the 6th Division together with some Brits and New Zealanders.

It could only be a matter of time . . .

•

Sound travels a long distance in the desert. With few obstacles between the source of the sound and the far horizons, there is little to stop it rolling on and on, so perhaps some of the nomadic Bedouin heard the sounds of the distant singing coming from around the fire that flickered between massive hulks of Panzers, parked in a protective circle — in the classic *laager* fashion that travellers through Africa had used since time immemorial — with the Afrika Korps sentries posted far enough out that they would get fair warning in the unlikely event of an attack. For these men of the 5th Light and the 8th Machine-gun Battalion, it was a part of the day when they could be as close to 'relaxed' as they were likely to get while in the middle of a campaign. After a long day of jolting along a rough road that showed no mercy for tanks on metal tracks with precious little suspension, when your body had been bounced around so badly in the furnace-like box of the tank cabin that you were bruised all over your back and you knew that once again that night you would have to sleep on your front, still, *welche Wohltat* — what a relief — to stop and camp like this, to eat, drink some blessed water, enjoy the camaraderie and forget the horrors of the day. And yes, even to sing in full voice a song — almost a kind of hymn — that had been written for this very campaign.

Heiss uber Afrikas Boden die Sonne glüht.
Unsere Panzermotoren singen ihr Lied!
Deutsche Panzer im Sonnenbran,
Stehen zur Schlacht gegen Engeland

Es rasseln die Ketten, es dröhnt der Motor,
Panzer rollen in Afrika vor.

Hot over the African ground, the sun is glowing.
As our engines sing their song!
Panzers in the blazing sun,
Stand in battle against England.
The tracks rattle, the engine hums loudly,
Panzers are rolling forward in Africa.

And certainly, while on this occasion Rommel was not with them —
and was likely in his caravan planning the next day's move — he was not
forgotten, as they warmed into their favourite song of all: *Unser Rommel*
(Our Rommel).

Mit uns im Kampf und im Siege vereint,
marschieren Italiens Scharen.
Bis einst die Sonne des Friedens uns scheint,
und wieder gen Deutschland wir fahren.
Doch wenn mich die feindliche Kugel fand,
so lasset mich ruhen im Wüstensand,
und rühret noch einmal die Trommel,
Vorwärts, vorwärts mit unserem Rommel.
Vorwärts mit unserem Rommel.

Together with us in battle and victories,
the Italians are marching.
Until the sun of peace will shine for us,
and we will return to Germany.
But if an enemy shot hit me,
So let me rest in the desert sand,
and play the drum roll once again.
Forwards, forwards with our Rommel,
Forwards with our Rommel.

•

The general optimism of such men, there in the African desert and steadily
closing in on their destination — even as, that night, they finally made their
way into the tents they had carefully coated in a mix of clay and sea water to
blend into the desert environment in the daylight[8] — was in stark contrast to

the mood of the British back in Cairo, which was getting grim. The surest sign of which way the wind was blowing in the war was the Egyptian bartenders. In February, when the Allies had been sweeping all before them and it was obvious that Britain would be a power in Egypt for many years to come, nothing was too good for any Allied servicemen, up to and including drinks on the house and warm smiles all around.[9] Now the mood had turned surly, and that will be exactly 50 piastres, please. Now it looked as if the British and their allies would soon be all swept away, so there was little further point in being pleasant.

And yet, and yet ... at least there was still time to get themselves ready.

On 30 March, Neame received a personal cable from Wavell in Cairo noting that some reports had come through of a large body of German forces landing in Tripoli that he should be aware of. Wavell regretted that none of the reinforcements that Neame had requested would be available for another eight to nine weeks at the earliest; but, that situation notwithstanding, Neame's task was 'to delay the enemy's advance over the 150 miles from Agheila to Benghazi for two months'.[10]

Still, not to worry *too* much. Because against all that, Wavell had done his calculations and felt confident in assuring Neame that 'I do not believe that Rommel can make any big effort for at least another month'. (True, Wavell had by this time received some warning from his Intelligence service that a large number of enemy convoys had been pushing into Tripoli, but as he later recounted, 'the Information was so poor and vague that I largely discounted it'.[11])

In this estimation that the Afrika Korps would not push forwards in the short term, Wavell had indeed read the desires of Berlin's German High Command like a book. Because, by any measure, it *was* insane for Rommel to push forwards, and Berlin already had specifically stated just that, with von Brauchitsch himself having told Rommel on his trip back there a week earlier, 'The British are far too strong for a single light division ... You will have to wait until the 15th Panzer Division arrives in May.'[12] And though Wavell, of course, wasn't aware of the details of the specific conversation, he did have access to the work of the Allies' key code-breaking unit in Britain's Bletchley Park — a 581-acre estate in Buckinghamshire, between Oxford and Cambridge, containing some of the finest and most eccentric mathematical minds in the country — which had intercepted and decoded many of the cables flying between Berlin and Tripoli, and these indicated that there was no question of early attack. What neither Wavell nor the German High Command in Berlin had figured on, however, were the desires of the maverick Rommel himself. Whatever else, he was not an orthodox fox.

For the following morning, 31 March 1941, Rommel effectively cut the Afrika Korps loose, instructing the German 3rd Reconnaissance Unit and 5th Panzer Regiment to attack what proved to be the British 2nd Armoured Division, situated just south of Marsa el Brega. Rommel had been counselled by some of the braver members of his senior staff not to do so — on the grounds that all of their reconnaissance had told them that the British had been very busy digging themselves in — but the man leading the Afrika Korps would hear none of it.

'We've got the enemy on the run,' he told his Chief of Staff. 'And we must capture Marsa el Brega before it becomes more of an obstacle. *Wir greifen an!* We attack!'[13] And attack they did, launching at exactly 0944 hours. The results, from the British point of view, were appalling.

When the Panzers came up hard against the British Cruiser and Matilda tanks for the first time in this campaign, it was quickly apparent that it was not a fair fight. Because there had been no transports to get the British tanks to the front, the Cruisers had trundled there under their own considerable steam, all the way from the port of Tobruk, some 450 miles away, and had consequently started the battle with gearboxes, transmissions and whole engines so shot to pieces that the chances of them shooting other things to pieces were always minimal. But, still, that wasn't the major problem. The simple reality was that the clapped-out Cruisers, with their inch-thick armour and two-pounder 'pop-guns', going up against the Panzer IIIs and IVs, with their two-and-a-half-inch (65-mm) thick armour and, respectively, 50-mm and 75-mm guns, was the rough equivalent of trying to stop a charging rhinoceros by hurling flaming marshmallows at him. True, it turned out that the German anti-tank guns, the 37-mm PAKs (as in, Panzer Abwehrkanone), were equally so useless against the Matilda tanks — their shells simply bounced off — that the German soldiers came to call their anti-tank guns '*Panzeranklopfgerät*', mere 'tank door-knockers', but the Panzers themselves more than compensated for this weakness.[14]

It was possible that the British tanks could do some damage to those Panzers if they got up close enough to fire right in their ears, but they were never able to. For the final factor in the result was that the German tank commanders proved to be vastly more canny than their British counterparts, with the Commanding Officer of the 5th Panzer Regiment's 2nd Battalion, Colonel Herbert Olbrich, shining in the way he led his behemoths in an outflanking attack on the entrenched British defensive positions.

From the other flank, Rommel personally organised an attack by the 8th Machine-gun Battalion, and by seven o'clock that evening all British resistance was wiped out, and Marsa el Brega had fallen to the Afrika Korps — with the rapidly descending night now only just held off by the small pillars of blazing British tanks strewn across the battlefield. A few lucky ones had escaped behind the shield of a minefield, but the rout was all but total.

Not least of the British problems had been the total German domination of the air. The famed German war correspondent Freiherr Hanns Gert von Esebeck was able to give a very graphic account for his readers at home. 'Stukas hover like white butterflies, high up in the dark blue sky. Now they turn, tilt over up front and howl out in high tones in the fall. In the dark roaring of the hits and the engines, the high rattle of the machine guns mixes in. It is an unforgettable picture, certainly unforgettable for the soldiers under fire. Because now plane after plane swings and circles and hovers. Poison yellow and grey-black fountains jump up. Again and again the Stukas start an attack, then come down very low above us, shudder towards us in a greeting, and pull steeply up for a new fall onto the enemy's positions.

'The attack rolls on and it is no different from any of the other attacks of the German infantry on the battlefields of the last two years. Only that the khaki shirt has the place of the grey field jacket, that the men are *braungebrannt*, suntanned from Africa's sun, and that their helmet is sand-coloured.

'El Brega ... is tightly in our possession. For the first time, General Wavell's Libya army has felt the toughness of German weapons. It will have to expect some more of this ...'[15]

Most importantly, with the German victory came the wonderful bonus to the attackers of fifty precious armoured carriers and more petrol supplies![16]

It all prompted the typical response from Rommel to his troops: 'Push on!'[17]

•

Meanwhile, Sir Philip Neame, the Allies' most senior military man on site, had already made his move.

He had written a letter. Complaining to Lieutenant General Morshead about the conduct of the Australian soldiers.

Specifically, Neame took aim at those Australians in that same unruly 20th Brigade — composed of the 2/13th, 2/15th and 2/17th Battalions —

that he had wanted to keep without sufficient transport or firepower in the middle of the very 'billiard table' that was even then falling to the German armoured attack.

Beginning with a curt 'Dear Morshead', Neame complained of some of his own recent interactions with Australian soldiers . . .

Since the 20th Infantry Brigade of the 9th Australian Division was moved to the Regima area, numerous disgraceful incidents have occurred in Barce. Drunkenness, resisting military police, shooting in the streets, breaking into officers' messes and threatening and shooting at officers' mess servants — even a drunken soldier has come into my own Headquarters and disturbed my staff.

This state of affairs reached a climax yesterday when the streets were hardly safe or fit to move in . . . I consider it disgraceful that I and my staff should have our attention and time absorbed by these disciplinary questions at a time when we have to consider fighting the Germans and Italians . . .

I did not mention it the other day, but I must tell you now that the C.I.G.S. and the C. in. C. when visiting me here were accosted in the street by a drunken Australian soldier. I myself have had the same experience in Barce . . .

I am at a loss for words to express my contempt for those who call themselves soldiers who behave thus . . .

Your Division will never be a useful instrument of war unless and until you can enforce discipline . . . And all the preparations of the Higher Command may be rendered useless by the acts of an undisciplined mob behind the front.[18]

The letter went on for many pages and finished with Neame threatening to report the whole matter to General Blamey.

Morshead's response, in supremely military language, was reminiscent of an instruction Australia's second Prime Minister, Alfred Deakin, gave to his secretary after receiving a letter from the Premier of New South Wales threatening to withdraw from the Federation of Australia: 'Tell him to go to hell — three pages.'[19]

When Morshead fronted Neame later in the day he used formal military language and was ruthlessly polite, but he allowed there to be no misunderstanding as to the force of his fury. The 9th Division commander felt very strongly that Neame had a prejudice against Australians to begin with; that he was part of the British 'Old School' which maintained that Dominion troops could only ever be any good if they were broken up and put under individual British command; that this whole attitude now permeated that of Neame's staff; and that, in any case, he was sure Neame was vastly exaggerating some minor disciplinary problems with a few Australian soldiers and trying to define an entire brigade by them.

In the case of the drunken Australian heading into Neame's headquarters, Morshead happened to know that he had been accompanied by two equally drunk British soldiers, and in his letter the Australian general expressed full confidence that, when the time came, his men would perform very well indeed. As Morshead's notes of the day reveal, he took the view that: 'Without in any way condoning any offences I cannot help but feeling it's the same old story of giving a dog a bad name. And we rather sensed the cold shoulder [at Neame's headquarters in Barce]. All this to me is so puerile. Several instances have occurred where incidents have been excitedly reported to us and on investigation proved unfounded.'[20]

As to Neame's threat to report the whole matter to General Blamey, Morshead told him he needn't bother, as he, Morshead, would *definitely* pass on Neame's outrageous letter to Blamey and quite possibly to Neame's superior, Wavell, as well. (Put that in your pipe and smoke it, mate.)

Overall, Morshead took the whole matter in his stride, far more concerned with the weightier matter of how exactly to stop Rommel. Personally, Morshead was developing a growing sense that whatever problems his troops might cause when on the grog, there seemed to be every chance that they would be just like they were in the Great War — superb — once the real fight was on.

•

The essence of the military doctrine of 'probing attacks' is similar to that of exploratory surgery. Rather than a full-on assault, the probes are initially tentative, carefully trying to work out where the defence's strong points are, and using that information to guide the later, *real* attack.

Rommel's small problem in this first part of April was that with every probe his troops were only collating weak points of the Allied defence, and just about nowhere was showing up as a strong point. Every time the German, and even Italian, forces went forwards, their primary obstacle seemed to be the dust in their eyes generated by so many Allied wheels churning up the ground in retreat. Air reconnaissance had it that every bit of Allied traffic they spotted in the Western Desert appeared to be moving east at pace.

More than once, Rommel asked himself: Why didn't they turn and fight?

•

Why didn't they turn and fight? It was a question troubling not just Rommel but more and more of the Australian and British forces, as the orders kept coming through to fall back, retreat, retire and fight rearguard actions only. Having dispatched his letter to Morshead, Neame was now following closely the order of Wavell to abandon any ground that he didn't consider worth fighting for, and to do everything possible to keep his forces intact. In fact, so cognisant was Neame of Wavell's instruction that he even sent a message to Major General Michael Gambier-Parry, saying, 'Do not commit the 2nd Armoured Division to counterattack, without reference to me.'[21]

Gambier-Parry — a rather effete officer of the English Old School, what? — was dismayed. He managed to get a message back, pointing out that the right moment to counterattack might only be a fleeting one and that he therefore 'urged seriously' that the right to counterattack should be left to his own discretion, especially in circumstances where communications were so difficult; but by this stage it was all getting to be rather beside the point as the Afrika Korps continued to flood forwards, no matter what blocks they encountered. Gambier-Parry's failure to both assert his will more strongly, and to use effectively what little latitude he did have, did not surprise many in the senior echelons of the British military who were familiar with his situation. They had been amazed at his appointment to command of the 2nd Armoured Division from the first, and everything they had seen since had confirmed to them that he simply wasn't up to it.[22]

•

By four o'clock on that afternoon of 2 April, another former Allied stronghold, the good-sized town of Agedabia, had fallen to Colonel Olbrich's 5th Panzer Regiment — and it was a particularly significant place because the town was effectively the starting point for six tracks that fanned out across the desert and into the mountains to the west. Neame had tried to thwart the German advance by again placing what was left of the 2nd

Armoured Division — comprising all the tanks that had not been destroyed or disabled and as much of the motorised infantry it could muster — in their path, but the Germans had simply been too overwhelming in numbers and too skilled in their manoeuvres to be stopped. Before withdrawing, as instructed by Neame, the 2nd Armoured Division had still lost another six tanks while the Afrika Korps had only lost three.[23]

The Allied retreat in the face of the Afrika Korps was now in full swing, and what the Diggers would ever after refer to as the 'Benghazi–Tobruk Handicap' — essentially, a race to see who could get to Tobruk first. Giving extra propulsion to the Afrika Korps and their Italian Allies was a real problem with water supply. It was so scarce behind, all the way back to El Agheila, they almost had to go on to be sure of getting more ahead . . .[24]

•

Back at Tobruk, the 2/23rd Battalion continued to dig in, in the company of other garrison units, with all of the soldiers conscious that the war was heading their way and there was a high likelihood that in short order many thousands of retreating Allied soldiers would be with them in Tobruk, either using it as a Dunkirk — a place to get away from the Germans by using the port facilities — or as a place to turn, fight and make a stand.

Among the 2/23rd, as ever, John Johnson had been doing his duty — in the previous week or so he had organised and manned a guard detail to ensure that a munitions warehouse was absolutely secure — though still finding time to write to his precious family, giving them his own news, and responding to theirs from previous letters . . .

Fancy our baby being 10 lb weight now & doesn't our lovely baby Sylvia just adore her. Tell my Sylvia with the Brown eyes that Sylvia is Daddy's big baby girl & Josie with the blue eyes is Daddy's little baby girl. And how Daddy loves them. I suppose my boy Des doesn't go to school yet? I will get a surprise when you write & say he goes to school . . .[25]

Up on those front lines, where everything that could be taken for granted at home was rare as hen's teeth, John was glad to have a pen, as plenty of his mates only used pens for addressing their envelopes, scrawling the letter itself in pencil, and could be frequently seen pausing in their letter-writing to sharpen their pencils on their bayonets.

As to his own activities in Tobruk: apart from the relatively mundane hours of guard duty, John and his mates had also been busy getting involved in what would subsequently famously be known as 'the Bush Artillery'. This artillery was predicated on the notion that there was no reason why it should be just the artillery blokes who had all the fun plus the chance to fire guns at the Germans and Ities. In those first days of April in Tobruk, lots of ordinary soldiers, cooks, bottle-washers, drivers and all the rest decided to capitalise on the fact that the town was chock-a-block with abandoned Italian armaments — mostly 40-mm anti-tank guns, with a few heavier field guns as well — and more ammunition for them than you could poke a burnt stick at. So it was that the Bush Artillery boys decided to roughly learn how to set the weapons up, load them, aim them and fire them, so that if the worst came to the worst they would have at least some chance of giving Jerry one for his bloody corner.

Careful, though. Just in case the whole damn thing blew up on you, it was best to have a lanyard of telephone wire, sometimes 100 feet long, to 'pull the trigger' — or whatever it was — to fire the damn things.

Sure, a lot of the weaponry had been partially disabled by the Ities before they left, by removing the sights and so forth, but it was far from destroyed.

So it was that a lot of the non-front-line Australian soldiers then in Tobruk used whatever spare time they could garner to set the guns up the best they could, sight the brutes by looking straight down the barrels and develop the idea that when a tank or something like that came into range, they could *let the bastard rip*!

Now, if they missed the first time they'd just have to chock the barrel a bit up or a bit down, and they'd get their range that way. At one point when John Johnson and his mates were trying to get the hang of it, their first shell had been way too low, and after hitting the desert 200 yards forward of the barrel, it then, as John told Josie in a letter, 'bounced across the desert like a kangaroo', to the roars of their own laughter.[26] Never mind, they soon tried again and soon started to get it right.

It hadn't been in any textbook they'd come across, it hadn't even been discussed at places like Bonegilla, Puckapunyal or Ingleburn, and there might well have been one or two of the more pukka British blokes around who thought it wasn't quite *cricket* to use the Italian guns in that fashion, but no one on the Australian side could see any reason why they shouldn't have a crack at it.

Not to be left out, some of the blokes of a notably mechanical bent turned their attention to another idea. Why not secure some of the Italian anti-tank guns onto the back of a couple of tabletop trucks? That way you could be kind of like a tank without the armour, but still a lot faster and more manoeuvrable than a tank, and maybe if you were quick enough you could get in, have a go at the German tanks and get the hell out again before they quite knew what had hit them! There were logistical problems, of course, in terms of ensuring that the very act of firing the gun wouldn't tear it from the back of the truck, but after some quick experimentation with bolts and extra beams crossways on the truck, mixed with a couple of practice rounds into the ocean, they thought they might be in shape to give it a bit of a burl if it came to it . . .

•

With control of Agedabia, an attacker was suddenly given a choice of many ways in which to advance his forces. And, despite his orders, Rommel was sorely tempted to go on with it. After all, why not?

Yes, Generale Gariboldi had sent him a furious message saying, 'Your attack on Agedabia was in contradiction to what I ordered. You are to wait for me before continuing with any advance.' But that was only Gariboldi. In Rommel's view it was the height of presumption for the Italians to try to tell him what to do when they were so totally dependent on German arms for their very existence. And while the dictates of Berlin carried a lot more weight, Rommel had built an entire career on spontaneous, rapid action; taking advantage of opportunities as they presented themselves and then presenting higher command with an extraordinary *fait accompli*. Yes, he had been specifically ordered by Berlin not to advance anywhere near this point before the end of May, but that was only an order from people well distant from the front. In this case, it seemed to Rommel that, by obeying orders and stopping at Agedabia, all he would be doing would be giving the British time to dig in, stock up and make a future advance all the harder and more costly to the lives of his men; whereas by pushing forwards now, *immediately*, he could keep his momentum going, with the prestigious prize of Benghazi just up ahead. Now *that* would make headlines in Berlin!

Fascinating. After the Afrika Korps had successfully stormed one more British position, the German war correspondent Freiherr von Esebeck came across a carefully camouflaged tent in which which he found a lot of letters to the Tommy soldiers from their families at home. The first thing he noted was that the most recent were from late the previous year! As he subsequently remarked on to his readers:

'The connection to the island that rules the sea is broken. What do the soldiers, the sergeants, the lieutenants and colonels know of the events at home? The letters that we look through are not encouraging for soldiers, who far away from their homeland on foreign ground are supposed to fight for a goal that for them could not be clear at all. And how may the sense of war reflect in the head of an English bricklayer, a teacher or a mechanic, when for months he doesn't know anything else other than that the war in the motherland had become a terrible truth.

'Even if you do not hear anything from me, writes the wife of a sergeant, still you know that I am thinking of you. When it is time to leave off writing here, it is because I need to go to the air raid shelter. And I must go early, because they close the doors early, it is so full. We must go into the shelter — what can we do? Already there are many people who have lost their homes. Last night it rained bombs. I could tell you the destruction they brought, but it is wiser to be silent. All that we know is that the Jerries are throwing their bombs again.'

Esebeck had little sympathy, as he made clear to his readers:

'And so it goes on. Letter after letter describes life in London in London's cellars and speaks of destruction and fires. The German attacks since then have not only continued, but increased. England wanted the fight. She has received it and it is without doubt useful when also the English soldier in Africa knows it . . .'[27]

•

Prime Minister Winston Churchill — who had himself fought in the North African terrain four decades earlier, in the Omdurman Campaign, and therefore fancied himself an even greater expert on this matter than most — continued to be dismayed at the German advance and, as he was ever wont to do, cabled Wavell to that effect. Noting that the prospect of a British withdrawal from Benghazi was 'most melancholy', he went on:

```
I cannot understand how the enemy can have developed any
considerable force at the end of this long, waterless coast
road . . . If this blob which has come forward against you could
be cut off you might have a prolonged easement. Of course, if
they succeed in wandering onwards they will gradually
destroy the effect of your victories. Have you got a man like
O'Connor or Creagh dealing with this frontier problem?[28]
```

The last issue of whether it would have been far better to have Richard O'Connor in charge instead of Neame was a question Wavell had already been wrestling with. As a matter of fact, on this very afternoon of 2 April — after sending a message to O'Connor that he wanted him to take over the following day — Wavell was flying to meet with Neame to discuss the situation.

The Commander in Chief of all Allied armies in the Middle East was of heavy heart, and uncomfortable both physically — in the cramped but draughty bomber — and emotionally, as he realised that he and his command really had totally underestimated the force that Rommel could generate, and the speed with which the German could move it forward. Still, one thing gave him strength. It was a poem that had been printed in an Egyptian newspaper he had with him, penned by Londoner Greta Briggs during the Blitz, and the poem began . . .

> *I, who am known as London, have faced stern times before,*
> *Having fought and ruled and traded for a thousand years and more;*
> *I knew the Roman legions and the harsh-voiced Danish hordes;*
> *I heard the Saxon revels, saw blood on the Norman swords.*
> *But, though I am scarred by battle, my grim defenders vow*
> *Never was I so stately, nor so well-beloved as now . . .*[29]

Reading the words over and over again, Wavell began to feel better, thinking that perhaps, despite everything, there was still the matter of great British resilience to count on, that while they had taken many hits in the previous days, weeks and months, they were a people who had proved over the decades and centuries that they could suffer serious setbacks and still triumph. This slightly more upbeat mood did not last long, however. For once he was back on the ground and again dealing with Philip Neame, a clear schism in their views soon emerged.

Wavell wanted to again place the 2nd Armoured 'Division' — because by this time it was a division in name only — between the Afrika Korps and Benghazi, while Neame wanted to relocate them inland to prevent the Germans moving east across the desert and so doing to the defenders the same devastating thing that O'Connor's forces had done to the Italians. Wavell was less concerned by the possibility of the Germans turning east, assured as he had been by GHQ Intelligence that the Afrika Korps' vehicles were not designed for it, and that 'it would take them months of experience to become desert–worthy'.[30]

In any case it was all effectively too late, as Neame had already decided that Benghazi just couldn't be held and had given the orders accordingly. In his words, Benghazi 'had no strong defences like Tobruk, was overlooked by a line of hills within artillery range, and was impossible to supply by sea', and should not be held because, as he later recalled, it 'was by this time of no military use to me whatever, and I had already given orders to implement the very complete demolition scheme which I had prepared there'.[31]

In the meantime, the 2nd Armoured would try to block the desert passage by moving inland towards the crossroads of Mechili, while the Australians of the 2/13th and 2/15th dug in northeast of Benghazi would try to stop the Germans coming along the coast road — on the off chance that Benghazi was not enough for them, and they *still* wanted to come on. (Though frankly, Neame couldn't believe they would and nor, for that matter, could Gambier-Parry.)

Wavell reluctantly agreed to Neame's plan, but also told Neame that he had sent for *Sir* Richard O'Connor — the hero of Operation Compass had been knighted just a few days previously for his valour in the conquest of Cyrenaica — to help organise the defences. After holding a meeting with Neame one more time in the midst of this crisis, Wavell was now convinced that he really had made a mistake in appointing him to such a large command in a field of battle and a type of warfare in which he had no previous experience, at the expense of a commander like O'Connor, who was a proven performer of the first order in such a domain. The view that Neame just wasn't up to it was confirmed for Wavell when he was quietly taken aside by Neame's Brigadier General Staff, John Harding, who begged to have O'Connor take over immediately.[32]

As Wavell would later recount in a private letter, when it came to Neame in the middle of this battle, 'he seemed to . . . never to have any idea whatever where his troops were, or to make any particular effort to find out, although he always remained perfectly calm and never lost his head'. If this was galling, as Neame had been appointed at Wavell's own insistence, almost equally galling was that the other appointment he had insisted on, that of Gambier-Parry, was also turning into something of a disaster as, in Wavell's view in the same letter, the Commanding Officer of the 2nd Armoured was 'equally inept in his handling of his Command'.[33]

•

Nevertheless, as it turned out, no matter what General Wavell said, when O'Connor arrived he was strongly against the sacking of his good friend Neame as the Commander of all forces in Cyrenaica, to be replaced with himself. The brilliant O'Connor was so insistent that 'changing horses in mid-stream would not really help matters', that Wavell was obliged to agree to leave Neame in his post, and accept as a compromise measure having O'Connor installed as Neame's adviser only. (Perhaps one other factor in O'Connor's extreme reluctance, however — as he himself later acknowledged — was that he could not pretend that he 'was happy at the prospect of taking over command in the middle of a battle, which was already lost.'[34])

•

The following morning of 3 April, at his command post just 270 kilometres by road south of where Wavell and Neame had been meeting, Rommel gathered his senior commanders to him and informed them that they were to continue the advance at pace. To conduct it most expeditiously, he told his men that from this point they would be dividing into three groups. One group would head immediately up the coast road to Benghazi, and there was even an expectation that they would meet no resistance whatsoever, as Intelligence had already received one unconfirmed report that the British had abandoned the town. Meanwhile, Rommel personally would take a mixed German–Italian force to cut a path deep through the desert, heading east towards the British stronghold of Mechili, just 210 kilometres southwest of Tobruk, a place particularly significant because the Germans would be able to replenish their water supplies there. Finally, the plan was for Streich to lead his 5th Light Division, including Colonel Olbrich and his Panzers, over the parallel track pioneered by O'Connor's force a few months earlier, with a view to attacking Mechili from another angle.

At this point it was, again, only General Johannes Streich who had the courage — and sufficient counterweight of authority — to try to put the brakes on Rommel's plans. Streich pointed out to Rommel that his own men of the 5th Light Division were exhausted, and the trucks and Panzers in desperate need of maintenance, and that before proceeding they needed at least four days to build up the oh-so-crucial supplies before trying to push on.

'Ridiculous!' Rommel burst out. 'We are not going to let success slip away just because you reckon you're short of petrol and want time off to grease the vehicles. Take petrol from the non-essential trucks; they can catch up later. As for the maintenance, it will have to wait.'[35]

Rommel's plan was for all available trucks to unload, make a dump right there and be sent back — driving around the clock — to get ammunition and gasoline from the dumps further back. The 5th Light could load itself to the gills with such supplies as it had now, and by the time they were running out the first of those trucks should be back to them, so they could keep going again!

Still Streich demurred, causing Rommel to explode: 'This is the way to save bloodshed and to conquer Cyrenaica!'[36]

Reluctantly, because the only alternative was outright insubordination, Streich agreed.

•

It was at a spot just south of Benghazi, as the forward elements of the Afrika Korps were on the approaches to the crucial Benina airfield . . .

Amid all the shimmering heat of this terrible desert day, with many signs that the retreating British and Australians had only recently abandoned their positions, the armoured column of the Afrika Korps came to a halt almost as one on this large, amazingly flat and barren surface. With infinite relief, desperate for air not cooked to a dusty crust by the confines of their mobile ovens, one by one the hatches opened and red-faced, sweating German tank commanders appeared, looking for all the world like rabbits popping their heads out of burrows. Most of them, for so long immersed in their own dust clouds — as the wind had very unfortunately blown from behind them — were still wearing the gas masks which they found had helped them to breathe marginally better. Now they could mercifully take them off and suck in the slightly fresher air, hot as it was, their sweaty faces never redder, and not for the first time they looked around in vain for any sign of cheery palm trees, the image of which had optimistically been attached to the sleeves of their uniforms and was surmounted by a swastika on the very tanks they drove. But, alas, not a single one. Just endless, endless desert.

But . . . what was that sound? And that *vibration*?

For, even as they emerged from their tanks, the air was rent by an excruciating *gggggggrating* sound, as suddenly their tanks began to lurch downwards at all angles. And then, appalled, these men newly arrived from Germany realised what was happening. The flat, dusty 'desert' they had been traversing was in fact just the sand that covered a dry salt-lake bed; and, while crossing it at speed had been no problem, from the moment they had stopped, the law of gravity had begun to act upon them. In no time, all of fifteen tanks had sunk into the salt right up to their axles. What manner of land *was this* that they were in?[37]

And still it got worse. They were no sooner moving again — after a fearful labour which involved those few unstuck Panzers towing the others out — than they came under attack. The problem was not the shells from the British Cruiser tanks; just as they had in the previous encounters over the last few days, these simply bounced off. A worse event happened after the Panzers had seen off that attack and sent the Cruisers scurrying. At the front of one of the Panzers there was suddenly an enormous explosion.

Was war das?!?!

They'd hit a mine. Before the other Panzers could be warned, two others had also hit mines, blowing their tracks off. It was then that a warrant officer from one of the Panzers, supremely inexperienced, jumped from his stricken vehicle to have a closer look ... and landed on a fourth mine.

Afterwards, they could only find his cap ...

•

The three prongs of the Afrika Korps nevertheless continued to fan out on that morning of 3 April and press on, as difficult as it was. One thing complicating it all was that, although all those in the vanguard had been issued with beautifully designed Italian maps, the markings on them proved to have very little to do with the actual lie of the land. Points marked down as settlements proved to have either been blown away by a sandstorm or covered up by it, and sometimes even when the Germans found the spot, it proved to be no more than the well-marked grave of a pilgrim, when what they wanted was not dusty bones, but *Wasser!* water! Still, they kept moving as quickly as they could ...[38]

In the face of this advance on all fronts, confusion reigned supreme among the Allied forces in North Africa. To stop the Germans they would have had to have been well manned, well equipped with good communications and great transportation, and all of it backed by the will of their immediate military leadership to hold their ground, come hell or high water. Instead, none of those conditions was met. Many of the tanks that might just possibly have helped to stop the Panzers were back in the Delta getting much-needed maintenance work — as were a lot of the trucks; they had no heavy artillery to speak of, and the Allied signals infrastructure was so devastated that on several occasions General Neame had been obliged to place calls via the Benghazi telephone exchange, which was worked by

Arabs. Without smooth communications, the once good-sized army became just so many isolated units, few of which were any match for the Germans, and beyond all that Neame continued to give orders to those units he could reach, to keep falling back and keep themselves intact.

Inevitably, in the urgency of the moment, mistakes were made. At one point, when some British tanks of the 2nd Armoured Brigade were approaching Msus — an old Italian desert fort near Benghazi that had been converted into a major supply depot — they were stunned to see the petrol dump they had been relying on to keep going blow up before their eyes. Having received a report that tanks were heading his way, the man in charge of the petrol had presumed they were German tanks, and so had given the order to torch the lot. Many vehicles and tanks simply had to be abandoned because of it, while the others were left with no choice but to revert to the coast road, where there was some chance of getting more petrol.

By that night Benghazi had indeed fallen, and watching from the hills to their northeast, the 2/13th could see great plumes of black smoke. As it turned out, the arrival of the Germans was a great mercy to the surviving Italian settlers, for in the brief power vacuum between the British leaving and the Afrika Korps arriving, some of the local Arabs had taken the opportunity to settle some accounts with the colonists. With long memories — which included the time when their land had been taken at the point of a bayonet by Italian forces — now was the time for revenge, and they didn't miss the opportunity, killing some of the men and raping some of the women.

The Germans and Italians kept moving, even as the British and Australians kept retreating — under orders.

•

On that night of 3 April — just as he had continued to do every night when he was away from her — Rommel wrote to his wife. On this occasion the wonderful words just flowed out of him . . .

Dearest Lu,
We have been attacking since the 31st with dazzling success. The staff people in Tripoli, Rome and possibly Berlin will be possibly astonished. I have dared to proceed against earlier orders and directives, because I saw an opportunity. In the end they will give their approval and I am

sure that anyone would have done the same in my place. The first objective — planned for the end of May — has been reached. The British are on the run ...

Our losses are unusually light. It has so far been quite impossible to take stock of the material we have captured. As you may imagine, I cannot sleep for joy.

Which was as well, as there remained a heavy scene to get through that night before he would even get his head close to the pillow. For in the short term it was not Rommel's superiors in Tripoli, Rome or Berlin that he had to worry about so much as his nominal superior on site, Generale Gariboldi, who had at last caught up with the runaway German general in Agedabia and was now pounding on the door of his caravan.

Furious as only an Italian general can be when he feels that his will has been not only thwarted but totally ignored, Gariboldi demanded to know what the German had been *thinking* when he had first allowed his men to proceed to this point, and then sent them advancing from there against Gariboldi's specific orders! When Gariboldi was angry, his impressive white moustache not only bristled more but seemed to grow in size, taking on a life of its own to the point that it looked every bit as outraged as the words coming from the mouth beneath.

At first Rommel tried to placate the Italian, saying, 'There's no cause whatever for concern about our supply situation',[39] but Gariboldi would not be calmed and, if anything, became more upset at Rommel's refusal to back down. Both the Italian soldiers who had accompanied the Italian commander on his trip forwards, and the German soldiers whose job it was to guard Rommel, could clearly hear the heated voices coming from within, and it was obvious that neither man was holding back. One of Gariboldi's main objections was that Rommel's actions were in direct contravention of his orders, and that even if Rommel wanted Gariboldi to change those orders, he could not do so until he received clearance from Rome.

Rommel countered that, while he acknowledged that Gariboldi was above him in the command structure, it altered nought the fact that as the commanding officer of the forward troops he, Rommel, had to be trusted to take the opportunities where he found them, and the British retreat presented such a colossal opportunity that only a fool would not take it. As he put it: 'One cannot permit unique opportunities to slip by for the sake of trifles.'[40]

Trifles? *Trifles?* Desperately now — albeit also with rising anger — Gariboldi noted the absurd tenuousness of Rommel's supply line, and that the further he proceeded, the closer that line got to rupturing.

Rommel returned with a statement that he was certain that his men could live off the land, using dumps they had captured together with the supplies that were continuing to be rushed forwards to them. Still Gariboldi would not back off — and neither would Rommel.

The furious meeting continued for all of three hours, until they were interrupted by a tentative knock on the door. It was a nervous German signalman with a decoded message for Rommel from German High Command in Berlin — specifically, from Generalfeldmarschall Wilhelm Keitel. Excusing himself momentarily, though not leaving the caravan, Rommel quickly digested it.

It seemed that Keitel, too, was extremely concerned at the rate of Rommel's advance and, knowing just how thin and fragile the Afrika Korps' supply line was the further it got from its Tripoli base, Keitel emphasised once again that Rommel's forces were there in an essentially defensive and not offensive capacity and that the Führer himself had directed this. Accordingly, Keitel wrote:

```
The resultant offensive operations with limited objectives
may not be expanded further than weak forces permit
before the arrival of the 15th Panzer Division. Above all,
an endangering of the open right flank, which would
necessarily arise in the case of a pivot movement in a
northerly direction on Benghazi, must be avoided.⁴¹
```

Rommel finished reading the communication and then beamed broadly.

'It is from the Führer,' he said triumphantly. 'He has given me complete freedom of action ...'⁴²

In this game of bluff poker, Rommel had himself just claimed to be holding four aces, and from the moment Gariboldi accepted the ruse, the Italian was left with no choice but to leave the trailer and skulk away into the night.

And now, committed as never before, Rommel became a complete whirlwind of activity. A week earlier, Churchill had most inappropriately compared the lead forces of Rommel to 'the head of the tortoise'. It was, then, a metaphor that did not even come close, and applied even less in the first days of April. For in many ways the performance of Rommel's men from this point on was similar to his efforts the previous year in France, when his 7th Panzer Division had become known as the *Gespenster-Division*, or 'ghost division', for their ability to disappear and then show up at a point where they couldn't possibly be yet. Now, moving along three approaches to Tobruk — the coast road, the inland route and a track further south — still Rommel's forces were here, there, everywhere, with but one thing in common: every time they were advancing, and with extraordinary rapidity at that.

CHAPTER NINE

First Strike

I sniff through the country like a fox . . .
ERWIN ROMMEL, WHO BECAME KNOW AS THE DESERT FOX

Menzies saw Australia only as part of the larger British Empire. He could not envisage Australia without the Empire, and the defence of the Empire as a whole and particularly its heart, Great Britain, could not in Menzies' mind be completely separated from the defence of Australia. Though Menzies would push hard to obtain planes for Australia, he would not use his position to undermine basic British strategy if such a change would lay Britain open to greater risk. So British ministers found they could quickly abort Menzies' claims for equipment for Australia by graphically describing the position in the mother country.
AUSTRALIAN HISTORIAN DAVID DAY[1]

Trucks coming.

But there was no panic for the men of the 2/13th, still dug in on a tactically strong possie on the Er Regima Pass, where they had been for well over a week. For the last few days there had been plenty of Allied trucks coming through, all heading east in a thickening stream, and the 2/13th's job was to simply stay where they were and make sure that, when the Germans and Italians came, they could provide a nice welcoming party and ensure that the retreating Allies got safely away before they pulled out themselves.

For his part, in the meantime Lieutenant General Morshead was more than merely frustrated, and not just at the difficulties of keeping under his basic control a 9th Division that was now spread out over 250 miles — a crawling convoy that was part caterpillar and part sitting duck. Even more aggravating was that he could make neither head nor tail of the movements of the British armour in the face of the German advance, as it seemed to move to its own whim. Willy-nilly, stock-still, vice-versa, versa-vice, nilly-willy. And nor was Morshead capable of altering that whim, with his every attempted communication to General Gambier-Parry obliged to proceed via Neame's HQ, where it seemed to disappear and never emerge on the other side.

Either way, if Neame was directing the movements of the British armour, it was crazy. If he wasn't directing them it was crazier still. And reconnaissance was hopeless. Sometimes reports would come back saying a German column had been sighted at a certain spot, and Morshead would position what little Allied artillery he could muster to block it — only to find that it was the *British* 2nd Armoured Division! Other times it was the reverse, and the situation, in Morshead's view, was completely intolerable.

At least he was far from the only one feeling it. On Wavell's brief visit to his senior officers in the front line, the old man at least had the grace to personally say to Morshead, 'I am very sorry to have put you in this mess. You were quite right in your appreciation and we were wrong.'[2]

As to Morshead's own battalions of the 9th Division, he stayed in touch with them the best he could, but the reality was that the problem he had foreseen a fortnight ago, insufficient transport to move his men — and even then it was not 9th Division transport and had to be begged for — was critical.

•

Another awful reality was that the air support for the retreating troops was totally inadequate for the job at hand. General Philip Neame later wrote: 'I could count the available aircraft on the fingers of my two hands, while we had to face about a hundred German fighters, and a hundred German bombers, with the same number of Italian. Three sorties daily of Hurricanes, and on one day, only one was available for reconnaissance.'[3]

Still, what sorties they were! For, despite the meagre number of fighters available, the withdrawing troops really did owe a lot to, in particular, the RAAF's No 3 Squadron, commanded by Squadron Leader Peter Jeffrey. In their frail Hurricanes, those magnificent men in their flying machines — often outnumbered five to one — hurtled back and forth above the retreating Allied troops, defending against whatever Luftwaffe attacks there might be, and fearlessly attacking the German and Italian pursuers on the ground, with many strafing attacks launched on tanks, transports and troops. True, even with the support in the last few days from the RAF's No 73 Squadron, there was nothing the Hurricanes could do, so few were they, to turn the tide on their own, and as each of their forward airfields fell to the enemy, their range of operations had to be pulled back accordingly. And yet, in general their actions were crucial in providing some resistance to an

Afrika Korps that was otherwise completely rampant, delaying the Germans just long enough to allow the troops on the ground some desperately needed time to get themselves organised.[4]

•

With reports coming back to Rommel from his own aerial reconnaissance, that all across Cyrenaica British vehicles were seen to be moving in an easterly direction, he was momentarily surprised. *Still* the British weren't going to offer any serious resistance? Did they think that he was far better manned and equipped than he really was? Had they made their estimations and decided that it would be wiser to cede territory than to stand and fight for it? If so, so be it. He would give them even more reason to panic. As ever, Lieutenant Heinz Schmidt was right there beside him when he gave his very simple orders: 'Panzers to the head of all formations! Rear vehicles to raise dust, nothing but dust!'[5]

It was typical Rommel. Simple, brilliant, devastating to the enemy, and taking advantage of conditions unique to that battlefield, it all helped to build his momentum. In the desert, enemy observers would only be spotting the lead vehicles in the convoy anyway, and after that would judge the size by how much dust was generated. By putting the Panzers at the front, the enemy assumption would have to be that there were *hundreds* of tanks bearing down on their defensive positions . . .

And so it proved. The sheer speed of the Panzers — despite the fact that in some parts the road was so bad that the men called it a *Wellblechpiste* (corrugated iron road)[6] — was staggering, as was the amount of territory they ate up.

Back in the Great War his men used to say, 'Where Rommel is, so is the front . . .' and nothing had changed two and a half decades on. Throughout, the German General was right near the prow of the action, such as it was, observing, commanding, harrying, guiding his forces for maximum thrust, insisting that they keep going.

No excuses were accepted. Rest? You can rest later. Maintenance needs? Just do enough to keep going, and that can be sorted out later. Petrol run out for the Panzers? Well, get it from some of the trucks and let the trucks sort themselves out. Keep going!

Because Rommel certainly was . . .

Not for nothing did his own soldiers sometimes refer to him as '*General der Autobahn*', the General of the Highway, and to the road they were advancing on as '*die Rommelbahn*', as Rommel's car became so familiar to them, buzzing back and forth. Or perhaps that was him in the plane that had also been swooping around near the front troops and was now landing on the desert, just over yonder? (In a similar fashion, the wide publicity given to Rommel's activities had seen a new word emerge in the German language: *rommeln*, which meant 'to overwhelm, and to confound an opponent through fast and decisive action'.[7])

Always, visits and contacts with his troops galvanised the ranks ... as painful as it might sometimes be on first contact. The Commander of the 8th Machine-gun Battalion, for example, Lieutenant Colonel Gustav Ponath — a courageous and well-respected forty-three year old from the small village of Hanswalde in northeast Germany — had been shocked one day to be woken just after four o'clock in the morning by the bellowing Rommel getting him and his men out of his swag, as he 'chases us forward out of touch with the battalion across the stony desert'.[8]

Forward, forward, always forward. There was to be no delay, no time for something as weak as sleep, or anything else. All — *all* — must be sacrificed to the need to press forward, and Rommel particularly wanted Ponath and 250 of his best men to be at the forefront, because it was always his firmest principle that you put your best men forward to the point where they could do the most damage.

As Lieutenant Schmidt would later write: 'The General inspired all ranks with enthusiasm and energy wherever he appeared. He could not tolerate subordinates who were not as enthusiastic and as active as he was, and he was merciless in his treatment of anyone who displayed lack of initiative. Out! Back to Germany they went at once ...'[9]

While the English referred to someone being 'bowler-hatted' when they were sent on their way from the battlefront, the Afrika Korps had a far more scenic expression, appropriate to their environment. Where is Fritz? He has been sent 'on his camel'. Home, because he was just not up to it.[10]

•

And, at last, this really was wonderful country to fight a war in. With the newly arrived Australian troops, Chester Wilmot had by this time left the hurly-burly of Athens far behind, and they were now well out into the Greek countryside, heading north to try to form a defensive line to block the invading Germans somewhere up near the northern border.

One thing Wilmot — and, indeed, all of the Australian troops — noticed as they headed through the fields in this burgeoning spring, was the number of women doing serious, heavy farm work. Where were their men? As it happened, many of them were right where the Australians were heading — up in the north, readying to battle the Germans as valiantly as they could with ancient weaponry borne forwards on wagons pulled by bullocks.

And yet even the heavy farm work wasn't enough for many of these women. For a lot of them were also busying themselves, with their children, working on the very roads that the Australians were proceeding on. With hoes, picks and shovels, they were widening them, repairing them and throwing gravel down to make them firmer and easier for the Australians to get to the Germans on, pausing only long enough to wave cheerily as the soldiers passed.

'We realised,' Wilmot told the ABC listeners at home, 'that here there was a nation at war — a people who knew that their free existence was at stake and were fighting and working from the front door to the front line ...'

With the troops, the radio correspondent kept moving north, while the news started to filter through that an ever bigger body of Germans was now moving south towards them ...

•

Blood. Edmondson blood. Everywhere. And there seemed to be just about nothing that Elizabeth Edmondson could do to stop it, as it just kept gushing out of this man she loved. Her husband, whom she frequently referred to as 'JW', had been working with a steel wedge on their farm, and a splinter had come off it to slice one of the major arteries in his leg, clean. The blood just kept coming out of him, and Elizabeth momentarily despaired that she could ever stop it. Finally, though, bit by bit, by pressing the wound closed with one hand while she quickly wrapped a bandage around it with the other, she managed to stop the flow, get him stabilised and to the doctor. He would be okay, but would have to stay in Liverpool hospital for the next few days. Elizabeth would have to tend to the cows that night and was in a right state. If only Jack were here ...

Her mood worsened the following day, when the *Sydney Morning Herald* reported that the Germans had attacked the Allied lines and already entered Benghazi. That was somewhere around the area where her Jack was, and that night she poured out her feelings in her diary:

I feel so very fearful as I know how little Jack spares himself. He would so completely forget himself as if he just didn't count. I get the shivers when I think of it. There is no one I can even talk to. I would not worry JW.[11]

That same day Jack was with the rest of the blokes of the 2/17th Battalion, positioned just behind the Er Regima Pass being held by the 2/13th, all of them feeling frustrated. They were aware that things were happening, that the Germans were coming, that some units were pulling back, that there was going to be a 'big blue'; but in their own neck of the woods there was very little trouble to this point. Jack, together with his best mate, Athol Dalziel (a quietly spoken police officer from Perth he'd got very close to over previous months), and the other blokes in his section who he'd come to know like brothers — 'Snowy' Foster, Ron Keogh, Ted Smith, 'Splinter' Williams and Ron Grant — continued to stare to the west. Like them, Jack was hoping for some sign that they'd get a crack at the Germans; but so far ... nothing, nothing at all. In any case, in a forward position to them it was the 2/13th that would get the first crack at the Jerries.

•

Those poor bastards.

As the big Panzers moved to within sight of the Benina airfield just on the outskirts of Benghazi, the last of the Hurricanes of the RAAF's No 3 Squadron took off, heading east. Only shortly afterwards they passed close over the heads of the men of the 2/13th Battalion, dug into the slopes of Er Regima — suddenly rising 400 feet from the plain — who were now cheerily waving their hats up at them in farewell.[12] The Australian pilots waggled their wings in turn, as cheerfully as they could, but they knew better than most just what their own Aussie soldiers would soon be up against. The pilots had seen from the air over the previous few days just what kind of devastation the Panzers were capable of wreaking, and now feared that their countrymen were going to face it in full on the ground. It couldn't be long before the two forces clashed, and the Australians started copping it ...

And indeed. For the previous two days, the thick flow of retreating Allied troops heading past the 2/13th Battalion had started to thin to a trickle as the bulk of the defenders between the Australians and the Afrika Korps passed by. Just that morning a truck full of Tommies had torn through — all the soldiers with haunted eyes — stopping only long enough to tell them that as far as they knew they were the last, and the Germans weren't far behind, and good-luck-and-see-you-later!

Now it was mid-afternoon of 4 April, a scorching hot day, and the men of the 2/13th Battalion kept their eyes glued to the black road ribboning out of the shimmering coastal town 15 miles to their southwest. Sometimes that black road would be lost in the shimmer as it melded with the black of the smoke now billowing from Benghazi, but then it would come back clear, and all eyes would focus again.

Among them, Bert Ferres and Bill Walmsley were acutely aware that at long last they might be able to see some of the action that they had so long been hungering for. They had engaged in heavy training for nearly a year now, felt ready to handle the Germans' best punches and throw a few of their own, and they wanted it to be now. Bert, though he felt confident in his own right, knew big Bill was as game as a bull ant, and drew added strength from the fact that, if it came to it, they would be fighting shoulder to shoulder. Real soldiers — not just pretend ones who had only trained without ever actually fighting.

There!

Just a little after two o'clock they saw something, crystallising and then fading in the vibrating light ... crystallising ... fading ... getting clearer now ... much clearer ... clearer still ... *Germans*. On trucks. With tanks. So it was done. The Krauts were on their way, and the 2/13th was going to be the first battalion to have a crack at them in the whole war.

The job assigned to the 2/13th, and it was a big one, was to delay the brutes coming up that slope for the rest of the day, to give the remainder of the 9th Division time to get away. If all went well, reinforcements would shortly arrive and in the early evening — when it could finally be rustled up — transport would come for them and they could make their own escape.

To stop the Germans, the Australians didn't have much bar their own courage, the thrill of at last turning to stop and fight, and a few scattered weapons, including four 4.5-inch howitzers that they had managed to borrow along the way from Britain's 51st Field Regiment and a couple of captured Italian mortars.

Their three rifle companies, plus a machine-gun company from Britain's Royal Northumberland Fusiliers (composed of hard-as-flint Geordies from the far north of England, near the Scottish border), were now stretched across a 9-mile front which offered just about nothing in terms of cover — all shaly rock and shrubs stunted by the glaring sun and cruel, hot wind, but at least it was better than a billiard table — and the mood was quiet and steely. Checking ammunition. Bayonets. A few muffled prayers from those who believed that the same God who had presided over this dreadful war to date might in this case look upon them benignly. Everything they'd learned at the camps at Ingleburn and Kilo 89 and Julis, every bond of trust they had formed with each other, was about to be put to the test.

It was just before 4 p.m. when the Germans were close enough to hear.

And then, just half an hour later, coming hard at the Australians — most pointedly at the 2/13th's D Company, which was astride the main road — were the advance elements of the 3rd Reconnaissance Unit, with two waves of eight tanks each coming ahead of twenty armoured cars and perhaps 3000 soldiers on a few dozen lorries. Over the previous few days these elite German soldiers had been at the prow of the Afrika Korps and not come close to faltering.

Noisy now. Extremely noisy. The growls of menace coming at the Australians up the hill from the Panzers started to turn into angry roars as the engines of the German vehicles showed the strain. Getting closer.

Then the moment came. Somewhere out on D Company's right flank as they faced the attackers, a Digger, holding one of the Italian long-range mortars that had been salvaged against the specific instructions of General Neame, had the supreme honour of being the first member of the Australian Imperial Force to fire a shot against the German Army in World War II. And it was just like Corporal 'Ned' Kelly had taught them back at Ingleburn: 'You drops the bomb in here and *whoooosh!* out she comes . . .'

Out she bloody come all right, and — with their other mortars and howitzers soon playing in symphony — in no time at all they'd dropped a mortar right on the noggin of one of the light tanks, knocking it, *kaputt*, out of the battle!

Just who it was on the German side of things similarly honoured to be the first to fire on the Australians was never clear; it was only certain that there were many contenders for the prize. For, seemingly from everywhere now, German shots and shells rumbled and exploded around the Australians, even as the German infantry had scattered everywhere, foraging up the hill, trying to outflank, do them in. It was *on*.[13]

For all that, the 2/13th held their ground, firing, reloading and firing again.

At one point, the 2/13th's mortar platoon was seen to be firing so hard and fast that, while one man was holding onto the barrel to try to stop it from shaking to pieces, another man was lying across the base plate trying to steady its foundations, while the third kept aiming the best he could and firing the bloody thing. One way or another, though, they were able to keep it firing.

As the battle raged, with the Germans continuing to try to push their way up the hill and the Australians throwing everything they had down at them — trying to hold them at least until just after dark, when their transport would arrive to ferry them back to the rest of the Allied forces — one action was particularly notable. Just when one of the German tanks had appeared to break through and all might be lost, a Digger with the much-maligned Boyes Anti-tank rifle managed to stop it, literally in its tracks, with a singularly well-placed shot. For once, the bloody thing worked! Then, when the German tank crew jumped out, Private Stephen 'Curly' Eland charged down the hill at them, firing his Bren from the hip as he went, killing one of them and capturing another three.[14]

Not a bad effort from a man who, up until just a year before, had been a humble and anonymous butcher from Strathfield, in the western suburbs of Sydney.

These common men of the free countries . . .

Alas, Eland was to be killed only a short time later, as the Germans, by sheer weight of numbers and firepower, continued to press their attack.

With B Company, Bert Ferres and his mate Bill were now called to move across the escarpment to get to the point where the Germans had focused their attack, and to help to support D Company, but it didn't quite work out as planned. For in the approaching dusk they were just scrambling towards their besieged mates when they heard a cry — 'Here they come!' — and in nothing flat bullets started flying all around them, as they threw themselves to the ground. D Company had mistaken them for German soldiers!

'Cut it out, you silly bastards!' roared one of the forward B Company soldiers. 'It's us!'

Luckily, no one had been hurt, but it had been a close-call.

•

Back in Cairo at this time, Lieutenant General John Lavarack, the Commander of Australia's 7th Division, had received an odd order. He was really only passing through the Egyptian capital with his troops on the way to Alexandria, where they were to embark for Greece, when he was urgently summoned to go and see General Wavell that evening. When

Lavarack presented himself, the British general quickly got to the point. What he wanted to know was, what did Lavarack think of *not* sending the 7th Division's 18th Brigade on to Greece, but instead sending them to help defend Tobruk?

Wavell did not frame it in the shape of an order — as there were political sensitivities to the military relationship between Great Britain and Australia to tread delicately around — but made it equally clear that it would be very much to his liking if Lavarack would accede to the request. After some more discussion, the distinguished Australian military man agreed that the 18th would go to Tobruk, and he would go with them.

It was unfortunate that there was no time to consult the commander of Australian forces in the Middle East, General Blamey, but that was just the way it was.

Still, Blamey was furious when he found out, while attempting to direct the campaign in Greece. For him it was, once again, a flagrant bloody example of British high-handedness when it came to dealing with Australian troops — breaking up an entire division and doling his men out as it suited, without referring to him, as Britain had agreed to do when the war had started. This approach had to stop, and he felt himself to be just the man to make it stop, as soon as the immediate crisis was over.

•

The 2/13th found itself in a spot of bother, but more or less managed to sort it out. For when neither the reinforcements nor the transport arrived as expected, the only way of survival was for the battalion to slowly pull back, leapfrogging each other down the road, company by company, and also using the enveloping darkness to their advantage. By now the Germans knew that they far outnumbered the defenders, but because at this point it was a lot more difficult to work out where those defenders were, they had to proceed with caution. At last, just a little over an hour before midnight, the rumbling of trucks behind signalled that the 2/13th's relieving transport was nearby, and the men managed to pile on board and get away — less some ninety-five of their fellows, killed, captured or lost. With no fewer than eighty men to a truck, space was even tighter than on some of the train carriages they had seen in Bombay, and for hours Bert was only able to get one foot solidly down on the truck flat-bed. Generally, the mood of the 2/13th was positive, notwithstanding their losses. For the first time they had been tested, had actually fought with the Germans, had given as good as they got, and probably a bit more besides.

•

On a track not so far away, on one of the Australian trucks also nudging forwards into the gloom that night as the 2/24th Battalion was pulled back from Tocra, Private Ivor Hancock was sitting beside his mate Frankie Barlow, each huddling into the other in the middle of a night as cold as it was black, with the only punctuation points to those conditions being the many fires burning by the side of the road as various ammunition, fuel and food dumps were put to the torch before departure by other units. There were so many men and so few trucks, with space at such a premium, that everything not absolutely essential simply had to be dumped and burned, and even the bit of flat space atop the roof of a truck was claimed by men hanging on for grim death.

Speaking of which ... as they continued to rumble forward, it wasn't just the bitter cold that was making Frankie shake but the fact that he had himself just survived a near-death experience. While he was on the truck, the end of the rifle he had slung around him had caught on the webbing of a truck coming the other way, suddenly hurling him backwards, and if the webbing hadn't broken he would have been dragged to his certain death. Ivor did his best to calm Frankie, telling him that it was obvious that his number wasn't up, that the main thing was that he had suffered no damage; but still, every now and then Frankie would shudder — almost like a big mongrel dog shaking itself to get dry after jumping out of a creek — over the thought of what might have happened to him. He bloody well didn't want to die in this war, flaming well wanted to get back to his people at home on the farm in Victoria, that's what he wanted to do.

Through it all, their truck kept slowly rumbling forward the best it could. In such conditions, nothing could tarry. Even if a good vehicle was stopped by virtue of a flat tyre or dirty spark plugs, there was just no time to fix it — so it was set on fire with the rest while the occupants scrambled across any passing tailgate that would have them. Frequently these Allied trucks would burn right beside the shattered remnants of Italian trucks and tanks, still lying there following their own disaster at the hands of O'Connor's men a bare month before. No joke, both Ivor and Frankie were becoming ever firmer in their view that this was a strange kind of war ...

Behind, they could hear the rolling dirty thunder of explosions as engineers blew up bridges and tried to cause landslides across the roads to slow down the Germans. At least, they hoped it was their own engineers causing those explosions and not the Germans themselves. It wasn't that they didn't want to fight the Krauts — far from it — but not bloody well now, not in this frozen darkness where they hadn't had a chance to dig in and prepare for the encounter that must come. Most frustrating was when there'd be a hold-up and one of the drivers would take the opportunity to nod off, and then have to be roused when the blockage was clear. You could lean on the horn, of course, but, as much as possible, the retreating Allied troops were trying to keep as quiet as they were invisible, with their lights off; no one was quite sure where the Germans were, as the Allied soldiers continued to the east, which they could tell because the Pole Star — which they'd learned about — remained throughout on their rough left.

At dawn, the mobile chaos that Ivor and Frankie were a part of became a little clearer in contour. Along the road, cars, trucks, motorcycles, tanks and armoured vehicles were bumper to bumper, sometimes six abreast, each trying to nose its way along a road that often had huge holes blown out of it, courtesy of German bombers. Thank Gawd for what was left of the RAAF boys, because somehow it was Australia's own fly-boys who had managed to keep the Luftwaffe off the ground forces in this most exposed part; but it was obvious to all that if the German planes did arrive in force then the Australian high command would have to get Shit Creek Paddle-makers on the blower in a bloody big hurry.

And yet, when any of the vehicles did try to move ahead of the pack or dodge blockages by venturing off the road and trying their luck on the desert proper, they were always brought undone by either soft sand or sharp stones and they, too, had to be abandoned.

As the sun kept rising in the morning sky, so the Australians kept moving. Through the night, many of the men had admittedly been torn between shame at turning tail and *wonderment* that the Germans and Ities were fighting with them for this nowhere bit of the globe in the first place. But, with the fast-rising African sun, it seemed to be shame that was winning hands down. Most wanted to turn and fight. Make a stand somewhere. Show the bastards what they could do! Were they really going to just be chased off the desert by the Germans and hop on a ship back home? And what would they tell the kiddies then, when they asked what did you do in the war, Dad? Were they going to have to live with that for the rest of their days?!

Still, they kept moving. Sometimes German armour would be spotted on the far horizon, apparently coming at them in a flanking movement. But on each occasion the Pommy blokes on the crews of the 25-pounder guns would, smooth as you like, pull out of the convoy, take their sights on the

Germans and send just enough shells raining down upon them to keep the bastards away, before moving back into the line.

•

It had been a close call, but they had done it. On the previous afternoon of 4 April, a good chunk of Australia's 2/3rd Anti-tank Regiment, together with another chunk of the 3rd Indian Motor Brigade — valiant Indian soldiers, with trucks, commanded by British officers — had tentatively made it into the inland fort of Mechili, sitting astride the key crossroads of that part of North Africa, unsure of whether it was in their own or German hands. Happily, it proved to be already occupied by a missing squadron of Brits, the 18th Cavalry, who'd been out of touch and feared captured for a few days, and together they all settled in — only to find that, on this morning of 5 April, they were already under siege. At the very least it was clear that they were surrounded by scattered German forces who were taking pot shots at them from a safe distance — hardly a concerted push, but it was obvious that the Allies had beaten the Germans to Mechili by only a matter of hours. (In fact, Rommel himself appears to have recognised that it would likely be a close-run thing. Having been told by the Luftwaffe that Mechili appeared to be free of British forces for the moment, he got a message through to the commander of his most forward forces: 'Mechili clear of enemy. Make for it. Drive fast. Rommel.'[15] Shortly thereafter, spotting from the air that one company had stopped for no reason that he could determine, Rommel, flying above them in his Fieseler Storch plane, dropped a note on them: 'If you do not move right away, I will come down. Rommel.' They got moving right away.)

Now that the Allies had got there first, though, it was going to be their job to hold the fort against what was sure to be a rising tide of Hun, as more and more of the brutes flooded forward. The fact that the Jerries didn't launch on them right away could only mean that, by their own estimation, they were insufficient in numbers and firepower to force a victory — but that situation was unlikely to last for long.

The British, Australian and Indian soldiers set up their defences the best they could, determined to hold Mechili at all costs, and conscious that the longer they held those crossroads and their crucial water supplies from the Germans, the more time they would be giving to the 9th Division to make its way to relative safety down the coast road, without having the Germans at Mechili push north to the coast and cut it off before it got to Tobruk. The one thing the Allies wouldn't be lacking was their own supplies, as

Mechili had been essentially set up as a supply dump for the 2nd Armoured Division, and was now capable of sustaining 10 000 men for thirty days.

It was as well, by the by, that Mechili had a plentiful water supply, as on the first night there some of the Diggers from the 2/3rd Anti-tank Regiment accepted an invitation from the 3rd Indian Motor Brigade to dine with them, and top of the menu was curry. Hot curry. In all of their born days none of the Diggers — nearly all of whom had been raised on bangers and mash, or steak and three veg — had ever tried curry, and it *didn't* go down a treat. It was nice of the Indians and all, but the evening finished with the Diggers pouring canteen after canteen of water down their gullets in the hope that the bushfire in their throats and stomachs could at last be put out.[16]

Speaking of the 2nd Armoured Division, however, where the hell were they? The strong expectation was that they should have arrived at this point two days previously, and yet there was no sign. Nor, of course, could they be contacted. The Mechili garrison would just have to wait for some sign, or a message to get through; and in the meantime, hold the fort ...

•

The deeply troubled feeling just wouldn't leave Elizabeth this Palm Sunday. Her husband was still in hospital — there wasn't even a bus to get her there to see him — and the only way she could take her mind off things was to do hard work on the farm and then knit like fury into the night, the rhythmic clicking of the knitting needles still not keeping pace with her tumbling thoughts.

She'd noticed that the Germans always seemed to pick Sundays for their special atrocities, and whenever there was trouble the British always seemed to throw the Australians into the toughest situations, using them as cannon fodder, just as they had done at Gallipoli.

Did other people feel like she did now? Why was her Jack there, in the front line, and not, say, home like the Grimsons down the road, who had contributed absolutely no one to the war effort!

•

One measure of Rommel's extreme keenness to attack was an altercation he had with General Johannes Streich late on the afternoon of 6 April, just 25 kilometres to the west of Mechili. From the perspective of the Afrika Korps, if the Allies could be blasted out of there then the way to the east would be clear, and there would be every chance that they would be able to cut off many of the Australian and British troops retreating on the coast road. So, yes, Rommel was set on launching an all-out attack on Mechili, and he wanted to use General Streich's 5th Light Division to do it.

However, when, in response to Rommel's stated plans, Streich again made the very reasonable point that the core of his division — which is to say, the Panzers themselves — had not yet arrived, Rommel was still keen that they attack anyway! Streich, by this time more than merely wearied by Rommel's incessant insistence that everything had to be sacrificed on the altar of pell-mell *schnell*, demurred, saying it would be better to wait until the Panzers arrived.

When Rommel still would not let up, going so far as to accuse Streich of *cowardice* for his reluctance, Streich could not help himself and lost his temper.

Pointing to the hard-won Knight's Cross around his neck, he roared, 'Nobody has dared tell me that before. Withdraw that remark, or I'll throw this at your feet.'[17]

Rommel, surely realising he had gone too far, withdrew the charge.

For all that, neither man particularly bothered to hide from the other his antipathy. Streich, a Prussian, spoke in the clipped and educated tones of the *Hochdeutsch*, the purest form of the German language spoken by most of the ruling class — rather like 'Oxford English' was in Britain; and, indeed, he had about him something of the air of one who was born to rule. Yet here was Rommel, speaking the common language of the common man, somehow in a position of power over him![18]

But power Rommel did have, and he had made the decision: the Afrika Korps would keep advancing.

•

At almost the same moment, another key decision was reached in Cairo. In the face of complete disaster, with their forces totally routed in North Africa by the mainly German troops and no sign that Rommel was easing up, the British Foreign Secretary, Anthony Eden, had a meeting with Chief of the Imperial General Staff Sir John Dill, and General Sir Archibald Wavell, together with the Commander in Chief Mediterranean, Admiral Sir Andrew Cunningham, and the Air Chief Marshal of the British Middle East Air Forces, Sir Arthur Longmore.

After the bare preliminaries, they got to *the* key question: in the face of this rampant German force, was it going to be possible to hold Tobruk? It was not just a question of whether or not the Allied units on site, and arriving, would be strong enough, but also of whether the garrison could be maintained over a long period of time. Should they cut and run completely, or commit every resource they had to holding the most important port between Alexandria and Tripoli?

In this, it was Admiral Cunningham's view that was critical. For while it was one thing for the troops to have the wherewithal to hold Tobruk in the short term, the reality was that, unless the navy undertook to supply them in the long term and actually deliver, they'd inevitably have to surrender within weeks, if not days.

What would Cunningham say?

When Robert Menzies had met Cunningham six weeks earlier on his trip to the Middle East, he had described him in his diary as 'slim, red-faced, blue-eyed, radiating optimism, faith in his ships and his men. This is the No 1 personality I have so far encountered on this journey. Compared to him, Lord Chatfield [Admiral of the Fleet] is a stuffed shirt.'[19] Fortunately, it was a combination of that optimism and faith in his ships and his men that shone through now ...

For when the good admiral spoke, there was a sense that he both knew the gravity of what he was committing to, and the fact that they could, literally, deliver.

'Yes,' he said simply. 'We can do it.'

It would take many ships and fantastic effort to shift supplies to Tobruk from Alexandria, but he felt both that his men were up to it, and that militarily it was a risk worth taking. (Upon first spying the Australian troops in the Middle East, Admiral Cunningham had reported back to London they were 'magnificent material' and 'the most lively and undefeated fellows I have ever had to do with'.[20])

The decision was taken, then: Tobruk it was to be. Once again, there was no time to confer with General Officer Commanding the AIF in the Middle East General Blamey, who had his hands full in Greece. Still, they felt sure he'd be fine with it once the urgency of the situation was explained, and that there was really no choice. They had to move, and move *now*.

Troops and supplies even then just about to head for Greece were stopped at the docks and redirected — notwithstanding that, on that very day, Germany had formally declared war on both Yugoslavia and Greece, and within ninety-five minutes of that declaration bombs had begun to fall on Belgrade, and a short time later on the Athens port of Piraeus. Neither the declaration nor the attack had been unexpected, but for now it was the troops in North Africa who had to remain the primary focus, in the hopes of avoiding complete catastrophe. The alternative was to give the Axis powers one more crushing victory and possibly the Suez Canal itself, and that was completely out of the question.

All in to Tobruk, on the double, and last man in to shut the gate. Then lock it — '*Cry havoc, and let slip the dogs of war . . .*'

•

Long, long had they suffered, but now was the time of their redemption. It was at Neame's former headquarters of Barce, just 90 miles northeast of Benghazi, that four Diggers of the 2/17th Battalion were told that a food dump was about to be blown up, so if they liked they could eat anything they found there and take away with them as much as they could carry. In no time at all the Diggers were hoeing into enormous tins of large black cherries, pineapples, sausages, the lot — much of it previously retrieved from the Italians. It had been *months* since their stomachs had had the pleasure of taking in that kind of rich food, and every mouthful was a delight . . . at least for the moment. Quite what their digestive systems would make of it remained to be seen . . .

•

In many ways the approaching Germans really were reminiscent of a bushfire back in Australia. Long before an actual sighting of flames, the air was simply full of flight and approaching menace, and it was in just such an atmosphere that Generals Neame, Morshead and O'Connor met on the evening of 6 April in the small town of Marawa, where Neame had moved his headquarters in the face of Rommel's advance. Outside the tiny, dowdy building in which they met on the edge of the town, Allied traffic continued to rumble and grumble past, fleeing to the east.

Every bit of information the generals had from reconnaissance and the passing parade indicated that their worst fears had been realised: the Germans had cut inland, and were proceeding quickly. It was not a question of stopping them so much as working out the best way of getting as many troops as possible to safety.

The meeting concluded, something else now took their urgent attention — that was, to get themselves out. The dark night had descended, the Germans were getting closer with every hour and, with discretion the better part of valour, it was time to regain their own front lines, wherever they may be at this point. (It was genuinely far from sure.)

The three commanders took two separate routes, with Morshead following one road, and Neame and O'Connor another, which they thought to be more direct. In the latter car, a big Lincoln Zephyr, it was Neame who took the wheel in the place of the driver, trying to navigate and keep to the road by the light of the moon alone, as it was too dangerous to have the lights on. And it was while looking at the moon that O'Connor began to feel uneasy. If they were heading in the direction they should have been, then the moon should have been positioned more or less ahead of them to the left. But it wasn't — it was well out to the *right*, meaning that the direction Neame was taking them in was dangerously to the north. And suddenly there by the side of the road was a sign board stuck on a petrol tin![21] The suggestion was put to Neame that they should stop, reverse and look at the signpost, to work out where they were, but Neame wouldn't hear of it. Time was of the essence, he said, and besides, he knew exactly where he was going. This did little to abate his fellow general's growing alarm.

Once O'Connor protested; twice he protested; and on the third occasion he was successful in getting Neame to hand the wheel back to the professional driver in an effort to move back on track.

The two British Generals now dozed off to sleep in the back seat, only to be woken at around three o'clock in the morning with the car suddenly lurching to a halt, accompanied by the sound of someone shouting.

What the *hell* was happening?

'I expect it's some of those bloody Cypriot drivers, sir,' the driver offered and, indeed, that initially seemed possible because the shouting clearly was in some kind of foreign gibberish. And then they realised — it was *German*. They had been nabbed. Both men quickly tried to remove the many badges of high rank they had upon them, but it was too late.

'*Raus! Raus!*' the German soldiers roared at them as they pulled the doors of the car open. Get out! Get out!

The Germans who had pinched them — just a small way from the Derna airfield, as it turned out, were the crack troops of Lieutenant Colonel Gustav Ponath's 8th Machine-gun Battalion, and it did not take them long to work out just what kind of prize catches they had, either.

It is the stuff of subsequent legend — albeit perhaps apocryphal legend — what happened next.

So the story goes, when Neame and O'Connor were taken back to Rommel's headquarters some 50 miles to the west, they arrived just as his officers were sitting down to breakfast.

'Does anyone here speak English?' O'Connor thundered, most assuredly not in the manner of a man who had just been taken prisoner.

When one rather timid, bespectacled officer put his hand up that, yes, he spoke English, he was rewarded by O'Connor roaring at him, 'Well, damn you for a start!' And nor did it improve O'Connor's mood any to be told shortly after the capture, by other German officers with a grasp of English, that Rommel's aim was, in their own words, 'Egypt and far beyond!'[22]

Unfortunately, a long period of imprisonment beckoned for both Neame and O'Connor, though in late 1943 they would escape together from their Italian prison camp, and O'Connor would return to active service, adding some more glorious chapters to his military reputation.

As for Morshead, though deeply upset to hear news of their capture, he had no doubt where the blame lay, as he subsequently wrote in a letter to his wife, Myrtle:

I was very sorry O'Connor was captured. But I was not far behind Neame and O'Connor and they should have been off hours before, as I should have been, but Neame was the cause for the delay as he had spent the fateful day chasing Gambier-Parry's show and not finding it.[23]

•

Just a couple of hours after Neame and O'Connor had been captured, General Gambier-Parry at last slipped through the German perimeter around Mechili, with the news that the rest of the severely depleted 2nd Armoured Division had cut back to the coast road in need of fuel. (For some reason no one could ruddy fathom, the supply dump at Msus had been blown up, and the 2nd Armoured just didn't have the juice to get to them.) The General held out some hope that a lot of them could still make it, but gave no promises, which was as well. For when the rest of his 'division' did finally arrive a few hours later, there was just one Cruiser tank, a motorised rifle regiment, a 25-pounder gun, a troop of Royal Horse Artillery and the Division HQ. In short, although it wasn't the twenty-five tanks they had been hoping for, at least it was *something* . . .

Twice the Germans called on the Mechili garrison to surrender, with the most interesting appeal arriving on the evening of 7 April. The written demand, signed by Rommel himself, was brought by a senior German officer and promised the Allies the 'full honours of war' if they laid down their arms and came out with their hands up — though precisely what the 'full honours of war' meant, no one was sure.[24] (Just quietly, though, it was pretty impressive that Rommel himself was out there, as his reputation had preceded him.) Still, given that the officer bearing the message had made it clear that Rommel was keen to have a reply as soon as possible, Gambier-Parry ensured he kept Rommel waiting a good four hours before telling him his considered answer: 'No.'

But by late in the night, as the shelling on the garrison was growing intolerable, it was obvious that the situation was becoming hopeless. If they stayed much longer they would be captured or killed, which would serve no one. By this time they were getting some support from a few planes of the RAF and even fewer of the RAAF, who had been magnificent in harassing Mechili's German besiegers; but it was not going to be enough to change the result of a real battle if it came to it.[25]

Besides, it was the view of General Gambier-Parry that the job had now been done, that they'd held Mechili long enough, blocking the German advance by the inland route, and that by this time his own 2nd Armoured Division and the 9th Division proceeding by the coast road to Tobruk would already have arrived. Therefore, it was the job of the Mechili garrison to get itself out, and get to Tobruk. Gambier-Parry's decision was that at dawn the following morning, 8 April, they would attempt to break through the German cordon surrounding them by essentially doing a Blitzkrieg in reverse. Classically, Blitzkrieg involved bringing maximum force to bear on a certain point of a perimeter to get *in*, but Gambier-Parry wanted all his tanks and trucks to fire up and head to a spot on the eastern perimeter going *out*, at which point they would try to get away from the German pursuers and make their way to Tobruk. Behind them they would leave a valiant rearguard, which included men from the 2/3rd Anti-tank Regiment. So get the guns primed, lads, the trucks loaded, the tanks full and some sleep if you can. We'll attempt the breakout at dawn.

•

It was just like cracker night at home, only this wasn't any fun at all. An hour before the break of day on the morning of 8 April, John Johnson and his mates were woken by the roar of aircraft and distant explosions. As one, they leaped from their swags, with their rifles at the ready, to see what they could see …

It was the Luftwaffe, attacking Tobruk's port and harbour surrounds with everything it had in it, which was plenty. The Australian soldiers sat spellbound, given a grandstand view as Stuka after Stuka hurtled screaming from the sky, going into all but vertical dives on their targets of wharves, warehouses, water plants and ships before unleashing and then pulling out at the last moment. (Just an instant later, from huge yellow flashes sprinkled in catastrophic clusters around the port, enormous licks of flame vaulted skywards to meet the next Stuka hurtling down, but never quite getting there.) To complete the impact of the moment, all of it was mixed with the roar of the garrison's own Ack-Ack fire, trying to put up a blanket of flak and tracer bullets for the brutes to run into. And then there were the garrison's own planes, the blokes from the RAAF's No 3 Squadron and the recently arrived RAF's No 73 Squadron, both of whom had scrambled from Tobruk's tiny El Gubbi airfield — situated just back from the harbour on a plateau only a foot or two larger than the runway — and now getting amongst the hurtling Huns. Now, every few minutes or so, there would be a kind of *crump!* as one or other of the planes was blown from the sky and hit the desert floor — always a slightly different resonance to the more vibrant sound made by a bomb exploding.

Soon it was all over. The Stukas had spent their venom and gone, less a few of their number. The Hurricanes limped back to El Gubbi, also less a few, to fight another day. Around the harbour, various fires licked away.[26] Christ, those Stukas looked powerful. (And sounded the same. Each one was fitted with an air-powered siren screamer that let out a blood-curdling shriek to wake the dead, at its most horrifying the instant the plane went into a dive to release its bombs. That way, whoever the bomb didn't hit would at least be half scared to death.)

•

Now!

On Gambier-Parry's signal, tank and truck engines simultaneously roared into life, heavy fire was laid down upon the selected point on the perimeter, and together they put the pedal to the metal, hurtling forward, as the shocked German troops, now fully awake, scrambled to return fire.

Coming towards the Germans was a rough 'box formation' of men and machinery, more or less as Gambier-Parry had planned, with the heavier armoured vehicles and one tank on the prow of the breakout, while on the flanks and rear, making a rough box behind, were the thinner-skinned trucks. On the layer inside and right in the middle were those with the thinnest skin of all — soldiers — many on the back of lorries, a few running forwards. Almost as if nature was in tune with the mood of the moment, a sandstorm was whipping through, and the billowing clouds of dust raised by the churning vehicles and artillery fire from both sides were soon sweeping to all parts of the battlefield, adding to the general confusion.

They were through!

At least most of them were through. Inevitably, the Germans recovered from the first shock and soon laid down a withering fire on the sides of the box, meaning that, while the forward elements soon had the worst of the fire behind them, others were now caught in it. In his own armoured command vehicle, General Gambier-Parry turned back in an effort to see if he could help extricate those who were caught, and in all but an instant he and his senior officers were also engulfed in heavy fire.

Even as others raced away, though, those in the rearguard of the 2/3rd Anti-tank Regiment trained heavy fire on the Germans, so as to keep them occupied and give the other blokes as much time as possible.

In a particular part of this rear battle to take Mechili, a Panzer Mark IV, with seven smaller Panzer Mark IIs — described by German historian Wolf Heckmann as 'like chickens around a mother hen'[27] — was attacking a defensive position on the western perimeter of the fortress proper. To the infinite surprise of the men in the Panzers, some of the defenders had not run at their very sight, but had kept up a steady stream of fire. This didn't really matter to Lieutenant Albrecht Zorn, in command of the all-but-invulnerable Mark IV with its booming 75-mm short-barrelled cannon. Sighting a handy target away to his right in the anti-tank ditch — some soldiers firing an ineffectual anti-tank gun at them, with its pathetic little rounds simply bouncing off — Zorn directed his driver to go across to it. Watching this behemoth coming his way, the commander of those soldiers — an Australian gunner from Mudgee by the name of Vince Rayner — told his men to hold their ground and keep firing! (Not that any of those men were under any illusions, for all that, about the power of their own gun, which the Australians usually referred to as 'pea-shooters' or 'popguns'.)

Look, it *was* a bit grim that their shots were being deflected off the astonishingly thick hide of this German beast — shrieking now, with the combined sound of its hideously roaring engine and the tracks grinding through the sand that was now spewing out from all angles, even as it got larger in their vision, all black crosses, radio antennae and Nazi pennants — but it was the principle of the matter. Neither Vince nor his mates were going to bloody well give way.

And now Zorn gave his orders to the driver. Crush them. Take the tank right up to the ditch and then down into it. The Mark IV lurched forward, closing now to within 20 yards of Rayner.

It had been Zorn's considerable experience that, at that range — with the vision of the Panzer's 75-mm cannon and two Spandau machine guns, both roaring fire, combining with everything else — those few defenders who hadn't by this point run for their lives would shit their pants, but for whatever reason these defenders still held their ground, even though their death was now all but certain as the tank came straight for them.

In the stress of the moment, however, Zorn's driver made one critical error. That is, he did not engage the Panzer in its lowest gear as it went over the edge of the ditch. Had he done so, the tracks of the tank would automatically have followed the precise lie of the land as it flowed over the edge down into the ditch. But, in the higher gear, the tank momentarily hung over the edge of the ditch before gravity took it downwards, and for just a split instant the soft underbelly of the Panzer was exposed — a mere half-inch thick, instead of the three times that thickness it boasted over most of its framework elsewhere.

And the Australian was not one to let an opportunity pass.

'Give him one more up his arse!' Rayner roared as the gun fired off one last shot for the money.[28]

The effect of such a shell penetrating a container it could not subsequently escape, bang-bursting from side to side like a red–hot marble in a steel tin, was of course devastating, and on one of its catastrophic ricochets it took off Zorn's left leg before removing his driver's head. And as artillery rounds from the other Panzers fell all around these Australians, all were hurled backwards with most of them injured, including Rayner, who had severe lacerations to his legs. Sadly, their bravery did not alter the course of the battle, and Mechili soon fell to the Afrika Korps — with over 2000 prisoners taken, including 100 Australians and Major General Gambier-Parry himself. Those prisoners included Vince Rayner and the survivors of his gun crew, but they had certainly demonstrated that dogged bravery in the face of overwhelming firepower stood some chance.

•

Only a short time later, Rommel landed his Storch plane on Mechili's airstrip, positively *beaming* that the last effective obstacle between the Afrika Korps and the British and Australian forces now congregating at Tobruk was gone.[29] *And* they had captured another British general to go with the two already in the bag! That gentleman, he was told, was secured in one of Mechili's buildings, and before anything else Rommel went to have a brief, courteous conversation with him. As Rommel was one of the few German generals who was a stickler for the rules of the Geneva Convention, even such an English silver-spooner as Gambier-Parry, still bristling at the sheer indignity of his capture, found it hard not to like him; and, despite their military enmity, the English General certainly had his professional admiration for what his German opponent had achieved in North Africa to this point.

To the collected POWs as a whole, Rommel now had a few words, assuring them that they would be treated fairly, but he also couldn't resist adding a touch of vaingloriousness by telling them, 'Today is the 8th of April. By the 15th I will be in Cairo, by the 30th I will have the Suez Canal, and where will your British Empire be then?'[30]

(And pleased to meet you, too, Herr General.)

Then Rommel moved off to have a look at the remarkable command truck that Gambier-Parry had been using, which — exactly like the ones that had been used by Generals O'Connor and Neame for most of the campaign, and captured with them — had been purpose built for desert conditions with high axles, large, spongy tyres designed to get a grip on the shifting sands, and high-quality radios inside. With a quick swastika painted on their fronts, and nicknamed '*Mammut*' (Mammoth) by the troops, they would henceforth be perfect to head on down the *Rommelbahn* in. (Significantly, this was one of the few concessions to swastikas that Rommel made. While most Afrika Korps trucks and tanks displayed them as a matter of course, and he was happy to have them painted on top of his vehicles to prevent attack from the Luftwaffe, he never had swastikas on display in his headquarters, and strongly discouraged his staff from displaying them.[31])

On the instant, though, Rommel was right there as the vehicles were being emptied of their inventory of equipment, and something caught his eye. It was pair of large sun-and-sand goggles, which pleased him from the first.

Smiling, he picked them up and said, 'Booty — permissible, I take it, even for a General.'

Indeed. He put them on, just above the gold-braided rim of his cap peak, and they remained there ever after, for all his time in the African desert.[32]

Now, there was little time to waste. Every military instinct Rommel had told him that speed was of the essence, that the enemy would be in complete disarray and there would never be a better time to attack than immediately.

•

For those members of the Afrika Korps' 8th Machine-gun Battalion, who had now taken Derna, the pleasure on this day was almost surreal. As recorded by one of their number, Lieutenant Erich Prahl: 'Here is the Africa of our dreams: palm trees, gorgeous heavy scented blossoms in many colours and snow white houses. Arabs in oriental colourful robes, but also in Italian and English parts of uniforms, want to sell us eggs, oranges, dates, lemonade and cakes. Others push towards our vehicles with handmade and decorated slippers, scarves, rings, necklaces and metal plates. This is the orient from "1001 Nights". This delightful oasis is bordered by the dark blue sea — we could almost think of ourselves as sailors of Sinbad. An old saying comes to mind: "Here it is good, let us build huts here ..."'[33]

But no. This was not a time for hut-building, and the German soldiers had to take their cue from the thousands upon thousands of tiny swallows that had arrived in Derna on that same day, on their annual pilgrimage north from Africa up to Germany and surrounding countries.[34] The swallows tarried no longer than was necessary, and neither could the soldiers — as wistfully as they might have been looking at the direction the lucky swallows were heading in — for Rommel's orders had now come through. After they had replenished their supplies of water, petrol and provisions from the captured dumps, they were told by their commander, Lieutenant Colonel Gustav Ponath — his otherwise proud Prussian features now raggedy-haggard — that they were to move forwards to Tobruk at all possible speed. Reluctantly, the German soldiers started their engines and moved east, not quite knowing what to expect of this place they were heading towards.

•

Out in the desert, those who had escaped from Mechili now headed for Tobruk at all speed. Initially they had, as feared, been hotly pursued by several German armoured vehicles, but mercifully a severe sandstorm suddenly blew up, and in all the murk they managed to shake them — dust falling off everywhere as they did so — and keep going towards Tobruk. It was possible that there were German ambushers ahead, but they would just have to deal with that when or if they came to it ...

•

The horror, oh, the *horror*!

It was true that wartime delivered many grisly and horrible sights, but mostly you were able to turn away and look at something else. The sad thing for the driver of the truck bearing more retreating troops was that there was no choice. He *had* to look, had to keep his eyes peeled right on the road to redemption ahead — and what did he see? *What did he see?*

Four Australian bums, *mooning* him, that's what he bloody well saw. Four Diggers from the 2/17th Battalion with clearly severe dysentery, hanging off the tray of the truck in front and holding on for grim life as they tried to ease their tortured bowels.

Yes, this manoeuvre of theirs was probably necessary, as there was no time for stopping with the Germans right on their hammer, but it was no less disgusting because of it.

In trucks not so far behind came blokes like Austin Mackell, Jack Edmondson and the rest of the 2/17th Battalion, most of them highly annoyed that they were obliged to retreat without yet being able to fire a shot in anger. That morning their company commander, Captain John Balfe, had told them that if they didn't get a hurry-on, they'd be having their breakfast with the Germans; within minutes, they were on their way. He was good like that, Balfey — no nonsense, straight to the point, but a good little bloke with a good way of expressing himself that didn't get up blokes' noses. They reckoned he was the best company commander in the 2/17th.

Yet now here they were in the back of a truck, always in the middle of a man-made sandstorm, freezing their bollocks off at night and boiling by day, all while being battered from side to side, as it seemed to be a point of honour with the driver to hit every pothole between them and Tobruk. Would that they could get somewhere, anywhere, so they could dig in and face the German brutes.

Too, the fact that much of the last stretch into Tobruk consisted of hundreds of hairpin bends — known to the Diggers as 'devils' elbows' — meant that at one point the column of Allied vehicles heading east extended for 15 miles. Slowly, inexorably though, the convoy proceeded, with the surest sign that they were getting close being a huge mural on the western wall of one of the white Italian houses by the side of the road — left there by one of the 6th Divvie Diggers — depicting an enormous beer and a horse-racing scene, with a caption reading, '*Abbotts Lager: A good drink but bloody hard to get.*'

That mural was well known to be just 15 miles or so to the west of Tobruk, so it couldn't be long!

And, indeed, it wasn't.

For at last they were here. Piling out of the truck, the men of the 2/17th were battered, bruised and exhausted, but so immensely glad to be here that some of them could even raise a cheer. At last they could fight. Still, where exactly was 'here'?

For many it looked like the last spot on earth worth defending. As far as the eye could see through the swirling dust, there were just camel-thorn bushes and rock, camel-thorn bushes and rock, on and on. This was Tobruk?

The best they could work out, they were to man a section of the perimeter near Post R33, whatever that was. Some of the men went into the posts while others, like Jack Edmondson's section, went into trenches beside the main posts looking out over the wasteland on the other side of the wire ... that almost seemed to be sullenly gazing back at them.

To this point, as many in the 9th Division were keenly aware, their key distinction as a fighting unit was that they had retreated a greater distance, with greater speed, while still staying substantially intact, than any other fighting unit in history.[35] At least here, in Tobruk, it seemed they might be a fair chance of making a stand.

•

Meanwhile, at this time in North Africa, it was hardly exaggerating to say that all roads led to Tobruk. From the west, as Morshead and his men of the 9th Division rather expertly leapfrogged each other along the track winding back to Tobruk, they were joined by three regiments of British field artillery which had been engaged on the front line around Marsa el Brega, but had wondrously managed to get themselves and — most crucially — their precious 25-pounder guns out and into Tobruk. From the south came those of the Australian 2/3rd Anti-tank Regiment who'd been able to get away from Mechili, together with another anti-tank battalion from the Royal Horse Artillery — both of them having narrowly escaped the clutches of the Germans at Mechili in the company of the 3rd Indian Motor Brigade. From the east came such crucial units as the 107th Royal Horse Artillery, which had been on a training exercise by the Nile Delta when their signalmen were woken in the middle of the night with the news that the regiment's presence was required at Tobruk, and by dawn they were on trucks heading west, desperately trying to get there before the ruddy Germans and Ities closed the road.

•

And they also came in by sea. In Cairo, the word had gone out urgently to get the right men in the right ships with as much of the right weaponry as could be carried in one rushed trip. Most crucially, the same brigade of the 7th Australian Division — Morshead's original 18th Brigade — which Wavell had stopped from embarking for Greece was rushed in by ship together with every unit of Ack-Ack artillery, field artillery, Matildas and Cruisers that could be scraped together in depots and workshops. Hurry! Hurry! Hurry! No time to tarry, we'll send the rest of the stuff later. *Go! NOW!*

From the air, the Hurricanes of the RAF's No 73 Squadron flew in and were soon joined by some Lysanders of No 6 Squadron — as many as could be spared and a few that couldn't quite be, but were sent anyway.

William Shakespeare had once famously written that there is a 'tide in the affairs of men', and all across North Africa that tide was heading straight towards Tobruk from all points.

Still, others were close to missing that tide, and had to scramble to make it.

Out on Alexandria Harbour, for example, an English captain of the 7th Royal Tank Regiment by the name of Rea Leakey was enjoying his brief leave in a yacht, in the company of a friend and two lovely nurses, when he saw a strange thing.

There on the shore was a man from his regiment who, as far as he knew, was meant to be engaged in tank training exercises hundreds of miles away. And the fellow was walking towards a ship! Curious, and perplexed, Leakey lightly jigged the tiller to see if he could come closer and get a better look at what kind of ship it was. Into its massive shadow, he looked up at its rail to see on it many of the men of his regiment chortling down upon him. That did not last long. Suddenly his Commanding Officer peered over with a face like thunder, and he was not long in letting some of that thunder out: 'Get back to Cairo immediately, Leakey!' he ordered. 'Pick up the truck we've left you and follow us to Tobruk. Get going now, you haven't a moment to spare!'[36]

Leakey got going, on the spot. Farewell, my love.

•

Still they came from Germany too. For at that very time, coming from the north, high above the Mediterranean, some 3500 veteran German soldiers — being transported in 208 Junker-52s — were also heading in the rough direction of Tobruk, albeit via Tripoli. They were the men of the 15th Panzer Division, coming in as the vanguard of both the rest of the men of the division and all of their heavy equipment, called in by Rommel with some urgency as soon as it had become apparent that the British were falling back with such haste. As ever, the German general's instincts were that, when the enemy gave way, they had to be hit with everything available — but the problem was that he simply didn't *have* the men he needed to properly consolidate.

And yet here they now were, flying towards the African coast at the rate of some 350 miles per hour, their mood one of grim determination — despite the fact that, before taking off, they had all been issued with life jackets and given instruction on what to do if they were shot down and found themselves floating in the Mediterranean. They were elite troops who had never known defeat, and for good reason: to a man they were superbly trained, and equipped, and in many ways had been raised to accomplish precisely the kind of task that was now being set them — to advance the cause of the Fatherland through force of arms against whatever the British Empire could throw at them.

As a matter of fact, there were some of those hurtling British things now. Just north of the African coast, with the glistening waters of the Mediterranean still sliding by beneath them, the convoy was suddenly set upon and strafed by British planes, presuming perhaps to get some fairly easy kills among the lightly defended Junkers. But those British pilots had not figured on the German troops inside, one of whom was the 21-year-old from Stuttgart, Rolf Völker. After a year in the regular German Army, he had joined the Afrika Korps just a month before, as one of the *Panzergranadiere* of the *Schützenregiment* 104, which had been undergoing intensive training in Baumholder in western Germany between the Saar and Mosel rivers. Like all the rest of the men, Rolf's mood to this point had been far from cheery, as the ride had been so bumpy that every one of them had thrown up, and that stinking vomit was now sluicing around on the floor of the plane they were all sitting on with their kitbags and ...

And now they were under attack!

In short order Völker and his fellow soldiers had taken fire axes to their own cargo hold to get out some of the light machine guns and their ammunitions drums — all of their heavy weaponry had been left in Italy in their rush to get to North Africa — and then used those same axes to break the planes' plexiglass windows before returning some serious fire, with Rolf personally taking over the machine gun in his plane. The British planes soon disappeared. If there was a way to triumph, these were the sort of men who would find it, rather in the image of their Commander, General Heinrich von Prittwitz und Gaffron.

A military professional of aristocratic birth — in fact, from a long line of distinguished German officers — he was just over fifty years old and considered an able commander of such an august body of men, admired particularly for his capacity to be totally ruthless in the pursuit of victory, to find a way to win the day.

His reputation was very good, and it was likely for this reason that he had no sooner landed in Tripoli than Rommel had sent for him to come forward at once, as he needed his leadership abilities for a task he had in mind.

•

All up, the stage was now set.

After millennia of Tobruk slumbering peacefully in the sun, punctuated by the odd outbreak of violence as two competing regional powers struggled for control, the tiny town was now the focal point of a coming major battle between many faraway powers. The pride of the British Empire was inside, while the Hun was at the gate outside, and the Italians not far away ...

The battle was not for Tobruk for its own sake, but because it was a hinge of history; because whoever controlled it over the next few weeks and months could help guide the fortunes of entire nations struggling for control in this whole world war.

CHAPTER TEN

All Set

While this is so, it should be remembered that the adventurous spirit,
which leads to exuberance such as we saw in Tobruk this day,
is the very quality which gives the best Australian troops their
initiative and dash in battle.

CHESTER WILMOT IN HIS ABC REPORT[1]

I'm proud to be an Aussie, there's something different about them.
The Hun fights with grim determination, the Tommies fight by numbers,
but the Aussies tear about like kids at a picnic, swearing and laughing
the whole time. They knock some bastard, then lean against a rock
and roll a cigarette . . .

A YOUNG DIGGER IN TOBRUK TO HIS MOTHER[2]

Good news!

German intelligence reported that a flotilla of Allied ships was making its way towards Tobruk from all parts of the Nile Delta and Alexandria. Rommel read the reports with grim satisfaction. Clearly, those incoming ships could only mean that the British were doing in Africa exactly what they had done all over Europe, most notably at Dunkirk: cutting and running. It was not surprising — in this war so far, it was what they had done best whenever it came to fighting the Germans — but it did make the matter of taking Tobruk all the more urgent. The key would be to get inside and capture all the British, Australian and Indian troops, apparently some 30 000 in total, before they could get away. If Rommel could achieve this, then there was no doubt that it would outshine every other feat in his brilliant career so far.

That included, of course, his triumph of the previous year, which had an uncanny resemblance to the present situation, albeit on a smaller scale. With his Ghost Division of the 7th Panzers, Rommel had broken through to St Valéry, on the French coast, where they had cornered 4000 French troops and 8000 British troops of the 51st Division, together with four Allied generals. Just as the British were preparing a smaller version of Dunkirk, Rommel had brought his artillery forwards to the heights of the western side of the harbour and fired just enough salvos to make it clear that those 14 000 troops had no choice but to surrender or be blown to bits. And so they had surrendered. With that previous success in mind, Rommel now asked Major General Heinrich Kirchheim — who had come to Africa simply as an observer for the OKH, but was now to be roped in for a new task — to go on ahead to Tobruk and reconnoitre the spot near Tobruk Harbour where the Afrika Korps could do exactly that when the time came.[3]

Why not simply look at a detailed map of Tobruk and its surrounding areas, to find the best spot to set those guns up? Because, despite Rommel's best efforts, and that of his staff, the Germans simply had not been able to secure any layouts of Tobruk detailing what the topography of the land was, where the strong and weak points were, or where the batteries, the minefields or even the worst of the anti-tank ditches were! Given that their Italian allies had been in possession of the town only two months before, it would have seemed a fairly simple matter to find such maps, but … *nein*, and *no, no, NO!* Somehow their Italian allies had failed to take any maps of Tobruk and its defences with them when they had scarpered.

Even without the maps, the imperative for Rommel was to keep pushing hard, whatever the obstacles; and, just as he had roped in Major General Kirchheim, he also ordered the newly arrived General von Prittwitz to take charge of a combined force of the 8th Machine-gun Battalion, the 3rd Reconnaissance Battalion and a couple of companies of the 605th Anti-tank Battalion, together with some artillery provided by Italy's Brescia Division, and pursue the British down the coast road.

•

The one thing never in question, however, was the need to gain access to Tobruk one way or another — and the option of just leaving the Allies inside and moving on to Egypt in force was never contemplated. For the real problem was supply.

Now that the lead units of the Afrika Korps were some 1400 kilometres east of Tripoli and nudging towards the Egyptian border, they were gorging on 44 000 tonnes of supply every month, including the supplies they were stockpiling for the future move into Egypt. The Luftwaffe needed 9000 tonnes, and the Italians needed 63 000 tonnes. And yet Tripoli alone could only cope with unloading 45 000 tonnes … which was where Tobruk came in, as it possessed the only decent harbour, not to mention coastal freshwater supply, for hundreds of miles. What is more, given that the principal road from east to west went right through Tobruk, it meant that if the Allies weren't dislodged, all that would be left for the Afrika Korps would be to reroute their supply lines out into the desert, pushing on some 100 extra kilometres to the shifting sands to the south — with all the risks and drain on energy that such a manoeuvre entailed. Finally, while so ever the Allies held on to their garrison, there would always be the risk that they would break out at any time and strike at Rommel's entirely unprotected flank, completely cutting his forces off. There was nothing for it: Tobruk *had* to be taken, and quickly.

Though Wavell and all of the British command in Cairo were devastated at the capture of Neame and, perhaps more particularly, the valiant O'Connor, there was simply no time for misery. With all possible speed, Wavell flew to Tobruk on the morning of 8 April with Lieutenant General John Lavarack, and together they moved to get the situation in hand. It was Wavell's decision that Lavarack was the best man for the job to replace Neame as Commander of all the Allied forces in Cyrenaica, with the defence of Tobruk as Lavarack's most immediate goal; and it was equally at Wavell's suggestion that Lavarack agreed to make Morshead the Commander of Tobruk itself.

And yet it was a measure of the extraordinary conditions this war was fought in that, between the time Wavell and Lavarack took off in their Lockheed Lodestar from Cairo and landed at Tobruk, such a terrific dust storm had blown up that, although the pilot managed to get the plane down, it was one hour before the senior officers on site could find them — sitting out the storm in the plane on the runway — to properly greet them. Nevertheless, once located they were soon whisked away to the battered house near the centre of Tobruk that was temporarily being used as a headquarters — chosen because it boasted a big blackboard on its first floor — and they were almost immediately joined by Morshead, who had himself just made it inside the perimeter after having overseen the successful withdrawal of the bulk of the 9th Division from points west. Wavell greeted the Australian warmly and — recognising just how right Morshead had been three weeks earlier, when he had said that the Germans were in all likelihood on their way — repeated that he (Wavell) was very sorry with the way things had turned out, and that Morshead and his men should find themselves in this situation.[4]

They all then got down to brass tacks, nutting out just how they were going to tackle the task of holding Tobruk. Prime Minister Winston Churchill had noted the gravity of the situation, and had sent a cable the day before, which included a singularly firm desire:

Tobruk seems to be the place to be held to the death without thought of retirement. I should be glad to hear of your intentions.[5]

Churchill added that it would be simply intolerable for any individual unit in Egypt to withdraw, 'unless 50 per cent casualties are sustained'.[6]

Now, though it had to be noted that Churchill, in London, was always very big on such magnificent phrases as places being 'held to the death' and, equally, that Wavell was yet to see that particular cable, the fact was that for once Wavell was in full agreement with the Prime Minister.

In Wavell's estimation, so long as Tobruk was held, Rommel simply would not dare — nor, perhaps, even be capable of launching an all-out attack on Egypt with his supply lines stretched so long.

To finish the conference, Wavell's words were designed to impress upon them just how isolated they were and just how hard they were going to have to work to hold it: 'Remember. There is nothing between you and Cairo ...'

Then, turning specifically to the junior of the two Australian Generals, he said, 'Morshead, I rely on you to hold Tobruk for eight weeks to enable me to get a force together to come to your relief.'[7]

Yes, sir. Very good, sir.

End of meeting. After lunch, Wavell was back on his plane and gone, winging his way to Cairo, which he eventually reached, albeit only after being twice forced down in the desert when the engine of his plane malfunctioned. Lavarack and Morshead and their men were on their own, and it was up to them.

•

Back in Cairo, the alarm at the way things were heading was now palpable and, though GHQ had expressed confidence that Tobruk could and would be held, still Wavell wasn't taking any chances, ordering the rest of the Australian 7th Division to go to Mersa Matruh, to help bolster the defences of the frontier.

•

Having detailed maps of the battleground was one of the most important of Lieutenant General Morshead's military touchstones. As one who had known the horror of landing at Anzac Cove twenty-five years earlier in the wrong spot, a mile and a half from where he was intended to be — meaning the maps he and his men had possessed were useless and they were therefore proceeding 'blind' — the General was aware of the potentially disastrous consequences of trying to do without the maps. It was with this in mind that, as soon as he had arrived in Tobruk, he had sought out maps of the port and its perimeters, and he had been most relieved to get his hands on them.

Fortunately, Morshead was able to profit from the same maps that O'Connor had secured before the first siege of Tobruk ten weeks before. Now, by using the maps and engaging in a lot of on-site recces, Morshead, Lavarack and a handful of senior officers began planning in detail how they would set out their defences. The key question was: should they place their men in the old, outer ring built by the Italians — proceeding in a rough arc with an average radius of 9 miles from the harbour — which meant defending a very long arc of about 28 miles? Or should they bring the men in closer, to the bare beginnings of another defensive ring that was in the process of being constructed?

The latter had been Wavell's suggestion, on the reckoning that in that way the defensive line of the fortress could be a lot shorter, and therefore the density of men they could put in that line all the greater. After looking at how well the old Italian defences were holding up, however, and how far the construction of the second ring had proceeded, Morshead and Lavarack decided to place the troops on the outer defensive ring. To begin with, by choosing that outer ring they would be able to keep the enemy artillery so far away from the harbour that it would not easily be able to pepper the lifeline of supply. There was, as well, an even more cogent reason: in reality, the inner ring was still little more than a few hastily constructed stone walls and shallow trenches built in spots that the Italians had considered the British invaders would be most likely to take, while the outer ring remained impressive.

Yes, some of the posts were in need of repair, and the anti-tank trenches, particularly, needed further digging out, but they were defensive positions that the Italians had spent years constructing, and Morshead and Lavarack felt that when they were held by committed Australians, they would be formidable defences indeed. It was true that the Italians had usually put between twenty-five and fifty men in each post, and the Allies would have only ten to fifteen Australians, but they would just have to find a way to manage. It wasn't ideal, but one of Morshead's favourite aphorisms was that he'd 'rather command a hundred men with their tails up than a thousand men with their tails down', and he felt that by putting Australians in the defensive positions rather than Italians, he was doing that very thing ...

•

With the decision to hold Tobruk now firmly made, the stream of Allied soldiers heading towards the town thickened, and yet travel in those parts soon became extremely difficult. For, upon his departure, Wavell had not taken the sandstorm with him, and for the rest of 8 April — as well as all of the next day and into the night, that swirling hell had worsened to the point that some of the Italian settlers who had been taken prisoner said it was the biggest such storm in their memory. The Diggers didn't doubt it, because one thing was certain: it couldn't get any *worse*. To be sure, some of them were from parts of the outback where they reckoned that in a bad blow, the crows flew backwards to keep the dust out of their eyes, but none of them had ever seen a sandstorm like this ...

In fact, the Diggers preferred the Arabic word for a sandstorm, '*khamsin*', as one way or another this was not 'sand' as they knew it to be, the way Bondi Beach had sand. This sand was finer than talcum powder, so fine that gravity had no more than barely a ghostly grip, and it could stay suspended and be swirled around in the air for hours. And while the khamsin was blowing it was like being in a dry, brown fog, a fog that attached itself, insinuated itself, through the tightest confines and penetrated *everything*. Whatever part of a man's skin was exposed was soon covered in a thick, dull patina of dust; the moisture of every orifice soon became a muddy mess; your hair became a wretched filter for the filthy air, with obvious results; and your clothing was several pounds heavier for all the fine dirt it was carrying in every fibre. Your wristwatch stopped working because the dust got into that too; and, most importantly, the same applied to gun mechanisms — so cleaning them became more important than ever. Men continued to work through it the best they could, phantom figures barely outlined in the swirl of what looked to be the 'twilight world of the dead'... and — *there!* — a figure would come forward, seeming like a goggle-eyed monster lurching out of the gloom. Sure, wearing gas masks was uncomfortable, but at least they helped you breathe a little easier and you didn't have to squint your eyes so terribly just to get a little vision.

Still they kept digging into the stony ground, conscious that every shovelful gave them further protection as their trenches got deeper and the walls higher. Sometimes, such digging could turn up treasures like an old shard of pottery or somesuch to remind you of just how long civilisation had been in these parts, but there were occasional nasty surprises that could shake a man to his bones. Out on the western perimeter, for example, Private Arthur Smith of the 2/9th Battalion was with his mates digging down, and making surprisingly easy headway, when — *oh Christ Almighty!* — his pick suddenly penetrated something soft and stinking. Gawd help us all, it was a recently buried Italian corpse, to judge from the remains of the tattered uniform.

They covered the poor brute up again, and decided to dig their trench a little further away, and a bit more tentatively this time. There but for the grace of God . . .

Sometimes, as the khamsin kept blowing and blokes fell exhausted to the ground, they would curl themselves into almost a foetal position, as they saw the camels do, in the hope that that would provide some relief. Others learned from the Arabs themselves, and covered all of their face with a wraparound cloth, leaving only the eyes exposed, and tried to keep working, simply by keeping their slits of eyes turned away from the direction of the storm.

In such circumstances it was only just possible for the trucks bearing troops and supplies to keep coming into Tobruk, but keep coming they did.

•

Nearly there now. Captain Leakey had barely stopped moving since he had been plucked out of Alexandria Harbour four days earlier, and nor had the wheels of his truck stopped turning. It had been a hairy trip, racing against the time when the Germans would surely cut across and secure the road on the eastern approaches to Tobruk, and prevent any further Allied reinforcements by land. The risk of a German ambush was considered so great that, at one point, Allied military police had actually closed the road heading east, but Leakey and a friend who had accompanied him to share the driving duties ignored the closure and insisted on continuing regardless. The result was that, after sharing the steering wheel around the clock, he and his comrade were at last on the approaches to Tobruk, and in fact got in with just moments to spare. With German armoured cars roaring from behind, they made it through to be greeted by some grinning Australians moving aside some barricades for them, with their sergeant saying, 'Come in, you Pommy bastards!'[8]

•

By midnight on that night of 9 April, the khamsin was so bad that when new arrivals got out of the back of the truck, each man had to hold onto the belt of the man in front of him. Heads down, they clawed their way through the storm to the blessed barracks that awaited them. Throughout the night, if any needed to go to the toilet they would wait till enough of them needed to, and out and into it they would go again. (Consequently, blokes really had to be busting before they went.)

By four o'clock on that morning of 10 April, the storm had abated a little, and yet that only meant that sometimes the exhausted soldiers were now seeing things they didn't want to see.

For it was at exactly that hour that one of the men in one of the trucks of the 2/48th Battalion that was making its way to the perimeter thought he heard some kind of rumbling noise and poked his head out the window to have a look.

Oh ... Christ.

'For God's sake, get a move on!' he told the driver.

'Why, what's wrong?'

'There's a German tank up our bum!'

And there bloody well *was*, too. A big Panzer tank, rumbling right at them and nearly in range to fire off a shot.

With the arrival of that last company of the 2/48th, the 9th Australian Division was effectively forming up in the one place at the one time for the first time, with three brigades of infantry — the 20th, 24th and 26th — all settling in, together with the 18th Brigade of the 7th Australian Division, and some 12 000 British and 1500 Indian soldiers to bring the numbers up to about 27 000 soldiers defending. The question now was just how to best place them, to not just keep the Germans and Italians at bay but to really *hurt* them.

•

Dreaming of Germany. Of days in the sunny upland meadows, walks with his wife, playing with his children, them playfully tugging on his shoulder ... less playfully now, *really* tugging on his shoulder ...

Oh. It was Rommel.

And he was angry. Those natural humour lines on his face could instantaneously be placed at the service of a deeply unpleasant snarl when he was unhappy, and this was just such an occasion. In Rommel's army, clearly, one did not sleep — one attacked! At the least one was preparing to attack, and no other activity was acceptable. Rommel was insistent that von Prittwitz must instantly be up and about, ready to lead his men in battle, and *not* let another Dunkirk happen! Did he not realise that time here was of the essence, and every hour that they delayed meant more men and military materiel that the Allies would spirit away?

Raus! Raus! RAUS!

The previous plan had been for von Prittwitz and his men to go from their present position, 50 kilometres west of Tobruk, skirt the fortress and attack from the east, but now Rommel changed his mind. Immediately if not sooner, he wanted a direct attack: straight down the road and overwhelm the Tobruk defences from the west. (This despite the fact that, as Rommel later acknowledged, 'We had at that time no real idea of the nature or position of Tobruk's defences.'[9])

In mere minutes von Prittwitz was up and out, on his way, trying to shake off the fatigue that comes with a long journey in such a short time, and acclimatise himself to the infernal heat of Africa, so different to the temperate climes of Germany. Up ahead, somewhere, lay the first of the defences he and his men would have to overcome to successfully storm Tobruk and prevent the British escaping. All he knew was that Rommel had *insisted* that with no time lost for probing or reconnaissance, his combined forces had to attack Tobruk from the west. Rommel had also told him that the coastal road was secure up until at least 12 kilometres out of Tobruk, and that point was still 3 kilometres ahead. The mood in his small party was confident, with one of the men expressing the hope that Tobruk would be undefended.

'With luck,' he said, 'the Australians will have left their stocks of beer behind. So it's just as well we're getting a thirst up.'

•

The tone for the defence of Tobruk was spelled out by Lieutenant General Morshead on the morning of 10 April in his Order of the Day, which had echoes of the famous signal given by Lord Nelson in 1805 before the Battle of Trafalgar to the effect that 'England expects every man to do his duty' — a signal that was credited with stiffening the sinews of the men as they responded with alacrity, putting the French to the sword.

But Morshead's style was a lot more prosaic and to the point: 'There will be no Dunkirk here. If we have to get out we will fight our way out. There is to be no surrender and no retreat.'[10]

It was typical Morshead. Few oratorical flourishes, no attempt at appealing to higher instincts, just a direct statement as hard and unyielding as Ayers Rock.

Yes, they had their backs to the sea, and yes, they were surrounded by the Axis powers. But jumping on a boat and getting the hell out simply wasn't an option. There was to be only one way: the Germans and their Panzers might have knocked over all of Europe; the Italians might have run rampant through many of the countries of north and eastern Africa — but this time they were all going to be facing blokes using a different kind of gumption.

That same morning, the Commanding Officers of every battalion and every ancillary unit gathered at Lieutenant General Morshead's headquarters, which had been set up in some deep tunnels on the escarpment leading up to Fort Pilastrino. They were there to see Colonel 'Gaffer' Lloyd, the General's second in command, whose job it was to give them a briefing on the lie of the land as near as it could be reckoned, as well as to assign each of them to the specific part of the perimeter that Gaffer and General Morshead had worked out it would be their job to defend. The mood among these senior officers was tired — many of them had been able to snatch only a few hours of sleep over the previous few days — but purposeful. Despite the relative disaster of the last few days, though, they had made their way into Tobruk mostly intact, and the best news of all for them was that their retreat was over. They were now going to *stand and fight*, and the officers formed a tight circle on Gaffer, rather like the rough, tight circles he was now showing them on a map ...

For there they could see the port of Tobruk snuggled neatly into the wavy lines of the Mediterranean coast and the penetrating finger of the harbour; and there were the circular contours of the 137 concrete perimeter posts that had been so effectively built by the Italians over the past ten years, which, in the garrison's evolving lexicon, became known as 'the Red Line'. Inside that again, about 2 miles back, was another ring of defences known as 'the Blue Line', which would be both the fall-back position should the Red Line be penetrated and the place where those in reserve for the front line would be situated — able to bring fire on any enemy tanks that got stuck in the minefields in front of them, or any enemy sappers who tried to clear a passage through those minefields.

In broad brush strokes, Gaffer divided the 30-mile perimeter into three sectors, with each brigade to take one: the 26th Brigade taking the west, the 20th Brigade to be spread along the south, and the 24th in the east. Gaffer was a forthright man, described by Chester Wilmot as 'big and bluff, with a manner that is a strange mixture of bluntness and friendliness'[11] — perhaps another way of saying that he was particularly Australian in his approach to military leadership. Naturally, then, he was speaking to these senior officers in the confident and direct manner of one who was not going to brook any kind of debate on these orders, for the simple reason that he knew they were all up to it, no matter how difficult it might appear at first blush.

And where was he?

The way the plan worked, it would mean that six battalions would take a rough 5 miles between them of the Red Line, while another three battalions would be placed just behind them on the Blue Line as a reserve, ready to go should the need arise. Similarly, each of those battalions on the front line would have three companies manning the posts between them, while another company was to dig in just half a mile behind that line as a reserve.

As to the crucial British artillery, it would for the most part be situated just inside the Blue Line, far enough back that it could be protected, but close enough to the front line that it could easily direct its fire on all those who would seek to crack the Tobruk nut.

Even as the meeting was breaking up, though, the need for speed in properly setting up the defences was demonstrated by a key event on the only hill on the western perimeter of Tobruk, where some of the 2/28th Diggers, observers on the rough slopes, noticed three German armoured cars approaching their positions.

The only guns on hand were two old Italian units salvaged for the Bush Artillery, with the troops manning them being a party of transport drivers and pioneers. But no worries ...

With not the slightest hint of panic, the two ranking officers on site conferred as the men on the guns hung on every word, keenly aware that they were now on the edge of some real soldiering.

The rounds were in the barrel, the fuses were primed and everything seemed to be sighted more or less right — as the approaching vehicles moved to within a distance of 500 yards — so there was nothing more for it than to give it a burl.

'Shall we open up?' Lieutenant Dick Lovegrove, the Transport Officer, asked Captain Tony Tunstill, the Quartermaster.

'Yes, please, if you don't mind,' replied Tunstill in the distinctly calm, polite manner for which he was always known.

'All ready boys, let 'er go!'[12]

'With that unconventional fire order,' the 2/28th Battalion History recorded, 'the first shot was fired in defence of Tobruk. It came out of an Italian field-piece which was without sights and which was manned by infantrymen with a week's training in the art of gunnery.'[13]

There was an almighty roar — quite shocking to some of the men not used to being this close to an exploding gun — a flash of flame from the end of the barrel, and then ... some 200 yards ahead of the lead vehicle, a sudden huge spout of dirt indicated where their first shell had landed. For that first shot — because the gun had not been properly dug in — the vibrations caused by the firing of the artillery made the whole thing wobble and fall, with the sandbags surrounding it toppling forwards as well.

Again, though, no worries. While one team worked getting that gun back up and properly dug in, another team of the Bush Artillery worked to get the second gun going, and this time with a slightly different angle ...

'Cock 'em up a bit, boys,' suggested a British Gunnery Colonel who had stopped by to give them a bit of advice on this occasion.[14]

And ... *heave.* All hands on the barrel, they managed to lift the second Italian gun a couple of inches, put in half a brick to keep it up there, and then get another round down the barrel.

And ... fire! This time the shell landed right between the two leading vehicles, which now faltered uncertainly.

Guter Gott, what was happening? They certainly had not expected this kind of reception. Now, as the Bush Artillery of the 2/28th kept firing, the German convoy turned tail and left.

Ah, but they would be back, or at least some of their mates would be. Just half an hour later, up at the point that the 2/28th's A Company was dug in by the Derna Road entrance to Tobruk, someone saw something new. Over the previous few days it had been A Company's job to check in the last of the competitors of the Benghazi–Tobruk Handicap, but straightaway this was different. First they heard a kind of earth-shaking rumbling, and then they saw a mass of armoured German vehicles approaching!

Perfect. Roughly prepared for just such a thing, the Diggers had not long before finished manhandling into place five aerial bombs they'd found in an abandoned Italian warehouse, and wiring them into the superstructure of yonder bridge which crossed the deep gully of a wadi on those approaches. Ah, what a positive pleasure it was to now blow the bastard up![15]

Still, it was not long before the Germans came on again, looking to find a way over the wadi. Well, again the Australians were ready for them ...

•

Motoring fairly fast down that same road just a short time later, General von Prittwitz and his immediate escort barely had time to realise something was amiss. Suddenly, after coming around a corner, up ahead they saw some men of their 8th Machine-gun Battalion stopped on a slope leading down to a bridge that had been blown up, appearing to wave them down, yelling, '*Halt! Halt!*'

Von Prittwitz would have none of it, though, and shouted back, '*Los, vorwärts! Der Feind haut ab!*' — Let's go! The enemy is getting away![16] And yet there was only an instant between that exchange and what happened next . . .

For one of the Australian gunners of the 2/28th Battalion Bush Artillery — still dug in on the other side of the ravine and intending to hold off the Germans for as long as they could — was unable to believe his luck. All morning he had been hoping for an appropriate target for his captured 47-mm anti-tank gun, 'held together with string', and now here was a German vehicle coming straight down the road!

This particular gunner let the vehicle keep coming, as its driver was obviously oblivious as to what lay before it. Steady, steady . . . *now* . . . he pulled the lanyard connected to the firing mechanism.

There was a sudden jerk; an explosion of sound, fury and light; and then the anti-tank round — powerful enough to pierce light armour, let alone the tin can of a staff car — was satisfactorily speeding right towards its target . . .

It is likely that von Prittwitz never knew what hit him. A simple blinding flash, then blackness, instantly — and eternally.

Dreaming of Germany. Of days in the meadows, walks with his wife, playing with his children.

The vehicle was destroyed, and von Prittwitz and his driver with it.

A skirmish lasting for about three hours then ensued, with various of the German armoured vehicles trying to find their way into Tobruk, only to be blocked and blasted at every turn by serious artillery fire they had not been expecting. And even though the Germans were able to extract some revenge by firing on the dug-in batteries, by the time they had headed back down the road whence they came, they were minus a couple of armoured cars and seven trucks. And they were carrying the shattered remains of one dead General.

•

When General Johannes Streich heard shortly afterwards what had happened to his colleague, he was both devastated for von Prittwitz and appalled at the senseless waste of his life that had resulted from being pushed forwards too quickly with too little knowledge of where the defences lay — in Streich's view, breaking the cardinal rule of military attack. Both emotions seized him so strongly that he instructed his driver to pursue Rommel's command vehicle, which, inevitably, was right in this area of the front line and had passed them a short time before. A brief chase ensued, which finished with yet one more furious confrontation between the men. As it turned out, Rommel already knew of von Prittwitz's death and seemed to be more concerned on the instant with the insanity of Streich chasing him in a captured British vehicle.

'How dare you drive after me in a British car!' he roared at Streich. 'I was about to have the gun open fire on you!'

'In that case, you would have managed to kill *both* your Panzer Division commanders in one day, *Herr General*,' Streich replied.[17]

•

Elsewhere around the ring of posts, the preparations of the Australian defenders were frantic as the newcomers, particularly, got to grips with properly digging themselves in. Just like when the khamsin arrived, what had started as a few whispers of wind had soon turned into a stiff breeze, before howling across the landscape and picking up everything as it went; and now there was a growing expectation that the winds of war that had already stirred around Tobruk would soon be blowing a gale right where they stood, and they were going to have to be ready ...

Some defensive work had already been done as, to his credit, Neame had given orders several weeks earlier that the Tobruk defences be revitalised against the day they might need the town as the Allies' fall-back position, but there still remained a great deal to do.[18]

Working quickly but a little more carefully, whole companies of sappers laid out fields of mines, keeping detailed maps as to which tracts of land were seeded with such death and destruction, based on where it was estimated they would be likely to bring the greatest harvest. Some of the mines were anti-personnel; others were designed specifically to break tank tracks; but all were potentially lethal in their effect. The sappers worked on, each man conscious that every mine sown was another thorn in the German side that would hopefully draw blood, and it wasn't only those few Indian soldiers now within the perimeter who'd be able to give the Afrika Korps curry, that was for damn sure!

Meanwhile, others of the Australian front-line troops, like the 2/13th's Bert Ferres and Bill Walmsley, stripped to their grimy waists and, sweating like *bastards*, busied themselves with digging out those anti-tank ditches which in some parts had become partially filled with sand, as well as clearing out as much as possible of the debris and filth that had been left by the Italians in the posts. (The graffiti on the walls saying things like 'British Pigs' and '*Viva Il Duce!*', they could live with, but the slithering vermin and — more particularly — the aged Italian excrement had to go.[19])

At least Bill was a tin miner by trade and was notably good with a shovel in his hands. One thing he and Bert particularly concentrated on was filling sandbags and putting them around the rim of their post, as it was obvious that when the real shooting and shelling started, they didn't want flying chips of concrete to be added to all the shrapnel which would already be heading their way. In fact, ideally the sandbags would stop the shrapnel, cold as a spud. At least, they hoped so . . .

Around and about, others worked at repairing the many barbed-wire obstacles and filling sandbags and placing them just in front of their firing positions to provide an added shield. All the while the chief cooks and bottle-washers and their ilk began to transport canned food up to the front lines and deposit it in the same dumps that were also accommodating the growing water and ammunition stores, while they also worked out how hot food was going to be transported to the men on the perimeter when the battle started to heat up too. An especially important task was set for the engineers: to get the two water-pumping stations that the Italians had damaged before leaving up and running again, as well as what was left of the electrical power system.

Many was the time in all these ventures that the right equipment wasn't available to do the job the way it was meant to be done; but on such occasions, like the good farm boys that a lot of the Australians were, they knew that all that was needed was to find the right bloody way to do it — and it *could* be done. It was fair dinkum *amazing* what could be achieved simply with fencing wire and elbow grease and a bit of good ol' Aussie gumption. True, it was something of a worry that they were bloody short on anti-tank and Bren guns and their 30-round magazines — and there was no time to build up any serious dumps of ammunition near the front lines — but they would just have to make the best of it.

Still, one more thing was crucial. At the front of each post, most of the platoons established a small listening post, about 100 yards out into no-man's-land, consisting of a small hole into which a man could secrete himself at night and be all ears until sunup. At the slightest sound of something in the darkness, it was the job of that Digger to haul on the end of a long, strong piece of string, the other end of which would be attached to a large casing shell back in the post . . .

Further back, the signals system was rather more sophisticated. A big believer in the importance of having effective communications during battles, Morshead had insisted that Signals put enormous effort into gathering every bit of shattered Italian cable that it could get its hands on and then re-laying them. He wanted, and got, the cables laid in a spiderweb leading from his own Divisional Headquarters at the centre out to all Brigade HQs — and thence to the HQ of the battalions and from there to the companies based in the posts on the perimeter. In that manner Morshead would be able to keep precise track of just what was happening all along his front lines and move his forces around accordingly.

Yes, there was likely to be a problem when German artillery began to rain down, as a lot of those lines would be destroyed, but it would then be the job of Signals to repair them as quickly as possible. In the meantime it would be the task of runners — usually very athletic soldiers capable of covering ground like an emu stung by a bee on the bum — to keep going back and forth, doing the job that the signal cables were incapable of.

With the spiderweb of communications working, standard procedure would be meticulously observed, with each forward company being contacted every half-hour and the officer at Divisional HQ asking, 'Sitrep?' (Situation report?)

If all was as it should be, the answer expected was 'Sitnor' (Situation normal). If any other answer, or no answer, was received, the Duty Officer was immediately notified.[20]

•

On and on the men worked, against the clock, against the attack they knew was coming. Always they had the sense that the enemy might emerge at any moment from the billowing dust clouds; happily, though, on this day the only beings that emerged from the hazy horizon to the west and south were stragglers who'd been left behind in various rearguard actions, but were now making their way to safety. They were quickly looked after with water and food and, if they were still strong enough, immediately put to work, for it was a time when every one of them who could do something was obliged to.[21]

They kept working. For those in the 2/13th Battalion, particularly, it seemed weird that, just a few days before on the escarpment, with the Germans coming at them, the sun had just dawdled while they had prayed for it to be dark — and now that they were racing against time to get ready before the Germans arrived, the sun was tearing across the sky.

So too for the mighty British gunners — the true professionals. While the Diggers worked up front, the Pommies worked up back, cleaning their guns, stowing their ammunition and working out their arcs of fire, how each gun would cover for each contingency, and how each one could cover for another that was knocked out. Too, they were careful to dig their guns down as far as possible — generally about 2 feet, before putting up something of a sandbag wall of about the same height — so that while their capacity to fire would be unimpeded, they would be protected against the fire of any tanks that did manage to break through. Passing Australian soldiers who saw them at it were well satisfied.

Having the Bush Artillery up front was one thing, but all of the Australians were very conscious that, when it came right down to it, it was the Pommy gunners who were going to be crucial to them all being able to hold the fort.

•

Over on the western side of the perimeter, Ivor Hancock was settling in with the men of the 2/24th Battalion. It was a measure of how well the Italians had constructed and camouflaged their defensive posts that, in searching for them, many of the men of the 2/24th had to effectively do 'emu bobs' — walking forward 100 abreast, with 10 yards between each man — across a given bit of terrain.

Soon, like the other battalions on the front line, the 2/24th were busy building up their own defensive trenches between the posts, which included an awful lot more digging and — in classic Australian fashion — when it was time to pitch in, *everyone* pitched in, including some of the most senior officers.

So it was that late on the afternoon of 10 April, the 2/24th's second day in Tobruk, an extremely pukka British Artillery officer, a Captain, turned up on the front lines with his batman in tow, looking every inch the part of a great military commander surveying the forward defences. Thanks, no doubt, to the midnight labours of the batman, the shorts of the captain had a crease in them, the shirt was spotless, the boots were highly polished and the Sam Browne belt positively gleamed. To complete the look right down to the last 't', the Brit had a map case slapping against one thigh while against the opposing hip rested his service revolver, attached to a lanyard around his neck. (Seriously, he would have done an Italian officer proud.)

Which was fine for him but clearly, to his dismay, none of the Australians gave a flying fuck. As Australians under Australian command, it was neither here nor there to them that a British officer had turned up. They had a serious job to do and were getting on with it.

Finally, however, the British chappie could bear it no longer and, stopping right in front of one Digger who was going flat out and completely ignoring him, rather theatrically cleared his throat. When the Digger looked up, the captain spoke and, in the yarn that would go right through the battalion over the next few days — and even be recalled decades later — their interaction proceeded along the following lines ...

Pommy Captain, in the very plummy English public school voice of one who had always known he was just born to rule: 'I've heard you Orstralians are a most undisciplined lot, but surely you know enough to salute an officer?'

Whereupon the Digger straightens up, leans nonchalantly on his shovel and coolly surveys the Pom. Then, without a word, he turns his back to him, picks up his shirt, puts it on, does up the buttons, tucks his shirt into his shorts and turns back to the Captain, showing for the first time his epaulettes — which signify that, instead of a mere nameless Digger, the man in question is actually a *Major*.

The colour drains from the Englishman's face, before it all comes rushing back in a blush ... and then drains again. To this point it has been simply inconceivable that one who carried so high a rank would be found doing something so lowly as digging. But now the Australian speaks: 'As you can see, Captain, I am a Major. What is more, I am the Commanding Officer of these men, and let me tell you they don't even salute me, never mind about you. Now, as I outrank *you*, stand to attention and salute.'

The British Captain, blushing once more, immediately snaps off a very smart salute, whereupon the Major dismisses him with a very curt 'Piss off'.

Which the Captain promptly does, trailed by the batman who, throughout, had stood like an Easter Island statue with only his ears flapping, not knowing whether to laugh or cry — or wet his pants as a compromise. The one thing that *was* certain was that he had never heard anything like it. The way these Australians did things was so different from the British way that it was sometimes bloomin' incomprehensible.

The Major? He took his shirt off again and went back to digging the trenches with his men.

Geez, the 2/24th Battalion — who'd always taken the view that saluting Pommy poofta officers only encouraged 'em — loved that story.

•

A certain group of vehicles was going to be crucial to holding Tobruk — apart from tanks — and that was the Bren carriers. They were lightly armoured vehicles with open tops — as close to tanks as Australia possessed — and it would be their job to ferry supplies from the depots and warehouses beside the harbour right up to the front line, possibly under fire; and to give whatever support they could while there by using their Bren guns, evacuating the wounded back to the regimental aid posts, and then going again.

Just before the sun went down on that afternoon of 10 April, John Johnson took delivery of his carrier, which he promptly christened 'Walwa'. It had been a difficult few weeks for John, not just because he was missing his family terribly — it had now been eight months since he'd seen his wife or children, and his newborn he had never seen — but also because it was becoming increasingly apparent that this thing he was involved in wasn't just a lark to get some land, but a real war. Just quite what they were on the edge of here he wasn't sure, but it looked likely to be a donnybrook to beat them all, to judge from the ferocious flocks of German aeroplanes he had been observing over just the last couple of days, unleashing death and destruction by the ton and then winging on their way. Now, while he was every bit as brave as the next man, John was acutely conscious that this wasn't just about him — it was about his wife and children and the fact that he *had* to get home to them intact, and sleep once again safe in the little cottage beneath the Murray moon, or else . . .

Or else he didn't know what. Without him as a provider, there could be no alternative but his family sinking further and further into poverty.

Anyway, at least he had his great friend, Pat Joy — who had just taken delivery of his own fine carrier — to talk things over with. Over the last few months, John had become ever more close to his Walwa friend, and the two were always looking out for each other, sharing their weapon pit, food, water and tent, as they swapped news from home. In action they tried to work in tandem with their carriers whenever possible, and in downtime frequently headed off together to look for the other Walwa man in Tobruk, Alan Kelly, who had played that haunting reveille on their last morning at home. Each man to the other was the closest thing to home there was in all of North Africa, and it just felt right.

•

That night, Rommel retired to the quarters that had been prepared for him in one of the many white-walled houses that the Italians had built by the roadside; this particular building was distinguished by the fact that one of the passing Australians of the 6th Division had, at some point, painted an enormous mural on the western face of that wall, depicting what was clearly the Digger's favourite beer together with scenes of horse racing and some kind of salutation about Tobruk being not too far away that Rommel couldn't quite decipher.[22]

First things first, though. Before settling down for the evening meal and planning the following day's attack, it was necessary to bury the unfortunate von Prittwitz in the garden of the premises. If Rommel felt any guilt at this tragic death or remorse over his argument with Streich, it did not particularly show, though he did at least comment at one point, 'Perhaps we went too far, with too little.'

•

In his own makeshift headquarters in a dilapidated house just back from the harbour, Lieutenant General Morshead worked through most of the night, pausing only at three o'clock in the morning to write to his wife that, although they were in 'a tight corner', he'd been in tight corners before and felt every confidence that he and his men would get out of this one, too.

And yet if they did fail, it would not be for lack of energy from the General and his staff. Beneath a single naked light bulb, with maps all set out on what had been a kitchen table, they continued to work out precisely where to place their available forces.

Behind his second line of defence, Morshead established 'a mobile reserve' whose job it would be to stem any penetration that made it through either the first two rings of defence or — and this was important — tried to arrive by parachute or via the harbour itself by way of boats. Morshead ensured that these three battalions of infantry really were mobile in more than name only, with plenty of trucks to carry both the men and the anti-tank guns. In terms of mobile armour, Tobruk boasted just four Matildas and thirty Cruisers, and they too would be deployed in a central position, ready to move to where they were most needed, while most of the anti-aircraft guns would be situated around the harbour, as it was a fair bet that that was where enemy bombers would focus their attention.

The instructions that Morshead gave to all were commendably clear: even if the German attack was to push through between the posts, the posts were still to be held at all costs, while the Germans were to be stopped by the forces on the inner ring and the mobile reserve would move to stem the breach. In the meantime, if any of the Germans did breach the line, his orders were an Australian classic: 'You'll just have to chuck them out again.'

If, despite everything, the Germans *still* kept coming, then Morshead's approach was reminiscent of the one enunciated by Winston Churchill after he delivered his famous 'We will fight them on the beaches' speech in the House of Commons the year before, just after Dunkirk had been evacuated. On that occasion, while the thunderous applause was still rolling around the famously august chamber, Churchill had breathed to the man beside him, 'We'll beat the bastards over the heads with broomsticks if we have to.'

So too on this occasion ... Morshead issued orders that if the Germans were to break through all the outer defences and make their way towards the harbour, then every man in the garrison who could fire a gun — from chief cooks down to bottle-washers, from Commanding Officers down to their drivers — was to get his hands on anything that could fire, point it at the Germans and Italians, and pull the trigger. When the bullets were exhausted, they were to go for the bayonet. One way or another, not only was Tobruk not going to fall cheaply, but every fibre of Morshead's being seemed to say it *would not fall at all*.

For, notwithstanding the fact that Rommel was an acknowledged military genius who had never suffered defeat on the battlefield, and he had at his disposal Panzers that had never been stopped before, Morshead was not without confidence — and nor were his men ...

•

As to Rommel personally, although he had a few worries on this morning of 11 April — mainly that such a ragtag bunch of survivors could hold out against the military might that he had assembled — he was very keen to begin the full-blown attack and get it over and done with. His forces had now arrived in strength around the perimeter, including, most importantly, the 5th Light Division. This last had been devastating in the Polish and French campaigns and had at its core seventy light Mark II Panzers, eighty medium Mark IIIs, seventy heavy Mark IVs and twenty-five armoured cars, together with sundry units of motorised machine-gunners, artillery, anti-tank and the crucial ten-man platoons that looked after the precious 88 mm anti-aircraft guns, all of which were borne forward by a kind of armoured tractor.

In short order Rommel had a conference with Streich, whom he found with his Mammoth in a wadi near El Adem, and by this time Rommel's adjutant, Schmidt, had been with the German General long enough to know his intense intent even before he expressed it. For Rommel had a way of standing when he was set on attack come what may, attack if on top, attack if struggling — *attack!* — that was almost like a boxer ready to throw a killer blow. With his compact torso ramrod straight above coiled legs ready to spring, Rommel would thrust his chin forwards, and more often than not have his arms up and ready — albeit instead of his hands being clenched, they were holding his Zeiss binoculars, trained on enemy fortifications, as he worked out where the punch should land for optimum effect.

And sure enough ...

'We must attack Tobruk with everything we have,' Rommel now told Streich in a voice that brooked absolutely no discussion, 'immediately your Panzers have taken up their positions, and before Tommy has time to dig in ...'[23]

•

It did not take long for those Panzers to be so disposed.

Just before noon on 11 April 1941, Good Friday, the men of the Afrika Korps who had swept past to the south of Tobruk and then veered north, cut the Bardia Road, which was the only land passage between the garrison and Cairo.

In an instant, Wavell's warning of three days earlier — 'There is nothing between you and Cairo' — was terribly out of date. Now there were Germans between them and Cairo.

With the roads to the west, south and east of the garrison now all cut, the Siege of Tobruk had begun.

CHAPTER ELEVEN

The Easter Battle

*When I first saw him I could not believe that this man was either an
Australian or a fighting general; he was too trim to be kin to the army of
toughs I was surrounded by, too, dare I say, 'prim', to be a leader of
fighting men. Then I heard the name these toughs had given to him,
'Ming the Merciless', and in their voices when they spoke it was the
nearest thing to awe that an Australian will allow.*

BRITISH SIGNALMAN FRANK HARRISON, ON LIEUTENANT GENERAL LESLIE MORSHEAD[1]

What we have, we hold.

MOTTO OF AUSTRALIA'S 2/17TH BATTALION

*Heaven help any force which meets those wild Western Australians.
It is not fair to let them loose in a war . . .*

AN UNNAMED AUSTRALIAN ARTILLERY OFFICER, 1941[2]

Time to rumble.

As part of a closely co-ordinated manoeuvre, General Johannes
Streich's group now approached Tobruk from the south, while the division
that had formerly been under the control of Heinrich von Prittwitz came
from the east, and to complete the enclosure with the Mediterranean Sea to
the north, some of the Italians of the Brescia Division came from the west,
making a show of force to keep the Allied defenders dissipated and guessing
where the real attack would come from. Still others from the Brescia were
set the task of pouring through the gap that would be made by the German
soldiers on the southern perimeter, holding it and widening it.

•

The primary emotions of the men of the Afrika Korps as they closed in on
Tobruk were a mix of fatigue — they had, after all, spent the previous three
weeks fighting both the ferocious conditions and the retreating British and

Australians — and the steely-eyed grim determination of men who knew they had a lot of killing to do, and it was now time to get on with it. What they didn't lack was confidence. After all, they were officers and soldiers of what was undoubtedly the most powerful, best-equipped army in the world, and in the previous eighteen months — through all of Poland, Belgium, Norway, Holland and France — their Nazi flag had always blazed forward, forward, ever forward. What chance, then, was a motley collection of Australians with a bunch of British and apparently some Indian soldiers going to have of stopping the likes of them?

So it was that, just after noon, the Germans began to get into position for the attack proper and await Rommel's word. Shortly after one o'clock, it came. And the word was: '*Angriff!*' Attack! Told once again by his air reconnaissance that the Tommies were beginning to escape via ship, just as they had at Dunkirk, Rommel knew that speed was imperative and sent his forward forces in. As to the others further back, the order to them was to, once again, '*Machen Sie Staub!*' Make dust! As before, all of it was designed to give an impression to the enemy of having more forces coming at them than they actually did.[3]

Streich's 5th Panzer Regiment was the first to draw fire when it moved forwards to the southeastern part of the perimeter, with infantry following up tightly, gauging just what kind of defence there was between posts R59 and R63. The short answer was: plenty.

•

For the well-entrenched Australians, and the British gunners behind, these German tanks moving around in broad daylight within range of their guns was manna from heaven, and everyone wanted their fair share. (And didn't those fellows in the 2/13th love hearing the Pommy shells whistling overhead, on their way to give Jerry a real hiding!)

Within the first hour of their appearance, five German tanks were left as smoking ruins, while the other tanks had withdrawn in dismayed disarray. As to the German infantry, they too had taken a lot of casualties, and Allied artillery observers with powerful binoculars had been satisfied to see that the stony ground seemed to exacerbate the effect that the explosion of their artillery landing caused. Not only was the impact of the missiles not cushioned by landing in soft sand, but the stones themselves appeared to become devastating shrapnel.

But there was more to come.

At three o'clock the men of the 2/13th were amazed to see 400 German soldiers approaching to within 400 yards of their positions. What the hell were they up to? Did these coves think that the sight of them alone would make the Aussies lay down their arms? Not on your bloody nelly, it wouldn't!

Taking careful aim, and awaiting their commander's signal — *Fire!* — the Australians lined 'em up and knocked 'em down. The Germans retreated some way, dragging their wounded with them.

Next time, you bastards, send in the *men*!

•

Instead, the Germans sent in some more of Colonel Olbrich's tanks, with seven of them soon appearing, sniffing around the area in front of Post R31 and probing the anti-tank ditch there, looking for a suitable crossing. For their trouble, the British gunners of the 1st Royal Horse Artillery still took great delight in using the tanks for target practice, and the Germans quickly disappeared in the same direction their soldiers had. Further back, the Italian soldiers of the Brescia Division — whose job it would have been to pour through had the tanks breached the defences — were stood down.[4] There was little grumbling.

Less sanguine was Erwin Rommel, who had been nuzzling along behind Olbrich's tanks in his Mammoth, and was quick to upbraid Olbrich upon his return: 'We failed today, because we forgot one of the elementary principles of war — concentration of effort. Instead of concentrating everything on a single point and bashing a hole through the enemy's line, you let yourself be stopped halfway up the slope, waiting like sheep for the slaughter. Next time it's going to be different! Every man in the Afrika Korps that can be got up here will be used in an all-out assault.'

And though indeed there was yet to be an all-out attack, still the confidence of the Tobruk garrison grew with each of these encounters. The Germans had come, they had seen, they had been pissed off!

Next, just after four o'clock, it was the turn of the men of the 2/17th to receive a visit. About 700 German infantry were seen approaching, and even when the artillery had opened up on them and scored some hits, still they kept on coming! To defend themselves, the men of the 2/17th at that point had only two Bren guns and a couple of dozen rifles — though, sadly, not a single anti-tank gun. The closest they could muster in that department were two Boyes anti-tank rifles — huge bloody things about twice as big as an ordinary rifle but guaranteed to do damage. Unfortunately, that guarantee was limited to the firer's shoulder. Still, they would just have to do, and the Australians laid down the fire upon the attackers.

•

Bullets, everywhere! Whining. Slaying. Carnage! Men crying out and falling. For the men of the Afrika Korps sent in on this ill-prepared attack, without maps or any idea of what they would be facing, it was an experience like they had never suffered before. Desperately they scratched into the ground, trying to get some protection, and then worked their way forwards in small leaps, trying to provide covering fire each for the other. But the accuracy of the *Scharfschützen* (snipers) among the defenders was incredible. Every movement brought fire upon them, and the screaming of hit *Kameraden* was unbearable.

Still, there was help, as two of their number were medics, and each had a big red cross displayed on his front and back. With enormous courage these medics now stood up and started to drag some of the wounded men back. Some of the others prayed that the good Lord would look down in peace upon the medics and that the defenders would not shoot them. Whether it was the Lord or something else, one way or another it seemed to work, for though the fire kept up on the attacking soldiers, the medics — who were much easier targets — remained untouched. Strange — it was almost like a brutal game, with rules being developed as they went along. It was like: 'Though we will do our all to kill each other, if we just wound each other we will do our best to let you live . . . to perhaps kill you another day.'

Bitterly, doggedly, the German soldiers managed to slowly advance in the face of the withering fire, and tried to return some of their own, but it was hard to even see where the fire was coming from, so well were the defenders secreted. At last, a few hundred yards out, the ground became a little easier to dig into, and it was even possible to make small 'shell scrapes' (shallow trenches) in which they could stop and bake awhile as the bullets continued to scorch the tops of their helmets as they simply lay there, mad with thirst, and wondered that it had come to this — and, more importantly, what the hell were they going to do now?

Where are the *tanks*?[5]

•

All up, to the Australians it seemed a strange, dislocated kind of attack, though there was no doubt that the German soldiers had a fair bit of intent about them. Despite the fire put upon them, the Jerries continued to forge their way forward in small increments, mostly under the cover of heavy machine guns they had set up behind them, and were soon approaching the anti-tank ditch, such as it was, and where they began to mortar every defensive post they could reach from that point.

Not long afterwards, a new threat emerged in the form of yet more tanks. There were seventy of the brutes, a mix of Panzer Mark IVs, IIIs, IIs and Italian M13s coming in waves of twenty, with one smaller wave of ten. They continued substantially unchecked, even through the British barrage, and came again right up close to where D Company of the 2/17th was dug in, and started firing upon it with both their 75-mm cannon and Spandau machine guns, with some ferocity. It was a worry, all right. At this point the anti-tank ditch was really that in name only, and it seemed at any moment that if the tanks made a concerted charge, they would be across it and right into the Australian defenders. All the 2/17th could do, meantime, was to keep pouring fire into them with everything it had, as little as that was. It was a real problem, because the 2/17th had no anti-tank guns of its own to reply with, and nor could its artillery help because the two sides were now so close together that any artillery from either side risked hitting its own men.

Fortunately, some four British tanks soon arrived and fired directly over the heads of the 2/17th at the Germans, who just as quickly returned fire, as the Australians hugged the earth tightly.

Still, with the kind of heat the brutes were now taking, on this occasion the Germans did not press their attack in the descending darkness, and soon sheared off towards the 2/13th front beside them, which then gave the tanks another tickle-up for their trouble before the rumbling, grumbling beasts withdrew entirely, wounded by their reception.

Though the 2/17th had lost one soldier killed, Private Arthur Beezley — who'd been hit by machine-gun fire — all up, for the Australians the whole thing still had the feel of a probe rather than a thrust, or a demonstration of power rather than a full attack, but it was enough.

Back at his 9th Division Headquarters, Lieutenant General Morshead kept collating all the information coming in and, together with his senior officers, began to form the view that if a massive German attack was on its way, it was likely to be launched on the Red Line at the precise point that the 2/13th and 2/17th Battalions were defending, with the 2/15th in the reserve position just behind. If so, there would be some irony that the Gods of War had decreed that the German attack would be striking at the same 20th Brigade that Neame had already deemed to be an 'an undisciplined mob', but Morshead strongly disagreed and felt his men would be up to any task handed to them.

It was still way too early to commit all of his reserve forces to stopping that, but certainly early enough to begin to move a few of them, and also to make detailed plans of just how they would deal with the Germans if any did cross the line at that point.

The problem Morshead and his senior staff were wrestling most with was: what would happen if the German tanks made it across the anti-tank ditches? The Australians had already learned that even the Mark III had the firepower to knock out a British tank with one of its 4.5-pound shells at a distance of well over 1000 yards, while the Mark IV's capacity meant that British defences and tanks even at a distance of *3000* yards were not safe. Against that, the few British tanks they had possessed nothing like that kind of force or projection, and could only be effective against those bastard behemoths at a distance well inside 800 yards. All of the Allied battle plans for the defence of Tobruk, therefore, had to focus on the need to allow the German tanks in *close*, to the point where they could be dealt with. They began to work on that very problem ...

In the meantime, there was to be no rest for the wicked — or the good. Certainly it was a garrison intent on defending to the last, but, as was typical of Morshead, a large part of its defence was to be aggressive. There was to be no mere waiting around for the enemy to attack; Morshead effectively wanted his men to get their retaliation in first, and with that in mind had issued orders for there to be vigorous patrolling in the anti-tank ditches and beyond the wire, to feel out the enemy and strike where possible, even as engineers and sappers worked throughout the entire night laying yet more mines. This aggressive patrolling immediately drew results, with a patrol from the 2/13th discovering a raiding party in the anti-tank ditch armed with its own version of Bangalore torpedoes and lots of explosives, clearly indicating it was in the business of blowing in the sides of the ditch to allow a passage for tanks. That threat was quickly neutralised, but it was obvious that, one way or another, the Germans were as serious as syphilis, and it was going to be *on*.

•

They were still there!

Dawn of Easter Saturday, 12 April 1941, revealed to the men of the 2/17th Battalion that the same German soldiers who had been trying to get at them the previous afternoon were still out in the desert, just 400 yards off the perimeter and strung out about 1200 yards across — small, slightly moving clumps in among the low shrubs that showed up in the binoculars. They were far enough away that mere bullets were unlikely to reach them; widely enough dispersed and well enough dug in behind the small rock shelters they'd constructed that artillery was unlikely to blow them away; but they were still there, all right! What manner of men were these?

Were they really going to lie there all day, frying in the desert, face down on the sand?

Yes, but in the first instance frying wasn't the Germans' main problem.

For there is cold, there is stone cold, there is *freezing* cold, and then there is the cold a man feels when waking in the desert after a long and terrible night totally exposed to its malice. Cold to the bone, cold to the marrow, so cold that death would have almost been a relief. Part of the problem for the men — apart from their exposure and inability to get any shelter at all — were the German uniforms. Singularly ill designed for desert conditions, they soaked up the morning dew, but then soaked up the last of any heat the human body had in it, until the only relief came through numbness. And speaking of relief, how did a soldier perform his morning ablutions, go on his *Spatengang* (spade walk) in such circumstances?

Exactly.

Upon arriving in Africa, the soldiers had been officially informed by their commanders that 'The desert will not prove large enough for a soldier to retire with a spade to a spot he has chosen himself',[6] but none of them had quite expected this. Yes, to lack of privacy, but they were now in a situation where simply by squatting they risked being shot! So they did the only thing they could, which was to defecate where they lay.

Not surprisingly, it was hell on earth, with one of the soldiers later commenting, 'You look at your watch at ten o'clock and look again four hours later and it's ten-fifteen.'[7] (At least in this regard, the Australians in their slit trenches were a little better equipped, being able to piss — and worse — in their empty bully-beef tins and toss them over the side.[8])

Nevertheless, despite all the many difficulties, of which effective ablutions were nearly the least, Lieutenant Colonel Gustav Ponath and his men stayed there — being roasted by the sun above and fried by the sand below — and even managed to bring fire to bear upon the perimeter posts in front of them without really coming on. Having advanced to this point against the Australian defences, it was their job to wait in that advanced spot with the flies and the scorpions until the order came through that it was time to launch a full-blown attack.

The attack would not come that day — at least, not on land — despite the fact that as the men of the 2/17th gazed out upon the prone German soldiers, they could clearly see great clouds of dust on the far horizon, indicating a massive movement of machines, probably Panzers. Fortunately, though, because the 2/17th were still without anti-tank guns, for the moment the tanks did not come forward. Not surprisingly, when seven anti-tank guns did arrive a little after the tanks had backed off, the collective confidence of the Australians in that particular part of the front line rose one more notch. From time to time one of Ponath's snipers would take a precise shot, trying to prevent those anti-tank guns from being dug in to become a feature of the defence, but the damage they inflicted was minimal.

Now, if the tanks came, the Australians would be more of a chance of making a proper fight of it. In mid-afternoon it was clear to the men of the 2/17th that the Germans were proceeding forwards, but a combination of accurate artillery fire and some forward probes by a couple of sections of the 2/17th drove them back again.

Nevertheless, just as the mighty khamsin always began with just a few filthy flurries of wind, so too was there a sense that the enemy was building to unleash an almighty storm upon them . . .

•

A similar dynamic was operating in the skies above. While many Axis planes came over, dropping bombs on selected targets — like the guns of the Royal Horse Artillery and facilities around the port area — Tobruk had organised plenty to greet them. A combination of the boys on the Ack-Ack guns and those supremely courageous half-dozen pilots left flying in the Hurricanes for the RAF's No 73 Squadron was able to give at least as good as it got. Operating from the tiny El Gubbi airfield, it took extraordinary courage for the RAF's pilots just to take off and land on a runway where there was no margin for error, let alone take on an enemy that was far superior numerically in the skies above, but they did it time and again. Just on that afternoon of 12 April, three enemy planes had been put where they belonged — blown to pieces, scattered on the desert floor.[9]

•

The mood among most of the Tobruk garrison then, as the African sun sank like a falling stone back into the desert at dusk, was one of cautious confidence. True, the Germans and Italians were yet to launch a full-on assault, but they had been probing, and each probe had been parried, frequently by soldiers getting their first taste of battle action. The point was that, even if the clashes to this moment had been mere warm-up overs for the true game that was likely about to begin, both the Australians and

English had looked the goods in those warm-ups. A night's sleep, and who knew what the morrow would bring?

•

Wretched Easter Sunday, 13 April 1941. With her husband, Will, so crook with his leg and all, Elizabeth Edmondson could not even have the solace of going to church, and so had to stay home throughout a day which just hung heavy. All she could do was pray for the day to end, and she did just that, watching the face of the big old grandfather clock and sometimes wondering how it could have moved so very little in what seemed like such a very long time. Usually a woman who liked air and light in her house, on this day Elizabeth pulled the pastel curtains closed in a half-hearted attempt to keep the world at bay. Precisely why that day was so tough she didn't know, just that, as she recorded in her diary that night: 'It was a woeful day and I could simply feel every nerve jangling . . .'[10]

•

Things were stirring. High above them on this Easter Sunday morning, the men of the 2/17th Battalion noticed a reconnaissance plane swirling around, like a vulture that had spotted a sick lamb. Then, at a distance of perhaps 2000 yards, men on motorcycles were seen escorting a staff car, and soon other staff cars pulled up. It looked very much like some kind of battle HQ was being established, and though it was right at the outer limits of the range of the little artillery they had, a few lobbed missiles later, they were delighted to see a staff car and two motorcycles explode. *That* would give the bastards something to think about! Nevertheless, it seemed fairly clear that the Germans were now ready to frame an all-out attack at their sector; and the feeling that all the movement to the front of the 2/17th sector just might be a harbinger of hell was compounded when a German plane swooped low, just above the range of their rifles, and dropped leaflets, so very gaily fluttering down upon them:

THE GENERAL OFFICER COMMANDING THE GERMAN FORCES IN LIBYA HEREBY REQUESTS THAT THE BRITISH TROOPS OCCUPYING TOBRUK SURRENDER THEIR ARMS.

SINGLE SOLDIERS WAVING WHITE HANDKERCHIEFS ARE NOT FIRED ON. STRONG GERMAN FORCES HAVE ALREADY SURROUNDED TOBRUK, AND IT IS USELESS TO TRY AND ESCAPE. REMEMBER MEKILI. OUR DIVE-BOMBERS AND STUKAS ARE AWAITING YOUR SHIPS, WHICH ARE LYING IN TOBRUK.

A pity. With so little water, and so much bloody dust, the Australians hadn't been able to do their laundry and just didn't have any white handkerchiefs left, so they'd have to fight — though at least those leaflets would come in useful for something else they had in mind, particularly those with enduring dysentery. Still, that plane was simply the first of many, as the 2/17th soon saw several other reconnaissance planes overhead, prowling around and surely looking for any weak points. Soon, armoured cars appeared on the hazy horizon, and then trucks clearly disgorging troops. Lots of troops. Artillery soon dispersed them, but they made no move to retreat. Before long, German machine-gunners advanced to within 1500 yards and started the eternal *dub-dub-dub* guaranteed to make sure every Australian in front of their fire kept his head down.

Things were warming up. At about five o'clock, artillery fire started landing all around the Australian post, and half an hour later tanks appeared just 500 yards off, together with infantry, advancing under cover of heavy machine-gun fire. Those blessed Pommies of the 1st and 107th Royal Horse Artillery soon dropped enough on the Germans' noggins to stop them and make them back off, but no one thought it was over, not by a long shot. The RAF's own reconnaissance soon reported that there were now 300 vehicles assembling just out along the El Adem road.

•

So they would not feel too left out, it was at this point that the men of the 2/24th Battalion on the western perimeter came under fire for the first time, with enemy mortars suddenly landing all around them. Where Ivor Hancock was situated the mortars kept up for half an hour, putting the wind up a few blokes, until they realised that the damage they were taking was actually fairly minimal. When mortars were used indiscriminately, the way the Germans or Ities were using them, it seemed that so long as you kept your head down in your own trench, you really had to be dead unlucky to be one of the unlucky dead. That could really only happen if the mortar bomb landed upon you in a hastily constructed open trench, where no measures had been made to give yourself even half-arsed protection. Ivor and his mates didn't like it, but they survived it all right.

As to attack by aeroplane, though, they weren't so sure. Later that same morning, just when things seemed to be calming a little in their sector, the lieutenant issued an order for enough water to be handed out to each man so that he could complete the armpit and crotch wash, already known as 'the Tobruk bath' — of which the deluxe version was when your mate wiped down your back with a damp cloth before you did the same for him.

Ivor was using the time to shave and was standing out in the open with a soapy lather, holding an Army issue steel mirror, when a distant drone turned into an ear-shattering roar, and a German Heinkel light bomber suddenly came screaming down upon them. Because there was simply no time to do anything else, all of the men hurled themselves into the sand face down, pressing their bodies as flat and low as they could into the bosom of Mother Earth — still while keeping their mouths open, because the theory was that if a bomb went off near you, that simple thing could stop your ear-drums from bursting. Mercifully, the Heinkel passed over and didn't return, and Ivor was able to get back to his feet, the lather on his face now entirely covered by desert sand. Shit.

•

Disagreements between officers in the German Army were rare. For the simple rule was that the officer with the most rank won every argument every time, while the officer with the inferior rank who wished to go on with the argument risked being accused of insubordination — with very grim consequences indeed.

And yet, at Rommel's HQ just a few thousand metres from the western perimeter of Tobruk, General Johannes Streich could bear it no more and felt he had to say something to convince Rommel of the folly of continuing this kind of helter-skelter attack on Tobruk.

It was already clear to Streich, as it was to another of his senior military colleagues, Major Wolfgang Hauser — who very courageously supported him — that the Australians and British were so well dug in, and so very determined to defend their positions, that there was simply no chance an attack would budge them to the point that Tobruk would fall. Rommel wouldn't even begin to listen. He was convinced, and he said so with some force, that the enemy was even then preparing a massive evacuation, and destroying much-needed supplies in the meantime. Just what evidence he had for that contention he did not say, but an officer of Rommel's rank didn't have to back up his own argument — it was enough that he said it was so.

Or it should have been. When Streich still went on with it, Rommel returned icily: 'It is not usual in the German Army for a service order to a unit to be answered by a counterproposal from the unit concerned.'[11]

Streich took the matter as far as he could without refusing outright to co-operate, but Rommel in turn was dismayed by what he later referred to in his personal notes as 'unwarranted pessimism' on the part of the 5th Light.[12]

Infuriated by Streich's attitude, Rommel decided to take over this area of the operation himself, selecting the men who would conduct the first part of the raid and organising them from there in every particular of the operation. The man to lead it, he decided, would be Lieutenant Colonel Gustav Ponath of the 8th Machine-gun Battalion, accompanied by some of his best men, and some sappers to take care of whatever mines they found.

And where was Ponath? Still out, sweltering in the sun, some 400 metres from the Red Line, just as he had been for most of the last two days. No matter. At last, though, the message got through and, crawling on his belly for the first part, Ponath made his way to Rommel and received his instructions.

Burned by the sun, exhausted by a furious fortnight without rest, the valiant Ponath agreed to follow orders and was soon making his way back to his men to properly organise the attack.

•

In Cairo, the unfolding events were watched with increasing attention by Wavell and his senior officers, with all of them aware of exactly what was at stake. If Tobruk fell, it would be a complete disaster, with Cairo and the Suez Canal threatened — and yet they were not without confidence that it could, in fact, be held. The tone was set by a message from Wavell to Morshead and Lavarack:

> Enemy advance means your isolation by land for time
> being. Defence of Egypt now depends largely on your
> holding enemy on your front. Am glad that I have at this
> crisis such stout-hearted and magnificent troops in
> Tobruk. I know I can count on you to hold Tobruk to the
> end. My wishes to you all.[13]

•

Just after six o'clock in the evening, Ponath and his men greedily drank from their water bottles and moved off, forty of them in all, carrying a mortar, eight machine guns and two small field guns between them.[14] Their assignment, at the pointy end of the German thrust, was to force the first breach in the enemy's perimeter through which the rest of the German forces — now massed just a short distance back from this point and awaiting orders to roll — could follow. It was, nevertheless, a measure of the kind of pressure they were under that, after Ponath had arrived back from meeting with Rommel, the process of getting all his forward forces apprised of what was happening had caused three messengers, one after the other, to be shot in trying to get the message through.[15]

That job had been done, though, and now it was time to execute the plan. To help them, furious artillery fire would pound onto the defenders at the wire for fifteen minutes, to force them to keep their heads down until the attacking force could get close.

Miraculously, given the high level of Australian awareness that the Germans were interested in their area, they found little resistance and were able to get all the way to the anti-tank ditch, and got to work on both it and the barbed wire, preparing a passage for the tanks.

As luck would have it, Ponath's group had foraged forwards at the precise spot where the Tobruk Red Line was at its most vulnerable, in the dead centre between two posts — in this case, posts R32 and R33.

Somewhere just after ten o'clock, Ponath's adjutant reported back to General Rommel and his senior staff. His men had got through, he said. They had snipped away the wire, deloused the minefields and found a way across the anti-tank ditch. His men were now digging in, waiting for the major attack to be launched.

Rommel was well pleased.

And now, in the manner of a man who has just demonstrated personally how a job should be done when it is done properly and it is now also for the subordinate to show that he too can do it, Rommel handed control of the operation back to Streich.

'I expect this attack to be conducted under your personal leadership and with the utmost determination . . .' he said. 'At your disposal, I will leave my aide, Lieutenant Schmidt . . .'[16]

From this point on, the German plan of attack was very clear, with all the forces near their starting line; Streich's 5th Light Division formed the prow of the attack, on either side of the El Adem road, right opposite the 20th Brigade. While the Italians would create a diversion by launching a small assault on the western side of the perimeter, the Streich force would break through on the southern side, and the plan was that by the morning of the 14th it would be right down by Tobruk Harbour, attacking the town just after the Stuka bombers had softened up whatever was left of its defences.

•

At Tobruk that same night, Corporal Jack Edmondson was manning a trench just beside R33, and making sure that if any of the marauding Germans came their way, he and the men he was in command of — 3 Section, 16th Platoon, 2/17th Battalion — would be well prepared. The last couple of days had been full-on, but Jack had performed well and displayed his usual quiet confidence. Other fellows liked fighting beside Jack, in part because they liked him a lot generally, but also because, as the generation before them had said about blokes like him at Gallipoli, 'He was a good man to have beside you in the trenches.' Right beside Jack on this night were Ron Keogh, Ted Smith, Splinter Williams, Ron Grant and Snowy Foster, good men all, and good soldiers. For the first hour after darkness descended, Jack talked to Bill and Ron about this and that and not much in particular, including what they had done on their last Palestine leave, but then the conversation ebbed as the fire upon them became heavier. All of them had a sense that things were about to heat up, which was prescient . . .

•

For, at around ten o'clock that night, the 2/17th's Jack Harris, who was rostered on for picket duty, was peering into the darkness only a short distance away from where Jack Edmondson and his men lay when a flare went up in its ever graceful arc before exploding against the stars and momentarily illuminating the terrain in front of him.

Immediately Jack saw them. A large group of men out in front and moving slowly towards Post R33. Quickly, but quietly, Jack alerted his section, and the Platoon Commander, Lieutenant Austin Mackell, was sent for. By the time he arrived, they could hear the men out in front speaking German, though at least it seemed they had stopped advancing and were starting to dig in . . .

Lieutenant Austin Mackell — known as 'Mummy' Mackell to his men for the reason that he was ever and always so solicitous of their health and welfare, and didn't mind talking to them about it at some length — now took control. Given that they were so heavily outnumbered and probably outgunned, the only way to fight was going to be getting close enough to the Germans so they could out-*man* them. After all, Lieutenant General Morshead had specifically said that 'If any Germans get through, you'll just have to chuck them out again!' and that was what Mackell's men were going to have to do *now*.

Since their days of arriving at Kilo 89, Mackell had impressed on the soldiers in his command that the Germans were no supermen — and now was the time to prove it. Leaving the post by its back entrance, Mackell jog-trotted over, bent at the waist, to where he knew he would find Jack Edmondson and his men in the darkness.

'The Germans have broken through the wire, Corporal,' he said grimly. 'I want you and your section to follow me back to the post as fast as you can.'

Jack did exactly that, with the other men wondering slightly why they were gathering in the post when that was surely the spot that *least* needed to be defended. But they soon enough had their answer.

'We've got a dirty job, boys,' Mackell said quickly, though there was no edge of panic in his voice. 'The Germans have broken through on our left front and set up a post about 20 yards inside the wire. Don't ask me how they did it without being spotted but the only thing that concerns us now is that they're there. I don't like it any more than the rest of you, but 3 Section is going to do a fighting patrol to try and wipe them out. We just can't sit here or we'll get plastered all night.'

This was a bit more like it! For, by all accounts, the response to this news was in no way one of trepidation so much as excitement. This was a lot closer to the stuff they had been trained for. This wasn't sitting in a rat hole; this was getting out and getting into them.

Jack was the first to speak.

'Do we know their numbers, sir?' he asked.

Mackell shook his head. 'No. But we can't afford to take out more than one of our sections, otherwise the post will be left too weak. Here's the plan. Strip your webbing. Bring your rifles with full magazines. Fix bayonets and take some grenades. We'll go round on their right flank and rush them in extended line. When we reach grenade-throwing distance, I'll order you down, throw your grenade and go in firing from the hip. Then use your bayonets … I don't need to tell you what the odds are — it won't be a training exercise. The post will cover us until 22.50. They'll make as much noise as possible to create a diversion. The rest is up to us. Synchronise watches.'

Jack looked at the special dust-proof watch bought for him by his mother at Ken's Jewellers in down-town Sydney — with a lovely engraving on the back — and it told him the time was 10.48 p.m. In two minutes flat, they were ready, and still there was no sign from the Germans, who were continuing to dig in, that they had any clue what was about to hit them. Bayonets fixed. Grenades secured in such a way that they wouldn't fall as the men ran, but would still be readily available when required. There were no handshakes or anything like that. This wasn't the charge of the Light Brigade; it was just a job that had to be done, and they were the men to do it. They knew they could count on each other, up to and including Snowy Foster, who was still only sixteen years old — he'd lied about his age to get in — but was every bit as much a fighting man as they were.

All set? Now! Mackell, with Jack Edmondson off his shoulder and the others following close behind, set off, spread out at a distance of about ten yards apart — meaning they were tight enough to stay together but not so tight that a good machine-gun burst would take out the lot of them. Getting faster now, they went on a low, crouching run to begin their loop to come in on the enemy's right flank, even as the blokes they'd left behind in the post opened up on the Germans, who returned fire immediately. The fact that the Germans were well-armed was highlighted by the curious crackling sound their Spandaus made with their high rates of fire. Less the dub-dub-dub the Australians were used to with their usual guns, and much more a *k-k-k-k-k-k-k-k-k-k-k-k-k-k-k,* with almost no pause between bullets. At least, though, the Jerries were copping plenty in return, to keep them pinned down ...

•

For, gathering what little shelter they could to themselves on the flat ground — by digging in and pushing up as much of a wall of sand around them as possible — even as they kept firing their Spandaus, the German soldiers were sweating, panting and a little desperate. The fire that poured upon them from the defenders was fierce. Then suddenly the firing stopped and there was a strange lull, in which the agonised groans of the Afrika Korps men who had been hit could now be heard for the first time. Now, one of the soldiers, panicking, screamed, '*Wo sind denn unsere Offiziere?*' Where are our officers?

Then, in the darkness, an angry voice, but muted by the needs of the moment:'*Haltet doch bloss eure Schnauze! Ich bin doch hier!*'[17] Keep your mouth shut, would you! I'm right here! hissed Lieutenant Schöllmann. And then the strangest thing ...

Out of the darkness, they could clearly hear the strains of a vaguely recognisable song, bellowed out by the defenders ...

'*It's a long way to Tipperareeee ...*'

Shouts in the darkness. Getting nearer ...[18]

ABOVE Erwin Rommel always set an example for his troops, constantly pressing the front line and frequently finding solutions, even in tough situations. No supplies, no water, no ammunition? 'See this dust cloud at the horizon?' he asked his troops, indicating the enemy's position late in the December 1941 battle for Tobruk. 'Get your water and supplies there!'

BELOW Mussolini greeting his troops. Invariably the Italians had the best-cut uniforms, with the officers looking especially dashing. The Germans later came to wonder whether such finery had any value on the front line.

ABOVE A view of Upper Bardia in February 1941.

LEFT Australian Prime Minister Robert Menzies (left) and British Prime Minister Winston Churchill met in London in March 1941. A growing band of critics in Australia were beginning to put it around that Menzies favoured being in London over Sydney, Melbourne or Canberra, and that was untenable for a man in his position.

ABOVE LEFT Generalleutnant Friedrich Paulus, who had a penchant for bathing twice a day and washing his hands between times, was known to some as 'Our Most Elegant Gentleman'. In April 1941, Hitler's Chief of the General Staff, General Franz Halder, ordered Paulus to fly to Rommel in North Africa to bring under control 'this soldier gone stark mad'.
ABOVE RIGHT ABC radio journalist Chester Wilmot described the war for Australian audiences back home with unparalleled skill. After his work in North Africa, Wilmot covered the fighting on the Kokoda Track.

BELOW Ivor Hancock third from left, carouses in Jaffa, Palestine, with fellow soldiers of the 2/24th Battalion. Hard men for the military police to handle when they had too much beer in them, the Australians would prove an even bigger handful for the Germans when they were stone cold sober.

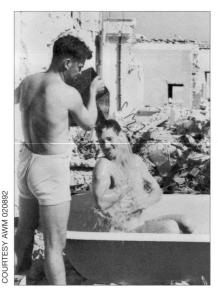

ABOVE Australian (left) and German soldiers — Rolf Völker and a friend (right) — bathing in the desert. The water ration was only 20 litres per man for washing himself and his uniform, but often it dropped to 10 litres or less. Frequently, the Australians would engage in a 'Tobruk bath', when your mate simply rubbed a damp cloth over your back while you wiped the rest.

BELOW LEFT Bombs landing in Tobruk harbour could throw fish up onto the wharves and shore. Axis soldiers denied access to the harbour had to make do with canned sardines so soaked in oil that they could also be used for lamps. **BELOW RIGHT** Rolf Völker and friend. From mid 1941 onwards, Afrika Korps soldiers often wore parts of Allied POW uniforms.

ABOVE Hill 209, or Ras El Medauuar, as the German referred to it. General Rommel said, 'Whoever is in possession of Ras el Madauuar can read the other's cards.' Much blood would be shed to get and retain this only bit of high ground within the Tobruk perimeter.

BELOW Bert Ferres and Bill Walmsley (in helmets) with members of the 2/13th Battalion and the Army Service Corps spent two weeks in this trench at the Salient, Tobruk, in 1941. **INSET** Every seven to ten days, Afrika Korps soldiers were allowed back from the front for twenty-four hours. Here, Rolf Völker and his great comrade Paul Lanz (standing) attend to mending and cleaning, during one such precious break.

COURTESY AWM 020699

ABOVE Tobruk, late September 1941. Men of the Army Service Corps, 9th Division, were used as infantrymen for a long period, and among other things guarded the rugged east coast sector, where the line of defence met the Mediterranean in a series of deep and narrow wadis.

BELOW After a day's rattling journey in a Panzer of up 220 km over rough terrain at an average speed of 16 km/h, men's backs and bones ached so much that they would often be obliged to sleep on their bellies that night in an attempt to recover.

PHOTO BY ROLF MUNNINGER

ABOVE At the end of May 1942, German supply vehicles and parts of the leadership were surrounded near Bir el Harmal, as the Allied forces pressed in. **INSET** Rommel, besieged and under pressure, looked for a way out, as his troops awaited his commands, and NCO Rolf Munninger took this photo.

BELOW A large part of Rommel's leadership was his conviction that there was always a way to triumph, and it was only a matter of finding it. He *felt* he could succeed, and that confidence invariably rubbed off.

ABOVE Anti-aircraft guns being fired at night against the ongoing attentions of the German and Italian bombers.

BELOW With temperatures of up to 55 degrees Celsius during the day and 'freezing cold' by night, the troops' other constant companions in the desert were thirst, hunger, snakes, scorpions, fleas and flies. **INSET** A drawing of a spontaneous cease-fire between German and Australian soldiers, during which, for an hour or so, they shook hands, talked the best they could and shared cigarettes.

•

Back at the post, the boys were smother-firing, hurling everything they could at the Germans to keep their block heads down and keep them distracted as long as possible, so the patrol could get close enough to do their job.

Unfortunately for the patrol — Jack now running hard and focusing on the back of Mackell, just in front of him — some wild shots in their rough direction from the cluster of Germans told them that their departure had been spotted. Still, by making an even wider loop than they'd planned, there was no doubt they'd moved out of the Germans' sight, even if the Germans would surely be waiting for the kind of attack they were now putting into operation. Still they moved quickly, the tiny fireflies in the distance allowing them to keep their exact bearing as to where the invaders were, their every shot a spark flickering in the darkness.

Getting closer now. The night was neither pitch dark nor well illuminated by the moon, but a kind of twilight world between. Just 250 yards away now and closing fast.

Suddenly bullets started whining all around them, with the closest ones whistling so close they near seared their ears. The tracer bullets now looked like sparks from an oxywelding machine, albeit not nearly so benign.

The seven Australian soldiers went in a dead sprint, zigzagging a little as they ran, firing furiously in the knowledge that the more lead they sent the Germans' way, the better their own chances of surviving. Back at R33, the rest of the blokes continued to do their part superbly, firing at the Germans with everything they had in them. Still, the German fire kept coming . . .

•

The thing about being shot is that, while the bullets pierce you instantaneously, often the realisation of what has happened takes longer. So it must have been for Jack Edmondson as a raking machine blast hit him first with two bullets across the stomach and two in the neck. Right beside him, another bullet severed Ron Grant's rifle sling, while yet one more put an enormous hole in the bottom right-hand pocket of his jacket, still without touching Ron at all.[19]

Jack, however, was hit, and hurt, but still not so devastatingly in the first instant that he couldn't do the job he had come to do, and that was to take out the nest of Germans. Despite being hit, he kept going and threw himself to the ground with the others just 50 yards from the Germans, pressing their bodies into the ground and sucking desert with their every breath. Jack knew he was hit, all right, but said nothing. For the Germans, at ground level themselves, it was a near impossible task to nail Mackell and his men at that angle, but still that wouldn't save the Australians — they had to finish the job. With that in mind, at Mackell's command they got the grenades out of their belts, removed the pins and held the little bombs tightly. Mackell checked his watch. In one minute, the fire from their own post would stop, and then they would be on their way.

Waiting. Waiting. Waiting.

Now!

An instant after the fire from R33 stopped, Mackell yelled, 'Right, boys!' and he and his men were up on their feet and charging forwards, firing as they went. At a distance of perhaps 40 yards out, the wild-eyed Australians started yelling, swearing and shouting — in fact, trying to sound as if they were coming a hundred strong instead of just the seven brave souls that they were. It was a cry that was instantaneously taken up by the men back at the post. For the Germans it must have momentarily seemed as if they were now being charged from two directions, and some of the German fire switched back to the post.

Just 30 yards away now, and the time was right. Following Mackell's lead, each man released the catch on his Mills grenade — meaning they were seven seconds from exploding — and made ready to throw, almost as if they were in the outfield back at school and the wicketkeeper was behind the stumps depending on them for a possible run-out, as the batsman hared towards the stumps.

In the soft desert night, six grenades suddenly lobbed skywards, heading straight for the Germans, their timers ticking away. The Australians were now close enough to see that there weren't a dozen of the Germans at all, but at least *forty*. The only good thing was that some of the German defenders, even as the grenades continued on their arcs, were now turning and running away.

The grenades landed and exploded almost simultaneously, bodies flying skywards silhouetted by the flash, and the screams of the survivors providing their echo. The toll was terrible. In short order, Captain Frank, leader of the 2nd Company, was severely injured, while Lieutenant Hofer of the 7th Company fell and died. Others, just nameless soldiers in the night, bled their last into the desert sands.[20] Not that all the German resistance was quelled — while some more of the Germans cut and ran, others held their ground and kept firing at the oncoming targets, who now loomed a whole lot larger in their sights.

•

With the Australians right upon them, even more of the Germans began to scatter, but now Mackell's men were in the thick of them, bayonets flashing even in the wan light of the moon, with Mackell being particularly voluble as he slashed and shot at them, screaming at the Germans in the manner of a man who had found trespassers on his property and wasn't going to stand for it any more: 'Get back to your lines, you bastards!'[21]

The remaining Germans, though, were valiant, fighting back hard with everything they had in them, which was plenty.

And Jack? He was in there with the best of them, despite his wounds, and the other blokes in this attacking Australian section were equally busy. Somewhere in the flashing action, one German could be heard to scream 'Please, it is peace, *s'il vous plaît!*'[22] right before someone got him and he gurgled his last, and then another German shouted in a despairing, thick accent, 'Wife, children! Wife! Children!'[23] before he too was sent to the great beyond.

But suddenly, Mackell was in real trouble as he slid his bayonet into one German and the damn blade wouldn't come out. The dying German had him in a death grip, concentrating the last ounce of his earthly soul on holding Mackell around the legs, while another German was coming straight at Mackell from behind. Mackell had just time enough to call out 'Jack!' and within an instant Jack Edmondson was at his side.

Just ten seconds later Jack had bayoneted both Germans dead, before going after yet one more who was trying to get away and also bringing him to ground. Mackell, meanwhile, without his bayonet — it had broken off inside the dead man — was using his rifle as a club, swinging wildly at every German within range, and cracking heads as he went.

And then all was quiet.

And for Jack . . . it was all somehow . . . darker . . . or lighter . . . or sort of ebbing and flowing between the two. He wasn't sure, but he felt strangely light-headed, almost as if he was floating away. In any case, the job was done.

With a dozen Germans dead at their feet, most of the Australians were just feeling mightily relieved to have come through the action alive, when they realised . . .

Oh, Christ. *Jack!* He'd been hit. Even in the soft light they could see the blood around his neck, and when they moved his hand away from his stomach where he'd been holding it, there was even more. Jack could speak, but not much, and the key was of course to get him to medical help as quickly as they could. While Mackell and Ron Grant scooped up every bit of German weaponry they could lay their hands on — including a Spandau machine gun, Mauser rifles and machine pistols — Doug Foster and Ted Smith lifted Jack as gently as they could and quickly got him back to R33.

Delicately, they pulled away Jack's shirt to have a look at his stomach and neck by the dull light of a lantern, and see if they could clean him up a bit. Oh, sweet mother of Jesus. Oh, Christ Almighty. Quickly it was apparent that Jack's injuries were even worse than they had thought. The bullets in the stomach were not flesh wounds but had taken him right in the guts, and one at least had blown clean out the other side, taking a chunk of the flesh off his back with it. So, too, did the big blobs of blood coming from his neck indicate that he was in a lot of trouble.

For all that, Jack remained conscious, and even cheerful. There was no expression of fear or complaint, and once they'd got him kind of laid up on a makeshift stretcher, he even encouraged them to get back to their posts and on to more urgent tasks.

Not bloody likely.

But there was no doubt it looked grim. At one point when Jack groaned that he needed to urgently have a crap, a bloke by the name of John Hedges — who had a very pronounced stutter — had a quiet word with his mate Jack Harris, as they stood there in a thick and sticky pool of Jack's blood.

'B-b-b-b-back home in Cooma,' John said, 'that's just what c-c-c-cows do when they're about to d-d-d-die. I don't think Jack is going to last l-l-long unless we can get him to a d-d-d-doctor.'

Jack's close friend Athol Dalziel now volunteered to do what had to be done, as concentrated German fire once again descended on them. That was, get Jack the hell out of this pit and straight back to the Regimental Aid Post, about half a mile away, where they had basic medical supplies and someone with at least basic expertise. Together with Bill Taylor, who also volunteered, they manoeuvred Jack's stretcher to the edge of the dugout and got ready to brave the bullets now pinging all around.

Ready?

NOW!

Alas, within just ten paces out of the shelter it was obvious that the only result of trying to run into that thick mist of machine gunnery would be getting all three of them killed, and Athol and Bill quickly scrambled back to where they'd started. Once they'd got him settled again, both men felt obliged to apologise to Jack, saying they were sorry, but it was just impossible to get him out right now.[24]

Jack just smiled and said, 'Don't worry about me, I'll be okay till morning. Now get back and give them hell . . .'[25]

For all that, Athol stayed with him, checking on him, wiping away the blood that kept oozing out and praying that by some miracle the light of the dawn, the dawn, the *dawn*, would see an upturn in Jack's fortunes.

•

Gott im Himmel.

Lieutenant Heinz Schmidt still wasn't quite sure what it all meant for Rommel to have put him with Streich for this attack, but he wasn't happy about it. Did it mean he was there as a kind of Rommel watchdog, to ensure that the general's instructions were followed? An adviser, perhaps? Just what *was* it that he was meant to be delivering to the war effort?

Now sitting inside Streich's own Mammoth in the middle of the night, as Streich issued some last-minute instructions outside before they got going, Schmidt had just a little time for reflection, and noticed on the bulkhead of the truck what he later described as 'a large Knight's Cross made of cardboard. But instead of the usual central swastika, it carried a sketch of a large black fly'. One of Rommel's senior officers explained that it was something of a running joke, with 'the "Knight's Cross" being awarded ceremoniously every evening to the inmate of the Mammoth who had "shot down" the largest number of the pestilential desert flies during the day.'

Schmidt liked Streich a great deal and had always found him a courteous and engaging German officer. This was as opposed to Rommel, with whom, he related, 'it was months before he called me anything but the formal Lieutenant, and only after he had decided I was more than a necessary additional limb did he address me by name, bother to find out my age, whether I was married, or, indeed, even to think of me other than as something that filled a uniform and answered a command. It was, in fact, almost strange, after a long acquaintance, to find the impersonal General actually human.'[26] One of the many odd things about Rommel was that, while he had a very easy way with the common soldiers and they, in turn, greatly admired and respected him for the fact that '*überall, wo es höllisch zugegangen ist*' — everywhere that hellish things went on — Rommel was always in the middle of them, there was little parallel in his relationship with his fellow officers, which more often tended to the cold and impersonal.

Against all that, looking at the caricature of the most prestigious Knight's Cross, defaced with the ugly drawing of the black fly, Schmidt lifted his admiration for Rommel a notch higher and, as he wrote, 'began to appreciate Rommel's more single-minded insistence that his subordinates should display initiative, aggressiveness, and hardness in the face of the enemy. He had no time for frivolity'.[27]

•

At 1.30 on the morning of Monday 14 April, Captain Rea Leakey was tapped awake by one of the chaps in his tank squadron with the news that their commanding officer was on the wireless, and wanted a word with him.

The news was bad: the Germans looked to be about to break through. It seemed their infantry had forced a passage through the Red Line astride the El Adem road, and tanks could be heard growling around on the other side. The expectation was that at dawn they would push through and head towards the town. Leakey was to gather his men and tanks and move to block them, backing up the artillery that he would find about 2 miles up the El Adem road from the perimeter.

Holding the transmitter tightly, he murmured his response. Yes, sir, very good, sir.

This was, after all, the very thing they had been trained for, notwithstanding the fact that at that moment Leakey was cold, exhausted and had a very empty feeling in the pit of his stomach. It was not easy to tell his group of tank commanders that they were about to put their lives on the line against a military force that had never been bettered in the war to date, but the job was soon done. And yet — only moments after he had finished speaking and they all began to move to their tanks to follow orders, to 'start up' and move into positions — suddenly one of his young officers who had newly joined the regiment simply broke down. Crying, he said he could *not* go into action, because he *knew* he would be killed if he did. Appalled, but still a little understanding, Leakey physically grabbed the shivering and now whimpering young man, took him aside and told him he had to pull himself together. He was an *officer* in His Majesty's Royal Tank Regiment, and he had to set an example to his men.

It didn't work. Still crying, the young officer kept repeating that 'I can't go into this action because I know I will be killed ... I *know* I will be killed ... I know ... I will be *killed*.'

Leakey gave him a swig of rum to give him some courage — to no avail, alas. Then he tried a softer tone, being understanding and gentle, but this only seemed to allow the officer the luxury of going to the point of complete collapse. Finally, as the minutes ticked by — with all the men, equally as cold and tired as this fellow, watching to see what would happen — Leakey was left with no choice.

He drew his revolver out of his holster, cocked it and pointed it at the young man's temple.

'All right,' he said in a voice that brooked no pity. 'Either you get into your tank or I shoot you for cowardice in the face of the enemy.'

Clearly, something clicked. For without another word the young officer pulled himself together, turned, went back to his tank and began giving orders to his men. In minutes the whole tank squadron was rolling, the roar of their engines still making no impression on the sound of the artillery, which kept hurtling in.[28]

·

Meantime, after Mackell had made sure that all his men were back, and that Jack was being looked after, he made his report over the signal wires to his commanding officer, Lieutenant Colonel John Crawford. Jack's terrible wounds notwithstanding, Mackell's exultation at the result of their action could not be hidden.

'We've been into 'em, and they're running like fucking bunnies!'[29] he reported.

And, indeed, those Germans they'd attacked really had run like bastards — those who had survived — but there remained plenty more where they had come from. For the battle for control of this part of the Red Line continued unabated and, if anything, increased in tempo. While it was one thing to take down the advance guard, it was quite another to stop the army proper coming behind it, and in the moonlight the men of the 2/17th could see that the German sappers had done their work and deloused the minefield on the other side of the wire from R33, even stacking the mines up neatly on the side![30]

At about a quarter past two in the morning, no fewer than 200 German soldiers made it through the breach and spread out, causing Captain John Balfe, who bore the responsibility for defending those posts, to make a hard decision. He sent up a Very flare calling for artillery fire to be brought down upon themselves *and* the Germans, trusting that, while in their own posts they would have a fair chance of surviving the pounding, the German infantry would take serious damage.

And so it proved. Within minutes of the flare splitting the night sky, some serious 'arty' brought down by those blessed Pommies of the Royal

Horse Artillery landed right upon the spot where they thought most of the Germans could be found.

It helped, but still the Germans didn't withdraw, and they were able to keep the small breach in the perimeter that they had forged open. They were so well dug in they were even able to threaten the posts on either side of R33, which was now under severe fire. By four o'clock in the morning, the situation had become even more urgent for the defending Australians, with reports coming back that many German tanks were congregating just in front of R41 near the El Adem road and were clearly getting ready to make an attack.

If they did, so be it.

All of the Australian infantry and British artillerymen defending knew Lieutenant General Morshead's order for what they should do if the German tanks breached the Red Line, and all now readied themselves to carry it out.

Lieutenant General Morshead himself was busy at that very moment, tweaking some more plans. He was, of course, wide awake in his fortified headquarters and following closely the course of the German thrust, as more and more reports came in over the signalling system on which such energy had been spent setting up. It now seemed all but confirmed that the enemy was indeed launching its Panzers on the southern perimeter, and from there it would in all likelihood try to proceed along the axis of the El Adem road to get to the harbour.

To counter this, Morshead and his senior staff had already made many moves, which included positioning two groups of Cruiser tanks, each a half-dozen strong, at a spot some 3 miles back from the Red Line, east of the El Adem road, where they were to await further instruction. Meanwhile, another unit of anti-tank guns was placed just half a mile to the west of those tanks, bolstering the men of the Royal Horse Artillery, at a point where Morshead was sure they would come in useful if the Germans did indeed penetrate.

From his headquarters, the orders flowed, both over the signal system and with runners as back-up, to ensure that when the curtain went up everyone would be where they should be and know their parts. They did, after all, want to put on a 'good show' and give the Germans a 'stiff go'.

•

Back in post R33, Jack's groans were growing weaker. Athol kept wiping away the blood the best he could, and yet was not surprised when the flow began to ebb, as he knew Jack simply couldn't have much left in him. If he didn't get serious medical help quickly, it was going to be bad, very bad.

•

Would the Germans even go on with the attack, though? Because of the actions of Mackell, Edmondson and their crew, together with the continuing furious fire from the 2/17th, the attackers had been unable to establish more than a very narrow bridgehead through the perimeter, restricting both their capacity to flow into the fortress in strength and to get out if anything went wrong.

The situation was so serious that there was even dissent. When Lieutenant Colonel Gustav Ponath was told by one of Rommel's senior officers that the attack was to go ahead, Ponath objected, pointing out the many difficulties and great dangers — especially those of continuing an advance into an area about which they had only the tiniest clue where the defences lay, and no heavy weaponry to back their attack.

The adjutant wasn't interested in discussing it.

'Divisional orders,' he fired off as a single shot, an argument in itself. Orders were *orders*, and they were not to be discussed — they were to be executed.

Still Ponath, a man who was as solicitous of his own soldiers' lives as Morshead was of his, would not back down. Sergeant Assenmacher of the 8th Machine-gun Battalion watched from a small way off — the outlines of the two senior officers silhouetted against the desert sand by the wan moonlight — as Ponath kept going at the adjutant, pointing out the folly of the operation. Like all the other soldiers, Sergeant Assenmacher was straining to hear every word, as a decision was made by which many of them would live or die ...[31]

'Divisional orders!' the adjutant repeated stonily, until Ponath was simply left with no choice but to follow those orders or face the consequences of refusing a direct order.

Equally reluctantly, General Johannes Streich, with Schmidt beside him, was now heading north in Streich's Mammoth towards the point where the Panzers were assembling for the attack. Streich's own Panzer — the one from which he could command the attack — rumbled along behind. Somehow though, in the soupy light, the Mammoth's driver missed the point on the road where they were meant to turn off, and they were suddenly under fire! Bullets ricocheted off the body of their vehicle and they could even see the tracers lazily coming towards them from the fortress. Both officers immediately abandoned their vehicle and jumped onto the back of the Panzer ... only to find it was turning around and they were exposed again with no protection whatsoever! One more mighty bound and they were taking shelter in a ditch by the side of the road, where they were quickly joined by the driver of the Panzer, after he had stalled and it seemed the starter motor was shot to pieces. Not only that, but with the bullets now pelting their tank so thickly that it seemed like they'd never be able to get out of this godforsaken place, the Panzer driver was making heavy weather of it.

When a salvo from British artillery burst nearby, showering them in dirt, the driver let out such a cry that Streich inquired whether he was hurt.

'*Nein, Herr General*,' the driver replied miserably. '*Noch nicht.*' Not yet.[32]

Despite the seriousness of their circumstances, General Streich could not stop himself from laughing. What was no joke, however, was that, pinned down as they were and effectively lost into the bargain, they now had no chance of joining the other Panzers in time for the major assault on the perimeter. Those Panzers would have to go in without him at the helm.

•

For his part, Rommel entertained few doubts, even making time to write his beloved wife, Lu, a quick letter by the flickering lamplight at three o'clock in the morning, as in the distance could be heard the rumbling of his Panzers getting into position.[33]

14 April 1941, 03.00

Dearest Lu,

Today may well see the end of the Battle of Tobruk. The British were very stubborn and had a great deal of artillery. However, we'll bring it off. The bulk of my force is now out of the desert after a fortnight of it. The lads stuck it magnificently and came through the battle, both with the enemy and nature, very well. We've even got water again ... [34]

•

More rumbling in the darkness. Roaring engines. Tanks. Probably fucking Panzers. A weird thing about the acoustics of the desert was that somehow, because there were no obstacles for sound to hit, it just sort of rolled around and thus seemed to come from everywhere. So, for the Diggers of the 2/17th and 2/13th in particular, it sometimes it looked as if the Panzers had already broken through and were coming from *behind* them. But steady, Eddie. They knew that wasn't bloody possible, as if there had been a break-in elsewhere surely the communications system would have kicked in and they would have been told. So they held their positions, peering into the darkness, knowing only that, whatever it was, and from whatever precise direction it was coming, it would soon be upon them and they would be in a fight for their lives.

In his own position on the front line with the 2/13th, Bert Ferres was among the first to discern in the gloomy darkness the even darker shapes of tanks, their very blackness seeming to highlight their look of pure, creeping evil. He was quick to warn the rest of his section. Some big bloody Panzers were on their way . . .

•

Guter Gott, what was going on? For all the Australians' concern at the growing mass of German tanks, the attackers were not without their own serious worries. To get that many tanks in formation in this low light, with a fog now as well, would have been hard enough on a parade ground, but to do it on rough terrain that no one was familiar with — in total radio silence while enemy artillery took stabs in the dark at them — was proving to be a near impossibility. Worse, the engineer guides whose job it had been to direct the tank drivers to the breach in the anti-tank ditch had got lost and first up led them to the wrong spot. Even more worse, one of the vehicles guiding the tanks had a defective light that kept flickering on and off intermittently, like a small mobile lighthouse flashing in the gloom.[35]

In the lead tank, the commanding officer of this, the 5th Panzer Regiment's 2nd Battalion, Colonel Olbrich, fumed. Just where General Streich was he had no idea, but in his absence it had been up to Olbrich to take overall command of the operation. Thirty minutes had already been lost between waiting for Streich and then trying to find the right path, and in that time they had lost their chance at attacking in a co-ordinated fashion with their own fire support. Had Olbrich had that most precious of all things — a map — he would have been able to see that, while the breach that had been made for them was right by R33, they had been instead guided to R41, two-and-a-half miles to the east, where the ditch was totally impassable! And now that they *had* found the right spot at last, the word came back that the gap was only wide enough for one tank to go through at a time.

Still, as just the first glint of the dawn started to show in the eastern skies, at 5.20 a.m. Colonel Olbrich gave the order and the fifteen tanks under his direct command started rumbling forward, in the best formation they could muster, through the breach in the perimeter just south of R33, dragging anti-aircraft and anti-tank guns behind. As ever, in strict tactical formation the Mark IVs went in the lead, with the thinner-skinned tanks behind, fairly protected from whatever enemy artillery there might be directly in front, though they weren't expecting much. Not long afterwards, another twenty-three tanks of the 5th Panzer Regiment's 1st Battalion — a Panzer battalion that had already rolled ruthlessly through Poland and France — also came through the gap in the same formation.

•

Steady now. Steady. Steady. Keep it coming. Keep it coming. Keep it coming . . .

In their slit trenches and posts, the Diggers let the tanks rumble past, the vibrations shaking the ground all around them as they hugged it tighter. Their strict instructions, oddly enough, had been to let the tanks go unmolested — and not give away just what their positions were — and it frankly hadn't been that difficult. Firing mere bullets at beasts like that would have been like trying to bring down rampaging bullocks with darts. It would have done nothing but enrage them, and you would most certainly have had to face the consequences.

In the wake of each tank now came a couple of dozen German machine-gunners, most of them walking briskly, though some were riding on the backs of the tanks themselves. Again, while the time would shortly be upon the Australians to fire on the machine-gunners, the key was to not give away their positions, yet.

For those same Australian soldiers in their slit trenches and on the flanks of this German thrust, it was now an extremely difficult thing to be presented with clear shots at the Jerry soldiers passing before their gun sights, but that is what they had been told to do, and that is what they bloody well did. They held their fire, even as the German infantry divided up into those proceeding with the tanks, and those whose job it was to guard the bridgehead that had been secured and, if possible, to widen it further. The time to have a go at those bastards would soon be upon them, but it was not yet — not while the tanks were still within cooee.

As to the German tanks themselves, formed up with the thickest-armoured to the fore, they suffered little damage because at that distance the British 25-pounders simply did not have the velocity to penetrate the thick armour. Yet that was expected, and the plan was always to bring the tanks to within a range of 600 yards, where the Brits really could wreak some devastation.

Up ahead, a good mile back from the Red Line, the soldiers of the 2/3rd Australian Anti-tank Regiment and the Royal Horse Artillery watched the German tanks move forward with an odd impatience. Further, my pretties, ah yes, further, further still . . .

Inside those German tanks, the mood was the familiar one of grim satisfaction, just as it had been over the last two short weeks of offensive action, when they had regained in North Africa all the territory bar Tobruk that it had taken the British *months* to wrest from the Italians. Despite the hassle of a couple of hours earlier when they had not known quite where to go, it was now exactly like it had been going through Poland and France. Once the first line of defence crumbled, the rest of the defence crumpled, cowering away from such a show of might. No fortress had ever withstood them. And nor had the British. In all of Norway, Belgium, France and the Western Desert so far in this war, the British had always retreated, and even if they did have their colonials from Australia with them, there was surely no reason it would be any different this time.

Besides, the tank commander had been informed by the German Intelligence Section before embarking on this mission that the enemy was demoralised, exhausted, with few munitions left, and was getting ready to evacuate. With a good attack here they could capture a lot of them, while the others would scramble onto the boats, where the Luftwaffe could take care of them.

Sure, there would still be the odd pockets of brave souls prepared to take the Germans on, but they too would soon be wiped out. Still, there were some minor worries . . .

For only a couple of kilometres after crossing through the wire, Sergeant Assenmacher, sitting atop one of the tanks, suddenly noticed something up ahead in the first flush of light of the dawn. The something looked rather like *guns*, about 800 metres in front of him, covered in camouflage nets. He pointed it out to Lieutenant Krampe, who said not to worry — it was probably Italian tanks which had themselves penetrated, or maybe even the men of one of their own units had somehow got ahead. Sergeant Assenmacher wasn't so sure, though, because as he gazed through his binoculars, he could swear that they were indeed artillery which seemed to be pointing right at them, and he soon passed on the first of these concerns to the tank commander, even as the men and tanks continued to move forward . . .[36]

•

And now was the time.

As soon as what appeared to be the last of this wave of tanks had gone through and rumbled into the distance, the men of the 2/17th and 2/13th opened fire on the German infantry that had been left behind to guard the bridgehead, while the forces further in lined up on the troops on the Panzers, with both lots of Australian defenders causing carnage.

At one point, when some Matilda tanks arrived to help take out the German infantry, a Digger from the 2/13th called out to the commander, 'Whop it up 'em, mate.'

'We'll certainly do that, Aussie,' the commander replied in an upper-class English voice while continuing to plough forward.

'This,' the Digger later reminisced fondly, 'characterised the typical British soldier. Nothing seemed to faze him. He had a job to do and he would do it to the best of his ability, come what may. I developed a deep and lasting respect for the "Poms", as we lovingly called them, while in Tobruk.'[37]

Meantime, the Australians at the perimeter also opened up on the crew of three German anti-tank guns that were being hauled up towards the wire. The German crew was followed by more German soldiers who were trying to get some large field guns through — including extraordinarily long-barrelled 88-mm guns that the Australians had never seen before. While the Germans were pinned down, another group of the 2/17th went after cleaning up those German soldiers who had not been wiped out by the initial attack. Now that the head of the German spear had been broken from the main shaft, the job ahead was to destroy it.

CHAPTER TWELVE

To Fight Another Day . . .

The war in Africa is quite different from the war in Europe. It is absolutely individual. Here there are not masses of men and material. Nobody and nothing can be concealed. Whether in battle between opposing land forces or between those of the air or between both it is the same sort of fight, face to face, each side thrusts and counter thrusts. If the struggle were not so brutal, so entirely without rules, one would be inclined to think of the romantic idea of a knight's tourney.

EXTRACT FROM LIEUTENANT JOACHIM SCHORM'S DIARY, 16 APRIL 1941

The light was now exquisite, with the fading moonlight mingling beautifully with the first flushes of dawn. From a great distance, the Pommy gunners of the 1st Royal Horse Artillery, situated about a mile southwest of the El Adem crossroads, stopped pounding the breach in the Red Line once it was clear that no more tanks were attempting to come through — and now picked up a bead on the dust cloud about a thousand yards away and closing, that was indicating where the German tanks could be found. As the Poms began to rain down fire upon these tanks, they achieved immediate results with still more damage to the German machine-gun crews.

The tanks lurched forward, eager to find their persecutors, firing their machine guns with tracer bullets as they came on, though regularly shuddering to an agonised halt to fire their 75-mm cannon ... before sullenly starting forwards once more. Such was the collective fire coming from the tanks that, more than one of the British gunners was reminded of Guy Fawkes night at home. A happy thought for the British was that the tracers, particularly, allowed them to determine just where the tanks were in the cloud, and the focus of the British fire was much less fractured because of it.

Still the tanks kept coming, however, and they started rumbling to the east before straightening on a course parallel with the El Adem road heading north, just as Morshead had thought they would. Their destination of the 'Kings Cross' crossroads was an obvious one and, while they would be unlikely to take the El Adem road itself — as they would have expected ambushes to be set up along it — by keeping within sight of it, the tank commanders were more easily able to orientate themselves.

Knowing their rough direction, the thirty-two 25-pounders of the 1st and 107th Royal Horse Artillery, and the artillery of the AIF's 2/3rd Anti-tank Regiment — now all directly in the Germans' path, and right on the Blue Line — stopped firing. Again, for them there would be a time to give away their positions, but it was not this time.

•

In his command post, Morshead followed all the incoming reports with some satisfaction, noting that so far all seemed to be going according to plan. Yes, the Germans had forced a narrow passage through the Red Line, but it was nothing his men couldn't deal with. His chief concern up to this point had been to determine if this was really all their activity. There was always a possibility that this was a mere feint on the Germans' part, designed to make him rush his resources to one point while the real attack emerged from elsewhere, but by now it was absolutely clear: this was the real German attack, all right, and it was therefore time to commit his own forces of tanks. Those orders went out, and only a short time later the Cruiser tanks from the 1st Royal Tank Regiment began to close on their quarry. Just as Morshead had planned, they would be attacking the German flank from the east, with the rising sun right behind them and hopefully blinding the German gunners.

•

Though taking some fire, still the Panzers grimly made their way north towards the Tobruk town proper. Again, though the first flurry of hits upon them back at the perimeter had been harrowing, German confidence overall was rising as the worst of the fire seemed to have suddenly fallen away and they were closing in on their destination. At a point about 4 kilometres inside the perimeter, the terrain they were covering was substantially flat, before heading up a slight rise . . .

Unbeknownst to most of them, however, waiting on the other side of the rise, and about 600 yards back, the British gunners of the Royal Horse Artillery and the Australians of the 2/3rd Anti-tank Regiment were waiting and getting ready to fire at them over open sights . . .

As they waited, many of the men of 425 Battery, 107th Regiment, in that Royal Horse Artillery were still thinking of a speech that had been given to them shortly before by their Commander, Captain Graham Slinn. The good Captain had not minced words. He had wanted them to understand that if they failed to do their duty at this point and did not stop the Panzers, then Tobruk would likely fall, meaning that Cairo would likely go with it, and after that Suez and perhaps the whole Middle East. Nothing less than the fate of England and the free world was in their hands . . .

While speaking, Captain Slinn had been reminded of a couple of lines from Henry V's famous speech at Agincourt, when 24 000 French soldiers were about to fall upon just 5800 English. Nearing the end of his rousing speech — which had included the immortal lines 'We few, we happy few, we band of brothers; for he today that sheds his blood with me, shall be my brother' — King Henry had said a few words that were absolutely appropriate to the moment, and Slinn now uttered them to his own English soldiers as the battle knell sounded . . .

'You know your places; go to them, and God be with you . . .'[1]

•

Almost within firing range now.

The growl of the approaching Panzers was ever so slightly muted to the British by the fact that it was rolling to them up and over the small hill, but within minutes there was a sudden surge in the sound as the top of the Panzers themselves came into view, growing larger with every yard they progressed. Slinn's men awaited the signal . . .

Now!

Right then a glorious cacophony of fire rained down upon the leading German tanks, with the first shot taking the turret off the first Panzer, a 22-tonne Mark IV containing the Battalion Commander. The second shot struck sparks off the flanks of the next tank along, without penetrating.

Sergeant Assenmacher's worst fears were realised. Those cannon he thought he had spied a few hundred yards back were now blazing away at them, and were either killing his comrades atop the tanks outright, or damaging the tanks themselves, most particularly shattering the tracks of the tanks, one after the other. Instantly the men jumped off the imperilled vehicles and fired back the best they could . . .

Of course the surviving Panzers, too, returned fire immediately, seeking to destroy their persecutors, but a measure of the British guts came when one of their guns indeed sustained a direct hit on its shield — designed only to protect the gun crew from the blast of their own departing artillery fire, and not a shell coming the other way. When this German shell hit, five of the six-man crew were blown apart. And yet just as one man had survived, so had the barrel of the gun itself, the firing mechanism and the round that had been in the barrel. Now, seemingly an instant after the hit, the one Pommy survivor was seen to be hurling his dead comrades out of the way to give himself some space, and *still* got the shot away.[2] Around him, the other guns kept hurling fire towards the Germans as never before, with the whole situation turning on whether they could blow up the tanks before the tanks could blow up them. In the normal way of firing, a 25-pounder would release two missiles a minute for 'slow', three for a 'normal' and five for 'intense'. In a situation like this, where it was absolutely life or death, the rate went up to twelve a minute, and the bottom of the barrels started to glow red as the heat from one launch never got a chance to dissipate before the next one.

And so it went. Both the German tanks and the British gunners continued to go at each other, though the tanks, being well above ground, were at a decided disadvantage, given that they presented a much better target than the British artillery, which had so carefully been dug below ground with only the barrels protruding above the desert floor. Under normal circumstances those anti-tank guns could have been dealt with by the men of the machine-gun battalion that always accompanied the Panzers; but, as the tank commanders were now acutely aware, those men were now nowhere to be seen. Where were they?

•

Otherwise engaged.

Back near the Red Line, the Australian attack had gone in on the German soldiers who'd been left there to hold the gap open. Bitter fighting followed, with rifles, bayonets, machine guns and grenades all coming in handy, though it was some time before the Germans realised just how dire their predicament was. For, far from thinking *they* were the ones in trouble, in broken English they began to demand that the Australians surrender! The tanks had gone through, they said; Tobruk had fallen, and it was time for the Australians to save themselves.

The reply of the Australians was of the vulgar two-word variety. They continued to close in on the German infantry, reaping a terrible harvest of dead, until around a hundred of Rommel's men took shelter in an abandoned house a few hundred yards inside the perimeter.

•

Gott, give them strength. Never in their lives had the men in the Panzers faced anything like this. Mostly resistance would fade at their mere sight, and always in the past, once they had broken through an initial defensive barrier, things would be comparatively calm. But . . . not . . . this . . . time. This time the Germans were being assailed from all sides and, for reasons they were still unaware of, they were getting no support whatsoever from their own infantry, the machine-gunners who were meant to help protect them in just this kind of fix. In his own Mark IV tank, Lieutenant Schorm was in command of four others in his crew: the gunner, loader, driver and radio operator. Now he was desperately trying to follow the barked radio commands of his squadron leader — 'Anti-tank gun at nine o'clock, British tank at five o'clock!' — and work out where to direct his fire, even as armour-piercing shells whizzed by and things were getting more perilous by the minute.

At one point, just as he was barking to his driver to 'Turn right — no, turn left!' the driver had shouted back, 'The engines are no longer running properly, brakes not acting, transmission working only with great difficulty!'[3]

All of the other surviving Panzers were in much the same position. What could Colonel Olbrich do in such circumstances, in the face of such a fusillade, with five of their number now no more than smoking ruins? Precisely what Morshead and his commanders thought they would do, which was to go back over the rise and move with the lie of the land to the right of their original path, seeking a way around and away from those deadly guns in an effort to outflank them.

Unfortunately for the Germans, however, that flank was only too well covered, as that was where Morshead had positioned more of the mobile anti-tank guns of the Royal Horse Artillery and some of the Cruiser tanks, which were now coming into play.

•

For his part, Captain Rea Leakey and his Royal Tank Regiment of five Cruisers were just on the approach to their position — it had taken them a long time to traverse the distance in the darkness — when a lorry screamed to a halt in front of them and an artillery officer jumped out. 'For goodness' sake, turn right and come to our help!' he yelled. 'My battery is being attacked by German tanks and the guns are being overrun. Look! They are only 500 yards away!'

And sure enough, in the direction the officer pointed towards, there were the Panzers about to overwhelm the battery in question. If they got through there would be nothing between them and Tobruk proper.

Leakey's squadron swung into action immediately, charging straight at the massed Panzers, with each tank commander issuing instructions to his crew.

'Driver, halt. Gunner, 2-pounder — traverse right. Target tank. German Mark III. Four-five-zero yards. *Fire!*' The tank would jolt slightly as the cannon fired, and it would begin again, the commander guiding the driver to put the tank where it needed to be, and the gunner turning the range drum to the desired distance and direction before firing, with the cabin of their rolling iron box quickly filling with the acrid fumes of burning cordite. It soon got so thick that in his own tank Leakey could barely see his loader, Adams, working like a demented Trojan in a Stygian hell, loading shell after shell into the breach, each of which was soon hurtling on its way into the Panzers. Leakey's squadron was blessed with a full minute of free fire into the Panzers, scoring many direct hits, before the Germans realised where the fire was coming from and turned to give them some back, the blaze of their cannon visible and getting bigger, brighter and more lethal with every yard they came forward.[4] Now the two waves of metal monsters started to come together from opposite directions.

Just to Leakey's left, the Cruiser piloted by the young officer who had been convinced he was going to die took the brunt of the first of the German fire, being hit several times in succession and immediately 'brewed up' — tank terminology for exploding so badly that those inside had just a few seconds to make their escape or they would be incinerated in a tank that would shortly be a real oven. Even while continuing to fire, Leakey had a few split seconds to monitor who got out — the gunner, the driver, the loader, the ...

No, no one else. The young officer he had forced into the tank at gunpoint had been right — he really had been killed. And then another Cruiser was hit, and in an instant one of the escapees of this one was out, wounded, dragging himself along the ground with machine-gun bullets peppering all around him.

'Driver advance, turn slightly left,' Leakey commanded, trying to give the man cover, but in doing so showed the Panzer gunners the wide-on view of his Cruiser, and so presented twice as big a target profile, which they weren't long in hitting. In an instant a German shell had penetrated Leakey's tank and removed most of the gunner's chest, and at that point it was time to scramble. One of the other crew members had also been killed, but the other had got out and was lying by the tank with a sickly grin, and his right leg hanging by a few threads. Leakey got him onto his shoulders and carried him to a trench, where the lad spoke for the first time.

'Cut it off, sir, it's no use to me ...'

Leakey did exactly that with his penknife, and only a short time later an Australian from a carrier turned up, stemmed the massive bleeding of the wounded man the best he could under the atrocious circumstances, got him in the vehicle and took him away. (A curiosity of quite a few of the medical orderlies on the Australian side was that they were conscientious objectors — strongly opposed to war, but mercifully not opposed to helping save those who engaged in it.)

As to Leakey and his crew, they had done their duty and scored their hits to the best of their ability, and it was now for the others to do the same.

•

Which they were. For in the meantime the tank battle had continued to rage, with the Panzers also being attacked by the other squadrons, which in short order had knocked out a further four tanks.

As confusion reigned supreme among the Germans, the Australian and British gunners kept pouring shells and bullets onto them, even as back at the Red Line the men of the 2/17th's B Company kept up a withering machine-gun and rifle fire on the breach, preventing any German or Italian cavalry coming to one of their fellows' rescue.

Up above them all, the valiant Hurricanes of the Royal Air Force and Royal Australian Air Force were acquitting themselves wonderfully, though heavily outnumbered by both German and Italian planes. Two enemy planes were shot down for the loss of one Hurricane. Two of the Italian planes that crashed narrowly missed taking out some of the German tanks — a pity, as for the defenders there would have been some poetic justice there.

•

At this time, just 90 metres back from the breach, an angered and even stunned Erwin Rommel was desperately trying to get the Italian soldiers of the Ariete Division to follow up, to pour through the gap and consolidate the ground he thought had been won, before sowing confusion behind the Australian and British lines.

While Rommel's own command post tried desperately to get in touch with him — it was all but unprecedented for a German officer of his rank to have moved so close to the front line that he was no longer in communication — the German general vainly tried to force the passage through. He approached to within 90 metres of the bridgehead, which was a crazy risk for him to take, as the British artillery soon rained down fire so close to him that a bit of shrapnel cut the aerial of the signals vehicle — but Rommel had never been one to guide a battle from reports only.

In any case, by this time the 'breach' was effectively that in name only. Yes, the concertina wire had been blown, the minefields deloused, and the anti-tank ditch filled in, but so heavy was the fire now being laid upon the gap that it was nothing short of suicide to try and cross it, even if Rommel had wanted to go further. Furious at his impotence, the German General had no choice but to go back to his own command post.

•

Jack Edmondson was holding on, but only just. Throughout the long and terrible night there had been a constant stream of visitors to his side, in the post to which he had first been carried; they included Austin Mackell, who had been able to formally and fervently express his gratitude to Jack for saving his life. Mostly Jack had been able to acknowledge their presence, but as his lifeblood continued to seep from his awful wounds, so too did he become progressively paler and less responsive. When the first grey streaks of the coming day ripened into the dawn twilight proper, Athol Dalziel could see that Jack was dying. And it seemed Jack knew it too.

Summoning some strength, Jack told his best friend that after he died he wanted Athol to have his writing case, which he would find back in his kit.

Dalziel replied, as evenly as he could muster, 'I'll keep it for you until you get out of hospital.'

Jack grinned and said, 'No, Athol, thanks all the same for trying ... I know hospitals are no good to me now ... Tell mother I am thinking of her ... Tarz, give my love to the folks ... and good luck, old boy.'[5]

Athol stood up and looked down on Jack lying before him, gazing up at him with a dull-eyed, half-comatose look.

He had to turn away for fear Jack would see his tears, and finally had to leave that part of the enclosure so that Jack wouldn't hear him crying.

Athol was relieved by another soldier from their company, Johnnie Durig, and, as Johnnie told Athol later, at about quarter to seven Jack just closed his eyes, even as his breathing started to get a bit raspier, as if by deep breaths alone he might be able to compensate for what was happening elsewhere in his body.

And then, about seven o'clock, with the sounds of the battle still raging in the near distance, suddenly from Jack came ... nothing. There was no breathing, no movement at all, and when Johnnie lifted his comrade's hand to check, it was clammy and dead. He was gone.

•

The time was nigh.

Just half a mile away from where Rommel had pulled back in frustration, the hundred German soldiers who had taken shelter in the abandoned house only a couple of hundred yards inside the perimeter had stopped calling upon the Australians to surrender, and were coming to realise what kind of predicament they were in. Still heavily outnumbered, they were taking a lot of fire, and considered that their best hope was to hold on until their Panzers — surely nearly victorious by now — could return to kill their persecutors. The Australians, however, were not going to give them that time.

With the sun now well up and the heat of the day soaring, it was time to bring the issue to a head. From the south, a former bank clerk from Sydney's Neutral Bay by the name of Sergeant Bob McElroy gathered his men to him and they launched an attack, running forwards and firing as they went, with other soldiers covering them. Fifty yards away they hurled their grenades towards the Germans and followed them up with a bayonet charge.

It was too much for many of the Germans. Despite the fact they still had ten machine guns and a mortar, it appeared that their nerve broke. While some started to run, others threw down their weapons and pleaded for mercy.

Eighteen Germans were killed with another eighteen taken prisoner, with the rest getting away to be mopped up by the other platoons. The job had been done.

•

Amid the Panzers, carnage continued to reign as they took simultaneous fire from the guns of the 1st, 3rd, 104th and 107th Regiments as well as the 2/3rd Anti-tank Regiment and the Cruiser tanks, and assorted distinguished units of — ladies and gentlemen, please put your hands together and let's hear it for — the Australian Bush Artillery!

As these lead tanks of the 2nd Battalion, 5th Panzer Regiment, were now blocked to their front, and on their flank, they could only turn around . . . to come face to face with the tanks of the Regiment's 1st Battalion, which had followed them in! Rommel's orders to the next wave of tanks had been to 'pursue the retreating enemy' to the west, but there was now no doubt that the enemy wasn't retreating.[6] Neither Panzer battalion knew quite what to do, as this had never happened before; and they had certainly not done this in drills, for the simple reason that Panzers never turned around — they only went forwards.

But not this time, sport.

The *coup de grâce* was delivered by the trucks upon which the 2-pounder guns had been secured. At a distance of about half a mile, these trucks roared in on the flanks of the German tanks, fired several salvoes, and roared off again before the tanks could get a bead on them. Not only did they score some direct hits on the German tanks, but the trucks were fast enough to get away again before they could be nailed by return post.

The resultant chaos was compounded by the fact that, in the heat of all the battle, some of the turrets of the surviving German tanks had now got stuck, grinding to a halt and refusing to respond to the tank's controls. They had needed maintenance, had not received it, and this was the result. Colonel Olbrich, finally, was left with no choice. It did not come easily to a German tank officer to give the order to retreat, but it was now clear to him that staying was not an option. With British tanks and artillery and Australian anti-tank regiments firing at them from all sides, and with their losses already severe, he felt he had no choice.

His order crackled across the radio to the headsets of the other tank commanders: '*Rückzug!*' Retreat!

Such an idea was not obvious to the worthy Lieutenant Colonel Ponath, who, with two of the companies from the 8th Machine-gun Battalion, was still in action and, shouting over the roar of the battle, tried to get Colonel Olbrich to stay and fight it out. A furious conversation ensued. Colonel Olbrich refused, saying his own tank was down to its emergency reserve of ammunition, the others were the same, and they *had* to go — but he could at least offer Ponath a lift upon his own machine.[7] Ponath declined, asserting forcefully that the Tommy resistance was nearly done and that if the tanks just kept going, they would win the day!

Olbrich was through arguing, however. He disappeared into the turret, pulling the tank lid firmly down on top of him, and in short order was roaring away with the other tanks. Now, with the decision taken, it wasn't quite every man for himself — but there was certainly a mad rush of German tanks and infantry, away from the *Hexenkessel* (witch's cauldron),[8] as Lieutenant Schorm would later describe it.

And now in all the dust, smoke and confusion, something happened that was a first for World War II, and indeed a first since the swastika had initially begun to spread like a stain across Germany, Europe, the Middle East and

North Africa. For now, you bloody beauty, those who had been taking Nazi flags forward had been given a beating like a red-headed stepson, with the result that those flags were now heading back down the same path whence they had come. (And in many ways the complete chaos of the Panzers was understandable. In all the training the commanders had done, they had practised many methods of framing an attack on a position or an enemy armoured brigade, or to defend against the same. They had spent months in training on how to go forward in correct formation, and whole weeks on the theory and actuality of *Absetzbewegungen*, which were specific sideways and backward movements, but they had never been trained on how to retreat.[9])

In the resultant maelstrom, it wasn't necessarily easy for the Australian and British gunners to pick out individual targets. But, then again, they didn't need to, as the surviving tanks churned and burned their way haphazardly back towards the perimeter, with their infantry hightailing it after them.

Back at the Red Line, Sergeant McElroy and his men, together with the rest of the 2/17th Battalion, saw the tanks coming and got ready. As one now, when the tanks came within range, the Australians and British just fired everything they had, from mortars to rifles to Brens to anti-tank weapons to grenades to 25-pound shells, into the heart of the billowing dust clouds churned up by the tanks, clouds that were soon mixing with the smoke of their destruction. Though unable to sight specific targets, the Diggers still felt some confidence that the retreating Germans were now stacked tightly enough that they'd have to hit *something*. And, between them, they mostly did.

Inside those tanks, the surviving Germans revved their engines for all they were worth, desperate to find an exit from this hell and appalled, as they turned tail, to see the scores of dead German soldiers lying by the very anti-tank guns they had been in such terrible need of. On the left flank of the exit as they got close they could see the Italian anti-tank guns, but no dead bodies around them — the Italian guns appeared to have been simply abandoned. The Germans kept scurrying, many of them with screeching metal as damaged tracks hurtled around the damaged sprockets which were exposed to the artillery fire.

As the last of the surviving Germans did make it through the perimeter — past two further Panzers that had been destroyed just outside the wire — so exultant did the Australians manning post R33 and its surrounds feel that it was all that Captain Balfe could do to stop his men charging through after the enemy, firing all the while; though he did allow them to go after the German soldiers who had tried to take refuge in the anti-tank ditch.

•

Meanwhile, 1.5 kilometres back from that ditch, Lieutenant Colonel Ponath and his men, abandoned by the Panzers, were in a desperate situation. They had no cover to speak of, were surrounded and in the position — entirely unaccustomed as they were — of being totally outgunned and outnumbered. Worse, the Australians who surrounded them were now taking no chances and were simply, strategically, moving in and picking off the German soldiers one by one, taking their time now that the departure of the tanks meant that there was no need to take risks . . .

A good officer, Ponath knew that the only way out was to fight their way out, and it had to be done quickly, before their own ammunition was used up. Rallying his sixty surviving soldiers, then, it was at his call that the men of the 8th Machine-gun Battalion made a dash towards the gap, firing as they went. Yet they had not travelled more than 20 metres before a single bullet dropped Ponath, shot through the heart and falling dead at the feet of his appalled troops, even as many other men were also hit and the calls for medics abounded. With Ponath's death, though, the fight seemed to instantly fade from the battalion, and the next most senior officer, Captain Bartsch, bowed to reality and gave the order for his troops to cease fire, drop their weapons and surrender, signalling what his orders had been to those who were shooting at them.

With their surrender, Bartsch stood with his hands up, whereupon a man with the insignia of an Australian major also stood up and stepped forward from where he had been shooting at the Germans. The two walked towards each other until face to face and then saluted each other. Then the Australian reached into his vest to pull out a cigarette case, which he proffered to the German, saying, 'Good fight.'[10]

Professionals to the end, the Germans — who were now being surrounded by beaming Australian soldiers with what seemed to the prisoners like unnervingly long and vicious bayonets — had not just simply thrown down their own weapons, but had disassembled them and thrown the separate parts all around. Nothing, however, could change the fact that they really were now prisoners. As that realisation struck home, some began to cry in part fury and part humiliation, but it is recorded in the 8th Machine-gun Battalion history that at least their Australian captors quickly offered them cigarettes and a cup of tea to make them feel better about it all, before taking them to the prison yard.

•

As to the Panzer commanders who had also been rounded up once they had escaped from their stricken vehicles, some were sobbing while others remained defiant, with one of them openly threatening, 'You will pay for this.' Most appalling to many of them was the bitter fate that had denied what they felt was their destiny: to participate in the *Endsieg*, the final victory, that they all felt sure was coming.

And mixed with it all was great confusion.

'I cannot understand you Australians,' one of the Germans told his captors. 'In Poland, France, and Belgium, once the tanks got through the soldiers took it for granted that they were beaten. But you are like demons. The tanks break through and your infantry still keep fighting.'[11]

In the whole range of the Germans' experience, they had never come across anything like this, and it had never even entered their heads that they might be so ignominiously captured. Them? The master race? How had this happened?

•

How had this happened?

Rommel was a gentle man when writing to his wife and son, and was usually at least courteous to most of his staff. But his fury when he felt let down by his underlings was something to behold, and this was just such an occasion.

With the surviving tanks all around now disgorging their shattered crews, Rommel was soon joined at his headquarters by Colonel Olbrich and General Streich, with the former reporting that under the murderous British fire he had had no choice but to order his Panzers to withdraw and that ... unfortunately ... they had had to leave the infantry to look after themselves ... and he was all but certain they were lost.[12]

Rommel whirled on General Streich and roared at him, 'Your Panzers did not give of their best, and left the infantry in the lurch!'

General Streich placated his superior officer the best he could, despite some internal angry feelings that surely approximated Rommel's own — yet they were directed not at his men, but at Rommel himself.

Managing to control his own emotions, though, Streich replied, 'Herr General, the Panzers would have reached their objectives despite strong anti-tank fire, if the whole sector had not been protected by deep and well-camouflaged tank traps.'[13]

Rommel would not accept any reasons for such a debacle.

As later described by his adjutant, Lieutenant Schmidt, Rommel was unforgiving because he considered that Streich and his men had committed the gravest of all military errors — they had lacked *resolve*.

'He gave vent to his anger openly,' Schmidt recounted, 'and used words, such as presumably only one general may use to another ...'[14]

At this point Rommel completely refused to believe that most of the 8th Machine-gun Battalion had either been captured or wiped out, and insisted that they must still be inside the perimeter fighting for their lives.

He tried to get the Italian Ariete Division to mount a rescue mission, but it soon became obvious that the Italians had lost all stomach for the fight. It was one thing to order an attack and quite another to actually have it happen.

Down at the harbour, meantime, forty German dive bombers had suddenly appeared at just after 7.30 a.m., clearly intending to be part of a synchronised attack — in classic Blitzkrieg fashion — to link up with the confusion caused by the tanks ... but there were no tanks there to meet them. The garrison's Ack-Ack gunners knocked four Stukas out of the skies, while another two were brought down by the valiant Hurricane fighters.

Just a short while later it was all over, and quiet again descended on the battlefield, with each side counting their dead, tabulating the missing and caring for the wounded. It took a lot more time to count on the German side than it did among the men of the Tobruk garrison.

Between them, the Germans and Italians had had 150 of their number killed, just under 500 wounded and another 250 taken prisoner. Of the thirty-eight tanks they had launched into the fray, a devastating seventeen had been destroyed, while many others had been severely damaged. The losses of the Tobruk garrison were comparatively light: twenty-six men killed, sixty-four wounded and two tanks and one aircraft.[15]

Most importantly, they had given Germany the bloody big smack in the mouth it so desperately deserved.

•

While in Tobruk's 9th Division Headquarters the mood was one of slightly cautious euphoria — they had seen off the first of the major German assaults, though there remained the question of what was to follow — one person was not euphoric at all: the august but now slightly forlorn Lieutenant General Lavarack. Despite the victory, he had just been cabled by Wavell that Cyrenaica Command, of which he was the Commander, no longer existed;

the whole thing was to become Western Desert Force, including all the forces not only in Tobruk but also the troops placed back near the Egyptian border, which were preventing Rommel's troops from continuing east.

The unstated problem was that, because Western Desert Force had so many British units in it, it simply would not do to have an Australian commanding it, so Lavarack would have to go back to commanding the 7th Division, minus the 18th Brigade, which was to stay in Tobruk. Within hours the worthy Lavarack had been flown out, leaving Morshead in sole command.

•

You bloody beauty.

Among the men of the 2/17th and 2/13th Battalions that had been on the front lines, taken the brunt of the German attack and emerged victorious — up against the bloody German Army, with Panzers and more guns than you could poke a stick at — there was now a general muted wonder at what they had come through. With just the tiniest fraction of that level of achievement in civilian life — as in, winning a football grand final — they would have held a party, clapped each other on the back, made speeches and told each other war stories until late in the night about specific moments in their battle for victory. But this was not like that. Soldiers who had performed the most extraordinary acts of valour didn't even mention it.

To look at Bobby McElroy, sitting there cleaning his rifle — he who had so bravely led the charge on the Germans holed up in the abandoned house — you wouldn't know that he'd just done anything out of the ordinary at all. Nobody was saying, 'Three cheers for Bobby!', hoisting him on their shoulders or even doing anything so benign as asking him for details. But blokes knew, all right. He'd done well. They'd all done well. Really well, and put on a 'good show'.

And now that so many of them had been effectively blooded in action, they felt stronger, almost — as trite as it might sound — like a cove who has lost his virginity may suddenly feel more of a man and comport himself more confidently thereafter. The loss of mates like Jack Edmondson was upsetting, certainly; but somehow, in the hurly-burly of everything else, there was no time to focus on that, because more important than grieving was the need to continue to survive. Now was the time to check ammunition belts, grab a bite of something to eat, have a kip if you could and get ready for whatever the bastards might throw at you next time.

Mixed with the Australians' own quiet pride at what they had achieved, however, was a great deal of admiration and gratitude for what the Pommy gunners had achieved behind them. Without them the game really would have been lost, and no man was slow to acknowledge it. As was so often the case, it was Chester Wilmot who was the first to find the words to accurately sum up the situation: 'It is broadly true that while the perimeter was occupied almost exclusively by Australians, the bulk of the supporting weapons were manned by British troops. This was an ideal combination. The dash and daring needed by the front-line troops ... was provided by the Australians. The steadiness and dogged reliability, required especially of the field and Ack-Ack gunners, came from the British.'[16]

Or, in the words of the Diggers themselves, they were bloody beauts!

•

That afternoon, General Streich went to see Colonel Olbrich to discuss the morning's events — and perhaps to compare notes on their thoughts about General Rommel — but could only find Olbrich's second in command, Major Ehlert, who had some distressing news for him.

Herr Rommel wanted to organise another attack.

In response, Streich was simply speechless. What and with whom exactly was he going to attack?

The 5th Panzer Battalion was, literally, shot to pieces and in no shape whatsoever to go forward again, while the 8th Machine-gun Battalion — which had lost 700 soldiers in the last two weeks — had all but ceased to exist as a functioning entity. Far from attacking again, it was Streich's private view that if at that very moment the Australians had sallied forth with their guns blazing, they could have knocked over the entire Afrika Korps.[17]

In the end, Rommel was left with no choice but to try to mount an attack with the Italian Ariete Division, which had at last moved up to the starting line, but that too came to nothing, even though Rommel accompanied them to try to give them steel. As Rommel later described it, 'Southeast of Gasr el Glecha, they received a few rounds of artillery fire from Tobruk. The confusion was indescribable. The division broke up in complete disorder, turned tail and streamed back in several directions to the south and southwest.'[18]

The whole thing proved to be a fiasco.

•

All up, Streich was not the only one who was unhappy with the way Rommel had handled things. In his own tent, Major General Kirchheim — recovering from having been wounded himself, just a short time before von Prittwitz had been killed, and near the same spot — wrote a detailed letter to the head of the OKW, Generalfeldmarschall Wilhelm Keitel, giving an account of what had happened and the essential futility of the attacks on Tobruk. He maintained — and said so in strong language — that unless these attacks stopped immediately, the 5th Light Division would effectively cease to exist and the Afrika Korps would be beaten. Then he sent it to Berlin, where it would be received with some interest ...

•

That Monday, 14 April 1941, had been a terrible day for Elizabeth Edmondson — so bad that, as she confided to her diary, she felt sure she would never forget it. First her older sister Ada had tried to get her to go to the Royal Easter Show to take her mind off Jack, and she'd almost had to be rude to make Ada understand that she just didn't want to go. And then, somehow, the silent scream she'd had inside her for so long came out in a way that surprised even Elizabeth. Stuffy the cat had been pawing at the back door and just wouldn't stop howling — Stuffy, who usually never even gave a miaow! Elizabeth had let him in to settle him, but then he simply ran from room to room through the house howling such a weird howl, like Elizabeth had never heard from him before. Finally, as she told her diary: 'I just could not stand it so I scragged him and sat him on a little table outside the back door. He sat there for a while still howling. So I shut the doors. Apparently he went somewhere as he wasn't here for tea and didn't come inside tonight.'[19]

Things were not as they should be and Elizabeth felt strongly something was very badly amiss. It wasn't just that she was worried that Jack was okay, because that was pretty much what she thought about all day, every day, but nor had she ever felt so uneasy ...

•

Far to the east of Tobruk at this time, things were happening that at least gave Rommel some good news for the day. He received confirmation that the forward forces of the Afrika Korps had captured both the town of Sollum, right on the Egyptian border, and the Halfaya Pass just to its east, both of which were of enormous strategic significance. In that whole area, Sollum and the Halfaya Pass boasted the only two roads that led from the high plateau of Libya 60 metres down to the low plains of Egypt; whoever controlled them controlled both the gateway to Egypt (if you attacked from the west), and the gateway to Libya (if you attacked from the east). If you didn't control those two points, the only way to proceed was to swing on a long, low loop through the open desert, 80 debilitating kilometres to the south. On a day when things had not gone at all according to plan, it was at least something to seize upon with triumph, and Rommel did so with an iron grip.

•

In London at this time, Australian Prime Minister Robert Menzies was not himself, in a town that was not itself. Whatever Menzies' growing band of critics was saying about his love of London over and above Melbourne, Sydney and Canberra, he was not enjoying his time there. The whole place was drab and grey, with all the colour and gaiety gone. Once-bustling squares were deserted; houses bombed to pieces; sandbags in doorways; ground-floor windows bricked up; death around many a corner. No more leisurely strolling about the Charing Cross Road bookshops or sauntering in Piccadilly, as he had loved to do. Gone, all gone.[20] These 'dark and hurrying days' in London, as he described them in his diary, were in fact not to his liking at all. He missed his wife, Pattie, and his daughter, Heather, terribly.

As to his political life in the capital of the British Empire, it seemed to provide little but constant irritation and frustration, and never more so than on this day. For on 15 April, while Menzies was attending a meeting of the War Cabinet, Winston Churchill blithely noted how wonderful it was to have the Australians in Tobruk, as the Allies would be able to use the town as a launching pad from which they could break out, and attack the Axis forces.

'Tobruk *must* be held as a bridgehead or rally post,' said the British Prime Minister, 'from which to hit the enemy . . .'

It was at this point Menzies could no longer contain himself.

'With *what*?' he asked fiercely.[21]

There was no doubt these were desperate times and the question was a very reasonable one under the circumstances. In Greece, in a campaign that Menzies had personally approved, the Australian PM now had 42 000 Australian soldiers just holding on. In Tobruk, 15 000 Australians were surrounded. At a later point, Menzies pushed the issue again with Churchill, wanting to know what the contingency plans were if things went wrong in Libya. Churchill would not hear of things going wrong and, in his view, to plan for defeat would be to invite it. What if the Army were to hear of it? Why, they would be demoralised![22] As it happened, to a certain degree the highest echelons of the Allies' leadership in the Middle East were already demoralised, with Wavell himself noting lugubriously, 'Winston is always expecting rabbits to come out of empty hats.'[23]

And yet, so it went. On and on and on.

'The Cabinet is deplorable,' Menzies wrote in his diary of the experience of seeing Churchill and his senior ministers up close. 'Dumb men, most of whom disagree with Winston, but none of whom dare to say so. This state of affairs is most dangerous. The Chiefs of Staff are without exception Yes Men, and a politician runs the services. Winston is a dictator; he cannot be overruled, and his colleagues fear him. The people have set him up as something little less than a God, and his power is therefore terrific.'[24]

Menzies was not the only one to gain such an impression, with Sir John Dill the year before having written to his friend General Lord Gort, 'The War Office is, as far as I can see, in complete chaos and the situation in Norway as bad as I expected ... I'm not sure that Winston isn't the greatest menace. No one seems able to control him. He is full of ideas, many brilliant, but most of them impracticable. He has such drive and personality that no one seems able to stand up to him ...'[25]

Certainly not the Australian Prime Minister, try as hard as he might. The sober reality of Menzies' experience since arriving in London and beginning his high-level consultations, was that he had achieved almost precisely ... nothing. Nothing bar one more flood of fine words from Winston about how very committed Britain was to defending Australia, how Menzies and his ministers shouldn't worry themselves about the spectre of an increasingly militaristic Japan joining the war on the side of the Germans, and how imperative it was that Australia send even more troops to defend the Empire. But of British ships, aeroplanes and resources to help bolster that defence of Australia — the prime reason the Australian Prime Minister had come to Britain in the first place — the closest Menzies could get was the promise of a handful of planes that Britain didn't want anyway!

(And, in fact, Churchill was already totally committed to prioritising the placement of Britain's limited resources in the European war to defend Britain well ahead of the needs of the far-flung and ultimately pruneable reaches of the Empire that Australia represented. So committed, in truth, that he had already secretly instructed a British delegation to Washington to tell the Americans that if they were to come into the war, they had to understand that beating Germany in Europe was the prime consideration and they would not be expected to 'come and protect Singapore, Australia and India against the Japanese'.[26] As to the aircraft that had been promised to Menzies for the defence of Australia, Churchill was so unhappy when he found out that this decision had been made by one of his ministers that he tried to have it reversed, arguing it was 'most unwise to fritter away aircraft to Australia, where they would not come into action against the Germans'.[27])

In light of Menzies' own failure to secure anything of substance to show for his trip, he felt so disconsolate about it all that he confided to Dill that, with the way things stood, it was barely worth him daring to return home and that instead he 'might as well go for a trip to the North Pole'.[28] In fact, just the week before he had been told by the Australian High Commissioner in London — who had been in particularly close contact with key people at home — that his whole political future rested on him coming home with either a cast-iron promise from Britain or, better still, cast-iron weaponry in the form of ships, planes and guns. And yet the sober reality was that he really had precious little to show for his efforts.

The true absurdity of his situation, though, was that while his political fortunes in Australia were hanging by a thread, his stocks in Britain were enormous, with the press generally lionising him, humble Britons asking him for autographs wherever he went, and even a low murmur emerging that if Churchill proved unequal to the task of guiding the Allied war effort, then there really could be a place for a man like Menzies to take a far grander role. After all, the influential journal the *Daily Sketch* had just written, in reference to him, that the British Empire was a 'single entity, and we must have, we need to have at the heart of it the best talent that any part of it can provide ... Often before in the history of our island we have been able to say that the hour has brought forth the man. Perhaps the Empire will have a chance of saying that, too.'[29]

All up, Menzies decided to remain in London a little longer. Perhaps he could secure something more solid from Britain; perhaps something would break his way politically; but, whatever else, it was clear that momentous decisions were shortly going to have to be taken concerning the besieged

Australian troops, and he did not want to leave those decisions to Churchill and his Yes Men. It was important that his own voice, an Australian voice, be heard on such matters.

For once.

•

Of all the jobs in the war, this was surely the worst. Slowly rumbling around just behind the front lines ... a truck was now moving with men inside effectively on 'death detail'. Their job was to go from post to post, trench to trench, and take away the broken and shattered bodies of those who had paid the ultimate price, from both sides. For there were Germans who needed to be buried also and their bodies were treated with respect. Often men who just hours before had been fighting each other as if their lives depended on it — because they had — now lay beside each other in death, as peaceful as you please.

One of the men assigned to this detail was John Johnson, in his carrier 'Walwa', and it near broke John's heart to do it, carefully lifting up the broken bodies and putting them in the rear of the vehicle to take them to be buried. Of course they couldn't feel anything but, somehow, treating them gently like that was a matter of respect. He was careful not to mention such a task to his family in his letters home, as it would so upset them, but still ...

This gathering of the dead was a dreadful job, universally hated, but like so much that happened at Tobruk it simply had to be done, and so it was.

On the morning of 15 April, they buried Jack with full military honours in Tobruk War Cemetery, with Colonel John Crawford and some of his senior officers attending with the chaplain. As deep as they could get him, Jack lay beneath a simple wooden cross on which were painted the words:

NX 15705

CORPORAL JOHN HURST EDMONDSON.

KILLED IN ACTION. 14.4.41.

As stark as such an inscription was — and despite the fact that plenty of other soldiers were buried in the cemetery that same morning — the death of Jack Edmondson was not regarded as just one more of many. Rather, the very heroism of the action that had killed him — and because it was Jack, a very popular, well-known bloke — seized the imagination of the garrison, and the story of the manner of his death went from company to company, battalion to battalion, and eventually around the whole garrison. Colonel Crawford even recommended to his superiors in Cairo that Jack be awarded a medal for bravery. After all, a bloke couldn't do much more than charge a dugout full of Germans against overwhelming odds and kill four of them — of whom three were done after he copped the shots that would shortly be taking him to Jesus — could he? He could not. Crawford sent the recommendation.

•

Yet there was little time for anything other than getting ready for the next attack, which they felt surely must come sooner rather than later. This included careful patrolling *outside* the wire, and on the afternoon of 16 April, three Australian Bren carriers of the 2/48th were in no-man's-land just to the southwest of Tobruk when they saw ahead of them an entire battalion of Italian infantry heading their way. Jesus. Chucking screaming U-ies — just as so many Australian youths had first done when learning to drive on the farm — the men raced their vehicles back to their own lines to sound the alarm.

Furious activity ensued, with every man jack in the area who could fire a rifle, or fire bush artillery, getting into position, and sure enough ... sure enough ... soon the Italians appeared on the far hazy horizon, marching towards them like ghosts out of the Dreamtime ...

And yet what was that behind them?

Tanks! *Panzers*.

Twelve of them. They almost seemed, if you didn't know better, to be herding the Italians forward!

Whatever the case was, the point was to make the Tank Commanders rethink their advance and, with that in mind, the Australians began to lob shells into the Italians' midst.

An instant later, it happened. Almost as one, the Italians were seen to storm towards the garrison — albeit being careful to throw down their weapons first — and now had their hands held as high as they could while their legs pumped furiously. En masse, they were surrendering, preferring the safety of a cage inside Tobruk to the dangers of continuing to try to assault it from outside. Behind them, the disgusted German tank officers — so suddenly left on their own — were seen to direct some of their fire into the backs of the departing Italians, their so-called allies.

Certainly it was not the finest moment of Italian arms, but calling it cowardice would not adequately cover it. The essence of the problem was that most of the Italian soldiers simply didn't believe in what they were doing in the first place. Give their lives for this godforsaken bit of dirt, just so Mussolini could prance and preen? No. It was one thing for Mussolini to rant and rave from the balcony of his *palazzo* and promise a new Roman empire, but quite another to actually give their lives for such a thing. A lot of the German soldiers, it appeared, really believed in that kind of *merda*, but the Italians most assuredly did *not*. An enormous number simply hoped to survive the war, and if the best way to do that was to become a prisoner, then so be it. So they kept running towards the Australian lines, and 803 of them were taken prisoner.[30]

All up, the Italian attacks on the western perimeter of Tobruk on 15 and 16 April came to nothing other than a swelling of the already long Italian prisoner list — which was great news for the Allies on the one hand, but on the other it meant Rommel had 3000 fewer relatively useless mouths to feed while Morshead had 3000 more totally useless ones draining his already meagre resources.

•

At ten o'clock that same morning, General Rommel, with two of his staff, visited the shattered remains of the 8th Machine-gun Battalion, in their position guarding the southern perimeter of Tobruk. After asking for a report of current battle strength and being informed that of the 1400 soldiers who had begun the African campaign, there were now just 300 left and able to go into battle, still he showed no sign of despair.

In fact, drawing himself up, he told the men straight out: '*Lassen Sie den Kopf nicht hängen . . . das ist Soldatenschicksal*' — Don't let your heads hang down, this is the destiny of soldiers.[31] He went on: sacrifices must be made, and the fact was that the battalion had fought terrifically so far, and with the award of the *Ritterkreuz* (Knight's Cross) to the late Colonel Ponath for his services in leading the 8th Machine-gun Battalion, this had been acknowledged. (The news of the award had come through on the very evening after he had been killed.[32]) None of them should be in any doubt that the successes they achieved in Africa would be of crucial significance to the outcome of the war, and that the losses of the battalion would be refilled in a few days, and weaponry and equipment would be replaced.

From energising the men and lifting the morale in an astonishing fashion — many Afrika Korps soldiers were awestruck just being around Rommel — the General wanted to make clear to them why it had all gone wrong. It seemed to him, he said, that they had secured too narrow a breakthrough. Instead of this, he said — and illustrated his points by slashing lines on a map — they should have rolled up from both sides and in that way secured *Rückenfreiheit*, a safe area behind them, so that troops could pour through the gap without fear of attacks being launched on them from behind. When Lieutenant Prahl was courageous enough to point out to Herrn General that, after they had made the break, the 8th Machine-gun Battalion had simply had no further men to widen the breach with, Rommel said that next time they would be provided with those men.

And, make no mistake, there would be a next time. Soon. Then he was gone.

Shattered though they were, somehow the visit by Rommel helped. As recorded in the 8th Machine-gun Battalion's War Journal: 'We, the few who are left, will gather all our actions and all our power to create a powerful battalion again, based on the model of the previous one . . .'[33]

Soldiers die, but the battalion, the battalion, lives on . . .

•

The commanders in Berlin, following the action the best they could by virtue of Rommel's official reports and such unofficial reports as came from the likes of General Kirchheim, were now getting worried and annoyed in fairly equal measure. It was all very well to be nudging Egypt's borders in that daring manner by possessing Sollum and Halfaya Pass, but what about *Tobruk*? And how long could Rommel sustain the crucial supply line for his attack on Egypt if Tobruk wasn't taken?

For the moment, Rommel did not seem to share their concerns. For, extraordinarily, despite the German Army having suffered its first defeat in this war, Rommel still didn't seem to understand, according to the letter which he wrote to his Dearest Lu on the very evening that almost an entire battalion of Italians had surrendered. It included the lines: 'The enemy is embarking. We shall therefore soon be able to take over the fortress.'

•

Not today, though, mate. Or tomorrow.

For, late the following morning, Rommel, truly desperate for a breakthrough, hurled into the fray the only remotely intact unit he had left — the Ariete Armoured Division — which *still* had not seen any serious action after their aborted attempt of a few days earlier. (That notwithstanding, the Ariete had taken a terrible pounding in the war to date, with only ten tanks out of the 100 it had started with now serviceable.

The rest were strewn between Tripoli and Tobruk in various states of disrepair and destruction.)

Yet in one of those tanks, right near the front, Mario, a former mechanic from Milan, was heading towards his destiny, ready to wrest Tobruk back from the Australian and English invaders who had come here to take from Italy what Italians had built up.

He moved the tank forwards into full throttle, and was just closing in on the western perimeter of Tobruk, when there was a sudden, blinding explosion. Somewhere up ahead a gun had lined him up and a missile had gone straight through his tank. Alas, as often happened with the design of the Italian tanks, the shot then had insufficient energy to go out the other side and instead bounced around inside like a red-hot ball bearing in a biscuit tin, until it was spent.

In a split second, the body of one of Mario's crew slumped against him, and for the rest of his days Mario would remember his friend's head bowing down, blood all over it, 'from which an eye hung by yellowish threads'.

Mario's own right arm was gone, and he collapsed. His war was over, and though fortunately he was pulled from the shattered tank and saved by an Australian medic, he was soon a Prisoner of War. He had done his best.[34]

And so had his colleagues in their tanks, but the impact on them all was much the same: all but total destruction. Put simply, the Italian tanks were jam tins on tank tracks and just not constructed sturdily enough to withstand even the most basic fire.

•

The reality was that, with the Tobruk garrison having successfully seen off every attempt to break its defences by land and air attack, in the short term Rommel was left with little choice but to try to blast the Allies out using a combination of heavy artillery and heavy bombing. An important target was the harbour, with the reckoning being that if the Germans throttled the Allied supply, the wretched defenders couldn't last long. So it was that, starting shortly after the Easter Battle was over, enemy air raids now became a constant, and the Ack-Ack boys were kept busy night and day, with waves of forty bombers at a time coming in to do their worst. The Diggers coped, mostly, though sometimes it wasn't easy . . .

•

Everybody loved Billy Wright, one of the great characters of the 2/17th Battalion. A natural comedian, with a laugh like a Gatling gun, he was always happy, always upbeat, and was something close to the life and soul of the battalion. And could he tell stories! One blessed afternoon, just after the Easter Battle, when the battalion had been pulled out of the front line — and the men were taking some momentary R and R down in the pristine waters of the harbour — someone asked Billy what was it he used to do, anyway, back on civvy street?

Well, Billy was upfront with them, and told them without any embarrassment whatsoever that as a matter of fact he was a safe cracker, and he even told the gathering about some of the jobs he did, including one in Pyrmont where he'd blown the blessed safe clear out into the street!

The men listened, enthralled. Back in Australia, if a bloke had told them he was a common criminal there would have been a great deal of unease — and quite likely a phone call to the local coppers. But here it was totally different. Maybe Billy was a criminal; here and now, though, he was first and foremost a Digger, one of *them*, a brother in arms, and all the rest was just background. It just so happened that his was a very colourful background.

He finished telling them the yarn, and they all went for a bit of a dip happily, noting as ever how extraordinarily blue the water was even close up, and yet when you dived into it, the crystal clarity exposed a whole, wonderful, underwater world . . .

•

What happened then is recorded in 9th Division veteran Jack Barber's book of Tobruk reminiscences, *The War, the Whores and the Afrika Korps*.[35]

For high, high above the bathing boys at that moment — at an altitude where they were no more than all-but-invisible specks — a group of Stukas gracefully rolled over and began to plummet to the earth, screaming down upon the Diggers and unleashing their bombs. Men scrambled to get out of the water and find shelter, somewhere, *anywhere*!

The last man out of the water was none other than Billy himself, and as he ran up the beach desperately looking for shelter, the wail of a bomb right above was reaching a climax, leaving him no choice but to dive headfirst into a curiously narrow trench just ahead, only an instant before the bomb landed and exploded, hurling shrapnel, rocks and debris above the prostrate Diggers as the planes went on their way.

As always after a bomb had exploded, there was a moment of stunning, ringing silence, and then through the fog of war, of dust and smoke, a nude figure suddenly appeared and raced like a mad thing back down to the water, diving in and out, the head going up and down like a demented seal, taking a big gasp of air, disappearing and then shooting up again, shaking itself every time. 'Geez, it looks as if Billy has lost his marbles,' said one Digger by the name of Beau.

'Yeah, well, if he has, he won't find the buggers out there,' replied his mate Jimmy.

'Why would ya get out of the trench and go back for a swim with all those bloody Stukas working the joint over?' asked Beau. It was a good question.

'Now the buggers have gone home, let's get an answer from Billy himself,' said Jimmy.

As they rushed down to the water's edge, Barber recounted, they were greeted by the loudest and longest string of obscenities ever heard on a waterfront, which was saying something in Australian terms. Finally Billy came out of the water, sucking for fresh air like a man who has just escaped drowning, and explained himself.

'When I dived into that slit trench I got the message loud and clear. It wasn't a slit trench at all, it was a bloody *shit* trench. The bloody trench was full of it.'

A great shudder wracked his whole body again, as if a fresh wave of horror had just broken over it, before he could continue.

'I dived into the bastard headfirst. Christ, I can still taste it. I've heard of blokes landing in the shit, but geez, not headfirst. Christ, I'll never be the same again.'

Needless to say, for the many soldiers who heard this account, the tears of mirth were now streaming down their faces, and it was some time before they could compose themselves to get back to their post.

CHAPTER THIRTEEN

The Battle Builds

*Battles and campaigns are won by leadership — leadership not only of
senior but of junior commanders — by discipline, by that knowledge
begotten of experience — knowing what to do and how to do it — and by
hard work. And above all that, by courage, which we call 'guts', gallantry,
and devotion to duty.*

GENERAL LESLIE MORSHEAD[1]

*This bloody town's a bloody cuss,
No bloody trams no bloody bus,
And no one cares for bloody us,
Oh bloody bloody bloody.*

POPULAR POEM AMONG THE TOBRUK GARRISON[2]

As it happened, Billy wasn't the only Australian in the shit that day.
For in the annals of the Australian Army, it would long stand as one of
the most famous commands ever given. With the German Army now
engulfing his forces in Greece, Brigadier 'Bloody' George Vasey made his
decision, and announced it in uniquely Australian terms:

'Here we bloody well are, and here we bloody well stay. And if any
bloody German gets between your post and the next, turn your bloody
Bren gun round and shoot him up the arse.'[3]

True, translated into militarese by his Brigade Major, this became 'The
19th Australian Infantry Brigade will hold its present positions, come what
may', but the spirit of the command remained intact.

Sadly, the magnificence of that resolution alone was not enough and,
faced with total annihilation unless they gave ground, the Australians were
in fact obliged to withdraw.

Despite fighting magnificently in Greece, the Australians of the 6th
Division, together with the New Zealand Division and ancillary units from
Britain, were simply outnumbered by an implacable, superbly well-organised

enemy that had planned this campaign for a long time, while they had figuratively been thrown in at the last minute.

All up the Allies boasted only 58 000 men, together with 70 000 men of the Greek Army, while the Germans had put an overwhelming twenty-five divisions against them, of which eight were armoured divisions, a total of roughly 400 000 soldiers.

Perhaps most significantly, the Germans had all but absolute control of the air over Greece, with almost 1000 planes thrown into the battle, while the RAF could muster just eighty serviceable aircraft at the best of times. Tragically, the prior British commitment given to Robert Menzies, that adequate air cover would be provided to give the Australian troops a 'fighting chance', had just not been met. And still it got worse. After Yugoslavia surrendered on 17 April, the flow of German troops into Greece quickly became a full-blown flood as more and more of Hitler's front-line troops were freed. (One who was not surprised at the debacle was Winston Churchill. Even though he was the one who had insisted that the Australians and New Zealanders be sent to Greece in such large numbers, he had thought from the beginning that the probability of failure was high.)

Still, despite the Allies being plainly overwhelmed by the huge number of German troops, watching the battles from close up, Chester Wilmot was able to report at least two positive things to his Australian audience.

'From what I saw and heard, I am convinced that if our troops meet the Germans on anything like equal terms, they will be able to defeat them just as they defeated the Italians.'

Too, there was this: 'If Hitler eventually enters Athens himself, he will barely find a mile of the road from the Yugoslav border to Thermopylae and beyond which hasn't its plot of little white crosses on German graves.'[4]

Nothing, however, could change the bottom line. Though Hitler didn't, in fact, enter Athens, the result was the same. Despite noble resistance, the swastika was soon flying triumphantly over the Acropolis, even as Australian, British and New Zealand troops continued to scramble towards safety. The Greek campaign had been a complete disaster for the Australian and the rest of the Allied forces — at its conclusion 320 Australians, 291 New Zealanders, and 146 British had been killed, while another 6480 were captured and hundreds more were cut off from their units and left to fend for themselves, with 50 662 in total managing to escape German clutches, 26 000 of whom landed in Crete, where they intended to make a new stand. Before leaving, however, the Allies were obliged to destroy almost all of the equipment they had brought with them, from tanks to trucks to artillery to ammunition — everything that their brethren in North Africa were then most in need of.

•

In the absence of such equipment in Tobruk, the Australians continued to make do with what they had, rather in the manner of many of their forebears, who for generations had scratched out a living in the Australian scrub. So, just as the boys of the Bush Artillery continued to work wonders with abandoned Italian guns that they would find, shine and haul to the front lines, others were developing new applications for everyday things, all the better to help the general war effort with . . .

A helmet, for example, could be used for everything from a cooking pot to a shovel when some serious digging was needed, to a pillow and even, *in extremis*, a toilet. Shaving mirrors? By now they were no longer mere items from the troops' few surviving toiletry bags. No — under Morshead's instructions they were gathered in and reconfigured so that, put together with carefully cut bits of plywood laid out by the carpenters, they became — ta-DAAA — periscopes![5] In this fashion, front-line troops wanting to have a peek at what was happening out in no-man's-land could first go 'up periscope' instead of putting their heads up and maybe getting them shot off by snipers, as had already happened too many times. Oh, and in spots where the ground was so rocky that you couldn't even build a decent protective wall, it was found that when you took bags of rotten Italian flour and mixed the stuff with sea water, the result was that it hardened into something capable of stopping a shell, let alone a mere bullet. (As the Diggers themselves said, 'If it's stupid and it works, it ain't stupid.')

In this man's army, even *condoms* you had left in your wallet — because God knew there was no outlet for conventional use in these parts — were terrific to put over the top of your rifle to keep out the dust, which was a continuing problem. The signallers also found condoms superb for encasing key wire-joins and keeping them safe from the elements. Meanwhile, some of the mechanic blokes had come up with a you-beaut scheme to keep the crucial Vickers guns on the backs of the carriers cooler than otherwise. Just by rerouting hoses from the water-jacket of the guns, see, to the radiator of the carrier, you could keep firing for a much longer time![6] And even then, if water for either the jacket or the radiator was running short you could always — and they often did — piss in them. (Sure, the Vickers weren't the equal of the German Spandau, as they weighed about ten times as much and had only half the rate of fire, but it was worse where there was none.)

Nothing, really nothing, was wasted, up to and including the propellers of crashed Stukas, which the troops found were excellent for the battalion dentist to melt down and turn into tooth caps.[7] Others grabbed the rear part of the Stuka cockpit, and mounted it upside down on a heavy foundation. Now, by putting your Ack-Ack gun through the opening at the rear, you had protection all around, even as you attempted to bring down more Stukas.

Somehow or other, these Australians were capable of making a wigwam for a goose's bridle out of shoelaces and old rope if the need arose ...

•

While the general mood of the Tobruk garrison at this time was optimistic, Morshead didn't have any hesitation in ordering his engineers to wire all the water facilities, ammo dumps and fuel supplies with explosives, so that if the worst really did come to the worst, they could send the whole lot sky-high and let the Germans and Italians inherit nothing but debris.

Mostly, though, the efforts of the Allied troops were trained on ensuring that they wouldn't have to do anything of the kind, because their defences would be so strong that they simply wouldn't crack, whatever Rommel threw at them. With this in mind, Morshead focused on re-laying the minefields, and at his insistence mines were now laid inside the Red Line as well, clearly marked for the defenders but hopefully a total surprise for whatever enemy forces might try to get through. After careful consideration of the most likely point of attack, Morshead and his senior officers designated precisely where the precious mines were to be laid, and it was done.

•

A small parenthesis here. As an instructive cultural quirk, it is interesting to note the difference in the way that the Australians and the Germans laid out their mines. A captured German manual reported on by Chester Wilmot gave specific instructions for how mines should be deployed.

Laying of Un-Camouflaged or Open Section Minefields.

First type: Mine-laying from column of threes: one Teller mine to one metre.

The section commander gives the command: 'Lay mines without camouflage from column of threes-Double.' The left-hand man in each file marches ten paces. The right-hand man marches twenty paces. The centre man in each file remains stationary. All make a right turn. The section commander gives the command: 'Lay first mine.'

> *Execution: Each man lays the mine in his right hand on the ground between his feet . . .*
>
> *The section commander then gives the command: 'Lay second mine.'*
>
> *Execution: Each man takes ten paces forward and five paces to the left and lays the mine as before. Each man buries his second mine first, i.e. the mine he laid last and then his first mine.*[8]

The Australian method by contrast was far more to the order of 'This'll do. Put 'er in there, mate. She's right.'[9] Close parenthesis.

•

Together with the minefields, Lieutenant General Morshead situated gun emplacements covering them. This was so that, if it came to it, the attackers could not easily do to the Australian defenders what the Australians had done to the Italians when they were attacking Tobruk back in January. Morshead wanted all German delousers trying to neutralise the minefield to be dealt with summarily (i.e. shot dead).

•

It stated it right there, black on white. Her son had been killed. The box had come with the morning post to her home in the little German town of Naumburg (Saale), and in big letters it had inscribed upon it by the field post office, 'Property of Leutnant Albrecht Zorn, killed in action'. Inside was the boot of his left foot.

Nein, nein, NEIN! She simply refused to believe that her son was dead.

And she was right. Though it would take much wailing and many phone calls to sort it all out, there had actually been a terrible misunderstanding. After the confrontation between Zorn's Panzer and Vince Rayner with his anti-tank gun, each man had been retrieved by his own medical corpsmen. Rayner was whisked away to a field hospital, while Zorn was soon high above the Mediterranean in a Junkers being taken to Italy. It was in the wake of the battle that the Sergeant Major of Zorn's 4th Company had arrived and found, right beside the wrecked Panzer, a leg with a boot on it, and on the boot was written *Leutnant Zorn*. Thinking, not unreasonably, that the rest of the worthy lieutenant had simply ceased to exist, he had arranged to have the boot cleaned, wrapped and sent to the home of Zorn's mother in Naumburg (Saale) . . .

•

It was Friday, 18 April and if it wasn't one thing for Elizabeth Edmondson on this wretched day, it was another. Nothing went right. For no reason at all the car wouldn't start, and with her husband, Will, still injured from the farming accident, she had to push the wretched thing — right until the point that she nearly collapsed — and was just able to get it started by rolling it down towards the dam. She got it to the garage, only for them to say they couldn't see anything wrong with it. Then she went to see the doctor, who gave her a similar diagnosis. He could see that she wasn't well, but he couldn't work out why. Then she got to the thing that she always dreaded most. She got the *Sydney Morning Herald* and scanned its account of the fighting in Greece and North Africa — where the battle was terrible — and then the casualty lists . . .

Mercifully, there was no sign of Jack in the list, but what worried her sick was an account of a bayonet charge in Tobruk — headlined AIF PATROL TRIUMPHS. TOBRUK AREA TANKS DRIVEN BACK — in which a Lieutenant and Corporal had taken prominent parts on Easter Sunday night. Of course there were no names, but Elizabeth felt a stab of ice in her heart. She just *knew* the Corporal was Jack and said as much to her husband when she passed it on to him. He would neither agree nor disagree, but Elizabeth didn't care — nothing could persuade her that it wasn't her Jack. And nor did she care that the *Herald's* account had it that there were no casualties in the bayonet charge. She just felt in her bones that all was not well with her son. The weather was the perfect adjunct to her mood: rainy all day, with miserable clouds that just kept coming and coming and coming. Stuffy hadn't turned up yet. Will looked around and kept calling for him, but he had not come home yet. He just wouldn't come home.[10] The rain didn't let up.

•

By this time, the men were starting to get used to the ways of Morshead, and had nicknamed him 'Ming the Merciless', after a favourite comic-book character in the *Flash Gordon* strip they were all familiar with at home. When confronting a particularly troublesome problem — which was extremely frequently in Tobruk — Morshead would scrunch up his face in a fashion that made him look quite Asiatic, and the ruthless approach he took to solving those problems also fitted with the moniker. (Morshead had a way of just *looking* at subordinates who had let him down, such that they swore ever afterwards they had seen right through Ming's eyes to the hot fires of hell, and there was no life in there.)

Still, whereas in the comic strip Ming was the feared emperor of the planet Mongo, in Tobruk Morshead's men were coming to have great respect for their leader. Though he was definitely not a man to engage in informalities with, all sensed that he was as tireless in getting the garrison properly organised, and with as many supplies as he could blast out of Cairo, as he was totally merciless in attacking the Germans.

The thing they most treasured him for, though — and this was no small thing — was that he clearly valued *their* lives. Time and again Morshead would show up unannounced at their front lines and cast what was clearly a very experienced eye — they all knew he'd been at Gallipoli — over their defences, and woe betide any platoon or company that had not taken every possible precaution to dig themselves in as deeply as they could, or positioned themselves in such a fashion that the enemy's job of killing them was made any easier than it had to be. Morshead was particularly keen that there be many defensive trenches between the posts, so as to be able to maximise the garrison's defensive firepower. Wherever feasible, such trenches were constructed about 2 yards wide and as deep as possible — usually a yard or so. The process of digging them was constant, and Morshead would always glow positively when he saw them well done and well manned.

When it came to discipline, however — not following his orders to the letter or meeting the exacting standards that he had set — Ming really was merciless, and made no apology for it. As he later explained to Chester Wilmot, while there was a popular belief that the Australian soldier chafed under strict discipline, it was his own view that, so long as it was applied in the right way, it was the key ingredient that the Australian soldiers needed to be effective.

'Without it,' he told Wilmot, 'there is nothing to bind the strong personalities of the Australians into an organised fighting force.'[11]

Morshead, therefore, insisted on strict discipline, and his charges were the more effective because of it. And because he always gave off such an air of confidence, they also, inevitably, became all the more confident in their own approaches.

•

For the Diggers in Tobruk, contact with the outside world was now more highly valued than ever, and none more so than that from a strange bloke who was showing up on the German propaganda station broadcasting in English, a station which the Diggers would tune into as often as possible for a bit of a laugh.

Known colloquially as 'Lord Haw-Haw', this cove came on the radio day after day and started to whine on and on about all the wonderful German successes and Allied setbacks and, while some in Britain found it upsetting when he displayed a most unusually detailed knowledge of what was happening in their country, right down to what time was showing on damaged clock towers — meaning the country must be awash with spies — those in Tobruk had no such worries.

As a matter of fact, the best thing of all was when Lord Haw-Haw gave Tobruk a mention, not long after the 'Easter Battle' as they were already referring to it — a sure sign that what they were engaged in really was important, if someone in Berlin could give a bugger! But wait, it got better still . . .

Did yers hear? According to Haw-Haw, Tobruk was now being held by 'the sons of sheep herders', these 'self-supporting prisoners of war'[12] who were now surrounded by the mighty German and Italian armies, and were caught like 'rats in a trap . . .'

'These rats of Tobruk,' he had sneered. 'Living like rats, they'll die like rats.'

The Diggers reeled. Looked at each other. Laughed. The 'rats of Tobruk'! They loved it. It was perfect. In fact, make that the 'Rats of Tobruk' with a capital 'R'! In no time at all, what Lord Haw-Haw had said about them moved from one post to another, bounced around and circulated from there — in fact, from Rat hole to Rat hole! Morale was lifted no end. Not only was what they were engaged in important enough for someone in Berlin to try to sap their morale, but they had been given an absolutely perfect sobriquet that they would genuinely treasure for ever afterwards.

The Rats of Tobruk they were then, and they intended to give Lord Haw-Haw *plenty* to talk about and choke over in the coming months, however long this bloody thing might last.

•

Another priority was to ensure that, despite the bombing on the harbour, as many supplies as possible could get into Tobruk to feed the many hungry mouths, and that every mouth in Tobruk that was not strictly necessary could be moved out. And there was only one way to do that . . .

With every road into the garrison now teeming with the enemy, and the skies perpetually buzzing with the angry hornets of the Luftwaffe, it was far from certain just how long the garrison could hold on. However, there was equally no lack of certainty as to just who and what Tobruk's lifeline was: the brave men in the ships of the Royal Australian Navy. And despite the fact that Hitler would go on to deride them as 'Australia's old tin-cans',[13] and Lord Haw-Haw as the 'scrap-iron flotilla', many of those ships performed so magnificently during the course of the siege — most notably, in the first few months, the *Voyager*, *Vendetta*, *Vampire* and *Waterhen* — that the mere mention of their names would inspire toasts from those who knew even a part of what they had achieved.

They were soon joined by the *Stuart* and the *Parramatta*, and two ships of the Royal Navy, the *Decoy* and the *Defender*. For all of them, the two keys were courage and speed: courage to be there in the first place, and speed to get out as fast as they could.

For Tobruk Harbour — if you made it there down 'Bomb Alley', as the last 30 miles of the approach to the harbour were now called — was likely the most dangerous stretch of water in the world at the time. As such, the more you could limit the time in there, the better it was. Ships that had taken a combination of soldiers and swarming Egyptian labourers a full three hours to load in Alexandria Harbour — with endless cans of bully beef, bully beef, yet more bully beef and, most precious of all, 'every description of sudden death packed in tin or box; gun and rifle ammunition, land mines, grenades, detonators, demolition explosives, bombs, cases of petrol and kerosene'[14] — were frequently unloaded in thirty minutes flat in Tobruk. To do it, every able body on the ships and the wharves lent a hand to get the munitions and foodstuffs up and out of the hold and onto the two 'lighters', the small launches specifically designed for taking cargo.

That done, the ships would then take on whatever and whoever needed to be moved the other way, especially POWs, non-combatant servicemen and Libyan refugees, helping to reduce the strain on the town considerably. (Those ships also took out only the grievously wounded Allied soldiers, as if you were only lightly wounded, it was expected that you could recover in the Tobruk Field Hospital and then get back to your post.)

•

It was a moment that Lieutenant Heinz Schmidt would never forget. Just beyond the Red Line on the western edge of the Tobruk defences, there was a small hill; and on this day, right near the top, Rommel was lying on his belly all alone, with shells going back and forth over his head and some bursting quite close, but still he was not turning a hair. With his hat perched on the back of his head, the German General was studying something quite intently, with his binoculars never wavering from a particular point.

Keeping his head well down, and slithering close to the ground, Schmidt crawled up beside him.

'Ras el Medauuar,' Rommel muttered.[15] Schmidt glanced quickly at his map to get his bearings, and then crawled a small distance away to get better shelter behind a pile of rocks before looking again. From their vantage point, the ground sloped gradually downwards to a very thin bit of flat ground, before sloping upwards again, equally gradually. And on the far crest was, as Schmidt later described it, 'a triangular shaped ruin of stones surmounted by a close network of barbed wire. Considerably further back is a higher mound of stones.'[16]

Both men kept gazing intently just beyond the barbed wire and, even as they were watching, they could see some of the Allied soldiers moving around along the perimeter. Something seemed to overcome Rommel at their very sight — almost a primitive huntsman's urge, almost as if it was against nature that enemy soldiers could be within his sight and not be dealt with ...

'Lieutenant!' he commanded Schmidt. 'Orders to the Panzers! Attack the stone ruins ahead — two Panzers through the northern wadi, two through the southern wadi ...'

Schmidt did as he was bid, and in short order the two closely watched the result: mayhem. No sooner had the Panzers got close to the ruins than a murderous fire descended upon them, and shortly thereafter it also started lobbing very close to where Rommel and Schmidt were observing. Reluctantly, they had to retreat. There was going to be no easy way into Tobruk.[17]

•

Time and again, examining the lie of the land with his practised military eye, Morshead's attention was drawn back to two bumps on the landscape. The first rose about 100 feet from the flat track which ran all around the western perimeter and was known as 'Hill 209', for the Trig Point 209 marking it as 209 feet above sea level — and the summit was distinguished by an enormous pile of stones, all that remained of a Roman fort that had once sat atop it. The Italians had already had a go at storming it on 17 April, just a couple of days after the Easter Battle. In many places on the earth's surface, 'Hill 209' would be no more than 'Bump 2', if that. Yet such was the flatness of the desert terrain that it was capable, figuratively, of making mountains out of molehills, and as Hill 209 was the highest bit of ground within the Red Line, it was clearly a valuable bit of real estate.

The second bump was what the men called 'Carrier Hill', about a mile outside the southwestern perimeter, almost but not quite looking Hill 209 in the eye. If Rommel did have designs on attacking Hill 209 (although he knew it as Ras el Medauuar) — and Morshead felt sure he did, because that is precisely where he himself would have attacked had he been in the position of the Afrika Korps. Then putting heavy resources behind and on Carrier Hill was a sure prelude, given that it was the one part of the terrain around Tobruk where the enemy could get close to the Red Line and remain fairly well hidden. And there was no doubt that the enemy already occupied it with a large battery of guns, because it was from there that a constant stream of missiles was falling upon the Tobruk garrison. That situation would have to be attended to, and Morshead gave the orders, both for the lee side of Carrier Hill to be cleaned out and for the defences around Hill 209 to be strengthened ...

•

Again, Menzies, still in London, was unhappy. He had just seen a list of the major posting of senior officers in the Middle East and there was no mention of the senior Australian officer on site, General Blamey. Australia was to contribute some 40 000 men to the Middle East and yet their senior man there was not to be given a senior position in the British command structure? He didn't think so.

Menzies summoned the Chief of the Imperial General Staff, General Sir John Dill, to Australia House and expressed himself freely. This grasping of Australian soldiers but rejection of Australian officers could not go on. If Dill 'had any generals in that area who are as good as Blamey, then they must be very good indeed,' he said pointedly. Dill had to understand the situation, 'that if the Australian public learns that Blamey, whose troops have so shone in the Middle East campaign to date, has been overlooked in the senior command structure, there will be a very strong reaction indeed'.[18]

Dill promised to look into it, and was as good as his word. In short order, upon being evacuated from Greece, Blamey was appointed as Wavell's Deputy Commander in Chief Middle East, while still remaining the General Officer Commanding of the AIF.

•

Far, far away in his dugout in Tobruk, and writing a letter to his family at much the same time, John Johnson was focusing on communicating to his family not his fears but, rather, all of his love for them ...

How is my Sylvia Rose & my Josie Jacqueline. Not forgetting all my men. I'm expecting a letter from John any time & hope he is well and happy. How old is Alex. How are you Al old boy last letter I got from home you were not too good. I do hope you are well again. It's time I had a letter from each of you so see if you can save your ninepences & drop me a line all of you. How are you Donald my duck. I suppose you are still quacking away as it were. Don't forget to write. Hello Barry can you hear me. Are you still growing bigger than ever. Good luck & write soon. Day Len, still smiling Lenny Penny & don't you ever get wild and stop smiling as you were meant to smile always. Every time I think of you I imagine you smiling. Write soon & tell me the news. Day Des Peter how are you & when are you going to start school. I suppose you won't start till Xmas. Cheerio my Des Peter. Hello my darling Sylvia Rose. How are you my little sweetheart & do you look after Josie & rock her in the pram. I want Mummy to tell you all that I want to say to you tonight when you go to bed. Cheerio my loved ones. I will conclude now with best wishes & love to you all from your loving Dad. Did you all get an egg for Easter. Remember me to Gran & Dad & Morris & the Stewarts. There were two swallows perched on the beam on my towel & I won't put them out tonight as they are scarce here & a night hawk might get them.
Tons of love to Mum (Josie)
Dad.[19]

Still, he had a job to do, and the following day it was going to be a big one. The orders had come through, and in a combined action the 2/48th would take out Carrier Hill and the 2/23rd would do the same for the Italian forces dug in around the Derna Road positions to the north. The 2/17th would also have a role to play in the south.

John Johnson's job was to take 'Walwa' into the heart of the battle, to first provide covering fire for the men of his own 2/23rd Battalion and then help to remove whatever casualties there might be.

For both battalions the rough plan was the same: to circle around and attack the Italian battalions from behind, so driving them towards the Red Line.

In the misty dawn of 22 April, both the Australian battalions moved off.

For the ninety men of the 2/48th Battalion, the initial plan had been to have the added protection of three Matildas from the 7th Royal Tank Regiment — the noise of which would hopefully be drowned out by a Lysander plane buzzing closely overhead — but when the tanks became separated from the infantry in the morning mist, the 2/48th attacked anyway.

The Italian batteries confidently lobbing artillery into Tobruk from the lee side of Carrier Hill suddenly found themselves under attack from an unexpected angle, and the subsequent action was short, sharp and very bloody. The Italians had no time to turn their heavy guns on the charging Australians, but poured machine-gun fire on them. The 2/48th never faltered, firing their Brens from the hip before using their bayonets.

By eight o'clock the action was over, with the Italian forces on Carrier Hill substantially destroyed, many of their guns destroyed, heavy casualties inflicted, and sixteen officers and 352 lower ranks captured.[20] The men would be taken away for interrogation — although it wasn't always easy to bridge the language divide. (However, one of the German officers captured in these days of raids and counter-raids had enough command of English to say out loud what he had in all probability been aching to say for the last ten years, with little safe opportunity to do so. He said — and he put some force into it — '*Fuck Hitler!*'[21] But far more important than him was a map that had been captured in the raid, clearly indicating the enemy's intent to attack the obvious: Hill 209.[22])

For the 2/23rd Battalion the going was much tougher, with the Italians astride the Derna Road providing much hardier resistance.

At the crucial point in the battle, Italian machine-gun fire, artillery and mortars poured onto the 2/23rd's C Company, exposed in open space with no way out but to charge. The Australians charged, supported by the men in four of their carriers, who tried to give as much protection as possible while also pouring in their own fire.

Although hit by anti-tank fire, John Johnson's 'Walwa' carrier managed to keep going in the maelstrom, providing the covering fire required of it and picking up wounded Australian soldiers — rescuing fourteen of them from the 2/23rd's C Company alone, before heading back to the Australian lines and the Regimental Aid Post.

The final 'bag' for the 2/23rd was ninety Italian prisoners, with about twenty 'kills'.

•

No sooner had Rommel heard of the attack on Carrier Hill than he rushed there, with as many forces as he could muster on short notice, to try to save the situation — and he was appalled by what he found. Where were the six Italian tanks that had been positioned there, so they could defend that very position against any Allied attack? For reasons unknown, the Italian commander on the ground had sent those tanks to the rear, leaving his own men denuded of serious defence. As Rommel walked among the detritus, with vehicles and motorcycles still burning furiously and precious shattered guns lying around — although some did seem salvageable — he was furious. Why had the Italians not fought, not defended themselves?

'Needless to say,' he later wrote, 'I was not very pleased at this curious behaviour in the face of the enemy.'[23]

•

After the Battle of Carrier Hill, things between the two armies began to settle down for a few days, as both sides girded themselves for the next big battle. The same could not be said for what was happening in the air, as both the German and Italian air forces outdid themselves trying to pound Tobruk into submission.

As Lieutenant General Morshead would later recount, that last week of April was daily marked by 'waves of up to forty dive bombers, escorted by fighters, attacking target after target, paying special attention to the brigade in reserve, Pilastrino, port installations and most of all to shipping in the harbour . . .'[24]

As some defence for the Diggers against the Axis bombers' domination of the air, it was clearly necessary for the men on the ground to make both themselves and their armaments as invisible as possible, at least when viewed from 10 000 feet above. After some experimentation, it was found that a certain blend of dull yellow paint most approximated the colour of the desert sand, and in short order both trucks and guns were plastered with that paint. Careful, though, for it was equally realised that the desert was far from being uniformly that colour; so it was decided that, particularly for the guns with the longer barrels, a stripe about halfway up of light brown or green would most likely look like a tuft of bush or somesuch from that height.

But what of the telltale shadow that would be cast by, especially, some of the bigger trucks? How could you camouflage a dark shadow on the desert floor? The short answer was that you couldn't, but by painting the largest vehicles a kind of creamy white, with the odd splotch of light brown or green, the feeling was that the lighter colour of the truck would 'neutralise' the darker shadow, and from the air it would all kind of blend in. That was the theory, anyway.

The Germans? Some of their tanks were painted coal-black, the better to meld with the night, while others had the more traditional camouflage patterns, but it was not vastly important either way, as there were no Allied bombers to worry about.

•

Wonderful news!

A letter. A letter from Jack, which he'd written three weeks earlier. Certainly, it was a bit of a worry that for the first time he was acknowledging that the conditions were bad, that there wasn't a lot of food, and he had to make one water bottle last for a whole two days, but the main thing was that Elizabeth had contact. As to the conditions Jack was dealing with, Elizabeth couldn't do much, but she went straight down to the Liverpool Post Office and posted him a parcel of Horlicks milk tablets, chocolate milk biscuits and some cigarettes.

•

In Berlin, General Franz Halder, the Chief of Staff, was more than merely worried about the fate of the Afrika Korps — he was seriously annoyed. No matter what efforts he and the German High Command made, none of it seemed to have any effect on Rommel. The headstrong general appeared to believe in his own destiny to the point that he considered himself to be above any of the restraints that Berlin placed upon him.

On the night of 23 April, Halder wrote in his diary:

Rommel has not sent us a single clear-cut report all these days, but I have a feeling that things are in a mess. Reports from officers coming from his theatre, as well as a personal letter, show that Rommel is in no way up to his operational task. All day long he rushes about between the widely scattered units, and stages reconnaissance raids in which he fritters away his forces. No one has a clear picture of their disposition and striking power. Certain only is that his troops are widely dispersed and that their striking efficiency has considerably deteriorated. The piecemeal thrusts of weak armoured forces have been costly ... Air transport cannot meet Rommel's senseless demands, primarily because of lack of fuel; aircraft landing in North Africa find no fuel there for the return flight ...[25]

Things were not helped when Rommel's report did arrive the following day containing yet more urgent demands for reinforcements, and this: 'Situation at Bardia, Tobruk graver from day to day as British forces increase.' In this case, Halder was not the only one to be unhappy: one of Hitler's own staff noted in his diary that night, in reference to the reaction aroused by Rommel's report: 'Führer uses very strong language ...'

•

Perhaps the worst of it was that none of this was terribly new. Even before the Easter Battle had begun, Halder had noted in his diary that Rommel had been 'preposterous in his demands' for more resources, and now those demands were getting more preposterous by the day, with more and more Axis ships coming under Allied attack in the Mediterranean. The situation looked so grave that Halder now decided the only way to get a better grip on it was to send one of their own, the *Oberhauptquartiermeister* of the OKH, Lieutenant General Friedrich Paulus, to North Africa to both assess the situation and, far more importantly, to 'bring Rommel under control'. Halder had been quite impressed with the work that Paulus had done in planning the invasion of Poland, and thought there were few assignments he could give the General that he would not be capable of. Noting, too, that Paulus and Rommel had been Company Commanders together in the same regiment in the late 1920s, Halder was of the view that Paulus was 'perhaps the only man with sufficient personal influence to head off this soldier gone stark mad'.[26]

•

And yet, at almost the same time as Halder was writing in his diary, Rommel was having a meeting with an apparently mollified Generale

Gariboldi and his chief of staff, Generale Mario Roatta, at Sollum, where Rommel had been busying himself consolidating the forward defences of his forces looking over Egypt. Rommel had wanted to take Gariboldi on a thorough inspection of the front-line positions, right up close to the point where he could even see the guns of the enemy, but suddenly talk of an important meeting that Gariboldi simply had to attend at Cyrene had popped up and the Italian general decided, with regret, that he wouldn't be able to go the front line after all.

Before taking his leave, however, with great pomp and ceremony, Gariboldi bestowed upon Rommel Italy's highest decoration for *coraggio* and farewelled him with the following words: 'Thank you for your wonderful achievements. All the measures you have taken are correct. I would have done exactly the same.'[27]

It took a man as experienced as Schmidt to pick it up, but Rommel *fiel fast vom Stuhl* — nearly fell off his chair in surprise.

On their way back to Bardia, Rommel's eyes twinkled and he said with a mischievous smile, 'I wonder what it is that is so urgent at Cyrene?'

As Rommel wrote to Lucie that night:

I was awarded the Italian Medal for Bravery. I am also supposed to be getting the Italian Pour le Mérite. What a trivial business it all is at a time like this . . .

Once Tobruk has fallen, which I hope will be in ten days or a fortnight, the situation here will be secure.

How are things with you both? There must be a whole lot of mail lying at the bottom of the Mediterranean.

P.S. — Easter has slipped by unnoticed. [28]

•

One more air raid over Tobruk, although this was one that would long stand out in the memory of the garrison. For, over the previous three days, the fighter planes that the Tobruk garrison could throw into the air to defend itself had gone from three to two to now just one, though there were a couple of others under repair and almost ready for action. But this one ready to go was a Hurricane, under the command of just about the last pilot left standing.

What would that bloke do now that he was just one against dozens of German planes? Why, he took off, surely knowing he was going to his certain death.

One of the defenders, Sergeant Bill Porter of the 2/9th Battalion, would later tell his son that in his whole life he had never heard louder cheering, as every man jack of the garrison who witnessed the departure yelled and clapped their appreciation of his extraordinary bravery as he took off, even as they followed his fortunes thereafter. He took down one — *You beauty!* — and then another — *Go, mate, GO!* — until the inevitable happened. From behind, a Messerschmitt lined him up and cut him to pieces. The cheering stopped as they watched the brave pilot tumble from the skies, into that sudden distant *crump* of a plane hitting the land at speed, followed by enormous billows of black smoke. No parachute appeared.[29]

•

The next day, Anzac Day 1941, it happened. The other two surviving Hurricanes of The RAF's No 73 Squadron, now repaired, flew east out of Tobruk — hopefully to safety — leaving just one plane behind in an underground hangar for the purposes of reconnaissance only — while the Germans had six airfields operational within 25 miles of Tobruk and so many planes that on a bad day they could block out the sun.

Yet, while those defending Tobruk took a terrible pounding from German bombs, the happy reality was that Morshead's insistence that the Diggers put such serious energy into digging in had a happy result. For, as the Tobruk Commander subsequently wrote in a letter home to Myrtle, 'slit trenches are really effective and our 9th Division casualties from bombing are surprisingly low. Bombing frightens much more, infinitely more than it kills. In war, morale is everything.'[30]

Helping keep that morale high was the attitude of the Diggers themselves, with one remark by a Private McDonald being well celebrated for the spirit it displayed: 'I don't like dive bombers, they're such noisy things.'[31]

The only real advantage in having so little of their own air support was that they didn't really have to waste any time determining whether the plane overhead was one of theirs or one of the other fellow's, and you could even tell whose. If it was way up high it was in all likelihood Italian and it wasn't worth wasting your ammo; if it was coming in low, it was a dead cert to be Luftwaffe, and it was time to start firing with everything you had ...

•

It was 26 April 1941 and Elizabeth Edmondson had had a particularly difficult couple of days. The day before had been Anzac Day and this year, for once, she and Will had done nothing to observe it. Will was still on crutches, making it too difficult for him to move around and, besides that, Elizabeth was just not feeling strong enough to go out herself. She still had this creeping sense of dread, like she was afraid of something without being able to say exactly what it was, though she certainly knew that it made her very cold inside. To try to shake it off and warm up her insides a little she had had first one brandy and then another one, even as she tried to keep busy by making a couple of rich fruitcakes for Jack and getting them installed in special cake tins.[32] She filled in the cracks with molten chocolate and sealed the tins, ready to send them off in the post the following day, and then got to her most feared but compulsive exercise of the day: reading the papers. The news had been very bad, with affirmation that the German Army was in full cry in North Africa and advancing on a place called Tobruk. The report had not said that the Australian Army was bearing the brunt of it, but Elizabeth just knew it was. And indeed one clue came in the *Herald*, in which it was recorded that in London, the editorial in *The Times* on Anzac Day had been:

'As the war has gone, a disproportionate share of the fighting has fallen on the Australians and New Zealanders. Their own wish, dictated by obvious geographical consideration, was from the beginning to make the Middle East — especially the protection of the Suez — their principal military preoccupation. Few Australians, for they are a nation of fighting men, regret that their soldiers have been given an opportunity so early to add fresh lustre to the glorious record of which the first page was written 26 years ago . . .'[33]

Personally, Elizabeth was not quite so sure.

And now, this morning, she was just preparing to go down to Liverpool Post Office to send off the fruitcakes when there was a knock on the door. She opened it to find that there was a telegram for her from the Australian Government, and it was marked *Personal Acknowledgment of Delivery*. In the barest instant, the fellow who brought it to her was gone . . .

Time stopped. Trembling, she opened it to find a sheet of crisp pink government paper:

Time Lodged 8.40 p.m. 25th April 1941.

Liverpool 26th April '41.

It is with deep regret that I have to inform you that NX15705 Corporal John Hurst Edmondson was killed in action on the 14th April and desire to convey the profound sympathy of the Ministry for the Army and the Military Board.

Minister for the Army.

P. Spender.

Weakly, barely able to make a sound, she called for Will to tell him the news.

Their Jack was dead.

•

In her comfortable house in the town of Wiener Neustadt, Frau Lucie Rommel was in for a small shock when the mail came this morning. For this letter from North Africa with the familiar military stamps was not from Erwin but someone else, in a hand she did not recognise. What could it be? Trouble? Quickly, she opened it. Ah. It had been written by one of her husband's senior staff, Schräpler — a sure sign of how totally exhausted Erwin must be, because in their whole life together he had never deputised someone else to write his letters — and it was basically to bring her up to date with the situation:

22 April 1941

Sehr geehrte Frau Rommel,

I realise that there is a possibility that it may cause you a shock to receive a letter bearing my name as sender; nevertheless, I am taking this risk in order to give you the assurance that all is well with your esteemed husband.

He will have had little time for writing during the past few days, as they have been very full for him, and very worrying too. His endeavour and the desire of every one of us to be not only in, but far beyond Tobruk, is at the moment impossible to realise . . .

We have too few German forces and can do nothing with the Italians. They either do not come forward at all, or if they do,

run at the first shot. If an Englishman so much as comes in sight,
their hands go up. You will understand, Madam, how difficult
this makes the command for your husband. I am certain, however,
that by the time this letter arrives you will not have much longer
to wait for the special communiqué announcing the capture of
Tobruk, and then things will begin to move again . . .
    Signed
    Schräpler.[34]

•

The whole thing was a nightmare, from first to last.

While it was possible to make fairly good time all the way from Tripoli
to within about 12 kilometres of Tobruk, 1700 kilometres to the east, from
that point on the strain on the mostly Italian drivers of the Afrika Korps'
supply trucks was appalling. They were obliged to make a long detour
through the desert well to the south of where the Australian and British
garrison was blocking them, so engines were constantly overheating; there
was no water to spare to cool down the radiators, and sometimes the petrol
in the tank would get so hot it would just vaporise. Frequently the trucks
became bogged down in the soft sand, and then other trucks would have
to use chains and ropes to drag them out, often getting bogged themselves
— which then meant still more trucks were required to get them all out.
At other times sharp stones would get caught between the double wheels
of the lorries and quickly cut both tyres to shreds. Sweating in the searing
African sun, trying to find something hard enough on which to put the
jack to lift the truck and the 2 tonnes of supplies on board, they'd change
the tyres, only to have it happen again. And then they'd more often than
not have run out of spare tyres and they'd have to sit there — *Dio canne!
Puttana de merde!* — until another truck came along and lent you one if
you were lucky.

The result of it all was that for every day Tobruk was held, Rommel's
supply line was pushed closer to the breaking point. And it was taking
2 litres of petrol — in terms of the return trip as well — just to bring 1 litre
of petrol to the front. The port of Benghazi was closer, of course, than
Tripoli, but it came with many problems. To begin with, it was only a tiny
port; but, most significantly, it was a lot further for the ships to make safe
harbour from Italy, and was so beset by attacks from the Royal Air Force
and Navy that the Italians refused to attempt it.

It all meant that, although by 26 April Rommel's forward forces of the Afrika Korps — and, indeed, Rommel himself — were right at the Egyptian frontier and well dug in, there was no way they could go further unless they lanced the agonising boil in their side that Tobruk represented. So long as the garrison held, the Afrika Korps were sapped of strength, and Rommel now readied himself to launch another full assault on the garrison, this time having learned from the mistakes that were made during the Easter Battle.

•

As to Tobruk's own situation of supply, it too remained perilous and was only sustained by two things: the derring-do of the Captains and crews of the supply ships, and the sheer courage and tenacity of the Ack-Ack boys down by the harbour, who continued to hurl explosives skywards at the waves of German and Italian bombers that constantly tried to pound Tobruk into submission.

The key skill in Ack-Ack fire was to determine at what height the attacking planes would likely come, and then set the fuse on the shells accordingly so they would explode and send out flak at approximately that altitude. And the other important thing, obviously, was to continue firing no matter how much the bombs exploding all around might sometimes knock you from your feet with their concussion waves, make the ground beneath you rear in an angry wave, fill the air with smoke and screams, and put you in the midst of a searing hell from which there might seem to be no release — none of that mattered, so long as you *kept firing*.

It took no small amount of courage to do so, of course, but fortunately courage was in plentiful supply, and besides, the Ack-Ack crews could see the sense of it. With the Stukas screaming down upon them in almost vertical dives before unleashing their bombs, it stood to reason that the more shells that were sent straight up to meet them, the more chance there was that they could get the Stukas before the Stukas could get them.

In order to try to dilute some of the bombs, the Ack-Ack crews built makeshift guns well away from any of the real Ack-Ack. Every bomb that fell around those dummies was another bomb that didn't fall near the real McCoys.

As to the supply ships that continued to run the gauntlet of Bomb Alley, they had the admiration of every man in the garrison, perhaps best expressed in the manner of an army padre who was celebrated for the way he said grace: 'For what we are about to eat, thank God and the British Fleet ...'[35]

And so said all of them.

•

Lieutenant General Friedrich Paulus arrived at General Rommel's headquarters outside Tobruk on the morning of 27 April 1941. In this particular situation, the relationship between these two high German commanders was tenuous at best, and they only just managed to touch fingers from opposite extremes. Rommel was an impulsive, decisive, battle-front commander who was in his element with shells, bullets and tanks all around. Paulus, a year his junior, was an extremely considered, deliberate desk soldier who had risen to eminence by his ability to administer an enormous body of men and manage difficult relationships between powerful men — as well as formulate solid battle plans on map boards (as he did, most notably, during the invasion of Poland, at Halder's behest). Rommel could go days without bathing, or even eating, if the exigencies of battle demanded it; Paulus was referred to by some colleagues as 'Our Most Elegant Gentleman' for the fact that he liked to bathe and change clothes twice a day and was fond of wearing gloves to keep his hands free of dirt. He was, in short, precisely the kind of officer Rommel liked least.[36]

And yet, though Paulus was nominally Rommel's superior and had been sent to North Africa as a representative of the OKH, to effectively bring Rommel to heel and make sure that his impulsiveness was kept in check, it was not simply a matter of giving an order. For Rommel was Germany's greatest hero, second only to Hitler, and had to be treated with respect — the more so because Paulus had an almost slavish regard for Hitler and felt the German leader, 'whether he understood him or not, was sacrosanct, the highest Commander'.[37]

On their first meeting in Africa, thus, Paulus settled in Rommel's tent and listened carefully to how the Commanding Officer of the Afrika Korps planned to proceed from here. Paulus certainly accepted the logic that ideally the Tobruk garrison should be induced to surrender, but under no circumstances did he want to risk a repeat of what had happened a fortnight earlier, when the Korps had lost so many men and tanks for no gain.

And though it perhaps went against the grain for Rommel to explain his plans in detail — or to have to justify them — Paulus was relieved to hear that the situation had improved and that the Afrika Korps really was in better shape this time to force the issue.

For indeed, even as they spoke, the rumble in the near distance signified that the first of the tanks of the 15th Panzer Division had at last arrived from Tripoli and were rolling into the Afrika Korps encampments around

Tobruk. In addition, repair work on the surviving tanks of the last attack had brought the strength of the 5th Panzer Regiment back up to seventy-four tanks — just as the airfields in the vicinity were welcoming more bombers and fighters freshly arrived from Germany. On the Italian side, fresh artillery batteries had also turned up, and together with the German units, there were now thirty-five batteries with their guns trained on the point in the perimeter where Rommel wanted to send in his next serious attack.[38] That was on what the Tobruk garrison called Hill 209 and the Germans referred to by its Arabic name of Ras el Medauuar.

Though Rommel was not inclined to acknowledge having made any mistakes in the previous assault to launch the Easter Battle, he did now make it clear to Paulus that for this attack he wanted to completely overwhelm a whole section of the perimeter and roll in the Panzers and masses of men from that point. There was to be no small gap on which the British artillery could concentrate blanket coverage; this time they would be less a spear than a battering ram. And let there be no doubt: it really was the key spot to break into the defence because, as Rommel had already told his senior staff, 'Whoever is in possession of Ras el Medauuar can read the other's cards'.[39]

When Paulus averred that he felt he needed to have a look at the situation himself, Rommel was quick to oblige.

'Schmidt,' he ordered his subservient shadow, 'tomorrow you will accompany the general to the Tobruk front. You know the dispositions of the staff and will be able to give all necessary information.'

•

On this night back in Walwa, Josie Johnson sat writing a letter to her beloved husband on the family's prized bit of furniture — the round dining table John had made for her after they had just got married — and felt quite tearful. Every day she followed the news of what was happening in North Africa, specifically Tobruk, in both the newspapers and on the radio and she realised more than most that her husband was now right in the thick of it. Addressed as ever to 'My Own Darling John', she soon enough began to pour out some of her fears ...

One says, 'Thank God', when each day passes, as each day gone is one nearer to your return, for which I pray day and night. Darling I love you so and should the worst happen

I can't understand how I am going to go on my babies are all that will keep me going in that case. Darling what a woeful page this is, I am truly not like this all the time it is only when I hear that you are in danger I get morbid, but just the same motto 'Chins up and take it' still holds good for the soldiers' wives here in Walwa, we keep one another going, it's all we can do for each other, so we do it . . .

Gosh what confidences we will have to share when you return, which you are aren't you. I'd love to sneak on you and surprise you just as much as I would love you to sneak on me and surprise me just as much you did nearly twelve months ago on your first leave from camp.

Darling we will be true to one another to the end won't we I am sure of myself and doubly sure of you as I know you so well. Gee dear I love you and will even more if possible when you return to me to finish our lives together. I love you dearly and sincerely, do you remember that song . . .

My very own darling you will soon be home won't you I feel it in my bones and what a day my word that will be the day and what a day.

Lil & family have just been up and held me up. Darling we all send our very love to you your six boys and your baby girls and I send all my love and the kisses you have missed since our last letter. 'Chin up and take it', our motto Darling I think of you in every way in every minute of every day.

Au revoir my darling,

From Josie.

Love a million to my Darling Husband. I'm still smiling even through tears Dear.

Sleep tight my love.

Remember I am yours always.[40]

•

Some senior German officers would never have dreamed of sharing their private thoughts with an officer as junior as Schmidt, but General Paulus was not of their number. For some reason this acting chief of the OKH had quickly struck up an easy relationship with the junior Lieutenant of the Afrika Korps who had been ordered to show him around — to the point that the first words Paulus said to Schmidt when they had set off on the morning of 28 April were, 'Now we shall be able to talk more easily ...'[41]

Full of questions, he wanted to know not only of Schmidt's background but also as much as the Lieutenant could tell him, and show him, about the conditions the troops were fighting under at Tobruk.

In response, though Schmidt did not take the General right up to the front lines — where a well-aimed shot might take him out in the same manner as it had the tragic von Prittwitz — he did take him close enough for Berlin's representative to observe for himself the kind of artillery fire the forward elements of the Afrika Korps were having rained down upon them from the Tobruk garrison, the dust that constantly surrounded them, the difficulties of provisioning them and the inevitable result of shell-shocked and physically weakened troops that it occasioned.

Paulus was appalled, and said so.

'The troops around Tobruk are fighting in conditions that are inhuman and intolerable,' he declared, unconsciously tugging at his glove. 'I am going to recommend to Berlin that we withdraw to a strong position at Gazala, where our supply lines will be shorter. The troops will live under better conditions, and we shall be ensured greater reserves. As I see it, every man here is on duty without a break. Relief and the freshening up of troops is not possible. We must do something to remedy this state of affairs.'[42]

Schmidt was certainly interested to hear it, but equally did not take it as given that that was what would happen. As one who had seen Rommel in action over the previous two months, he felt sure that the Commanding Officer of the Afrika Korps would do what he always did when something was blocking his path — blow it away or find a way around it. In this case, Schmidt felt that Rommel was likely to be at his persuasive best in convincing Paulus that the only way forward was *Vorwärts*, into Tobruk, and not backwards, to Gazala.

•

And sure enough. Late that night, after hearing everything and reviewing Rommel's maps — at last the Italians had provided some decent ones of Tobruk! — Paulus agreed to the attack going ahead, though there was one issue on which he would not give way. When Rommel stated that he wished to bring German troops back from the Egyptian frontier of Halfaya Pass and Sollum so he could use them in the assault, leaving behind the

Italian troops to hold the positions won in the east, the senior officer was nothing if not direct.

'You have never ceased to stress,' he told Rommel, 'that the Italian troops are absolutely useless. In that case you cannot entrust the protection of your flank on the frontier to them alone. It is, after all, the key point for keeping up the encirclement of Tobruk.'[43]

For once, Rommel ceded. Since he had captured the Halfaya Pass in mid April, it had already been lost once before being recaptured, so it made sense to leave his forward troops in place there and make do with what he had on site at Tobruk. The main thing was that he had the go-ahead to launch the attack on Tobruk.

Back in Berlin, Halder was far from convinced that the right decision had been made, but he could hardly countermand Paulus, his senior man on site. Nevertheless, to his diary there was no need to be mealy-mouthed, and he spelled out his view in very clear terms: 'In my opinion this is all wrong.'[44]

•

Ivor Hancock, with his 2/24th Battalion, moved up to the Red Line defending Hill 209 on the afternoon of 30 April, to relieve the 2/48th Battalion. He and his platoon were allocated post R5 to man, and they quickly made themselves at home, throwing their sleeping gear and bags in the back of the post while sorting out their weaponry and ammunition stores up the front.

It gave Ivor no little comfort to be in this pit with his old mate Norm Graham, who had been with him from the first day of joining the Army, through all the camps in Australia, the journey to the Middle East, the camps in Palestine and now here. They had trained together, taken out women together, whored together, and now here they were, about to fight together for the first time. In this instance Norm was very proud to have in his possession a small captured Italian mortar that he promised to put to good use, even if, on the quiet to Ivor, he acknowledged that the damn thing was so bloody ineffectual that the mortar bomb it propelled would just about have to hit some unlucky bastard on the head before it would do any damage. Never mind — if the Germans actually got to them in the post, he could maybe use it as a club to crack their heads open with.

Also in their post were Corporal McKenzie, Dougie Smythe, Lou Gazzard and a couple of other blokes. In terms of weaponry, apart from the Italian mortar, between them they had one Bren gun, a heavy Vickers machine gun and a few rifles which wasn't much, really, to hold off the whole of the German Army, which was apparently about to descend upon them. But when Ivor was assigned the third of the circular pits that the bunker consisted of, along with the battalion knuckle man, Max the Axe, he immediately felt better. Yeah, he would have preferred Norm for friendship's sake, but of all the blokes he'd come across in this man's army to date, The Axe was clearly one of the best bastards to be alongside in a tight spot when the bullets started to fly, as it seemed they likely would ...

CHAPTER FOURTEEN

The Battle of the Salient

*The Australians, who are the men our troops have had opposite
them so far, are extraordinarily tough fighters. The German is more
active in the attack but the enemy stakes his life in the defence and
fights to the last with extreme cunning. Our men, usually easy going
and unsuspecting, fall easily into his traps especially as a result of
their experiences in the closing stages of the [Western]
European Campaign . . .*

CO MAJOR BALLERSTEDT, AFRICA KORPS, 2ND BATTALION, TO HIS SUPERIORS

*Berlin Radio made a fatal mistake in trying to jibe and scare the
Australian soldier into surrender. The longer the odds Lord Haw-Haw
offered against the Diggers' chance of getting out, the more heavily the
Digger backed himself.*

CHESTER WILMOT, RADIO BROADCAST, 1941[1]

It was time to give it another go.
Time for all or nothing, as Rommel's orders made clear:

> The Afrika Korps will force a decision in the battle
> around Tobruk during the night 30 April–1 May, by an
> attack from the west.[2]

Which was all to the good. Among most of the Afrika Korps the feeling
ran high that, while mistakes might have been made in their last assault on
Tobruk, this time they would get it right against an enemy that had surely
been weakened by the pounding it had taken over the previous two weeks.
This time they would have two armoured divisions going in, instead of
one, together with three Italian infantry divisions that could be thrown into
the fray. Combined they would have 50 000 men, 200 aircraft and some
600 armoured vehicles, a large chunk of which could be hurled at the

specific spot of the perimeter that had been carefully selected — the posts in front of Hill 209.

•

What the Afrika Korps would not have, however, was much of an element of surprise, because it simply had not been possible to prepare this attack on the treeless expanse of the desert without the garrison being aware. As a matter of fact, with the Germans now clearly readying for another tilt at Tobruk, Lieutenant General Morshead's own formal orders to all forward battalions were issued at much the same time as Rommel's:

> All positions are to be held at all costs. No withdrawals will be made. If positions are surrounded by the enemy, they are still to be held and will be relieved by counterattack. Tanks should be allowed to pass through to be engaged by anti-tank and field guns in the rear. Infantry following are to be engaged and defeated.[3]

In short, Morshead's rough plan was for his troops to do to the invaders the very same thing they had done on the last occasion.

•

For the men of the 2/13th, 2/7th and 2/15th Battalions late on that afternoon of 30 April, things suddenly were familiar, reminiscent of what had happened just over a fortnight earlier. Once again, on the far horizon to the immediate south of where they were defending the Red Line, on either side of the El Adem road, they could see massive dust clouds indicating great vehicular movement, and once again artillery fire rained down upon them, while something like fifty aircraft came over, alternately bombing and strafing their positions.

It looked very much as if Fritz and Giuseppe were gearing up for a major assault right on their very spot.

But in fact not long afterwards the feeling grew that maybe the Germans had learned their lesson the last time they tried, and the attack on the 20th Brigade this time was only a feint, as it was soon apparent that the blokes of the 26th Brigade a couple of miles to their west — defending a length of perimeter about 7000 yards in front of Hill 209 with two battalions, the 2/23rd and 2/24th — were copping it even more.

•

Were they what!

For Ivor Hancock and his mates, holding their positions with the 2/24th on the side of Hill 209, things started to really warm up from late in the afternoon of that last day of April 1941, when it became obvious that something big and very ugly indeed was stirring. For no sooner had they spied enormous clouds of dust rising and swirling skywards — signifying major activity in what had been no-man's-land to their west — than from above whole packs of Stukas were suddenly screaming down upon them, dropping their bombs both on the posts themselves and on the barbed wire and minefields that helped to protect them. And all this even while heavy artillery shells began to land all around. It was clear that the Germans now had a much better idea of how the perimeter's defences were organised, as each wave of Stukas attacked particular posts in tight groups, unleashing hell upon those below.

Though this wasn't the first time the 2/24th had been directly attacked, on this occasion the number of Stukas and the bombs they dropped was so overwhelming that, while the Ack-Ack kept going throughout, all the defenders on the Red Line could do was to crouch down in their posts and trenches and wait for the attack to finish, praying that they would not take any direct hits.

In his own post, R5, Ivor felt afraid — and not just that he might lose his life. He was afraid that his fear might show; afraid that in some manner he might let the other blokes down; afraid that, when the firing really started, he wouldn't be able live up to what they all knew was the very proud heritage of being an Anzac. And he wanted to see Jean again, and hold their child when it was born.

At least all the trembling was not his own, though; for as the bombs kept dropping closer, his whole post shook furiously as the tremors moved through each of them — but no substantial damage was done to R5. At least, not to the *structure* of the post . . .

The same could not be said for the morale of all the defenders. For not long after this serious bombing and shelling started, the most extraordinary thing happened. Max the Axe — the battalion knuckle-man, the hard bastard to beat all hard bastards, the one everyone said would be a good man to have beside you in the trenches — broke down! Instead of manning the third gun pit and waiting for a possible land attack, he had crawled into the sleeping recess behind. And now, with even the tiniest lull in the bombing, his plaintive sobs and prayers could be heard as he called variously on God, Jesus and Sweet Mary Mother of Jesus to save him and spare his life. Ivor listened, stunned like a mullet, and knew he would not have believed it had he not heard it with his own ears.

•

Watching through his binoculars from on top of 'Carrier Hill', Rommel observed the whole attack going in, with Schmidt by his side. For the most part he was satisfied, as it was evident that this time, with the overwhelming force he had assembled across a much broader line of the perimeter, headway was being made; but there was equally no doubt that the resistance put up by the garrison remained formidable. Even with all the Stukas and artillery there had barely been any diminution of fire coming from Tobruk, including, most notably, from the Australian sharpshooters, who were apparently the men manning the forward defences. As Rommel later wrote: 'The enemy fought with remarkable tenacity. Even their wounded went on defending themselves with small arms fire, and stayed in the fight to their last breath.'[4] (It wasn't, however, that the Australians were unimpressed with the Germans' own splendid effort, with one of those Diggers later recalling, 'If Jesus Christ himself had come down at that moment, none of us would have been surprised. It was like a bloody fanfare to herald the end of the world!'[5])

Rommel kept his binoculars trained, hoping for some sign of a breakthrough. Would these enemy soldiers never give up?

Still, there was to be no question of pulling back. Rommel was never one for pulling back.

'Schmidt,' Rommel said, 'work your way forward to Major Schräpler. He must consolidate and hold his present position. The attack will be reinforced and continued tonight.'

'*Zu Befehl, Herr General*,' Schmidt replied with instant acceptance of the task. And then he was gone, to do his master's bidding.

Still, of all the jobs!

It was no easy thing for Schmidt to work his way forwards alone, across open ground already hard won by German infantry that had provided covering fire for each other — and Rommel's adjutant was acutely conscious that just one bullet from a sniper and he was gone — but there was no choice.

'I made as much speed as I could,' Schmidt later reminisced, 'feeling every time I slowed down that Rommel's glasses were blistering the seat of my trousers. I reached Schräpler just before dark.'

•

Just before sundown in Ivor Hancock's post, his mate Dougie Smythe, a popular man in the section, just momentarily poked his head above the parapet to have a look-see at the immediate area and determine whether any Germans or Ities had yet penetrated their defences. (Their section hadn't yet organised themselves to make periscopes from shaving mirrors.)

It was really only an instant. But no sooner had Doug's head gone up than a shot rang out, and a German sniper — presumably waiting for that precise thing — fired off a single bullet and drilled Dougie straight between the eyes. Their comrade was hurled backwards nearly as fast as his brains, which splattered over the back wall behind him.

Corporal McKenzie, letting out a yelp, grabbed Smythe where he had fallen, but it was so obvious that nothing could be done that the others soon obliged McKenzie to let him go again. Tearfully McKenzie did so, as others dragged Dougie to the back of the pit and covered his body and what was left of his head with a blanket. There would be a time to grieve, but it was not now. Now was the time to take stock and work out just what their position was, and what they could do to strengthen it. What was clear was that they were under attack, as attested to by the bullets now whining all around, thicker than flies on a cow pat, and the artillery shells landing both before and even right *on* their post.

And yet while their post was able to withstand the artillery barrage, the same could not be said for the surrounding barbed wire, minefields and anti-tank ditch. With all the bombing and artillery fire, much of the barbed wire that protected the 2/24th from the German marauders had been blown to kingdom come, while the minefields in front of them were destroyed. Finally, the anti-tank ditches which had been so clearly delineated, marking a barrier over which a tank could not pass, in many spots had now been blown apart and the sides of the ditch had caved in, meaning that if a tank attacked at the right spot, it would have no trouble passing through.

Also severely threatened by the bombing was R5's lifeline: trucks bearing supplies to them, coming up from the port proper in the harbour. That evening, only a short time after Dougie Smythe had been killed, a truck carrying some more ammo and, most importantly, the condenser for the Vickers machine gun to cool it down — without which the weapon was all but useless — was on the approach to their post when it took an artillery shell right through the windshield and everything was blown sky high, including the company driver and the Quartermaster Sergeant.

The situation was grim and getting grimmer. Making everything worse in R5 was the fact that they were now totally out of contact with everyone, including the posts to their left and right. The bombs and shells had torn all of the signalling wire to shreds, and the fire remained constant enough that not even any of the runners whose job it was to cover that eventuality would attempt to get through. Whatever happened from this point on would be essentially up to them, without either guidance or help from the outside. Topping it all off, the moonless night was as black as death itself — almost like it was stalking them — and there was simply no way of knowing if the Germans were making their way through the posts or not . . .

Not surprisingly the morale of these isolated men on the forward lines began to wane somewhat — and in a few cases more than somewhat.

The query now was just when, after such an artillery barrage, the Germans would send in their tanks and infantry.

Not long after dark, Corporal McKenzie came into the pit where Ivor and Max the Axe were, and told them they must take it in turns — every two hours or so — to peer into the darkness and look for any signs that the Germans were on the move.

Ivor, knowing there was no way that the still terrified Max would sleep — and that he would need all his own strength to be at the maximum for whatever the Germans were about to throw at them — told the whimpering one that he was on the first watch and that Max was to come and wake him when he'd had enough. The Axe was now in such a state that he would have hurled himself to the floor if anyone had even *farted* loudly.

·

Whatever else, the German tank commanders would not be lacking in confidence in their coming assault. After all, how could they not triumph? They had total control of the skies, a massive superiority in artillery and tanks, a brigade of engineers, one and a half German machine-gun battalions to pour through the breach, and two Italian infantry brigades whose job it would be to roll up the flanks while the tanks and machine-gunners pushed on to the harbour.

In one of those tanks — waiting in a wadi just south of the perimeter for the artillery and bombing to soften up the defences before they got among them themselves — was Panzer Commander Joachim Schorm. An indication of his own confidence was a rare moment of indulgence he had enjoyed the evening before, drinking the last of his bottle of Chianti with the Commanding Officer of his tank unit. And why not? Yes, it was a little sad when they had put the last precious drops into their metal cups, but the main thing was they would have more in just a short time, and that it would taste even better because they would be drinking it in celebration. When they took Tobruk by high noon the following day.

•

It was Max the so-called bloody Axe again. He was breathing heavily, and shaking Ivor.

'The Germans,' he hissed. 'They're coming through the wire.'

In an instant Ivor was wide awake, had grabbed his rifle and leaped to his feet in one fluid motion, and he quickly followed Max back to their nest. Now peering into the murky darkness, he saw them too, flitting through the shadow. *There!*

Ivor fired off a couple of shots, but there was neither any return fire nor the sound of bodies thudding to the ground. Rather embarrassingly instead, there was a spray of sand right in front of his nose which burst back into his eyes. In the darkness he hadn't been able to see the rather large clump of dirt just outside their pit, and that is what he had been staring at — and probably Max too — when they thought they had been seeing Germans!

The whole damn thing was an illusion brought about by the dark night and their worst fears coming together at a time when they'd had the wind put up them.

Rather curtly now Ivor told The Axe to bloody well stay at his post, and to bloody well stop seeing things! Stupid bastard ...

•

From positions all around Hill 209 now as the night settled in, and the ground troops and tanks prepared themselves for their assault, the German and Italian artillery continued to pour in heavy fire, specifically targeted on the perimeter posts.

For the men of the 2/13th, 2/17th and 2/15th, it seemed an extraordinary thing this time to be *watching* a bitter battle instead of being right in the middle of it. Situated in the eastern lee of Hill 209, they were obliged to hold their own turf just as they had done before, scanning the murk for any sign that the Germans were about to attack them, but inevitably their eyes came back to what, to the untutored eye, might have looked like a not-so-distant fireworks display. Each shell-burst atop their mates' heads emitted a sudden flash, not unlike the big penny bungers on cracker night at home, just as the many flares sent skywards were reminiscent of the rockets that, as kids, they used to let off in milk bottles. The tracer bullets arcing lazily backwards and forwards? They looked just as if some giant hand was slowly drawing a sparkler across the sky.

It was perhaps merciful for them that, because Hill 209 was in the way, they couldn't see the results of the German bombs landing. The men in the posts of the Red Line, just along from where the attack was going on, were not so privileged. What suddenly worried them — as the Stukas continued to scream down and unleash their lethal loads, while the *dub-dub dub-dub* of the Spandaus went on without end — were what seemed in the gloom to be stuck Catherine wheels. Where once was darkness in an instant became a powerful *whooooosh* of flame leaping across space. Instinctively the Diggers down below knew only too bloody well what that was:

Fucking *flame-throwers*.[6]

•

Across a broad swathe of the perimeter, the German infantry was now moving in, and this time they were better prepared, trying to accomplish with *Flammenwerfen* what they had been unable to accomplish with bullets and bayonets: quelling the resistance in the posts. Fortunately, they didn't get far. The soldiers manning the flame-throwers on that dark night were like miners holding a candle at the bottom of a dark pit, with methane gas all around, just begging to be blown up. And so they were also perfect targets for every Australian within cooee and every British artillery unit — who didn't miss.

And then, at nine o'clock, another light — a green and white Very light — went arcing gracefully through the night sky. Morshead knew that it wasn't one of their own signals, so it could only belong to the attackers; and what it meant they couldn't know.

But Rommel did: it was the signal that a key part of the objective had been achieved and that what the British called Hill 209 and his army called Ras el Medauuar was now in their hands.[7] True, it soon turned out that, against all odds, a lot of the perimeter posts had held on, but they could be dealt with in due course. At least the Afrika Korps controlled the heights.

•

In that dark night, Morshead's 9th Divisional HQ was in a state of almost complete ignorance as to what was going on. Had the Germans penetrated the Red Line or not? Were the garrison's posts holding on, or had they already fallen? In the darkness, with most of the signal cables shattered by the shelling and simply nothing emerging from the outer side of Hill 209, there was no way of knowing. The runners that had been sent out either couldn't get through or had got through and seemingly couldn't come back. The minutes sadly struggled by like old blind men on a cliff path — slowly, painfully, with each one holding on to the one in front and behind, and *refusing* to let go.

Finally, just after three o'clock in the morning, news. One of the patrols that had been sent out on a reconnaissance mission now returned with five German prisoners.[8] These had been captured well inside the wire, and the likelihood had to be that there were plenty more where they came from.

Morshead himself was not awake when they arrived — and nor was he awoken at this point. Knowing that he would likely be needing all his strength for the fight on the morrow, and that his staff would wake him if there was anything he really needed to be made aware of, he had the discipline to turn in and conserve his energy for what was to come. So he was awoken at dawn with the news that the Germans were inside, but little else was confirmed. He waited to find out more before making his move.

•

And now there was more shouting.

Right at daybreak, Max the Axe burst into Ivor's sleeping alcove, screaming with joy: 'Tanks! Tanks! Our tanks have arrived!'

This Ivor had to see. If it was true, it was wonderful news indeed; maybe now they could make a fair fight of it. Certainly he could hear the roaring of engines but, peering into the thick mist, it was far from obvious where the tanks were. Oddly, though, over the angry growl of the motors now came an unfamiliar sound of indeterminate origin, and then bursting out of the mist appeared a herd of camels, panicked by forces unknown — though very likely sent by the besiegers with the hope that their massive flip-flopping feet would set off whatever remained of the perimeter mines.

Ivor had little time to muse on the idea when the first of the tanks appeared from out of the mist, a huge hulking monster rumbling up the hill, and this time there could be no doubt at all. The big black cross over a larger white cross on the sides said it was a *German* tank, not British. When Ivor quietly pointed out the insignia to Max, the big man lost it completely and went to pieces.

Running from the gun pit, Max now charged around and about the post, yelling that they quickly had to find something white to wave so they could make it clear they were surrendering. Out of the gloom, however, came the voice of another of the Australian soldiers in the post with them: 'You wave something white, mate, and I'll blow your fucking head off.'

In the deathly calm way it was said, there was no doubt that the soldier was serious — and somehow it got through to Max the Axe, because he immediately stopped in his tracks before again retreating to the sleeping alcove, presumably to get at the furthest possible point in the post from where the fire from the tanks might hit.

For the moment, however, the crisis passed when the first of the tanks veered away towards one of the other posts. What didn't veer away, though, was the German infantry, who were now coming thick and fast to judge by the number of bullets that were whistling around the Australians. It was bloody frustrating that they still couldn't clearly see the brutes — due to what turned out to be a very thick fog — but there was no doubt they were close.

In Ivor's post, the men kept up some fire in the rough direction of the Germans the best they could, though it was difficult from the moment their principal bit of weaponry, the heavy Vickers gun, jammed after just the first few rounds — all for want of the condenser which had been destroyed the night before. With Max nowhere to be seen, Ivor was alone in his post and firing his rifle. When his mate Norm Graham realised Ivor was alone he had come along to help, though it was a gesture only, as Norm's own rifle had been destroyed by mortar fire the day before. Still, Ivor felt better for having him there, as shell after shell started landing around their post again. The constant chatter of machine guns and whining of ricocheting bullets mixed with the screams of men who'd been hit and ... somehow ... though it was all so strange he wasn't quite sure if this was really happening ... he suddenly felt disembodied, like he was floating away, watching the whole thing on a giant movie screen, or even like they were all children playing a game. The sensation was so strong that a conscious thought even surfaced: 'How ridiculous and amusing ...'

Bzz... Bzz ... Bzz ...

Back to reality, if this actually *was* reality. The sound of a bullet flying past his ear, Ivor found, was like that of an angry bee buzzing by. The Germans were getting close now and Ivor's post was clearly a target. He had long wondered just what he would feel if ever he had an enemy soldier in his sights, with a bullet in the breach and his finger on the trigger. Would he be able to squeeze that trigger? Send a bullet hurtling from his barrel and KILL another man? And if he could do that, what would he feel?

Now, as the first of the German forces came into clear view, Ivor knew he was about to find out.

For just 150 yards away now, and closing slowly, a group of German soldiers was struggling up the misty hill towards the post. Carefully now, making sure to keep his own head down and as safe as possible, Ivor aimed his rifle at the group and picked out a particular soldier. He could have picked any of them, but he just happened to pick this bloke from the mass — some mother's son from somewhere, someone's husband, someone's father, it didn't matter. The only thing Ivor knew was that he had his sights right on the soldier's heart and now was the time.

Carefully, then, ensuring that he made no sudden jerk which would spoil the shot, Ivor gently squeezed ... harder ... and a little harder still until ...

In any other environment, the detonation of the bullet in the chamber would have made a colossal noise that could have been heard up to 2 miles away. Not on this occasion, though. In fact, such was the cacophony of catastrophe from the rest of the battle going on all around that the crack of Ivor's rifle attracted not the smallest bit of attention. But sure enough, down the hill, the soldier Ivor had selected suddenly dropped like a sack of spuds and subsequently made no movement. At the instant it happened, Ivor had the prescience to mentally note what he was feeling as he killed another man for the first time.

'Nothing,' he later noted. 'The moment passed and only that man's friends and relatives would feel something.'

Still the Germans kept coming. Still Ivor kept firing, and they kept falling. Still he felt nothing.

For others in the post with Ivor, though, it was quite the opposite. One gun pit over was Lou Gazzard, a primary school teacher back home in Condah, Victoria, a softly spoken man renowned in the battalion as a warm and sensitive fellow, with a wonderfully easy way with children — including whatever Arab kids they had come across; a bloke who had joined the Army because he had felt it was his duty to serve his country at a time of need, for such a just cause. Lou had been hit pretty hard by the death of his best mate, Dougie Smythe, the night before, but was now doing the job he had to do, still without hate in him. He was manning the one Bren gun they had, and covering a certain spot on the path up the hill that all the Germans had to traverse if they were to get to them. And, now that the Germans were in range, Lou had opened up all right, directly on them, and the enemy soldiers were going down in ones and twos and even threes. Like ninepins, men were falling and dying at Lou's hands.

And yet, as he kept slaughtering them, Lou began to sob uncontrollably and unashamedly, and even though he kept firing, he was heard to say, 'I will never teach another child ever again!'

It was a dreadful situation, but Lou had no choice but to keep firing, and nor did the rest of them have the time to console him in any way. All kept going. For Lou, though, the problems were becoming twofold. For it wasn't just his heart that was breaking. In fact, the barrel of his Bren was now so hot that it first began to glow and then distort, to the point that it started to bend up into the air. The Germans stopped falling to his gun and somehow, in this brief relief, they were at last able to bring some fire to bear on *him*. In an instant, a bullet from a German soldier came and drilled Lou clean through the head. He fell dead at his mates' feet.

•

Not far away at this time, Rommel was once again appalled. While he had some respect for Italian artillerymen, if not their guns, and a fair measure of respect for Italian pilots, he simply couldn't work out how to get the Italian soldiers moving. Now, pulling up just a few hundred metres back from where the breach had been made overnight, he was outraged to see members of the Ariete just beginning to unload their weaponry and ammunitions and prepare to move into the breach. Under the plan he had formulated, that should have happened hours ago! He shouted at one of his own men, Major Appel, to get the Italians moving, but it was to no avail. As Rommel recounted, 'with British artillery fire sweeping the whole area, the Italians crept under their vehicles and resisted all of their officers' attempts to get them out again'.[9] The real problem, he noted archly, was that 'The Italian soldiers had acquired a very considerable inferiority complex, as was not surprising under the circumstances'.[10]

What was it going to take to make them fight?

•

Back in Ivor's post, the situation was even hotter than before.

At one point, with bullets and mortars coming all at once, Ivor decided he needed to get a better idea of just how close the German infantry were and decided to risk a quick look above the parapet of his gun pit.

He put his head ... *up-then-down* ... and yet even in that moment it was enough for three Germans he had spotted nearby, manning a light cannon, to fire off a round which only narrowly missed killing him.

It was only shortly after this that Corporal McKenzie came along and, with a heavy heart, as the sounds of the battle raged all around, told them that the situation looked hopeless and there was no point in dying for nothing, so ... what did they think about surrendering?

Both Ivor and Norm Graham considered it for an instant and told him they would go along with the majority. If they wanted to stand and fight, that was fine with them, and they would fight with them. If they wanted to surrender, well, they understood and would go along with that too ...

Corporal McKenzie seemed okay with their response; and yet, only a few minutes later, when things went strangely quiet in their immediate vicinity, it was Norm who risked putting his head up above the parapet, only to see the rest of the men — including the weeping Max the Axe — being led away by German soldiers.

Christ Almighty. It suddenly felt like it was just the two of them left facing the whole fucking German Army.

What to do?

While they were trying to work that one out, Ivor decided to risk one more look himself, and poked his head up — only to find himself looking into the blackest bit of blackness there is in all the world: right down the barrel of a machine gun pointed straight between his eyes and, above it, a German officer peering down intently upon him.

It was a shocking moment, and as Ivor would later write of it: 'Most of us had grown up in the shadow of the "Aussie Digger" image, with many of our fathers having served in World War I. Being killed in action or being wounded had always been considered an option, but having to put up our hands, irrespective of the circumstances, had never been a consideration.'

And yet there was simply no choice.

In the international sign language for 'You've got me covered and I know it', Ivor put his hands above his head, as did Norm an instant later, and soon the two were led away to captivity, shortly catching up to the other men from their post who had surrendered.

From the shock of the moment, Ivor's memory ever afterwards would be hazy, but two things would stand out. One was sharing a cigarette with his captor, even as the gun stayed trained upon him, passing the ciggie back and forth between them — a strangely intimate act between men who had been enemies until moments before. And the other was the stunning image of Rommel himself, instantly recognisable, head coming out of the turret of some armoured vehicle, smiling down upon them and saying, with no malice and in what was perhaps a practised English phrase, 'Sorry, gentlemen, outflanked.'

Rommel regarded the Australian prisoners with particular interest. For three weeks these men and their brethren had been holding out against his Panzers, Stukas and artillery, and his finest troops, and he was eager to get a close-up look at them. He later wrote: 'A batch of some fifty or sixty Australian prisoners were marched off close beside us — immensely big and powerful men, who without question represented an elite formation of the British Empire, a fact that was also evident in battle.'[11]

These Australian prisoners were subsequently well treated. It was at Rommel's insistence that they received exactly the same medical attention as his own men, as prescribed by the Geneva Convention, in which he was a firm believer, and the code of which he had always strictly observed. It was for a very good reason that Rommel would later describe the whole Tobruk action — joined by the affirmation of soldiers from both sides — as a '*Krieg ohne Hass*', war without hate. (And certainly the fact that there were no women or children involved made that a lot easier. In Rommel's view the participants were all honourable men — albeit from different tribes — warriors all meeting on the flatlands by the water to sort this out.)

None of which alleviated Ivor's distress at the time. It wasn't just that he had been taken prisoner and was likely facing years in some camp, nor even that his ankle hurt like bloody hell. It was that while he and the other men from all the other posts had been standing around, they had been comparing notes, and Ivor heard for the first time what had happened to his mate — Christ, practically his *brother* — Frankie Barlow the night before. The way the other blokes told it, when the barrage had started Frankie had been sheltering at the bottom of the steps leading down into the bunker, and a shell had landed right in the gun-pit above and killed him, nearly blowing his head off in the process ... Ivor could barely believe it. Dead. Frankie ... *dead*. Frankie, who had been so relieved a month earlier when, while he and Ivor were pulling back from El Tocra, he had narrowly survived being pulled off that truck during the Benghazi Handicap, relieved because he had looked death in face and *survived* it! Now ... dead, after all.

And some other mates had been knocked, too. A few posts up, a Jerry tank commander had shouted from his turret, telling the Australians to surrender or he would blast them out of their pits. The response had been for one Australian to call back 'Well, bloody well blast us out, you bastard!'[12] And he had ...

The only thing that remotely cheered Ivor was the sight of Cocky Walpole turning up at the last moment — he'd been captured by the

Germans while running a message — which meant that, though he was a prisoner like them, at least he was alive. And Cocky was glad to see them too.

'Thank Gawd you blokes are here,' he said, his big mouth spreading into an enormous smile that near split his ugly mug in two. 'I thought they'd taken the Pole for a souvenir . . .'

•

And now, as the mist and dust raised by all the shelling had, at last, lifted, the situation became a little more defined. There on Hill 209, clearly visible, were forty Panzers! Back at Divisional Headquarters, Morshead's senior staff were collating information, and they informed the General that it seemed likely that the seven posts which could not be contacted, the ones on the other side of Hill 209, had indeed fallen to the enemy.

This was shortly followed up by reports from air reconnaissance that as many as sixty tanks were within the perimeter, while as many as 240 more tanks — two groups of seventy and one of 100-odd — were approaching along the Acroma Road![13] For Morshead, the situation remained most uncertain.

•

For Rommel, the situation remained most uncertain.

Yes, they had broken the initial defences and breached the Red Line. But the problem was that so many of the enemy strongpoints were still holding on against overwhelming odds; and while he was perpetually needing more troops to feed the attack and keep it going, it was not easy to get those troops inside while so many posts remained in Allied hands. At this stage he was still confident that Tobruk could be taken — and, certainly, once the Panzers got going again things should be sorted out quickly — but he was also more than a little shocked at how strong the resistance continued to be. He gave orders for the posts that had already been taken to be doubly secured with whatever troops were available, to prevent them being retaken by the enemy with a counterattack, and while one group of Panzers was to head east towards the town, another group was to stay back to help the troops clean out the posts on the perimeter.

•

Back at the Blue Line, just behind the point where the Panzers had broken through, the 2/24th B Company was heavily dug in and facing their fate with equal parts trepidation and resolution. For now the mighty Panzers were moving forward en masse, straight towards them and firing their cannon and machine guns nineteen-to-the-dozen, and it seemed likely that the game was up. They just couldn't stop these brutes!

But maybe the anti-tank boys could . . .

Firing from a distance of about 750 yards, the men of the 24th Australian Anti-tank Company — with next to no protection themselves — fired salvo after salvo directly into the massed Panzers and immediately knocked out a Mark III. Inevitably the Panzers turned upon them, but still the anti-tank boys kept firing, taking out two more Panzers until they were themselves wiped out. On such all-but-anonymous heroics does the fate of a battle often turn, but in this case the anti-tank lads had merely stung but not stopped the Panzers, which kept coming on to the 2/24th's B Company, who now seemed to be looking death right in the eye.

Then, just when all seemed lost, the most extraordinary thing happened. The tank at the front suddenly sprang a flame from its left track, and shook like a dog before belching black smoke from its belly, doing a quarter turn and shuddering to a halt. And then another tank did the same, and then another and then another!

Mines! By the grace of God, hail Mary, praise be to thee — she *does* exist, after all! — the Panzer squadron had come straight onto one of the most heavily laid minefields that Morshead had insisted be planted between the Red Line and the Blue Line, at the points he had considered most likely to suffer an incursion!

Around and about, other tanks had also hit mines and the whole Panzer thrust was literally stopped in its tracks, either because they had hit a mine or were petrified they were about to. In a rough approximation of what had happened in the Easter Battle, seventeen of them were now disabled.

In one of the as yet undamaged Panzers, the same Lieutenant Joachim Schorm who had been at the forefront of the Easter Battle as the whole thing had turned into a witch's cauldron, was once again shocked by the course of the events. He had just been proceeding with all the others, confident (as he'd written in his diary that morning) that today was the day 'we intend to take Tobruk', when the first shuddering explosion had taken place to the right of him. Artillery? No. *Mine!*

Schorm had immediately crackled advice into his radio: 'Commander Schorm. See if you can turn round in your tracks.'[14] But it was no good as those tracks were broken.

Then came an order from the squadron commander: '*Rückzug!*' Tanks to retire.

For the second time at Tobruk, and in World War II, Panzers were being turned!

At least, the best they could.

In fact, the only way out was for the undamaged tanks to back out over their own wheel tracks, the only part of the field they could be sure didn't have a mine. Others, however, stayed to cover the disabled tanks and ensure that those that could be towed back out would be.

Now the British artillery poured in high explosive shells upon them, until a wiser head issued the command to cease and desist — it was more important to keep the precious minefield intact than anything else, and they couldn't take the chance that their missed shells would effectively defuse the rest of the mines.

•

In the meantime, the other Panzer squadron had been working with the Panzergrenadiere to move south along the perimeter posts and take them out one by one — with mixed results.

As later recounted by German writer Wolf Heckmann, in one of those Panzers, Joachim Sänger and his crew were firing for all their tank was worth at the Australian defenders up ahead. And it was strange, Sänger reflected — always strange. In their time in the Panzers to date, it was a frequent occurrence for a man suffering from dysentery to squat over the hole in the Panzer floor where the shell casings were thrown out. But now, as ever once the action started, everyone forgot about dysentery and their sphincters tightened — the exact opposite of what they might have expected. They kept rolling forwards, furiously firing, when there was an explosion which shook the entire tank in such a fashion that the shuddering seemed to go on and on. Clearly they had been hit and the tank damaged, but whether or not that shuddering had been a death rattle, it was not yet possible to determine. What was immediately apparent was that their Panzer could move neither forwards nor back and that, now immobilised, they were coming under heavy fire, so it could only be a matter of time before they took a big hit that would kill them all. Operating more from instinct than rational thought, Sänger found himself pushing the lid of the tank open and frantically climbing out, desperate to get out, out of this infernal iron coffin, and make a run for it.

Running now, hard, trying to make sure that his boots got purchase on the oft-slippery desert sand. Spurts of dust were starting to kick up around his heels as distant gunners started taking their bead, and it could surely only be a matter of time before he was hit when suddenly the desert yawned open before him. A hole! Safety!

In a split second Sänger dived into what proved to be a quite massive cavern, only to find that there were others in there before him. Forty of them. *Australians.* They looked every bit as big as he and his German colleagues had imagined them to be — which is to say, really big — but still . . .

In one more split second, Sänger had again reacted instinctively and withdrawn a grenade out of his pocket, yelling 'Hands up!'

At the time, and ever afterwards, the reaction of the Australians to the German's threat to end all their lives if they didn't surrender to him would seem extraordinary to the German.

For instead of shooting him dead where he stood — easily possible with a single shot, and they still they would have had enough time to hurl his grenade away — the Australians did everything but laugh.

The first of them to speak was an enormous Digger who stepped towards Sänger and said with a grin, 'Just put that dangerous thing away, will you?'

Upon consideration — understanding the sense, if not the exact meaning of the words — Sänger did precisely that, and not one of the Australians made any attempt to take it off him. With the sounds of battle still going on all around them, the mood was even something akin to convivial, in the manner of strangers meeting under a tree to take shelter from the storm, though at least one thing really was dramatic. In the corner one of the Australians appeared to be dying, with part of his face simply shot away. His comrades explained, without rancour, that he'd copped it from a German machine gun.

Gott.

With a sudden shudder, Sänger realised that the Germans who had in all likelihood ended this Australian man's life were him and his comrades, and while it was one thing to fire off a hopeful burst in the rough direction of the enemy, it was quite another to see the result up close. Quickly, Sänger got out his own emergency first-aid kit and, with some of the other Australians helping him, set out to fix up the wounded man the best he could . . .[15]

All up it wasn't much, but it at least it made the poor fellow a little more comfortable, which was something — perhaps the main thing, given that he was surely going to die anyway. Too, the Australians seemed to appreciate the care and concern shown by the German, because presently the big man who had first greeted him in the dugout spread some butter from his homeland on a biscuit, together with some weird-looking black stuff that tasted sort of sour but nice, and said to Sänger very pleasantly, 'Better get used to Australian food; that's where you'll be going now, nice and safe.'

'Mmm-mm,' said Sänger, eating the biscuit and intoning in the universal language of one who is enjoying his tucker. 'But it's you who are the prisoner.'

In response, some of the Australians laughed. Fancy that Jerry thinking he was going to take them prisoner! Not bloody likely! Still, he didn't seem like a bad cove, and now they were quick to forgive. As a matter of fact, before long some of the Australians were crowding around him and pressing pieces of paper on him on which were written their home addresses and telephone numbers. One fellow even showed him pictures of his family, his farm and himself shearing sheep. 'Call my people when you get to Australia. You're a good chap, we'll look after you.'

Outside the battle raged, the artillery landing so heavily all around that they really were completely unsure whose territory this was.

The one thing that was certain on the German side was the order that had come from Rommel himself — 'The strongpoints taken will be held *at all costs*' — while for his part Morshead was still counting on his artillery to take out what tanks they could, and keeping what meagre tank resources he had in reserve.

•

In London, just a couple of hours later, the senior Whitehall mandarin Maurice Hankey had just bade his old friend Robert Menzies a fond farewell, before the Australian Prime Minister headed off on his plane trip home, and had turned to make his way along Park Lane and Hyde Park when he heard the sound of someone running behind him. It proved to be Menzies himself, with something to say.

One last time, the Australian wanted to give that dictator Churchill and the wretched Yes Men who populated the War Cabinet a work-over, and he knew he could trust Hankey with such potentially explosive remarks, as they were nothing on what Hankey had frequently said to him! (As a matter of fact, Churchill had always been one of the many common points of interest to the two, ever since Hankey had introduced the British and Australian PMs all those years ago at Churchill's country house, Chartwell.)

'There is only one thing to be done,' Menzies expostulated, 'and that is summon an Imperial War Cabinet and keep one of them behind, like Jan Smuts in the last war, not as a guest, but as a full member . . .'[16]

In fact, Menzies had in mind that one Commonwealth figure might perhaps replace Churchill altogether — and if it were him, Menzies, who took over then all the better — but it was probably not the best thing to say such a thing so nakedly, even if he knew that Hankey was a critic of the Churchill way. And yet theirs was not an idle conversation. That afternoon, Hankey consulted another senior Establishment figure about it, and on the strength of the response, Hankey called Menzies and encouraged him to go and see Churchill before he left, that very night, and put forward the idea of the Imperial War Cabinet and, whatever else, insist that Churchill cease and desist his dictatorial ways. Menzies said he was going to do exactly that . . .

•

Back at Joachim Sänger's post — with the mass of Australians taking shelter from the storm — the standoff continued as the battle raged all around, and they all waited to see who the ruling force upstairs would be. They didn't have to wait too long, as suddenly the barrels of many rifles and machine guns were pointing down upon them.

For a brief moment, time was suspended — and then the realisation sank in for them all.

They were German guns.

Again the situation had the makings of a bloodbath, but then the Australian captain shrugged his shoulders and the tension vanished. His men laid down their arms, for the simple reason that it was either that or be massacred where they stood. Much better to live.

Sänger, so recently their prisoner but now one of their captors, helped the Australians to pack up their coats, food and cigarettes. The one good thing about the situation for the Australians was that, now they were no longer isolated in a hole in the middle of the battle, their badly wounded cobber could get some serious medical help. Two of the Diggers got the wounded man sitting on their locked arms and, at German directions, carried him towards the facility the German doctors had set up — where, as Rommel had commanded, patients were dealt with according to the severity of their wounds, with no regard to be placed upon which uniform they wore.

Similarly, at many of the Regimental Aid Posts set up on the inside of the Blue Line, German and Australian soldiers who had equally given everything they had to hurting each other could now be found sitting side by side waiting for treatment in all but perfect equanimity.

Wanna ciggie, Jerry?

Dankeschön, mate.

•

Early in that afternoon of 1 May, the Panzers that had managed to extricate themselves from the minefield in front of the reserve 2/24th position now joined with the other tank squadron and thrust in a southeasterly direction, essaying to knock over the holdout perimeter posts — with five tanks firing on each post to keep the defenders' heads down, allowing the Panzergrenadiere to get in close — and then kept going to reduce those perimeter posts, one by one ...

In the face of such overwhelming force, the Australian soldiers were nothing short of magnificent, sticking to their guns long after the situation was clearly hopeless, and finding a way to keep the fire upon the enemy. In one notable episode in post R6, the German fire had been so fierce that a couple of machine guns had been knocked out; but, refusing to give up, a wounded corporal had got them quickly repaired again, using for a tool the only thing he had handy — a nail file!

By mid afternoon, Morshead took the hard decision to commit — after some limited armoured action in the morning — some more of the garrison's limited tank force to stop the Panzers. Always, his inclination had been to hold his own tanks until the last minute, as he was acutely conscious that if they were wiped out and the Germans got beyond the minefields, there would be simply nothing to stop them. But now it really seemed as if he had no choice. Reports came back in confirming that the Panzers were doing real damage and — as there were no reports of any other major thrusts at the Red Line anywhere — it was apparent that this was indeed the real focal point of the German attack, and there were unlikely to be other surprises elsewhere.

So Morshead made the decision. He sent in seven Cruisers and five tanks — specifically designed as anti-infantry tanks — to hold off the Germans and prevent them from skirting around the southern edge of the minefield and coming east again. In the furious battle that ensued, the Tobruk garrison lost two Matildas and two Cruisers were destroyed, with another Matilda severely damaged, while the Germans lost not just four tanks badly damaged but, crucially, momentum and morale.

It was far from an Allied victory, but the critical thing was that the Germans had been delayed, giving the garrison time to set up other defences. It was in much the same spirit that Morshead now took an even harder decision: to send in both the 2/48th Battalion from one side and the 2/23rd's D Company with carrier support (including Corporal John Johnson's carrier 'Walwa') from the other, to try to regain the ground that had been lost.

It was a move far from assured of victory, and Morshead knew full well that he was sending some of his men to their deaths — following the action of the morning by the 2/24th Battalion, a devastating 314 men were now missing — but in this crisis the Australian General's instinct was very strong that the most imperative objective they should try to achieve was to put the Germans back on the defensive at whatever price.

Even at the price of more men's lives . . .

•

For Rolf Völker, with his fellow soldiers of the Schützenregiment 104, there was much confusion. Just ten days earlier they had been freezing in the ice and snow of a singularly cold April in Germany, and now they were here in this hot and dusty hell on earth, trying to hold on to their hard-won territory of Ras el Medauuar. Confusion. Men going forwards, backwards. Machine-gun fire. Artillery shells. Roaring tanks in the gloom. Ours or theirs. Mercifully ours. News. Our men have been attacked. Many dead. No headway made. Mines everywhere. No breakthrough. Serious resistance. Australians ahead. Australians!?! What were *they* doing here? And instead of just resisting the German advance and trying to stop it, these strange men from far to the south were even *counterattacking*. This was not meant to happen. Men killed. Good men. Killed. How could they survive when, as the common expression among them went, '*die Luft ist eisenhaltig*' — the air contains iron. Rolf did not like it and, as he would later note, '*ich hatte Schiss*' — I was scared shitless, '*Ich war kein Held*' — I was no hero.

The worst of it was that there was so little cover in these conditions. Bullets and bomb fragments really were flying everywhere, and each and every one of the men would have taken shelter behind a blade of grass if there had been one — but there was nothing. All they could do was scratch whatever shelter they could from the desert and return fire the best they could. This was not like the Hitler Youth. This was not fun. This was not how it was meant to be. Somehow, in the middle of all the murderous madness, Rolf found himself thinking of his father. In the last war his father had been fighting with the Turks against the British, on the other side of the Suez, and now here he was fighting with the Italians against the British on this side of the Suez. All to what purpose? His father had never recovered from his own experience and had died just three years after the war was over, shortly after Rolf's birth. But would Rolf make it even that long? This was *verrückt* — crazy! He was sure he was fighting on the right side, for Hitler and for Germany, but not so sure whether this was the right place to be ...

To survive it all, some soldiers tried to carefully think things out. To Rolf's mind, they were the ones who died. He followed his instinct. Move quickly, head down, move again. All the drills they had done in their training helped to guide those instincts. But those who tried to move within the realms of conscious thought were sometimes paralysed by choosing an option, pausing just long enough to become a target. Move! Move! Move!

•

Robert Menzies got nowhere. When, at 10 Downing Street that night, the Australian Prime Minister broached the subject of the general inadequacy of the War Cabinet, Churchill couldn't agree more. 'You see the people by whom I am surrounded,' he growled, 'they have no ideas!'

Menzies gave up. There was nothing for it but to begin his long trip home to Australia, via America and New Zealand — acutely conscious as he was that he had precious little to show for the well over three months that he had spent away. And he was not the only one who had noticed, with his colleagues in the United Australia Party/Country Party Coalition Government, the Opposition, led by John Curtin, and, most damaging of all, the Australian electorate all becoming more perturbed by the fact that decimated Australian troops had had to be evacuated from Greece on an ill-conceived Menzies-backed venture, while other troops were under siege at Tobruk and looked to be only just holding on. In the Australian Federal Parliament, Labor MPs had hurled accusations that the British were guilty of 'cold-blooded murder' for sending Australians to Greece without sufficient weaponry or accompanying troops. The cry went up that Australian soldiers should 'never again ... be allowed to fight in such unfavourable circumstances'.[17]

And all of that while the likelihood of Japan entering the war was increasing by the day, and when he got home Menzies would not be bringing anything or anyone to defend Australia with. Not for nothing would there begin to be stirrings that Menzies was not up to the office he held, and that he needed to be replaced ...

•

In Tobruk it was now just gone dark. In the entire day of hard fighting, using considerable resources, the Afrika Korps had expanded its holding by only another five posts — to give them fifteen in their hands on the western perimeter — and now held a 4500-metre front to a depth of about 2700 metres on what had previously been the garrison's territory. The battle lines had now stabilised to the point where the newly acquired German territory was clearly marked out in the shape of half a football. This described, in Morshead's eyes, 'a salient', which is how those days in early May became known as the 'Battle of the Salient', and the area itself as 'the Salient'. This expansion of territory was all to the good for Rommel — but it had come at a considerable cost. Between them the Axis powers had lost 167 soldiers Killed in Action, a crippling 574 wounded, and they still had 213 Missing in Action, presumed killed or captured. They had twelve tanks destroyed as well, not to mention countless guns and huge amounts of munitions from a rare resource that was fast running out. Things were tough.

•

And getting tougher ...

As a matter of fact, back among the survivors of his own Panzer tank squadron, the same Lieutenant Schorm who just two days previously had noted in his diary his desire to help himself to some of the Australians' presumed stockpiles of Chianti would now be happy to get out of Tobruk with just his life, let alone getting his hands on some damn fool drink.

For, trying to inch his tank forwards along the southern perimeter in the late afternoon, looking for a way through that no longer seemed to be there, Schorm felt a rising desperation. No matter that the Afrika Korps had air superiority throughout, with their dive-bombers and twin-engined fighters bombing and strafing those who would try to stop them — still the British kept throwing tanks at them.[18] And then, when the planes had gone, the British artillery had started firing on them; and in all the dust and fading light, it was now next to impossible to work out who was friend and who was foe. All Schorm knew was that shots were coming from everywhere, their lives were on the line and they didn't even know who to fire upon to try to get out!

Suddenly, his radio crackled to life with a message. The initial breach the Afrika Korps had made in the Tobruk defences was now under attack, meaning they were in danger of being trapped inside the former perimeter. With the other Panzers, Schorm turned and raced back towards the gap ...

•

Desperate to claim back what had been lost, Morshead decided to send in the 2/48th Battalion to recapture the posts that had fallen.

Their Commanding Officer, Colonel Windeyer, was appalled when he received these orders, and said so. His battalion had no time to prepare a proper counterattack, no artillery support available, no tanks, and it would be a job even to gather his battalion in the one place at the one time — dispersed as they were along the Blue Line — let alone launch a serious attack.

At least he succeeded in getting Morshead on the phone, at which point the General laid it on the line.

'Listen, Windeyer,' he said, 'it is important that this be done, and done today.'

'That is impossible, sir,' Colonel Windeyer replied with some force.

'Why?'

'My troops are spread across miles of the Blue Line, and we just won't be able to get them to the start line on time.'

'Well, we will send trucks to enable you to do that, but I insist that it be done.'

'Very well, sir, so long as the trucks arrive we will be there, though I also request that we have tank support.'[19]

Morshead promised he would send whatever tanks he could after they had finished their actions on the southern perimeter, and there the conversation ended. Then Windeyer got cracking on his end, while Morshead did the same in Garrison HQ, ensuring that the 2/48th received the transport they needed.

Just after 7 p.m., the 2/48th had gone in to counterattack, with support from the 2/24th Battalion's B Company. Their mission was to recapture no fewer than 4500 yards of the perimeter now held by hardened German troops, a huge order for such a small number of men at the best of times, and these times were far from that. But they had been given their orders, and now got on with it.

Alas, alas. No sooner had the 2/48th got to its 'start line' in the last rays of the sun that evening than the German artillery atop Hill 209 simply lobbed shells down upon them, and continued to do so no matter which way they moved. From their exalted height, the Germans really could see much of Tobruk, meaning that it was nigh on impossible to launch a surprise attack on them, and every yard of advance would have to be paid for with lives.

Still the Australians kept going, despite suffering terrible casualties.

Again, in the midst of that maelstrom, it was frequently not clear to either side just who was who, and whether if you fired on a figure or form or flash in the dark you might not be getting one of your own — but what was clear was that the Australians did have at least partial success.

Lieutenant Schorm knew as much when, later in the night, he and his squadron of Panzers received one more urgent message: 'Australians have penetrated the defences between R1 and R7. Immediately counterattack and cover with tanks.'

He related in his diary:

Wireless message: 'Ready for action.' Oh hell! Where to? No idea. Italians argue and gesticulate wildly. I start by going as far as the gap, then turn right. No officer knows the position. Near R7 an Italian tank is burning. The Australians have gone back leaving 26 dead behind them. The Italians are absolutely in confusion. They have been under heavy artillery fire. Of 150 men occupying R7, there are more than 100 dead or wounded.[20]

In fact, the Australians had gone back. Despite their enormous courage and tenacity in continuing to advance against the overwhelming firepower ranged against them, the upshot was that the 2/48th was getting so badly shot up that it was soon clear that regaining all of Hill 209 was simply out of the question, and trying to hang on longer would have seen them all but entirely wiped out.

Further north, Corporal John Johnson and his men were soon once again in the thick of the action, with German bullets clattering off their armour. Their specific task was to try to retake the posts that had been lost overnight on the northern end of the breach that had been forced, as well as to provide relief to those posts in Australian hands that were still holding on. John Johnson's job, as well as commanding the vehicle, was to keep the heavy Vickers gun constantly in action, and give covering fire where he could. In that maelstrom of mortar and machine guns, it would only have taken one stray bit of metal to take out the man from Walwa and ... yet, somehow he survived it.

Overall, the counterattack on the Germans by Morshead's men had great benefits, despite their great losses. While the Germans had given their all to stop the Australians retaking the captured posts, they had been forced to abandon plans to expand the territory they had already secured, meaning that all of their momentum had been lost.

Whatever else, Morshead and his men had come a long way from Neame's prediction of just five weeks earlier that 'The 9th Division will never be a useful instrument of war'.

That certainly was not the view of the mauled Afrika Korps, who were now concluding that Tobruk might be a very tough nut to crack indeed. As expressed by Lieutenant Schorm in his diary that night:

> Our opponents are Englishmen and Australians. Not trained attacking troops, but men with nerves and toughness, tireless, taking punishment with obstinancy, wonderful in defence. Ah well, the Greeks also spent ten years before Troy.

The toughness of the garrison was a common theme, with another German tank commander being singularly frank in his assessment: 'What we experienced in Poland and the Western Front was only a promenade compared to this.'[21]

•

Ah, Poland.

If you cried, you died. Usually, with a bullet to the head.

For to cry was to show weakness, and the SS guards had specific orders to exterminate those who were too weak to go on working. Many of the Jews who had been rounded up in the purges in those countries occupied by the Nazis would be exterminated as part of Hitler's 'Final Solution', while others were just worked to death. In the Polish ghetto of Lodz alone, the Nazi occupiers opened no fewer than ninety-six factories, while elsewhere, all over occupied Europe, a similar system swung into operation. The Jews and other undesirables in the camps — including Gypsies, homosexuals and any who had shown resistance to Nazi rule — were taken every dawn to the factories, where they were forced to work at the point of a gun.

One such worker was a woman by the name of Rose Besser, a Jewess who was forced to work twelve-hour days putting the timing devices into German bombs at a munitions factory in Peterswaldau in Lower Silesia — the part of Poland that had first succumbed to the German invasion. Her work camp of 1300 female prisoners was ruled by female SS guards who ever and always showed a special bent for sadism, which sometimes included cutting back even further on the two slices of bread and bowl of watery soup that daily just managed to keep them alive. For Rose, each day was a nightmare of simply trying to survive, to keep working, with the only reward looking forward to returning to the barracks she shared with 250 other girls, where she could at least get some precious rest in a freezing bunk with straw for a mattress. Heating was provided by a single stove in the corner. Those who fell sick were removed from the barracks, taken first to an isolation room to give them some chance of a quick recovery: but if they did not recuperate, they were taken out of the camp and shot. Under such circumstances, resistance to the Nazi rule was almost unthinkable, but some exceptionally courageous prisoners of Rose's ilk would find a way to weaken the Nazis in their own fashion ...

Others though had no chance at all and, in 1941, perhaps the grisliest task of all for some prisoners at another camp in Poland, called Auschwitz, was to be forced to build a series of enormous ovens ... though at least they would be spared from knowing what those ovens would shortly be used for.[22]

•

There are lulls before the storm, lulls after storms, and in hurricanes and wartime even lulls during storms ...

It was just such a lull that descended on Tobruk in the early hours of 2 May, after the 2/48th had withdrawn, as both the attacking and defending forces spent the rest of a difficult and yet essentially quiet night preparing for what would surely be an enormous battle when the sun rose. And yet, the following day, the storm that resumed was not a man-made one of artillery shells, tanks and bullets, but a far more powerful one, of nature. The following morning the khamsin that hit — the Afrika Korps called it a *Sandsturm* — was so powerful that it all but entirely shut down all offensive operations from both sides. Launching attacks on each other was now out of the question. Rather, it was about getting through the next torturous minute, hour, day — trying to extract oxygen from air so filthy that it was like trying to breathe through a dirty blanket. In fact, though, even had the soldiers been capable of continuing, there was little chance their weaponry would have answered the call for long.

For, as both sides had soon learned, all artillery in such conditions had to be well covered because their mechanisms simply clogged up in thirty seconds if they weren't. You couldn't fire them even if you wanted to. These terrible conditions also exacted a heavy toll on the German tanks, particularly, and they were constantly breaking down.

So now both sides spent an uncomfortable day, with effectively only the Afrika Korps mechanics being able to make some limited headway in recommissioning some tanks, while among Morshead's men the khamsin allowed some precious time to lay yet more minefields at likely points of German penetrations, as well as bring some more anti-tank guns forwards.

•

In the meantime, in the Australian 4th General Hospital, down by the harbour, where his condition had suddenly worsened after he'd stopped some fragments from an explosive bullet four days earlier, one soldier, Private Allan Brines of the 2/15th Battalion, was suddenly moved from Ward 1 to Ward 4 — which was full of wounded Jerries, many of them with various combinations of legs and arms missing. Already feeling wretched, Allan became worried when, with even the slightest pause in the sandstorm, the Luftwaffe started dropping bombs around the place; but the Jerry in the bed next to him told him not to worry, as there was no way the Luftwaffe would bomb a building like this with a big Red Cross on the roof. And the German proved to be right, at least on this particular occasion, as, although there were plenty of bombs, none actually came close to the hospital.

The two got to talking, helped enormously by the fact that the Jerry spoke very good English, courtesy of a mother who was Canadian. Now, notwithstanding the fact that the medical care being extended to the German soldier was every bit as good as that being received by Private Brines, the Jerry confessed to being mightily annoyed at all of the Australian soldiers.

And why would that be?

Well, he explained, the German soldiers *had* to be there shooting at the Australian soldiers; they had no choice in the matter. Joining up with the armed services in Germany was compulsory, and the best you could hope for you if you didn't enlist was to end up in a concentration camp. So they had no alternative but to be in this godforsaken place shooting at the Australians. What, he wanted to know, was the Australians' excuse? Didn't Allan understand that this whole war was a problem between the 'Big Heads' of England and Germany, and that there should be more understanding between the workers of the different countries — and if that were so, there would be no more wars?

No, Allan didn't understand it to be all quite like that, but was very interested to hear the Jerry's perspective and careful to note the whole conversation down in his diary that night.[23]

•

It was on the road just outside Derna. Being escorted by German guards, Ivor Hancock and sixty-odd other Australian prisoners were in the backs of trucks, heading to another prison camp, when suddenly the road ahead was filled with the roar of powerful motorcycles. Almost as one, the guards and prisoners looked up to see a company of the Italian elite Bersaglieri Unit heading towards them — each man resplendent in an astonishing sun helmet with an enormous cockade of black rooster feathers coming out the top. At the moment of passing though, the lead motorcyclist and Commanding Officer of the unit recognised the cargo as Australian prisoners and — in an action which seemed designed to impress the Germans — made an extremely vulgar gesture which involved clapping his left hand down on his biceps, as his right fist was thrust upwards. Superbly trained, the troops behind did the same thing and the result had to be seen to be believed. First one, and then another rider wobbled — then one went down and they all went down, all over the road! For an instant the whole thing resembled a fowl yard after a dingo had just been through, with black feathers flying everywhere and general chaos. Of course, all the Australians burst out laughing, and first one German guard did too, then another, then all of them — and in no time at all Germans and Australians were roaring with laughter, the war forgotten for nearly a minute until composure could be regained . . .

•

In the midst of such crucial battles, with the fate of the entire garrison perhaps hanging in the balance, Morshead's position was excruciatingly difficult. He was acutely conscious that, based on his decisions, some men died and some men lived; some children became fatherless while others would be born in years to come because their fathers survived now; some women would become instant widows while others could be down at the docks in a few months' time looking up to the crowded decks for their loved one, and finding him; while some mothers would look for their boys in vain ever after.

These were not easy things to bear, but bear them Morshead did, with perhaps some comfort being gained from the fact that, due to his own wartime experience, he was never asking men to do what he had not done himself in the last war and, on that matter, had done time and time again. This was *war*, and while it was deeply regrettable that men died, he took the view that the only way to justify the sacrifice of the fallen was to make sure that they had given their lives in the cause of a great victory, and not a miserable defeat.

So, despite the losses that had been taken by the 2/48th two nights before and the difficulty of sending in yet another counterattack, he had reluctantly come to the conclusion that his forces would make another attempt to throw the Germans from Hill 209. Certainly, some of his senior staff in this position had respectfully counselled that the best thing to do at this point was to cede to the Germans the territory they had won, and pull back to the Blue Line behind, but Morshead would not hear of such a thing.

'I could not listen to these counsels of fear,' he told Chester Wilmot a short time later. 'We will never yield a yard unless they take it from us.'[24]

With that in mind, on the morning of 3 May, Morshead ordered the men of the 18th Brigade to prepare to counterattack that evening. His plan was that, while the 2/9th Battalion attacked the fallen posts from the south, the 2/12th would do the same from the north, while the 3rd Battalion of the 18th Brigade, the 2/10th, would complete the barrage by attack from the east.

Ideally — if all went absolutely perfectly — the two battalions would meet in the middle and isolate those members of the Afrika Korps who had set up well inside the previous perimeter. The Salient, then, would effectively be 'pinched' off.

•

Again, however, though the 18th Brigade fought valiantly and continued to follow orders and see through the attack, by half past three in the morning — when it had become abundantly clear that the plan hadn't worked — Morshead called it off, and by dawn the survivors of the 2/9th and 2/12th were back behind their lines, less the ten men killed and twenty-four missing they had left on a battlefield now deeply soaked with blood.

In fact, after these first three days of fighting the Australians had lost some 800 men killed, wounded and captured, while the Germans and Italians had lost some 954 of their own number. Yes, the Afrika Korps had captured some territory, but one German officer who was under no illusion that it was anything other than another bleeding wound in their side was General Paulus. Outside Tobruk, on the evening of 3 May, Paulus — after insisting to Rommel that the whole attack be called off — cabled a message through to General Halder in Berlin that 'the Tobruk operation must be regarded as terminated', as the gains made had been so inconclusive and the troops were now in bad shape.

•

At Morshead's headquarters, meantime, the mood was generally upbeat, despite the thwarted attempt by the 18th Brigade to reclaim the Salient.

Yes, they had ceded to the Germans some minimal amount of ground on the edges, but the main thing was they had *held them off*. If the area possession of the Tobruk garrison was roughly the shape of half a football, then what had been won by the Germans was no more than a minor dent in it — about 3 square miles of the total 134 square miles held by the garrison — and in any case there was a great expectation that the football would fill once more as they hurled the brutes out again.

In any case, the Powers That Be were under absolutely no illusions as to the importance of what Morshead's men had achieved.

In a stunning moment for the General, shortly after this second major battle for Tobruk was over, he was handed a cable on 7 May:

> To General Morshead from Prime Minister England.
>
> The whole Empire is watching your steadfast and spirited defence of this important outpost of Egypt with gratitude and admiration.

And Robert Menzies, still en route home to Australia, took a similarly laudatory view in his own cable to Morshead the following day:

> I have been watching with pride the magnificent performance of you all at Tobruk. Against odds you are, I believe, putting up a fight which will live in our history and I am confident that you will win. I feel it is a great honour to be not only your Prime Minister, but your friend. Please convey to all ranks the greetings and thanks of Australia.[25]

This was, in fact, a bit of the good news that Menzies needed right then, as he already knew that the political times he faced when he got back to Australia were likely to be very troubled indeed. The same day the Prime Minister had sent the cable to Morshead, the Opposition Leader, John Curtin, had spoken strongly in the Advisory War Council — a bipartisan body designed to unite Australia's policy on defence before it emerged into the public domain — to the effect that as Opposition Leader he vehemently opposed further Australian troops going to the Middle East. Curtin had thought it wrong-headed from the start, was pessimistic about the chances of the British Empire holding on there and bitterly critical of the fact that Menzies had clearly not succeeded, on his trip to Great Britain, in getting Churchill to put more of Britain's fleet into Singapore. Broadly, Curtin was more than ever concerned about the possibility of Japan entering the war, and while he accepted that the defence of Britain was of paramount importance, he questioned whether 'this should be wholly accepted from the point of view of requirements of Australian defence'.[26] As in, why are our men in such a precarious position defending essentially British interests when our own country looks to be in an increasingly shaky defensive position and our men have already been decimated in Greece and Crete — suffering a shocking 8000 casualties in those campaigns alone? (One of those casualties, entirely anonymous to Menzies but dear to family and friends, was the same Jack Tully who had warned Elizabeth Edmondson how much Jack was suffering with asthma while in camp.)

In such a political environment, any serious blow falling upon the Australians in the Tobruk garrison would have been devastating for Menzies, and he was keenly aware of it — perhaps the more so because he had himself been in Tobruk only shortly after the Australians had taken it from the Italians, so he knew how vulnerable it truly was.

Very much aware of those stirrings, Menzies wrote in his diary as his plane winged home 'neath the dark skies of the Tasman Sea, that the 'sick feeling of repugnance and apprehension ... grows in me as I near Australia. If only I could creep in quietly into the bosom of the family and rest there.'[27] Nor was this terribly downbeat feeling something he bothered hiding. At his first press conference when once again on Australian soil, he gave fair vent to such feelings.

'I come back to Australia,' he declared, 'with just one sick feeling in my heart, and that is that I must now come back to my own country and play politics. I think that it's a diabolical thing that anybody should have to come back and play politics — however cleanly, however friendly — at a time like this.'

Well, he was just going to have to get used to it.

CHAPTER FIFTEEN

The Diggers Dig In

Es ist noch nie ein Meister vom Himmel gefallen.
There has never been a master who has fallen from the sky.

A GERMAN EXPRESSION MEANING 'DON'T GIVE UP!'

Today you and I are not only part of history, we are history in the making.
For years we have enjoyed, almost without effort, almost without thinking,
freedom won for us by others who endured; treasures of art and letters not
painted by ourselves; free speech and enfranchised thought earned by
unknown heroes in forgotten days. Today, the guard and safety of all those
things depends on us. The heritage of the ages is in our keeping. We are not
creatures of Destiny, but Destiny itself. Without us all that is decent and
kindly and holy will perish from this earth.

EXTRACT FROM A GHQ PAMPHLET REPRINTED IN 2/48TH NEWS SHEET

How is the position of the front line determined in any given battle? Essentially it is situated at the point where the power of the attacking force to move forward is roughly equal to the power of the defensive force to thwart any such progress. When those forces are roughly equal, the front line is stable. When they are unequal, it moves.

On such a key military dynamic did the fate of Tobruk now rest in that first half of May 1941. Rommel's men had forced the defences of the garrison right to the point where Morshead's men had at last been able to stop them, and both sides were now digging in furiously and rushing reserve forces forwards. In Rommel's case this was to secure the ground that had been so hard won with German lives, while Morshead was still determined that the Germans would not only go no further, but also be hurled from the ground they had stolen.

One of the battalions called in to hold the line was the 2/13th, who relieved the 2/1st Pioneers in the second week of May and took over the earthworks they had been constructing, all of it done at night.

Theoretically such constructions had to be undertaken in as near to absolute silence as possible, so as not to give away your general position to any artillery that might care to lob a few shells down on their heads, but this was not always possible ... for either side.

As a matter of fact, it is recorded in the 2/13th Battalion history that, as the battalion was taking up its position on the edge of the Salient, the Australians became extremely conscious of the fact that, as while they were doing everything they could to keep quiet, one of the enemy working parties just a few hundred yards away was using a wheeled tool that kept putting out very irritating squeaks. Finally, one 2/13th B Company man could bear it no more: 'Standing on the edge of his fire position, he cupped his hands and let forth a stentorian bellow, "For Gawd's sake, grease that bloody barrow!"'[1]

But, no joking, the Germans knew soon enough that a different kind of battalion was on the job when the dawn came. Before leaving, the 2/1st Pioneers — whose speciality was constructing things rather than occupying front-line positions — had advised the 2/13th lads that a favourite trick of the Germans was to have some of their soldiers stand up out of their trenches and shake their blankets at first light, to tempt the Australian soldiers to have a shot. Then, when they did, the Spandau gunners would open up on yers — so just be careful, hear?

The 2/13th, with a death's-head grin, thanked the Pioneers for the advice and made their own plans. The following morning, at the first flush of dawn, sure enough instead of the sound of a sparrow farting came the ugly chatter of the Spandaus and before their very eyes were German soldiers, within range, shaking their blankets out, practically daring them to have a go and give away their positions so the Spandaus could find them.

The 2/13th didn't have to be asked twice. From their lines came the crack of rifles of Australian soldiers who had been waiting for just this moment — bugger the Spandaus, they had positioned themselves so that they had both maximum protection and freedom of fire — and they didn't miss their marks. German survivors slept in dusty blankets thereafter, because that was the end of blanket-shaking in broad daylight for the duration. Unlucky German soldiers, though, were wrapped in those same blankets, beneath the sod, for ever more. A singularly aggressive tone on the front lines of the Salient had been set, and it was the 2/13th who helped establish it.

•

Back at Walwa, they were holding a 'Diggers Ball' — to properly send off to the AIF some newly recruited local soldiers — and right in the middle of it there was real trouble. It started with one of the Coughlan boys, Ian — a big, strapping fellow who, although he had not joined up, still saw fit to attend, and plenty of folk took a dim view of that.

As a matter of fact, someone had already taken such a dim view of his lack of service that they'd anonymously sent him a white feather in the post, suggesting that, as he was obviously a chicken, the feather must belong to him. Coughlan was far from happy about it, and may have been looking for trouble from the start.[2]

Now, precisely what happened just after ten o'clock — when the beer had flowed freely and everyone was loosened up — was subsequently the subject of much dispute, but there were three basic versions, each with the same outcome. The first account was that Ian Coughlan had propositioned the attractive Josie Johnson on the dance floor, knowing that her husband had been away a long time ... and she had responded by slapping him hard across the face. The second was that Josie had accused him of cowardice for not enlisting and given him the slap across his face as a rather appropriate exclamation mark to her previous remarks. And the third was that Coughlan had accused her of sending him the feather, which she had strongly denied and given him the same kind of exclamation mark for good measure. Whichever way it happened — you'd never believe it — the following day Coughlan marched down to the police station and had Josie charged with assault! Walwa was in an uproar.

That wasn't the end of it, though. As soon as Josie's father-in-law heard that Coughlan wanted to go on with it in a court of law — a big, healthy bloke not brave enough to serve his country in war but still happy to seek the defence of the law from the small slap of a soldier's wife whom he had propositioned — he knew what had to be done. He had to do what his son John would have done, had he been there and not fighting and proudly serving his country in North Africa ...

Ol' Pop gathered his horse from the top paddock, harnessed her into the gig and drove off to the butter factory where Coughlan worked, intent on giving him a good thrashing.

Coughlan wouldn't come out, however, and the factory people ordered Johnson senior off the premises. Not to worry: the town school teacher, Mr McMillan, said he was the man to do the job, and was as good as his word. Cornering Coughlan up behind the hotel toilets a few nights later, he gave him a hiding he would never forget.

Still Coughlan didn't drop the case.

•

Life on the front lines of the Salient settled into a kind of unreal, deadly pattern where the nightly struggle was to survive, dig and kill — not necessarily in that order.

Daytime was rather more problematic, as both armies slumped back, exhausted after the exertions of the night, while still keeping up a constant flood of fire on anything that moved on the barricades opposite, and the sun beat down relentlessly. In such circumstances, lying in shallow depressions that could all too easily become shallow graves if you got your head just a centimetre above the parapet, with whatever meagre water supplies that had managed to get to the front lines, the only thing to do was to lie motionless all day long. (The weird thing, under such circumstances, was that after just a couple of drops of something like water, your whole mood could lighten and change — whereas in the old days at home it was quite possible to knock back six cold schooners of beer and still feel morose.)

Not the worst of it all — though it was close — was the indescribably putrid smell that hung like a shroud of cloud over both armies, due to the fact that many men on both sides were suffering from dysentery, and that all too often the dead bodies of soldiers lay stinking and bloating in the sun just a small way in the *Niemandsland* — no-man's-land — that separated them.

Strangely, on the Australian side of things, despite the conditions being so awfully tough, there was little whingeing. The bulk of the men had been raised on the legend of Gallipoli, and the general consensus — as a frequent topic of conversation — was that the blokes at Anzac Cove and thereabouts had probably done it tougher. See, at Gallipoli they'd had the Turks firing right down upon them from on high, all the time, and even if you wanted to take a crap you had to go up and down these great bloody big hills, see? At least their immediate terrain was fairly flat, and at least they were defending a strong position and not attacking like the Aussie soldiers had been doing in Turkey in the last war. Things were grim, sure — but they could have been grimmer, so let's soldier on!

•

In their own front-line positions with the 2/13th, Bert Ferres and Bill Walmsley had more or less settled in the best they could and got down to business. Directly opposite them, about 250 yards away, was a German shooter they nicknamed 'Spandau Joe' for the fact that his bloody Spandau — set up on a tripod, with pretty much only its death-spitting barrel showing above the surface — just about never seemed to stop, and they both swore to do him down if ever they could get a bead on the elusive brute. At night Spandau Joe used tracer bullets, and blokes reckoned they were so thick going overhead that you could bloody well read a letter by them.

Spandau Joe was going to be a tough enemy to take out, but Bert and Bill at least got busy on the task, using their Bren gun during the night and sniper rifles during the day. Bert, particularly, was by this time an expert marksman and, crucially, possessed the extraordinary patience required to keep his rifle trained on the German positions for hours at a time, looking for the tiniest sign of careless movement that would give him a chance to kill them for their trouble — without being killed himself as he fired the shot. Many was the time he would squeeze off a shot and just a split second later Spandau Joe would send bullets flying just inches over his head. Other times, Bert would send sniper fire just a whisker above Spandau Joe's position in the vain hope that he would nail him when his guard was down and his head momentarily up. To try to stop Joe seeing what their own position was at night, Bert and Bill set up a system whereby they put two bayonets stuck upright in the ground just in front of their position, with a sandbag slung between and the muzzle of their gun just behind, with the flashes hopefully being hidden from Spandau Joe. Alas, in no time at all the sandbag had caught alight, meaning that Joe was all over them in an instant, *pouring* in the fire. Hmmm. What about if they pissed on the sandbag first? Bert and Bill tried that with, alas, much the same result, except that this time it took a little longer to catch alight . . . with a terrible stench now filling the trench . . . and to top it all, Joe gave them an even bigger cheerio this time!

Ultimately neither succeeded in killing the other, but did horrible damage to opposing ranks just the same.

During those long days, Bert didn't even stop to have a drink from his water canister, preferring to bury it as deeply as he could in the sand beneath him, to cool it down so he could enjoy it in the evening. With every confirmed kill — and he had several in those middle days of May — Bert would carve a notch into the butt of the rifle.

Observing this, his Sergeant advised him against it on the grounds that if the Germans ever captured him and saw the notches, they would be sure to exact a terrible revenge instead of merely imprisoning him — but Bert refused to stop the practice. Though he'd only left Australia a little over six months earlier, and had only really seen action for the first time six weeks before, he was an entirely different man now to the mere seventeen-year-old boy he had been in Sydney. These days, no one questioned his young age any more. He was a soldier of the 2/13th Battalion and that was all there was to it, and a damn good soldier at that. His standing with the rest of the blokes hadn't been hurt from the beginning by the fact that he was one of the few to give his cigarette rations to mates — Bert had been too poor back in Australia to pick up the habit — but those free cigarettes had little to do with the respect he was held in now. Some blokes shrank in front-line positions and some blokes grew. Bert Ferres, for all his still-youthful visage and slim physique, was one of those who grew — not that he even particularly knew what his mates thought, or took any pride in it. He was too busy looking for careless Germans and making more notches in his rifle butt.

•

All up, the only living things that were truly joyous in those parts at this time were the fleas, who never worried about anything so constricting as front lines but simply went everywhere all the time.

On your face, in your kit, down your shorts, in your socks — everywhere. Slapping them provided some satisfaction, but made absolutely no impact on their general population. Sometimes, in desperation pure, both the Diggers and the Germans would set fire to a few gallons of diesel on the floor of their dugouts, thinking that would fix the pests, but ...

But if anything there were even more of the little bastards after such exercises than before, almost as if they were attracted by the distress signals and gloried in them.

Thousands of them? No, by now there were *millions* of them!

•

And yet there were other, very real, distress signals going up at this time, of an entirely different calibre. For one who had been less than impressed with the way the Germans had launched their second major attack on Tobruk was General Paulus, who, despite having personally approved the attack, filed a report noting the grim situation that the Afrika Korps found itself in. Not only had it not gained a lot of ground in the Battle of the Salient, it was now critically short of both fuel and ammunition.

'The crux of the problem in North Africa,' Paulus cabled to the German High Command in Berlin, 'is not Tobruk or Sollum, but the organisation of supplies.'

The reality was that the Afrika Korps needed 24 000 tonnes of supplies a month just to survive, and another 20 000 on top of that to go on the offensive[3] — and in that merciless desert it was simply using up a lot more than was coming in. It was the view of Paulus that Rommel — a *Schwäbischer Dickschädel* (pig-headed Swabian), as he referred to him in private correspondence[4] — was simply too impulsive, keen to attack whatever the cost, and unless he was reined in he would be a great drain on resources needed for a major, forthcoming campaign.

The German High Command put the Paulus report together with Rommel's own cabled report on the Battle of the Salient — though the latter was careful to fudge a little, saying 'casualties cannot yet be assessed' — and reacted immediately. A blistering rebuke was sent to Rommel to the effect that he must halt his wild attacks and strictly adhere to the limits that had been laid down for him. It was completely unacceptable to sustain the losses he had, and he must be under no illusions that he would soon be able to replenish what he had lost in terms of either men or materiel.

Both cables were deeply embedded in the code that had been embraced by Germany just before the war, and sent out on the special machines used for such transmissions. As explained by German author Wolf Heckmann: 'The Enigma apparatus contained a number of cylinders, which could be turned in relation to each other and contained all the letters of the alphabet. Before a message, "in clear" was fed in and the drums were turned according to a pre-determined key. Provided the recipient of a radio signal knew how the cylinders were set at the transmitting end, his appropriately programmed Enigma receiver would turn the macédoine of letters into a clear text, and at lightning speed.'[5] Put more simply, if you typed a word like 'HELLO' into the keyboard then the letters — say, AZRWK — would be generated, depending on how the cylinders were set. At the receiving end, with the cylinders set to the same code, the Enigma machine would turn AZRWK into HELLO.

Fortunately for the Allied cause, these communications, like so many others, were effectively snatched from the skies and, still in code, sent to the Bletchley Park manor northwest of London. Here those same eccentric mathematical minds who had been working in secret for months — referred to by Churchill later as 'the golden geese that never cackled' — went to work on cracking the code, using what in later years would be looked back upon as the great granddaddy of the modern computer, until bit by bit the essence and even precise detail of the message became clear, together with all the other communications that were similarly being daily decoded. After being examined by expert assessors — whose job it was to sift through the mountains of transcripts in order to work out the importance of each item, and who on the strictly controlled list should be advised of its contents — these communications quickly found their way to both Churchill at 10 Downing Street and, in this case, shortly thereafter to Morshead in Tobruk — in the latter instance brought to him by an emissary from Cairo who made a special trip so as to not risk their own message being intercepted, thus letting on to the Germans that their code had been cracked.[6]

•

Wonderful. On the strength of this intercepted report, Churchill formed the view that Rommel and his Afrika Korps were indeed on their last legs, and if they could just be attacked in the right place and at the right time — yesterday — they might very well collapse. Churchill was quickly in contact with Wavell, requesting him to mount an immediate counteroffensive.

With *what*, then, Prime Minister?

Churchill had already taken measures to fix that. Against the wishes of most of the Admiralty, he had insisted a couple of weeks earlier that an enormous supply convoy, code-named 'Tiger' — bearing 295 tanks and forty-three Hawker Hurricane fighters — be sent directly from Britain, through the Strait of Gibraltar and *across the Mediterranean*, where German submarines and Italian destroyers prowled, to Alexandria to be placed at Wavell's disposal. As opposed to sending the convoy all the way down around the tip of Africa and then up through the Suez Canal, this journey would shave just under six weeks off the trip, even if it was a whole lot more dangerous.

•

It had been an extremely dangerous trip, of extraordinary nature. On the night of 10 May 1941, having flown in his Messerschmitt 110 all the way from Germany, Deputy Führer Rudolf Hess had come out of the clouds over the east coast of Scotland and proceeded to navigate the best he could from the roads and rivers he could see below in the moonlight. Hess, the Hitler loyalist to beat them all — or so it had seemed — was on a stunning mission, apparently without the blessing or even knowledge of Hitler (though there would later be great speculation on that matter). Now nearing his destination and realising that there was no landing ground where he had hoped, he parachuted out of the plane, letting it crash-land, and tumbled from the heavens into the field of a Scottish farmer by the name of David McLean.

Having heard the crash of the plane, McLean ran out to find a disoriented pilot with a parachute trailing behind.

'Who are ye?' McLean asked plainly. 'British or German?'[7]

With no hesitation, Hess replied in thickly accented English that he was German. Nevertheless, he said he was 'not an enemy Nazi, but a British friend'.

What could McLean do? He took the pilot back to his house and offered him a cup of tea. Once a little more composed, the strange man asked to be taken to see the Duke of Hamilton (whose path he had crossed five years earlier, at the Opening Ceremony of the Berlin Olympics in 1936). McLean thought it rather a better idea to bring in the Home Guard, two of whom promptly arrived and — though both were reeking of whisky and one was wildly waving around a World War I pistol he had with him — took the foreigner into custody and began to question him. After a cluey officer of the Royal Observer Corps, Major Graham Donald, arrived a short time later and joined the questioning, the Home Guard pair was incredulous when this officer asserted that the man they had before them was none other than Rudolf Hess, Deputy Führer of Germany!

Whoever the man was, he insisted he was there on 'a mission of peace', and continued to request that he be taken to speak to the Duke of Hamilton. Bit by bit — most particularly when the stunned Duke duly arrived the following morning to have a private interview with him — it all came tumbling out ...

The stranger acknowledged that he was Hess, said that he had met the Duke at the Berlin Olympics five years earlier, which is why he had sought him out, and that he had an important message to impart. He maintained that Hitler didn't want to destroy Britain at all — he only wanted hegemony over the nations that lay substantially to the east of Germany. Hess desired the Duke — whom, he had understood from intelligence in Berlin, was an opponent of Winston Churchill — to facilitate his meeting with a group of British parliamentarians that would not include Churchill (for both Hitler and Hess thought the British Prime Minister was a warmonger) and he hoped something could be worked out!

Unlikely.

When the Duke of Hamilton finally managed to get to the Prime Minister that night, Churchill was holding court at a dinner party in a sixteenth-century mansion just outside Oxford. Ushered into the magisterial presence, the Duke was asked by Churchill to say what it was that was so urgent that he had been interrupted in this rather irregular fashion. The Duke begged to offer that it was of the nature that it would be better if he divulged it to the Prime Minister alone, and was soon enough with Churchill and just one other: Sir Archibald Sinclair, the Secretary of State for Air, who had been at the dinner party. He began the story.

As detailed in Peter Padfield's book on Hess, the Prime Minister was understandably enough 'rather taken aback' by what the visitor was claiming.

'Do you mean to tell me,' Churchill said slowly, 'that the Deputy Führer of Germany is in our hands?'

The Duke of Hamilton said that was exactly his impression, and followed this up with some photos he had brought with him, for Churchill to judge for himself. Both Churchill and Sir Archibald agreed that it did indeed look rather like Hess, but Churchill wasn't about to let that alter his plans for the evening. He had guests, and they had been promised a film.

'Well,' he finally said, handing the photographs back, 'Hess or no Hess, I am going to see the Marx Brothers!'[8]

And so he did.

In Germany, Hitler followed the advice of his Propaganda Minister, Joseph Goebbels, and released a message writing off Hess as a madman who had acted entirely on his own.

So, on the face of it, what could the British authorities do once the identification of Hess was confirmed?

The obvious. Having now under lock and key the Deputy Führer of the very nation they were at war with — a co-architect of the many atrocities and acts of aggression they had sworn to fight against, and who clearly now had no authority to negotiate on behalf of Germany — they effectively threw away the key.

In the meantime, though, the emotions aroused around the world by Hess's flight were extraordinary. In Walwa, Josie Johnson's heart soared. It was possible, just possible, she told her children, that the war was coming to an end, and Daddy would be coming home!

•

Despite heavy air attacks, the Tiger convoy did indeed arrive in Alexandria on 12 May, having lost 'just' one transport carrying fifty-seven tanks and eleven Hurricanes. The most important thing was that some 250 tanks had got through, meaning that Wavell would have strong

ABOVE The high-velocity German 88-mm gun, designed as an anti-aircraft weapon, was at Rommel's behest used against British tanks. It proved to be master stroke, and the British forces were devastated. At one point, a captured British Tank Commander complained, 'It's not *cricket* to use anti-aircraft guns against tanks.'

BELOW A Panzer Kampfwagen II light tank with a 20-mm cannon, hit by a 'Molotov cocktail'. The tank weighed nearly 10 tonnes, carried three crew and had a range of 200 km. Due to its light weight, it was often used for reconnaissance. **INSET** German tanks leaving a trail of destruction and desperation.

ABOVE After being captured by Australian soldiers, Italian POWs headed off to their makeshift prison camp. Australian soldiers were staggered by the number of luxury items, such as coffee percolators and silky white handkerchiefs, that the Italians left behind them.

LEFT Coffee for a British POW. Prisoners from both sides were usually treated well by their captors in this 'war without hate', and in field hospitals Allied and Axis doctors often operated side by side, focusing their attention on the most in need of medical attention, without regard to nationality.

ABOVE The Australian Prime Minister Robert Menzies at Tobruk shortly after its initial capture by the Australians early in 1941. The fact that he had seen Tobruk himself, and its tenuous defences, always made him slightly pessimistic about the chances of the Australians holding it against a determined Axis attack.

BELOW The author's father, Peter McCloy FitzSimons, who was with the 9th Division from its formation, took this photo while he was with his Ack-Ack unit at an AIF training camp in Palestine, late in 1940.

ABOVE Tobruk, October 1941. Lieutenant General Morshead with General Kopanski, the Commander of the Polish forces in North Africa. There was great respect and friendliness between Polish and Australian forces at

Tobruk. **BELOW** This 1000-pound bomb fell 20 feet from an anti-aircraft gun post, and mercifully didn't explode. The bomb was made in Czechoslovakia, using slave labour, which sometimes nobbled its product. One such 'bomb' was found to contain concrete and a note saying 'Good luck to the Czechs'. **INSET** Lord Haw-Haw in action.

ABOVE The first reaction of many new arrivals in Tobruk was 'Is this what we are fighting for?' Yet before Tobruk the Axis forces had never lost a battle; after Tobruk they won very few more.

ABOVE A woodcut showing Allied soldiers leaving Tobruk via ships in the harbour, just visible by the starlight — and yet not the tiniest sliver of moon, as such exercises were always carried out on moonless nights for fear of Axis bombers.

RIGHT Always after the battle, the Germans carefully buried their dead comrades. The palm leaves on this dead soldier's grave indicate he was a member of the Afrika Korps, whose badge also featured a palm leaf.

Deutsche Reichspost

Aus dem Felde 45/44 a. 15. 10. 44 15.34 Uhr

* 42 Telegramm

15. 10. 44 19.00 Uhr

Ulm Schindler

Amt Herrlingen

Telegramm des Führers

An Frau

    Lucie Rommel

Herrlingen bei Ulm Donau.

Übermittelt
16.10.44 19.30

Herrlingen Schindler

Nehmen Sie zu dem schweren Verluste den Sie durch den
Tod Ihres Gatten erlitten haben mein aufrichtiges Beileid
entgegen. Der Name des Generalfeldmarschall Rommel wird für
immer mit den Heldenhaften Kämpfen in Nordafrika verbunden
sein.

          Adolf Hitler.

ABOVE After Rommel's death, Adolf Hitler sent a cable to Rommel's widow, Lucie, 'honestly' regretting her loss. He wrote: 'Take my honest sympathy for the heavy loss which you have suffered through the death of your husband. The name of the Generalfeldmarschall Rommel will be for ever connected with the heroic fights in North Africa' — Adolf Hitler.

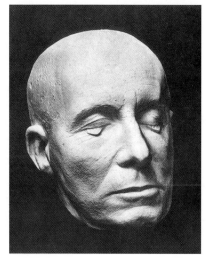

LEFT Rommel's death mask.

ABOVE In 2005 Rolf Völker travelled to North Africa and laid flowers at the Tobruk war memorial (a model of which stands in Sydney).

LEFT Lieutenant General Sir Leslie Morshead died in late September 1959, just a few days after turning seventy. His funeral was the biggest ever seen in Sydney, with his coffin borne on a gun carriage through streets lined with tens of thousands of people. Among them were thousands of the Rats of Tobruk, with one noting, 'He was the greatest Rat of them all.'

ABOVE Jack Edmondson was the first AIF soldier to receive the Victoria Cross. His grave is in Tobruk.

resources in reserve for the major operation he had planned against the Afrika Korps a few days hence.

In Tobruk Harbour that day, the gunboat HMS *Ladybird* was not as fortunate as most of the fleet in the Tiger operation. Caught at the western end of the port in broad daylight when a wave of Luftwaffe bombers arrived on a raid, it was all but immediately sunk as much of the garrison looked on, powerless to do anything. Still, just before abandoning ship, her captain, Lieutenant Commander Blackburn, signalled Lieutenant General Morshead, 'One wicket down for Yorkshire, nine more to go yet. Play up Australia, we will catch them on a sticky wicket.' Morshead replied: 'Great innings by *Ladybird*. Sorry that it has ended. We will beat them on any wicket.'[9]

And yet the courage of those British seamen, at that time and at that place, had to be seen to be believed.

An Australian soldier from the 2/15th Battalion by the name of Pulsford was there when some of the survivors were brought ashore, and later recounted: '*Ladybird* was an old friend of ours. Her work up and down the coast had earned her a great name among all the troops, and many times we had heard the shells from her guns screaming over our heads to crash into the Hun positions outside the perimeter. But no more — for today her end was near ... We ran down to the beach and watched those men from *Ladybird* being brought ashore, many being carried with great pieces of skin and burnt flesh hanging from their chests, arms and legs ... One giant of a man was standing there stripped to the waist with a great hole in his side from which the blood was running down his body and legs to the ground. In a clear calm voice he turned to the others and said, 'Never mind, mates, we'll have another bloody ship next week.' I turned away from this little group of men blasted and burnt and dying but still possessed of a spirit that could not be crushed by bombs or fire. And to me these men will always represent the men of His Majesty's Navy, possessing the calm courage that is beyond description.'[10]

•

Another day, another long letter.

This one was written on 13 May, and though Josie was careful to make only an oblique reference to what had happened with Ian Coughlan at the dance — as she knew it would upset John so — there was no such reticence about the love she expressed for her faraway husband, just as she had in every letter she ever wrote to him, as he did to her. She finished this letter with that love in full flow:

All our boys send their very best love and are writing to catch Friday's air mail, so look out …

My darling your baby girls just adore their Daddy. Sylvia gets your photo and shows it to Josie Jacqueline and says 'here's your Daddy.'

Darling I love you so, love me and the world is mine. Goodnight my darling.

From your adoring wife,

Josie.

Goodnight my love.

Sleep tight my love.

'Remember,' I am yours, 'Always.'

Darling forever I'll Remember.

'Til the Lights of London Bloom again.[11]

The following day, John Johnson began his own letter to his family,

My Dear Ones at Home.

All well still I hope as I am OK at present. I received your letters Sylvia & Des & Len and was so pleased to hear from you & hope you will all write again. Fancy you going to school Des. Isn't that great you must be growing like anything. Good old Don also got a beaut haircut from Mum. It would be a beaut but don't tell Mum I said so. Ha! Ha! I can't barrack for any particular 'house' in the school sports either Barry but I hope you had a good day & you all won. I have a few more coins to send home & will first chance …

And finished it …

How are my baby girls getting on. My dear Sylvia Rose & my little Josie. The snaps of her were lovely & I think she is a dear little chicken. Isn't she big & such long hair …

Love to Gran & Dad & remember to all our relations & friends.

Tons of love to you all from your ever loving Dad.[12]

And so the Tobruk days settled. Broadly, from the crystal clarity and crispness of each cold dawn, the climbing sun brought with it such a shimmer of arcing heat that the features of the more distant desert landscape melted into each other, and stayed like that until the sun began to sink quickly into the Mediterranean once more, at which point every physical thing regained its own shape from the shimmer and stood clear in the quiet desert twilight.

Too, the power of those conditions was such that, as detailed in the 2/17th Battalion diary, they 'imposed a degree of regularity on siege arty programs, for only in the early mornings or late evenings could guns be ranged onto targets by observation, or the effectiveness of their fire be gauged. As each new day dawned, the guns of both sides saluted it and, as it departed before the oncoming night, they saluted it again.'

By this time, many of those urgently dug holes of five weeks earlier had been expanded and made far more comfortable. If you were really lucky and could keep digging down, it was sometimes possible to make a little cubbyhole — just like when you were kids, but better — and get some iron bars over the top on which you could put sandbags, and live an all but entirely underground existence. You could pop up, fire off your shots through the slits you'd left in the sangar for that purpose, and then head back underground when the artillery fire came to find you or the Luftwaffe left its usual calling card of big bloody bombs hurtling down.

After the bombers had left, the Australians would emerge from the trenches, do their best to clean up whatever damage had been done and go back to what they had been doing in the first place: sweltering. At least there was apparently some chance that they would shortly be relieved ...

•

Alas, 'Operation Brevity', as the planned action to relieve Tobruk by land was called, was not destined to go down in the annals of British history as one of the greatest feats of arms that the Allies had known. The plan was for the operation to be launched on 15 May, and so to capitalise on the happy joint circumstance: while Winston Churchill had General Paulus's word for it — and beautifully decoded at that — that Rommel and the Afrika Korps had been terribly weakened by the Battle of the Salient, the Allies were suddenly flush with newly arrived tanks which would give them the reserves they needed, once they were all unpacked and made operational.

In broad brush strokes, the plan was that while the forces of Brigadier General William Gott would push to the west from the Egyptian frontier at

Sollum with the aim of securing Fort Capuzzo, which lay just over the border, Morshead and his men would make a feint of breaking out of Tobruk and attacking the Afrika Korps from the west, thus hopefully soaking up some of the German heat before getting safely back behind the Red Line.

And yet, even though the orders for Morshead were issued on 8 May, the vagaries of communication between Cairo and Tobruk were such that the Australian general didn't receive them until the afternoon of 13 May!

Still, Tobruk did what it could.

On 14 and 15 May, Morshead ensured that there was considerable radio chatter coming out of his garrison, in the manner of an army that was stirring itself for action. More importantly, on the morning of 15 May he ensured that there was a constant movement of tanks and trucks just within the perimeter, as if they were about to launch on a great breakout, firing hard on the Axis forces outside their perimeter, just as they had done at Mechili ...

That part of it might even have worked — but the thrust of General Gott did not.

Almost effortlessly, it seemed, Rommel's forces skilfully parried the thrust and shot up the enemy armour, and the British were obliged to withdraw from Fort Capuzzo the next day, managing only to hold on to the Halfaya Pass. At least for the moment ...

•

As Rommel had now twice been thwarted in serious assaults on the Tobruk perimeter, it was obvious that winning the campaign in North Africa would require a long haul; and of the many things that would have to be organised to accomplish it, making that long haul easier was paramount.

In the presence of Schmidt, Rommel was briefing a senior officer who had just joined his staff, and was giving him what he considered to be a crucial assignment.

'What would you say to a proper road — round Tobruk? Then we should not miss the coast road through the port which those damned Australians now deny us.'[13]

The plan was greeted with enthusiasm, especially by the Italians, who quickly set to with a will, using their own engineering skills and the manpower of their troops, most of whom were more than happy to trade a rifle on the front line for a shovel in the desert. (And whatever else, as Schmidt dryly noted, 'There was an ample supply of stone in the rocky desert, and no especial shortage of sand.'[14])

Following the rough outline that Rommel had drawn on the map, the road quickly started to take shape in a wide loop around Tobruk, with a particularly significant point being a small knoll called Ed Duda, about 20 kilometres southeast of the Red Line. Rommel's basic plan from this point was that, once the road was finished, he would build up his forces and supplies from the Halfaya Pass at the northern end of the Egyptian border — he even then had plans to recapture the pass from the British, and expected to launch his troops within a week — to Sidi Omar, about 40 kilometres to the south. With a broad mine belt in front, that would be his basic shield against an attack from Egypt — further ensuring the isolation of Tobruk, which he could then reduce without fear of being attacked in the rear.

Rommel had also decided he was going to need a change of personnel, and embarked on something of a purge of senior officers whom he felt were simply not up to it — starting with none other than General Streich. Streich was to be sent 'on his camel' back to Germany.

In the process of dismissing the entirely unmoved General, Rommel said, 'You were far too concerned with the wellbeing of your troops.'

Streich replied, with no little dignity: 'I can imagine no greater words of praise for a Divisional Commander.'[15]

And then he went. He was, however, to have the final word with his superiors in Germany. Back in Berlin, the extraordinarily suntanned officer was interviewed by the Army Commander in Chief, Oberbefehlshaber Walther von Brauchitsch, who, surveying a bulging folder of correspondence and reports from unhappy officers in North Africa — including reports from Rommel — came to the point.

'Was it so hot down there that you all just got on each other's nerves?'

General Streich replied, pointedly referring to the difference in the role played by Rommel in one World War to the next: '*Nein, Herr Feldmarschall*. But one thing's got to be said — there's a big difference between being a brave and adventurous Company leader and a Field Commander of great genius.'[16]

•

Christ.

Real trouble. Early in the morning of 17 May, one of the 2/23rd's companies had launched an attack to try to relieve their besieged comrades in Post S9, but it had gone badly wrong. Some of the soldiers were trapped, pinned by heavy fire, and needed help in a real hurry. Just after seven o'clock, John Johnson and the rest of the crew of the 'Walwa' carrier, with

Jim Swinton as the driver and Vern Scott as the third crewman, received orders to go forwards, to evacuate the wounded.

They went, and were soon not too far from the forward position, the pings of bullets off their light armour telling them that at least the enemy didn't seem to have heavy anti-tank weapons — for the moment. The German machine-gunners and snipers situated on the escarpment overlooking S9 had, however, clearly won the day, insofar as whatever Diggers were in the area were clearly keeping their heads well down, if they were alive at all.

The carrier crew were able to pick up one walking wounded, and get him safely inside the carrier, but that was it. Still, S9 itself had to be checked to see if there were Australian wounded inside, and John Johnson took responsibility for the task the only way he knew how — which was to leave the relative safety of the Cruiser and get into the post itself. He did so without mishap, while Jim Swinton kept 'Walwa' circling the post until John re-emerged, to make sure they would at least be a moving target if there were still snipers in the area. There he was . . .

Post S9 was empty, and John Johnson had now come out, so Jim drove the carrier over towards him. Everything was, suddenly, remarkably still, as if they were the last men left on earth. Only a light wind had been flickering across the desert, but now it too had dropped to nothing, and everything was as silent as the grave.

At this moment, somewhere in the position higher up on the escarpment about 500 yards away, a German sniper took careful aim as John climbed back into the carrier, and drew a bead.

The sniper squeezed the trigger and one can't help wondering, under the circumstances, precisely what his emotions were at the time that the shot was fired. Was it agony, or were his feelings much as those of Ivor Hancock a fortnight earlier in roughly parallel circumstances: 'Nothing. The moment passed and only that man's friends and relatives would feel something.'

In any case, the bullet hit John Johnson in the spinal cord, just below the neck line, severing the cord, but not killing him. He fell back onto the desert, his face to the skies. Jim Swinton and Vern Scott jumped from the vehicle to retrieve him, but a hail of machine-gun bullets all around instantly stopped that plan. What to do? Jim quickly jumped back into the carrier and manoeuvred the vehicle so it was between John and the direction they thought both the sniper shot and the machine-gun fire had come from, and this time the plan worked. They were able to scoop John up and get him into the carrier, before racing back to the nearest aid post, which was known as Fig Tree for the fact that it was situated in a cave beneath just about the only living thing in the entire area — a massive fig tree . . .

John was still alive when they got there, and still able to speak.

'Look after my family . . .'[17] he said before lapsing into unconsciousness. In such circumstances, the Army doctors in the Regimental Aid Post had to make tough decisions. With limited resources, they had to try to save only those who could be saved, and ease the passage of those who couldn't. One look at John's wound and they knew he had no chance. He was given a dose of morphine to ensure there was no pain and, shortly afterwards — even though he had been put in a 4-ton armoured ambulance and sent to a better-equipped hospital back towards the harbour — John Johnson, beloved husband of Josie, devoted father of eight children then being tucked into bed in the cottage in Walwa, died.[18]

He was buried that evening just as the sun went down, which was around the same time as his great friend, and fellow Walwa man, Pat Joy, was also killed while trying to retrieve some wounded in his carrier. In turn their great mate, Alan Kelly, was also killed on this day. They reckon that Alan had been so game that in his attack he had overshot Post S7 and had gone as far as Post S4 with his men before being overwhelmed by the German counterattack. Alan had lost his life fighting a rearguard action to let his comrades get away — and yet his own body was so terribly blown apart that there was nothing left to bury where he would likely have preferred to have rested, near his mates Pat and John.

At the end of that devastating day for the 2/23rd Battalion — with twenty-five killed and 140 other casualties — there had been no change in the position at the Salient. They had neither lost, nor gained, ground.

•

The conversation was just winding up.

'*Jawohl* . . .'

. . .

'*Nein* . . .'

. . .

'*Danke schön* . . .'

. . .

'*Auf Wiederhören* . . .'

On this afternoon of 19 May, in his office based in a massive bunker in the heart of Berlin, General Franz Halder put the phone down after an extremely upsetting conversation. On the other end of the line had been General Friedrich Paulus, just returned from North Africa. Paulus, himself dismayed by what he had to impart, told Halder that he had just talked with *Generaloberst* Alfred Jodl, the Wehrmacht Chief of Operations and confidant of Hitler, and had been firmly told the Führer's view on one particular matter was paramount. That was, whatever else happened, Hitler did not want Rommel to be hampered in any way by any Berlin directive.

General Halder could barely believe it. Somehow, despite everything, Rommel still enjoyed the Führer's confidence! How could it be?

(The answer, in essence, was that, just as Rommel could not stand the timid restrictions placed upon him by the General Staff, Hitler also found them extremely annoying, and had an innate sympathy and admiration for Rommel's front-line derring-do and willingness to attack no matter what. This admiration for Rommel was such that the situation for Halder soon worsened when, despite everything, Hitler made Libya the province of his own OKW, not the OKH, and promoted Rommel to command a newly constituted group, '*Die Panzergruppe Afrika*', of which the Afrika Korps was just the largest part.[19])

•

In and around Tobruk, then, the two armies faced each other, staring over their gun sights across no-man's-land, the minefields, the tank ditches and barbed wire, trying to work out just what the enemy was up to.

There were, yet, many differences between the German and Australian soldiers.

While the Germans were indeed marvellously equipped, superbly trained and prepared to be carefully calibrated cogs in an extraordinary fighting machine, they were still suffering terribly. For, as cogs, they were not at their best when suddenly changed conditions called for independent action and thought, rather than merely instant obedience to orders from on high. Nor was the German war machine, as it turned out, nearly so effective when it got the grit of the desert in it.

The Diggers, on the other hand, were generally hardy types, independent by nature, used to making it up as they went along and finding a way to get the bloody job done, even when the answer wasn't immediately apparent. The great Australian war historian C.E.W. Bean had written that a typical soldier in the previous war was 'A bushman in disguise, and if the wild pastoral life of Australia makes rather wild men, it makes a superb soldier.'[20] One generation on, nothing had changed.

In fact, for at least one observer, just looking upon the Australian soldiers was enough to create echoes of the famous story about what the Duke of Wellington had said when reviewing his troops not long before the Battle of Waterloo.

'I do not know what effect they will have on the enemy,' the Duke is said to have commented, 'but, by God, they frighten me.'

Plus — and this was no small thing — there was something in the psychological make-up of the Australians whereby they were never so strong as when they had their backs to the wall and were being pushed around by a bully who thought he had them cornered. Oh yeah? Well, cop *this*, mate.

In many ways the Germans couldn't quite understand the Australian approach. Like the Italians, they were stupefied that every Australian against them was there as a — can you believe it? — volunteer. And for the Australians' part, they just didn't get the German approach, which thought dying for their so-called bloody 'Fatherland' a high calling. None of the Australians was bloody well going to get his head shot off for nothing, and any German bastard who was going to try it was going to have to bloody *work* for it.

Yet even amidst all the killings, there was equally the bare beginning of a faintly fraternal relationship between the two armies, even if their primary intent remained fratricide. On one notable night, the Australian soldiers of the 2/13th could hear the Germans mockingly singing 'We'll Hang Out our Washing on the Siegfried Line' to them, and then laughing. How's your washing going now on our Siegfried Line, you Ossie bastards? On another night the Australians clearly recognised the wonderful melody of the Christmas carol 'Silent Night', which the Germans sang in their own language (which was, in fact, the language it had been written in). Not to be outdone, a Sergeant Major of B Company stepped up and sang the carol in his own manner — a magnificent baritone that rolled over no-man's-land and left no soldier untouched — as the Germans listened with what seemed like a reverential silence. Certainly, this shortly earned the good Sergeant Major a stern rebuke from on high, to stop 'fraternising' with the enemy, but no one cared. It had been a wonderful break in an otherwise bleak existence.[21]

And there would be at least a few more ...

For sometimes a weird kind of thing would also happen at around ten o'clock at night, when the Australians' 'tucker truck' would arrive to deliver the long-awaited evening meal. After the truck was parked a safe distance away, the tuckerboxes would be carefully carried forwards and delivered to the front-line positions. No one was quite certain who started it, but Bert Ferres would never forget it. The thing was, just before dinner was served, you'd quickly bang your 'Dixie' dish with your metal mug above your head in a split second, to indicate you were about to eat. If the timing was right, you'd hear the *ding-ding* coming back from the Germans, to indicate they were about to have their evening meal too, and both sides would knock off the war for half an hour or so, to have their din-dins.

And then, at least slightly refreshed, and with something in their bellies, they'd get back into the business of killing each other.

•

One of the things in the Diggers' favour was Leslie Morshead himself. Plucky, resilient, patient, he was born for leadership in such a static situation. Rommel, on the other hand — who was so devastating amidst all the confusion that occurred in open battle, who could hit and then hit again and again before hitting one more time from a flank that was completely unexpected — was not born for this exercise. Blitzkrieg was his forte, while *Sitzkrieg*, settling in for a long siege — was something that drove him to distraction. And the same could be said for his men. They were the Afrika Korps, either in the Panzers themselves, or Panzergrenadiere, trained to operate in the lee of massive machines that were perpetually on the move.

And while the German Army had indeed been well trained, the reality was that there was no training they could ever have done which would have prepared them for the horrors of holding their positions on that particular patch of ground opposite the Australians. At the point where the Germans were situated, the desert's massive underlying limestone base reached up to just a couple of inches below the sand — like a lurking monster of the deep — and it meant that every inch of trench literally had to be scratched into that monster's head. For the most part it simply couldn't be done to any depth, and that meant that the only way the soldiers could survive was to lie flat in whatever tiny shallow they had clawed out, and not move *a single muscle*, as the sun belted down all day, heating the air to the high 50s and the sand up to 75 degrees Celsius. In heat like that you even had to have most of your gun under your body — to protect it from the sun, because otherwise it would become too hot to touch and be totally useless if you were called quickly to action. Christ, it was uncomfortable.

Worse than everything? The black flies from hell that crawled all over them were craving exactly what the soldiers craved, which was moisture, and yet while the soldiers' own mouths felt like someone had left the Dead Sea Scrolls in them overnight for safekeeping, the flies found enough moisture there to crawl inside their lips for a drink. Of course then you'd scrunch down upon them and they would, literally, taste like *Scheisse*. (No wonder their doctors had determined that the flies were terrible carriers of all kinds of tropical diseases and infections that were cutting a swathe through the men. No wonder, either, that in those conditions apparently harmless scratches from the thorny camel bush simply refused to heal, turning into festering ulcers as the flies laid eggs in the tiny wounds.)

But not a muscle now. Any man prone to giving way and swatting one of the flies in the conventional manner risked instantly becoming a target for one of the wretched Australian snipers, and that thought if nothing else focused a man's mind uncommonly well. Come the night, at least they could move around a little — usually with everything fairly quiet, bar the odd punctuation points of some bomb-happy bastard firing impotently in the distance — but again the lack of a trench meant that the bitterly cold desert winds went right through them, chilling to the core of their core.

•

In short, Rommel and his men together were now like a champion boxer locked with a powerful opponent in a telephone box. The Germans and Italians had no room to manoeuvre — hated every moment of it, but there didn't seem to be any way out. All they could do was to keep hitting as best they could, and hope that their opponent would fall. And the trouble was not just that this opponent did not fall, but he kept hitting back — and hurting them.

For there was one thing Morshead made very clear to his men after those first two battles of Tobruk, and the expression of it came best after he had spied an article from a British publication with the headline TOBRUK CAN TAKE IT!

Morshead's response was immediate.

'We're not here to *take* it,' he thundered, 'we're here to *give* it!'

He meant it too. And so did the men. Neither Morshead nor his Diggers had any interest in just sitting there, waiting for the Germans to come at them, and they were much more disposed to getting out there and going at the brutes. They weren't going to simply consolidate their defences and give the Germans time and space to have another go at them; they wanted to get in tight on them and unleash some body blows of their own. They wanted to make sure, among other things, that Rommel was never close enough so he could launch an attack that was a complete surprise, nor so he could slowly, bit by bit, encroach on the garrison's territory. As Morshead put it in a subsequent conversation with Chester Wilmot: 'From the first day, I determined that no-man's-land would be *our* land.'[22]

So it was that from the beginning of the siege, but particularly from early May onwards, many, many patrols were sent out into no-man's-land on a nightly basis — to the point that every night at least half the men on the Red Line journeyed through the wire. Some patrols were purely for reconnaissance purposes: working out where the enemy's defences lay, what some useful targets might be and gathering information as to how many armed men they could expect to find when they got there. A bonus would be if they could bring back a prisoner — preferably a German one, as Italian prisoners were so thick on the ground it was already less of a problem of how to extract information from them as how to adequately feed them all.

Either way, it was then the job of the fighting patrol to take advantage of any information so gleaned and move out to kill and maim as many of the enemy as possible, as well as disabling any of its armaments that could not be carried away. But if they could be carried away then all the better, as German artillery was very highly prized — there being a special pleasure for the Diggers in taking guns that had been pointed at them and turning them around to face their enemies. (Seriously, there was no sweeter sound in the world than the sound of a German gun you had captured and then turned back upon the Germans.)

Such patrols worked well for the Australians on many levels. First, and perhaps most importantly, the patrols located enemy positions, enabling the Pommy artillery fire to have something precise to aim at.

Preparation for such patrols was painstaking, with most emphasis going on making the men as invisible and as quiet as they could be. Dark clothing and blackened faces and hands took care of the first part; but as to sound, the key was to ensure that nothing, but nothing, could clink against something else metallic when you were out there. In the frozen crystal night air of the desert, even the tiniest noise would travel an enormous distance, and with sentries in the night primed to listen, a single sound could mean the difference between a successful mission, and death and destruction.

Another consideration was to have the right footwear, either using specially designed desert boots with soft soles or, failing that, putting thick woollen socks outside your boots as well, so there would never be the crunch of stones sailing to a sentry's ears.

One other measure was crucial. While it was important for security purposes, in case of capture, to remove any personal letters or badges identifying your particular unit, it was even more important to ensure that the unique AIF sun badge on your lapel was there, free and unfettered. For the stories were already legendary of Australian soldiers in the dark desert around Tobruk thinking they were totally alone, then suddenly feeling a knife to their throat as another hand patted around their shoulder. Always, it was a member of the 18th Indian Cavalry Regiment — ghost-like in their capacity to move around silently at night, and devoted knifemen — and once the badge was found, everything was okay.[23]

'Australian. You go now ...' would come in a thick Indian accent, and then, like the Phantom in the comic strips, the Indian would suddenly disappear back into the dark night.

More than one Australian on the receiving end of such treatment wished he'd worn the brown underpants after all ... but those Indians were no joke, and they had completely terrorised the Germans, and even more, the Italians. (A story that circulated among the Australian soldiers, albeit of dubious authenticity, was very telling. The story went that on one occasion, finding three Italians asleep at their posts, the Indian soldiers quietly slit the throats of two of them while letting the third slumber on — the reckoning being that when he woke up he would have a story to tell the other Italian soldiers for *months* afterwards, which would ultimately do more for the war effort than killing him outright.)

And the Indians were proud of their handiwork, too. In their camp they had strung up a wire, and on the wire were threaded what at first glance looked to be dried and shrivelled bits of apple or somesuch, but on closer inspection proved to be human ears![24] And it wasn't the Romans who'd lent them an ear — it was the Germans and Italians. Dead ones. Every time one of those Indians killed a German or Italian, he sliced off the right ear of the corpse as proof of the kill — or as a souvenir. Who knew?

•

While the Australians never got into that kind of souvenir hunting, it wasn't long before they became extremely proficient in these patrols, right to the point where some of the more confident Diggers could even be blasé. On one celebrated occasion, a 2/23rd Battalion patrol had crept to within 100 yards of the enemy when a dog started to bark. (The Italians had recently introduced to their camps guard dogs — German shepherds, of course —

to give them some modicum of protection, or at least warning, against the wretched Australians.)

As recorded in the battalion history: 'Most of our chaps nearly had heart failure. They froze to the ground, expecting every moment to see the enemy come charging at them. Nothing happened, however, and after about ten minutes the dog stopped and it was deemed advisable to continue. Imagine the feeling of the platoon commander when he discovered that one of his men had fallen sound asleep, and had to be shaken violently by the shoulder before he could be awakened. "A fellow's got to make up his loss of sleep somewhere," he grumbled.'[25]

Each patrol filed a detailed report at the end of the night, noting precisely where it had proceeded and the information gained, all of which was tabulated on a constantly updated map at Battalion Headquarters, so that a precise view of exactly where the enemy was situated and what it was doing could be assured at all times.

During such patrols, the problem of navigation was an acute one. On a moonless night, on a surface as flat as a billiard table, there were no landmarks to steer by, and the only way you could get your bearing was by examining the stars, just as the first sailors had.

Still, once you got the hang of it in the northern hemisphere, it wasn't too hard. All you had to do was pick out the Big Dipper — which was about as easy as finding the Southern Cross at home — go a bit to the right of it and there you'd see the North Star, which was always pretty much due north no matter what time of night it was. On nights where there were no stars or moon, one simply had to keep to a straight course and count out precisely how many paces you'd gone before turning, and then trace exactly the same number of paces back. Despite all that, patrols certainly did get lost, in which case a different scheme would be worked out to help to guide them home. Some battalions had a system whereby when patrols were well overdue, they would fire a single tracer bullet skywards at regular intervals — though that wasn't good enough for the 2/15th. Its preferred method was to get one of its fellows, a keen saxophonist who had brought his instrument all the way to Tobruk, to stand just inside the Red Line and play a cheery version of 'Waltzing Matilda' or 'Roll Out the Barrel' into the desert night.

·

The German soldiers talked of it, always fondly, as *den Nordstern*, the North Star. Twinkling above the lip of the horizon, it was easily identifiable; always there, bright and cheery even in the middle of the coldest, darkest night.

And when you found it and looked towards it, you knew you were looking in the rough direction of home, and somehow that helped.[26] Most importantly of all, though, Rolf Völker and all his fellow soldiers found that the star was crucial for exactly the same thing as the Australians did — by following its unchanging bearings, you could always find your way back to your *Kameraden*.

•

Life settled down to an uneasy rhythm. During the day, it was time to either dig or sleep. During the blessed night, you could dig or go on patrol. Some of those patrols were out into no-man's-land, others went back and forth along the perimeter, making sure no other enemy battalions got through. A part of this latter kind of patrol was doing what was called 'love and kisses'. One platoon would move out from its post to go along the Red Line, to the point where the responsibility of another platoon took over. There it would see two sticks lying side by side (love). As a sign that the platoon had been there, the men would change the sticks to cross each other (kiss), and so the sticks would remain until the other platoon arrived and changed them back.

Love and kisses. If the other platoon arrived and found that the sticks hadn't been changed, that was a clear sign something was amiss and they would fix bayonets and carefully head off into the night to check that the other platoon was all right.

•

Have yers *heard?!?!*

They reckon there are some spies here at Tobruk?! Dinkum! There was this Australian Lieutenant, see, and he was always saying he was going up to the wire to observe the Germans, but a couple of the signallers got suspicious, followed him and watched him closely. They saw him sending flashes to the Jerries using a shiny tin, so they carefully wrote down a record of the flashes and took it back to HQ. Next time the bloke goes up to do this kind of caper, a single shot rings out and the Lieutenant falls down dead, shot through the heart from a place unknown, but they reckoned it was one of our coves who got him.

And there was another bloke caught like that, also spying for the Jerries, so they took him to a room, told him he'd been caught and left him in there with a revolver and a bullet, telling him to do the right thing. A minute later the shot goes off, and it was marked down officially as 'Killed in Action'. I'm telling you, it's dinkum![27]

What about Lord Bloody Haw-Haw, too? How do you think he knows so much about us, right down to what battalions are in here and who our Commanding Officers are? He's got someone inside here, I'm telling you! The other day when I was listening, he even knew when the reinforcements were arriving from Alex and what battalions they were joining! True!

Actually, no, it wasn't; however, such rumours flourished in an environment where not only was secrecy in all things important but Diggers spent many long hours of boredom staring at the desert, and any half-arsed yarn was often good enough to repeat and hey, why not, embellish, no matter if it lacked the tiniest shred of proof. Once the rumour was on the 'latrine wireless' they may as well have stapled it as solid news to the forehead of just about every hard-bitten bastard on the front lines — which was all of them.

Cairo was under attack from the Jerries. No, it wasn't; Tripoli was under attack from our boys and the Brits. They say that Rommel has been killed. No, they say that Rommel was actually seen through the field glasses of one of our observers just yesterday, standing in his car looking right at our bloke with *his* field glasses, but by the time we got any artillery on him, he'd bloody well scarpered! The Germans were apparently putting together thousands of paratroopers in Sicily who were going to be landing on us shortly and they were going to have specific orders to take no prisoners.

In response to such rumours swirling and counter-swirling, many battalions came out with their own news sheets — effectively small newspapers — in which not only were the goings-on of the battalion reported along with amusing anecdotes, et cetera, but also rough accounts of what the BBC news service had said the evening before in its nightly round-up of what had been happening in the war and around the world. You could follow what your mates in Greece, Singapore and Syria were up to. And what was happening at home? Was Menzies going to hang on as Prime Minister, or was that other cove by the name of John Curtin going to take over?

Known by the men as 'furphy-flushers' — with 'furphies' being the term used to describe the false rumours that were notoriously started by drivers of the water carts, made by J. Furphy & Sons, as they went from battalion to battalion in the Great War — the news sheets were an instant hit, and not just because they gave the soldiers the good oil on what was happening in other parts of the war as well as their own neck of the woods. For the rags also chronicled the day-to-day lives of the soldiers on the front lines, recounted great shaggy-dog stories, and whatever else the editors could come up with to fill them.

•

Another morning, another slew of reports that came in of damaging Australian raids the night before, creating havoc in German and Italian lines. Despite being upset at what was happening and the failure of his own troops to stop these incursions, the professional soldier in Rommel deeply respected the spirit of such raids, and at one point he commented to his adjutant, Lieutenant Schmidt, that the Australians manning the perimeters were 'the best of soldiers', and that perhaps the thing he most admired (as frustrating as he found it), was their ability to carry out ruthless reconnaissance raids night after night.

Still, he just couldn't quite fathom their extraordinary bravado at other times either. On one occasion Rommel was well forwards with Schmidt when one of their machine-gunners opened up on an Australian position.

'Our troops,' Schmidt recorded, 'stared in astonishment when one Australian coolly seated himself on the parapet and waved his broad-brimmed hat at us as a stream of machine-gun bullets splashed by ...'[28]

What manner of men *were* these?

•

Sometimes the furphy-flushers would offer up drawings of attractive women, in part by popular demand, and in part because it was maybe worth reminding these blokes that their existence on this earth really did have a lot more to offer than just bullets, brass, sand and latrine duty.

It was true that in a place like this a man's libido wasn't quite what it was once cracked up to be, but one thing was for sure: no one ever complained that too much of the rag was being taken up with these drawings and not enough given over to how well the Hun was going in Europe. Still, for some Diggers such illustrations weren't strong enough medicine and there was always a fairly brisk trade along the trenches of what were known as 'perv books': novels of fairly light pornography — often with such exotic titles as *Maidens by the Nile*, *Slave Woman* and *Bordello Bazaar* — that had been picked up in such places as Cairo and Alex, and carefully cached since, together with the '*feeeelthy* pictures' that still survived.

Well, a bloke had to pass the time in some fashion beyond just waiting for the next bloody attack, and for plenty of them reading perv books was

as good a way as any. Sure, after a while the thing started to lose its power
— and you'd be reduced to reading your cigarette packet, just for
something fresh — but then you could swap your dog-eared copy for
another bloke's, and so it went.

Not that the soldiers were without spiritual guidance, for all that. Each
battalion had its own Padre, and these individuals were generally highly
valued by the men — with one rider. In the words of one of the clerical
corps, after the war: 'They liked the Padre to be as straight in his talking to
them as they were in talking to one another. They were quick to sense
reality in a man's religion, and when they knew it was there they responded
to it. They did not carry a lot of useless theological baggage; such faith as
they had was real and vital . . .'[29]

Of all the Padres, one in particular was most popular. He was an old
Salvation Army fellow who used to wander around with a wind-up
gramophone and play music for the men, as well as always having a friendly
word. True, the Padre often received strange requests from the Diggers to
play the Egyptian national anthem — *ah, the memories!* — whereupon they
would sometimes get a rather glazed expression . . . but that was their affair.
(And, in fact, daydreaming about women at least helped to pass the time. As
recorded by one of the furphy-flushers, the following conversation took
place between two Diggers in late May, in the middle of a discussion about
what they would do when the war was over:

'Well, Blue, what's the first thing you'll do?'

'Have a coupla jumps.'

'Then you'll eat a slice of apple pie, I s'pose?'

'No fear — take me bloody pack off.'[30])

•

The increased firepower of the Ack-Ack notwithstanding, by early June
1941 the danger to shipping by the Luftwaffe was so acute that the only
way to keep it going was to move to night-time shipping only.

On any given night the ships of the 'scrap-iron flotilla', whose turn it was
to run the German gauntlet, would start loading in Alexandria at midnight
and then slip the surly bonds of the harbour just before dawn, doing 20 knots.
The aim was to be well away from the shore and prying eyes by sun-up. Into
the sea of blue they could then turn to the west, towards Tobruk, staying just
beyond the vision of the shore but feeling reasonably secure until such times
as they cleared the Allied front lines at Mersa Matruh. From that point on
they were more or less on their own and in enemy territory, with that

aloneness only occasionally leavened when one of their own fighter escorts would drone overhead. When those escorts left, the Captain would more often than not call to the engine room for full speed ahead, cranking up the old tubs to as high as 27 knots as they went on the terribly dangerous last 200 miles into Tobruk, of which the final 30 or so, down 'Bomb Alley' in the dark, were most hair-raising: the Luftwaffe patrolled heavily in those parts, snarling back and forth, looking for the phosphorescent wake made as the tubs churned forward, and swooping down accordingly when they found it.

For the men on those ships, it was a weird kind of thing to make your way into a harbour where, in the menacing moonlight, you could see poking from the waters the many masts and funnels of the ships that had passed this way before you, now standing silent sentinel to their watery graves beneath. Sometimes it was almost like an aquatic version of an elephant graveyard, a place where the big ships had come to groan and die. Eerie. And yet, there was little time to ponder on such melancholy thoughts because, as always, there was a need for *speed*.

Once the ship was into the jetty or anchored, the process of unloading would begin immediately, with the men on deck frequently passing the cargo hand to hand from the hold and throwing it down to the many willing hands below.

Say, hurry! The tiniest glimmer of light to the east which might signal the approaching dawn could push the ship's company into a complete frenzy, as they hurled everything overboard in their eagerness to get away, and strapped in tight those wounded or ill soldiers who were coming back with them.

Now the cargo hold was at last empty of munitions, the galley and cabins full of the new chums, and the skipper on the bridge was champing at the bit, straining his eyes to ensure that all was shipshape and ready to go. And now the reports came in.

'All secured for sea, sir!'

'Main engines ready, sir!'

'Right-oh, No 1. Thanks, Chief. Yeoman, make a signal to *Parramatta* — "Weigh and follow me out." Forecastle! Heave in! Cox'n, ring on the engines!'[31]

And then they would suddenly be away from the jetty, throbbing forwards, straining for the open sea.

All hands on deck and all else being equal, they wanted to be up to 150 miles away from Tobruk by sunup, and have only a few nervous hours to get through before an Allied fighter patrol from Mersa Matruh would come out and escort them back to safer waters. Usually then they could get in to

Mersa Matruh by about 2 p.m., so they could unload the wounded, load up the cargo hold once more and head back to Tobruk to do it all over again!

By co-ordinating their timing with other ships making the same run, it could be assured that most nights Tobruk would be getting some kind of a top-up in its supplies. And yet, even after the munitions, food and so forth had been safely deposited onto the wharves by Tobruk Harbour, there was still an enormous job o' work to be done to get the crucial supplies out to the front lines. Almost around the clock, a fleet of trucks ground its way down to those docks to be loaded up, whereupon they would growl and roar their way up the escarpment to any one of a hundred forward positions that might be assigned to them — and being obliged to take their chances with enemy artillery while still aware of just what sections of the road it was best to go full throttle on.

(One soldier would fondly long remember the instructions from the truck driver to him and his mates as they were about to be carried to forward posts across a patch of ground where German artillery fire was frequently heavy. 'So if youse blokes put yer heads down,' he said, 'I'll put my foot down, and we'll see how we go!' Jesus, they were game bastards.)

•

Despite all that effort and risk, however, it wasn't as if the end result for the Diggers on the front line was anything special. In fact, far from it.

For the Australians on the front lines, the staple during the day was one can of bully beef with twelve hard Army biscuits — and they really were *hard*. Like the gypsy recipe for owl soup that involved boiling an owl and a rock in a big cauldron of water and only removing the owl when the rock was soft, it was one thing to have biscuits, and it was quite another to be able to break them up into small enough portions to get them into your stomach. The best that could be done was to soak them overnight in water — or tinned milk if you were lucky enough to have any of that — mix it all up into a kind of porridge and call that breakfast. On a bad day, though, all you'd have was what the soldier's knew as a dingo's breakfast, which was a bit of a scratch, a bit of a fart and a bit of a look around.

As to more substantial evening fare, the base of this was the endless tins of M.V. (Meat and Vegetable), in which Australian beef killed long, long ago — in fact, quite possibly by Captain Arthur Phillip himself and the men of the First Fleet — was put together with what had supposedly once been carrots, peas and potatoes, but for now tasted for all the world like pebbles, mush and mud. But it did keep a man alive. Just. True, there was the occasional variation to this diet — if you were down by the harbour and had a spare grenade, you could throw it in and 'go fishing' by collecting the stunned fish, while up on the front line the only change was if you could shoot down an Italian carrier pigeon, which always tasted exquisite. In case you did get any food like that, or wanted to boil a billy, the system relied on a 'sand stove' — essentially, a 4-gallon tin of sand with petrol poured into the sand and lit. Not only did it generate a lot of heat, the best thing of all was that it emitted no smoke.

•

The Germans and Italians did little better. The common gruel for both armies of the Axis powers was cans of extremely tough tinned beef — mostly tendons and cartilage — marked A.M., nominally for *Administrazione Militare*, though the German soldiers maintained it really stood for *Alter Mann* (Old Man), while the Italian soldiers were equally convinced it stood for *Arabo Morte* (Dead Arab).[32] Together, they agreed it stood for *Achsenmist*, loosely translated as 'Axis shit'.[33]

There were also cans of sardines that some supply genius had thought would go down well in temperatures of over 40 degrees Celsius, but were in fact so inedible that even starving men found that the cans were more useful as lamps — simply by making a small hole in the lid, feeding in a wick which soaked up the oil and lighting it.[34]

The greatest deficit for both sides was in fresh fruits and vegetables; without them, diarrhoea and liver complaints were soon entrenched. Those suffering from the former could often be seen holding their stomachs as they made variably successful and unsuccessful dashes for the latrines, while those with liver complaints were frequently seen holding one side of their stomach only just above where their livers lay ...

•

It wasn't just the flies themselves, which continued to swarm in the millions; it was that nothing pleased the infernal insects more than weeping sores, particularly the 'desert sores' that were starting to show up on the bodies of the soldiers. The AIF doctors noted that they seemed to be most prevalent among those working in the field bakeries, men who were always in desperate heat, while the drivers and mechanics of the trucks, who were always covered in grease, barely suffered at all.[35]

(One point of debate among the Diggers was how to treat the sores, with some coves maintaining that the only thing to do was to follow

Australian male tradition by ignoring them entirely, while another group said it was worth using some of your precious water on them just to try to keep them a little clean and free from infection. The only thing that both schools of thought agreed on was that they wouldn't try the method used by the local Arabs, which was to piss on your own wounds . . .[36])

•

Though flies were also a terrible problem for the Afrika Korps, as were fleas, in the list of its hates neither of these came close to scorpions, mostly green ones and black ones. Though these dreadful little beasts weren't capable of killing, their sting was agonising and could throb for two days and nights before there was the slightest diminution of pain. The newly arrived Afrika Korps reinforcements soon learned that their first act, every morning, was to get their boots and turn them upside down, to make completely sure that their toes weren't about to give a scorpion its breakfast. Hence, a strange amusement that started to develop . . .

Sometimes, in what little downtime they had, the men a bit back from the front would get a big scorpion and put him on the sand, surrounded by a circle of a few dribbles of petrol, before setting the fuel alight. Always, the scorpion would charge around, looking for a way out, before realising that it was trapped. Then — and this was the good part — as the men would cheer at the climactic moment, it would sting itself and commit suicide.[37]

•

They were on fire. At least, the men of the Afrika Korps on the front lines of the Salient felt as though they were on fire, burning up beneath an African sun that pushed temperatures up to 55 degrees Celsius, with no relief in sight.

Wasser! Wasser!

Issued just half a litre of water a day, it was a classic example of the German expression '*ein Tropfen auf den heissen Stein*' — a drop onto a hot stone — and even in the evenings when the sun went down, thirst remained the main topic of conversation. A few of them, for example, had read books by the famous German writer Ernst Löhndorff, including *Hell in the Foreign Legion*, and passed on to the others a valuable secret therein: that simply by sucking on two or three little pebbles throughout the day, you could stimulate your salivary gland to produce a little more moisture for your mouth, and that seemed to work, at least a bit.[38]

Another Foreign Legion trick that was tried by the Afrika Korps was to set up your tent at night so that it would collect the dew, and though that helped minimally, it was of course all too little to meet their needs. While there were strict rules as to what kind of water they could and could not drink, in practice the Afrika Korps soldiers drank any kind of water they could get their hands on — right to the point that at, various stages of the siege, the thrill of capturing an enemy vehicle was not just for the vehicle itself, but for the water that could be found in its radiator ...[39] Similarly, after battles on the front lines with Australians, the most prized booty was neither their guns or grenades or bullets, but their water canisters.

And yet, sometimes, there was simply no relief. Rolf Völker was one of those soldiers on the front line driven half mad by the thirst, while others were driven fully mad and, after at last securing a canister of water, jumped to their feet to better let it roar down their throats — only to be shot on the instant by enemy snipers, now that they presented such an inviting target. Others drank their own urine in a vain attempt to find relief. Men died with throats and stomachs scorched by their own piss. This was not how it was meant to be.

Even at night-time there was no relief. In the desert dusk, the sun fell like a stone from out of the sky and down with it went the temperatures, falling to near freezing just hours after the sun disappeared.

•

All up, it was a good catch. One of the Australian patrols had captured a German tank commander by the name of Lieutenant Joachim Schorm, and he had with him a diary containing, in explicit detail, just what had happened on the German side of things during the Lieutenant's part of the Easter Battle and the Battle of the Salient. Once the pages were translated, Morshead devoured them for information, and was most heartened by their tone. As he wrote to his wife, Myrtle:

We cracked them a good deal harder than we thought. We knew that we had given the Germans a bloody nose but evidently we did more than that. Very encouraging and very satisfying. Still the German is game and I've no doubt that he will come again and adopting different tactics. Whatever he does and however he does it, he will get a warm reception and, I trust, a still bloodier nose.[40]

•

The decision was never in question. Whatever goodies — pouches of tobacco, socks, scarves, tins of sausages and camp pie, dried fruits and so forth — that arrived from the Australian Comforts Fund were to be shared equally between all the defenders of Tobruk, even the Pommies. Though it was quite true that the Brits didn't seem to have an equivalent to the Comforts Fund — nor the Indians, for that matter — the only thing to do was to make them all honorary Australians for the duration.

Through such gestures the warmth of feeling between the various nationalities in the Tobruk garrison continued to grow, based on a foundation of already enormous respect. Prior to the war, many of the Australians had never even met an Englishman, and tended to associate the race with such prickly characters as Douglas Jardine, who had captained England to Ashes fame in the Bodyline cricket series of a decade before. Jardine fitted well with the popular prejudice that the Poms were mostly a bunch of woolly wooftas with toffee on their noses, a plum in their mouths, and quite possibly a carrot up their bums; but, as the Diggers found, these blokes were not like that at all. Regular blokes — with funny accents, true — but by Gawd, they had some pluck in them! To see their artillery going at it even when under extreme bombardment, to see their tanks throttling forwards to the fray even when severely outnumbered, was to realise just what kind of guts they truly had. So, sure — when the ciggies and scones were handed out, the Brits had bloody well earned the right to be honorary Australians.

The attitude of the Brits towards the Australians was along the same lines. They were a seriously weird mob, these colonials, and there was no doubt about that. Firm friends referred to each other as 'bastards' while sworn enemies were '*real* bastards'; rank seemed a matter of complete indifference to them; and, generally speaking, in these circumstances their uniforms meant nothing to them. Apart from their shorts, most of them were naked much of the time, and there seemed to be surprising familiarity between officers and common soldiers — with a Private not only prone to ask a Captain if he had the makings of a cigarette, but the officer handing over the paper and tobacco if he had some, with no offence taken! True, when it came to things like what they called their 'tucker', the Aussies just couldn't be trusted: one British Ack-Ack battery was obliged to post a sentry every night just to guard its precious mascot, a sheep known as Larry the Lamb, from Australians who clearly had no affection for him whatsoever — and even *boasted* that they could have slit Larry's throat, gutted him, sliced and diced him, and had him sizzling on the barbecue in less than five minutes flat.[41]

But could they *fight*! The respect the Tommies felt for the Australians grew in tandem with the respect that the Australians felt for them, as they worked so hard to do Fritz down. The men of the 2/13th, for example, became particularly close to the men of the Northumberland Fusiliers, with whom they frequently fought side by side, and then often quartered beside whenever they were given a rest from the front line of the Salient and put in the Fort Pilastrino area. It was there that the relationship really developed, with the Geordies usually calling out jovially upon the very sight of the 2/13th men, 'Here come those Aussie Fookers!' or 'Hello, you colonial bastards!' To this the Australians would reply, 'You can't do without us, you Pommy bastards!' or sometimes 'Scottish misfits' for variety; but the warmth that grew between the two outfits was immense and longlasting.[42]

A similar dynamic came to operate at officer level, where initial suspicion soon changed to great respect. In one episode at this time, the King's Dragoon Guards sent one of their number, Lieutenant Williams, to join Lieutenant General Morshead's staff as liaison officer.

'Liaison officer from the KDG, sir!' he said as he presented himself to the Australian, snapping off a smart salute.

'KDG? What sort of a mob is that?' Morshead replied, looking him up and down.

'King's Dragoon Guards, General — raised in 1685, before Captain Cook first sailed to Australia.'[43]

It was the beginning of what would be a very strong relationship between the two.

•

Strangely, though, the relationship between the enemy combatants also continued to grow after a fashion. One night in mid June, Rolf Völker was on a detail with his fellow soldiers of Schützenregiment 104, doing what they did most nights — trying to thwart the continuing Australian patrols in their constant quest to steal back the posts that the Afrika Korps had won at such cost. It wasn't easy — it never was against the Australians, whom Rolf had come to admire for the great courage of their attacks and the fact that they somehow seemed to be *of* the desert and not merely *in* the desert like the Germans. (Ideally, the Afrika Korps themselves would have had the strength to attack the Australians, but simply didn't possess the numbers, so all they could do was defend against them.)

Suddenly, just down from where Rolf and his comrades were involved in a fearful *Schiesserei* (firefight), furious fire came from unseen assailants.

Rolf was personally okay and able to withdraw to the German lines with most of the others, but it was soon clear that there was a real problem. Not all of the men had made it back, and out of the night came the pitiful moans of the severely wounded who'd been left behind. Though it was a terribly dangerous thing to do, Rolf and seven of his comrades went out into the wan moonlight, spreading out to see if they could retrieve some of their own. And yet, it was one of those things ...

In the confusion of it all, the only man he and a couple of his friends could find was an unconscious Australian, and they had just put him on the stretcher to take him back to get medical help when they almost bumped into a handful of Australian soldiers on much the same mission! Sadly, the Australians were carrying, on a bit of tent canvas they had suspended between them, a dead German soldier. Somehow, though, the sheer humanity of what they were all engaged in overwhelmed everything else. Neither Rolf and his comrades, nor the Australians, made any aggressive move, though all were heavily armed, and had any of them gone for their guns or grenades, the likelihood was that there would have been a complete bloodbath. And yet, with every passing second as they all stared at each other, tension lessened. Soon enough, via hand signals, they arrived at the point where they were able to do the obvious, all without a single word being exchanged. That is, they swapped stretchers.

Now bearing the weight of one of his own, the closest of the Australians nodded his head and — after jutting one leg out to keep the stretcher flat — touched two fingers to his helmet as a kind of personal, but not military, salute to the Germans, and was followed in this by his mate.

Rolf and his *Kamerad*, bearing their own dead weight, returned the rough wave. A sort of understanding was emerging — yes, they were enemies on the battlefield, but when the battle was over they were first and foremost humans, acting in a hopefully humane way to each other.

Now, with a last unspoken cheerio, both groups returned to their own lines. For the next two hours, not a single shot was fired, ensuring that both sides had the time necessary to get their wounded away, and bury their dead ...

CHAPTER SIXTEEN

Manoeuvres Political

There they were, the German army, having more or less conquered all Europe,
yet the Tommies could not be driven from this tiny speck of Africa . . .

GERMAN HISTORIAN WOLF HECKMANN DESCRIBING THE POSITION
AT END OF MAY 1941[1]

Screwball tells us that when he was out on patrol the other night, he
spotted a dago on the skyline. He told the officer in charge of the patrol,
who said, 'Garn, it's only a petrol drum!' Nothing daunted Screwball
who came back a few minutes later and said 'Y'know that drum we
passed a little while ago?' 'Yes,' said the officer. 'Well, it's still there,
and it's talking to another one!'

FURPHY FLYER, 11 AUGUST 1941

Chester Wilmot was mightily annoyed.
He had just completed a very detailed, and savage, critique of the failed Allied defence of Crete — decrying the total failure of the British command to have prepared any fixed defences that the Australian and New Zealand forces could have fallen back upon in the face of the overwhelming German tide — only to find that his report had been CENSORED by that same British command!

And now General Wavell had read the report and Wilmot had been summoned to the Commander in Chief's office in General Headquarters. Of course the radio correspondent went immediately, as he was eager — apart from everything else — to meet the most powerful military figure in the Middle East. And yet, within seconds, he was profoundly disappointed.

This old man was Wavell? So short and stooped; so grey and jowly? One eye had been lost in action in the last war, lurking deep within its socket and an eyelid drooping over it, while the other just stared out rather unnervingly. After Wilmot sat down Wavell stood up, and paced back and forth, and talked — but not in the incisive manner that the ABC journalist would have expected from such a high military leader.

At least the Commander in Chief was frank, however, admitting from the first that everything Mr Wilmot had written was quite right and that the defence of Crete *had* been a debacle; that a fair measure of it had been his own fault; but equally maintaining that to print such a detailed critique would be giving the enemy valuable information and much material for damaging propaganda, while also stirring up a lot of entirely unnecessary trouble between Britain and the Dominions.

Chester stood his ground, insisting that there was already a great deal of ill will from the Dominion troops towards the British High Command; and when Wavell asked him why that was, the Australian gave it to him straight, based on what he had observed himself since being back in Cairo from Greece, and from many conversations with others.

He told Wavell: 'The general opinion among Australian and New Zealand officers and men who come into contact with GHQ is that the British in Cairo are not taking the war seriously; are not working all-out, are not working as hard as the men in the front line ... it is amazing and appalling to Australians that this GHQ can close down completely from 1.30 to 5.30 every afternoon; that the average working day for Middle East officers is not much over seven hours.'[2]

Entirely unfazed, even when Wilmot recalculated that they worked for only *six* hours, Wavell replied mildly, 'Well, I'll look into that ... If what you say is true, something ought to be done about it, though I don't think that people can do much work in this climate in the afternoons in summer ...'

Wilmot left, appalled at such lassitude from the heights of leadership down. He had a strong impression that in the whole Middle East there was a disproportionate number of Australians doing the fighting and dying, while too many British officers were pushing pens around for a few lazy hours before heading off for cocktails.

•

The job was done. On 26 May Rommel's troops attacked Halfaya Pass, and on the following day the British were forced to withdraw from their positions. A good part of the German success was built on the fact that Rommel insisted, with some ferocity, that his troops employ the same tactic that had worked so well for him in France, by using the 88-mm Ack-Ack guns in an anti-tank capacity. The results were stunning, with the British tanks completely devastated without ever quite knowing what was hitting them.

Never a man to rest on his laurels, Rommel now embraced this kind of system with alacrity so his troops would be more than ready for the British when next they tried to retake the strategically key position. Putting his engineers to work with his sappers, Rommel had his crucial Ack-Ack guns dug well down into pits. And that was not all: the 88s were put in a U-shaped formation so that any enemy tanks that could be lured in would be attacked from three sides. Still not satisfied, he insisted that small, desert-coloured tents be put over the tops of the guns in order that the guns would appear to be just a few more dunes in a whole desert sea of them.

All up the effect was so strong that, as he later recounted, 'with their barrels horizontal, there was practically nothing to be seen above ground. I had great hopes of the effectiveness of this arrangement.'[3]

Though Rolf Völker and his comrades had been pulled momentarily out of Tobruk for this attack, the instant it was won they were sent straight back. A victory at Halfaya Pass was great, but it changed nought the central equation. The Allied forces at Tobruk *had* to be defeated.

•

German and Italy had to be defeated. And Australia had to play its part. Up on the stage of the Sydney Town Hall, the Australian Prime Minister, Robert Menzies, was in rare form, exhorting the faithful and the doubtful alike — as the press scribbled notes and the radio people broadcast his words across the land — that the nation had to awake from its torpor and push to an all-out war effort in the manner that their soldiers are already doing in North Africa.

'First of all let me say something to you about our troops in the Middle East. I felt, as you would wish me to feel, that it was proper that when I was in the Middle East, I should visit if possible, every unit of the Australian forces ... It was not always easy to catch them, because they were very busy catching others ...'

A magnificent speaker when in full cry, the Town Hall turned electric as the Prime Minister warmed to the theme of how well the troops had been doing, the things he'd seen them doing, the things that they had said and what others had said about them.

'These Australian troops of ours, known all over the world, admired all over the world as the greatest troops in the world, have in them a simplicity, a gentleness, a warmth of heart that you might well take as our example in the tasks that they have left us to do in Australia.'

And those tasks were many, and it was for all Australians to take them up, to help the soldiers in a unified fashion make a greater war effort and display greater unity.

'GO TO IT!' he exhorted, to thunderous applause.

The following day the *Sydney Morning Herald* marked it down as 'the most stirring speech of his political career'.

Which was to the good. As Menzies knew better than most, though, that it was going to take a whole lot more than merely good speeches to turn both his and Australia's precarious positions in this war around ...

•

It was a letter from one of his beloved children ...

Walwa. Vic.

Sunday 1 June 1941.

Dear Dad,

I have got a new jumper. And I have got some new socks. Down at the bottom I have put some things I have learned I got Christianed today. I'm well I hope you are too. We enjoyed Jack being home. Here is a picture of my socks and jumper. This is my petrol truck which Johnny bought me home. We all attend Sunday school every Sunday. Gosh, I bet you have good fun over there, it's just the place I'd like to be at kiss kiss kiss kiss kiss

Look on back

Your Loving Son

Desy Peter

(Len helped Des to write this letter.)

•

Every morning, early, the same thing: Elizabeth Edmondson would emerge from a night of nightmares in which visions would come of Jack lying, dying, bleeding into the hot sands of Africa — and then she would come crashing into full consciousness. These were not mere nightmares, things that would go away with the dawn. This was all real. Jack was dead. He would never come home again. Where was he? He was lying, *rotting*, beneath the North African soil.

Now every day for Elizabeth meant more trawling through the depths of her misery, with seemingly every little thing she saw in the house, around the district and in town reminding her of him. That chair was where he used to sit with the cat, Stuffy, on his lap. That doorway was the one he would always come through, smiling so beautifully at her very sight. His dog kept looking hopefully at the farm gate, as if it really believed that Jack would soon be coming through it. That paddock, the one they used to always go for their long walks in. Everything but *everything* made her think of him, and nor was it something she tried to push away. She *wanted* to think only of him. Of course, she cried every day till she could cry no more, while still being often touched by the kindness so many people extended to her, the visits they made and letters they sent.

Letters she particularly treasured were ones from soldiers who were with Jack in Tobruk, and the one she corresponded with most eagerly was his great friend Athol Dalziel, who had been with him when he died, and who had taken responsibility for gathering Jack's personal effects — his letters, collar badges, watch, pens and so forth — to send back to Elizabeth and Will.

In a letter dated 2 June 1941, Dalziel referred to one of the previous letters Elizabeth had written to him:

You said at times, you think you loved Jack too much. I loved him too, but I could not love him enough. He was everything that I hope I can be when I am his age. In fact everyone that came into contact with Jack loved him.[4]

Also touching was the way he came to sign his letters to her,

Love,
Athol

almost as if he was trying to extend to her the living love that her son would have if he had been alive.

Athol's own mother came all the way from Melbourne to visit, as did the parents of Austin Mackell, bearing the specific message that Jack was adored by his men and that they were more determined than ever to achieve victory because of his death, and that Austin was acutely conscious that he would ever afterwards owe a debt that he couldn't repay. (Elizabeth seemed to take those assurances well enough, though Mrs Mackell couldn't help but feel a certain coldness from her, almost as if, well ... almost as if the poor woman might have felt that her Austin was somehow responsible for Jack's death, which was plainly ridiculous.)

As to the many other communications the Edmondsons received from soldiers in Jack's battalion and members of their families, Elizabeth did what she could in response, including sending to Jack's section in Tobruk parcels of woollen socks, sweets and the like to be shared out among his comrades.

Her husband, Will, remained devastated by the death of his beloved boy, but one thing bucked him up — a letter written by Jack's Commanding Officer, Colonel John Crawford. It was a very personal letter, but it contained most gratifying news.

'Jack's extreme gallantry,' the Colonel wrote, 'was such that I submitted a certain recommendation for an Award of a Decoration by the General Officer Commanding Middle East. My recommendation has now been returned with a suggestion that the circumstances were such as to warrant a posthumous award of the Victoria Cross. I have now submitted such a recommendation, and have every hope that it will be granted. If so, it will be the first award to a member of the AIF.'

Will was agog. A Victoria Cross! The British Empire's highest award for military valour, established by the mighty Queen Victoria herself! And if Will's son was in fact awarded it, he would be the first Australian to receive it in this war. Of course, in no way did it make up for Jack's death, but it was something, all right, and Will was thrilled, even if they were exhorted not to say anything at all, to anyone, until it became official.

Elizabeth, while pleased for Jack, was too deep in her own grief to be lifted by the prospect of the award itself, but she at least noted how much it seemed to lift Will and that was something. She supposed.

•

Strange.

As far as young Len Johnson knew, in his whole life George Hughes had never done anything to help anyone but himself, and yet on this day George had suddenly turned up at Walwa Public School to pick up the Johnson kids of school age. And now here he was, grim-faced, driving them back home. Um, thanks, Mr Hughes. When they arrived, their mother wasn't there, though they could see on the front veranda some of the gay presents she must have bought them on her shopping trip to Albury. Since their dad had been in the Army, things really had been a little bit easier financially. Anyway, one of their neighbours told them that mum would be back soon, apparently, as she was down at the post office, where some telegram for her had arrived.

Then the front door opened, and their mother came in, holding baby Josie in one arm, with little Sylvie toddling along by her on the other side, and young Barry ... holding her other hand and crying, crying, crying, as if he was fit to bust. Then their mother just told them, straight out: 'Dad has been killed in the war.'

From there everything went sort of wonky, with most everyone crying and wailing and cuddling their mother and being cuddled in turn, and people coming and going, and tea being made and more crying; and right in the middle of it all, one of the Stewart kids came over saying he wanted his marbles back, he must have his marbles, he wouldn't leave till he had his marbles and finally their mum gave him one of the presents for Barry she'd just got in Albury — a bag of marbles — just so he would go away. And then someone else came and took Len over to the Zuber place — a miserable pack of bastards — to maybe have some dinner while Josie went to tell her husband's parents and his brother what had happened; but no dinner came and young Len would never forget a question from one of the Zubers — *When are they going to pick him up and take him home? He can't stay here* — and he decided then and there that he would never set foot in their place again, and he never did either. And Barry, who was with his mother, Josie, when she told Grandma, would equally never forget Grandma sort of collapsing and crying out, and calling for 'My baby, my baby, my baby'. Somehow the whole family was back together again that night, less Dad, but nothing was ever the same.[5]

•

It was time to give the relief of Tobruk one more go.

This one, pushed hard by Winston Churchill and reluctantly executed by General Wavell, was called Operation Battleaxe, and was launched on 15 June with a frontal attack from the east by the 4th Indian Division and the 4th Armoured Brigade on the Sollum–Halfaya Pass axis, while the 7th Armoured Division swept around the flank of the Axis positions.

Alas, Rommel and his men and Panzers were effectively waiting for them, and by doing everything they could to lure the British tanks onto their carefully prepared and dug-in 88-mm anti-aircraft guns — positioned as anti-tank weapons in tandem with constantly working a concentration of the Panzers to the British flanks — they simply cut Wavell's forces to pieces.

At Halfaya itself Rommel's 88s destroyed all but one of a dozen Matildas, while four of the six Matildas in the next wave were disabled by carefully laid mines. Once his guns and mines had done their work, Rommel sent in his Panzers to mount devastating counterattacks for which the British simply had no answer.

A similar episode occurred just outside Capuzzo, where, in one celebrated manoeuvre, Rommel established a dummy camp at the bottom of a small depression, with well-dug-in 88s ready to blast whoever came — and they didn't have to wait long. Within hours British reconnaissance had spotted the camp, sent the tanks in … and were destroyed for their trouble, with the 88s capable of knocking out the British tanks at a distance of over a mile! (A new practice among the 88-mm German gunners was to paint a white ring around the barrel for every enemy tank destroyed — in the manner of a gunslinger of the Wild West cutting notches into his pistols — and there would be many rings painted that night.) In the meantime, Rommel's Panzers then mopped up whatever British resistance remained. Halfaya Pass thereafter became known to the Allies as 'Hellfire' Pass, and the horror of it would not be forgotten …

•

Another small parenthesis here. At a later point in the North African campaign, one of Rommel's most senior officers, Oberleutnant Gerhard Graf von Schwerin, used exactly the same tactic of turning the anti-aircraft guns on British tanks to all but completely wipe them out. 'One of the tank commanders,' von Schwerin recorded, 'asked me if he could see one of the weapons responsible for the wholesale destruction of the British armour. So I took him across to see the 88-mm AA Battery. The Englishman looked astounded as he turned to me and said indignantly but seriously, "But it's not *cricket* to use anti-aircraft guns against tanks!"'[6]

This was not a one-off. A short time later, after another encounter between the British and the German armoured forces, General Rommel's adjutant, Lieutenant Schmidt, overheard a conversation between a German interrogator and a young English tank driver. As recounted by Schmidt:

'In my opinion,' said the Englishman, with an unfriendly glance at a nearby 88, 'it is unfair to use [anti-aircraft] flak against our tanks.'

A German artillery man who was sitting on his haunches nearby, listening to the interpretation, interjected excitedly: 'Ja, and I think it most unfair of you to attack with tanks whose armour nothing but an 88 will penetrate!'[7]

Touché. Close parenthesis.

•

The bottom line was that, in the open field, in his element, Rommel invariably knew of more ways to thwart an opponent than the opponent knew to counter him. Within two days, Wavell — with ninety-one of his tanks now destroyed, 122 men killed, 588 wounded and 259 missing — signalled Churchill: 'I regret to report the failure of Battleaxe.'[8]

Churchill regretted it too. He received the news while down at his country residence of Chartwell, and was so upset by it that he wandered in the surrounding valley for several hours, disconsolately pondering what must be done next.[9]

A strong feeling that had been growing in him for some time began to crystallise. The fact was, the British Prime Minister simply did not like Wavell and never really had. There were many things that had strained their relationship, but one that was notable had occurred the year before, after Churchill had sent Wavell a blistering cable over the apparent inactivity of one of the British Generals under his command in the Somalia campaign, noting the lack of British casualties as a sure sign of that indolence.

Wavell had vigorously defended the General in question and served up to Churchill a highly presumptuous and almost insolent rebuke. He begged to inform the Prime Minister that 'A heavy butcher's bill is not necessarily evidence of good tactics . . .'[10]

Churchill had been incandescent with rage then, and although that antipathy had softened to the point where they could again work together, it was ever and always something bubbling under, and the latest episode seemed to point to a certain indolence on Wavell's part. Certainly, Sir John Dill had always defended Wavell to Churchill, saying that the PM had to 'back him, or sack him . . .'

Which rather raised the point. For finding, as Churchill later described it, that he had 'a tired fish on this rod and a lively one on the other', Churchill decided to move on the 'tired fish' (Wavell), and replace him with the 'lively one': General Sir Claude Auchinleck.

Wavell was shaving on the morning of 22 June when there was a deferential knock on the door. It was his adjutant with a cable from Churchill, and Wavell asked the aide to read it out as he continued to shave. After a few salutations, the Prime Minister got to the point:

> I feel however that after the long strain you have borne, a new eye and a new hand are required in this most seriously menaced theatre . . .

Even while continuing to shave, Wavell briefly interrupted his aide at this point, saying with seemingly perfect equanimity, 'The Prime Minister is quite right. This job needs a new eye and a new hand . . .'[11]

•

Though the news of Wavell's effective dismissal from his post was kept secret for the moment, even had it been known it would not have run close to the biggest news of the day. For in the early hours of that very morning three German Army groups — 117 divisions, comprising over three million German soldiers and more than 3300 tanks — had begun to move across the Russian border on a front from the Baltic to the Black Sea, and were essaying to move on Moscow.

Operation Barbarossa had begun.

As it happened, many of the men on the inside of the Tobruk perimeter were not at all perturbed by the news, as witnessed by a couple of paragraphs in the 23 June edition of the 2/13th Battalion news sheet:

'Now comes the joyful tidings that Germany is in such dire straits that she is compelled to attack her powerful neighbour. Whatever the outcome of the present conflict between Russia and Germany, the result must be in our favour. Every shell fired by a German gun in this Russian conflict will be one less fired at us; every German soldier killed will be one less for us to destroy.'

It was a measure of both Rommel's astuteness as a military commander and his basic honesty to his men as a leader that he not only agreed with that analysis, but said so. For some time later, when the first part of the Barbarossa campaign was reported as being very successful and some of his senior officers were celebrating, Rommel broke in quietly.

'Meine Herren,' he said with sadness, but force, 'I would love to be as excited as you are. But we cannot win a war on two fronts. I don't know any more how this war can be won.'[12]

And yet, despite the fact that Rommel's own views on the likely outcome of the war had started to turn towards pessimism, and despite the problems he had personally borne with the ongoing resistance shown by Tobruk — which continued to thwart his grand plan to take Cairo and the Suez Canal — the German public continued to adore him and devour the wonderful stories of the fearless German general rampaging through the North African desert and beating the British at nearly every turn. His victory in Operation Battleaxe had played very well and by this time his renown was such that he was regularly getting as many as forty letters a day from across the social spectrum of Germany — though Schmidt couldn't help but notice that a lot came from hero-worshipping boys, and many, many from girls and women, asking for a photograph.[13]

Few were left disappointed. This was because, together with the regular lots of bullets, bayonets and food that got to the Afrika Korps at the end of the exhausting supply line, room was also made for large cartons of postcard portraits, and it was a point of honour with Rommel to personally autograph each one, while Schmidt would formulate a letter of reply that Rommel would also sign.

'I was always amused, when he signed letters,' Schmidt later wrote, 'to see the tip of the General's tongue protruding and comically following in the air the outline of the unusually florid flourish of his pen when he completed the bold "R" in his signature.'[14]

Rommel was also assiduous in cultivating the affection of the German press and pursued something of an open-door policy with them — frequently dining with them, answering all their questions and happily posing for photographers in a suitably grand stance to make their work easy for them.

The difference in Rommel's approach to that of Morshead could not have been more marked. The only young person Morshead was interested in writing to was his daughter, Elizabeth, and while he was co-operative enough with the Australian press, there was never the slightest sign that he had any interest in nurturing his legend. If anything, quite the reverse.

On one famous occasion when Chester Wilmot passed to him the account he had written of the opening of the Battle of the Salient, the correspondent went on to tell ABC listeners of the Australian General's response.

'I was surprised at his frank self-criticism,' Wilmot recounted. 'He queried one point and said ... "You're making excuses here ... don't excuse this battalion ... they didn't do well in this fight ... say so." Then again ... "It would have been better if I had used all my tanks there. I didn't handle my tanks well that day."'[15]

•

It was the night before Josie Johnson was to appear in the Walwa Magistrate's Court on the charge of assault that had been brought against her by Ian Coughlan. With all of Walwa in uproar over the whole affair, the visiting stipendiary magistrate stayed at the Bridge Hotel in the nearby town of Jingellic so as to avoid contact with anyone involved in the case or, indeed, any case he was due to see on the morrow with the two local magistrates, Hanna and McHarg. It was for the same reason that the magistrate drank on his own that night down one end of the bar, well away from the local yokels; but the publican, Edgar Holt, didn't miss him. A great friend of the late John Johnson, Edgar chose his moment and then said loudly to the other drinkers, 'Poor Mrs Johnson at Walwa won't get a fair go tomorrow with Hanna and McHarg on the bench.'

Well, he never. The following day, against the vociferous protests of the aforementioned, the visiting magistrate stood down the two local magistrates for the Johnson case and presided alone. After hearing it all, his gavel banged down twice and he gave his verdict to the exhausted but still proud woman before him: Josie Johnson was bound to keep the peace for twelve months, but she would have no fine to pay. Case closed.[16]

•

Oh the sheer *relief*. After weeks of being on the front lines, at last in these final weeks of June some of the soldiers of the Afrika Korps were pulled out and allowed to drive in small groups to the coast for swimming. That such pleasure still existed on heaven and earth, after what they had been through! Peeling off their sweaty, dusty clothes for the first time since early May, they frolicked in the Mediterranean like naked babes, soaping themselves down and revelling in that wonderful feeling of being clean. But look .. !

The curious thing was that, even as they continued to bathe, much of their suntan faded with the soap, and some of their old selves began to emerge again.[17] A similar process occurred as they washed their clothes in the ocean, with the clothing becoming not only brigher but also thinner as all the dirt washed away. Best of all, whereas in Germany it could take days for clothes to dry in the soupy sun, here all was dry in no more than thirty minutes!

Would a spy in the hills now spot them as German? Not necessarily. For, by this time, many of them were wearing substantially British uniforms anyway. Most preferred the airy olive shirts of the Tommies — their pants were heftier and more able to stand up to wear and tear — and the thick rubber-soled shoes the English wore were regarded as superb. For quite a few of the Germans, only the cap and field shirt that the Wehrmacht had issued them with remained in their general outfit but, because there was little difference in both sides' colours and there were more serious issues in the desert, there was never a problem. Afrika Korps chic was precisely this mix of uniforms.

And now, with clean bodies for the first time in months and clean clothes for the first time in even longer, the German soldiers listened in on captured British radios, and for the first time heard the 'victory news about the campaign against Russia that began on 22 June'.[18]

While the younger soldiers exulted at the news, the older ones became a whole lot more pensive ...

•

What the hell was going on here?

There were leaflets fluttering down from the German planes. In big, bold black lettering they read:

> **AUSSIES After Crete disaster, Anzac troops are now being ruthlessly sacrificed by England in Tobruk and Syria. Turkey has concluded pact of friendship with Germany — England will shortly be driven out of the Mediterranean. Offensive from Egypt to relieve you totally smashed. You cannot escape. Our dive bombers are waiting to sink your transports. Think of your future and your people at home.**
>
> **Come forward — show white flags and you will be out of danger!**
>
> **SURRENDER!**

Yeah, right. What was that line they used to love when they were training in Palestine again? That's it!

'Tel Aviv, Tel Agib, Tell 'Em to Get Fucked ...'

An example of the attitude taken by the garrison was when a Digger tacked the leaflet up to the flagpole in the main square and wrote upon it in big black letters, '**Come and get it!**'[19]

Indeed, there was going to be no easy victory for the Germans here. If they wanted Tobruk, they really would have to come and get it.

•

They were going to come and get it.

A Führer directive that was released to the highest echelons of his military command at this time formalised the fact that Rommel still had Hitler's full support and that 'With regard to North Africa, it will be important for Tobruk to be eliminated, to create the basis for the continuation of the German–Italian attack against the Suez Canal.'[20]

The Führer had spoken, and that was effectively the end of the argument. From that point on, the flow of men, munitions and heavy armour coming across the Mediterranean towards Rommel started to increase as he began to build towards the critical mass he needed to finally fix the Tobruk problem, once and for all. Yes, there remained some possibility that the Allies would launch their own attack from Egypt, but it remained Rommel's view that such a prospect only made the taking of Tobruk doubly important, as his own capacity to resist would be increased exponentially once his supplies started to flow through Tobruk Harbour and he didn't have to invest such a large number of men just to keep the garrison under siege. And nor could he simply leave the garrison untouched, as it would then be a simple matter for the Allies to launch crippling raids on his supply line, through the desert to the south. While the Allies were there in numbers, the Axis had to be there, too.

•

Yet, well away from the Tobruk garrison itself, other pressures continued to grow to remove the Australians from it, and nowhere were those pressures felt more than on the person of Robert Menzies, who was now deeply worried.

For, despite all of the British High Command's optimistic predictions of forthcoming relief, it was now clear that Operation Battleaxe had been not just a failure but a disaster, and once again the fate of the 15 000 Australian soldiers in Tobruk looked to hang in the balance. With that in mind, on 21 June Menzies wrote a highly confidential cable to Thomas Blamey, passing on his base concern — 'I am most disturbed by the failure at and about Sollum' — and putting some queries.

Yes, it was slightly irregular at this time for an Australian Prime Minister to communicate so directly with the highest-ranking officer of the Australian Army — without going via the British military authorities — but Menzies felt it had to be done.

He justified the irregularity to Blamey by noting, slightly conspiratorially, that 'I am cabling you direct because I have great confidence in your judgment and would like you to let me have urgently the answers', and also that 'views which I received from London may be unduly coloured by wishful thinking, and I still feel that they constantly underestimate the enemy. That is why I would welcome your own full and frank view.'

As to his questions, they were relatively straightforward.

1. What is your own assessment of the enemy's strength
and our own on the Western Desert front and our
respective capacities to increase and maintain such
strength?

2. Are you satisfied that the garrison at Tobruk can hold
out? Should we press for evacuation or for any other and
what course?

The Australian Prime Minister summed up the nub of his political
problem crisply:

A disaster at Tobruk, coming on top of those in Greece
and Crete, might have far-reaching effects on public
opinion in Australia, and a reverse in Egypt itself would,
I think, produce incalculable difficulties in Australia.

Too, there was the risk that if Tobruk went bad, those critics of the
government — who had been multiplying like the very Dickens lately,
despite the fact that Menzies had continued to give good speeches —
would accuse it of being 'passive or insufficiently strong'.

Blamey replied shortly afterwards that Menzies need not overly concern
himself just yet, as he was sure that Tobruk 'could be held for the present',
and yet he too was rapidly coming to the conclusion that it would not be
wise to leave the Australian soldiers in the garrison for too much longer.

What had been an initial commitment of just two months had already
turned into three; and the way the British High Command referred to the
situation, it was clear that they had no plans to change things any time soon.
Which might have been fine for them, but it certainly wasn't fine with
Blamey, who had been mightily annoyed to begin with to discover that,
although he was nominally Wavell's 2IC, he had precious little real power to
influence the course of events. It was still a matter of great irritation to
Blamey — and the more so after the debacle of what had happened in
Greece — that Australian forces were, as he put it, 'scattered to the four
winds' throughout the Middle East, allocated according to the whims of the
Brits, and not under one central command as the Australian Corps. And the
Brits couldn't even begin to understand the need for that!

As Blamey put it in a formal letter to the GHQ Chief of the General
Staff on 4 July — in which he reminded him of the contents of the cables
between the British and Australian governments which had set out the

conditions under which Australian soldiers were engaged — there were plenty of British officers who had a 'fundamental misconception of the relationships between the forces of the Empire'.[21]

But beyond Menzies' political worries and Blamey's concerns over the Australians' place in the Middle Eastern command structure, the other salient reason to bring them out was the matter of the declining health of the garrison's men.

When, for example, in those dead dog days of early July, Lieutenant General Morshead was called back to Cairo to discuss with the senior officers of GHQ, including General Blamey, the situation in Tobruk and was asked about the condition of the soldiers' health, he chose his words carefully. (And if he was sitting slightly uncomfortably, it was not the question that troubled him so much as a piece of shrapnel he had taken in the buttocks just days before, when a shell from one of the long-range German guns that the troops had nicknamed 'Bardia Bill' and 'Salient Sue' landed within 75 yards of him.)

Morshead's view was that, while all of the garrison was in good heart and morale remained fairly high, there was no doubt that the continuous strain and arduous work under such difficult conditions in such proximity to the enemy really were starting to show. The health of the men remained passable — and was even remarkable, given their ordinary diet and constant lack of water — but the medical officers had reported to Morshead that the stamina of the entire garrison was waning and their powers of resistance weakening. Most of the front-line troops were now complaining of desert sores that never seemed to quite heal, just as even minor cuts and abrasions were so often becoming infected that the medical staff couldn't keep up.

On average, the front-line troops had lost a stone in weight since they arrived in Tobruk, with some men having lost as much as 2 stone. And indeed, back in the furphy-flushers, the running gag was that some blokes had lost so much weight that they had to take three steps before their trousers started to move![22]

Morshead pointed out that his remarks applied equally to British and Australian troops and that he would be most unhappy if, in the event of his 9th Division being relieved, British units had to remain.[23]

The response of the British leadership to all of the Australian concerns was nothing if not consistent: too bad.

Personally, Wavell's rather dour successor, Auchinleck, was never much given to matters of debate in matters military. The way he saw it — which was the only way that counted — the whole thing was straightforward.

Given that the Allied forces had already made two failed attempts to relieve Tobruk by land, they would be unlikely to try again until they had overwhelming force, and that would not be achievable before November. That left relieving the garrison by sea, and Auchinleck was unwilling, saying that unnecessarily sending thousands upon thousands of both the incoming fresh troops and the outgoing veteran troops through Bomb Alley was simply a risk he was unwilling to take.

Though Blamey began to fume, he contained himself for the moment.

It was clear that Auchinleck just didn't get it either! And while the Australian had had many differences of opinion with Wavell, he had at least liked him personally — which seemed unlikely to be the case with the new chap.

•

Rommel wrote to Lucie:

5th July 1941

... I usually spend a lot of time travelling; yesterday I was away eight hours. You can hardly imagine what a thirst one gets up after such a journey. I'm hoping that my flight to the Führer's HQ will come off in about a fortnight. It's no good going until the Russian affair is more or less over, otherwise there'll be scant regard for my interests.

I was glad to hear that Manfred is now getting on in mathematics. It's all a matter of the method of teaching. I'm also very pleased about his other successes in school ... [24]

•

It was something that was troubling to the doctors of the Afrika Korps. In such conditions, with a poor diet and so little water, there was only so much that the human body could stand — and, before their very eyes, the soldiers in their care were starting to fall apart. Many complained of a complete lack of appetite, while others were beset by vomiting and diarrhoea. On a simple physical basis, living and fighting in the desert required more energy than could be provided by the meagre food supply, so something had to give, and it was their bodies. Diphtheria proved to be a terrible problem, as were jaundice and tropical ulcers. Heatstroke was a constant menace. The strangest thing of all was something that was not easily discussed by the doctors under the circumstances. But ... well ... it was all but impossible not to note the preponderance of blond hair in the sick tents.[25] Despite Hitler's claims about the inherent superiority of the Aryan race in all things, it seemed possible that the more purely Aryan your blood, the more inclined you were to keel over in these parts from heat exhaustion alone.

•

Guards up ahead. Armed guards. Pacing back and forth. Guards who were looking out for precisely the threat that Bert Ferres and another Bren-gunner mate of his by the name of Bob Thomson posed. But that was too bad. Slithering on their bellies, the two 2/13th Battalion soldiers kept edging closer, silent as a slit throat, until the moment was right ...

Now! At the very moment when the guards were at the far ends of their circuit, the young Australians scampered forwards and were soon taking their pliers to the rolls of barbed wire that lay between them and their target: the tucker dump down by Tobruk Harbour. Certainly, they risked courtmartial by so doing, but for Bert and Bob it was practically a matter of life and death for their platoon. They simply couldn't get enough food via the tucker trucks, and it was in their nature to do what had to be done to fix the problem, whatever the consequences and whatever regulations might say about it. Besides which, this kind of exercise was as nothing compared with going out on a patrol near German lines, so they had plenty of confidence.

After loading themselves up with whatever they felt they could carry the 7 miles back to their posts — sausages, tins of stew, biscuits — they were again on their way. (Bert personally came to be so good at the caper he could tell what kind of food was in a box just by shaking it.) Bugger the guards. The main thing was they had some grub for the platoon, and they were able to do this caper time and again, though only ever when they were posted well back from the front lines and could afford to be away without risk to the main defences. In their platoon, when Bert and Bob announced they were 'going to look for some firewood', you knew that by sunup either you'd be eating heartily or the platoon would be missing two men who were in serious trouble.

•

It was now time for Morshead to be leaving Cairo, and getting back to his post at Tobruk, which was no bad thing. While it had been fine, for a day or two, to be back in a place where he could see grass and trees, he couldn't help but feel that it just wasn't quite right to be there, staying at the luxurious Shepherd's Hotel while all his men were still in Tobruk, and most of them in front-line foxholes. This feeling had been rather exacerbated when he had been obliged to go on something of the regular Cairo social round that was part of the military rhythm of life there: drinking champagne during a four-course meal with Thomas Blamey and his wife at their Cairo residence; playing golf at the splendid Gezirah Club, again with Blamey; and embarking on a long series of lunches and dinners, one of them silver service beside a swimming pool. Certainly there had been important meetings — he had much enjoyed speaking with both Wavell and his successor, Auchinleck, and felt it had been valuable to be able to talk to them personally about the situation in Tobruk. But all up, as strange as it might sound to someone well removed from the environment, it felt good to be going back to the rather more ascetic purity of the desert.[26]

•

It was the most extraordinary thing. Jack. Jack Edmondson!

He'd been awarded the *Victoria Cross*!

When the news of the award broke in that first flush of July 1941, it was greeted with joy and wonder by the garrison, a deep sense of the honour that had been done them all, and pride in Jack. As Captain John Balfe of D Company wrote in a letter to his wife in Sydney's South Hurstville, 'All can speak well of the dead, but I have said of him while he was still alive, that he was a really decent, good, clean chap. The first AIF VC. If ever there was a medal earned, Jack earned his.'[27]

As for the people of Australia, there was great exultation, and awe, that one of their own should be so recognised, and for such a remarkable act of bravery. A manifestation of the public excitement came when Sydney's *Sunday Telegraph Pictorial* devoted an eight-page lift-out to Jack's life and times, together with many baby and childhood photos.

Too, Mr and Mrs Edmondson were pictured in front of a photo of Jack in his soldier's uniform, with the 'grey-haired, soft-spoken Mrs Edmondson' saying, 'I am no more proud of my son because he has won the VC. I have always been proud of him. Jack would have regarded this award as an honour to the whole AIF.'

As to the actual presentation of the award, it occurred at Sydney's Admiralty House, where Governor General Alexander Hore-Ruthven, 1st Earl of Gowrie, graciously presented Elizabeth Edmondson with the medal, saying, 'I feel it is a very great honour, to hand you, on behalf of his

Majesty the King, this Victoria Cross, which has been so nobly earned by
your gallant son. I convey to you my sincere condolences on the loss of this
splendid young Australian, who gave his life for his King and country in the
hour of her greatest need.'[28]

•

One of the most popular of the furphy-flushers by this time was the *Tobruk
Truth*, with its motto of 'Always Appears', produced by a former journalist
by the name of Sergeant Billy Williams at the behest of his superior, Area
Commander of Tobruk, Lieutenant Colonel Thomas Cook, whose idea it
had been. Many battalions previously had rough news sheets, but now the
idea began to be refined, with the first editions being 'Roneoed' on
Gestetner machines, using the back of Italian Army forms.

In the great traditions of the free press, fierce competitors of the *Tobruk
Truth* soon emerged in the form of other news sheets from individual
battalions, with perhaps the most notable being *Mud and Blood* from the
2/23rd. Put out initially by the Staff Sergeant from Battalion HQ, it
operated from a newspaper 'office' that was no more than a hole in the
ground, slightly protected by a sandbag wall. With a radio and a candle that
sputtered in rough tandem, and a typewriter that had been in use since the
days when Noah first went looking for a couple of aardvarks, *Mud and Blood*
had also been an instant hit.

Though in the early stages of the newspaper the copy was written
almost exclusively by the editor, more and more contributions started
coming in from the Diggers themselves. Not only did this unearth some
lively writing, but it was a great morale booster to the men, giving them
firstly an occupation to be involved in during downtime that didn't involve
killing fleas. But ...

Hang on, now *there's* an idea!

One of the many competitions held by *Mud and Blood* was to see who
could catch the most fleas, or their equivalent. The scale, as determined by
the commanding officer who got into the spirit of things, went like this:

One bug equals 3 fleas.
One rat equals 10 fleas.
Three lice equals 1 flea. (Easier to catch by far.)
One gazelle equals 300 fleas.
One Itie prisoner equals 200 fleas (plus all 'catch' found on him.)

Bravo, of course, to the Commanding Officer who'd come up with such a scale, but the notion of 'freedom of the press' to criticise without fear or favour was still strong enough, even on the battlefield, that the editor did not hesitate to upbraid him. For, in the view of the editor, it was outrageous that a gazelle was considered the equal of 300 fleas while an Itie prisoner only got you a paltry 200, when everyone knew that an Itie was much fleeter of foot than the gazelle and consequently harder to catch.[29]

Who won?

Well, it proved to be as hard to work out as Chinese calculus, with all the disputes and carry-on, but in the end victory was awarded to D Company, which was a good thing. Otherwise an even bigger controversy would have ensued. Their win had been based on the fact that they had indeed bagged five Itie prisoners, but because one of those prisoners had been judged notably scrawny — and this was where tempers risked flaring — only 150 fleas were awarded for him.

For its part, the 2/24th's *Furphy Flyer* warmed to a similar theme, with the following joke creating much merriment: '"Tony, you're a parachute soldier, eh?" said the Commanding Officer to the captured Itie. "And you were dropped from the big new plane that just flew over?"

'"Yessir," nodded Tony. "New typo plano. Carry 50 men, but only one parachutist."

'"And what," asked the Commanding Officer, "are the other 49 for?"

'"Wot you tink?" replied Tony. "Why, they're needed to push out the parachutist!"'[30]

•

Basta! Basta! Basta!

Enough! At a certain point in mid July, the Italian soldiers in the front lines of the eastern perimeter of Tobruk, dug in around the Bardia Road, really had had enough of patrolling no-man's-land, because it seemed that every time they went out they were being ambushed, killed and captured, if not by the Australians then by the hideous Indians. The result was that, for sanity's sake, many of them would merely pretend to go on patrol, but as soon as they were out of earshot of their own front lines, they would simply sit down and wait for the appropriate hour to return, spending the time to make up stories of what they had seen.

To thwart this, the Italian officers soon came up with a new scheme. Each patrol had to build a stone cairn at a designated distant point which would be proof, when their officers examined the spot by binoculars the following morning, that they had been there.

It was a system that worked well for a few days only. For, while the men of the 2/48th were admittedly momentarily confused by the sudden appearance of the cairns — thinking them to be either artillery range markers or some kind of booby-trap — it wasn't long before a newly captured Italian prisoner told them everything. What to do?

Have some fun with it . . .

In the first flush of dawn, the Diggers would go out and dismantle the cairns, all the while fondly imagining the havoc this would cause back in the Italian front lines as patrols would swear blue to their senior officers that they really had been out there and done the job, alas now with no proof. Ah, how the Australians laughed.[31]

•

Those wretched Australians.

They never let up in their constant whingeing and whining about the need for their soldiers to be relieved from Tobruk. How they weren't healthy any more. How there was a growing likelihood that the Germans would attack again and the Australians wouldn't be strong enough to resist them this time. How they wanted all the Australian soldiers under the one command. How because some exchange of cables in the early part of the war meant the British Government *had* to observe the Australian request, and not merely consider it on its merits. As if there wasn't a bloody war on! Some of the anger was aimed at Robert Menzies, who, on 20 July, had written to Churchill noting that he regarded having the Australian units all together under the one command as 'of first-class importance', and that the Australian Government would be most pleased if the British could see their way clear to getting the troops out at their soonest convenience. Most of the anger, however, was aimed at bloody Blamey, who was never quite so diplomatic about putting forward his views.

As a matter of fact, Air Marshal Sir Arthur Tedder, responsible for all of the Allied Air Forces in the Middle East, pretty much spoke for the general British view when he described Blamey as being no more than 'really a rather unpleasant political soldier'[32] at best, and refused outright to use his planes to get the Australians out. For his part, the Commander of the Navy's Mediterranean Fleet, Admiral Sir Andrew Cunningham, allowed it as a possibility, but stated that he would far prefer not to have to do it. King George VI himself was perplexed, noting 'how different the Australians seemed to be to any of the other dominions', most notably in that 'in Australia they were always being critical'.[33] In fact, the British High Commissioner to Australia, Sir Ronald Cross, was himself rather critical of the Australian politicians he was dealing with, and exacerbated the already tense situation by — in the words of Churchill's Dominions Secretary, Lord Cranborne — 'lecturing Australian Ministers as if they were small and rather dirty boys'.[34]

As to Auchinleck, his view was that 'old Blamey' simply didn't understand that this was no longer trench warfare on the Western Front in France — as he had been used to in the Great War, where there had been an argument for keeping massive formations like an entire corps intact — but modern warfare, old boy, where really the biggest unit of military currency he cared to trade in was brigades. As one who was under almost daily pressure from Churchill to launch an enormous attack against Rommel, Auchinleck felt that the last thing he needed on his plate right now was to lose 15 000 of his front-line troops for no good purpose that he could see. (Most particularly when he had already told Winston Churchill on 15 July that one could not count on holding Tobruk beyond September, anyway! Could he lose so many front-line soldiers at a time like that? He could not.[35])

And, finally, Auchinleck had little interest in justifying himself and his decisions to an officer of lower rank. All things considered, he had no hesitation in saying as much to Blamey in a tense conversation between the two at General Headquarters Middle East.

'I want the Australians to stay in Tobruk,' Auchinleck told Blamey, before adding the dart. 'You must support me as my Deputy.'

'I am your Deputy,' Blamey replied evenly, 'but I am also General Officer Commanding AIF. I want them relieved.'

'Talking of reliefs,' Auchinleck said, now with menace, 'if you take that tone I shall be compelled to ask for your relief.'

'Go ahead and do it . . .'[36]

And there the conversation ended. For the moment . . .

Churchill? He completely ignored the cable from Menzies, though it was reluctantly decided as a compromise measure to replace the Australian 18th Brigade with the first arrivals of the Polish 1st Carpathian Brigade. The 18th Brigade would be missed and no mistake — as they had been Tobruk Trojans throughout the siege — but they would have to be sent on their way to see if *that* would settle the Australian blighters down a bit!

●

In a hurtling Stuka, screaming down from out of the skies above Tobruk, the Luftwaffe pilot chose his moment well, releasing the bomb at the exact moment in the dive when the chances of an accurate hit were at the maximum, while still allowing time to haul back on his 'stick', flatten out from the dive, and regain altitude to safety. Always, at the moment of release a pilot could feel a sudden surge as the plane engines roared in appreciation of the lighter load, and get a reckoning of the likelihood of hitting the target — in this case a gun emplacement right by the harbour. And this time the pilot knew he was on the money, as he could see the bomb hurtle down, straight towards the gun and the feverish crew who had been doing their all to bring him down.

For those ten men of the Ack-Ack crew, there were just two to three seconds' warning: a whistling sound that increased in pitch and volume the closer the bomb got to them. Because this one was all but right on top of them, they had never heard such a loud whistle, and perhaps some of them even knew that the bomb was going to hit before it did ... but, still, there was no time to run.

The point of impact was just a few yards from them, close enough to practically vaporise their bodies and leave only the gold fillings in their teeth as proof that they had once existed — and yet ...

And yet it didn't explode. Instead the bomb simply burrowed down into the ground, and all the Diggers on the Ack-Ack gun felt was something like a strong earth tremor as the gun jolted upwards and the land on which they stood suddenly jumped around. Never mind. They kept firing, mindful of the most important lesson they had learned in previous months — the best defence of all was just to keep firing, irrespective of what the enemy were dropping on them.

Later, though, there was an explanation for why the bomb had not gone off. When the bomb disposal squad had arrived and carefully opened up the bomb, it was to find a note on which words had been scrawled by some worker in one of the Nazi-controlled factories in occupied Europe: *Keep it up Tommy. This is the best we can do for you now.*[37]

(This was not the first time such a thing had happened. Just before Anzac Day of that year, the 2/15th had taken an enormous bomb falling right among them, which also hadn't exploded. When carefully opened, it proved to contain concrete and a note saying 'Good luck to the Czechs.' With their last sips of filthy water for the day, the 2/15th toasted those brave Czechs three times through.[38])

It was a problem that Chester Wilmot had been wrestling with for some time, and now he thought he might be on the edge of resolving it. Since arriving back in Tobruk after his brief sojourn in Cairo, and beginning the long process of talking to the officers and Diggers about just what had happened so he could file knowledgeable reports for the ABC — and perhaps for a later book that he had in mind — he had been seeking to define just how it was that these men had managed to accomplish their most extraordinary feat of arms. After all, with little training, lesser weaponry and an extremely insecure supply line, the Diggers on the Red Line had confronted elite divisions of the best-trained, best-equipped, most brilliantly led army the world had ever seen, and stopped them cold. Not as a one-off, but now for months on end! How had this been possible?

On this day Wilmot thought he might have come up with the right words, and by pure happenstance his close friend, the great Australian war cameraman Damien Parer, was there to record him writing them, pointing his camera over Wilmot's right shoulder as he typed . . .

The spirit which has made Australia is the spirit which has held Tobruk. The inspiring and binding force in Australian life isn't tradition or nationalism or social revolution. It's quite a simple thing. Henry Lawson called it MATESHIP . . . the spirit which makes men stick together. In Australia by sticking together, men have defied drought, bushfire and flood. In Tobruk they've scorned hardship, danger and death, because no Digger would ever let his cobbers down. In Tobruk for the first time in this war the Germans were thrust back by a spirit that even tanks and dive-bombers could not conquer.[39]

Late on the evening of 1 August, after Lieutenant General Morshead had finished his simple dinner at his HQ, he made a moonlight tour of the most forward positions of the Salient. It was something he liked to do as often as he could, arriving unannounced to see what state of preparedness his men were in and so keeping everyone on their toes — and he was deeply respected by his men for the fact that he wasn't an armchair General directing things from the safety of his bunker — but this particular tour had a specific purpose.

The men on the front line were about to launch a serious action and he needed to be sure that the last, tiniest detail that might mean the difference between success and failure had been attended to.

What was clear from the start was that it was not going to be easy. In fact, as he recounted to Myrtle in a letter he wrote the following day: 'It was a long trek in the moonlight . . . it reminded me much of the active sections in Gallipoli and France, with the almost continuous machine-gun fire and a certain amount of artillery and mortar fire, and again, the usual amount of Very lights. But in the last war, we moved about in deep trenches . . .'

Here, there was no such 'luxury', as all his men could do was slither around in whatever tiny shallow they had been able to scratch out, against an enemy that was clearly in exactly the same position.

Still, he told Myrtle with some relish, 'I enjoyed seeing the men in the posts so keen and alert. It's not much of an existence being fired at all day and night and the posts can hardly be described as home away from home. The country is terribly rocky and only by the use of drills and explosives can any depth be obtained. Consequently I am sometimes amused at our title of fortress. But it is a fortress when it comes to the men holding it . . .'[40]

As to what was about to happen: '. . .we are having a battle at 3.30 in the morning against the Germans this time, and we intend "going them the works". As you would expect, a good deal of thought and preparation has been devoted to it and I hope that we meet with full success. I'll let you know as much as I can about it later.'[41]

•

In a rough repeat of the plan pursued in the early days of May, Morshead's orders on this occasion were for four platoons of the 2/43rd Battalion to attack posts R7, R6 and R5 from the south, while D Company of the 2/28th would go at posts S6 and S7 from the north, and hopefully help pinch off the German penetration represented by the Salient. And yet, whatever Morshead's confidence in the coming operation, it was not necessarily shared by his men. In fact, one of the 2/43rd, Lieutenant Dick Hamer, wrote in his diary before the attack: 'Heavy casualties are certain, and I have no real hope of success; further, there are certain to be booby traps thickly strewn near the post, which our recce patrols can't get close enough to locate, nor our engineers to de-louse. And to attack this with one under-strength company, of whom 40 are newly arrived reinforcements, and 7 minutes' artillery preparation!'[42]

However, just before the 2/43rd moved off, the artillery barrage laid down on the posts they were attacking was so enormous that another member of the battalion noted, 'It was the heaviest artillery strike ever employed in Tobruk and the earsplitting concussion of this and the counteraction which it provoked was so shocking and so intense that the machine guns, normally so loud and staccato, were barely audible as a faint puttering undercurrent. I can remember feeling that my centre of consciousness had left my stunned body and was standing apart from it looking on.'[43]

And yet, depite their hope that no one would be still left alive among the defenders in the posts they were about to attack, as soon as the 2/43rd moved off at three-thirty on the morning of 3 August, the enemy artillery now effectively returned serve as a devastating hellfire of shells started to burst among them. The two forces of Australians kept going anyway, protected a little by Vickers machine-gun fire from the Northumberland Fusiliers and yet more of their own artillery barrage — both designed to ensure that the German defenders would keep their square Teutonic heads down until the Australians could get close enough to knock 'em off.

•

Alas, apparently the Germans had been prepared for just such an attack, as they had fortified their positions with heavy minefields, enormous barbedwire entanglements and enough defenders that the advancing Australians were met with such withering machine-gun fire and artillery that they were cut to pieces, allowing only a very few to get through and try their hand at cleaning the Germans out.[44]

Though the Australians fought tenaciously and held on, even when it was obvious that they were both outnumbered and, most importantly, outgunned, the result was carnage. In the case of the 2/43rd Battalion, of the well over 100 soldiers who had attacked, only a couple of dozen came out unscathed just after dawn when the order came through to withdraw. Where were the rest? Many killed, certainly, but also many wounded, still out there in the middle of no-man's-land — and from the plaintive cries of soldiers they could hear, there were a lot in the latter category.[45] The 2/28th had been similarly devastated.

The injured could not simply be left there, with a very strong understanding among all Australian soldiers that if you went down in battle then, come hell or high water, your mates would find a way to get through to you if it could possibly be done, and sometimes when it didn't really seem possible at all. So now something had to be done — but what?

It was out of the question to send in another fighting force, as it was clear from what had happened that such a move would all but automatically result in more killed and wounded at the hands of the well-entrenched Germans. In addition, it would not be dark for at least another twelve hours, and many of the wounded would be dead by the time the men tried to sneak in and get them out under the cover of darkness.

This called for extreme measures to be taken, and the pastor for the 2/43rd, Father Tom Gard, decided it was up to him and a couple of the soldiers. With a Sergeant by the name of Wally Tuit and stretcher-bearer Keith Pope, he grabbed a truck from behind the Blue Line and slowly drove it forwards; and with a very nervous Wally sitting on the bonnet waving a Red Cross flag, they nudged their way into no-man's-land. Every moment Wally thought might be his last, acutely conscious that at that instant there were probably 200 rifles and machine guns pointed right at him, and it would only take one shot and he was done for . . . but the louder sound of the Australian soldiers crying out for help now that they were closer kept them going. Steady, mate, steady, keep 'er going, slowly . . .

There!

From the German lines suddenly appeared an officer, walking towards them in a strangely circuitous route, albeit with his hand up in the international signal for 'Stop', as he shouted something that sounded like 'Halt, Minen!'

The Australians did halt, and then Father Gard walked forwards, offered the officer a cigarette and, in extremely broken English from the latter, the two began to talk, as for a brief blissful moment it felt, and it was so, that on this part of the planet the war had stopped.

And indeed. The reason the officer had come out really had been to give the Australians an important warning. Their truck was heading straight for a minefield and if they had not stopped immediately they would have been blown apart. He soon organised for one of his men to emerge from his shelter and guide the truck through so they could pick up the Australian dead and wounded, while he busied himself organising for a German ambulance to come from behind Hill 209, to also pick up the German dead and wounded. In short order a small posse of soldiers from each side had emerged, tentatively at first, and then with a little more enthusiasm, and the men were mixing and mingling, exchanging cigarettes and conversing the best they could, even as the gathering of the fallen continued. In this process, Germans helped Australians and Australians helped Germans, each with the other's wounded, as well as the gathering of the dead. It was an extraordinary thing to be standing side by side with a man you'd done your utmost to kill just a few hours before, with no ill will. And then you could even be helping onto a stretcher a man you had yourself shot, as his best mate thanked you for your trouble — but that was the way it was for both sides.

As later described by one of the Australian soldiers: 'It was as though two armoured combatants had paused to raise their visors and for one moment had glimpsed human faces behind the steel.'

From further back other soldiers on the front lines, while not going forwards, at least emerged from behind their small fortifications and waved at each other. It was a friendly, uplifting moment for two sides which had both been severely bloodied. When the Australians of the 2/43rd attempted to account for everyone, it turned out that of the 137 attacking troops, 106 were casualties, with twenty-nine killed, sixty-nine wounded and eight missing. But then they were informed by the Germans that four wounded Australians had been captured in the early hours and were being well looked after by German doctors, so the figures were adjusted accordingly. (Often the explanation for missing men was that they had taken direct hits from artillery shells and there was simply nothing left to find.)

The end of this purely local 'armistice' came when the last two men left on the field — Sergeant Wally Tuit and the original German Lieutenant who had warned them they were heading for a minefield — stood and saluted each other before retreating to their respective corners to begin the battle once more. (Though perhaps that German Lieutenant's true sympathies were shown by the manner of his salute, with Wally Tuit later telling Chester Wilmot, 'he gave me the salute of the *Reichswehr*, not of the Nazis',[46] the Reichswehr having been the old-style German Army before the Nazis had fully taken over.)

Tragically, when on their own part of the battlefield the 2/28th had tried for a similar armistice, the Germans had fired warning shots around the vehicle bearing the Red Cross, as they believed it might be actually disguised just so it could bring supplies forwards — the situation complicated by the fact that the 2/28th were still holding, just barely, onto Post S7. Though the rest of the 2/28th fought to get through to them, it was not possible, and the men in S7 had to subsequently surrender.

Lieutenant General Morshead's broad feeling on the Australian side of the battle was contained in a passage he penned to Myrtle the day afterwards: 'Well my dear, it was a hard battle and our troops fought very gallantly, with great determination and vigour. Although we did not meet with the success hoped for, we did have our successes and we did give the Germans some really heavy blows.'[47]

It was nowhere near as heavy, however, as the blow the Germans had given them, and in hindsight it is clear that the attacks were misconceived from the first. There was just too little knowledge of the defences that lay before them and insufficient firepower to force the issue in the Australians' favour.

•

For those not involved directly in the siege, there was still a great amount of work to do — most specifically, training. At Rommel's insistence, and frequently under his personal supervision, formations of Panzers now went through endless manoeuvres with elite and artillery units in the desert well to the east of Tobruk, refining the optimum method of operating to maximise both their lethal and defensive capacity in desert conditions. The forthcoming attack on the garrison, Rommel had decided, would be undertaken in the daylight, on the posts on the southeast corner, with the artillery laying down a barrage lasting approximately three hours, focusing on the perimeter posts themselves, the Allied artillery positions inside the fortress and the command posts further back. When the tanks began to move forwards, artillery units would go with them to protect the flanks of the Panzers and take out designated targets as decided by the tank commanders, all of it supported by the Luftwaffe operating in a highly co-ordinated manner. In these desert manoeuvres, the Panzers stopped the practice of advancing one behind the other as they had done in Europe, where that was considered the way to proceed down a road. Instead they came on in waves of small, rectangular formations, with the depth of each wave being roughly four times its width, as it had been worked out that this was the quickest way the Panzer divisions could cover country while still being able to rapidly get themselves into battle formation when the need arose.[48]

Two tactics that they practised were the ones that had been so successful to this point. The first was to have the anti-tank guns working in tandem with the tanks, with the blessed 88s frequently operating from the front line. Eventually they became so practised at this that the 88s were capable of stopping and firing so quickly before moving forwards again that the whole tank attack was not delayed at all.

The second tactic was to have the Panzers manoeuvre in such a way that the Allied tanks could be lured back onto 88s dug into key positions. Again and again and again, they kept going until Rommel was satisfied that, should there be a major tank battle, his men would be more prepared than ever.[49]

•

And still the bloody Australians weren't satisfied!

Having received no response to his cable to Churchill on 20 July, Menzies sent another cable early in the second week of August, informing the British Prime Minister that the Australian War Cabinet was 'considerably perturbed' by General Blamey's report of a 'definite decline in health resistance' of the troops at Tobruk, and reaffirmed that he wanted the Australians *out*. Of course, the safety of the soldiers was paramount, but another factor was also important. With his own political stocks continuing to slide, Menzies needed some good news — any good news — to announce to the Australian public; to be able to announce that the Tobruk garrison was now safe — with no possibility that the debacle of Greece and Crete would be repeated — really would have been something.

Alas, in response Churchill did much as he had done before, which was ... not much. As the British Prime Minister later acknowledged in his memoirs, his instruction to Auchinleck was that, no matter what the Australians wanted, 'not to prejudice the defence of Tobruk by making a needless relief'.[50]

In fact, when Auchinleck briefly returned to London at this time and had an audience with his Prime Minister, Churchill said as much to him in person and assured him that so long as he did the militarily best thing for the war effort, he — Churchill — would handle the political side of things and settle Prime Minister Menzies down ...

After all, there could be little doubt where Menzies' true heart lay in this difficult matter, as just a few days previously he had been quoted in the London papers exhorting his fellow Australians to a greater war effort and to be 'true children of magnificent Britain from where we come'.[51]

Sometimes, Menzies came across as being more British than the British — and, certainly, the criticism had continued to grow among his Australian constituents that his political ambitions lay closer to Picadilly than Parliament House, Canberra, and that his firmest desire was to go back to London. Which was a bit much from a man exhorting everyone else to roll up their sleeves, bend their backs and pitch in to help the all-out war effort in *Australia*.

•

Tobruk, up ahead.

For Adam Mrozowski and his brother soldiers of the Polish 1st Carpathian Brigade, it was not only a long, long way to Tipperary, as they still loved to sing. Rather, for all of them it was the end of a long journey, and yet the blessed beginning of doing the thing they had been yearning to

do, and training towards, since the first day of autumn in 1939: fighting
Germans. On a night in mid August, they stole through the small signal
lights that marked the entrance to Tobruk Harbour, glided into the jetty at
the port, and within moments had silently slipped from their ship like the
angels of vengeance they felt themselves to be — even as the first
Australians to be relieved from Tobruk, the 18th Brigade, quickly embarked
on the same ships. The Australians headed out of the harbour and into the
Mediterranean proper, while the Poles looked to move to the front lines.

But, look, first, why don't you blokes 'ave a cup of tea?

Many of the Polish soldiers actually would have preferred, and even
demanded, to get started on the killing of Germans right away — please,
which way are they? — but were prevailed upon to settle down, take off
their rather absurd-looking pith helmets, have a cuppa and get their
bearings. They were assured that there would still be plenty of Germans to
go after in the morning, don't you blokes worry about that, and you may as
well get this down yer gullets.

Now, as they would soon learn, having a cup of Tobruk tea was a
unique experience. The reason it was so piping hot and yet you had to
drink it as quickly as possible was because sipping and savouring was out of
the question — to Adam's palate it tasted like cat's piss, and he would not
have been at all surprised if it actually was.

But to work. Their first task next morning was to take over the
positions of the 18th Brigade, and though the Poles proved to be fine
soldiers, it was not as if there weren't a few 'teething' problems at first. For
one thing about the Poles no one could help noticing was that they just
weren't interested in the Italians. Time and again when faced with Italians
in the distance, the soldiers of the 1st Carpathian Brigade would do nothing
but ignore them with contempt. But let just one German shake a leg at a
distance of anywhere up to a thousand yards and the Poles instantly came
alive, electricity flowing through their very beings, as they did everything in
their power to bring the Jerry down. The memory of what had happened
to their country in 1939 and since was seared into them, as it would be
forevermore — and these bastards were going to pay.

A similar dynamic operated with the scattering of Polish surgeons who
had now joined some of the field hospitals.

On one occasion it was noted by one of the leading Australian surgeons
that whenever German wounded were brought into their makeshift theatre,
a particular Polish surgeon would refuse to have anything to do with them,
right to the point of insubordination.

Finally, the Colonel in charge of the hospital unit sent for the Polish surgeon and put it to him straight: 'Captain … you must deal with the wounded as they are brought in, irrespective of race.

Captain: 'Is that an order, Colonel?'

Colonel: 'Yes, Captain, it is.'

Captain: 'Very good, Colonel, I will obey you but you must understand that with regard to the Germans, my mortality rate will be 100 per cent …'[52]

They knew what the Germans had done, and were continuing to do to Poland, and would neither forgive, nor forget.

•

Indeed, far, far to their north at that time, many German soldiers were flooding through occupied Poland on their way to get to the heart of Russia. On one of those trains, the eighteen-year-old Henry Metelmann noted that the further east they went through the devastated country, the worse the conditions became. The villages visible from the railway line were decrepit, their inhabitants filthy, the cars they drove primitive.

To young Henry it seemed to affirm, in many ways, exactly what Hitler had been saying all along: the Germans really were a superior race, and these people really did live like pigs — *Untermenschen*.

Still, some things did trouble Henry; things he just couldn't shake off. One was when their troop train stopped at a station and on the other platform was another train with closed cattle cars. Those cattle cars had barbed wire all around to prevent the occupants getting their hands out. But …

But then one pitiful woman managed to speak to the German soldiers, saying over and over '*Brot* … *Brot* …' (Bread … Bread …). Despite Henry and his comrades having absorbed Nazi indoctrination virtually with their mother's milk, and then at schools, in the Hitler Youth and intensive army training, something stirred in their souls, and they asked the SS soldier who was guarding them, 'Would it be all right to give her some bread?'

'Nein!' the SS man replied sternly. 'They're bloody Jews and they were fed only a couple of days ago.'[53]

Soon the trains went their different ways. Henry's one towards Russia; the Jews' likely towards Auschwitz. Still, Henry couldn't shake a bad feeling about it, and it would not go away. It was one thing to fight on a battlefield, killing enemy soldiers, but quite another to see this kind of treatment of defenceless people.

He was to get a similar feeling some time later when, with his regiment, he got into Russia and the weather became progressively colder the further east they went. By the time they had reached the Crimea, it was downright freezing. As Henry would ever after recall, in the twilight of one frozen day they arrived in a small village of one-room cottages with earthen floors. It wasn't much, but it was where they would have to sleep for the night. Henry's Sergeant pushed open the door of one cottage to find a young mother with three small children hiding behind her skirts.

'Raus!' the sergeant roared. Out!

'This is our home,' the woman replied in a half-strangled gurgle of misery as her children started to cry. 'Where can we go?'

That wasn't the Sergeant's problem. He said *out*, and he meant it. While the German soldiers, including the troubled Henry, settled down in front of the cheery fire, the woman was obliged to roll up everything she could carry, dress her children as warmly as she could and then go out the door. Henry looked out the windows — there was the woman with her three young ones, each of them with a bundle of belongings on their head, standing forlornly in the snow.

Yes, for tonight the Germans had their Lebensraum (living space), but at what cost?

One who had no doubt that the right thing was being done was Hitler himself. His firm belief was that the 'biological basis' for Soviet Communism was the Jewish people, and it was only by their extermination that the Communists could be brought to heel. And he did mean exterminate. This was to be no ad hoc attack, but a systematic slaughter of all those — including women and children, and the old and infirm — who had Jewish blood. So it was that after the German Army had moved through and conquered the territory, mobile 'killing squads' trailed in their wake and simply rounded up the Jews and shot them. It was a process that in the first few months alone of the German invasion of Russia would kill over 200 000 Jews.

And still, Hitler was not content to stop there.

At a later point, in the North African campaign, when soldiers from a Jewish unit were captured by Rommel's forces, Hitler sent a direct order that they were to be 'immediately liquidated'. Rommel reacted furiously to his senior officers, saying, '*Das kommt gar nicht in Frage* [This is out of the question]. *Fertig, aus* [Finished]*! Keine Diskussion* [No discussion]. These are regular prisoners of war and will be treated as such. We are soldiers, conventions are in place, and we will go by them. These men are not our enemies, they are our adversaries.'[54]

As ever, on Rommel's watch there was to be *keine Schweinereien passieren* — no piggy business, no unfair play.

So instead the Jewish prisoners were handed to the Italians, who treated them the way the Italians treated all prisoners in World War II, which was substantially well. Killing Jews was Hitler's obsession, but Mussolini did not share it, and nor did his people.

•

Whether it was a bit of bomb or a bullet that came flying their way, Rolf Völker was never quite sure, only that it came from the newly arrived Polish forces, who seemed to fire upon the Afrika Korps at all times of the day and night. And whatever it was, it had torn the belly from one of his fellow soldiers, a friend he had been with from his first days in the barracks in Germany, to the trip to North Africa, and all his time at Tobruk. And now his friend was not only scrabbling in the dust with his intestines spilling out all over and dragging behind him as he tried to crawl back to some shelter, but he was begging Rolf to '*Erschiess mich! Erschiess mich!*' Shoot me! Shoot me!

Rolf wanted to. It was obvious that his friend would not live, and equally obvious that to go out into the fierce fire to try and rescue him would be nothing less than suicide. So to shoot him dead would perhaps be the best thing. But he just couldn't do it!

'*Und Du willst mein Kamerad sein?!*' his friend now goaded him. And you want to be my comrade?! '*Erschiess mich!*' Shoot me!

Rolf kept looking, mesmerised, horrified, appalled, disgusted at his own weakness in not being able to do it.

'*Erschiess mich!*' Shoot me!

Rolf wept but still could not do it, just couldn't bring himself to end his friend's life. The result was that over the next ten minutes all he could do was watch, as the life ebbed out of this man, this soldier, his friend, with only the waves of agony that seemed to shudder through him every few seconds signalling he was still alive, until finally, mercifully, they too stopped, and he was dead.

•

On 23 August 1941, in a letter to his wife, Morshead penned the following passage:

I've got used to being without ordinary amenities but I cannot get used to being without you. This is a lonely life being a man apart, friendly enough with all but unable to make a real friend of any particular one. And there is no let up, no relaxation, always drive, drive, drive. It cannot be otherwise or as I see it, it should not be otherwise. Fortunately I have a good team which pulls together.

Which was indisputable. The team at home, though, on the political front, had long since ceased to pull together and had instead turned to pulling Robert Menzies apart, as in those desperate days of late August 1941 his hold on the Prime Ministership proved to be very fragile.

Desperate to placate the growing band of critics, on 26 August Menzies wrote to Labor leader John Curtin, formally offering Labor a share of power in a wartime coalition.

'Your letter,' Curtin replied, 'indicates that you are not now able as PM to give Australia stable government.'

It was an irrefutable assertion, because it was no more than the simple, unvarnished truth.

Within two days, Menzies had resigned the Prime Ministership and the leadership of his United Australia Party. After a joint UAP–Country Party meeting to elect a new leader, he was replaced as UAP leader by Billy Hughes, and as Prime Minister by the leader of the Country Party, Arthur Fadden. Still, political stability was far from assured, and it was for a very good reason that the new Prime Minister Fadden didn't move into the Lodge.

'You'll scarcely have enough time to wear a path from the back door to the shithouse,' one of his more earthy colleagues advised him.[55] After all, the two Independents upon whom the Government relied for its hold on power were getting closer to John Curtin every day, and it could only be a matter of time ...

•

Ever the master of political persuasion, Churchill gave it one more shot. In a cable to the new Australian leader, the British Prime Minister noted that even if he'd wanted — and he didn't — to get the Australians out of Tobruk, it was 'physically impossible' for it to be done any time soon, as 'only half could be removed during the moonless period of September and the other half would have to be removed during the latter half of October ...'

All that aside, though, there was something even more important.

'I trust, however, that you will weigh very carefully the immense responsibility which you would assume before history by depriving Australia of the glory of holding Tobruk till victory was won, which otherwise by God's help will be theirs for ever.'

Fucking fleas!

CHAPTER SEVENTEEN

End Game

It was the end of the war, and the AIF were on parade. First came the 6th
Division, war worn and grim. No chocolate soldiers there! Then the 7th,
also showing marks of a hard campaign. Then the 8th, all spruce and neat
in their natty tropical suits, and finally, the 10th, who had been charged
with the defence of Australia — looking as if they had just come from the
tailors! Crowds cheered, flags waved and Mr Spender's chest swelled with
pride. Suddenly, Mr Fadden said, 'I say! Spender! Where is the 9th
Division?' Mr Spender's face grew pale. He clutched his head and said,
'GOOD GOD! I FORGOT! THEY ARE STILL IN TOBRUK!'

FURPHY FLYER, 2/24TH AUSTRALIAN INFANTRY, 6 SEPTEMBER 1941

Little wonder the boys were called the Rats of Tobruk. For all the dreary
desert and rocky hills were pock-marked by thousands of holes from out of
which popped the Rats. As they saw us approaching many rubbed their
eyes to the sunlight, squinting towards us with their grins spreading wider
as they emerged from their holes. Some wore tin helmets, others wore
shabby slouch hats; all were in shabby khaki that merged so well with the
desert ground. Some poked their heads back down the holes to yell, 'The
Navy is here,' up beside them would pop dark, bewhiskered, grinning faces.
Then the waving of arms with shouts of 'Hullo there, the Navy!' and
'Struth! It's good to see you any time.'
One wag called: 'How bout a pot of ale at the Ship Inn . . .?'
We would squat down and spin yarns . . . not about war but about well-
known cabarets at Alexandria, and then more softly of our dear old
homeland. For Aussie was sweet to all of us . . .

'THE COUNT' PETTY OFFICER, 'ON PATROL ROUND ABOUT TOBRUK'[1]

General Thomas Blamey had at last had a complete gutful of the
infernally superior British attitude. The Brits simply refused to
understand that when it came to the disposition of Australian soldiers, it was

the *Australian* Government and the *Australian* military authorities who had, first and foremost, to be consulted.

Blamey's thoughts on the subject had been well encapsulated in a letter to the Australian Minister for the Army, Percy Spender, on 8 September 1941: 'It seems quite impossible for the ordinary English officer to appreciate the position from our point of view, and once any Australian unit gets into the command of a UK formation, it's like prising open the jaws of an alligator to get them back again.'[2]

Well, this had to stop. Blamey didn't doubt that it would have suited the British military leadership to treat Australian soldiers the same way they treated their own soldiers — simply giving them *orders* and ensuring that those orders were properly executed — but what they failed to understand was that Australia was not merely a company of soldiers there to do mighty Britain's bidding! For the previous two months Blamey had fought a constant series of skirmishes with the likes of first General Wavell and then his successor, General Auchinleck, about the need for Australian soldiers manning the Tobruk garrison to be relieved, and he had been totally backed by the Australian political leadership. And yet, with the exception of the 18th Brigade, all the Australian soldiers concerned remained exactly where Churchill and Auchinleck wanted them: still in Tobruk, still at their posts, still keeping the Afrika Korps at bay.

And now it had come to this.

At a meeting of Blamey and Auchinleck at GHQ in Cairo, Auchinleck had mentioned rather offhandedly that, despite Blamey's wishes, Tobruk could not be relieved as it was 'not a feasible proposition'. The logistics were too hard, he said; the operation would be too dangerous; and, apart from everything else, it was Auchinleck's view that no such operation was actually *necessary*. The other British Services Commanders in Chief heartily agreed, there's a good chap, and would not be swayed even when Morshead spoke up and supported Blamey. Auchinleck offered another regiment of Matilda tanks to help reinforce the troops. Morshead thanked him, but begged to suggest that those tanks would be unlikely to change the central dynamic.

Finally, Blamey could stand it no more. He had long had it within him to tell his superior officer a couple of home truths, and it was apparent that now was the time.

'Gentlemen,' he said, considering his words carefully, 'I think you don't understand the position. If I were a French or an American commander making this demand, what would you say about it?'

'But you're *not*,' replied Auchinleck, clearly mystified by just what Blamey was getting at, and trying to bring him back to the main point. Auchinleck had already said that the Australians would not be moved out of Tobruk, and Blamey was not French or American, so what was there left to discuss?

Still, Blamey would not back down.

'That is where you are wrong,' he returned evenly to Auchinleck. 'Australia is an independent nation. She came into the war under certain definite agreements. Now, gentlemen, in the name of my government, I demand the relief of these troops.'

He was *what*?

Demanding the relief of the Australian troops from Tobruk.

Demanding, of a superior officer, that a particular course of military action be taken? In another place, at another time, that alone would have been enough to have Blamey court-martialled, if not taken out and shot. But the reality, as Blamey was obviously aware, was that the situation had changed. Britain really had made a firm agreement with Australia at the beginning of the war as to the conditions under which Australian soldiers could be used, meaning that Blamey was now holding four aces and a joker.

Auchinleck, extremely reluctantly, could see no way out.

'Well,' he said finally, 'if that's the way you put it, we have no alternative . . .'[3]

It had been a long and arduous process, but it seemed that the job was finally done. The British leadership had been *made* to understand that the same characteristics that formed Australians into such formidable soldiers in the field also made them difficult to push around off it.

The meeting continued as best it could, with the heat of the previous conversation still doing nothing to warm an atmosphere that had turned decidedly cool.

Cool enough, in fact, that Blamey thought that his actions might well have made him 'the most hated man in the Middle East' — not that he gave much of a damn . . .

•

And yet Blamey was not alone. For now Prime Minister Fadden made reply to Churchill's cable, putting it all in very diplomatic language, but the essence of it was that as Australian Prime Minister he was prepared to take his chances with history giving him a bad report card, and he insisted the Australian troops be withdrawn:

It is vital to the Australian people to have concentrated
control and direction of its expeditionary forces. We do
not consider it unreasonable to expect that by this date
effect would have been given to this principle . . .
    We do not consider military considerations put
forward by the Commander in Chief outweigh case for the
relief of the garrison.

Finally, Churchill could stand it no more and, with infinite annoyance, cabled Auchinleck to the effect that the Australian Government could not be moved and the War Cabinet was therefore left with no choice but to accede to their and General Blamey's request and, indeed, move at least the next batch of Australian troops out in the next moonless period. (The British Prime Minister was, after all, the man who would shortly be making the much celebrated comment that 'There is only one thing worse than fighting with allies and that is fighting without them ...' and the strain between Britain and Australia was now such that this was precisely what Britain was risking.)

Auchinleck — despite his prior acknowledgment to Blamey that he was left with no alternative and would follow through — was appalled that it really had come to this, and was inclined to offer his resignation on the grounds that the Australians clearly had no confidence in his military judgment as it pertained to the Middle East in general and Tobruk in particular. A furious round of meetings and discussions at Whitehall then ensued, with most of that fury continuing to focus on the perfidious Australians.

The Minister of State, Sir Oliver Lyttleton — who had previously counselled Churchill to leave the Australians in Tobruk, no matter how much they protested — thought that it most certainly wasn't Auchinleck who should go, but General Blamey. After all, how could they continue with a situation in which Auchinleck's second in command had so openly worked against the desires of his superior officer, and seemingly won the day?

Churchill, though he freely conveyed to Sir Oliver that he was 'astounded' by the Australian decision to depart, expressed the view that to relieve Blamey would 'injure the foundations of the Empire'. Nevertheless, the British Prime Minister was quick to confirm to Auchinleck that he still enjoyed the complete support of the British Government, and tried to soothe him by noting that Fadden's own government was under severe pressure from a 'bitter opposition, part of whom at least are isolationist in sentiment'.[4]

As it happened, it would soon be Churchill's lot to deal with that 'bitter opposition' in an entirely different form, as on 3 October, having lost the support of the two Independents in Parliament, Arthur Fadden was forced to resign as Australian Prime Minister and the Labor Party's John Curtin became Australia's third PM in six weeks.

•

Bert Ferres was told by his Sergeant to go back from the front lines, to Company HQ, to pick up another roll of barbed wired. He'd find a 'reo' there, a new soldier who was joining them as a reinforcement, and he could help carry the wire.

No problems, Sarge. But then, on the way back with the reo, a sudden burst of tracer in their rough direction meant they had to hurl themselves to the ground. For Bert that kind of thing was nothing, and once it was over he jumped to his feet again, saying to the reo, 'C'mon, she's right now.' But the young fellow wouldn't get up.

'C'mon, let's go,' Bert repeated, a little more forcefully. 'It's safe.'

There was still no movement and it soon became apparent that nothing would move the young fellow, though he was physically unhurt. Bert returned to the Sergeant alone, carrying the barbed wire himself. Then the Sergeant went back, threatened the reo with everything under the sun and moon, but still he remained, sucking the ground. So he was arrested and sent back to HQ. Funny thing was, this particular bloke was a boxer, and a very good and brave one, but he just couldn't bear being shot at. Nevertheless, instead of the reo being court-martialled and sent home in disgrace, the medical officer took pity on him and installed him as his batman, a position he filled honourably.

•

It wasn't the military good news that Rommel wanted to hear — that his soldiers had by some miracle at last overwhelmed Tobruk's defences and taken prisoner all its valiant defenders — but it was something, all right. On 8 October he received a letter from his publisher, Voggenreiter, informing him that the royalties from the large edition of his book about infantry tactics, *Infanterie Greift An*, now totalled 25 000 marks![5] He couldn't wait to tell his wife, his Dearest Lu, and did so promptly ...

Certainly, such a thing as book sales was trivial compared to the outcome of the war he was engaged in, but for Rommel it was extremely important, as the sales helped secure the finances of his cherished wife and child, no matter what happened to him. And if he did survive this war, he had a fair measure of hope that all the notes he had taken of all the campaigns he had been involved in would provide him with another bestseller, which would hopefully free the family from financial worries forevermore.

•

It was near mid October 1941, and as a group the men of the 2/13th and 2/17th had never looked at the moon so much as each night, you bloody beauty, a sliver was sliced from the silvery orb until it had almost disappeared altogether. You bloody *beauty*! The 'dark' was almost upon them and, as they all knew and endlessly discussed, the dark was when the convoys to get them out of there would arrive. And given that the vast bulk of all the other Australians had gone, it surely — *surely* — had to be their turn to go next.

And sure enough . . .

Finally, the word did come through. The ships were coming, and night after night more troops of the 20th Brigade were spirited away, piling onto the same ships that brought their replacements. By this time the methods of getting the incoming troops off the ships had become a little more sophisticated, with many of them sliding down a long board onto the wharf or, indeed, any other firm surface that was handy, such as any exposed deck of an otherwise sunken ship.[6] *Hurry! Hurry! Hurry!* was the muted cry. On and off these ships in the night, the incoming British soldiers and outgoing Australian soldiers were like ships in the night, passing each other briefly, with perhaps just a grunted 'G'day' and 'Good luck' having to pass for a greeting and farewell. One night while Chester Wilmot was watching, the ABC journalist was able to observe 300 troops with full kit disembark from one ship in the space of ten minutes.

To facilitate the changeover, Lieutenant General Morshead ensured that, while the Red Line remained fully manned and ready to thwart any attack, the outgoing and incoming troops moved from and to positions in the Blue Line.

On his own last day in Tobruk before leaving that night — filing up a gangplank and immediately moving to the bow of the ship to gaze back — Morshead had gone to visit as many of the units under his command as possible to thank them for their sterling service. To British units he made the point in a formal letter that it had been his own desire that they be relieved with the Australians, but that he had unfortunately been overruled.

That uncomfortable fact apart, he did then, and would afterwards, look back upon Tobruk with legitimate pride. He and his men had been charged to hold it for two months, had in fact held it for seven, and he had been proud to hand command to Britain's General Ronald Scobie of a garrison that was all but entirely what he had been given to defend.

With Morshead went the 9th Divisional HQ.

•

Cablegram Winch 1 LONDON, 26 October 1941, 12.20 p.m. MOST SECRET. From British Prime Minister to Australian Prime Minister.

　　Re: your 682 of 16th October.

　　TOBRUK. Relief is being carried out in accordance with your decision which I greatly regret.

At last the word came through to the men of the 2/13th. Now in those last days of October, they too were to pack up their troubles, and anything else that would fit, in their old kitbag — while abandoning all heavy weaponry and the small comforts that made life in the trenches bearable — as just after sundown trucks would be coming to take them down to the port. At last, their ship was going to come in!

All that remained was to hand over their positions to a battalion of Poms drawn from Yorkshire and Lancashire, and farewell their old friends from the Northumberland Fusiliers just down the way — the last of whom embraced them warmly, told them they were 'lucky fookers'[7] and that they looked forward to meeting up with them again, perhaps in Alex, Cairo, Jaffa or wherever. Anywhere, any time, it would be good to see them again.

You too, you beauts, and see yers.

And then it was down to the docks with their heavy packs on, smoking, talking softly, and waiting, waiting, waiting. Right beside them, the 2/15th Battalion was also packed and ready to go, with some officers from the 20th Brigade Headquarters. The whole lot of them had been taken by barge out to a partially sunken ship, the deck of which was being used as an alternative wharf, and because that deck was on an angle the whole thing was rather uncomfortable.

Still waiting.

In the darkness, in such circumstances, with every ear straining to hear the throb of distant engines coming up the harbour towards them, it was no surprise that there were many false starts, with lots of men swearing blind that they would know that sound anywhere and the ships would shortly be appearing — and one or two had even claimed to be able to discern the shapes coming at them from out of the gloom — but by the time midnight came, there was no denying it: something must have gone wrong. Even if the ships arrived right now and the men piled on at record speed, it was going to be dangerous because they wouldn't be far enough away by the dawn to have any measure of safety from the Luftwaffe, and the rumours began to circulate. The ships hadn't even left Alexandria. They had left but had been bombed. One of them had been torpedoed and the others had stayed to pick up survivors ...

Finally, just after one o'clock in the morning, the 2/13th's 2IC, Major Colvin, gave them confirmation: not only hadn't their ship come in, but it wasn't coming in. The HMS *Latona* had been sunk by dive bombers, with the loss of twenty-four sailors and seven soldiers, and the other ships in the convoy had stayed to help. The 2/13th men were to hoist their kitbags once more upon their shoulders and move back.

Wouldn't it. Bloody number 13! They knew it was unlucky, and now there was the proof! Standing with his mate Bill Walmsley, Bert Ferres could barely believe it. To be so near, and yet so far! To have it all snatched away from them when just about every other bastard they'd come here with who'd survived to this point had shot through. And they weren't the only ones feeling the pain of it all, for the men of the 2/15th were equally pissed off.

Despite the orders for strict silence, the rumbling grumbling of the men was like a dirty wave, sluicing back and forth over the lot of them in the darkness. After everything they had been through, all the risks they had taken and survived, just when it looked like they were going on the same well-deserved break that all the other battalions had gone on, they were still bloody well here! Not untypically it was one of the blokes who had been waiting with them, a poet by passion if not profession, who best encapsulated the mood in a verse he wrote on the spot, which included the lines:

And when the word was passed around
That we were not to leave the place:
The phrases coarse and words profane
Were really a most sad disgrace;
One word the very buildings shook.
(The Tommies rhyme it with Tobruk.)[8]

Some blokes swore the poet was every bit as good as the great Banjo
Paterson — which was not surprising, as the man was in fact Banjo's son
Hugh.

For all that, the mood of the 2/13th worsened the following day when,
instead of being on the high seas with the wind in their hair, the sun on their
faces and the prospect of the night-time joys of Alexandria up ahead, they
were back in bloody Tobruk right in the middle of the worst khamsin anyone
had ever seen. With no carefully prepared position to go to, no homey little
hole in the ground like they had left just two days earlier when they had been
pulled out of the line, all the 2/13th could do was to lie down on the ground
with (as they had lately learned) their head into the wind, so the dust
wouldn't go straight up their nostrils, and wait it out. It lasted for two days, by
which time Bull Burrows astutely judged the mood of his men and insisted to
General Scobie that it would be the best for everyone if the 2/13th was put
straight back into the front line. That way, at least, they could take out their
anger on the Germans and Italians instead of having it just fester inside.

•

Within two days the men of the 2/13th were back on a different part of the
front line, up on the Derna Road sector, with no tobacco, on Tommy
rations and attached to a battalion of the Polish 1st Carpathian Brigade.
Those coves had bugger-all English, but could they fight! From the first, the
Australians liked them and their eagerness to get into the action, whatever
the risks.

Still, they were a strange bunch and no mistake. On the one hand they
were very formal, constantly saluting each other and carrying on, but on the
other they were quick to laugh and try out some of their bastard English,
which the Diggers appreciated. And while they had a tendency to plaster
pictures of the Virgin Mary all over their digs, there was no doubt that they
had little interest in turning the other cheek to those who had done them
and their country wrong.

As a matter of fact, a great deal of amusement could be had on occasion
if you were lucky enough to be around the Poles when they were listening to
the BBC Bulletin, waiting for stray bits of news about what was happening in
Poland, as well as the German invasion of Russia, which they were obsessed
by. The reason is contained in the 2/13th Battalion history ...

'There was a team of Polish soldiers over there tonight ... It was an
education to watch them. When the announcer was giving news of the
fighting on the Russian front, he mentioned that so many thousand

Germans had been killed. The Poles cheered lustily — and that is not to be wondered at. But when he said that so many thousand Russian soldiers had been killed, the Poles cheered just as lustily. It's tragic for the poor blighters, but it's hard to guess who they'd rather see win on the Eastern Front . . .'[9]

One who worked closely with the Poles at this time was Bert Ferres, as he took them out on patrol, and he came to admire greatly their bravery and willingness to mix it with the Germans, even if he never had the first clue as to what they were yabbering about in their odd language. If Bert wasn't quite himself at this point, it was because of what had happened to his great mate, Bill Walmsley. Only a fortnight after they should have been on the ship taking them to the safety of Alexandria, Bill had been knocked when he trod on a booby trap while out on patrol and died shortly afterwards. The bloke who was with Bill at the time, Clarrie George, had cried when telling Bert about it, something which struck Bert as odd. He was himself personally upset, because he had really liked Bill a great deal and he missed him already, but he didn't feel like crying about it. Bert's emotions ran more to a kind of cold anger: anger that such a good life had been so uselessly wasted; anger that he hadn't been with Bill at the time to maybe help keep him out of harm's way; anger that they hadn't gotten away on the *Latona* to safety, in which case Bill would still be alive; and anger at the bloody Germans who were the reason they were in this godforsaken part of the world in the first place . . .

•

All was quiet now, and much, much cooler.

It was the time of the early evening when the thermometer in the desert plummeted from the raging heat of the day to bitter cold, on this evening of 14 November, and Colonel John Crawford of the 2/17th Battalion did up another couple of buttons of his coat as he slipped quietly through the gates of Tobruk cemetery in the dusk. No guns were firing either near at hand or in the distance, and the only sound was the rather mournful sighing of the soft wind moving through the hundreds and hundreds of simple white crosses. He was alone, and this was purely personal.

The Colonel had received confirmation that the 2/17th would be pulled out that night — leaving only their sister battalion of the 2/13th as the Australian presence in the garrison — meaning he was in his last hours in Tobruk, and he and his men would shortly be on their way. At least, most of his men would be; some would be staying here in the cemetery, for ever, and it felt right to Crawford that he should say goodbye to them. Which he now did, standing in front of grave after grave, recalling what he knew of the men themselves; how he'd first got to know them; the training he had put them through; the actions he had sent them out on; the situations they had been killed in; and the letters he had subsequently had to write to their parents. It was no easy thing to recall many of the painful details, knowing that in some ways it was the decisions that he had taken that had sent these men to their deaths, but it certainly felt right to be here.

In front of Jack Edmondson's grave, now, he paused longer.

Poor Jack. From the beginning he had stood out as a good cove, if a bit quiet; a good soldier, though not one who had ever sprung immediately to mind as likely to cover himself in glory in a heroic action. And yet there lay Jack, one of his men, the first Australian winner of the Victoria Cross in the whole war, a soldier whose name would be recalled well after the rest of them were long forgotten, and whom the 2/17th would for ever be proud to call one of their own.

Goodbye, Jack. And God bless you.

Finally, Colonel Crawford turned and walked away, the one man upright and moving in a field of the horizontal and still.

One last look back at the cemetery gates — 'they lay in peace for their long "Stand-Down",' he later described it — and he was gone. His men remained, occupying a part of the world that would be always Australian.

Then onto the ship, and out ...

Standing on the stern of the ship, looking back at Tobruk as it disappeared into the dusk, one young soldier shyly asked the correspondent from the *Sydney Morning Herald* standing beside him, 'Do you think they'll think at home that we're as good as the Anzacs?'

The response of the journalist on the instant is not recorded, but his answer to the *Herald* readership, after noting the question, was unequivocal ...

He belonged to a battalion which had held a front of 6000 yards on which sometimes 5700 shells had rained in on one day — one shell to almost every yard. Bombs had burst among them, fighters had sprayed bullets like rain, enemy tanks had rolled relentlessly against them, and incredibly been crumpled and hurled back. These men had suffered dust storms, heat, fleas, flies, sleepless nights when the earth shook with the enemy's bombardment ...'[10]

Yes, they were as good as the Anzacs.

Only a few hours later, the convoy steamed into Alexandria Harbour in bright sunshine, and proceeded past many ships of the British fleet that were based there. As every ship from Tobruk passed, each British ship was 'dressed' — with all flags and signal bunting flying — with every crew member standing along the side of his vessel and formally saluting the troops who had held Tobruk for eight months, against all odds.[11]

•

By late October 1941 the situation in North Africa had become delicately poised. With no major actions having occurred between the two enemies for the previous five months, both sides now had supplies substantially replenished, including reinforcements of fresh troops and new squadrons of tanks — even if, in Rommel's case, that supply line had recently been severely threatened, with no fewer than forty of his supply ships having been sent to the bottom of the Mediterranean since July, by Allied air attacks. (On the strength of it, his troops had taken to mocking Mussolini's famous claim that the Mediterranean was *mare nostrum*, our sea, and insisted that instead it was 'the German swimming pool'.[12])

Against that, at Rommel's headquarters reports had continued to flow in of convoy after convoy of Allied ships arriving, bringing men, munitions, guns and tanks to the Nile Delta; and the German general's finely honed military instinct sensed that in all likelihood the Allies would launch a major offensive against his forces, quite probably to relieve Tobruk.

While Rommel didn't think such an attack was imminent, his response, typically, was to make plans to attack the Allies first, and no matter that both the Italian and German High Commands were firmly opposed. They were *always* opposed to such offensives, perpetually worried about their lines of supply and all the rest. That, he felt confident, could be overcome, most particularly if he could capture some Allied supply dumps to make up for the supplies he had lost to the ocean.

His rough plan was to launch his attack on the Allies on the morning of 14 November, and he continued to place a large chunk of his forces, Germans and Italians both, on the Egyptian frontier, running from Sollum 40 kilometres south to Sidi Omar. This was both his shield against any attack from the east and his starting point for his own thrust when all was ready, and his men were feverishly working to make it so.

Another concentration of the more than 400 tanks he had at his disposal (of which 150 were Italian) would be built up just outside the southeast corner of the Tobruk perimeter, ready to penetrate when the time came and finally, definitively, lance the boil that had been causing Rommel and his men such pain since those days of mid April six months earlier. And they would be able to count on air support from around 300 aircraft, of which just under 200 were Italian.

•

Rolf Völker and his friends could always easily tell the *Neuankömmlinge*, the new arrivals to the Afrika Korps — of whom there had been a progressively greater stream lately — and not just because they generally appeared so much healthier, without the oft-haunted eyes of the Korps veterans who had suffered and seen more than they thought possible in recent months. For, too, it was the recruits' uniforms which stood out, particularly their hats which, because they had not been bleached bland by endless months of the sun and sand, practically shone green. For many of the new ones, the fact that they stood out in this fashion made them so uncomfortable that they soon learned to dip their hats into a pot containing a mixture of the pills they had been issued against gas attacks, Losantin, as this had proved to be the best way to make the fabric look instantly aged and worn.[13] Teaching them to think like the more experienced veterans took longer, but *die Alten* (the old ones, as in, the veteran soldiers) did their best to teach them as quickly as they could. In these parts the new ones had to learn not only to live off the land, but to understand the land.

When the ground was rocky and made of crushed stones, it was good for motorised movements but awful during artillery fire and bomb attacks, as dig work was hardly possible. When the ground was sandy, the effect of the grenades was substantially lowered; however, vehicles got stuck and cover holes were hard to build, because the sliding, drifting sand only allowed the scraping of flat hollows.[14] If you wanted to dig a hole or a trench, then look for the tiny telltale marks left where the real desert rats had dug their own holes, as that was invariably in the softer ground.

In the meantime, by mid October it was obvious to even the common soldiers that something was stirring.

Again and again, those men of the Afrika Korps not actively engaged in holding Tobruk were being put through their paces in endless training sessions focused on attacking dummy fortress positions. The older heads of the battalion picked it immediately — they were preparing for another major assault on perimeter posts like that of the Easter and Salient battles. As they trained, medical officers moved among them, looking to weed out those who were physically no longer up to such an assault.[15] Nominally the order was that only soldiers who were 100 per cent fit would be allowed to attack, but because it soon became apparent that no one fitted such a description, the doctors had to look for the mostly fit ... enough.[16]

At least this time they would have good maps, and know exactly where they were going to make the breach on the southeast corner; and with the prospect that their long-awaited victory over the garrison might now be at hand, morale was surprisingly high. High enough, in fact, that among some of the battalions a new song became very popular, sung to the well-known tune of *Feuert los!* (Start firing!) The refrain went:

Wenn wir in Kairo einmarschieren, mit Hurra und Gebrüll,
Vorbei an Rommel defilieren,
Dann stehn sogar die alten Pharaoenen still!
Wenn wir auf Pyramiden steigen und zum Baden lockt der Nil,
Und wenn alle Rohre schweigen: Dann ist das DAK am Ziel!

When we march into Cairo, with Hurrah and with war-cries,
March past Rommel,
Then even the old Pharaohs stand still!
When we climb up the Pyramids and the Nile tempts for a bath,
When all barrels are quiet: Then the Afrika Korps has reached
   its aim![17]

•

In Egypt at that time a similar state of intensity gripped Auchinleck's Allied forces as they worked towards the launch of their long-planned campaign to sweep Rommel and his men entirely out of North Africa. Codenamed Operation Crusader, it was to be accomplished by the newly formed 8th Army, under the command of General Sir Alan Cunningham — the brother of the Admiral who had earlier in the year so impressed Menzies, Sir Andrew Cunningham.

All up, Auchinleck had assembled a force of 700 tanks, 600 aircraft and just under 120 000 men — three times the number of soldiers used by O'Connor earlier in the year — including some of the finest fighting men that the British Empire boasted. The 8th Army consisted of the 13th Corps, made up of the 2nd New Zealand Division, the 4th Indian Division and the 1st Army Tank Brigade, together with the 30th Corps, which had the 1st South African Division put together with the 7th Armoured Division and the 22nd Guards Brigade. Still, with a combined force that size, it was the devil's own job to get the supply dumps built up, as with the Luftwaffe so strong in the waters just south of Italy, particularly, it was now out of the question to bring supplies through the Mediterranean, and everything had to come the long way around the Cape of Good Hope and then up through the Suez. Moreover, all the plans had to be synchronised, and all the forces moved into position and told exactly what they had to do, with secure lines of communication between them; all up the days of British GHQ working only six to seven hours a day, as Chester Wilmot had witnessed in May, were long forgotten. Aware that Rommel's own supplies were building up, Auchinleck feared that the Axis powers would attack first, and he was desperate to deny them the first strike. All else being equal, Auchinleck wanted to launch his campaign somewhere around mid November, and would have if the long-awaited 1st South African Division hadn't in fact arrived last and late, which forced him to delay things for a few days. But elsewhere the plans for the push continued feverishly.

•

To the intelligence officers concerned, the photographs were deeply troubling. Provided by the Luftwaffe, they clearly showed that the British had built a railway line to 75 miles west of Mersa Matruh, and it didn't take a lot to work out why they would do such a thing. It could only be to facilitate supply to their forward troops, and they would only have gone to such an effort if an enormous campaign was planned. Could it be that an Allied attack was imminent?

Strangely, Rommel not only did not want to see the photographs, he positively refused to.

'I will not look at them,' he said, throwing them to the ground.[18] He was convinced that the British would not attack until December at the earliest, and by that time he would have attacked them, so their own plans were all but immaterial. Besides which, he was at least a little distracted, not only with the massive organisation involved in getting his own forces ready to push on to the Suez Canal, but also because he wanted nothing less after that than to push north up into Iraq and stop the flow of oil to the Russians!

In addition, on a personal level, after many months, he was at last going to be able to see Lucie on a quick trip to Rome, which he had organised as a break before launching his campaign.

Meanwhile, on that newly constructed railway line, the Allied supplies continued to move forwards, ready for the Allied campaign to begin, and by the middle of November just under 30 000 tons of such supplies had been secreted in carefully selected and secluded spots in the desert, well away from the main tracks. This was not just so the British would be able to relieve Tobruk but also because Auchinleck's overall plan was to keep going thereafter, sweeping Cyrenaica clean and continuing all the way to Tripoli. For both men it was extremely frustrating, as both were desperate to be the first to attack, and yet neither wanted to go until ready. For his part, Auchinleck was extremely reluctant to launch until he felt he had roughly double Rommel's forces in place, and he kept delaying the attack accordingly, while Rommel equally was obliged to push back his own attack date until he got the final sign-off from Berlin, which also remained obdurate.

So it was that the Allied trucks and trains kept pushing forwards around the clock, even as Rommel's men kept bringing their own munitions and food supplies forward ready to launch their own attack.

•

It was going to be a race, and not just any race.

It was *the* race, the one all Australians cared about, no matter where in the world they were or what they were doing. The Melbourne Cup.

War or no war, it was still going to be run, and on the front lines at Tobruk where the Diggers were concentrated, the bets flowed thick and fast, with any number of blokes who hadn't even set foot in Australia for a year somehow claiming to be experts on which horses were in form and which were out-and-out dogs. And other drongos listened to them!

Working off a list of names which been cabled especially from Australia for the troops, some said Skipton was a dead cert, while others thought Velocity was the go. Still others, though, said they were all drongos who had no bloody idea whatsoever, wouldn't know their arses from their elbows and that Triggerman — perhaps the sentimental favourite among the Australian soldiers for his name alone — was a practical certainty. Some blokes had direct bets with each other, while others engaged in platoon sweeps. In the latter case, each Digger would put in a couple of bob and so have the right to pull from the Sergeant's helmet the scrunched-up name of one of the horses in the field. True, they wouldn't be able to listen to the race, because for some reason the bloody BBC wasn't going to cover it — and they *knew* they couldn't count on Lord Haw-Haw to do the right thing — but the word was that they would know the result within hours, once Australia cabled it through to Divisional Headquarters and it came down their signal wires from there. This was important, much more important than anything else they could think of right then, apart from maybe getting home themselves some time in the next few months ...

•

The word went around the 2/13th quickly. Something's happening — and it's no furphy, even if you won't see anything about it in any of the battalion news rags. Some of the old Diggers of the battalion, who were veterans of the Great War, had been invited to Bull Burrows' headquarters for a drink to mark Remembrance Day, 11 November. While there, they'd got some good news and some bad news from the Bull, on the quiet, like. The bad news was that they weren't going to be taken out that night after all, as had been mooted. The good news, though, and it was a bloody beauty — to make most blokes as happy as the few who'd put their money on Skipton to win the Cup and come good at 8/1 — was that the push was on! In just over a week or so, the long-awaited British surge from Egypt into Libya was going to happen, with their newly constituted 8th Army attacking from Sollum, while forces from Tobruk would break out and try to link up with them. If all went well, the siege would be lifted and the Germans and Ities routed!

True, it was unlikely that the 2/13th themselves would be seeing a lot of action, as it had been agreed between GHQ and AIF leadership that because of the political sensitivities they would only be used as a last resort; but it was something, all right.

•

Out on the western perimeter, Adam Mrozowski and his brethren were in a truck loaded to the gunnels with mines, heading off to do what they had been doing an enormous amount of lately, which was setting up the minefields on which the Germans would hopefully blow themselves apart when it all started.

Somewhere in the distance a German artillery battery had clearly got them in range, because one second the truck was rolling along merrily and the next a flurry of shells was dropping all around. Adam and his fellow Polish soldiers did the obvious thing, which was to leap from the truck and try to take whatever shelter they could on its lee side, away from where the shells were coming from ... and were therefore sucking closely the desert dust just as the next truck, full of Australian soldiers, came along.

Ah, how the Australians laughed.

'Chickens! Chickens!' they roared, even going so far as to imitate the actions of chickens, which the Poles had come to understand was an Australian way of saying they were lacking a certain something when it came to what the Aussies also called 'guts' and 'gumption'.

Still, no hard feelings. For even as the Australians were doing their impromptu pantomime of a farmyard run amok, the German artillery now drew a bead on *them* and, just as quickly as it had happened to the Poles, shells began landing around the Aussies. Understandably, under the circumstances, the Australians didn't react immediately; but when a shell landed right on the bonnet before mercifully not exploding, and ricocheting off into the distance, the Australians had had enough. Leaping from their truck like they were competing in the hop, step and jump in the Olympics, the Australians were soon sucking the same dirt right beside the Poles, who were now, in turn, in hysterics.

Ah, how the Poles laughed.

'Chikuns! Chikuns!' they imitated the Australians, and their previous jerky fowl movements, even while lying prone. 'Chikuns! Chikuns!'

Soon the Australians started laughing too. The Poles liked them a lot, but Madonna, they were a weird mob.

•

Rommel may have discounted the possibility of an early British attack on his forces in Cyrenaica, but Berlin had not.

When Rommel, now in Rome, heard that Berlin was getting jittery, he wasted no time in getting Feldmarschall Alfred Jodl, the Wehrmacht Chief of Operations, on the phone.

'I hear that you wish me to give up the attack on Tobruk,' his first biographer, Desmond Young, records him saying. 'I am completely disgusted.'

Jodl did not back off, even if Rommel was still Hitler's favourite General, and replied that, yes, he did have concerns about an imminent British attack. When Rommel insisted, saying that even if the British did attack first, his forces were strong enough to thwart them, Jodl moved to cover himself should things go wrong.

'Can you guarantee that there is no danger?'

'I will give you my personal guarantee!' shouted Rommel.

The delightful presence of Lucie notwithstanding, the mood of Rommel was little improved that night, when reluctantly — as it was his fiftieth birthday the following day — he and Lucie accepted the hospitality offered by his Italian hosts to see a special screening of the popular Italian film *On from Benghazi*. This detailed the extraordinary success of the Italian Army across North Africa six months earlier, all without showing a single German soldier!

'Very interesting and instructive,' Rommel commented dryly afterwards. 'I often wondered what happened in that battle.'[19]

•

On the night Rommel was so wondering, however, two British submarines, the *Torbay* and *Talisman*, surfaced in a quiet inlet on the northernmost part of the North African coast. A unit of British commandos, led by Lieutenant Colonel Geoffrey Keyes of the No 11 Scottish Commando, came ashore and made their way towards Sidi Rafaa, a small town just to the west of Cyrene, on the road to Tobruk. Their target was the two-storey Prefettura building which, their intelligence had informed them, housed the headquarters of Panzergruppe Afrika, and Rommel himself. During a storm shortly after midnight on 17 November, this group entered the building by force, hoping to eliminate Rommel and the nerve centre of the German command. Alas for them, even though Rommel was not there — and, in fact, even if he had been in Africa he would not have been there, as he had found that particular spot way too far from the key battlefield — the building was well defended, and Keyes was killed in the ensuing skirmish, along with four German soldiers.

When Rommel returned from Rome via Athens shortly afterwards and learned of this attempted assassination, he ordered that Keyes be buried side by side with his own men who had lost their lives in the action, all of them with full military honours.

And if he was not able to attend the burial himself, that was for a very good reason . . .

For, as it turned out, in the early hours of 18 November — just a few hours before Rommel arrived back at his African headquarters, then in Gambut, situated just to the west of Sollum — Operation Crusader had begun in earnest, with the whole of the British 8th Army pushing through Mussolini's wire to successfully sweep around Rommel's southern flank below Sidi Omar.

Led by the mighty 2nd New Zealand Division, the 13th Corps charged straight down the coast road as it set out to reach the besieged garrison at Tobruk. Meanwhile, the 30th Corps turned to the northwest and parked itself at a place called Gabr Saleh, ready to take on Rommel's frontier forces when they surely emerged and came west to try to retrieve the situation — even as from above the heavens opened as never before and rain, real rain, lashed down upon both the attackers and defenders. A real storm for the ages. The most amazing thing? That was when the rain at last paused, the sun came out and within hours tiny little blossoms bloomed all over, making the desert simply awash in riotous colours, almost as if God had spilled his paint palette. Both defenders and attackers were stunned, noting — even as their tank tracks crushed ever more blooms — just how beautiful it all was.

Within Tobruk itself, last-minute preparations were under way for the 'breakout', the moment when tanks and men would sally forth, tally-ho, from the southeast corner and right at the Italian defenders they expected to find there. In so doing, they would be attempting to reach out an armoured hand towards the other armoured hand that was reaching out for them from Egypt. If they could meet and grasp, each would be able to draw strength from the other.

What the soldiers launching from Tobruk didn't know at that point, however, was that even as they were preparing to burst forth from that corner, so too were Rommel's men preparing to attack that very spot in an action planned for 23 November, and from the night of 15 November the Germans had begun to move into position, right behind a thin layer of Italians who could at least serve as alarm bells if the Allies broke out first.

•

Though taken by surprise by the Allied attack, and too slow to appreciate its extraordinary dimensions, Rommel looked quickly to the upside. Always in his element in the open field, he fancied his chances against the best the 8th Army could throw at him, and if it could be destroyed he would be able to take Tobruk at his leisure. Gathering as much information to him as he could about the positions of the Allies, Rommel became a typical blur of movement.

Now, in that swirling desert war, at any given moment 'the front' was an academic question only as the Axis and Allied forces constantly sallied, thrust and parried across an enormous swathe of the land. At one point there were as many as five separate fronts — in fact, as Rommel himself thought of it, the whole thing was more akin to a naval battle than anything else.

'Gentlemen,' Rommel's adjutant Schmidt records him telling his officers, 'the struggle in the desert is best compared with a battle at sea. Whoever has the weapons with the greatest range has the longest arm, exactly as at sea. Whoever has the greater mobility, through efficient motorisation and efficient lines of supply, can by swift action compel his opponent to act according to his wishes.'[20]

As a result, so fluid was 'the front' that neither side could be sure if it was before it or behind it at any given moment, and with Germans frequently using captured British trucks and vice versa, and even sometimes the uniforms of their enemy, the situation was further confused.

At one point Rommel himself was even able to slip into an Allied field hospital where, typically, wounded British and German soldiers lay side by side. Shown around by the ranking surgeon, who later said he thought his guest was Polish, Rommel promised that the supplies they needed would be sent to them — as they subsequently were — and drove off into the dust.

And if the vast, swirling sea was a desert, so too were there 'islands', represented by the small knolls that rose above the flat sands, important because whoever was the king of the castle atop those knolls could also be a very dirty rascal indeed to an enormous expanse of terrain around. Most particularly, there was great significance in five of those knolls situated 6 to 12 miles outside the perimeter to the southeast of Tobruk, as it was obvious to both sides that control of them would help to determine the fate of Operation Crusader.

For, not far from those knolls was the alternative road that Rommel had had the Italians build in a loop around Tobruk, to facilitate the flow of supplies still coming from Tripoli and going to Rommel's mass of forces to the east.

Clearly any push to relieve Tobruk coming from the east would come along that *Achsenstrasse*, Axis Road, just as the breakout from Tobruk to join up with the relieving forces would soon be upon it. It was for precisely this reason that in his last weeks in command of Tobruk Morshead had insisted that the knolls closest to that southeast corner be established as Allied strongholds. The plan was to keep a 'free corridor' reaching out into the desert towards the relieving forces, so that the Allies would be able to launch attacks on the German supply lines when the time came. The most important knoll of all was the furthest one out at 12 miles, Ed Duda, as it was the closest to the Axis Road. If the Axis controlled the knoll, they could attack an Allied relief effort, and if the Allies controlled it, the knoll would be the obvious first point of contact for that helpful hand coming west towards them. Who controlled Ed Duda had perhaps half the battle won in that area . . .

•

In Cairo now, Lieutenant General Morshead followed the course of the battle as closely as he could from radioed reports, concerned especially for the fate of the remaining Australians there, the 2/13th Battalion, and whether they would or wouldn't be thrown into battle. For, despite the agreement that the Australians would only be used as a last resort, as the battle raged and Rommel's men continued to notch up successes, it was obvious that that point was being reached . . .

At least Morshead was able to pause long enough on 21 November to attend a ceremony at GHQ in which he was honoured by the leader of the Polish forces, General Sikorski, who bestowed upon him the high accolade of the Polish Order of *Virtuti Militari*, and congratulated him with a formal kiss on each cheek in the European fashion — something that rather shocked Morshead at the time; but then it was straight back to following the course of the battle.

And there was indeed much to follow.

For on that very morning, at 0620 hours, a strong force of assembled British units called TOBFORCE had broken out of Tobruk using mobile bridges thrown across the anti-tank ditch set at R67 and R69; surged through channels in the minefields that had been carved just for them, and attacked the assembled Axis forces situated atop the nearest knolls (known to the garrison as 'Butch', 'Jill' and 'Tiger') even as the 30th Corps had reached just 15 miles southeast of Tobruk to Sidi Rezegh. Named for the tomb of a Muslim saint who had lain there for centuries in a small white-domed building, its military significance came from the airfield to be found just a mile or so from the tomb.

The fighting to control these knolls was bitter and bloody. To the shock and amazement of TOBFORCE, after the first Italian resistance had been overcome they suddenly came up hard against extremely well-armed German soldiers, who wasted no time in attacking them with enormous strength. The only way TOBFORCE could hold on to what they had so bitterly won was to keep sending out from Tobruk reserve battalion after reserve battalion, and the 2/13th watched them go with great interest. They were following the battle the best they could and, though they couldn't be certain, there seemed some possibility that they would soon be called upon. At least, they hoped so.

•

November the 23rd was an important day in the German calendar of 1941, as it was the day of the annual *Totensonntag*, the Sunday of the Dead. In peacetime this was traditionally a day of grief, remembrance and reverence for those who had died, especially including those who had given their lives in Germany's war. The feel of the day was always one of a heavy shroud of silence, punctuated only by pealing church bells throughout the land.

However, for those Germans in North Africa in 1941 in the middle of this war, it was a day of grief for entirely different reasons. Rather than remember those who had died decades before, they were grieving for those who had died just minutes and hours earlier, and trying desperately to avoid joining their number.

For Rolf Völker, for example, who was in the thick of the battle for control of Sidi Rezegh, it was a day of burning tanks and vehicles, and fighting the urge to vomit from the stench of the burned bodies of his comrades. And there were no church bells — only the constant chatter of machine-gun fire, artillery shells landing and exploding, and grenades bursting all over as the British 8th Army tried to force its way through to Tobruk. And they were using American 'Honey' tanks — the nickname for the American M3 Stuart with 37-mm guns, which was notably powerful, fast and reliable in desert conditions — the first time the weight of American munitions on the British side was beginning to tell in battle.[21] Though at one point the men of Rolf's regiment were almost cut off, somehow they managed to fight their way out. How Rolf personally survived it he would never know, although he sometimes fancied it was his mother's prayers.

•

As to the tank warfare, while the Honey tanks did cover an enormous distance in the first instance, it was not long before Rommel counterattacked against the first of the British thrusts, using two of his Panzer divisions to create havoc among the Allied forces. In these battles, it was the admiring estimation of Rommel's own tank commanders that their superior officer was applying the highest rule of the tank tactic of the veritable father of German tank warfare, Generaloberst Heinz Wilhelm Guderian: '*Nicht kleckern — klotzen!*' Which meant that once the battle is begun and you are committed, you don't hold back; you give it everything you have at full power ...

On the strength of it, the 8th Army was soon being torn apart. There might, just possibly, have been a Commander who could have matched Rommel's capacity to manoeuvre to advantage in the open field, but that man was not General Sir Alan Cunningham.

From the beginning, Rommel kept his own tank forces concentrated on working in slick cohesion with machine-gun regiments and artillery, while Cunningham's forces were widely dispersed and frequently without either infantry or artillery.

Well equipped, superbly trained, the Panzer divisions managed — most particularly in the four-day battle at Sidi Rezegh — to destroy about 530 of the British tanks, even as Tobruk itself continued to be bled white with men sent to hold those crucial strongholds. They were crucial because it was those very corridors that defined the 'corridor' that the relieving British armour of the 30th Corps was supposed to be travelling down to lift the siege.

How had Rommel done it? In his later classic work on Tobruk, Chester Wilmot recorded the German commander telling a captured British tank Brigadier after the battle, 'What difference does it make if you have two tanks to my one, when you spread them out and let me smash them in detail?'[22]

Instead of Rommel attacking Tobruk directly at this point, however, when he was right on top, the German decided on a high-risk course of action that no one — not even his own senior staff — had even conceived of, let alone thought to attempt. Leaving a holding force at the gates of Tobruk, Rommel now gathered the bulk of his Panzers to him and, in a high-speed crazy dash, sent them charging to the east, through the border wire between Cyrenaica and Egypt, and into the back areas of the Allied advance, sowing havoc in the enemy's supply line and communications system, before perhaps even continuing the charge towards the Suez Canal, provided all went well and they could replenish their supplies from enemy dumps . . .

Rommel went with his instincts; one of his great aphorisms, almost as if he really was a boxer, was: 'It is often possible to decide the issue of a battle merely by making an unexpected shift of one's own weight.'[23] He was also of the view that there can be a psychological moment in each battle called a *Hexenkessel* (literally a witch's cauldron) at which point one of the protagonists is so overwhelmed he gives up, and that his own best chance of creating this condition in the 8th Army was to attack them where they least anticipated it.[24]

And well might it have worked, too, had the British panicked and drawn back their forces to try to stave off the threat behind them . . . which they almost did. For, even the night before Rommel made this stunning move, Cunningham, the Commander of the 8th Army, had signalled to Auchinleck that in his view it was foolhardy to continue the campaign. Both his men and his tanks had simply been cut to pieces by the forces commanded by Rommel, and total decimation awaited if they continued.

It was then that Auchinleck made the riskiest decision of his career. Even while Rommel's forces were on their charge to the east, Auchinleck gave Cunningham specific, written orders. While he acknowledged that the option of withdrawing had to be examined, there was another way . . .

```
The second course is to continue to press our offensive
with whatever means are in our power. There is no
possible doubt that the second is the right and only
course. The risks involved in it must be accepted. You
will, therefore, continue to attack the enemy relentlessly,
using all your resources, even to the last tank . . .²⁵
```

Such instructions could not have been clearer, and yet when Auchinleck came to the view that Cunningham still didn't have his heart in it, he summarily replaced him with his own Deputy Chief of Staff, Lieutenant General Neil Ritchie, who had indeed promised that he would fight to the last tank. While Ritchie may not have had a lot of experience with tank warfare, he was a fighter, and that was the most important thing at this point.

•

One key success, for the Allies at least, was when news came through on 26 November that the 1st Essex Battalion had wrested Ed Duda from the Germans, while nearby Bel Hemed and Sidi Rezegh had also been secured. This meant that, although at great cost, the hand had been stretched out from Tobruk east into the desert, and there really was a corridor for the 8th Army to reach towards themselves.

And . . . there! In the distance, not long after the Essex had reached the heights of Ed Duda, they saw three red Very flares exploding in the night sky to their northeast, the arranged signal that the 8th Army was indeed close and fighting its way towards them.

Now, at last, the outstretched fingers of the two armoured Allied gloves reaching for each other in the desert did meet and touch, when at one o'clock on the morning of 27 November the 19th New Zealand Battalion and a squadron of British tanks fought their way through to Ed Duda. By the following day Major General Alfred Godwin-Austen, the Commander of 13th Corps, whose troops had broken through, was able to send his famous cable to Cairo: 'Corridor to Tobruk clear and secure. Tobruk is as relieved as I am.'²⁶

Yet there remained a good deal of fighting to get through to see if that relief really was momentous, or perhaps only momentary.

Far to the east now, Rommel's Panzer divisions were exhausted by their long forging-and-fighting journey through the desert, and with petrol supplies running low — in their rush they had passed mere kilometres to the north of two enormous 8th Army supply dumps in the desert — they were left with little choice now that the 8th Army had refused to turn back and engage them. Unable to remain where they were in Egypt without any substantial targets to attack, and also without the capacity to keep moving on to Cairo and the Suez Canal (they had only sixty-five tanks left of the 200 they had started with), the only option was to turn back and proceed to the area around Tobruk, and attack the 8th Army there ...

Rommel's charge to the east had always been a high-risk ploy, but it clearly hadn't worked. He now set himself to recover, to take what forces he did have, and retrieve the situation by smashing those outstretched fingers and dividing the Allied forces once more.

27 Nov. 1941.

Dearest Lu,

The battle has now been raging in the desert around Tobruk and in front of Sollum since the 19th. You will have heard from the communiqué more or less how it has gone. I think we're through the worst and that the battle will be of decisive importance to the whole war situation.

I'm very well. I've just spent four days in a desert counter-attack with nothing to wash with. We had a splendid success.

It's our 25th wedding anniversary today. Perhaps it'll run to a special communiqué. I need not tell you how well we get on together. I want to thank you for all the love and kindness through the years which have passed quickly. I think, with gratitude to you, of our son, who is a source of great pride to me. With his splendid gifts he should go far.

All for now.

Our next move is already beginning ...

Erwin [27]

At last, the 2/13th was needed once more. Based inside the Blue Line around the Pilastrino area — its job had been to act as a mobile reserve only, ready to move to counter any attempted Red Line penetration — the men had spent most of the last two weeks frustrated at their own inactivity, obliged to watch as unit after unit had gone out beyond the wire, getting stuck in with mixed results. But now ... now, maybe, it was their turn.

The first sign came at six o'clock on the evening of 28 November, when their Commanding Officer, Bull Burrows, came back from a meeting with the brass with a spring in his step and a glint in his eye that could only mean one thing. Action.

After the two previous failed attempts, this time the 8th Army had got through and was close to reaching Tobruk in force. The remaining obstacle was the Germans threatening to take the most important piece of high ground outside the southeastern perimeter — Ed Duda, situated right by the newly constructed Axis Road. If the Germans gained it, they could prevent the relief of the Tobruk garrison; while if TOBFORCE could hold it, not only would the siege be effectively and definitively lifted, but Rommel's whole supply line and even his line of retreat would be threatened.

There was only one way, and that was for the 1st Essex Battalion, which was then holding Ed Duda, to be reinforced and the Germans beaten off. Given the past valiant record of the 2/13th, and that it was the last battalion left in reserve, General Scobie had no choice but to call for The Bull and ask him if he would agree to send his men in. Before the British General knew it, he had a man called Bob for his uncle. For the old Australian Colonel had responded heartily and with no hesitation: 'Sure. We'll see to that for you ...'[28]

Upon his return The Bull had given the orders and that was that. Within two and a half hours the 2/13th was on its way, piling into the trucks that had been sent and moving *outside* the Red Line! Not long afterwards it stopped at the first stronghold, Tiger, which had been taken a few days earlier by the 2nd Battalion of Scotland's magnificent Black Watch (which, after each man had been given a good tot of rum before heading off, had been led into the key battle by the second in command playing the bagpipes, before he was killed).

At Tiger, each soldier of the 2/13th was issued with a 'sticky bomb'. These were essentially grenades encased in a gluey substance, of frankly indeterminate value, but the hope was that with them the troops would have some defence against any of the tanks the Germans might send their way. (All they had to do was get close enough to the tank to stick the bastard on, and detach their own hand before it blew up!)

Okay, now back on the trucks, boys, and let's go. It was now bitterly cold as the battalion moved softly forwards to its destiny. The men had been in this position before, of course, and — if it can be accepted that it really is possible to say 'the battalion feels ...' without exaggeration — there was a very definite feeling abroad among the 2/13th. Resolution, certainly, and equally some trepidation as to what might await them ... But the predominant mood for the men, after nine months of personally surviving battle after battle, while seeing many of their comrades fall, was an almost sanguine feeling in the opinion of one Digger who put it like this: 'The first feelings of being scared left me, and the feeling of "what's to be will be" came to me.'[29]

Sure, it was possible that they now had just hours to live but, as battle-hardened veterans, they had learned enough to know that being anxious about that fact wasn't going to help things, and the best thing to do was to continue to attack with everything they had in them. They kept moving — slowly, slowly — trying to make as little noise as possible ...[30]

At midnight they were unloaded and took up positions around and about some British tanks on a dip in the desert in the lee of Ed Duda, which would shortly become known to the troops as 'Murder Flat', and for very good reason ...

For no sooner had the sun first started to peek over the horizon the next morning than there was a series of sudden explosions off to their high right, followed by the piercing whistle of a whining shell heading their way and descending ... descending ... descending ... to land ... *where?*

Oh Christ! Right in the middle of them. *Oh Christ!* They jumped in all directions, running for cover. For a few seconds flat the 2/13th received salvo after salvo of 110-pound shells into its middle, which were coming from Germans well dug in on a neighbouring ridge. When the first volley landed some blokes were blown to pieces, with their bedding and their rifles and their sticky bombs all hurtled skywards, and their souls continuing in that direction thereafter.

Somehow the trucks had dropped them in the wrong spot, so close to Ed Duda that they were within artillery range!

As Private George McFadyen of the 2/13th later wrote to his uncle, describing the action:

'Jerry had a big battery on the high ridge on our right overlooking the flat we were on, he had our range to a "T" and did he feed those guns! I could see the muzzle blast, the guns were so close. We had no cover — only the tanks, and they drew the crabs. Boys were hit all around — calling for stretcher bearers, calling for mates. How we weren't all done over I shall never know.

'One shell landed near me as I was making my way towards a tank. I was carrying all my kit, rifle, 500 rounds and a Vickers gun. As I hit the ground I could feel the hot blast of the explosion. My strength left me. I couldn't move my arms or legs. The last I remember was being helped into a tank by the crew. I came round some time later feeling very sick but a bit of strength returning. I was having a smoke and coming to when a Tank Commander stuck his head in the Tank and told the crew, "We go over the bags at 11.30 with the Aussies" — and me like that. I pulled myself together a bit and collected my kit and made off to find my section. I found the boys in a bit of a hole all set to go.'[31]

Those same Aussies were just hoping to at least stay alive until 11.30 a.m., when they would have a chance to get their own back in the attack, and all scratched as much of a grim shallow into the desert floor as they could, hoping to find some shelter from the shrapnel. And so they waited, even as the tanks warmed their engines readying to go, but the Germans didn't let up their shelling even for a moment. How much ammo did those bastards have up there? The short answer was 'plenty', and the shells kept landing among the tanks and the men. Retreat was no possibility, as that would make it even harder to regain this patch of ground they had already 'won' in the darkness. What most of the Diggers and the tank Commanders wanted to do was bring it on, get on with it, get to grips. Alas, word came through — for reasons best known to the British commanders — that the attack was to be postponed for three hours. There was nothing the men could do but hug even tighter to Mother Earth the way they had once hugged their own mothers as babies, and hope they could last it out.

At least the Germans were soon copping a bit back on their own account, as a couple of big batteries of Pommy artillery opened up behind and — you bloody beauty — shells started landing on high, making a 'soft, tearing, rustling sound as they went over our heads', as Private McFadyen described it.

It soon became apparent that Ed Duda above, which they thought was still held by the 1st Essex Battalion, had now fallen, and shell-shocked survivors of that outfit, who all but rolled down the hill to them, soon told the Australians through glazed eyes that they'd been overwhelmed by a squadron of fifty German tanks supported by infantry. Suddenly, the mission of the 2/13th had altered. Instead of just reinforcing the Tommies of the Essex Battalion, it was going to be the Australians' job to win back the summit of Ed Duda, and the fate of the entire battle possibly hinged on them doing so.

Soon they could even see the German tanks peeking over the lip of the plateau of Ed Duda, and in no time at all the Pommy tanks were moving, forward-ho and straight up the hill at 'em, soon disappearing over the top, with only the sounds of their heavy Vickers machine guns and 2-pounder cannon going nineteen-to-the-dozen coming back to the 2/13th. Then, a hideous explosion and a big black column of smoke indicated that at least one of the Pommy tanks had copped it, as again shells started landing among the soldiers back on Murder Flat . . .

Word came back that the Germans had sent in forty of their own tanks and that, for the moment, it was to be the tanks that had to sort it out, while the 2/13th was to once again go to ground and survive the ongoing arty the best it could. After dark, the tanks that had survived the German attentions thus far returned for a quick breather. And now, at last, the 2/13th was told that its time really had come, because when its own twenty tanks went back up the hill, it would be going with them.

It was a curious thing to be down below, watching the German soldiers furiously digging in on the heights of Ed Duda, in the spots between the many Mark IVs and Mark Vs that would also be waiting for them, but the Australians still fancied their chances and were anxious to get started on them.

A couple of hours after dark, the men of the 2/13th B and C Companies lined up right at the foot of the rise in a long line — about 160 of them in total, standing in bright moonlight, going up against what later proved to be about 450 dug-in Germans. Always at such moments there are last-minute adjustments to be made, and so Corporal Earl Walsh from Coffs Harbour was not all that surprised to be asked by Captain Michael Graham of B Company to move from 10 Platoon to 12 Platoon, as 12 Platoon was shy a couple of Corporals. Yes, sir, no problem, sir, and Corporal Walsh moved just a little to his right because of it.

Now Colonel Burrows stood out the front of his men, holding his Tommy gun, and notable among many other things for the fact that he was pretty much the only man jack among them who did not have a helmet on, but had kept his slouch hat. The word from the Colonel came down the line: 'Fix bayonets.' It was all, somehow, eerily reminiscent of their stint back in Palestine when the day's training exercises would be about to end and they would have to attach their bayonets before charging up Sheepshit Hill, 'cept this was now for real, and there were Germans with their own guns and tanks waiting for them at the top.

And one more thing from The Bull: 'Give a good shout when you go in . . .'

Alas, just seconds before they were to start there was a sudden whistling getting ominously higher and higher in pitch as all of them tensed, waiting for it to land, just knowing it was going to be bad . . . and then an artillery shell landed right among B Company's 10 Platoon, blowing many of them apart. Of twenty-six men in that platoon, only eight were able to get up on their feet again and join the line, with six brave soldiers killed outright. Men were now screaming, dying, calling for help, even as the telltale streaming arc of spark of a Very light went up skywards just ahead of the Australian troops — the signal they'd been waiting for — and exploded in a peal of ethereal green across the night sky.

The dead were dead, and the wounded of 10 Platoon would have to wait, as the men of 11 and 12 Platoons right beside them were now already moving forwards, gritting their teeth, averting their eyes and ignoring the cries of their brethren . . . but now more set than ever on getting to grips with the enemy. One of those resolutely marching by was Corporal Walsh, who looked on, appalled at what had happened to the comrades he'd left just minutes before to go to 12 Platoon. For the rest of his days he would never forget the horror of hearing the cries of one of his friends, a bloke they all called Clancy, screaming at the top of his lungs, 'Shoot me! Shoot me!' And maybe Corporal Walsh might have too, for mercy's sake, but like everyone else he knew what his job was now, and it wasn't to try to stem Clancy's bleeding.[32]

•

And . . . chaaaaaaarge!

As one, they started screaming, 'The Australians are coming!' — a cry that was met with one of alarm by the German soldiers unfortunate enough to be in the front line of the defence, who cried to their fellow soldiers, '*Die Engländer kommen!*' even as, to the amazement of the Australian attackers, some broke and began to run.

Tearing up the hill now, mortars started to land among the Diggers, but at least the British tanks of the 32nd Brigade were out in front, firing tracers and shells and giving at least as good as they got. They were also aided by fire coming from the gunners of the Royal Horse Artillery, to the point that some of the German tanks began to withdraw!

Still, however, enough remained that, as Private McFadyen wrote: 'Jerry's tracers were splashing off the sides of our own tanks, sending them in all directions and things were starting to get a bit mixed. I remember hearing bullets buzzing past and laughing at the small buzzing things after the heavy shelling we just had that day. Tommy guns and Brens went into action on my right. We landed in a trench full of men.'

'"We're New Zealanders!" someone shouted. Our boys answered, "We're Aussies!"'

And then together across the ridge, they went at it — dinky-di ANZACs at last — with McFadyen recording that, amidst all the explosions and gunfire, he could hear 'Kamerad!' and 'Mercy!' in high-pitched voices coming from his right, as some of the lads got serious with their bayonets.

Meantime, to the north of McFadyen, Bert Ferres was also tearing up the hill, with no one at all on his immediate left. It just so happened that if all the Australian soldiers at the bottom of the hill had been numbered 1 to 160, then Bert would have been number 1, so that he was especially conscious of what lay out to his left, as he would be the first in the line of fire. Which is why he saw them first ...

•

Further up the hill but well out to the left, Bert suddenly saw a broad mass of Germans — perhaps a hundred of them — who were starting to fire straight across into the 2/13th's otherwise unprotected flank, meaning that Bert had only one option. Operating more in the realms of urgent instinct than conscious thought, he grabbed three of his mates and charged straight at the Germans.

Firing his Bren gun from the hip straight into the mass, he could barely miss, and perhaps the fact that his bullets caused such immediate carnage meant that the Germans lost their nerve, for before his very eyes some of the soldiers started to break and run while others went to ground. One way or another, the fire that was coming upon the Australians was not as heavy and devastating as it might have been, and as Bert and his men got closer to the Germans — and their fire became consequently more accurate — it was obvious that the Germans had little fight left in them. Bert had no sooner called upon them to surrender, using the only German words he knew —

'Handy hock oda ik sheessa', as in, '*Hände hoch oder ich schiesse*' ('Put your hands up, or I'll shoot!') — than most of them did so. Again, most of them were mesmerised by the length of the Australian bayonets, but some German soldiers continued to do what they had been trained to do, which was to pick their weapons apart and throw them every which way before surrendering.[33] In short order, Bert Ferres and his men had been able to take some twenty-five of them prisoner. It was an action that would earn for Bert the highly coveted Military Medal, for displaying such great courage and leadership.

There were many other acts of great bravery on Ed Duda that night. Out on the right flank, Sergeant John Searle was with five of his men when they came straight upon a pocket of heavy resistance, and at this point a less experienced section might have gone to ground. But not Searle and his men — they too tore directly at the enemy, firing as they went, and had the satisfaction of seeing the Germans panic, turn and run. Searle was later awarded the Distinguished Conduct Medal for his leadership and bravery.

All up, within half an hour of the charge beginning it was over, and the 2/13th had taken the knoll and over 167 prisoners with it. To be sure there was a fair bit of mopping up to do, but after what they had already been through, that felt like nothing.

In the immediate aftermath of the charge, those Germans who had surrendered had to be disarmed and taken away, and it was in the course of this that one highly celebrated exchange took place. As recorded in the 2/13th Battalion history, just after the runner for C Company, Private Clarrie Jones, had captured a German captain, his new prisoner demanded to know where the charging troops that had just overrun him and his comrades were from.

'We're Australians,' Jones had replied proudly.

'No,' the German officer replied, 'you must be English, because all Australians have left Tobruk.'

Indignant, Jones insisted that they really were Australians, and in the moonlight even showed him the badge he wore on his uniform, with the AIF emblem and the word '**Australia**' clearly visible.

Still, the German wouldn't believe him, insisting: 'Ach, you are ze English, just dressed up in Australian uniforms to frighten us!'[34]

•

And, in fact, there was still a fair bit of frightening of Germans to be done by Australians that very night in those parts. So rapid had been the taking of

Ed Duda that, throughout the night, German supply trucks and staff cars kept nudging forwards, thinking they were heading to an outpost still in their hands, and were obliged to put those hands up for their trouble before being led away.

Too, when the sun rose the following morning, the most extraordinary thing for the Australians atop Ed Duda was that a great German camp was clearly visible on the flats below, with tents, kitchens, groups of soldiers marching back and forth, and mobile repair shops working on tanks. Clearly, they also had no idea that the heights before them were in Allied hands — but they didn't have to wait long to find out, with a unit of the Royal Horse Artillery giving them a wake-up call that German survivors would be a long time in forgetting, as shells soon rained down upon them and the whole thing was turned into a dusty carnage.

Not that the 2/13th's part of the battle was done as, now desperate to retrieve the situation, Rommel flung in battalion after battalion to retake Ed Duda and surrounding posts, isolate Tobruk once more and ensure that his own supply line was secure ...

•

In response, the Australians simply dug in and weathered the storm, taking on all comers; though one sad episode occurred in the first daylight hours of 1 December, just as Bull Burrows was poring over a map with his 2IC, Major Colvin. They were working out the precise co-ordinates of a mass of enemy tanks that was on its way towards them when there was a sudden whistling of an incoming 210-mm shell, which landed and exploded only a few yards from where they were sitting. Fortunately — or not — the shrapnel hit The Bull in the head — most certainly the hardest part of him — and though he was badly wounded, and carried away on a stretcher, he did survive, with Major Colvin fortunately suffering only minor injuries.

Still the Australians held on over the next two days and nights as yet more attacks came in upon them, and they never gave an inch until relieved in the first wee hours of 3 December by a British unit — the 4th Battalion of the Border Regiment.

A sign of how the men felt at this point, after their five days of holding on for grim death, is in their battalion history: 'Never did we dream, during those weary months of siege, that we would ever welcome a return to the perimeter, but it was with a feeling of relief that we finally passed through the perimeter wire to take over a position from the Durham Light Infantry, astride the El Adem Road.'[35]

•

The situation for the Afrika Korps was now beyond desperate. When, at one stage, one of Rommel's senior officers complained that his men were all out of water, ammunition and supplies, Rommel pointed to an ominous smudge in the distance.

'See this dust cloud at the horizon?' he said. 'Get your water and supplies there ...'[36]

In short, the British had what the Germans needed, and if the latter wanted it, they would have to go and get it from them. Certainly it wasn't ideal for the Afrika Korps to at this point effectively be turned into a *Zigeunerarmee* (gypsy army), living off the land and fighting for whatever else it needed, but it at least let it keep going — at this point some 70 per cent of its vehicles were captured British trucks — when otherwise all would have been lost.

And yet, by 7 December it was obvious to a deeply disappointed General Erwin Rommel that the best hope of his troops was to live to fight another day, and he began to pull his men out, unit by unit, to fall back upon a carefully prepared fortified position at Gazala, 60 kilometres to the west of Tobruk.

(On that same day, the Japanese bombed Pearl Harbor and the war quickly moved into another phase entirely.)

The real breakthrough, on 9 December, came when the Carpathian Brigade managed to take back all of Hill 209, as the German and Italian forces had melted away during the night. Rommel, having lost 60 000 men killed, wounded or captured from his original force of 100 000 before Crusader had begun, simply couldn't go on with it. For its part, the 8th Army had lost just over 18 000 men of its original force of 118 000 soldiers, but had at least emerged victorious.

For finally, the signal went out from the garrison's HQ, that operations in the Tobruk area were officially over, the troops did not have to 'stand-to' and they would not even need a password if they wanted to cross the perimeter.

What an extraordinary feeling for the 2/13th, especially, having been under siege themselves for no fewer than 242 days without a break, to now be able to wander about in broad daylight, right near the perimeter and even out into no-man's-land, and what's more to have a good stickybeak in the area where the Germans had been dug in, all without fear of shells and machine-gun fire!

And yet their mood wasn't elation pure, as might have been expected. Yes, it seemed they had survived and would soon be heading to relative safety, which was wonderful, but mixed with all that there was a great deal of sadness for their fallen mates, the blokes who had 'taken the count', many of them just near the final bell, too. To this point the men hadn't properly been able to allow themselves the luxury of grieving, as that would have compromised their readiness for the coming battles, but now they were able to pause, remember, and let at least some of their feelings out.

More than a few went down to the cemetery to say their final goodbyes to the mates they would surely soon be leaving behind; and, sure enough, it was shortly official. They would be pulling out — by truck, if you please — and in just a day or two. For the 2/13th, the fact that the lads of the RAAF, their own blokes from Oz, soon turned up and they were able to catch up with some of the latest news from home somehow proved that the whole thing wasn't a dream. The siege truly was over, and they really would be leaving before long! When it was confirmed on the evening of 15 December, they gathered every Very flare they had and sent them skywards, making a real 'bunger night' of it.

Even as they exploded, a series of messages for the 2/13th had begun to arrive from other units.

From Colonel Nichols — Essex Regiment.
    Happy Hunting 2/13th. Wish to keep up our connections after war. Good luck all.
    Nichols.

Another message read:

1 Royal Horse Artillery to 2/13th Battalion.
    Farewell, off at last, see you soon we hope good luck all.
    C.O. 1 RHA.

And, finally, one from the RAAF No 3 Squadron that went down particularly well.

Best of luck will keep an eye on you over the desert.
    From the boys 3rd Squadron RAAF.[37]

And then the cattle trucks came for them. As one, they piled on, and just after seven o'clock on the morning of 16 December 1941, the 2/13th

Battalion — the unit which had the honour of being both the first and last Australians to fight the Germans in the Tobruk campaign, and which had acquitted itself magnificently between times — went through the roadblock on the perimeter on its way back to Cairo. One more sign that the men's feat, and their valour, was recognised by the garrison as a whole was that the common Tommies on the roadblock saluted them as they passed — the ultimate compliment from one group of enlisted men to another, a gesture of profound respect.

Good on you, you Diggers.

Thank you, you Tommies. And see yers.

The last of the 9th Division, thus, to pull out from Cyrenaica, behind them they left 832 dead, had suffered 2177 wounded and had lost 941 as prisoners ...[38]

Of course, as the trucks began to pull east, east towards Palestine, each man strained for his last look at the tiny town by the sea as it began to disappear into the dust behind them.

Five hard days' travel later — including a massive cheer when they crossed the Egyptian border and saw the first tree many of them had seen in months — they arrived back in Palestine and were taken on the back of yet more lorries to a camp that had been especially prepared for them at Hill 69.

As the 2/13th moved through the lines of their two sister battalions, the 2/15th and 2/17th, many of the men came out to clap them in, and there were shouts of 'Good on you, 13th!'

Somehow, it was simply in the air. Many a man was then and there reminded of how it had been just a little over a year before when, still wet behind the ears, they had gone marching, marching, marching, out of Ingleburn camp on their way to Bathurst, past many of the same soldiers. Then, as they had marched out the gates of Ingleburn, their new-found soldierly grimness had become somewhat relaxed and they had allowed themselves a grin and a cheer in answer to the hearty farewell. Now, despite their exhaustion — and some of the enduring sadness as they thought back to the blokes who had been with them back then who were not with them now — again their mood lightened, as they returned the cheers.

This wasn't 'home' as they had long dreamed of home, but it was as near to home as they could get while out on the battlefield. And by God they had earned their rest.

Epilogue

Veni, vedi, vici.

JULIUS CAESAR

Had there been no Tobruk, we would have lost Egypt and would
eventually have been driven from the Middle East . . .

LIEUTENANT GENERAL LESLIE MORSHEAD, 1947[1]

For a fortnight or so after their return from Tobruk, the 2/13th were effectively the toast of the AIF in the Middle East. Wherever they went and their insignia were spotted, they were slapped on the back, cheered on and asked what the last days there had been like. When out and about in Tel Aviv on leave they couldn't buy a drink, and were hailed by one and all as 'the Fighting 13th'. There would be little time to enjoy it all, however, as in short order, together with the 2/17th and the 2/15th, they found themselves freezing on mountains in Syria — moved there to block any possible attack on the Suez Canal from the north — and thus had exchanged the flies, fleas, dust and dysentery for sleet 'n' snow, shivering and trying to make sure their trigger fingers didn't get frostbite.

In the meantime, though, with Japan's entry into the war at the end of 1941, Australia's 6th and 7th Divisions were, via a circuitous route, eventually called home to help protect their country against a possible Japanese invasion, and with them went General Blamey — leaving Lieutenant General Morshead in command of all Australian forces in the Mediterranean theatre.

At the point when the Japanese were at their most threatening — as they were marching inexorably down the Malayan Peninsula in the first weeks of 1942, getting closer and closer to the British citadel and symbol of the far-reaching power of the British Empire in Asia that was Singapore — the man with the overall responsibility for the Allies' defence was none other than General Sir Archibald Percival Wavell. After his command in the Middle East, Wavell had been made first the Commander in Chief of India and then, after the Japanese had bombed Pearl Harbor, Commander in Chief of British Troops in the Far East; and in this situation, things must have seemed rather familiar. For, once again, Wavell was desperate for support from Britain that never quite got there, and yet there was always an abundance of stirring words from He Who Must Be Deferred To.

On 10 February 1942, in the kind of language that gave the word 'Churchillian' its punch, the British Prime Minister essayed to give mettle to his men from afar, asserting that Wavell and his officers should abandon any 'thought of saving the troops or sparing the population. The battle must be fought to the bitter end at all costs. The 18th Division has a chance to make its name in history. Commanders and senior officers should die with their troops. The honour of the British Empire and of the British Army is at stake.'

On balance, however, Wavell decided that it would be better if the men of the 18th Division lived, and in the face of overwhelming Japanese force, Singapore was surrendered to them on 15 February 1942. Wavell himself had visited Singapore for the last time five days earlier, and soon returned to India with the aim of using British forces there to liberate Burma from the Japanese. When this venture failed, Wavell was once again replaced in his military role by none other than General Sir Claude Auchinleck.

Nevertheless, in the curious way the British often have in such situations, Wavell was actually nominally promoted all the way up to the rank of Field Marshal, and became in fact a peer of the realm as Viscount Wavell of Cyrenaica and of Winchester. Finally he was appointed Viceroy of India, a post he occupied with great distinction until 1947, when he was replaced by Lord Louis Mountbatten. Wavell died on 24 May 1950. His experience after the battle for Tobruk in 1941 could not have been in greater contrast to the way things turned out for Erwin Rommel . . .

•

After consolidating at their fallback position of Gazala and then Agheila, Rommel and his Afrika Korps soon swept east again the next month, and in June of that year once more placed Tobruk — held at this stage largely by South African troops — under siege.

This time the nut cracked in two days, and on 21 June 1942 Rommel was at last able to drive down Tobruk's main street at the head of his conquering army. A few minutes later he was with one of his aides, Rolf Munninger, on the first floor of the Albergo Tobruk — the hotel where he intended to set up his new headquarters — when a drunken British officer burst in.

'More beer!' he roared. 'I must have more beer!'[2]

Ushered away, and sobered up, that officer was informed that the situation had rather changed, and he would be unlikely to be getting more beer for some time to come. An interesting point in the circumstances of the fall of Tobruk was highlighted by Rommel's greatest modern biographer, David Fraser, in his book *Knight's Cross*: 'The South Africans had asked that the considerable number of black prisoners should be segregated from the whites, a request Rommel turned down flatly, saying that the blacks were South African soldiers, had fought alongside whites, worn the same uniform and they were all captives together.'

More important than the 33 000 prisoners that now came to Rommel were the 2.5 million gallons of precious fuel, and 2000 vehicles of various descriptions. Churchill, when he heard — right in the middle of a meeting with US President Franklin D. Roosevelt in Washington — was devastated, outraged and vindictive all in one, beginning his caustic remarks by noting, 'There is a difference between defeat and disgrace.'

Though Rommel was instantly made a Field Marshal in recognition of his success at Tobruk — with the German propaganda ministry now designating him as the unbeatable *Volksmarschall*, or 'people's marshal' — neither he nor the Afrika Korps would be able to enjoy Tobruk for long. (And indeed, as Rommel wrote to Lucie: 'Hitler has made me a Field Marshal. I would much rather he had given me one more division.')

For, now that Tobruk was secure, Hitler gave the order for the Afrika Korps to move on to attacking Cairo and the Suez Canal. They got to within 96 kilometres of Alexandria before they were stopped in September 1942 by the forces of Britain's 8th Army and the mighty 9th Division, both under the overall command of General Bernard Law Montgomery (known as 'Monty' to one and all), who had replaced General Auchinleck the month before. (In those darkest days of the war, with Allied defeat abounding, there was even the possibility that Churchill would lose a vote of no confidence in the House of Commons, and the British Prime Minister was so desperate for a major victory — any victory — that he was daily pressing Auchinleck for another major offensive against Rommel. When Auchinleck steadfastly refused, maintaining that he would not be rushed into it until his troops were ready, Churchill did to him exactly what he had done to Wavell the year before, and replaced the reluctant general with one who appeared more willing.)

After Rommel and his forces had been stopped in this battle, General Montgomery took over, and using both his predecessor's plans *and* his insistence that the counterattack should not be launched until all was in readiness, prepared the killer blow. At last all was ready. In late October

1942, Montgomery's combined Allied force counterattacked, broke through, and turned Rommel and his men westwards once more. In this famous second Battle of El Alamein, Morshead's 9th Division — with the 2/13th and 2/17th once again right in the thick of the action, together with, most notably, the 2/24th, 2/48th and 2/23rd Battalions — was once more outstanding, with Montgomery later saying of them that they were 'the best fighting division I have known'.[4]

That Battle of El Alamein also saw the beginnings of a major rift between Rommel and Hitler.

At the height of the battle, a point when it was apparent that Montgomery's forces were likely going to overwhelm Rommel's and the Afrika Korps was beginning to withdraw, Hitler — in almost classic Churchillian fashion — cabled the nation's greatest military hero and demanded 'victory or death'.[5]

Orders from the Führer were not ignored lightly, and though Rommel briefly halted the advance, he knew that victory was not achievable on this occasion, and had no interest in death either for himself or his men. In November 1942 Rommel briefly left the Afrika Korps to fly back to Germany to have a face-to-face meeting with his most superior officer of all, and Hitler completely lost his temper, screaming at his Field Marshal that Rommel had refused to follow orders, and he had no interest in Rommel's ideas of a tactical retreat to get the Afrika Korps out, intact, without having to surrender and be captured.

'You suggest exactly the same as the Generals did in Russia!' Hitler roared. 'I didn't do it and remained in the right. Here I also will not do it, because I have to consider the political consequences.'

Rommel would not back down.

'If we remain in North Africa,' he replied, reasonably, 'the destruction of our army is inevitable. With just rifles, we cannot fight against tanks.'

Hitler then exploded and, in the words of one of his officers who witnessed it, threw Rommel out of the conference room, as if he was 'a *begossener Pudel* [soaked poodle]'.

Still, relenting slightly, Hitler then ran after Rommel, mumbled half an apology and said by way of expiation, 'Our nerves are all a bit strained.'

The meeting continued, and though Hitler refused to countenance withdrawal, he did agree to send more supplies to North Africa.[6]

Rommel was left with no choice. He flew back to Africa and continued the withdrawal anyway, fighting a series of brilliant rearguard actions, not unlike those the 9th Division had executed against the Afrika Korps a year earlier when moving east to Tobruk. Throughout, Hitler never let off in his demand that Rommel and his men stop retreating, but was steadfastly ignored. On 11 November 1942, Tobruk was abandoned by the retreating Germans and the Allies were once again in possession.

There were many twists and turns along the road, but the final result was that, although the Field Marshal indeed succeeded in getting a quarter of a million German and Italian soldiers back to Tunis, the weight upon them soon doubled when a combined American and British force landed in Morocco, Algeria and Tunisia for Operation Torch, and began to move east towards Tripoli and the Afrika Korps — while the British continued to push from the other direction. Hitler's promised fresh supplies never arrived. By this time the Afrika Korps had, literally, changed their tune, with the soldiers sometimes singing their old song, albeit with new words:

> *Es klappern die Knochen,*
> *Es streikt der Motor*
> *Bomben fallen aufs Afrikakorps!*[7]

> The bones clatter,
> The engine strikes
> Bombs are falling onto the Afrika Korps!

Berlin had not the slightest sangfroid about it, however; panicked at the prospect that the man who was still a hero of the people, whatever differences they might have had in recent times, was going to be taken as a POW, Hitler ordered Rommel back to Germany, and he reluctantly went in March 1943 — just before most of the Afrika Korps and the Italian forces were captured.[8]

•

By early 1944, General *Sir* Leslie Morshead — knighted by the King for his services in defending Tobruk — had been promoted to Commander of the 1st Australian Corps, and commanded it both in Papua New Guinea and in Borneo. That 1st Australian Corps had also contained the 9th Division which once again covered itself in glory in the battles it fought in New Guinea.

After the war Morshead returned to civilian life and resumed his work as a shipping executive, becoming the manager for the Orient Line. He died on 26 September 1959, just a few days after turning seventy, and the month after he had registered the crowning achievement of his commercial life by succeeding Charles Lloyd Jones as Chairman of David Jones Ltd. His funeral was the biggest ever seen in Sydney, with his coffin borne on a gun carriage through the streets lined with tens of thousands of people. Among them were thousands of the Rats of Tobruk, come from all corners of Australia to wear medals proudly won under his command, and to pay tribute — one noting, 'He was the greatest Rat of them all'.[9] Every one of his pallbearers was a distinguished Australian general.

For Morshead's military epitaph, no one has done better than the one provided by Frank Harrison in his book *Tobruk: The Birth of a Legend*: 'For Morshead, Tobruk had been a triumph. His steadfastness under attack had been infectious. He had met everything that Rommel could throw at him, and had inflicted two defeats on the man. They were to meet in the field twice more and on each occasion Morshead would repeat the treatment. If Rommel had a nemesis ... it was Morshead.'[10] As to Morshead himself, his own view on Rommel is instructive. In a speech at Victoria Barracks in Sydney on 11 June 1947, he said, 'Rommel was a very aggressive and thrusting General, energetic, always on the ball. He drove his troops hard and he was impatient. He was ambitious and inclined to be spectacular personally and militarily, and there was a good deal of the politician in him. I would say that his military knowledge was not very profound. There were two principles which he clung to: counterattack quickly and exploit early success. He overdid both.'

For the last word on Morshead, one should go to a passage written by Chester Wilmot for the *ABC Weekly* on 21 November 1942, even though Wilmot (or his editor) scratched out the passage before publication: 'The bases of his success, I believe, are his strong insistence on discipline, his determination to retain the initiative and the offensive spirit, his attention to detail and his searching self-criticism.'

•

Morshead was otherwise engaged, however, on the other side of the world when, in the first months of 1944, Field Marshal Rommel was back in active service and in charge of the Wehrmacht's Army Group B, situated in northern France, Belgium and Holland, readying the defences against the Allied invasion that the German High Command knew would not be long in coming.

By this time Rommel had become convinced not only that Germany could not win the war, but also that Hitler was simply not capable of extricating the country intact from it. And he was not alone. In the highest reaches of the German Army, others had reached the same conclusion, and while Rommel was on service in northern France, he was approached by a small, clandestine cabal of senior officers saying that Hitler needed to be assassinated and that it would be Rommel's duty to take over as head of state after Hitler had gone, and to get Germany out of the war. Though Rommel did not reject the idea outright, he did no more than listen, and in fact counselled the conspirators against launching the coup in Berlin, as there would be no ready supply of disaffected German troops to follow them.

In the meantime, Rommel was soon fully occupied in trying to stop the unstoppable — after the Allies did indeed invade France, on D-Day, 6 June 1944 — and was his usual blur of military movement, constantly careering around his front lines and exhorting his troops to greater effort while also ensuring that those efforts were well placed.

Taking the risks he did, there was always a high likelihood that he would be wounded or killed, and on 17 July 1944 Allied fighters dived down and strafed the Field Marshal's car, causing it to crash at high speed. Rommel escaped with his life, albeit with four fractures in his skull, shrapnel in his face and a paralysed left eye, and he was soon recuperating at home. His fifteen-year-old son, Manfred, was granted leave from the anti-aircraft battery he had been drafted to, so he could spend time with his father and, most particularly, read to him.

Only three days after Rommel had been wounded, though, the same group that had approached him months earlier now tried the infamous assassination attempt on Hitler — putting an exploding briefcase near where it was presumed the Führer would sit — but succeeded only in wounding him and enraging him further. When that conspiracy consequently began to unravel, Rommel's name emerged as one who had been consulted.

The scene was set ...

On the morning of 14 October 1944, a closed train carriage arrived in the small and picturesque western German town of Ulm bearing inside an enormous floral wreath, proclaiming Rommel as a hero of the German people.

At high noon, in a leafy avenue in the village of Herrlingen, just outside Ulm, two Generals of the SS came to the home that Field Marshal Rommel and his wife and child had moved back to in 1943, after his return from Africa. They asked to see the Field Marshal alone, and he agreed, asking Manfred to leave the room while Lucie waited in their bedroom upstairs, and the young lad chatted in the kitchen with one of Rommel's adjutants who also happened to be there, before going to his own room to colour in some maps.

In Rommel's study, the two SS Generals now presented the Field Marshal with surely as stark a choice as any man has had to face. It was not so much death or glory — which Rommel had faced many times before and had always emerged on the glory side. This time, the SS Generals made clear, his choice was either death *and* glory ... or ... a short life and disgrace, together with the incarceration and ruination of his wife and child.

They knew what he had done, they told him, and that he had been involved with those who had tried to assassinate Hitler.

Therefore, either he came with them now and quickly took some cyanide pills they had with them — in which case he would be dead in just three seconds, whereupon it would be announced he had died of natural causes and would be given a glorious state funeral — or he would be arrested, tried for treason in the *Volksgericht*, the so-called court of the *Volk* in Berlin, and executed shortly afterwards. In the latter case, he was to understand that his wife and son would also be interned as enemies of the State. Furthermore, he should know that the house was surrounded with armed men with orders to shoot to kill.

Precisely what Rommel made of such a choice will, of course, never be known, but surely built into his calculations was that his chances of actually facing the court and being allowed to freely speak from the dock about what he thought of Hitler were nil. One way or another, death was coming, and it was clearly better to take the first option they proffered.

After a quarter of an hour, the meeting was over. Excusing himself, Rommel went straight upstairs to Lucie to tell her the situation, say goodbye and leave her for ever.

Young Manfred, now worried by the sudden black mood that had enveloped the entire house, but uncertain what was going on, entered his parents' bedroom a few minutes later to find his father standing in the middle of the room, ashen-faced.

'Come outside with me,' Rommel Snr said to his beloved son in a tight voice which was totally unfamiliar to Manfred.

And then, back in Manfred's room, the father told the son ... 'I have just had to tell your mother,' he began, slowly, 'that I shall be dead in a quarter of an hour.'

At Manfred's shocked reaction, the Field Marshal acknowledged something of his own feelings on the matter, while also making clear that there was no alternative.

'To die by the hand of one's own people is hard. But the house is surrounded and Hitler is charging me with high treason.'

Though completely stunned by this news, the son would for ever remember the following words, dripping with sarcasm: 'In view of my services in Africa, I am to have the chance of dying by poison. The two Generals have brought it with them. It's fatal in three seconds. If I accept, none of the usual steps will be taken against my family, that is, against you. They will also leave my staff alone.'

'Do you *believe* it?' Manfred interrupted.

'Yes,' Rommel Snr replied. 'I believe it. It is very much in their interest to see that the affair does not come out into the open. By the way, I have been charged to put you under a promise of the strictest silence. If a single word of this comes out, they will no longer feel themselves bound by the agreement.'

'Can't we defend ourselves . . ?' Manfred interrupted.

'There's no point,' he said. 'It's better for one to die than for all of us to be killed in a shooting affray. Anyway, we've practically no ammunition.'

Manfred, too, was obliged to reach the same conclusion as his father. There was no way out.

Then the Field Marshal began to make his final arrangements — which included putting a leather overcoat over the Afrika Korps uniform he had donned for the initial meeting — and soon he was ready . . .[11]

With Manfred by his side, he walked out the front door and down the garden path. He shook his son's hand at the garden gate and told him to look after his mother. The two Generals were standing by the car, with the door opened for Rommel, and now greeted him with their right hands in salute. Rommel ignored them, and rather just climbed into the back of the car, followed by the Generals, and it then pulled away, purring malevolently up the hill.

Frau Rommel watched from the upstairs window, weeping, as the green car took her husband to his death.

It stopped in a small forest just a kilometre or so away, and then one of the Generals got out of the car with the SS driver and walked away, while the other General gave Rommel the pills.

A little over fifteen minutes after the Field Marshal had left, the phone rang in the Rommel household. One of the Generals gravely informed Lucie that her husband had had a stroke, undoubtedly due to the injuries he had suffered during the fighting in France, and though he had been rushed to hospital . . . he was terribly sorry to inform the Rommel family that the brave Field Marshal Rommel was dead.

The following day, Hitler sent a cable to Lucie Rommel:

Take my honest sympathy for the heavy loss which you
have suffered through the death of your husband. The
name of the Generalfeldmarschall Rommel will be for ever
connected with the heroic fights in North Africa.
Adolf Hitler

Rommel was buried with full military honours, in a colossal state funeral. One thing neither Rommel's son nor wife could help but notice was the expression on his death mask, one they had rarely seen before. It wasn't fear; not anger, nor even the agony of one dying a terrible death.

It was *contempt*. Complete contempt.

The death certificate stated he had died of a heart attack.

After the funeral, his ashes — for the Nazis were quick to cremate him — were buried in a sunny spot in the beautiful cemetery at Herrlingen, and he lies there still, beside his beloved Lucie, who died in 1971. Their son, Manfred, went on to become a highly respected politician, including becoming the Mayor of Stuttgart, the city in which he now lives in quiet retirement.

•

Another who had been caught up in the fallout from the Hitler assassination attempt was General Franz Halder, Rommel's longtime enemy in the Wehrmacht, who fell out with Hitler over the way the war was being conducted in Russia and was subsequently moved aside. On 23 July 1944, just two days after the assassination attempt on Hitler, Halder was arrested by the Gestapo, charged with being one of the conspirators and sent to Dachau. In fact, this was the best of all possible places to be for a senior German General when Liberation came and the hunt was on for Hitler's cronies — as whatever Halder had done in the early part of the war, the fact that he had finished it in Dachau as an official enemy of the Führer automatically moved him closer to his liberators. He was called as a witness at the Nuremberg trials, giving valuable evidence against his former colleagues, and lived until 2 April 1972.

•

Meanwhile, General Friedrich Paulus had an extraordinary rise and fall. Before his trip to North Africa in April 1941, attempting to bring Rommel into line, Paulus had been heavily involved in the planning and then organisation of Operation Barbarossa, the German invasion of Russia. When that began to go bad — with many of the German Generals killed, injured, imprisoned or dismissed — there was a need for more Generals to be sent from Germany, and Paulus was one of them. So it was that on 5 January 1942, Paulus — whose previous highest battle command had been a rifle company three decades earlier — between the wars — took charge of Germany's 6th Army, composed of 250 000 soldiers. Under his command the situation went from bad to worse. A year later, in the infamous siege of Stalingrad — with his forces almost destroyed by the cold of winter, hunger and a Russian resistance so fierce that he was suffering casualties at the rate of 20 000 soldiers a week — Paulus was presented with a choice: surrender his forces or suffer complete annihilation.

After consultation with Berlin, Paulus chose to fight on, even though the situation was clearly hopeless. On 30 January 1943, Hitler made him a Field Marshal, on the reckoning that no Field Marshal would ever surrender his forces. But on 24 January, Paulus sent Hitler a personal message:

> Troops without ammunition or food. Effective command no longer possible. 18 000 wounded without any supplies or dressings or drugs. Further defence senseless. Collapse inevitable. Army requests immediate permission to surrender in order to save lives of remaining troops.

Hitler replied almost immediately:

> Surrender is forbidden. 6th Army will hold their positions to the last man and the last round and by their heroic endurance will make an unforgettable contribution toward the establishment of a defensive front and the salvation of the Western world.

And that was that. Just a few months earlier when Rommel had been presented with a similar order from the Führer, he had disobeyed and his men had been saved. But this was an entirely different man. When Hitler commanded, Paulus obeyed. Right to the end. On 31 January, Field Marshal Paulus got his final message through to Adolf Hitler:

> The 6th Army, true to their oath and conscious of the lofty importance of their mission, have held their position to the last man and the last round for Führer and Fatherland unto the end.

Only hours later, Russian troops stormed his headquarters and found he who had once been known as 'Our most elegant gentleman', lying sick in a filthy bed. At the request that he surrender, Paulus did all that he could, which was to nod — and shortly afterwards 100 000 Germans were taken prisoner, of whom only some 6000 would survive the brutal Russian prison camps to see Germany again. As to Paulus, he too was taken prisoner and subsequently held under a kind of house arrest in Moscow. For two years his Soviet captors pressured him to renounce Hitler and be part of the leadership of a movement against him. Paulus resisted until after the assassination attempt, when he did speak out, which so infuriated Hitler that the surviving son of Paulus — another had been killed in the war — was thrown into a concentration camp and his entire family was interned under the Nazi doctrine of *Sippenhaft*, which maintained that a whole family could be held responsible for the 'crimes' of just one member.

Paulus remained a prisoner of the Russians for the next eleven years, and finally returned to what by that time had become Communist East Germany, where he worked with the infamous Stasi security force. His wife had died just four years earlier, and the two had never been reunited since their last meeting before the disastrous Stalingrad campaign. In 1955, Paulus contracted motor neurone disease and he died in a Dresden clinic in February 1957, at the age of sixty-seven.

•

Though sent 'on his camel' back to Germany by Rommel, General Johannes Streich's war was not over, and he continued to serve in various roles until captured by the Americans near the end of the war. Released from the POW camps in 1948, it wasn't until 1976 that he re-emerged on the public record when the controversial British historian David Irving later tracked Streich down to an old people's home outside Hamburg in northern Germany, and reported that he was not the kind who had held a grudge against Rommel for all those years.

'He was,' Irving reports, 'a spry, slightly built, soldierly figure of eighty-five — neatly dressed, going deaf, eating dainty cakes in a circle of elderly ladies who cannot have asked him very often to recite those dramatic weeks with Rommel ... The conversation was not very productive, but it did bear fruit later. Out of the blue came a lengthy sheaf of close typescript, written by Johannes Streich many years before but never published, entitled "Memoirs of Africa". The war diary of his 5th

Light Division has also turned up in private hands, and bears out Streich's version in every detail.'

Streich died peacefully a year later, at the age of eighty-six.

•

Rolf Völker was still in North Africa in October 1942, and was wounded in the Battle of El Alamein, when splinters of a hand grenade thrown by a Scottish soldier hit his back and buttocks. And, in overview, he had been one of the lucky ones. Of the 195 men who had arrived with him in North Africa eighteen months earlier, there were now just eight left, as the others had been killed, wounded, captured or lost to disease.

After a period of convalescence Rolf returned to duty and, having joined the disastrous German campaign in Russia, was part of the retreat via Odessa to Romania. At one point, as the Wehrmacht retreated through Siebenbürgen, Transylvania — where a German colony had flourished for 800 years — he laid eyes for the first time on a blue-eyed, blonde seventeen-year-old girl by the name of Erika Penteker. Instantly smitten by her beauty and poise, his life was never quite the same again — and yet both of them would have a great deal of unhappiness ahead of them.

For Erika would soon become a refugee, and at the time was fleeing on foot with her younger sister, Gerda, before the invading Russians. Just after crossing the Austrian–Czechoslovakian border at Waidhofen, Gerda noted how hot and sweaty Erika was in the hot westerly sun and offered to walk in the lead. Erika accepted, and just an instant later a bullet from a Czech partisan eager to fire at anything and anybody that even looked German blew half of Gerda's head off. Erika screamed and wouldn't stop. Another woman was there with a baby, and put the baby in Erika's arms to try to calm her, but nothing would help.

Erika would suffer lifelong depression, with that tragic episode as its likely base ...

As to Rolf, he continued to fight for the German Army until, in early 1945, as the Allies and Soviets closed in on Germany from all sides, his own battalion was finally overwhelmed by the Americans of the famed Rainbow Division. It occurred just after Rolf and his comrades had crossed the Saar River and were vainly trying to make a stand in a bunker that was left from the old Siegfried Line. Rolf was taken prisoner one day after his twenty-fifth birthday, on 5 March 1945, and a terrible period of imprisonment followed, starting with his first internment in an American-run prison across the river in Steney, Germany.

Not long after his capture, his guards showed him photos they claimed were from concentration camps, photos of terribly emaciated bodies in stripey clothes — and they said this had been done by *Germans* working in a systematic way to exterminate all the Jews.

On the instant, Rolf refused to believe it and said so loudly, asserting that the photos must have been of Germans who had been destroyed by the many American bombs that had rained down upon German civilians, as he had seen with his own eyes bodies just like that — most particularly the burned corpses of women and children in Stuttgart.

A combination of Rolf's refusal to accept such proof, his blame of the Americans instead and the fact that his guards — many of whom had migrated from Germany to America and joined the US Army — had themselves been brutalised in Germany either before or during the war, and had lost dear friends at the hands of hated German soldiers whom Rolf now came to represent, made for a very unhappy result. Soon after, the situation was exacerbated when, instead of mere photos, the guards saw for themselves just-released Jewish prisoners, and the word spread of the true depths of cruelty and inhumanity that had been reached by the German Nazi system.

Ever afterwards, Rolf would recall being beaten up by his captors, and how he was put into a freezing confinement cage with spiky stones on the floor, barbed wire as walls and one blanket — giving him a choice between putting the blanket beneath as protection against the stones, while he froze, or alleviating the cold by having the blanket on top of him, while he lay on the cruel stones.

At one point, a guard asked him: 'Do you still believe in the *Endsieg* [final victory]?'

Rolf replied: 'Well, Hitler must still have something up his sleeve if he keeps on sending soldiers out ...'

Of course it was not to be, and soon enough Rolf came to understand that Germany was heading for an even more crippling defeat than it had suffered in the Great War. It was not just Germany, though, but also its soldiers who would be humiliated.

On another occasion, in prison in Saarburg, right by the border of Luxembourg and Germany, Rolf was dragged out stark naked into the courtyard and told by a drunken guard, '*Du Nazi-Schwein wirst jetzt erschossen!*' (You Nazi pig will now be shot!) The guard had a machine gun, and the terrified Rolf's only hope was that the man would aim straight enough to kill him outright, instead of leaving him there with an agonising slow-death shot to the belly. Fortunately, the guard had only wanted to scare him, exacting revenge on behalf of all those who had suffered at the hands of the German Army, and Rolf was soon dragged back to his cell.

Another episode at this time, in April 1945, when he was briefly imprisoned in Mailly le Camp, would stay with Rolf for life. In the agony of everything that was happening to him, one man alone working in the prison showed consistent kindness to him and tried to ease his situation. What was more striking still was that he was a Jewish man. Rolf sought to explain to him that he was terribly, terribly sorry about what had happened, and he wanted the Jewish man to know that he knew nothing, absolutely nothing, about that kind of atrocity going on. The man shook his hand, and said to him, 'I believe you didn't know anything about the camps.'

And then one day the man disappeared. When Rolf asked where he had gone, he was told: the Jewish man had gone to Dachau, where his father had been gassed during the war. And yet this man had never said a word to Rolf. Rolf was stunned. Here was a man whose entire people had been devastated by the regime that Rolf had been fighting for, whose own father had been killed, and yet he not only believed Rolf but had continued to show him kindness. It was all so very different to what he and all his schoolmates had been taught about Jews ...

Somehow the whole episode focused Rolf's mind even more on the horror of the Holocaust, and just how evil the regime he had believed in and fought for truly had been.

At least the behaviour of Rolf's captors as a whole improved markedly once it was established that Rolf had been part of the North African campaign in 1941–1942, followed by being in the Ukraine, Romania and Hungary in 1943, and had nothing to do with the concentration camps.[12]

•

And Lord Haw-Haw? For much of the war William Joyce continued to live a comfortable life in Berlin and in September 1944 was awarded the Cross of War Merit 1st Class. As the tide of war against Germany continued to rise, however, he began to drink heavily and his life to fall apart. During the final stages of the war, with the Red Army approaching Berlin, Joyce moved to Hamburg. He made a final broadcast on 30 April 1945, and though the Allies were closing in from the north, south and west while the Soviet Union was moving in from the east, Haw-Haw gave a last warning. He said that although Britain might in fact win this particular battle, nothing could change the fact she would finish the war a much lesser power than she had been, and the British Empire would ultimately cede to a Soviet Empire. He signed off with a final, defiant 'Heil Hitler!' and only a few weeks later was captured by British soldiers while going through a wood near Flensburg, on the Danish–German border.

Charged with treason, he was sentenced to death; while awaiting the gallows, he carved a swastika on the wall of his cell. His last message to go out on the public airwaves — just before he was hanged on 3 January 1946 — was reported by the BBC: 'In death as in life, I defy the Jews who caused this last war, and I defy the powers of darkness they represent.'

•

Far from having dominion all over Europe, by January 1945 Adolf Hitler's own Lebensraum was restricted purely to the Chancellery in Berlin and to the *Führerbunker* built right beneath it, as the Soviet forces closed in on the city from the east and the Allies from the west. For those first four months of 1945 he never left those environs — frequently issuing orders to German armies that had long ago been wiped out — until it became obvious that there really was only one way out, and it was not on this earth.

On the afternoon of 28 April, just hours after he heard of the fate of Benito Mussolini and his mistress Clara Petacci — shot, killed and hung heads down in the Piazza Loreto in Milan, before cheering crowds — Hitler decided on a different way of making his exit.

But first things first ...

That evening, with the Soviets just a matter of kilometres away, the Führer dictated to his secretary his last will and political testament, where he essentially asserted that *Mein Kampf* had been proved correct and everything that had happened since really was demonstrably the fault of the Jews. He also appointed Admiral Karl Dönitz as head of the state and Joseph Goebbels as Chancellor.

That done, shortly before midnight he married his longtime partner, Eva Braun, in a quick civil ceremony, but there would be no honeymoon. By the afternoon of 29 April, with the Soviets barely 2 kilometres away, he had his dog, Blondi, brought to him, and gave the German shepherd some poison capsules to see if they worked. To his grim satisfaction — because he abhorred cruelty to animals — Blondi was dead within a minute.

At two o'clock on the afternoon of 30 April, with the Soviets now just a block away, Hitler's chauffeur was ordered to bring 150 litres of petrol to the Chancellery garden.

Then, after Hitler and his wife had farewelled all those still left in the bunker, the two went into their private quarters while the others waited and the sound of the approaching Soviets got ever louder. At 3.30 p.m. a single shot rang out. When his two remaining high-ranking loyalists, Dr Joseph Goebbels and Martin Bormann, rushed in, they found Hitler dead on the sofa from a self-inflicted gunshot wound to his temple, with the poisoned Eva beside him. Their bodies were carried upstairs to the garden, doused with petrol and burned over the next several hours.

Below, most of the staff who remained immediately began to do what they had long wanted to do, but had refrained from because Hitler had always strictly forbidden it — they pulled out their cigarettes and began to smoke. Heavily. Long, burning draws into their lungs.[13] It had been a long war.

•

Rudolf Hess had an unhappy time practically from the moment he arrived in Great Britain after his amazing flight. He was in the Tower of London in the middle of May 1941 when he received word of the heights of Hitler's outrage at his action, which plunged him into the depths of despair, and he cried for an entire day and night.

At the conclusion of the war he was reunited with some of his former Nazi colleagues when he stood in the dock at the Nuremberg trials. Hess did not deny any of the accusations against him, but he did have one thing he very much wanted to say, and he took the opportunity before his verdict was read, clearly eager to set the record straight. 'For many years of my life,' he said, 'I had the privilege of working under the greatest man my nation has ever produced in its thousand-year history. Even if I could, I would not erase this part of my life. I am happy that I did my duty for the German people, my duty as a *National Socialist*, and my duty as the Führer's loyal adherent. I do not regret a thing. If I could start over again, I would behave just as I have behaved, even if I knew I would end up being burned on a pyre. Regardless of what people do in the future, I will stand before the judge of eternity. I will justify myself to him, and I know that he will acquit me.'

It must, nevertheless, have seemed like an eternity on earth before Hess could make those justifications as, after being found guilty on two charges, he was sentenced to life imprisonment and sent to serve it in Spandau Military Prison in western Berlin. At one point, some quarter of a century after being sentenced, Hess confided to the Director of the prison that if ever he were to get out, he would never again put a bird in a cage. But Hess himself remained in the cage until he could finally bear it no more. In the early afternoon of 17 August 1987, he was found hanging in a small garden shed on the prison grounds. As ever with a person of his fame, such a strange death resulted in myriad conspiracy theories — focusing on the fact that he was ninety-three years old and infirm and seemingly physically incapable of killing himself — but the bottom line was unchanged. A singularly troubled, and damaging, life had at last come to an end.

•

Winston Churchill, of course, stayed British Prime Minister right up until the end of the war in Europe — at which point, oddly, he lost the July 1945 election, upon the judgment of the British people that his talents for leadership were not ideally suited to peacetime. Nevertheless, he did again return to power as Prime Minister in 1951, at the age of seventy-six. Though he retired on 5 April 1955, just a few months after turning eighty, he stayed on as a much venerated Member of Parliament until six months before his death at ninety. He died on 24 January 1965, and Queen Elizabeth II accorded him a state funeral.

•

Despite his falling out with Churchill, Claude Auchinleck was promoted to Field Marshal in 1946, shortly before his wife left him for another officer. When he retired, Auchinleck moved to Marrakesh in Morocco, and lived quietly until his death in 1981, looked after in his latter years by a serving Corporal he had befriended, Malcolm Millward.

•

Bert Ferres stayed with the 2/13th Battalion throughout the war, seeing notably heavy action in New Guinea, where he again displayed outstanding courage, and he finished the war in Borneo. Since the day he had first sailed out of Sydney Harbour to war's end, he had only had two brief leaves back in Sydney, and the rest of the time had been spent fulfilling his duty. He married Lottie Hardy in 1949, raised two children and spent most of the rest of his professional life in the aircraft industry, including as a technical officer for the Department of Defence, ensuring that its planes were battle ready. He and Lottie are still going strong-ish, and now live in quiet retirement in the Hunter Valley, north of Sydney.[14]

•

Ivor Hancock was liberated from his POW camp in Germany in May 1945, and returned to Australia by ship to see Jean Coles for the first time in five years, and to meet his child, Dorothy. Having lived with the stigma of being an unmarried mother for most of the war, Jean was keen to be married and that little Dorothy be legitimised — so Ivor's feet had barely touched Australian ground before he was heading up the aisle towards his bride.

The bad limp he displayed on that occasion was not just a certain reluctance to be tied down to a marriage — whatever his moral obligation to Jean and his child — but also showed that his childhood ankle injury had so deteriorated during his time as a prisoner that he could no longer walk properly, and an eighteen-month stint in Melbourne's Heidelberg Repatriation Hospital beckoned while he started to try to re-establish his Australian life. While physically Ivor recovered from his war injuries, psychologically it wasn't so easy, and as he later recounted, 'It was many, many years before I was able to love or show affection to any other human being, this included my children who, sadly, meant absolutely nothing to me. I was only one of many ex-servicemen and women suffering from post-war shock and trauma, the full impact of which lasts through whole lifetimes ...' Further, in words that had much wider application than his own circumstances, Ivor would write that what he had gone through 'was to bring dreadful unhappiness and hurt to many people who didn't deserve it. *The casualties kept coming long after the shooting had stopped.*'

Ivor's trauma would manifest itself in many ways, from his suffering bouts of deep and near-suicidal depression to engaging in heavy drinking and wild philandering; but at least he was able to find a niche in which he prospered — as a radio broadcaster initially with Radio 3KZ in Melbourne. (His first acquaintance with the world of radio had come at the Heidelberg Repatriation Hospital, where a complete broadcasting studio had been established for the patients' use.) Great fame and riches were to be his, but it was soon without Jean and their three children, whom he abandoned to follow a visiting English cabaret singer to Sydney, where he joined radio station 2UW.

A further four wives followed, and as many radio stations in Sydney and Brisbane, as Ivor was never quite able to settle, even though his fame grew and he earned the nickname of 'The Steamroller' for his forthright nature. The doyen of Australian radio broadcasters, John Laws, remembers Ivor as 'a very strong radio-man, with an enormous fund of stories', and yet Ivor rarely referred back to his time at Tobruk.

One notable exception came in the middle of 1953 when, while behind the microphone, he commented with great favour upon the news that not only had five Victoria Cross winners from Australia and New Zealand been invited to attend the coronation in London of Her Majesty,

Queen Elizabeth II, on 2 June, but that on their way over they would briefly stop off at Tobruk and pay their respects at the grave of Jack Edmondson.

Ivor died in 2002, but he managed to write down his extraordinarily frank reminiscences beforehand, which I have drawn on extensively for this book.[15]

•

Also doing his bit for radio during the first part of Queen Elizabeth's reign was one of the most esteemed correspondents in the world, the great Chester Wilmot, whose career had continued to prosper both through and after the war. In 1942 he had distinguished himself with his reporting from the Kokoda Track, and two years later his widely hailed book *Tobruk 1941: Capture — Siege — Relief* came out to acclaim that was still not quite the equal of that which he received for his 1952 classic, *The Struggle For Europe*, which recounted what happened in the European theatre during World War II.

He was at the height of his career when, in December 1953, he visited Sydney to anchor an around-the-world radio program that preceded the Queen's broadcast on Christmas Day. From Sydney Wilmot introduced speakers from all over the British Commonwealth, before heading back to England and his wife and daughters. Tragically his plane crashed in the Mediterranean, and Wilmot was one of the thirty-five passengers killed. As truly one of the greats of Australian journalism, his name deserves far more reverence than it currently receives.

•

Another to suffer greatly from what he had experienced in the war was Austin Mackell, whose life had been saved by the courage of Jack Edmondson. Though Mackell had a happy family life with a loving wife and four children, and also had a successful career as a business executive, he was beset by severe depression which occasionally required his hospitalisation. He died in 1965.[16]

•

After the war was over, Vince Rayner was awarded the Military Medal for his feats in standing his ground as the Panzer roared towards him at Mechili, and managing to get off the shot — 'Give him one more up his arse!' — that destroyed it. But he was unable to collect the medal from the Governor General at Government House in Sydney on 11 September 1947, as he was too busy on the farm. So he sent his sister instead.[17] He died in 1981.

•

Captain Rea Leakey stayed in the Army after World War II was over and continued to rise through the ranks, also seeing active service in the Korean War, and he retired with the rank of Major General. In the 1990s he began to write his memoirs; the subsequent book, which was edited by noted English author George Forty and entitled *Leakey's Luck: A Tank Commander with Nine Lives*, was published in 1999, shortly before Major General Leakey died, peacefully, at the age of eighty-three, on 6 October 1999. His son David is now a Major General in the British Army.[18]

•

Elizabeth Edmondson mourned the death of her son, Jack, every day for the rest of her life, as did her husband, Will. Exhausted, in part because it was nigh on impossible to run the farm without his son, Will died in 1958. While Elizabeth held on to the home as long as she could — it was, of course, the place which held the most memories of Jack — by 1961 it was getting to be too much for her. Though her remaining energies had gone into tending the garden — most particularly the things she and Jack had planted together — finally she was persuaded by friends to sell the house and move into a nearby residence in Moore Street, Liverpool, together with her books, photographs, papers, letters, and some of the flowers and shrubs from her garden which she had transplanted. Sadly, however, her health failed rapidly; in early October 1961 she moved into the Masonic Home, Glenfield, where she died only three weeks later.

The house that the Edmondson family lived in all those years ago, Forest Home, is still there on what is now known as Camden Valley Way, all but unchanged while around it development has continued at a crazy pace. On 14 December 2005, at the kind invitation of the current owner, I had the great pleasure of walking past the jacaranda trees planted by Jack, which still stand, through the front door of the house and around its rooms, all of it right after I had attended the opening of the new high school in the area, the John Edmondson High School — the roof of which can be seen from the front veranda of Forest Home.

•

In 1985, Dariel Larkins of Turramurra in Sydney's northern suburbs found the diary Elizabeth Edmondson wrote during all the time Jack was away; it was among the papers of her own parents, Ward and Olive Havard, who were highly respected amateur historians. It was evident that Elizabeth had given the Havards, as friends and long-term neighbours across the paddocks, the diary, and other texts and photographs, to assist in the production of a souvenir brochure about Jack that came out in 1961, just before Elizabeth died. Recognising the historical significance of the diary, and after making a number of enquiries, Dariel contacted the Australian War Memorial, where the diary now resides. The texts and photographs were distributed between the AWM and the City of Liverpool Library.

•

Similar to Elizabeth Edmondson, Josie Johnson never recovered from the agony of losing her husband. Precisely the poverty John had feared for his family should he die, became their lot: they soon moved from their cottage in Walwa to a Housing Commission tenement in Melbourne, and struggled thereafter, with their lives moving to the rhythm of the pittance pension payments. The supreme sacrifice that John Johnson had paid for his country was not remotely repaid by the country to his family, as the money they received was simply never enough to properly make ends meet. Josie could not afford toothpaste or toothbrushes for her kids, or underpants for her sons. All she could do was keep them all warm and dry and at least secure in her love.[19]

Still, sometimes, passing her door late at night, her children would hear their mother sobbing in her bedroom, though she was careful to be as composed as possible in front of them, and was always so in public. Whatever her misery inside, she did not affect the manner of the grieving widow and focused her energies on working hard, keeping the family together and giving them as good a start in life as possible, despite everything that had happened. As later described by her youngest daughter, 'She ruled those boys with an iron hand belied by her diminutive figure. She was determined they would "do well". This was her grail. She carried it for Dad — a masterful legacy.'[20]

And they did do well, each in their own field, with John prospering as an influential Victorian public servant; Alex became a business manager in Melbourne and a company director; Don became an engineer, Len an army officer and farmer, and Des a successful businessmen; while Sylvia Rose was a highly qualified nurse and midwife, and Josie a teacher and university professor.

What of the fourth son, young Barry? He died in November 2005, at the age of seventy-three, two days before I made my first phone call to contact the family. As recorded in his obituary, published in the *Herald-Sun*,

Barry became a director of a timber company, fathered eight children to the same good woman, and the opening two paragraphs say something of the man John and Josie Johnson's son turned into: 'With his energy, drive and potential to represent the interests of large numbers of people in their battles for a better life, Barry Johnson could well have been a splendid federal Labor MP. Barry always had the wellbeing of the working man and his family at heart and stood up for what he believed was right.'[21] His father would have been proud, and on that subject the obituary also noted, 'Barry, born at Walwa, never got over the death of his father, John, in Tobruk, in 1941 ... What hurt Barry the most was that successive federal governments allowed a soldier's widow to live below the poverty line.'

The fifth-oldest son, Len, was also marked heavily by what happened to his father. In 1946, at the age of twelve, he had purposefully gone to 'Dad's drawer' — filled with letters, medals, a watch and personal belongings that had come back from Tobruk — and sat down and read all the correspondence between his parents, understanding for the first time the contours of the terrible tragedy that had occurred. He was filled with such an unbearable sadness that he resolved never to touch the letters again, as he simply could not bear the pain that came with them.

Despite the circumstances of his father's loss, however, Len joined the Australian Army as soon as he was old enough and ended up going to Vietnam, during which time he rose to the rank of Major. So it was that, thirty years after losing her husband in World War II, Josie once again knew that gripping fear with every knock on the door, every late-night phone call that might, just might, bring the dreaded news that he had been killed.

Happily, though, it didn't occur, and finally in late June 1970 she received the blessed news that Len was home safe, and back in Townsville with the 6th Battalion, Royal Australian Regiment. Her voice filled with love and relief, she told Len she would come up and see him within a few days — and yet, that too didn't happen.

For, just three days after that, it was Len who received the phone call, informing him that his mother had been in a car accident. She had been travelling with her daughter-in-law and two grandchildren when a tyre blew out, the car rolled and she was killed. The others were, mercifully, unharmed.

•

After the war, Adam Mrozowski, like so many of the Polish soldiers, could not safely return home as — far from having been liberated, as he and his comrades had hoped — their country was now under the yoke of the

Soviet Union. It was possible for him to return, certainly, but to then leave again would likely have been out of the question, and the word from their own people at home was, 'You are better to stay away', which most of them did. Adam remained at first in England, where he had been training to be a pilot with the Polish Air Force, and then headed to Australia in 1947.

With the help of the Rats of Tobruk Association, well over a thousand of the Polish 1st Carpathian Brigade — with nowhere else to go — were settled first in Tasmania, and then spread out from there. In 1959, Adam married local girl Leonie Flynn and with her raised two sons, both of whom naturally learned the words to 'It's a Long, Long Way to Tipperary'.

In 1969 came the phonecall for Adam: his father back in Poland was extremely sick and had only expressed one desire — he wanted to see Adam before he died. Could Adam come home?

Dare Adam risk returning, going behind the Iron Curtain at the very height of the Cold War? He decided that he couldn't refuse the dying wish of his father, and so he returned to Poland for the first time since he had left in June 1940. At the airport he was looking out for an older version of the slim, beautiful mother who had so long occupied his dreams and memories of his homeland, when a stumpy woman with grey hair and thick spectacles rushed up to him, put her arms around him and began weeping. After ten seconds of total confusion, looking for someone to explain or at least extricate him, Adam decided that *this* woman must be his mother.

And it was.

She took him to his father, who told Adam he had been waiting for him to come before he died. Just two days later, he did so.

In the time between that death and the funeral, a local military official turned up and formally required Adam to accompany him, so he could be questioned as to his past and his purpose in Poland. The questioning endured for seven solid hours, each one a reminder of why Adam had made the right decision to live in Australia and raise his family there — and not under a system where pissant officials like this could behave in such a dictatorial manner. As he was an Australian citizen by now, the Polish Government had no right to hold him there, but they left him in no doubt that they would have liked to.

Adam's wife, Leonie, died in 2003, and he — aged eighty-two at the time of writing — now lives in quiet retirement in the southern suburbs of Brisbane.[22]

•

After nine months of imprisonment in various locations at the hands of the Americans, Rolf Völker escaped a little before Christmas in 1945 and, after making his way back to Germany, became a fugitive in his own country. Moving by night, living off the land, he finally got back to his home in Stuttgart — where, ironically enough, he was helped by some Jews he met in a darkened square in the middle of the city who were preparing to emigrate to Israel. For a small price they gave him some properly stamped papers that would allow him to travel freely. Again, Jews were being kind to him, despite everything.

There were many Germans who had now washed their hands of the whole Nazi experience, maintaining that they had always been against it, but what made this all doubly difficult for Rolf was that he had *not* been against it. He had believed in the values of work and order; had believed that things had been generally better under Nazi leadership; and now he was forced to confront where it had all led. By March 1946 he no longer had to live as a fugitive, though, because the Occupying Powers had decreed that those who had fought for the German Army — with the exception of those to be tried for war crimes — would have no further penalties imposed on them.

However, the life for someone who had fought for the German Army was not easy in these post-war times. In broad terms, Rolf and his fellow veterans had gone from being heroes to being regarded as crippling and criminal embarrassments, and it would be several difficult years before he was able to resume his formal engineering studies and finally marry Erika in 1955.

A peripatetic life ensued as they travelled extensively in the Middle East — including a lot of time spent in the same Egypt that he had been fighting so hard to get to in 1941 — and they occasionally passed through Palestine, where he was shocked to see how bad it was for many of the refugees now fleeing Israel. Just where was it all going to end, and what was his own part in it? There were no easy answers, but it was something that was frequently on Rolf's mind. What was always clear to him was that it wasn't just Hitler who had killed the Jews — everything was connected, including him and those he had fought with, and all the others who had so enjoyed things like the Hitler Youth — and none of it sat easily.

Rolf now lives a relatively anonymous life in the suburbs of Stuttgart, an 86-year-old widower with one grown and loving daughter. Few people who see him meandering slowly with his walking stick along the main street know anything of his background fighting for the Afrika Korps, and yet in numerous ways, like so many of the soldiers who fought there on both sides, it remains the time in his life that ultimately defined him. His closest friend is a former British tank commander called Lawrie Brookby, who was part of the Occupying Powers after the war, and stayed on when he married a German woman. Together, Rolf and Lawrie go to Blackpool every year for the reunion of Lawrie's tank regiment, where the German man is, according to Lawrie, more warmly welcomed than he is. Lawrie also accompanies Rolf to Afrika Korps reunions and is close friends with many of the old soldiers.

The war record of other men of their age in Germany is stuttered over at best, totally hidden as the norm, and the men of the Afrika Korps are literally the only German military unit from World War II that is *allowed* to hold regular reunions.

The Afrika Korps still has about 700 men surviving and they have a strong Battalion association which does its best to keep its members in touch with each other. The major gathering every year focuses on the Sunday nearest to the anniversary of Rommel's death, where there is a brief ceremony followed by a lunch. Barring ill health, Manfred Rommel is a regular attendee. In 2004, on the sixtieth anniversary, there were some 3000 people gathered, and though when I attended myself on 16 October 2005 the numbers were not nearly so great, the warm feeling of the men of the Afrika Korps for Rommel had not abated. This was the last year that the veterans of the Wehrmacht would run it themselves, as in 2006 it is the modern German Army, the *Deutsche Bundeswehr*, who will conduct proceedings, and survivors like Rolf worry whether they will do it justice.

After the 2005 ceremony, I was invited to have lunch with twenty-five of the veterans, effectively the core of the Korps, and was struck by the similarity in ambience between their situation and that of the 2/17th Battalion, whose own reunion I had also been invited to attend a few weeks earlier in Canberra ...

The Australians had met in the Kangaroo Club on the outskirts of the Australian national capital in a room that, while fine enough, was right next to a very loud disco; it struck me as odd, and not quite right, that these noble survivors of the 2/17th should be making toasts to fallen comrades over the sounds of 'I'm a believer, I couldn't leave her if I tried', blaring from the disco next door ...

The restaurant in Ulm that the Afrika Korps used was equally fine, I suppose, but they did not have a room to themselves — and there were plenty of people on the long table next to theirs who knew nothing of those present, the sacrifices they had made to fight for their country — as wrong as their cause was — the toasts they were making and so forth. They were simply old men talking about an old war, a disgraced war that Germany had lost. But they still have each other, all these years on, comrades who *understand* what it was like, and what it has been like since, when their whole era has been dismissed by succeeding generations with a single word: 'Nazi'. End of conversation.

In Rolf's words: 'One can make every German *mundtot* [silent] when mentioning "Nazi", "Auschwitz" and "Holocaust". Concerning this, it is worse than in the Third Reich today, because nobody dares to say anything. One is looked at strangely. It is as if all Germans were criminals and all others were angels ...'

It is his view that, so torn asunder was Germany by the exposure of what it had done in World War II, there seems little room to acknowledge that there were good men fighting in a bad cause on one side and, even in nations that were on the victorious side of the war's ledger, there were adherents of the poisonous Nazi ideology. And he still believes that 'the Second World War started on the day that the Treaty of Versailles was signed'.

In terms of his own experience, both after his capture and in his subsequent life, Rolf has no time, he says, for '*böse Nachrede oder Hass*' (either defamation or hate). Rather, he wants 'peace and reconciliation ... but also truth'. And nor has he ever believed in an old Bedouin saying he learned in North Africa: 'Who believes one must always say the truth, should at all times have a saddled horse in front of the tent.'

In April 2005 Rolf embarked on a trip to Egypt with a group of English veterans. He was the only German participant, but their long-ago differences were completely put aside. Once, when they had gone on a search for shrapnel, Rolf had pointed out a certain area and said, 'If you dig there, you'll find a couple of tonnes in an hour ...' and had proved to be as good as his word! Oh yes, he knew all right the places where, six and a half decades earlier, they had said '*Die Luft ist eisenhaltig*' — the air contained iron — and the British veterans, in turn, had been able to show him where they had been firing on him from ...

In the final dinner, a toast was made to Rolf by his old adversaries: 'You came as a stranger and you left as a friend', and he treasures those words.

Strange, though. When he said to the old British soldiers that 'it is not easy to be a German soldier in Germany', they had nodded in what appeared to be a sympathetic understanding. For, all these years on, these former enemies of his at least knew that the Afrika Korps once stood for something.

He has no doubts: 'These days I receive more respect from the British than I do in Germany.'

•

Of course, the respect that grew between the Australian and British soldiers in Tobruk continued to flourish after the war, and it was never better expressed than in an episode that occurred when Don Bradman's Invincibles were touring England in 1948 and playing against Lancashire, in a benefit match for English batsman John Ikin. Bradman was ever a man who played to win, whatever the occasion, and when Ikin was on ninety, Bradman threw the new ball to the great Keith Miller. So the story goes, Miller — who had seen action in the European theatre of war as a fighter pilot — threw the ball back to Bradman in disgust, saying, 'Don't you know, he was a Rat of Tobruk!'

For Miller, that was enough. International fixture or not, a man who had served in Tobruk was to be treated with respect, and it was going to be a cold day in hell before Keith was going to send cricket balls whizzing past the nose of a Rat.

•

In military circles, the significance of what happened at Tobruk would not fade. As late as 1986, a young Colonel by the name of Ward A. Miller, working at the US Army Command and General Staff College in Fort Leavenworth, Kansas, would finish a learned treatise entitled *The 9th Australian Division Versus the Africa Corps: An Infantry Division Against Tanks — Tobruk, Libya, 1941*, examining precisely what could be learned from the way the garrison had been defended and attacked. In his view, it was a clear and classic demonstration of how, 'by employing all available assets in a combined arms effort, well-supported light infantry forces defeated a heavier armoured force'.

He concluded ... 'The Australians' epic stand at Tobruk had a major impact on the war because the Germans suffered a serious and unexpected reversal. The Tobruk garrison demonstrated that the hitherto successful German Blitzkrieg tactics could be defeated by resolute men who displayed courage and had the tactical and technical ability to coordinate and maximize the capabilities of their weapons and equipment in the defense.'

Despite Rommel's 1941 defeat at Tobruk, his military ideas would also retain an enormous amount of currency, and his book *Infanterie Greift An* is still studied in military academies around the world, including at the famous American military academy at West Point. In fact, the American General Norman Schwarzkopf reread his own copy of the book before planning the liberation of Kuwait in the first Gulf War, and told a reporter during that conflict that he kept his copy of 'Rommel's book' at his bedside throughout.

•

As to Tobruk itself, it is now all but totally unrecognisable from the tiny town it was, due in no small part to the fact that only a short distance to its south — in an area that looked to be among the most worthless real estate on earth — oil was discovered in the early 1960s.

People and capital flowed in, drills whirred down, derricks went up, pipelines went out, and it is now a town of about 100 000; Libya itself produces about a twelfth of the world's oil. If there is a new occupying power in the perpetual coming and going of rising and falling dominations, it is now the international oil corporations that hold sway — at a price nevertheless well paid to the government of the Libyan dictator, Colonel Mohamar Gaddhafi. Occasionally, with the increase of human traffic in those parts, there is a devastating accident where a grenade or mine that has lain there for well over half a century explodes at the touch of an innocent wanderer, but such tragedies occur less frequently now. As to the hulks of the burned-out tanks, they disappeared long ago, sold for scrap metal. As ever in that part of North Africa, nothing is left to waste.

•

Old soldiers who return to Tobruk — and they still do, in large numbers, because the place seems to exert a magnetic pull upon them — frequently go on visits out to the perimeter posts, and for the most part those posts are still out there in the desert, howling when the wind blows through them. Too, the men always go to visit the cemeteries, to pay their respects to those who have fallen.

The Commonwealth War Graves Commission Cemetery is there by the Bardia Road, even though it is now right beside an ugly industrial area, with noisy trucks going past all the time. Nevertheless, inside all is pristine and beautifully cared for, with many flourishing gum trees, and at the entrance stands a simple concrete memorial 7.5 metres high, displaying a marble slab which reads . . .

THIS IS HALLOWED GROUND,

FOR HERE LIE THOSE WHO DIED FOR THEIR COUNTRY.

AT THE GOING DOWN OF THE SUN,

AND IN THE MORNING, WE WILL REMEMBER THEM.

Many relatives of the fallen make their way to that cemetery, almost in the manner of a pilgrimage.

The greatest Aussie Rules figure of them all, Ron Barassi, arrived in 1984, to be physically close to the father he had not seen since he was just four years old, when Ron Snr had gone to war. On the night of 31 July 1941, the elder Barassi had relieved an exhausted truck driver and had shortly afterwards been killed by a bomb . . .

Somehow, as Ron Jnr stood alone before his father's simple grave — struck by the fact that he was now nearly twice as old as his father had been when he died — the sense of what he had lost, what his mother had lost, the years that his father should have had with them but didn't, simply overwhelmed him and he began to cry.

Once started, there was no stopping it, and he continued crying, almost as he had when he was five years old and the terrible telegram had come. He felt he could have stayed there crying all day, even while luxuriating in that feeling of wonderful *closeness* to his father that he simply didn't want to let go of. But finally he pulled himself together and said what he now realised he had wanted to say all along — perhaps the reason he had come here.

'Dad, I love you . . .'

•

Twenty years later came another visitor, on a similar paternal pilgrimage. It was Len Johnson, the fifth son of John and Josie, and there were many powerful forces that had propelled him to this point. Once retired from the Australian Army, where he had risen to the rank of Lieutenant Colonel — with his last command being that of the 2/4th Battalion of the Royal Australian Regiment — Len had decided to forego his previous vow never to read the letters between his parents again, and had begun to minutely research the circumstances of his father's death. For purely personal and family reasons, he had assembled the letters into a publication called *War Letters 1940–1941*, which, with the letters themselves, he sent to the Australian War Memorial. And yet that still was not enough. For decades now, Len had felt that it was not right that his father should lie alone in his grave, away from his family, without at least one of the family trying to get to him to make the final farewell.

And now he was here. With his own son, Damien, Len went all over Tobruk, seeking out the places he had studied for so long from afar. There was the harbour, as he had imagined it; the escarpments that climbed to the plain where the key battles took place; the spot where the 2/23rd Carrier Platoon had been based on the morning of 17 May 1941 before his father had gone on his last mission; and there . . . yes, there was Post S9. It was all but entirely unchanged from the day his father had gone inside looking for wounded Australian soldiers, right down to the ration tins and spent cartridge cases and an empty Bren gun magazine being heaped in a rubbish pile where the last soldiers had likely thrown them. Eerie.

Finally, in the late afternoon of this searing summer's day, he was walking into the cemetery where lay the father he had missed so desperately for over sixty years. Everything was quiet now, so quiet that he could hear the sound of the slight wind rustling the gum leaves overhead.

Len was immediately struck by how the mass of white headstones before him looked like so many soldiers on parade. He knew exactly where his father was, and now walked to it alone, as Damien dropped back.

Like them all, it was a simple grave, with a white headstone upon which is written:

VX42266 CORPORAL

J.L. JOHNSON

2/23 AUST. INF. BN.

17TH MAY 1941 AGE 38

WE WILL REMEMBER YOU ALWAYS
JOSIE AND FAMILY, MUM AND DAD

Right next to John Johnson, on one side was the grave of his great friend and fellow Walwa man, Pat Joy, while on the other was another friend, Stan Peters.

Somehow, standing at last before his father's grave, there was for Len an intense sense of unreality. So many thoughts, so many memories, all jostling against each other, treading on each other, hurting. The day they got the news; the tears of Mum; the move to Melbourne; the low, dull ache of missing Dad always and growing to maturity without him, wondering if he would have been proud of them and trying to live up to his memory so that he would have been proud, had he lived.

Had he lived ...

But he hadn't. Len wanted to cry, but this was not yet the time. Instead, he sat on the baked red–orange clay and told his father all that had happened to each and every family member in their lives: how I lost the book *Dumbo the Flying Elephant* you gave me, Dad — and to this day has never been able to look at another one as it is still too painful; how proud John would have been of how Josie had kept both the family together and his memory alive, despite the extremely rigorous hardships they went through; that Alex was himself dead now and that, Dad, you've got thirty-six grandchildren and they're all going well, full of brightness and promise ...

Still, though, Len didn't cry, as inexplicably the satisfaction of once more being with his father overwhelmed all else.

The next day he returned, and stayed there for some time, until in some indefinable way, a certain peacefulness came over him. Then he cried. Somehow, it was over.

The sun was going down, and the shadow from his father's headstone was long. He said goodbye, and walked out of the cemetery without looking back.

•

Those cemeteries have seen many such scenes over the years, and they will likely do so for many years to come. At least I hope so.

In Australia, at the time of writing, the name 'Tobruk' is still widely recognised as an iconic battle of World War II and the general understanding is that Australian soldiers did well; but apart from those who fought there and perhaps their immediate descendants, most detail has been lost from the wider public consciousness.

Allow me to say, if I have a chief hope for this book, it is that it will help the feats of the Diggers live again, as they deserve to.

A fair indication, I think, of how the legend of Tobruk has waxed and then waned is that after Prime Minister Robert Menzies visited Tobruk in 1956, it was nigh on another fifty-odd years until the next Australian Minister turned up, in the person of the then Trade Minister, and now Deputy Prime Minister, Mark Vaile, who visited in 2002.

Vaile made a special point of kneeling at the freshly restored headstone of Jack Edmondson.

On ya, Jack. We remember you, still ...

April–December 1941

Adv HQ 9 Aust Div

Rear HQ 9 Aust Div
9 Aust Div Int Sec
'D' Sec FSS
One Pl Aust HQ Gd Bn
9 Aust Div Emp Pl

2/12 Aust Fd Regt, RAA, plus Sig Sec
3 Aust A/Tk Regt (less 1 Bty)
71 L.A.D.

HQ RAE 9 Div
2/3 Fd Coy
2/4 Fd Coy
2/7 Fd Coy
2/13 Fd Coy
72 L.A.D.
No. 10 (Aust) Cam Unit

HQ Sigs 9 Aust Div
'J' Sec Sigs 7 Aust Div
2 Op Sec Sigs 1 Aust Corps

HQ 18 Aust Inf Bde Sig Sec
Platoon Aust Guard Bn
16 Aust A/Tk Coy
2/9 Aust Inf Bn
2/10 Aust Inf Bn
2/12 Aust Inf Bn
47 L.A.D.

HQ 20 Aust Inf Bde Sig Sec
Pl Aust Guard Bn
20 Aust A/Tk Coy
2/13 Aust Inf Bn
2/15 Aust Inf Bn
2/17 Aust Inf Bn
58 L.A.D.

HQ 24 Aust Inf Bde
Sig Sec
Platoon Aust Guard Bn
24 Aust A/Tk Coy
2/28 Aust Inf Bn
2/43 Aust Inf Bn
Under Command
2/32 Aust Inf Bn
76 L.A.D.

HQ 26 Aust Inf Bde
Sig Sec
Platoon Aust Guard Bn
26 Aust A/Tk Coy
2/23 Aust Inf Bn
2/24 Aust Inf Bn
2/48 Aust Inf Bn
78 L.A.D.

2/1 Aust Pioneer Bn

HQ AASC 9 Aust Div
9 Aust Div Pet Coy
9 Aust Div Supply Coln
7 Aust Div Supply Coln
9 Aust Div Amn Coy

MEDICAL
HQ AAMC 9 Aust Div
2/3 Fd Amb
2/5 Fd Amb
2/8 Fd Amb
2/11 Fd Amb
2/4 Fd Hygiene Sec

MISCELLANEOUS
9 Aust Div Pro Coy
9 Aust Div Salvage Coy
9 Aust Div Postal Unit
9 Aust Div Fd Cash Office

FORTRESS TROOPS
8 Aust Lt AA Bty

SIGNALS
4 Line Sec Sigs 1 Aust Corps

ORDNANCE
2/1 Army Fd Workshopps AAOC
No. 6 Rec Sec 2/2 AFW AAOC

TOBRUK SUB-AREA
MEDICAL
4 Aust Gen Hosp
2/2 Aust CCS

ORDNANCE
4 AOD AAOC

The following units were formed from 7 and 9 Aust Div Supply Columns and appeared in Orders of Battle subsequent to the one above:

- *No. 1 and 2 Tp Carrying Coys*
- *Area Transport Coy*
- *No. 1 and 2 Aust F.S. Ds*
- *9 Aust Div Res Tpt Coys*

The Order of Battle for September 1941 and October 1941 also included No. 10 Aust Camouflage Unit (formed from troops already in Tobruk).

Endnotes

CHAPTER ONE — In the Beginning

1 From an article in *Smiths Weekly*, 26/2/44
2 Winter (ed.), *Making a Legend: The War Writings of C.E.W. Bean*
3 Maughan, *Australia in the War of 1939–45: Tobruk and El Alamein*, p. 11
4 Young, *Rommel*, p. 32
5 Lucas, *Hitler's Enforcers: Leaders of the German War Machine 1939–45*, photo section
6 *Ibid.*, p. 148
7 Porch, *Hitler's Mediterranean Gamble*, p. 206
8 Farrell, *Mussolini: A New Life*, footnote p. 64
9 *Ibid.*, p. 72
10 *www.firstworldwar.com/features/tandey.htm*. See John Godl's work and the research he used: Chapman, 'Beyond Their Duty', *Sunday Graphic*, UK, December 1940; Colonel Earle, *The Green Howards Gazette*, UK, June, 1937.
11 *www.firstworldwar.com/features/aslowfuse.htm*: contribution by Simon Rees, updated October 2003
12 Strawson, *Hitler as Military Commander*, p. 20
13 Hughes, *Billy Hughes*, p. 77
14 Luck, *This Fabulous Century*, p. 30. For this and the story about the 60 000 dead Australians, there are various versions and words used, however the theme is always the same.
15 Irving, *Rommel: The Trail of the Fox*, p. 20
16 Strawson, *Hitler as Military Commander*, p. 23
17 Padfield, *Hess: Flight for the Führer*, p. 16
18 Farrell, *Mussolini: A New Life*, p. 12
19 Strawson, *Hitler as Military Commander*, p. 30
20 Padfield, *Hess: Flight for the Führer*

CHAPTER TWO — His Struggle

1 Adolf Hitler, *Mein Kampf*
2 Bosworth, *Mussolini's Italy: Life Under the Dictatorship 1915–1945*

3   Padfield, *Hess: Flight for the Führer*, p. 80

4   Coombes, *Morshead: Hero of Tobruk and El Alamein*, p. 75

5   Horner, *Blamey, The Commander in Chief*, p. 97

6   Horner, *Crisis of Command*, p. 17

7   *www.historyplace.com/worldwar2/hitleryouth/hj-prelude.htm*

8   *www.historylearningsite.co.uk/Nazis_Education.htm*

9   Based on a paper by Kesby, Harper and Kiddy, 'A Biography of John Hurst Edmondson VC', AWM 12334

10 *Sunday Telegraph* pictorial, 13 July 1941

11 Account written by Athol Thomas of Cottesloe, WA, dated 28 October 1955, held by the Australian War Memorial

12 Based on a paper by Konrad Kwiet and Olaf Reinhardt, 'A "Nazi" Assessment of Australian Racial Policy from 1935', in *Australian Journal of Politics and History*, 34/3 (1989), pp. 388–405

13 Heckmann, *Rommel's War in Africa*, p. 10

14 Farrell, *Mussolini: A New Life*, p. 7

15 Padfield, *Hess: Flight for the Führer*, p. xviii

16 *Ibid.*, p. 87

17 Coombes, *Morshead: Hero of Tobruk and El Alamein*, p. 81

18 Rommel, *Infantry Attacks*, p. 226

19 McDonald, *Chester Wilmot Reports*, p. 5

20 Parker, *Chamberlain and Appeasement: British Policy and the Coming of the Second World War*, p. 181

21 Charmley, *Chamberlain and the Lost Peace*, p. 141

22 *British Hansard*

23 *Ibid.*

24 *Ibid.*

25 Martin and Hardy (eds), *Dark and Hurrying Days: Menzies' 1941 Diary*, p. 4

CHAPTER THREE — A World at War

1   Gullet, *Not as Duty Only: An Infantryman's War*

2   *www.eyewitnesstohistory.com/ultimatum.htm*. The site refers to Paul Schmidt, *Hitler's Interpreter* (Heinemann, 1951).

3   Elizabeth Edmondson diary, AWM file 89/05/33, entry 8 January 1940

4   MacDougall, *Australians at War: A Pictorial History*, p. 164

5   *Ibid.*, p. 64

6   *www.worldatwar.net/article/australiaswar/index.htm*

7   Day, *The Politics of War*, p. 2

8   Moore, *Morshead: A Biography of Lieutenant General Sir Leslie Morshead*, p. 67

9   Lucas, *Hitler's Enforcers: Leaders of the German War Machine 1939–45*, p. 150

10 Moorehead, *African Trilogy*, p. 75

11 Lewin, *The Chief*, p. 127. Also, Young, *Rommel*, records (p. 95) that Rommel's library contained a well-thumbed copy of a German translation of Wavell's pamphlet on the art of generalship, *Der Feldherr* (Zurich, 1942).

12 Horner, *Blamey, The Commander in Chief*, p. 136

13 Charlton, *The Thirty Niners*, p. 47

14 Elizabeth Edmondson diary, AWM file 89/05/33, entry 19 April 1940

15 *Ibid.*, entry 8 January 1940

16 Letter written by Elizabeth Edmondson to Don Gibson

17 Elizabeth Edmondson diary, AWM file 89/05/33, entry 13 May 1940

18 *Ibid.*, entry 1 June 1940

19 Fearnside (ed.), *Bayonets Abroad: Benghazi to Borneo with the 2/13th Battalion AIF*, p. 5

20 Elizabeth Edmondson diary, AWM file 89/05/33, entry 4 May 1940

CHAPTER FOUR — **Rommel Rises**

1   Schmidt, *With Rommel in the Desert*, p. 85

2   Lucas, *Hitler's Enforcers*, p. 152

3   *Ibid*, p. 158

4   This editorial appeared in the *New York Times* in early June 1940, and was subsequently reprinted in a 9th Division news sheet in Egypt in 1942, where it was read and memorised by the author's late father, Lieutenant Peter McCloy FitzSimons, who was serving with the 9th Division of the Australian Imperial Forces at the time.

5   Connell, *Wavell: Scholar and Soldier*, p. 229

6   Parkinson, *The War in The Desert*, p. 9

7   Bosworth, *Mussolini's Italy: Life Under the Dictatorship, 1915–1945*

8   Fearnside (ed.), *Bayonets Abroad: Benghazi to Borneo with the 2/13th Battalion AIF*, p. 8

9   Aldrich (ed.), *Witness to War: Diaries of the Second World War in Europe and the Middle East*, p. 176

10 Heckstall-Smith, *Tobruk*, p. 11

11 *Ibid.*, p. 11

12 Details in a letter written by Sergeant Merrikin to Elizabeth Edmondson, after Jack was killed, held by Australian War Memorial

13 Pitt, *The Crucible of War*, p. 49

14 Interview with Ned McDonald, who was told this by Ken Hall of Army PR

15 Fearnside (ed.), *Bayonets Abroad: Benghazi to Borneo with the 2/13th Battalion AIF*, p. 10

16 *A History of the 2/17th Infantry Battalion 1940–1945: 'What We Have . . . We Hold!'*, p. 6

17 Pitt, *The Crucible of War*, p. 49

18 Heckmann, *Rommel's War in Africa*, p. 15

19 Day, *The Politics of War*, p. 85

20 Elizabeth Edmondson diary, AWM file 89/05/33, entry 30 September 1940

21 *Ibid.*, entry 5 October 1940

22 William Wordsworth, *The Prelude*

23 Johnson, *An Australian Family*, vol III: *War Letters 1940–1941*, p. 50

CHAPTER FIVE — **Enter the Australians**

1 Moorehead, *African Trilogy*, p. 82. Australian journalist Alan Moorehead was impressed when seeing Australian soldiers disembarking in the Middle East for the first time.

2 Heckmann, *Rommel's War in Africa*, p. 17

3 Elizabeth Edmondson diary, AWM file 89/05/33, entry 29 October 1940

4 Based on a paper by Kesby, Harper and Kiddy, 'A Biography of John Hurst Edmondson VC', AWM 12334

5 Moorehead, *African Trilogy*, p. 4

6 *A History of the 2/17th Infantry Battalion 1940–1945: 'What We Have . . . We Hold!'*, p. 10

7 Share (ed.), *Mud and Blood, Albury's Own: 2/23rd Australian Infantry Battalion*, p. 26

8 MacDougall, *Australians at War: A Pictorial History*, p. 182

9 *www.diggerhistory.info/pages-conflicts-periods/ww1/lt-horse/beersheba.htm*

10 Elizabeth Edmondson diary, AWM file 89/05/33, entry 30 September 1940. It is in this same diary entry that there is an account of him saying, 'No mother, I want to come home.'

11 *Ibid.*, entry 15 September 1940

12 *Ibid.*, entry 15 September 1940

13 Fearnside (ed.), *Bayonets Abroad: Benghazi to Borneo with the 2/13th Battalion AIF*, p. 37

14 Heckmann, *Rommel's War in Africa*, p. 27

15 Porch, *Hitler's Mediterranean Gamble*, p. 204

16 Based on an interview of Heinz Guderian by Basil Liddell Hart about tank warfare for his book *The Other Side of the Hill* (1948). Guderian was scathing about Halder's old-fashioned views.

17 Johnson, *An Australian Family*, vol. III: *War Letters 1940–1941*, p. 64

18 Hetherington, *The Australian Soldier: A Portrait of World War II*, Chapter 1, 'Education in the Desert'

19 Serle (ed.), *2/24th: A History of the 2/24th Australian Infantry Battalion*, p. 26

20 McDonald, *Chester Wilmot Reports*, p. 37

21 Barber, *The War, the Whores and the Afrika Korps*, p. 37

22 Diary of Australian soldier Norman Ellis Richard Freeberg of the 2/16th Battalion, AWM file PRO1410, entry 6 January 1941

23 Johnson, *An Australian Family*, vol. III: *War Letters 1940–1941*, p. 7

24 Elizabeth Edmondson diary, AWM file 89/05/33, entry 6 January 1941

CHAPTER SIX — Take Tobruk

1 Wilmot, *Tobruk 1941: Capture — Siege — Relief*, p. 59. Chester Wilmot notes the difference between the approach taken by Australian and Italian soldiers when it came to the gear they took with them.

2 Ronald Lewin, quoted in Porch, *Hitler's Mediterranean Gamble*, p. 196

3 Sherwood, *The White House Papers of Harry L. Hopkins*, vol. 1, p. 240

4 Heckmann, *Rommel's War in Africa*, p. 22

5 Cull and Minterne, *Hurricanes Over Tobruk*, p. 10

6 Wilmot, *Tobruk 1941: Capture — Siege — Relief*, p. 18

7 McDonald, *Chester Wilmot Reports*, p. 64

8 Wilmot, *Tobruk 1941: Capture — Siege — Relief*, p. 4

9 McDonald, *Chester Wilmot Reports*, p. 66

10 *Ibid.*, p. 67

11 Moorehead, *African Trilogy*, p. 79

12 Wilmot, *Tobruk 1941: Capture — Siege — Relief*, p. 20

13 Pitt, *The Crucible of War*, p. 148

14 Moorehead, *African Trilogy*, p. 82

15 Pitt, *The Crucible of War*, p. 159

16 Wilmot, *Tobruk 1941: Capture — Siege — Relief*, p. 40

17 *Ibid.*, p. 27

18 *Ibid.*, p. 45

19 *Ibid.*, p. 45

20 Young, *Rommel*, p. 17

21 Cull and Minterne, *Hurricanes Over Tobruk*, p. 44

22 Wilmot, *Tobruk 1941: Capture — Siege — Relief*, p. 60

23 *Ibid.*, p. 58

24 *Ibid.*, p. 54

25 *Ibid.*, pp. 45, 61

26 *Ibid.*, p. 48

27 *Ibid.*, p. 162

28 Masel, *2/28th Battalion History*, p. 28

29 Heckmann, *Rommel's War in Africa*

30 Day, *The Politics of War*, p. 107

31 As recorded in the *Mud and Blood* news sheet on 4 September 1941

32 Hetherington, *Blamey, Controversial Soldier*, p. 175

33 *Australian Hansard*, 20 April 1939

34 *Ibid.*

35 Martin and Hardy (eds), *Dark and Hurrying Days: Menzies' 1941 Diary*, p. 31

36 *Sydney Morning Herald*, 6 February 1941

37 Hetherington, *Blamey, Controversial Soldier*

38 Morshead was himself a great admirer of Lloyd's, and in a letter to his wife Myrtle on 10 June 1941 wrote: 'I don't think you have met Lloyd my right hand man. He is one of the ablest soldiers and one of the bravest I've been associated with. He has done a splendid job and I count myself lucky in having him. This is the first time he has had such a job, but he would do well in any capacity. He's the only right choice that my predecessor made.' Held by the Morshead family.

39 Bierman, *Alamein: War Without Hate*, p. 50

40 Irving, *Rommel: The Trail of the Fox*, p. 59. And yet, while Irving says that Rommel met with Hitler also, I can find no other evidence of that.

41 *Ibid.*, p. 99

42 *Ibid.*, p. 99

43 *Ibid.*, p. 99

44 Barker, *Afrika Korps*, p. 10

45 Baynes, *The Forgotten Victor: General Sir Richard O'Connor*, p. 118

46 Cull and Minterne, *Hurricanes Over Tobruk*, p. 63

47 Connell, *Wavell: Scholar and Soldier*, p. 330

48 Day, *The Politics of War*, p. 115

49 Maughan, *Australia in the War of 1939–45: Tobruk and El Alamein*, p. 4

50 Salter, *A Padre with the Rats of Tobruk*, p. 22

51 Neame, *Playing with Strife: The Autobiography of a Soldier*, p. 267

CHAPTER SEVEN — **Enter, the German General**

1 Parker, *Desert Rats: From El Alamein to Basra*, p. 9

2 Barker, *Afrika Korps*, p. 13

3 Liddell Hart (ed.), *The Rommel Papers*, p. 101

4 Firkins, *The Australians in Nine Wars*, p 197

5 Moorehead, *African Trilogy*, p. 76

6 Horner, *Blamey, The Commander in Chief*, p. 173

7 Long, *Australia in the War of 1939–1945: Greece, Crete and Syria*, p. 17

8 Heckmann, *Rommel's War in Africa*, pp. 4–5

9   *Ibid.*, p 8

10 Cited in Coombes, *Morshead: Hero of Tobruk and El Alamein*, p. 101

11 McDonald, *Chester Wilmot Reports*, p. 112

12 Fearnside (ed.), *Bayonets Abroad: Benghazi to Borneo with the 2/13th Battalion AIF*, p. 43. In the actual text of *Bayonets Abroad* it says 'miles and miles of blank-all', but the author, of less genteel disposition than the authors of *Bayonets Abroad*, has drawn the obvious conclusion that the actual Australian expression was used as a descriptive term at the time, as opposed to the sanitised version.

13 A brief account of those Bedouins is to be found at *ibid.*, p. 46.

14 Schmidt, *With Rommel in the Desert*, p. 13

15 Barker, *Afrika Korps*, p. 15

16 Interview with Afrika Korps veteran Wilhelm Langsam, 15 October 2005

17 Aberger *et. al.*, *Nur ein Bataillon*, pp. 78–79

18 From the speech delivered by Lieutenant General Morshead to a function held at Victoria Barracks, Sydney, in 1947. Copy held by the Australian War Memorial.

19 Elizabeth Edmondson diary, AWM file 89/05/33, entry 1 March 1941

20 Johnson, *An Australian Family*, vol. III: *War Letters 1940–1941*, p. 80

21 Maughan, *Australia in the War of 1939–45: Tobruk and El Alamein*, p. 27

22 Moore, *Morshead: A Biography of Lieutenant General Sir Leslie Morshead*, p. 75

23 Hall, *Tobruk 1941: The Desert Siege*, p. 31

24 Johnson, *An Australian Family*, vol. III: *War Letters 1940–1941*, p. 71

25 *www.australiansatwar.gov.au/stories/stories.asp?war=W2&id=154*

26 From the speech delivered by Lieutenant General Morshead to a function held at Victoria Barracks, Sydney, in 1947. Copy held by the Australian War Memorial.

27 Coombes, *Morshead: Hero of Tobruk and El Alamein*, p. 102

28 *Ibid.*, p. 102

29 Keegan (ed.), *Churchill's Generals*, p. 59

30 Neame, *Playing with Strife: The Autobiography of a Soldier*, p. 268

31 Moore, *Morshead: A Biography of Lieutenant General Sir Leslie Morshead*, p. 77

32 Coombes, *Morshead: Hero of Tobruk and El Alamein*, p. 103

33 Connell, *Wavell: Scholar and Soldier*, p. 386

34 Fearnside (ed.), *Bayonets Abroad: Benghazi to Borneo with the 2/13th Battalion AIF*, p. 48

CHAPTER EIGHT — **Attack!!!**

1   Heckmann, *Rommel's War in Africa*, p. 28

2   Barker, *Afrika Korps*, pp. 10, 37

3 Porch, *Hitler's Mediterranean Gamble,* p. 206

4 Connell, *Wavell: Scholar and Soldier,* p. 388

5 Heckmann, *Rommel's War in Africa,* p. 100

6 *Ibid.,* p. 99

7 Letter from Lieutenant General Morshead to his wife Myrtle, 26 March 1941, held by the Morshead family

8 Aberger *et al., Nur ein Bataillon,* p. 84

9 Young, *Rommel,* pp. 16–18

10 Neame, *Playing with Strife: The Autobiography of a Soldier,* p. 273

11 Letter From General Wavell to Sir Richard O'Connor, 27 June 1945, ref [4/3/1] in the papers of General Sir Richard O'Connor, held by the Liddell Hart Centre for Military Archives, King's College, London.

12 Barker, *Afrika Korps,* p. 18

13 *Ibid.,* p. 19

14 Aberger *et al., Nur ein Bataillon,* p. 91

15 Freiherr Hans Gert von Esebeck, 'Wie El Brega in unsere Hand fiel' ('How Brega Fell Into Our Hands'), *Die Oase* 8, 5 April 1941

16 Aberger *et al., Nur ein Bataillon,* p. 93

17 Parkinson, *The War in the Desert,* p. 42

18 Letter held in the Morshead papers, AWM file 3DRL/2632, item 2/2

19 Luck, *This Fabulous Century,* p. 20

20 Morshead diary, 31 March 1942, held by the Australian War Memorial

21 Maughan, *Australia in the War of 1939–45: Tobruk and El Alamein,* p. 55

22 As detailed in an interview with General Sir Richard O'Connor GCB DSO MC: recollections of the planning and conduct of the First Libyan Campaign, 1940–1941

23 Liddell Hart (ed.), *The Rommel Papers,* p. 109

24 As recorded in *Kriegstagebuch vom 8 Maschinengewehr Bataillon,* 3 April 1941

25 Johnson, *An Australian Family,* vol. III: *War Letters 1940–1941,* p. 85

26 *Ibid.,* pp. 85, 108

27 Freiherr Hans Gert von Esebeck, 'Briefe aus England: Die Heimat klagt an' ('Letters from England: The Home Country Accuses'), *Die Oase* 9, 6 April 1941

28 Maughan, *Australia in the War of 1939–45: Tobruk and El Alamein,* p. 57

29 Wavell (ed.), *Other Men's Flowers,* p. 97

30 Neame, *Playing with Strife: The Autobiography of a Soldier,* p. 278

31 *Ibid.,* p. 276

32 Baynes, *The Forgotten Victor: General Sir Richard O'Connor,* p. 133

33 Letter from General Wavell to Sir Richard O'Connor, 27 June 1945, ref [4/3/1] in the papers of General Sir Richard O'Connor, held by the Liddell Hart Centre for Military Archives, King's College, London

34 Connell, *Wavell: Scholar and Soldier*, p. 393

35 Barker, *Afrika Korps*, p. 22

36 Irving, *Rommel: The Trail of the Fox*, p. 71

37 Heckmann, *Rommel's War in Africa*, p. 41

38 Aberger *et al.*, *Nur ein Bataillon*, p. 93

39 Irving, *Rommel: The Trail of the Fox*, p. 71

40 Rommel, *Krieg ohne Hass*, p. 23

41 Maughan, *Australia in the War of 1939–45: Tobruk and El Alamein*, p. 66

42 Irving, *Rommel: The Trail of the Fox*, p. 71

CHAPTER NINE — **First Strike**

1   Day, *Menzies and Churchill at War: A Controversial New Account of the 1941 Struggle for Power*

2   Coombes, *Morshead: Hero of Tobruk and El Alamein*, p. 104

3   Neame, *Playing with Strife: The Autobiography of a Soldier*, p. 271

4   More on this can be found in Wilmot, *Tobruk 1941: Capture — Siege — Relief*, p. 79

5   Schmidt, *With Rommel in the Desert*, p. 28

6   Aberger *et al.*, *Nur ein Bataillon*, p. 87

7   Lucas, *Hitler's Enforcers: Leaders of the German War Machine 1939–45*, p. 157

8   Harrison, *Tobruk: The Birth of a Legend*, p. 20

9   Schmidt, *With Rommel in the Desert*, p. 42

10 *Ibid.*, p. 46

11 Elizabeth Edmondson diary, AWM file 89/05/33, entry 4 April 1941

12 Maughan, *Australia in the War of 1939–45: Tobruk and El Alamein*, p. 69

13 The account following comes from Fearnside (ed.), *Bayonets Abroad: Benghazi to Borneo with the 2/13th Battalion AIF*, p. 57

14 Maughan, *Australia in the War of 1939–45: Tobruk and El Alamein*, p. 73

15 Lewin, *Rommel as Military Commander*, p. 37

16 Interview with Keith Seccombe of the 2/3rd Australian Anti-tank Regiment

17 Irving, *Rommel: The Trail of the Fox*, p. 74

18 Bierman, *Alamein: War Without Hate*, p. 57

19 Martin and Hardy (eds), *Dark and Hurrying Days: Menzies' 1941 Diary*, p. 34

20 Day, 'Anzacs on the Run: The View From Whitehall 1941–42', *Journal of Imperial and Commonwealth History*, Vol XIV, No. 3, May 1986, p. 188

21 Baynes, *The Forgotten Victor: General Sir Richard O'Connor*, p. 136

22 Neame, *Playing with Strife: The Autobiography of a Soldier*, p. 281

23 Letter from Morshead to his wife Myrtle, 18 June 1941, held by the Morshead family

24 Silver, *Target Tank: The History of the 2/3 Australian Anti-tank Regiment, 9th Division*, p. 54

25 Latimer, *Tobruk 1941: Rommel's Opening Move*, p. 90

26 Johnson, *An Australian Family*, vol. III: *War Letters 1940–1941*, p. 88

27 Heckmann, *Rommel's War in Africa*, p. 43

28 *Ibid.*, p 61. In Maughan, *Australia in the War of 1939–45: Tobruk and El Alamein*, Rayner is quoted (p. 105) as saying the whole thing a little more delicately. 'We fired shell after shell at this tank and still it came on . . . I can remember the last order I gave. All thoughts of army drill were forgotten. I just gave the order: give him another one, the last one in the tail.'

29 Schmidt, *With Rommel in the Desert*, p. 34

30 Silver, *Target Tank: The History of the 2/3 Australian Anti-tank Regiment, 9th Division*, p. 66

31 Interview with Herrn Rolf Munninger, 15 October 2005, at his home in Stuttgart

32 Schmidt, *With Rommel in the Desert*, p. 34

33 Aberger *et al.*, *Nur ein Bataillon*, p. 98

34 Carell, *Die Wüstenfüchse*, p. 20

35 As noted in Serle (ed.), *2/24th: A History of the 2/24th Australian Infantry Battalion*, p. 48

36 Forty (ed.), *Leakey's Luck: A Tank Commander with Nine Lives*, p. 84

CHAPTER TEN — **All Set**

1 Wilmot, *Tobruk 1941: Capture — Siege — Relief*, p. 55

2 Latimer, *Tobruk 1941: Rommel's Opening Move*, p. 73

3 Heckmann, *Rommel's War in Africa*, p. 72

4 From the speech delivered by Lieutenant General Morshead to a function held at Victoria Barracks, Sydney, in 1947. Copy held by the Australian War Memorial.

5 Connell, *Wavell: Scholar and Soldier*, p. 404

6 Day, 'Anzacs on the Run: The View From Whitehall 1941–42', *Journal of Imperial and Commonwealth History*, Vol XIV, No. 3, May 1986, p. 190

7 From the speech delivered by Lieutenant General Morshead to a function held at Victoria Barracks, Sydney, in 1947. Copy held by the Australian War Memorial.

8 Forty (ed.), *Leakey's Luck: A Tank Commander with Nine Lives*, p. 86

9   Liddell Hart (ed.), *The Rommel Papers*, p. 122

10 Firkins, *The Australians in Nine Wars: Waikato to Long Tan*, p. 227

11 Maughan, *Australia in the War of 1939–45: Tobruk and El Alamein*, p. 12

12 Order recorded in Wilmot, *Tobruk 1941: Capture — Siege — Relief*, p. 93

13 Masel, *2/28th Battalion History*, p. 20

14 Wilmot, *Tobruk 1941: Capture — Siege — Relief*, p. 93

15 Masel, *2/28th Battalion History*, p. 21

16 Aberger *et al.*, *Nur ein Bataillon*, p. 101

17 Irving, *Rommel: The Trail of the Fox*, p. 78

18 Neame, *Playing with Strife: The Autobiography of a Soldier*, p. 280

19 Cull and Minterne, *Hurricanes Over Tobruk*, p. 74

20 Parr-Smith, *A Signaller's War*

21 Serle (ed.), *2/24th: A History of the 2/24th Australian Infantry Battalion*, p. 53

22 Schmidt, *With Rommel in the Desert*, p. 36

23 *Ibid*, p. 37

CHAPTER ELEVEN — **The Easter Battle**

1   Harrison, *Tobruk: The Birth of a Legend*

2   Quoted on the front page of the *Sydney Morning Herald*, 16 April 1941

3   Aberger *et al.*, *Nur ein Bataillon*, p. 104

4   Barker, *Afrika Korps*, p. 31

5   Aberger *et al.*, *Nur ein Bataillon*, p. 105

6   Hall, *Tobruk 1941: The Desert Siege*, p. 103

7   Barker, *Afrika Korps*, p. 37

8   *As I Remember It*, AWM MSS 1587, p. 26

9   Wilmot, *Tobruk 1941: Capture — Siege — Relief*, p. 96

10 Elizabeth Edmondson diary, AWM file 89/05/33, entry 13 April 1941

11 Heckmann, *Rommel's War in Africa*, p. 79

12 Liddell Hart (ed.), *The Rommel Papers*, p. 123

13 Firkins, *The Australians in Nine Wars: Waikato to Long Tan*, p. 233

14 Interview with Jack Harris of the 2/17th Battalion

15 Aberger *et al.*, *Nur ein Bataillon*, p. 107

16 Schmidt, *With Rommel in the Desert*, p. 44

17 Aberger *et al.*, *Nur ein Bataillon*, p. 111

18 *Ibid.*, p. 11

19 Based on Kesby, Harper and Kiddy, 'A Biography of John Hurst Edmondson VC', AWM 12334

20 Aberger *et al.*, *Nur ein Bataillon*, p. 111

21 Ron Grant's recollections, as printed in Kesby, Harper and Kiddy, 'A Biography of John Hurst Edmondson VC', AWM 12334

22 This is according to a report by Austin Mackell, quoted in the *Sydney Morning Herald*, 18 April 1941, p. 10

23 Account written by Athol Thomas of Cottesloe, Western Australia, dated 28 October 1955, held by the Australian War Memorial. Much of the detail within it is confirmed by other sources.

24 Letter from Athol Dalziel to Mrs Edmondson, held by the Australian War Memorial

25 Letter from Athol Dalziel to Elizabeth Edmondson, 17 September 1941, in response to her request for details as to the manner of Jack's death, held by the Australian War Memorial

26 Schmidt, *With Rommel in the Desert*, p. 88

27 *Ibid.*, p. 44

28 Forty (ed.), *Leakey's Luck: A Tank Commander with Nine Lives*, p. 91

29 Chapman, *History of the Sydney University Regiment*

30 Hall, *Tobruk 1941: The Desert Siege*, p. 70

31 Account by Sergeant Wilhelm Assenmacher in Aberger *et al.*, *Nur ein Bataillon*, p. 113

32 Schmidt, *With Rommel in the Desert*, p. 45

33 Liddell Hart (ed.), *The Rommel Papers*, p. 124

34 *Ibid.*, p. 124

35 From the captured diary of tank commander Lieutenant Joachim Schorm, AWM 54 423/4/69, entry 14 April

36 Aberger *et al.*, *Nur ein Bataillon*, p. 116

37 *As I Remember It*, AWM MSS 1587, p. 123

CHAPTER TWELVE — **To Fight Another Day**

1 Bierman, *Alamein: War Without Hate*, p. 80

2 Heckmann, *Rommel's War in Africa*, pp. 77, 82

3 From the captured diary of tank commander Lieutenant Joachim Schorm, AWM 54 423/4/69, entry 14 April

4 Forty (ed.), *Leakey's Luck: A Tank Commander with Nine Lives*, p. 92.

5 Papers of Elizabeth Edmondson, PR 89/56, AWM file 89/0533

6 Hall, *Tobruk 1941: The Desert Siege*, p. 70

7 Heckmann, *Rommel's War in Africa*, p. 82

8 From the captured diary of tank commander Lieutenant Joachim Schorm, AWM 54 423/4/69, entry 14 April

9 Aberger *et al.*, *Nur ein Bataillon*, p. 146

10 The details of this battle from the German perspective can be found, in German, in *ibid.*, p. 118

11 Firkins, *The Australians in Nine Wars: Waikato to Long Tan*, p. 232

12 Liddell Hart (ed.), *The Rommel Papers*, p. 125

13 Schmidt, *With Rommel in the Desert*, p. 43

14 *Ibid.*, p 44

15 Maughan, *Australia in the War of 1939–45: Tobruk and El Alamein*, p. 155

16 Wilmot, *Tobruk 1941: Capture — Siege — Relief*, p. 89

17 Heckmann, *Rommel's War in Africa*, p. 83

18 Liddell Hart (ed.), *The Rommel Papers*, p. 126

19 Elizabeth Edmondson diary, AWM file 89/05/33, entry 14 April 1941

20 Martin and Hardy (eds), *Dark and Hurrying Days: Menzies' 1941 Diary*, entry 11 March 1941

21 MacDougall, *Australians at War: A Pictorial History*, p. 344

22 Aldrich (ed.), *Witness to War: Diaries of the Second World War in Europe and the Middle East*, p. 285

23 Keegan (ed.), *Churchill's Generals*, p. 59

24 Aldrich (ed.), *Witness to War: Diaries of the Second World War in Europe and the Middle East*, p. 278

25 Keegan (ed.), *Churchill's Generals*, p. 55

26 Day, *The Politics of War*, p. 111

27 *Ibid.*, p. 123

28 *Ibid.*, p. 126

29 Day, *Menzies and Churchill at War: A Controversial New Account of the 1941 Struggle for Power*

30 Hall, *Tobruk 1941: The Desert Siege*, p. 113

31 Aberger *et al.*, *Nur ein Bataillon*, p. 120

32 *Ibid.*, p. 120

33 *Ibid.*, p. 121

34 Heckmann, *Rommel's War in Africa*, p. 100

35 Barber, *The War, the Whores and the Afrika Korps*, p. 79

CHAPTER THIRTEEN — The Battle Builds

1 Quoted in Maughan, *Australia in the War of 1939–45: Tobruk and El Alamein*, p. 11

2 Dennis *et al.*, *The Oxford Companion to Australian Military History*, p. 300

3 Braga, *Kokoda Commander: A Life of Major-General 'Tubby' Allen*, p. 134

4 McDonald, *Chester Wilmot Reports: Broadcasts that Shaped World War II*, p. 130

5 Hall, *Tobruk 1941: The Desert Siege*, p. 112

6 Wilmot, *Tobruk 1941: Capture — Siege — Relief*, p. 51

7 Parr-Smith, *A Signaller's War: Remembrances of a Young Person During the Years 1924 to 1940 and of a Young Soldier from 1940 to 1945*

8   Wilmot, *Tobruk 1941: Capture — Siege — Relief*, p. 196

9   *Ibid.*, p. 197

10 Elizabeth Edmondson diary, AWM file 89/05/33, entry 18 April 1941

11 Account from an ABC broadcast by Chester Wilmot on 16 November 1942, National Archives of Australia SP 300/4, item 208

12 Porch, *Hitler's Mediterranean Gamble: The North African and the Mediterranean Campaigns in World War II*, p. 231

13 Jones and Idriess, *The Silent Service*, p. 134

14 *Ibid.*, p. 134

15 Schmidt, *With Rommel in the Desert*: names Fort Pilastrino here instead of Ras El Medauur, but see note 39, below.

16 *Ibid.*, p. 39. Schmidt's account of this episode actually has it placed much earlier, but on the basis of other mistakes he has made, I think this is the correct timing. The timing in much of his book is confused — due, I suspect, to the fact that he wrote it well after the war was over.

17 *Ibid.*, p. 39

18 Horner, *Blamey. The Commander-in-Chief*, p. 210

19 Johnson, *An Australian Family*, vol. III: *War Letters 1940–1941*, p. 96

20 Figures from the speech delivered by Lieutenant General Morshead to a function held at Victoria Barracks, Sydney, in 1947. Copy held by the Australian War Memorial.

21 Wilmot, *Tobruk 1941: Capture — Siege — Relief*, p. 123

22 Details from the speech delivered by Lieutenant General Morshead to a function held at Victoria Barracks, Sydney, in 1947. Copy held by the Australian War Memorial.

23 Liddell Hart (ed.), *The Rommel Papers*, p. 130

24 Details from the speech delivered by Lieutenant General Morshead to a function held at Victoria Barracks, Sydney, in 1947. Copy held by the Australian War Memorial.

25 Burdick and Jacobsen (eds), *The Halder War Diary 1939–1942*, p. 374

26 Lewin, *Rommel as Military Commander*, p. 41

27 Schmidt, *With Rommel in the Desert*, p. 66

28 Liddell Hart (ed.), *The Rommel Papers*, p. 131

29 Information supplied John Porter, Griffith, New South Wales

30 Letter from Morshead to his wife Myrtle, 31 May 1941, held by the Morshead family

31 Fearnside (ed.), *Bayonets Abroad: Benghazi to Borneo with the 2/13th Battalion AIF*, p. 128

32 Elizabeth Edmondson diary, AWM file 89/05/33, entry 25 April 1941

33 *Sydney Morning Herald*, 26 April 1941.

34 Liddell Hart (ed.), *The Rommel Papers*, p. 130

35 Wilmot, *Tobruk 1941: Capture — Siege — Relief*, p. 256

36 A good account of the character and background of General Paulus and can be found in Mitcham, *Hitler's Field Marshals.*

37 Goerlitz, *Kleine Geschichte des Deutschen Generalstabes*, p. 381

38 Heckmann *Rommel's War in Africa,* p. 108

39 Schmidt, *With Rommel in the Desert*, p. 48. In fact, in Schmidt's account, Rommel says that whoever is in possession of Fort Pilastrino can read the other cards, but this does not make sense. Fort Pilastrino is not on such a high point that there could be any card-reading from there, while many months would be spent by both sides attacking and defending Ras El Madauuar/Hill 209 for exactly that reason. Having been there, I know Fort Pilastrino cannot be seen from outside the perimeter, while Ras El Madauur has exactly what Schmidt described, with the remains of the barbed wire, and the two mounds of stone. Thus, on balance, I believe Schmidt is confused on this point and meant to write that Rommel coveted Ras El Medauuar/Hill 209, which he certainly did.

40 Johnson, *An Australian Family*, vol. III: *War Letters 1940–1941*, p. 89

41 Schmidt, *With Rommel in the Desert*, p. 55

42 *Ibid.*, p. 60

43 Heckmann, *Rommel's War in Africa*, p. 108

44 Burdick and Jacobsen (eds), *The Halder War Diary 1939–1942*, p. 377

CHAPTER FOURTEEN — **The Battle of the Salient**

1 Account from an ABC broadcast by Chester Wilmot on 16 November 1942, National Archives of Australia SP 300/4, item 208

2 Firkins, *The Australians in Nine Wars: Waikato to Long Tan*, p. 240

3 Serle (ed.), *2/24th: A History of the 2/24th Australian Infantry Battalion*, p. 58

4 Liddell Hart (ed.), *The Rommel Papers*, p. 132

5 Hall, *Tobruk 1941: The Desert Siege*, p. 130

6 Schmidt, *With Rommel in the Desert*, p. 50

7 Hall, *Tobruk 1941: The Desert Siege*, p. 131

8 From the speech delivered by Lieutenant General Morshead to a function held at Victoria Barracks, Sydney, in 1947. Copy held by the Australian War Memorial.

9 Liddell Hart (ed.), *The Rommel Papers*, p. 132

10 *Ibid.*, p. 134

11 *Ibid.*, p. 132

12 From the reminiscences of Private Don J. Radnell, VX34693,
    2/24 Infantry Battalion. Kindly sent to the author by his family.

13 Details from the speech delivered by Lieutenant General Morshead to a
    function held at Victoria Barracks, Sydney, in 1947. Copy held by the War
    Memorial.

14 From the captured diary of tank commander Lieutenant Joachim Schorm,
    entry 14 April 1941, AWM 54 423/4/69

15 An account of this episode can be found in Heckmann, *Rommel's War in
    Africa*, pp. 111–113.

16 Aldrich (ed.), *Witness to War: Diaries of the Second World War in Europe and
    the Middle East*, p. 286

17 Day, 'Anzacs on the Run: The View from Whitehall 1941–42', *Journal of
    Imperial and Commonwealth History*, Vol. XIV, No. 3, May 1986, p. 189

18 Extracts from the captured diary of tank commander Lieutenant Joachim
    Schorm, April 1941, AWM 54 423/4/69

19 Maughan, *Australia in the War of 1939–45: Tobruk and El Alamein*, p. 217

20 Extracts from the captured diary of tank commander Lieutenant Joachim
    Schorm, April 1941, AWM 54 423/4/69

21 Wilmot, *Tobruk 1941: Capture — Siege — Relief*, p. 148

22 *www.cjnews.com/pastissues/98/june25–98/front2.htm*

23 From the diary of Private Allan John Brines QX6722B, COY 2/15Bn,
    entry May 2 1941. Diary held by family; copy sent to the author by the
    soldier's niece, Bev McAppion

24 Wilmot, *Tobruk 1941: Capture — Siege — Relief*, p. 112

25 *2/48 Battalion News Sheet*, Vol. 1, No. 11, 8 May 1941

26 Day, *The Politics of War*, p. 134

27 Martin and Hardy (eds), *Dark and Hurrying Days: Menzies' 1941 Diary*,
    p. 134

CHAPTER FIFTEEN — **The Diggers Dig In**

1 Fearnside (ed.), *Bayonets Abroad: Benghazi to Borneo with the 2/13th
   Battalion AIF*, p. 138

2 Johnson, *An Australian Family*, vol. III: *War Letters 1940–1941*, pp. 145–146

3 Porch, *Hitler's Mediterranean Gamble*, p. 230

4 Gorlitz, *Paulus, 'Ich stehe hier auf Befehl!' Lebensweg des Generalfeldmarschalls
   Friedrich Paulus mit den Aufzeichnungen aus dem Nachlass, Briefen und
   Dokumenten*, p. 46

5 Heckmann, *Rommel's War in Africa*, p. 49

6 Wilmot *Tobruk 1941: Capture — Siege — Relief*, p. 154

7 Padfield, *Hess: Flight for the Führer*, p. 205

8   *Ibid.*, p. 217

9   McDonald, *Damien Parer's War*, p. 145

10   Latimer, *Tobruk 1941: Rommel's Opening Move*, p. 63

11   Johnson, *An Australian Family*, vol. III: *War Letters 1940–1941*, p. 114

12   *Ibid.*, p. 115

13   Schmidt, *With Rommel in the Desert*, p. 67

14   *Ibid.*, p. 68

15   Irving, *Rommel: The Trail of the Fox,* p. 97

16   *Ibid.*, p. 102

17   Arnold, *Mother Superior, Woman Inferior*, p. 42

18   Johnson, *An Australian Family*, vol. III: *War Letters 1940–1941*, p. 112

19   Erfurth, *Die Geschichte des Deutschen Generalstabs von 1918 bis 1945*, p. 271

20   Coombes, *Morshead: Hero of Tobruk and El Alamein*, p. 17

21   Interview with Bert Ferres, 2/13th Battalion, East Branxton, New South Wales

22   Wilmot, *Tobruk 1941: Capture — Siege — Relief*, p. 218

23   Account taken from *Australian Womens Weekly*, 3 April 1943. Another reference for this can be found in Latimer, *Tobruk 1941: Rommel's Opening Move*, p. 90.

24   *As I Remember It*, AWM MSS 1587, p. 34

25   Share (ed.), *Mud and Blood, Albury's Own: 2/23rd Australian Infantry Battalion*, p. 70

26   From the published reminiscences of Dr Manfred Auberlen, a Medical Private, First Class, of the German Africa Korps

27   *www.australiansatwar.gov.au/stories/stories.asp?ID=47&war=W2&next=yes*

28   Schmidt, *With Rommel in the Desert*, p. 52

29   Salter, *A Padre with the Rats of Tobruk*, p. 37

30   From the 2/32nd Battalion, news sheet, *The Newt*, mid June 1941

31   Based on an account of such a departure in *H.M.A.S*, written by serving personnel of the Royal Australian Navy, p. 124

32   Schmidt, *With Rommel in the Desert*, p. 60

33   Interview with Afrika Korps veteran Wilhelm Langsam, 14 October 2005

34   Heckmann, *Rommel's War in Africa*, p. 125

35   *Medical Journal of Australia*, No.14, 2 October 1943

36   Details of this can be found in Parker, *Desert Rats: From El Alamein to Basra: The Inside Story of a Military Legend*, p. 8

37   Interview with Afrika Korps veteran Wilhelm Langsam, 14 October 2005

38   Aberger *et al.*, *Nur ein Bataillon*, p. 125

39   Interview with Afrika Korps veteran Wilhelm Langsam, 14 October 2005

40 Letter from Morshead to his wife Myrtle, 1 June 1941, held by the
    Morshead family

41 Wilmot, *Tobruk 1941: Capture — Siege — Relief*, p. 169

42 *As I Remember It*, AWM MSS 1587, p. 26

43 Heckmann, *Rommel's War in Africa*, p. 147

CHAPTER SIXTEEN — **Manoeuvres Political**

1   Heckmann, *Rommel's War in Africa*, p. 146

2   McDonald, *Chester Wilmot Reports: Broadcasts that Shaped World War II*,
    p. 176

3   Liddell Hart, *The Rommel Papers*, p. 138. There is frequent conjecture about
    when Rommel first started using the 88mm Ack-Ack guns in an anti-tank
    capacity in the African campaign, with the British generally claiming that
    this did not occur until the middle of June, during Operation Battleaxe.
    Nevertheless, in the authoritative Aberger *et al.*, *Nur ein Bataillon*, there are
    clear references to the use of 88mm guns briefly in the Easter Battle
    (p. 106) and also briefly during the first phases of the Battle of the Salient
    in early May (p. 165) — albeit on a very limited scale.

4   Letter from Athol Dalziel to Elizabeth Edmondson, 2 June 1941, held by
    the Australian War Memorial

5   Johnson, *An Australian Family*, vol. III: *War Letters 1940–1941*,
    pp. 128–129

6   Barker, *Afrika Korps*, p. 7

7   Schmidt, *With Rommel in the Desert*, p. 65

8   Connell, *Wavell: Scholar and Soldier*, p. 146

9   Lewin, *Rommel as Military Commander*, p. 47

10 Keegan (ed.), *Churchill's Generals*, p. 76

11 Connell, *Wavell: Scholar and Soldier*, p. 505

12 Interview with Herrn Rolf Munninger, 15 October 2005, at his home in
    Stuttgart (Munninger, one of Rommel's senior officers in the North
    African campaign, was present on the occasion)

13 Schmidt, *With Rommel in the Desert*, p. 72

14 *Ibid.*, pp. 39, 73

15 Account from an ABC Broadcast by Chester Wilmot on 16 November
    1942, National Archives of Australia SP 300/4, item 208

16 Johnson, *An Australian Family*, vol. III: *War Letters 1940–1941*, p. 146

17 Aberger *et al.*, *Nur ein Bataillon*, p. 130

18 *Ibid.*, p. 130

19 Wilmot, *Tobruk 1941: Capture — Siege — Relief*, p. 167

20 Kriebel, *Inside the Afrika Korps: The Crusader Battles, 1941–1942*, p. 19

21 Horner, *Blamey, The Commander in Chief*, p. 229

22 *Grubb's Gazette*, 2/48th Battalion news sheet, 9 June 1941

23 From the speech delivered by Lieutenant General Morshead to a function held at Victoria Barracks, Sydney, in 1947. Copy held by the Australian War Memorial.

24 Liddell Hart, *The Rommel Papers*, p.149

25 Aberger *et al.*, *Nur ein Bataillon*, p. 132

26 Letter from Morshead to his wife Myrtle, 12 July 1941, held by the Morshead family

27 Letter written by Captain John Balfe of D Company, 2/17th Battalion, to his wife in Sydney, held by Australian War Memorial.

28 Based on a paper by Kesby, Harper and Kiddy, 'A Biography of John Hurst Edmondson VC', AWM 12334

29 *Mud and Blood*, battalion news sheet, 7 August 1941

30 Hall, *Tobruk 1941: The Desert Siege.* p. 56

31 Wilmot, *Tobruk 1941: Capture — Siege — Relief*, p. 233

32 Horner, *Blamey, The Commander in Chief*, p. 244; *Australian Hansard*, 20 April 1939

33 Day, *The Politics of War*, p. 162

34 *Ibid.*, p. 165

35 Day, 'Anzacs on the Run: The View From Whitehall 1941–42', *Journal of Imperial and Commonwealth History*, Vol. XIV, No. 3, May 1986, p. 192

36 Hetherington, *Blamey, Controversial Soldier*, p. 179

37 Wilmot, *Tobruk 1941: Capture — Siege — Relief*, p. 277

38 From the diary of Private Allan John Brines QX6722B, COY 2/15Bn, entry May 2 1941. Diary held by family; copy sent to the author by the soldier's niece, Bev McAppion

39 McDonald, *War Cameraman: The Story of Damien Parer*, p. 111

40 Letter written by Leslie Morshead to his wife Myrtle, 1 August 1941, held by the Morshead family

41 Letter from Morshead to his wife Myrtle, 2 August 1941, held by the Morshead family

42. Combe, *The Second 43rd Australian Infantry Battalion: 1940–1946*, p. 60

43 *Ibid.*, p. 60

44 For further information on this, see Wilmot, *Tobruk 1941: Capture — Siege — Relief*, pp. 198–201

45 Details taken from an interview with Father Tom Gard, published in Cairns newspaper *The Leader*, 4 December 1983

46 Wilmot, *Tobruk 1941: Capture — Siege — Relief*, p. 200

47 Letter from Morshead to his wife Myrtle, 4 August 1941, held by the Morshead family

48 Kriebel *Inside the Afrika Korps: The Crusader Battles, 1941–1942*, p. 45

49 Lewin, *Rommel as Military Commander*, p. 55

50 Horner, *Blamey, The Commander in Chief*, p. 235

51 Day, *The Politics of War*, p. 153

52 Wilmot, *Tobruk 1941: Capture — Siege — Relief*, p. 201

53 Metelmann, *Memoirs of a Wehrmacht Private: Through Hell for Hitler*

54 Interview with Herrn Rolf Munninger at his home in Stuttgart, 15 October 2005

55 Day, *John Curtin: A Life*, p. 413

CHAPTER SEVENTEEN — **End Game**

1   Jones and Idriess, *The Silent Service*, p. 155

2   Hetherington, *Blamey, Controversial Soldier*, p. 181

3   *Ibid.*, p. 183

4   *Ibid.*, p. 242

5   As recorded in Liddell Hart (ed.), *The Rommel Papers*, p. 151

6   As recorded in Harrison, *Tobruk: The Birth of a Legend*, p. 158

7   *As I Remember It*, AWM MSS 1587, p. 35

8   Fearnside (ed.), *Bayonets Abroad: Benghazi to Borneo with the 2/13th Battalion AIF*, p. 160

9   *Ibid.*, p. 135

10 *Sydney Morning Herald*, 24 November 1941

11 Based on an account in Salter, *A Padre with the Rats of Tobruk*, p. 55

12 Heckmann, *Rommel's War in Africa*, p. 157

13 Aberger *et al.*, *Nur ein Bataillon*, p. 165; and interview with Rolf Völker

14 *Ibid.*, p. 161

15 *Ibid.*, p. 134

16 *Ibid.*, p. 134

17 *Ibid.*, p. 164

18 Lewin, *Rommel as Military Commander*, p. 57

19 Young, *Rommel*, p. 102

20 Schmidt, *With Rommel In the Desert*, p. 77

21 Aberger *et al.*, *Nur ein Bataillon*, p. 136

22 Wilmot, *Tobruk 1941: Capture — Siege — Relief*, p. 300

23 Lewin, *Rommel as Military Commander*, p. 46

24 Schmidt, *With Rommel In the Desert*, p. 112

25 Young, *Rommel*, p. 111

26 Heckstall-Smith, *Tobruk*, p. 170

27 Liddell Hart (ed.), *The Rommel Papers*, p. 168

28 Heckmann, *Rommel's War in Africa*, p. 210

29 *As I Remember It*, AWM MSS 1587, p. 35

30 Letter by George McFadyen, NX36681, of D Company, 2/13th, to his uncle, part of the original 13th Battalion, 17 January 1942, supplied to author by his daughter Dorothy Barnes

31 *Ibid.*

32 Interview with Earl Walsh, March 2006

33 Aberger *et al.*, *Nur ein Bataillon*, p. 80

34 Fearnside (ed.), *Bayonets Abroad: Benghazi to Borneo with the 2/13th Battalion AIF*, p. 153

35 *Ibid.*, p. 156

36 Interview with Rolf Völker

37 Fearnside (ed.), *Bayonets Abroad: Benghazi to Borneo with the 2/13th Battalion AIF*, p. 159

38 Maughan, *Australia in the War of 1939–45: Tobruk and El Alamein*, p. 401

Epilogue

1 From the speech delivered by Lieutenant General Morshead to a function held at Victoria Barracks, Sydney, 1947. Copy held by the Australian War Memorial.

2 Interview with Rolf Munninger, 16 October 2005, at his home in Stuttgart

3 Mitcham, *Hitler's Field Marshals and Their Battles*, p. 182

4 Article by Major General R.J.H. Risson, *Sunday Telegraph*.

5 Reuth, *Rommel*, p. 175

6 *Ibid.*, p. 76

7 Letter (with documents) from Rolf Völker, Stuttgart, 7 March 2006

8 Westphal, *Heer in Fesseln* (*Army in Chains*), p. 192

9 Coombes, *Morshead: Hero of Tobruk and El Alamein*, p. 233

10 Harrison, *Tobruk: The Birth of a Legend*, p. 162

11 *www.eyewitnesstohistory.com/rommel.htm*

12 Interviews with Rolf Völker, Stuttgart, 2005–2006

13 *www.historyplace.com/worldwar2/holocaust/h-death.htm*

14 Interview with Bert Ferres, 2/13th Battalion, East Branxton, New South Wales

15 Account in possession of family. Interview with Ivor Hancock's son Gary Parsisson

16 Interview with Austin Mackell's son Roger Mackell

17 Service record of Vince Rayner

18 Interview with General Leakey's son David Leakey

19 Johnson, *An Australian Family*, vol. IV: *Josephine Mary Johnson, A Steadfast Mother*; and interviews with Len Johnson

20 Arnold, *Mother Superior, Woman Inferior*, p. 10

21 'Stood Steadfast in Face of Bigotry, Bullying, Poverty', obituary of Francis Barry Johnson, *Herald-Sun*, 28 December 2005

22 Interview with Adam Mrozowski, Polish 1st Carpathian Brigade

Bibliography

Aldrich, Richard J. (ed.), *Witness to War: Diaries of the Second World War in Europe and the Middle East*, Corgi, 2005.

Arnold, Josie, *Mother Superior, Woman Inferior*, Dove Communications, Blackburn, Vic., 1985.

Barassi, Ron and McFarline, Peter, *Barassi: The Life Behind the Legend*, Simon & Schuster, Roseville, 1995.

Barber, Jack, *The War, the Whores and the Afrika Korps*, Kangaroo Press, Sydney, 1997.

Barker, Lieutenant-Colonel A.J., *Afrika Korps*, Bison Books, London, 1978.

Barnett, Correlli, *The Desert Generals*, Viking Press, New York, 1961.

Baynes, John, *The Forgotten Victor: General Sir Richard O'Connor*, Brassey's UK, 1989.

BBC Radio, 'Tobruk Truth: The Dinkum Oil', a daily summary condensed from BBC commentary, London, 1941.

Bierman, John and Smith, Colin, *Alamein: War Without Hate*, Penguin, London, 2003.

Bosworth, Richard, *Mussolini's Italy: Life Under the Dictatorship, 1915–1945*, Allen Lane (Penguin), London 2002.

Braga, Stuart, *Kokoda Commander: A Life of Major-General 'Tubby' Allen*, Oxford Press, South Melbourne, 2004.

Burdick, Charles and Jacobsen, Hans-Adolf (eds), *The Halder War Diary, 1939–1942*, Greenhill Books, London, 1988.

Carell, P., *The Foxes of the Desert*, translated by M. Savill, E.P. Dutton, New York, 1960; first published as *Die Wüstenfüchse*, Hamburg, 1958.

Chapman, Ivan, *History of the Sydney University Regiment*, Sydney University, 1996.

Charlton, Peter, *The Thirty-niners*, Macmillan, South Melbourne, 1981.

Charmley, John, *Chamberlain and the Lost Peace*, Hodder & Stoughton, London, 1989.

Christensen, George (ed.), *That's the Way it Was: The History of the 24th Australian Infantry Battalion, 1939–1945*, 24th Battalion (AIF) Association, Melbourne, 1982.

Collier, Richard, *Duce! The Rise and Fall of Benito Mussolini*, Collins, London, 1971.

Combe, Gordon, Ligerwood, Frank and Gilchrist, Tom, *The Second 43rd, Australian Infantry Battalion, 1940–1946*, Second 43rd AIF Club, Adelaide, 1972.

Connell, John, *Wavell: Scholar and Soldier*, Collins, London, 1964.

Coombes, David, *Morshead: Hero of Tobruk and El Alamein*, Oxford University Press, South Melbourne, 2001.

Cull, Brian with Minterne, Don, *Hurricanes over Tobruk: The Pivotal Role of the Hurricane in the Defence of Tobruk, January–June 1941*, Grub Street, London, 1999.

Cumpston, J.S., *The Rats Remain: The Siege of Tobruk, 1941*, Grayflower Productions, Melbourne, 1966.

Day, David, 'Anzacs on the Run: The View from Whitehall 1941–42', *Journal of Imperial and Commonwealth History*, vol. XIV, no. 3, May 1986.

Day, David, *Menzies and Churchill at War: A Controversial New Account of the 1941 Struggle for Power*, Paragon House Publishers, New York, 1988.

Day, David, *John Curtin: A Life*, HarperCollins, Sydney, 1999.

Day, David, *The Politics of War*, HarperCollins, Sydney, 2003.

Esebeck, Hanns Gert Freiherr von, *Héros du Désert: La Lutte en Afrique du Nord*, 1943. (No publisher listed, but it was released as German propaganda in occupied France in 1943.)

Farrell, Nicholas, *Mussolini: A New Life*, Weidenfeld & Nicolson, Great Britain, 2004.

Fearnside, G.H. (ed.), *Bayonets Abroad: Benghazi to Borneo with the 2/13th Battalion AIF* (2nd edn), John Burridge Military Antiques, Swanborne, WA, 1993.

Firkins, Peter, *The Australians in Nine Wars: Waikato to Long Tan*, Rigby, Adelaide, 1971.

Forty, George, *The First Victory: General O'Connor's Desert Triumph, Dec 1940–Feb 1941*, Guild Publishing, London, 1990.

Forty, George (ed.), *Leakey's Luck: A Tank Commander with Nine Lives*, Sutton Publishing, Phoenix Mill, 1999.

Glassop, Lawson, *We Were the Rats*, Angus & Robertson, Sydney, 1945.

Gullet, Henry, *Not As Duty Only: An Infantryman's War*, Melbourne University Press, Melbourne, 1976.

Harrison, Frank, *Tobruk: The Birth of a Legend*, Cassell, London, 1996.

Heckmann, Wolf, *Rommel's War in Africa*, Doubleday, New York, 1981.

Heckstall-Smith, Anthony, *Tobruk*, Anthony Blond Ltd, London, 1960.

Herington, John, *Air War Against Germany and Italy, 1939–1943*, Australian War Memorial, Canberra, 1954.

Hetherington, John, *The Australian Soldier: A Portrait*, FH Johnson Publishing Co, Sydney, 1943.

Hetherington, John, *Blamey, Controversial Soldier*, Australian War Memorial and the Australian Government Publishing Service, Canberra, 1973.

Horner, D.M., *Crisis of Command: Australian Generalship and the Japanese Threat, 1941–1943*, Australian National University Press, Canberra, 1978.

Horner, D.M., *High Command: Australia & Allied Strategy 1939–45*, Allen & Unwin, North Sydney, 1982.

Horner, D.M., *Inside the War Cabinet: Directing Australia's War Effort 1939–45*, Allen & Unwin, Sydney, 1996.

Horner, D.M., *Blamey, the Commander in Chief*, Allen & Unwin, Sydney, 1998.

Hughes, Aneurin, *Billy Hughes: Prime Minister and Controversial Founding Father of the Australian Labor Party*, John Wiley & Sons, Milton, Qld, 2005.

Irving, David, *Rommel: The Trail of the Fox*, Wordsworth Military Library, U.K., 1999.

Jackson, C.O. Badham, *Proud Story: The Official History of the Australian Comforts Fund*, F.H. Johnston Publishing Co., Sydney, 1949.

Johnson, Len, *An Australian Family*, vol. III: *War Letters 1940–1941: Letters Exchanged between VX 42266 Corporal John Leslie Johnson and his Family from his Enlistment in Melbourne in June 1940 until his Death in the Siege of Tobruk in May 1941*, Rock View Press, 2002.

Johnson, Len, *An Australian Family*, vol. IV: *Josephine Mary Johnson, A Steadfast Mother*, Longleat House Publishing, Brisbane, 2006.

Jones, T.M. and Idriess, Ion L., *The Silent Service: Action Stories of the Anzac Navy*, Angus & Robertson, Sydney, 1944.

Keegan, John (ed.), *Churchill's Generals*, Cassell Military Paperbacks, London, 1991.

Kriebel, Colonel Rainer and the U.S. Army Intelligence Service, *Inside the Afrika Korps: The Crusader Battles, 1941–1942*, edited by Bruce I. Gudmundsson, Greenhill Books, London, 1999.

Latimer, Jon, *Tobruk 1941: Rommel's Opening Move*, illustrated by Jim Laurier, Osprey Publishing, London, 2001.

Lewin, Ronald, *Rommel as Military Commander*, Barnes & Noble Books, New York, 1968; republished in 1998.

Lewin, Ronald, *The Chief: Field Marshal Lord Wavell, Commander in Chief and Viceroy, 1939–1947*, Hutchinson, London, 1980.

Lewis, Jon E. (ed.), *World War II: Over 200 first-hand Accounts from the Six Years that Tore the World Apart*, Robinson, London, 2002.

Liddell Hart, B.H. (ed.), *The Rommel Papers*, translated by Paul Findlay, Collins, London, 1953.

Lucas, James, *Hitler's Enforcers: Leaders of the German War Machine 1939–45*, Arms and Armour, London, 1996.

Luck, Peter, *This Fabulous Century*, Lansdowne Press, Sydney, 1980.

MacDougall, A.K., *Australians at War: A Pictorial History*, Five Mile Press, Noble Park, Vic., 2002.

Martin, A.W. and Hardy, Patsy (eds), *Dark and Hurrying Days: Menzies' 1941 Diary*, National Library of Australia, Canberra, 1993.

Masel, Philip, *2/28th Battalion History*, Perth 2/28th Battalion and 24th Anti/Tank Company Association, 1961; reissued 2000.

Maughan, Barton, *Tobruk and El Alamein*, Australian War Memorial, Canberra, 1966.

McDonald, Neil, *Damien Parer's War*, Lothian, South Melbourne, 2003.

McDonald, Neil, *Chester Wilmot Reports: Broadcasts that Shaped World War II*, ABC Books, Sydney, 2004.

Medical Journal of Australia, 1 August 1942; 24 October 1942; 18 September 1943; 2 October 1943.

Metelmann, Henry, *Memoirs of a Wehrmacht Private: Through Hell for Hitler*, Spellmount Publishers, Staplehurst, Kent, U.K., 2003.

Miller, Colonel Ward A., *The 9th Australian Division versus the Africa Corps: An Infantry Division against Tanks: Tobruk, Libya, 1941*, U.S. Army Command and General Staff College, Fort Leavenworth, Kansas, 1986.

Mitcham, Samuel W. (Jr), *Hitler's Field Marshals and their Battles*, Leo Cooper, London, 1988.

Moore, John, *Morshead: A Biography of Lieutenant General Sir Leslie Morshead*, Haldane Publishing, Sydney, 1976.

Moorehead, Alan, *African Trilogy*, Hamish Hamilton, London, 1944; Text Publishing, Melbourne, 1997.

Neame, Phillip, *Playing with Strife: The Autobiography of a Soldier*, George G. Harrap, Sydney, 1947.

O'Connor, Richard Nugent, Recollections of the planning and conduct of the First Libyan Campaign, 1940–1941: Imperial War Museum interview recorded 20 May 1974 (IWM, Department of Sound Records, Accession No. 000012/08).

Oxford Companion to Australian Military History, edited by Peter Dennis, Jeffrey Grey, Ewan Morris and Robin Prior with John Connor, Oxford University Press, Melbourne, 1999.

Padfield, Peter, *Hess: Flight for the Führer*, Weidenfeld & Nicolson, London, 1991.

Parker, John, *Desert Rats, from El Alamein to Basra: The Inside Story of a Military Legend*, Headline, 2004.

Parker, R.A.C., *Chamberlain and Appeasement: British Policy and the Coming of the Second World War*, Macmillan, London, 1993.

Parkinson, Roger, *The War in the Desert*, Granada Publishing, London, 1979.

Pitt, Barrie, *The Crucible of War: Western Desert 1941*, Jonathan Cape, London, 1980.

Porch, Douglas, *Hitler's Mediterranean Gamble: The North African and the Mediterranean Campaigns in World War II*, Weidenfeld & Nicholson, London, 2004; also published as *The Path to Victory: The Mediterranean Theatre in World War II*, Farrar, Straus and Giroux, New York, 2004.

Porch, Douglas, *Hitler's Mediterranean Gamble: The North African and the Mediterranean Campaigns in World War II*, Weidenfeld & Nicolson, London, 2004.

Quarrie, Bruce, *Hitler: The Victory that Nearly Was*, David & Charles, London, 1988.

Rommel, General Field Marshal Erwin, *Infantry Attacks*, 1937; Greenhill Books, London, 1995.

Royal Air Force, *Oculi Exercitus: A Short History to Commemorate the Anniversary of No. 6 Squadron, 31 January 1964*, printed in Nicosia, Cyprus, 1964.

Royal Australian Navy, *H.M.A.S.*, Australian War Memorial, Canberra, 1942.

Salter, J.C., *A Padre with the Rats of Tobruk*, J. Walch & Sons, Hobart, 1946.

Schmidt, Heinz Werner, *With Rommel in the Desert*, George G. Harrap & Co Ltd, London, 1951.

2/13th Battalion, ex-members of, *Bayonets Abroad: Benghazi to Borneo with the 2/13th Battalion AIF* (2nd edn), edited by Lt G.H. Fearnside, John Burridge Military Antiques, Swanborne, WA, 1993.

2/17th Battalion History Committee, *'What we have . . . we hold!' A History of the 2/17 Infantry Battalion, 1940–1945* (revd edn), Australian Military History Publications, Loftus, NSW, 1998.

2/24th Australian Infantry Battalion, *Furphy Flyer*, 1941.

2/32nd Battalion, news sheet, *The Newt*, mid June 1941.

2/48th Battalion, news sheet, vol. 1, no.11, Thursday, 8 May 1941.

Serle, R.P. (ed.), *A History of the 2/24th Australian Infantry Battalion*, Jacaranda Press, Brisbane, 1963; reissued 1986.

Share, Pat (ed.), *Mud and Blood, Albury's Own: 2/23rd Australian Infantry Battalion*, Heritage Book Publications, 1978; reissued in 2002.

Sherwood, Robert E., *The White House Papers of Harry L. Hopkins: An Intimate History*, Eyre & Spottiswoode, London, 1948–1949.

Silver, John, *Target Tank: The History of the 2/3 Australian Anti-tank Regiment, 9th Division, AIF*, Cumberland Newspaper, Parramatta, NSW, 1957.

Spowers, Allan, *The Story of the 2/24th Battalion (Wangaratta's Own): An Address Delivered at Wangaratta on 21st September 1946*, Pioneers' Memorial Trust, Wangaratta, 1946.

Strawson, John, *Battle for North Africa*, Bonanza Books, New York, 1969.

Strawson, John, *Hitler as Military Commander*, B.T Batsford, London, 1971.

'Stood Steadfast in Face of Bigotry, Bullying, Poverty', obituary of Francis Barry Johnson, *Herald-Sun*, Wednesday, 28 December 2005.

Toppe, Major-General Alfred, *Desert Warfare: German Experiences in World War II*, U.S. Army Command and General Staff College, Fort Leavenworth, Kansas, 1991.

Wavell, A.P. (ed.), *Other Men's Flowers: An Anthology of Poetry*, Pimlico, London, 2002; first published by Jonathan Cape, London, 1944.

Wilmot, Chester, *Tobruk 1941: Capture – Seige – Relief*, Angus & Robertson, Sydney and London, 1944.

Young, Desmond, *Rommel*, Collins, London, 1950.

German texts

Translations of passages used were provided by Sonja Goernitz.

Aberger, Heinz-Dietrich, Taysen, Adalbert von and Ziermer, Kurt, *Nur ein Bataillon*, Selbstverlag Walter Borchardt, Essen, 1972.

Esebeck, Freiherr Hans Gert von, 'Briefe aus England: Die Heimat klagt an' (Letters from England: The Home Country Accuses), *Folge* 9, 6 April 1941.

Erfurth, Waldemar, *Die Geschichte des Deutschen Generalstabs von 1918 bis 1945* (The History of the German General Staff from 1918 to 1945), 1957.

Generalfeldmarschall Rommel: Zum Ehrenden Gedenken, 1984.

Goerlitz, Walter, *Kleine Geschichte des Deutschen Generalstabes* (History of the German General Staff), 1967.

Gorlitz, Walter, *Paulus, 'Ich stehe hier auf Befehl!' Lebensweg des Generalfeldmarschalls Friedrich Paulus mit den Aufzeichnungen aus dem Nachlass, Briefen und Dokumenten* ('I'm standing here following orders!' Life of Field-Marshal Friedrich Paulus, with the Scripts from the Estate, Letters and Documents), Bernard & Graefe, Frankfurt am Main, 1960.

Kriegstagebuch vom 8 Maschinengewehr Bataillon (8th Machine Gun Battalion War Journal).

Reuth, Ralf Georg, *Rommel, Das Ende einer Legende* (Rommel, The End of a Legend), Piper, München and Zürich, 2004.

Rommel, Erwin, *Krieg ohne Hass* (War Without Hate), edited by Lucie-Maria Rommel and Fritz Bayerlein, Heidenheimer Zeitung, Heidenheim, 1950.

Westphal, Siegfried, *Heer in Fesseln* (Army in Chains), 1950.

Wieder, Joachim and von Einsiedel, Heinrich Graf, *Stalingrad und die Verantwortung der Soldaten* (Stalingrad and the Responsibility of the Soldiers), 1993.

Documents

These are listed below under their subject.

Auberlen, Manfred: extracts from the reminiscences of Dr Manfred Auberlen, a Medical Private, First Class, of the German Africa Korps, dated 21 November 1991.

Balfe, John: AWM collection, letter written by Captain John Balfe of D Company, 2/17th Battalion, to his wife in Sydney.

Brines, Allan: extracts from the diary of Private Allan John Brines QX6722B, COY 2/15Bn, entry 2 May 1941; diary held by family; copy sent to the author by the soldier's niece Bev McAppion.

Edmondson, Elizabeth: AWM PR89/056, papers of Elizabeth Edmondson.

Edmondson, John Hurst: AWM collection, 'A biography of John Hurst Edmondson VC', paper by Joanne Kesby, Jane Harper and Leanne Kiddy, written while they were students at Hurlstone Agricultural College.

Edmondson, John Hurst: AWM PR85/278 and PR90/101, papers of John Hurst Edmondson.

Edmonston, Jack: AWM document concerning the death of Jack Edmondson, written by Athol Thomas of Cottesloe, WA, 28 October 1955.

Hill, Alec Jeffrey, 'Er Regima: Baptism of Fire, *Wartime*, official magazine of the Australian War Memorial, 2004.

McFadyen, George: letter dated 17 January 1942, from George McFadyen, NX36681, of D Company, 2/13th, to his uncle who had been a part of the original 13th Battalion; a copy of the letter was sent to the author by McFadyen's daughter Dorothy Barnes.

Morshead, Leslie: AWM 3DRL/2632, papers of Sir Leslie James Morshead.

Morshead, Leslie: AWM PR3DRL 2632 item 3/2, Leslie Morshead's diary, January–July 1941.

Morshead, Leslie: AWM PR 00368 pt 5, papers of Sir Leslie James Morshead. (This is the copy of Morshead's speech notes, for a lecture on Tobruk he delivered at Victoria Barracks on 14 May 1947; it is extensive and fascinating – P.F.)

Parr-Smith, Leon: AWM PR01310, bound and illustrustrated typescript, 'A signaller's war – remembrances of a young person during the years 1924 to 1940, and of a young soldier from 1940 to 1945'.

Radnell, Don J.: the reminiscences of Private Don J. Radnell, VX34693 2/24 Infantry Battalion, kindly provided by his family, and sent to the author.

Schorm, Lieutenant: AWM54, 253/4/15, translation of German diary
    (2nd Lieutenant Schorm), captured in Libya; Appendix 'C' to
    6th Australian Division, Weekly Intelligence Bulletin, 15 Sept 1941.
Schorm, Lieutenant: AWM54, 423/4/69, translations of extracts from
    German diary captured near Tobruk; diary of Lieutenant Schorm, 5 Tank
    Regiment, April 1941.
Watkins, Leslie W: AWM MSS 1587, manuscript titled 'As I remember it'.

Interviewees

Bert Ferres, 2/13th Battalion, East Branxton, NSW
Doug 'Snowy' Foster, 2/17th Battalion
Jack Harris, 2/17th Battalion
Bill Noyce, 2/13th Battalion
Keith Secombe, 2/3rd Australian Anti-tank Regiment
John Searle, 2/13th Battalion
Adam Mrozowski, Polish 1st Carpathian Brigade
Wilhelm Langsam, Afrika Korps, Germany
Rolf Munninger, Afrika Korps, Germany
Rolf Völker, Afrika Korps, Germany
Len Johnson (son of John Johnson, 2/23rd Battalion)
David Leakey (son of Captain Rea Leakey, 7th Royal Tank Regiment)
Roger Mackell (son of Lieutenant Austin Mackell, 2nd/17th Battalion)
Gary Parsisson (son of Ivor Hancock, 2/24th Battalion)
John Porter, Griffith, NSW (son of Bill Porter, 2/9th Battalion)
Earl Walsh, Mona Vale, NSW (son of Corporal Walsh)
Mrs Dariel Larkins (friend of the Edmonson family)
Mrs Sue McGowen (friend of the Edmondson family)

Index

1st Australian Corps 497
2/3rd Anti-tank Regiment 225, 226, 303
   Mechili 232, 234, 239
   Tobruk, Easter Battle 293, 296
2/3rd Light Anti-Aircraft Regiment 177–178
2/13th Battalion
   Afrika Korps 220–221
   in Australia 61, 62, 64–66, 75, 84–85, 91, 100
   Battle of El Alamein 496
   Benghazi 205
   casualties 176, 222, 486, 492
   El Agheila 172
   Er Regima pass 187, 213, 218–220
   HMS *Latona* 462–464
   Kilo 89 (tented camp, Palestine) 104–105, 109
   Northumberland Fusiliers 417, 462
   Suez Canal 102
   Syria 493
   'the Fighting 13th' 493
   Tobruk 467
   Tobruk, anti-tank ditches 256–257, 258
   Tobruk, Battle of the Salient 351, 356
   Tobruk, Derna Road sector 464–465
   Tobruk, Easter Battle 266–267, 269–270, 290–291, 294, 309–310
   Tobruk, Ed Duda 482–489

   Tobruk, El Adem road 489
   Tobruk, front line of the Salient 383–384
   Tobruk, leave 491–492
   Tobruk, messages from other units 491
   Tobruk, Operation Crusader 472, 476–477
   Tobruk, pull back to 222
   Tobruk, siege ends 490–491
   Tobruk, sticky bombs 482–483
   weaponry 219
2/15th Battalion
   2/13th Battalion 492
   in Australia 65, 91
   Benghazi 205
   El Agheila 172, 175
   HMS *Latona* 462, 463
   Syria 493
   Tobruk, Battle of the Salient 351, 356
   Tobruk, Easter Battle 269
   Tobruk, patrols into no-man's land 406
   Tobruk, unexploded bombs 442
2/17th Battalion
   2/13th Battalion 492
   in Australia 61, 66, 84, 85, 91, 100, 107
   Barce 229
   Battle of El Alamein 496
   casualties 269
   El Agheila 175
   Er Regima pass 218

2/17th Battalion (*cont.*)
  Kilo 89 (tented camp, Palestine)
    104–105
  Marsa el Brega 172
  relieved 461, 466–467
  reunions 518
  Suez Canal 102
  Syria 493
  Tobruk 333
  Tobruk, artillery 395
  Tobruk, Battle of the Salient 351,
    356
  Tobruk, Easter Battle 267–274,
    278–285, 287, 289, 290–291,
    294, 301, 305, 309–310
  Tobruk, pull back to 238–239
2/23rd Battalion
  in Australia 79, 86, 92
  Battle of El Alamein 496
  casualties 399
  in Jaffa 142
  Mud and Blood 438–439
  in North Africa 174, 176–177
  Tobruk 200–202
  Tobruk, Battle of the Salient 351,
    370–371
  Tobruk, Italian forces Derna Road
    333–335
  Tobruk, patrols into no-man's land
    405–406
  Tobruk, relief of Post S9 397–398
2/24th Battalion
  in Australia 82, 94, 116, 118
  Battle of El Alamein 496
  British Artillery officer 259–260
  Furphy Flyer 419, 439, 456
  missing 371
  Tobruk, Battle of the Salient 351,
    352–356, 358–364
  Tobruk, Blue Line 364–366
  Tobruk, defensive concrete
    perimeter posts 259
  Tobruk, Easter Battle 274–275

  Tobruk, Hill 209 348–349
  Tobruk, taken prisoner 362–363
  Tobruk, the Salient 374
  Tocra pass 187, 223
2/28th Battalion 253–254, 255,
    444–445, 447
2/43rd Battalion 444–447
2/48th Battalion
  arrive in Tobruk 250
  Battle of Carrier Hill 333–335
  Battle of El Alamein 496
  Battle of the Salient 370–371
  Hill 209 348
  Italian stone cairns 440
  patrolling outside the wire 316
  the Salient 373–375
2nd Armoured Division (British)
  Gambier-Parry commands 171,
    172, 199
  Marsa el Brega 194–196
  Mechili 204–205, 226, 231–232,
    233–234
  Neame 199–200, 214
  pulls back to Tobruk 232
5th Light Panzer Division (Afrika
    Korps)
  Agedabia 199
  complement 147, 263
  Kirchheim 311
  Marsa el Brega 194–196
  Mechili 206–207, 227
  North Africa 192–193
  Streich commands 147
  Tobruk 263, 265, 266, 345
  Tobruk, Easter Battle 277,
    288–294, 295–297, 303–304, 310
  Tripoli 167–168
8th Machine-gun Battalion (Afrika
    Korps)
  capture Neame and O'Connor 230
  casualties 308, 310, 317
  Derna 237
  Marsa el Brega 195

North Africa 192
Ponath commands 216
Rommel 317–318
Tobruk, Easter Battle 276–277,
    289, 304, 306
von Prittwitz commands 244, 255
15th Panzer Division (Afrika Korps)
Afrika Korps 147, 185, 194, 211
Battle of the Salient 350–351,
    355–356, 358–359, 364–368,
    370–371
Blue Line 364–366
elite troops of 240–241
Ras el Medauuar (Hill 209)
    371–372
Tobruk 265, 344–345
von Prittwitz commands 147
18th Brigade
in AIF 6th Division 51, 72, 101,
    116
in AIF 7th Division 161, 221–222,
    240, 250
18th Brigade (2/9th, 2/10th, 2/12th)
2/9th Battalion 249
in AIF 9th Division 89, 161
relieved 441, 450, 457
the Salient 380
Tobruk 309
20th Brigade (2/13th, 2/15th,
    2/17th) see also 2/13th Battalion;
    2/15th Battalion; 2/17th
    Battalion
in AIF 7th Division 91
in AIF 9th Division 161
Benghazi, pull back to 179–182,
    186–187
conduct 196–198
El Agheila 172–173
Gambier-Parry commands 171
North Africa 163, 165–166, 169,
    171
Tobruk 250, 252, 269–270, 277,
    461

21st Brigade 143
24th Australian Anti-tank Company
    365
24th Brigade
AIF 9th Division 250
North Africa 161
Tobruk 182
Tobruk, defend eastern perimeter
    252
26th Brigade (2/23rd, 2/24th) see also
    2/23rd Battalion; 2/24th
    Battalion
in AIF 7th Division 106, 119
in AIF 9th Division 161
Benghazi 181
Gazala 182
Tobruk 250
Tobruk, defend western perimeter
    252
27th Brescia Division (Italian)
North Africa 125, 189–190
Rommel 147
Tobruk, Easter Battle 265, 267
von Prittwitz 244
132nd Ariete Division (Italian)
Afrika Korps 125, 147
North Africa 189–190
Rommel 301–302, 310, 318–319,
    361
surrender 316–317
Tobruk, Battle of the Salient 361
Tobruk, Easter Battle 301–302,
    305, 308, 310

A
Aboriginal policy 29–30
Abyssinia 31
Ack-Ack (Anti-Aircraft gunners)
    99–100, 233, 240, 272, 319, 343,
    416, 442
Adams (loader, Royal Tank
    Regiment) 300
Advisory War Council (Australia) 381

Afrika Korps *see also Die Panzergruppe Afrika*; Italian 10th Army
  3rd Reconnaissance Battalion 154, 188, 194, 220, 244
  5th Light Panzer Division *see* 5th Light Panzer Division
  8th Machine-gun Battalion *see* 8th Machine-gun Battalion
  15th Panzer Division *see* 15th Panzer Division
  27th Brescia Division *see* 27th Brescia Division
  132nd Ariete Division *see* 132nd Ariete Division
  605th Anti-tank Battalion 244
  On from Benghazi (film) 473
  Bersaglieri Unit 379
  captured 497
  casualties 266, 282, 303, 306, 308, 373, 490
  Feuert los! 469
  German Intelligence Section 293
  Neuankömmlinge 468
  in North Africa 170
  Operation Battleaxe 425–427
  Panzer Divisions 234–235, 270, 308
  reunions 518–520
  strength 147, 467–468
  supply 244–245, 318, 342, 388–389, 467, 490
  Totensonntag (Sunday of the Dead) 477
  training 448
  uniforms 271, 430
  weaponry 420–421, 425–427, 448
  Zigeunerarmee (gypsy army) 490
Agedabia (Libya) 199, 202, 210
AIF (Australian Imperial Force)
  1st and 2nd AIF 51, 65–66
  culture 4–5
AIF 6th Australian Division
  2/1st Battalion 130–131

2/1st Field Company 126
2/3rd Battalion 129, 130–131
2/4th Battalion 131, 133–134
2/6th Battalion 138
2/12th Battalion 57–58
18th Brigade *see* 18th Brigade
19th Brigade (2/1st, 2/3rd, 2/4th) 134, 138, 322–324
25th Brigade 89
Bardia 116–117
Beda Fomm 148
Benghazi 146
called home 493
Derna 140, 144–145
El Agheila 157–158
in Greece *see* Greece
move up into Libya 114
relations with AIF 9th Division 171–172
Tobruk 122, 125, 126–127, 134
training in Palestine 98–99, 104, 113
AIF 7th Australian Division
  2/13th Battalion *see* 2/13th Battalion
  2/15th Battalion *see* 2/15th Battalion
  2/17th Battalion *see* 2/17th Battalion
  2/23rd Battalion *see* 2/23rd Battalion
  2/24th Battalion *see* 2/24th Battalion
  18th Brigade *see* 18th Brigade
  20th Brigade (2/13th, 2/15th, 2/17th) 91
  25th Brigade 161
  26th Brigade (2/23rd, 2/24th) 106, 119
  called home 493
  in Greece 158
  is formed 60
  Mersa Matruh 246

AIF 9th Australian Division
  18th Brigade see 18th Brigade
  20th Brigade (2/13th, 2/15th,
    2/17th) see 20th Brigade
  24th Brigade see 24th Brigade
  25th Brigade 89, 161–162
  26th Brigade (2/23rd, 2/24th) see
    26th Brigade
  Australian Bush Artillery see under
    Tobruk garrison
  Battle of El Alamein 496
  casualties 135, 492
  changing composition of 145,
    161–162
  Morshead commands 144 see also
    Morshead, General Sir Leslie
  New Guinea 497
  North Africa 152, 163–165
  relations with AIF 6th Division
    171–172
  Tobruk, pull back to 232
  weaponry 175–176
Albania 97
Alexandria (Egypt) 83
Algeria 497
Allen, Arthur ('Tubby') 5
Allen, Major 'Bluey' 108
Allied code-breaking unit 194,
  389–390
Allied forces see British Allied Army
Anzac Day 13
Appel, Major 361
Aquitania (ship) 92
Arab population
  Arab urchins 103–104
  of Benghazi 177–178, 209
  of Derna 144
  in North Africa 1–2
  resistance to Italian colonisation 2
  treatment of desert sores 414
Ariete Division (Italian) see 132nd
  Ariete Division
Armstrong, Private Arty 109

Arras (France) 70
Asmis, Dr Rudolf 29–30
Assenmacher, Sergeant 289, 293, 297
Auchinleck, Field Marshal Sir Claude
  Blamey 434–435, 441, 457–458,
    459
  Churchill 427, 441, 449, 459, 495
  Commander in Chief of British
    Troops in the Far East 494
  Morocco 510
  Operation Crusader 469–470,
    479–480
Australia
  Australian troops, command
    protocol with Britain 55–56, 458
  Berlin Olympic Games (1936)
    32–33
  Britain declares war on Germany 48
  defence 24, 33–34, 39–41, 50,
    312–315, 432–433
  Fascism in 23–24
  fear of Communism 23–24
  federal election (1940) 88
  federation 2
  in Great War see Great War
  joins up 50, 77–78
  penny collections 112
  Treaty of Versailles 12
Australia (warship) 50
Australian Army
  AIF sun badge 405, 488
  army structure and ranks 63
  bayonet training 62
  command structure 50–51
  enlistment numbers 161–162
  infantry battalions 43
  kit 61
  marching 84–85
  medical orderlies 301, 319
  mess 80
  mortar training 64–65
  Personal Acknowledgment of Delivery
    141

Australian Army (*cont.*)
  rabbiting 133
  short arm inspection 82–83
  soldier settlement farms 66
  square bashing 63
  training bases 67–68
  training camp 61–64
  venereal disease 83, 117–118
  volunteers 137, 378, 401
  Wartime Secrets Act 119
Australian Comforts Fund 112, 115,
  416
Australian Corps 433
Australian Light Horse 103, 105
Australian War Cabinet 449
Australian War Cemetary (Gaza) 104
Austria, *der Anschluss* 36

B
Badoglio, Marshal Pietro 73
Balfe, Captain John 108, 238, 287,
  305, 437
Barassi, Ron 522
Barber, Jack 320
Barce (Libya) 153, 171, 197, 229
Bardia (Libya)
  Australian troops take 121, 337
  Bangalore Torpedoes 130
  Italians forces in 113, 116–117, 131
Barlow, Frankie 82, 106, 223, 363
Bartsch, Captain 306
Batory (as troopship) 94
Battle of the Salient
  2/48th Battalion 370–371
  15th Panzer Division (Afrika
    Korps) 350–351, 355–356,
    358–359, 364–368, 370–371
  Morshead, General Leslie 351, 370,
    415, 429
  Tobruk garrison 350, 352–364,
    372–373, 389, 395, 415, 429
BBC Bulletins 464–465
Bean, C.E.W. 4, 5, 400

Beda Fomm (Libya) 148, 151, 180
Bedouin people 166
Beersheba (Palestine) 105
Beezley, Private Arthur 269
Bel Hemed (Libya) 480
Belgium 68, 293
Belgrade (Yugoslavia) 228
Benghazi (Libya)
  20th Brigade withdrawal to 166,
    179–182, 186–187, 190
  Allied forces in 149
  Arab population 177–178, 209
  falls 209, 218
  Italians forces in 113, 146
  landmines 208
  Neame 205
  port 342
  Rommel advances 206–207
  salt-lakes 207–208
  Wavell 183
Bennett, Gordon 5
Berlin Olympic Games (1936)
  32–33, 391
Besser, Rose 376–377
Bird, Captain 163
Bismarck, Otto von 18
Blackburn, Lieutenant Commander
  393
Blamey, General Thomas
  AIF 6th Australian Division
    158–159
  AIF 7th Australian Division 222
  AIF 9th Australian Division 145
  Auchinleck 434–435, 441,
    457–458, 459
  Australian troops 456–457
  Australian War Cabinet 449
  decision to defend Tobruk 228
  defence of Australia 493
  Deputy Commander in Chief,
    Middle East 332, 433–434, 441
  General Officer Commanding
    2AIF 51, 332, 441

Great War 5
Menzies 158–159, 332, 432–433
Morshead 457
protocol with Britain 55–56, 458
Wavell 332, 435
White Guard (in Victoria) 24
Blitzkrieg 44, 69, 71, 232
Bombay (India) 102, 103
Bonaparte, Napoleon 1
Bormann, Martin 509
Borneo 497, 510
Bradman, Don 520
Braun, Eva 508–509
Brescia Division (Italian) *see* 27th
  Brescia Division
Brines, Private Allan 378
Britain *see also* British Allied Army
  Anglo–Polish pact 41
  Battle of Britain 101
  British Expeditionary Force 56–57
  Chiefs of Staff 50
  declares war on Germany 46–48
  defence treaty with Australia 50
  Fascism in 22–23
  Greece 97, 122, 123–124, 152, 160,
    161, 188–189, 323
  Italy declares war on Allies 73
  London blitz 202–203, 204, 312
  in Middle East 77, 101 *see also*
    Egypt
  military capability 33–34, 39, 41
  Munich Agreement (1938) 37–38,
    68
  protocol with Australia 55–56, 458
  Treaty of Versailles 12
  War Cabinet 160, 161, 312–313,
    368–369, 372, 459
British Allied Army
  1st Army Tank Brigade 469
  1st Essex Battalion 480, 482, 484
  1st Royal Horse Artillery 172, 267,
    274, 295–296
  1st Royal Tank Regiment 296, 303

1st South African Division 469,
  470
2nd Armoured Brigade 209
2nd Armoured Division *see* 2nd
  Armoured Division
2nd British Division 33
2nd New Zealand Division 469,
  474
3rd Indian Motor Brigade 225,
  226, 239
3rd Royal Tank Regiment 303
4th Armoured Brigade 425
4th Indian Division 113, 425, 439,
  469
5th Brigade 33
7th Armoured Division 148, 171,
  425, 469
7th Royal Tank Regiment 240,
  334
8th Army 469, 472, 478–480, 482,
  490
13th Corps 469, 474, 480
18th Cavalry 225
18th Division 494
18th Indian Cavalry Regiment 405
19th New Zealand Battalion 480
22nd Guards Brigade 469
30th Corps 469, 474, 477, 479
32nd Brigade 487
51st Division 244
51st Field Regiment 172, 219
104th Royal Horse Artillery 172,
  303
107th Royal Horse Artillery 239,
  274, 296–297, 303
Agedabia 199
armoured vehicles 33, 113, 195,
  236, 240, 270, 294, 299,
  370–371, 425, 478
Benghazi 146, 187
Black Watch 482
Border Regiment 489
casualties 146, 297–298, 490

British Allied Army (*cont.*)
  Durham Light Infantry 489
  El Agheila 157, 172
  Greece 322–324
  intelligence 155
  King's Dragoon Guards 417
  Marsa el Brega 194–196, 239
  Mechili 205
  No 11 Scottish Commando 474
  Northumberland Fusiliers 417,
    445, 462
  Operation Crusader 469–470, 472,
    474
  Operation Torch 497
  Polish 1st Carpathan Brigade 441,
    449–450, 453, 464–465, 490,
    515–516
  Royal Horse Artillery 239, 272,
    287–288, 293, 299, 487, 489, 491
  Royal Northumberland Fusiliers
    219
  Royal Tank Regiment 286,
    299–301
  South African troops 494–495
  TOBFORCE 477, 482
  Western Desert Force 112, 308
British High Command 432–433
British Troops Egypt (BTE) 152
British Union of Fascists (BUF)
  22–23
Brookby, Lawrie 518
Burma 494
Burrows, Colonel 'Bull' 64, 109, 464,
  472, 482, 485–486, 489

C
Capuzzo (Libya) 426
Chamberlain, Neville 37–38, 41, 42,
  48, 54, 68
Chatfield, Lord 228
Churchill, Winston
  Allied code-breaking unit 389–390
  Auchinleck 427, 441, 449, 459, 495

Battle of Britain 101
  Duke of Hamilton 391–392
  Dunkirk 263
  Fadden 454–455, 458–459
  Greece 123–124, 152, 161, 323
  Hess 391–392
  Menzies 39, 89, 124, 140, 312–313,
    372, 440, 441, 449
  Morshead 381
  Munich Agreement (1938) 38, 68
  Mussolini invades Greece 97
  North Africa 203
  Omdurman Campaign 203
  Operation Battleaxe 425, 427
  oratory 68, 149
  as Prime Minister 68, 510
  Singapore 494
  Tiger supply convoy 390
  Tobruk 122, 123, 246, 495
  War Cabinet 368–369
  Wavell 188–189, 203, 313, 390,
    427–428
Ciano, Count Galeazzo 73, 87
Citizens Military Force (CMF)
  21–22, 39–41, 49–50
code-breaking unit (Allied) 194,
  389–390
Coles, Arthur 88
Coles, Jean 83, 94, 162–163, 510–511
Colvin, Major 463, 489
Communism 14, 23–24, 452
Cona, General 148
Cook, Lieutenant Colonel Thomas
  438
Copland, Major John 131–132
Coughlan, Ian 385, 429–430
Country Party *see* United Australia
    Party/Country Party Coalition
Cranborne, Lord 441
Crawford, Colonel John 108, 287,
  315–316, 424, 465–466
Crete 323, 382, 419–420
Crimea 452

Cross, Sir Ronald 441

Cunningham, Admiral Sir Andrew 227–228, 440, 469

Cunningham, General Sir Alan 469, 478, 479–480

Curtin, John 88, 144, 175, 372, 381–382, 454
  becomes Prime Minister 460

Cyrenaica (eastern Libya) *see* Libya

Cyrene (Libya) 169

Czechoslovakia (Munich Agreement, 1938) 37–38, 68

D

Dachau (Germany) 502

Daily Sketch (UK) 314

Daladier, Edouard 37

Dalziel, Athol 284–285, 288, 302, 423
  2/17th Battalion 218

de Groot, Francis 23

Deakin, Alfred 197

Denmark 58

Derna (Libya) 113, 169, 189, 230, 378–379
  Afrika Korps captures 237
  AIF 6th Division 140, 144–145

Deutsche Arbeiterpartei (Germany Workers' Party) 13–15 *see also* Nazi Party

Deutsche Bundeswehr (Germany Army) 518

Die Panzergruppe Afrika 400, 474, 478–479, 481 *see also* Afrika Korps
  casualties 490

Diggers (term) 65

Dill, General Sir John 180, 181, 227, 313, 314, 332, 427

disarmament conference (1922) 50

Dixon, Sir Owen 55

Donald, Major Graham 391

Dönitz, Admiral Karl 508

Dorman-Smith, Brigadier Eric 152

Drexler, Anton 13–14, 15, 16

Dunkirk (France) 71–72, 263

Durig, Johnnie 302

E

East German Stasi 504

Easter Battle
  Morshead, General Leslie 415
  Tobruk garrison 415

Eden, Anthony 146, 152, 227

Edmondson, Corporal John Hurst ('Jack')
  2/17th Battalion 218, 238
  Australia at war 48–49
  background 3
  CMF 39–41, 49, 60
  commands 3 Section, 16th Platoon, 2/17th Battalion 278
  death and burial 302, 309, 315–316, 524
  education 19, 27–28
  enlistment papers 61
  health 60, 74
  home leave 89–91
  John Edmondson High School (Sydney) 513
  Mackell 108
  at sea 99
  Tobruk, Easter Battle 279–285, 287, 288
  training camp 80
  Victoria Cross 424, 437–438, 466

Edmondson, Elizabeth
  Jack 19, 59–60, 67, 74, 89–91, 98, 107, 114–115, 171, 311, 422–424
  JW ('Will') 217–218, 226, 272, 327, 424, 513
  Personal Acknowledgment of Delivery 340–341
  Victoria Cross 437–438

Egypt *see also* Suez Canal
  Afrika Korps at frontier 343
  Australians 103

Egypt (*cont.*)
  British interests in 2, 31, 83, 194,
    246
  Cairo 150, 155, 194, 437
  Die Panzergruppe Afrika 479, 481
  veterans 519
Ehlert, Major 310
El Abiar (Libya) 187
El Adem (Libya) 263
El Agheila 494
El Agheila (Libya) 148, 156–157, 158,
    168, 175, 179–182, 186
  Rommel attacks 188
El Alamein (Libya) 188, 495–496
El Kantara (Egypt) 103, 164
Eland, Private Stephen ('Curly') 221
Er Regima pass (Libya) 187, 213,
    218–220
Eritrea 31
Ethiopia 32
European colonialism 16

F
Fadden, Arthur 454–455, 458–459, 460
Fascism
  in Australia 23–24
  in Britain 22–23
  in Germany *see* Nazi Party
  in Italy 17, 30–31
  rise of 16–17
Ferres, Bert
  2/13th Battalion 85, 92, 100, 103,
    106, 222
  Borneo 510
  in CMF 40–41
  Ed Duda 487–488
  Er Regima pass 219, 221
  HMS *Latona* 463
  Italian pistol 176, 187–188
  joins up 62
  Military Medal 488
  New Guinea 510
  Polish 1st Carpathian Brigade 465

  raids tucker dump 436
  Tobru, 'reo' 460
  Tobruk, anti-tank ditches 256–257
  Tobruk, dinner in 402
  Tobruk, Easter Battle 291
  Tobruk, Spandau Joe 386–388
Foch, Marshal Ferdinand 76
Fort Capuzzo (Egypt) 396
Foster, Doug ('Snowy') 278, 280, 284
  2/17th Battalion 218
France
  British Expeditionary Force 56–57
  D-Day 499
  declares war on Germany 49
  Free French in Tobruk 128, 172
  German invasion 69–70, 72, 292
  German occupation 76–77
  Great War 4, 9
  Munich Agreement (1938) 38
  prison camps 77
  Rhineland 27, 31
  surrenders to Germany 75–77
  Treaty of Versailles 12
Frank, Captain 282

G
Gabr Saleh (Libya) 474
Gaddhafi, Colonel Mohamar 521
Gallipoli 3, 4, 247, 386, 444
Gambier-Parry, Major General
    Michael
  captured by Germans 235
  commands 2nd Armoured Division
    172, 205–206
  commands 20th AIF Brigade 171
  Mechili 231–232, 233–234
  Neame 199
Gambut (Libya) 474
Gard, Father Tom 446
Gariboldi, Generale Italo d'Armata
    147
  Rommel 155–156, 202, 210–211,
    337–338

Gaza (Palestine) 104

Gazala (Libya) 171, 182, 347, 490, 494

Gazzard, Lou 95, 348, 360–361

Generals and Generalship (Wavell) 55

George, Clarrie 465

George VI, King 37, 440–441

Germany 2
  airforce *see Luftwaffe*
  armistice 10–11, 53
  army *see Reichswehr*
  Berlin Olympic Games (1936)
    32–33, 391
  Britain declares war on 46–48
  Communism in 14
  declares war on Yugoslavia and
    Greece 228
  Enigma code 194, 389–390
  Greece 124–125, 228
  invades Belgium, Luxembourg and
    Holland 68
  invades Denmark and Norway 58
  invades France 69–70
  invades Greece 216–217, 322–324
  invades Poland 44–46
  invades Yugoslavia 191–192, 323
  Libya 124–125
  post-war 519–520
  propaganda 56, 146
  Prussian Old Guard 53
  reaches English Channel 73
  reparations 11, 19, 76
  Rhineland 27, 31
  territorial annexation 11, 16, 26, 45
  Totensonntag (Sunday of the Dead)
    477
  Treaty of Versailles *see* Treaty of
    Versailles

Ghemines (Libya) 187

Gleiwitz (Germany) 43

Godfrey, Lieutenant Colonel Arthur
  138, 145

Godwin-Austen, Major General
  Alfred 480

Goebbels, Joseph 169, 392, 508–509

Gort, General Lord 313

Gott, Brigadier General William
  395–396

Graham, Captain Michael 485

Graham, Norm
  Dorothy Poynton 83
  joins up 77–78
  at sea 106
  Tobruk 348, 359, 362
  training camp 81
  two-up 150

Grant, Ron 218, 278, 281, 284

Gray, Edgar ('Dunc') 32–33

Graziani, Marshal Rodolfo 83–84,
  86–88, 112

Great Britain *see* Britain

Great War 4–5, 6–11, 34 *see also*
  Treaty of Versailles
  Australians in 13, 51, 55, 60, 104,
    105, 153, 157
  Germans in 371

Greece
  AIF 6th Division 123–124, 152,
    158–159, 163, 164, 173, 175,
    312–313
  AIF 7th Division 158
  Allied forces 323
  Australian casualties 382
  Australian troops evacuated 372
  Britain 97, 122, 123–124, 152, 160,
    161, 188–189, 323
  British Army 322–324
  Crete 323, 382, 419–420
  Germany declares war on 228
  Germany invades 216–217, 322–324
  Greek Army 323
  Mussolini invades 96–97, 122
  Turkey 124
  Yugoslavia 124, 191–192

Guderian, *Generaloberst* Heinz
  Wilhelm 478

Gulf of Sirte (Libya) 156, 168, 170

H

Haile Selassie 32
Halder, General Franz 54, 185, 348,
   380
   Dachau 502
   Rommel 110, 336–337, 399–400
Halfaya Pass (Libya) 312, 318,
   347–348, 396, 397, 420–421
   'Hellfire Pass' 425–427
Hamer, Lieutenant Dick 444
Hamilton, Duke of 33, 391–392
Hancock, Ivor
   2/24th Battalion 118, 187, 223,
      259
   background 20
   education 28
   Jean Coles 83, 94, 162–163
   joins up 77–78
   POW 378–379
   radio broadcaster 511
   returns to Australia 510–512
   at sea 99, 106–107
   Tobruk, Battle of the Salient 352,
      355, 356, 358–364
   Tobruk, Easter Battle 274–275
   Tobruk, Hill 209 348–349
   training camp 81
   two-up 150
Hankey, Maurice 39, 368–369
Harding, Brigadier General Staff John
   205
Harris, Jack 278, 284
Hauser, Major Wolfgang 275
Havard, Ward and Olive 513–514
Haw-Haw, Lord see Joyce, William
Heard, 'Turk' 75
Heckmann, Wolf 366, 389
Hedges, John 284
Henderson, Sir Neville 46–47
Hennessy, Lieutenant 133–134
Hess, Rudolf 15, 18, 22, 32–33,
   390–392, 509–510
Hetherington, John 113–114

Hetzler, Dr Erich 56
Hitler, Adolf
   25 Point plan 16
   assassination attempt on 498–499
   background 8
   becomes Chancellor 25
   becomes der Führer 24
   Beer Hall Putsch 17–18
   commits suicide 508–509
   creates Gauleiter (district leaders) 21
   Directive No 22 124–125
   'Final Solution' 376–377
   France surrenders to 76
   Führerbunker 508
   Great War 8–10
   influence on Nazi Party 15–16, 30
   invasion of Poland 44–45
   Jews in Germany 22
   Jews in Soviet Union 452
   joins Deutsche Arbeiterpartei 14–15
   Lucie Rommel 501–502
   Munich Agreement (1938) 37, 68
   Mussolini 31, 96–97, 125
   non-aggression pact with Soviet
      Union 41, 54, 125
   Nuremberg Rally (1938) 36–37
   OKW 36, 110
   oratory 14, 15
   reoccupies Rhineland 31
   Rommel 35, 52–53, 110, 146–147,
      184–185, 400, 496–497
   Suez Canal 431
   Treaty of Versailles 15, 16, 17, 26
Hitler Youth 25–27, 451
HMAS Canberra 100
HMAS Parramatta 330
HMAS Perth 92, 100
HMAS Stuart 330
HMAS Vampire 330
HMAS Vendetta 330
HMAS Voyager 330
HMAS Waterhen 330
HMS Decoy 330

HMS *Defender* 330
HMS *Ladybird* 393
HMS *Latona* 462–464
HMS *Talisman* (submarine) 474
HMS *Torbay* (submarine) 474
Hofer, Lieutenant 282
Holland 68
Holt, Edgar 430
Hopkins, Harry 123–124
Hore-Ruthven, Governor General
    Alexander 437–438
Hughes, Billy 12–13, 39, 454–455
Hughes, George 424
Hungary 79–80

I
Ikin, John 520
India 314, 494 *see also* British Allied
    Army
Indra Puera (troopship) 99
Infanterie Greift An — Infantry
    Attacks (Rommel) 34–35, 53,
    109–110, 460, 521
Irving, David 504
Italian 10th Army *see also* Afrika
    Korps
  27th Brescia Division *see* 27th
    Brescia Division
  102nd Trento Motorised Division
    125, 147
  132nd Ariete Division *see* 132nd
    Ariete Division
  attacks British forces 87–88
  Australians 137
  Bardia 116–117, 121, 131
  On from Benghazi (film) 473
  casualties 121
  counterattack on 112–113
  Derna 144–145
  in Libya 55, 83–84, 86–88, 113, 156
  surrenders at Beda Fomm 148
  taken as prisoners 113, 121, 131,
    135, 136–137, 138, 146, 148

tanks 190
treatment of prisoners 453
Italian Navy 126
Italy *see also* Mussolini, Benito
  Fascism in 17, 30–31
  Great War 6–7, 34
  North African colony *see* North
    Africa

J
Jaffa (Palestine) 141–142
Japan 12, 140, 313–315, 372, 490,
    493–494
Jardine, Douglas 416
Jeffrey, Squadron Leader Peter 214
Jews
  concentration camps 506–507
  in Germany 22, 26, 30, 41
  in Hungary 79
  in Poland 45, 376–377, 451
  in Soviet Union 452
Jodl, *Generaloberst* Alfred 400, 473
John Edmondson High School
    (Sydney) 513
Johnson, Barry 514–515
Johnson, Jack 92–93
Johnson, John
  2/23rd Battalion 86, 174, 232–233
  joins up 66–67, 78–79
  leave before embarkation 92–94
  Len 151
  letters home 86, 111–112,
    173–174, 200–201, 333, 394
  in Port Said 120
  at sea 99
  Tobruk, Battle of Carrier Hill
    334–335
  Tobruk, Battle of the Salient 370
  Tobruk, battle to retake perimeter
    posts 375
  Tobruk, Bren carrier 261
  Tobruk, death detail 315
  Tobruk, killed at 398–399

Johnson, John (*cont.*)
    Tobruk, relief of Post S9 397–398
    Walwa mates 94–95
    War Letters 1940–1941 (Len
        Johnson) 522–523
Johnson, Josie 66, 78, 345–346, 385,
    393–394, 429–430, 514
Johnson, Len 424–425, 515,
    522–524
Jones, Charles Lloyd 498
Jones, Private Clarrie 488
Joy, Pat 92, 94, 261, 399, 523
Joyce, William (Lord Haw-Haw)
    22–23, 41–42, 56, 507–508
    'Rats of Tobruk' 329

K
Keitel, *Generalfeldmarschall* Wilhelm
    211, 311
Kelly, Alan 92, 94, 261, 399
Keogh, Ron 218, 278
Keyes, Lieutenant Colonel Geoffrey
    474
Kirchheim, Major General Heinrich
    244, 311, 318
Krampe, Lieutenant 293
Kreowski, Czeslaw 58–59, 79–80
Kuwait 521

L
Lang, Jack 23
Lavarack, Lieutenant General John
    commands 18th Brigade 221–222
    commands AIF 7th Division 221,
        308–309
    commands Allied forces in
        Cyrenaica 245
    Tobruk 245, 247
    Wavell 221–222, 276
Lawson, Henry 443
Leakey, Major General Rea 240, 249,
    286–287, 299–301, 513
Libya 2, 521 *see also* North Africa

Lloyd, Colonel Charles 'Gaffer' 145,
    252–253
Lodz (Poland) 376–377
Löhndorff, Ernst 414–415
Longarone (Italy) 7
Longmore, Sir Arthur 227
Loraine, Sir Percy 73
Lovegrove, Lieutenant Dick 253
Luftwaffe see also Reichswehr
    (German Army)
    Battle of Britain 101
    in Greece 323
    in Libya 157
    Mediterranean 469–470
    in North Africa 190
    in Sicily 149
    in Tobruk *see* Tobruk garrison:air
        raids
Luxembourg 68
Lyons, Joseph 39, 48, 88
Lyttleton, Sir Oliver 459

M
McDonald, Private 339
McElroy, Sergeant Bob 303, 305,
    309
McFadyen, Private George 483–484,
    487
Mackay, Iven 5
Mackell, Lieutenant Austin
    ('Mummy') 107–108, 278–284,
    286, 302, 512
    2/17th Battalion 238
McKenzie, Corporal Roy ('Macca')
    94, 348, 354, 355, 362
McLean, David 390–391
Manella, Generale Petassi 126, 132
Marawa (Libya) 229
Marsa el Brega (Libya) 172, 179,
    194–196, 239
Marx, Karl 16
Masaryk, Jan 38
Mauritania (ship) 72

Max the Axe (two-up organiser) 150, 349, 352–353, 355, 356, 358–359, 362

Mechili (Libya)
Afrika Korps 206–207, 231–232, 234–235, 512
falls 235
Neame 180, 205
Operation Compass 148
prisoners 235
siege 225–226

Mediterranean 77, 337, 390, 432, 467, 469–470

Mein Kampf — My Struggle (Hitler) 18, 25–27, 30, 125

Melbourne Cup 471–472

Menzies, Robert
Australian troops 142, 421–422
Blamey 158–159, 332, 432–433
Churchill 39, 89, 124, 140, 312–313, 372, 440, 441, 449
Cunningham 228
declares Australia at war 48–49
federal election (1940) 88
Great War 142–143
Greece 158, 323
Morshead 143–144, 381
political future 314, 381–382
resigns as Prime Minister 454
visits Tobruk 524
War Cabinet 368–369

Merrikin, Bill 80

Mersa Matruh (Egypt) 87, 165, 246, 410, 411–412
British railway line 470–471

Metaxas, General Ioannis 97

Metelmann, Henry 451–452

Miller, Keith 520

Miller, Ward A. 520

Mills, Sergeant 133–134

Millward, Malcolm 510

Mitchell, Bob 107

Monte Matajur (Italy) 6

Montgomery, General Bernard Law 495–496

Moore, Colonel 98

Morocco 497

Morshead, General Sir Leslie
20th Brigade conduct 196–198
33rd Battalion 4, 5
Allied code-breaking unit 390
Australian troops 327–328, 434
Australia's defence policy 33–34
background 3–5
Battle of Carrier Hill 332
Battle of the Salient 351, 370, 415, 429
Benghazi, withdrawal to 179–182
Blamey 457
Blue Line 461
Churchill 381
CMF 21–22, 33
Commander of 1st Australian Corps 497
Commander of Tobruk 245, 309, 402, 403–404
commands 18th Brigade 51–52, 57–58, 72, 101, 116
commands 33rd Battalion at Gallipoli 4, 5
commands AIF 9th Division 144, 145–146, 162
death and funeral 497–498
discipline 328
Easter Battle 269–270, 288, 415
Ed Duda 476
enlistment number 162
family life 21, 190–191
Great War 4–5
Hill 209 357–358, 364, 379–380
Marawa 229
Menzies 143–144, 381
mobile reserve 262–263
Neame 170–171, 172, 196–198, 213–214, 231
nicknames 327

Morshead, General Sir Leslie (*cont.*)
  Old Guard (in NSW) 24
  Operation Brevity 396
  Order of the Day (10 April) 251
  patrols into no-man's land 404
  Polish Order of *Virtuti Militari* 477
  re-lays minefields 325–326
  relieved 461–462
  retreat to Tobruk 239
  Rommel 198
  the Salient 373–375, 443–444
  Signals 258
  in Tobruk 134, 138, 247, 251
  Wavell 180–182, 214, 245–246, 276
  Williams 417
  Wilmot 429, 498
Morshead, Myrtle 5, 21
Mosley, Oswald 22–23
Mountbatten, Lord Louis 494
Mrozowski, Adam
  in Hungary 79–80
  in Jerusalem 178
  in Poland 45–46, 58–59, 75
  Polish 1st Carpathan Brigade
    449–450, 472, 515–516
Msus (Libya) 209, 231–232
Munich Agreement (1938) 37–38, 68
Munninger, Rolf 494
Murray, Brigadier John 145
Mussolini, Alessandro 17
Mussolini, Benito
  declares war on Allies 72–74
  Fascism 17
  Great War 7–8
  Hitler 31, 96–97, 125
  Il Popolo d'Italia 7, 8
  invades Eritrea and Abyssinia 31
  invades Greece 96–97
  Jews 453
  march on Rome (1922) 17
  Munich Agreement (1938) 37
  North Africa 317
  orders attack on Britain 84

  Rome–Berlin Axis 31, 55
  Rommel 148–149
  shot 508
  trinceresti and *la trincerocrazia* 8

N
'Nancy' in Cairo 150
Nazi Party *(Nationalsozialistische*
    Deutsche Arbeiterpartei)
  1932 elections 24
  Aryanism 16
  Australian Aboriginal Policy 29–30
  concentration camps 506–507
  as *Deutsche Arbeiterpartei* 15
  education and training policy
    25–27
  Hitler's influence 15–16
  Nazism 18–19
  rise in membership 22
  Sippenhaft 504
  swastika 15
Neame, Lieutenant General Sir Philip
  Australian troops 187, 196–198,
    269, 375
  background 153
  Benghazi 205
  captured by Germans 229–231
  Gambier-Parry 199
  Morshead 170–171, 172, 196–198,
    213–214
  North Africa 173, 209, 220
  O'Connor 205–206
  Tobruk 256
  Wavell 182–183, 194, 199,
    204–206
the Netherlands 68
New Guard and Old Guard (in
    NSW) 23–24
New Guinea 12–13, 497, 510
New York Times 71–72
New Zealand 49, 103, 113
  Greece 123–124, 152, 322–324
Nichols, Colonel 491

North Africa 123–125
  Allied forces 182, 208–209
  Italian colony 2, 147, 169, 183,
    189–190, 209
Norway 58, 293, 313
Nuremberg trials 502, 509

O
O'Connor, General Sir Richard
  captured by Germans 229–231
  General Officer Commanding
    British Troops Egypt 152
  Greece 151–152
  Neame 205–206
  Operation Compass (North Africa)
    112, 113, 147, 148, 158, 173,
    205, 223
  Wavell 204
OKH (Oberkommando des Heeres) 36,
  69, 110, 244, 337, 344, 346, 400
OKW (Oberkommando der Wehrmacht)
  36, 110, 311, 400
Olbrich, Colonel Herbert
  Agedabia 199
  commands 5th Light Panzer
    Regiment, 2nd Battalion 195
  Mechili 206
  Ponath 304
  Rommel 307–308
  Streich 310
  Tobruk 267
  Tobruk, Easter Battle 291, 299, 304
Old Guard and New Guard (in
  NSW) 23–24
On from Benghazi (film) 473
Orion (as troopship) 94
Ottoman Empire 1–2

P
Page, Earle 142–143
Palestine 98, 103–104, 115, 517
  Hill 69 camp 492
  Julis Camp 143, 145–146, 149–150

Kilo 89 tented camp 104–105, 109,
  115
Port Said 117–118
Die Panzergruppe Afrika 400, 474,
  478–479, 481 see also Afrika
  Korps
  casualties 490
Papua New Guinea 12–13, 497, 510
Parer, Damien 443
Paterson, Hugh 464
Paulus, Field Marshal Friedrich
  East German Stasi 504
  Halder 400
  invasion of Poland 54
  North Africa 337
  Operation Barbarossa 502–504
  Rommel 344–345, 347–348, 389
  Schmidt 346–347
  Tobruk 380, 388–389, 395
Penteker, Erika and Gerda 505, 517
Petacci, Clara 508
Pétain, Marshal Henri Philippe
  76–77
Peters, Stan 523
Piraeus (Athens) 228
Poidevin, 'Pudden Head' 81–82, 106,
  150
Poland
  Anglo–Polish pact 41
  Auschwitz 377, 451
  casualties 54
  German invasion 44–46, 53–54,
    292
  German occupation 58–59,
    451–452
  Lodz 376–377
  Paulus 337, 344
  Polish Army 45–46, 59, 75
  Polish Carpathian Brigade 80,
    178–179
  refugees 58
  resistance 45, 52, 515–516
  Soviet Union 54, 465

Ponath, Lieutenant Colonel Gustav 216, 230, 237
 awarded *Ritterkreuz* 317
 Olbrich 304
 Tobruk, Easter Battle 271, 276–277, 289, 304, 306
Pope, Keith 446
Port Said (Palestine) 117–118
Porter, Sergeant Bill 339
Poynton, Dorothy 83
Prahl, Lieutenant Erich 237, 318
Pulsford (2/15th Battalion soldier) 393

Q
Queen Mary (as troopship) 91–92, 98, 100

R
RAAF (Royal Australian Air Force)
 Bardia 117
 command of 50
 Luftwaffe 224
 Mechili 232
 No 3 Squadron 190, 214, 218, 233, 491
 Tobruk, Easter Battle 301
 Tobruk, siege ends 491
RAF (Royal Air Force)
 Bardia 117
 Battle of Britain 101
 Benghazi 342
 camouflage 176–177
 Greece 97, 323
 Mechili 232
 No 6 Squadron 240
 No 73 Squadron 214, 233, 240, 272, 339
 Operation Compass 113
 Tobruk 128
 Tobruk air raids 338–339
 Tobruk, Easter Battle 274, 301
RAN (Royal Australian Navy) 50, 330

'Rats of Tobruk' 329, 456, 498, 520
Rats of Tobruk Association 516
Rayner, Vince 234–235, 326, 512
Reichswehr (German Army) *see also* *Luftwaffe*
 5th Light Panzer Division (in France) 109–110, 292 *see also* Afrika Korps
 6th Army 503–504
 7th Panzer Division 69–70, 73, 212, 243–244
 15th Panzer Division *see* Afrika Korps
 15th Panzer Regiment (in France) 109–110
 16th Bavarian Reserve Infantry Regiment 8
 Alpine Korps 6, 147
 casualties 504
 Hitler Youth 25
 List Regiment 9
 Panzer Divisions 45, 53, 70–71, 195, 234–235, 307
 Panzergrenadieren 70
 salute 447
 Treaty of Versailles 11
Ritchie, Lieutenant General 480
RN (Royal Navy) 50, 71, 126, 128, 342, 393
Roatta, Generale Mario 338
Robertson, Brigadier Horace 134
Roman Empire 1–2
Romania 97
Rommel, *Generalfeldmarschall* Erwin
 abandons Tobruk 497
 advances on Benghazi 206–207
 assassination attempt on Hitler 498–499
 attacks Agedabia 199, 202
 attacks Egypt 495–496
 attacks El Agheila 188
 attacks Marsa el Brega 194–196

attacks Tobruk 212, 243–244,
    265–268, 345
Australian troops 362–363, 409
background 5
Barbarossa campaign 428
Battle of El Alamein 495–496
book *see Infanterie Greift An —
    Infantry Attacks*
breaks through to St Valéry
    (France) 243–244
'Cardboard Division' 188
career 22
commands 7th Panzer Division 69,
    73, 243–244
commands Afrika Korps 147 *see
    also* Afrika Korps
commands *Die Panzergruppe Afrika*
    400
commands *Führerbegleitbataillon* 52
commands Wehrmacht's Army
    Group B 498
Communism 14
Egyptian frontier 467
fall of Tobruk 494–495
forced to commit suicide 499–502
funeral 502
Gariboldi *see* Gariboldi, Generale
    Italo d'Armata
Gazala 490
goggles 236
Great War 6–7
Halder *see* Halder, General Franz
Hexenkessel 479
Hitler *see* Hitler, Adolf
invades France 69–70, 212
invades North Africa 154–157,
    184–185
in Italy 6–7
Jodl 473
leadership 168
Mechili 225, 231–232, 235–236
military tactics 6, 198–199,
    215–216, 475

Morshead 498
Mussolini 148–149
Olbrich *see* Olbrich, Colonel
    Herbert
Operation Crusader 475–476,
    490
Paulus *see* Paulus, Field Marshal
    Friedrich
postcard portraits 429
Schmidt *see* Schmidt, Lieutenant
    Heinz
Sidi Rafaa 474
Sitzkrieg 402
Sperrverband (blocking formation)
    147
Streich *see* Streich, General
    Johannes
swastika 236
Tobruk, Battle of Carrier Hill
    335
Tobruk, Battle of the Salient 350
Tobruk campaign 243–244,
    263–264, 266, 267
Tobruk, Easter Battle 307–308
Tobruk, Operation Battleaxe
    425–427, 428
Tobruk, Ras el Medauuar (Hill
    209) 331
treatment of Jews 452–453
treatment of prisoners 71, 236, 363,
    369, 495
Victory in the West (film) 146
von Prittwitz *see* von Prittwitz und
    Gaffron, General Heinrich
Wavell 55
wounded 499
Rommel, Lucie 7, 22, 147–148,
    209–210, 290, 338, 341, 435,
    473, 481, 499–502
Rommel, Manfred 22, 148, 499–502,
    518
With Rommel in the Desert (Schmidt)
    167

Roosevelt, President Franklin D. 123, 495

Russia *see* Soviet Union

S

San Giorgio (warship) 133

Sänger, Joachim 366–368, 369

Savage, Michael 49

Schmidt, Lieutenant Heinz
88-mm AA Battery 426
mentioned 215, 263, 308
Paulus 345, 346–347
postcard portraits 429
Rommel 167, 216, 285–286, 330–331, 347, 353, 396–397, 409
Schräpler 353
Streich 277, 285, 289–290

Schmidt, Paul 46–47

Schöllmann, Lieutenant 280

Schorm, Lieutenant Joachim 299, 304, 355, 365, 373, 375, 376, 415

Schräpler, Major 341–342, 353

Schwarzkopf, General Norman 521

Scobie, General Ronald 462, 464, 482

Scott, Vern 398

Searle, Sergeant John 488

Shirer, William 76

Short, Corporal Harry 159–160

Sidi Barrani (Egypt) 86, 87, 112, 176–177

Sidi Omar (Libya) 397, 467, 474

Sidi Rafoa (Libya) 474

Sidi Rezegh (Libya) 477, 478–479, 480

Siegfried Line (German border with France) 505

Siegfried Line (German–French border) 56–57, 401

Sikorski, General 477

'Silent Night' (Christmas carol) 401

Sinclair, Sir Archibald 392

Singapore 140, 314, 381, 493–494

Slinn, Captain Graham 297

Smith, Private Arthur 249

Smith, Ted 218, 278, 284

Smythe, Dougie 95, 348, 354, 360

Sollum (Egyptian–Libyan border) 87, 113–114, 312, 318, 338, 347–348, 396, 425–427, 467, 472

Somalia campaign 427

Soviet Union
Germany invades 186, 428, 431, 451–452, 464–465, 496, 502–504
Germany retreats 505
invades Germany 505, 508–509
non-aggression pact with Germany 41, 54, 125
Russians in Poland 54, 465, 515–516

Spender, Percy 457

Stalin, Josef 41, 54, 125

Stalingrad siege 503

Strathaird (troopship) 101

Strathmore (as troopship) 94

Streich, General Johannes
commands 5th Light Panzer Division 147
Mechili 206–207
'Memoirs of Africa' 504–505
Olbrich 310
Rommel 109–110, 168–169, 226–227, 255–256, 263–264, 275–276, 307–308, 397
Schmidt 277, 285
Tobruk 265, 266
Tobruk, Easter Battle 289–290, 291
von Prittwitz 255–256

Sudetenland 37

Suez Canal 54, 83, 101, 102–103, 113, 185, 229, 276, 431

Swinton, Jim 398

Syria 493

T

Tandey, Henry 9

Taylor, Bill 284

Tedder, Air Marshal Sir Arthur 440

Thomson, Bob 436

Tobruk — Capture — Siege — Relief (Wilmot) 512

Tobruk (Libya) *see also* Tobruk garrison

Abbotts Lager mural 238

Achsenstrasse (Axis Road) 396–397, 476

Allied plans for 122

Allied retreat to 224, 238–239

Allies storm 128–129

'Benghazi–Tobruk Handicap' 200, 254

Commonwealth War Graves Commission Cemetery 521–522

damage to 136

decision to defend 227–229

discovery of oil 521

El Gubbi airfield 233, 272

Fort Pilastrino 252, 417

harbour 123, 138, 165–166, 319, 330, 393, 411–412, 450

history of 1–3

Italian 10th Army in 88, 113, 126, 135–136

maps 128, 244–245, 247, 251, 347

sandstorms 245, 248–249, 377, 464

Tobruk War Cemetary 315, 465–466, 491

Tobruk garrison *see also* Tobruk (Libya)

1941 Melbourne Cup 471–472

ablutions 271

AIF sun badge 405, 488

air raids 232–233, 272, 335–336, 338–339, 352, 378, 393, 395, 410–412, 442

airfields 233, 272, 345

Allied strength 232, 239, 240, 250

anti-tank ditches 138, 139, 244, 247–248, 256–257, 270, 302, 354

Australian 4th General Hospital 378

Australian Bush Artillery 200–202, 253–255, 303–304, 324–325

Australian troops and Afrika Korps 220–221, 307, 362–363, 409, 486–487

Battle of Carrier Hill 332, 333–335

Battle of the Salient 350–364, 370–373, 389, 395, 415, 429

Blue Line 252–253, 296, 364–366, 461

bridge approach 254–255

casualties 447

communications 258

death detail 315

defensive concrete perimeter posts 139–140, 247, 252, 257, 266, 277, 278, 287–288, 291–292

defensive trenches between posts 328

desert sores 413–414

diet 412–413

earthworks 383–384

Easter Battle 265–285, 287, 288–297, 299, 301–310, 415

Ed Duda 397, 476, 480, 482–489

El Adem road 277, 286, 295–296, 351, 489

flamethrowers 357

fleas 388, 438–439

front line 383, 400

German leaflets 273–274, 431

gun emplacements 326

health 434–436, 449

Hill 209 (Ras el Medauuar) 331–332, 345, 351, 356–357, 364, 374, 490

Italian forces Bardia Road 439–440

Italian forces Derna Road 333–334

landmines 126–127, 134, 256, 270, 287, 325–326, 354, 365–366, 446, 472

Tobruk garrison (*cont.*)
　listening posts 257
　mobile reserve 262–263, 482
　navigation by night 406–407
　news sheets (furphy-flushers) 408,
　　409–410, 438–439
　Operation Brevity 392–393,
　　395–396
　Operation Crusader 472, 475–476
　Padres 410
　patrolling outside the wire 316
　patrols into no-man's land 404–406
　'Rats of Tobruk' 329, 456, 498,
　　520
　Red Line 252–253, 269, 277, 286,
　　287–288, 295–296, 298, 301,
　　305, 325, 332, 348, 351, 364,
　　461, 482
　Regimental Aid Post 284, 369, 399
　relief of Australian troops 441
　the Salient 373, 384, 399, 443–444
　scorpions 414
　scrap-iron flotilla 410–412
　siege ends 490–491
　supply 243, 317, 329–330, 343,
　　390, 392–393
　TOBFORCE 477, 482
　Tobruk Field Hospital 330
　Tobruk Truth 438
　tropical diseases and infections 403
　tucker dump 436
　tucker truck 401–402
　water 257, 414–415
　weaponry 201–202, 259, 261, 262,
　　348–349, 354–355
Tobruk: The Birth of a Legend
　(Harrison) 498
Tocra pass (Libya) 187, 223
Tovell, Brigadier Ray 145
Treaty of Versailles
　Germany signs 10–11, 13–14, 519
　Hitler 15–17, 26
　Rhineland 27, 31

Tripoli (Libya) 125, 151, 154–155,
　167, 471
　German forces land 194
Tuit, Sergeant Wally 446, 447
Tully, Jack 60, 382
Tunisia 497
Tunstill, Captain Tony 253
Turkey 2, 124

U
United Australia Party/Country
　Party Coalition 372, 454
United States 11, 101, 123, 314, 478,
　490, 495, 505

V
Vaile, Mark 524
Vasey, Brigadier George 322
Victory in the West (film) 146
Vietina, *Ammiraglio* Massimiliano
　133–134
Völker, Rolf
　Afrika Korps 468
　Battle of El Alamein 505
　Christliche Deutsche Jugend
　　26–27
　Halfaya Pass 421
　joins up 44–45
　returns to Germany 517–520
　Schützenregiment 104 241, 371–372,
　　417–418
　Sidi Rezegh 478
　taken prisoner 505–507
　Tobruk 415, 453
von Brauchitsch, *Oberbefehlshaber*
　Walther 146, 185, 194, 397
von Prittwitz und Gaffron, General
　Heinrich 147
　Afrika Korps 244
　blown up 254–255, 262
　commands 15th Panzer Division
　　242
　Rommel 250–251, 256, 262

von Ribbentrop, Joachim 30
  as Foreign Minister 46, 47, 56
von Schwerin, *Oberleutnant* Gerhard
  Graf 426

W

Walmsley, Bill
  2/13th Battalion 100, 106
  anti-tank ditches 256–257
  Er Regima pass 219, 221
  HMS *Latona* 463
  killed 465
  Tobruk, Spandau Joe 386–387
Walpole, 'Cocky' 82
  Cairo 150
  in Port Said 120
  at sea 106
  Tobruk, Battle of the Salient
    363–364
Walsh, Corporal Earl 485, 486
War Letters 1940–1941 (Len Johnson)
  522–523
War Savings Certificates 112
*The War, the Whores and the Afrika
  Korps* (Barber) 320
Waugh, Corporal Stanley 177–178
Wavell, Field Marshal Sir Archibald
    Percival 494
  Australian troops 103
  background 54–55
  Blamey 332, 435
  Churchill 188–189, 203, 313, 390,
    427–428
  Commander in Chief for the
    Middle East 54, 72–74
  Commander in Chief of British
    Troops in the Far East 493–494
  Commander in Chief of India 493
  French defeat 77
  Greece 152, 158
  Italian 10th Army 83–84, 87, 88
  Lavarack 221–222
  Libya 146

Morshead 180–182, 214, 245–246,
  276
Neame 182–183, 194, 199,
  204–206
O'Connor 204
Operation Battleaxe 425–427, 432
Operation Brevity 392–393
Operation Compass 112–113
Rommel 55
Tobruk 122, 227, 245, 247, 276
Viceroy of India 494
Viscount of Cyrenaica and of
  Winchester 494
Western Desert Force 308
Wilmot 419–420
Wegmar, Lieutenant Colonel 168
Wehrmacht *see* OKW
  (*Oberkommando der Wehrmacht*)
Weimar Republic 11, 14, 17, 19
Wellington, Duke of 401
White Guard (in Victoria) 23–24
Wilkie, 'Jock' 81
Williams, Lieutenant (KDG) 417
Williams, Sergeant Billy 438
Williams, 'Splinter' 218, 278
Wilmot, Chester
  background 36–37
  Bardia 116–117
  career 512
  Diggers 443
  Greece 164, 216–217, 323
  Morshead 429, 498
  Nuremberg Rally (1938) 36–37
  Rommel 479
  at sea 99–100
  Tobruk 127–129, 136–137, 310,
    461
  Wavell 419–420
Wilson, Alex 88
Wilson, General Sir Henry Maitland
  142, 158
Wilson, Woodrow 11–13
Windeyer, Colonel 374

With Rommel in the Desert (Schmidt)
167
World War I *see* Great War
World War II
Allied casualties 71, 173, 308
inevitability of 41
Wright, Billy 35, 319–321
Wynter, Major General Henry 144

Y
Ypres (Belgium) 9
Yugoslavia 124, 191–192, 228, 323

Z
Zorn, Lieutenant Albrecht 234–235,
326